credulity - readiness to believe
cognitive - knowledge (having)

*AN INTRODUCTION TO*

# Principles
# of
# Right
# Reason

*By*

HENRY S. LEONARD

*Michigan State University*

HENRY HOLT AND COMPANY

*NEW YORK*

*TO PRISCILLA AND KIP*

# *Preface*

This book is a consequence of more than twenty years of experience in teaching elementary logic and related subjects to college freshmen. Within that span of time, the author has experimented with a great variety of approaches, including the traditional, Aristotelian logic and the various sentential and first-order functional calculi of modern symbolic logic. In the course of those years, certain convictions were developed that shaped the pattern and content of this present textbook. Experimentation with the text in mimeograph during the last several years has helped not only to remove many pedagogic blemishes from the text, but to strengthen the author's conviction that the approach is pedagogically sound.

Among the convictions referred to above, one might mention the following:

1. The overwhelming majority of students taking a first course in logic will major in some other subject and in all probability take no further courses either in philosophy or in logic. Hence, the course must have its own internal integrity and must contribute to the student's educational development whatever his major academic interests may be.

2. The student who elects a beginning course in logic expects it to have some practical value as a means to improving his powers of rational thought. While the usual courses in logic contribute something to this end, they nevertheless fall woefully short of it for a variety of reasons. (a) Too few validating forms and types of fallacy can be learned in a term, or even in a year, to provide the student with adequate tools for the direct critical analysis of the deductive situations that he is

regularly confronting. For example, only a tiny part of the world's reasoning is done in syllogisms. (b) But even with all the logic in the world at his command, the problems of application and of critical evaluation are sufficiently difficult to demand more attention than the usual logic course can afford to give to them. (c) These problems of application and evaluation involve a variety of disciplines in addition to logic, such as methodology, theory of language, and general theory of knowledge. Thus the "principles of right reason" are far from being exclusively principles of logic. (d) Finally, most students will throughout their entire lives employ, for the symbolic vehicle of their rational processes, a natural language such as English, rather than a calculus such as those developed in symbolic logic.

A consequence of these convictions is *Principles of Right Reason*, a text that draws on logic, methodology, and semiotic without any effort to keep the three disciplines sharply distinguished, and that ties the whole together with considerations drawn from the general theory of knowledge. The aim is to provide the student with an *understanding* of the cognitive situation, the role of language, of deduction and of induction, with a continuous illustration of how these theories apply to the right guidance of reason. The hope is that this understanding and the illustrative applications will encourage the student to make for himself critical and evaluative applications even in situations that are different in character from any actually illustrated in this text. Numerous unsolicited comments of seniors and others who had taken this course some years earlier in their academic careers encourage the author to believe that this hope was not entirely misplaced.

There are some things that the author would change in the present text, yet it would appear to him foolish to delay its publication on that account. Rather, let it go out and let him hear from you.

\* \* \*

To acknowledge here individually the author's debts to all who have contributed advice, suggestions, encouragement, or other assistance would be quite impossible. The plan and program of this book have been so long in evolving that many conversations relating to it are now merged into the vague and general educational background of the author's own intellectual history. But he cannot refrain from citing the enormous debt owed to a long series of freshman classes that have studied under him and from whom he has learned much.

During the last four years, the comments and suggestions of six colleagues at Michigan State University, who have used the mimeographed version as the textbook in their own classrooms, have proved invaluable. The author's debt in this respect is especially great to Professors Lewis K. Zerby and John F. A. Taylor, and Messrs. William J. Callaghan and Joseph F. Lambert.

Professor William P. Alston of the University of Michigan has read the entire text, at least half of it in two versions, and his comments and suggestions have led directly to a large number of undoubted improvements both in general and in respect to numberless particulars. Professor John F. A. Taylor of Michigan State University generously read the entire text in proof and offered numerous suggestions for minor improvements and insertions that were extremely helpful. And the unfailing encouragement and assistance of the author's wife, protecting his leisure for the pursuit of this task and also contributing her own time, talents, and counsel in connection with a disconcerting variety of problems arising throughout its prosecution, have enabled him at long last to bring this volume into publishable form.

Other acknowledgments are due a small host of typists, who assisted in preparing either the mimeographed experimental text or the typescript of this final version, and to the Michigan State University Press, which manufactured the experimental mimeographed text.

H. S. L.

Okemos, Michigan
April 2, 1957

# Foreword
## to the Instructor

---

## I

This textbook has been devised for a course attended primarily by freshmen and sophomores who will not major in philosophy. Yet the author's experience with it through several years of use in mimeographed form has been that the course has noticeably contributed to the preparation of students who took further work in logic or in other branches of philosophy. They already knew what they were concerned to do. They already had a concern for analysis and an appreciation of what this involved.

But the experience with nonmajors has been most gratifying. It appears that the course has thrown new light upon their other college studies in their diverse fields of special interest, upon the methods of these studies, of research in these fields, and even upon the methods for evaluating presented subject matter.

## II

On the whole, the division of the book into units represents a division into feasible daily assignments. This is not true, however, for Part V, if the instructor expects his students to master that material rather than merely to acquire a general grasp of it as illustrating the possibilities of formal analysis. But the earlier units represent what, in the author's experience, freshmen can compass in a single assignment. Were the text used for more advanced students, an instructor might find that longer assignments would not be impractical.

Some topics have been treated in this book that an instructor might not wish to impose on freshmen in a one-semester course, but that he would consider thoroughly appropriate for a more mature class, for one with more specialized interests, or for one with more than a semester at its disposal. (We find that two quarters are not too long for the entire text.) Many of these items have been isolated and marked, so that any one or more of them may be readily omitted at the instructor's discretion without disturbing the continuity of the remaining text. They are printed in somewhat smaller type and are marked in the Table of Contents by a footnote.

On the whole, items so marked *prior* to Unit 32 are not intrinsically too difficult for freshmen, but constitute digressions or refinements that may be sacrificed for the sake of acceleration; those occurring in and after Unit 32 are more abstruse considerations than the freshman is likely to grasp without considerable help or to appreciate without more scholarly experience.

Still other omissions than those marked in the text might be made in Parts I to IV if an instructor wished to reserve a larger part of his course time for the study of Part V. The inclusion of a glossary makes such other omissions not so serious a handicap to reading later portions of the text as it might otherwise be.

## III

The reader will find numerous innovations in this book. These consist not only of a somewhat novel distribution of the space and time accorded to various topics brought together in a single text, but include as well genuine alterations and transformations of the theories thus brought together. To cite only a few examples: (1) The treatment of semiotic, particularly of the purposes of discourse, has affected and modified the account given to *meaning*. (2) The treatment of *extension* and *intension* is far from traditional. (3) The discussion of definition is more extensive than is customary, classifications such as *real* and *nominal* are reconceived, and the traditional rules of definition have been transformed and supplemented. (4) Finally, the discussion of inference and of proof is not the usual one. For one thing, it has been affected by the earlier stress on semiotic. For another thing, while much of the apparatus of traditional logic has been retained to provide a framework, it has been supplemented and its treatment has been modified by considerations that are usually reserved for treatment only in courses on symbolic logic.

All of these revisions of traditional theory have been undertaken in order that the values of the traditional approach might be preserved. They represent "updatings" of traditional theory that brought to bear upon such theory certain results of more modern study and research in related fields, such as semiotic and symbolic logic. It is the author's earnest hope that the most of these modifications will appeal to you as improvements and that not too many of them will strike you as disconcerting aberrations.

# *Foreword*
## *to the Student*

As you begin the study of this book, you will discover that it deals with many topics: language, logic, the methods of the sciences, what is a belief, a proposition, a true proposition, a justified belief. As it deals with many topics, so it will make contact with, and even overlap, many of your other studies: your courses in English composition, in science, in mathematics, psychology, and your other courses in philosophy. While such of those courses as you have taken may help to explain what you will read here, what is especially hoped is that what you read here will shed a considerable light on what you study, or will study, there.

For this book represents a course of study in the principles of right reason, of the means and methods that intelligent people have at their disposal for the resolution of problems and the effective organization of knowledge. No matter what the subject of one's inquiry might be, the efficient and effective methods for dealing with it remain much the same. It is for this reason that the course of study represented in this book will touch upon so many of your other studies. Indeed it is to be hoped that this study will contribute to making all of your studies throughout your college program more illuminating and more profitable, that you will "see" more clearly what your professors and your textbooks are trying to do and why they are going at it in the way that they do.

Such desirable results, however, cannot be attained without your making a deliberate effort to achieve them. For this purpose, your chief technique must be a continuous effort to *apply* what you study here. The situation is much like that of a student of a foreign language. If he does no more than his daily assignment, he will hardly learn to speak the language. He must practice from the very beginning the use of his newly discovered vocabulary and grammar, by using it to talk about whatever comes to his attention.

So here, the chief tools of study are understanding and practice. You will discover several new and unfamiliar technical terms in this book. Merely to memorize them and their explained meanings would be the poorest method of study. First, try to understand them. Then try to use the ideas they represent in analyzing all sorts of situations. As you do that, you will gain a greater understanding. And when you have done it, you will find that memorizing is either completely unnecessary or is very easily accomplished.

In short, conscientiously do the exercises as soon as you come to them. But do something more than that: look for other illustrations of the principles explained and for opportunities to apply what you study to materials that you discover in your other courses.

The Review Questions at the end of each unit should help you to make certain that you have properly identified and understood the important ideas developed in that unit. And the glossary at the back of the book should help you to recall the meanings of various new terms when these meanings may have slipped from your mind.

# Table of Contents

_____
* May be omitted without disturbing the continuity of the text.

---

* May be omitted without disturbing the continuity of the text.

_____

* May be omitted without disturbing the continuity of the text.

---

\* May be omitted without disturbing the continuity of the text.

_____

* May be omitted without disturbing the continuity of the text.

* May be omitted without disturbing the continuity of the text.

───────────

\* May be omitted without disturbing the continuity of the text.

# PART ONE

# GENERAL
# INTRODUCTION

# Logic, Methodology, and Language

## §1.1 Practical Problems

The life of a person, like that of any other kind of animal, involves a constant process of adjustment and readjustment to the world that surrounds him. We meet things in the world, and we do something about them: some we eat, some we talk to, some we build into other things, some we use as tools to aid us in controlling yet others, some we run away from, some we simply pay no attention to. What we do with these various things differs markedly from what a lower animal—a dog, robin, angleworm, or what not—does with them. How one person deals with them differs from how another person would have dealt with them.

By and large, our manner of dealing with the world is settled for us by our human instincts and acquired habits.[1] Most of our reactions are instinctive or habitual, at least in part, so that our responses are almost automatic. This determination of response by instinct and habit is even more complete in the case of the lower animals.

But even among the lower animals, and still more often among men, situations arise that require some response, while instincts and habits provide no determinate pattern of response. In such circumstances, the person or animal is face to face with a **practical problem,** a problem concerning what to do.

Consider this illustration. We sit down to dinner at a table with familiar silver before a plate containing familiar foods. Through the force of instinct and habit, and almost without any thought, we select the appropriate fork or spoon and commence eating. Our mind and conscious thought is directed toward the conversation with our host. But let there be an unfamiliar food—say, an inlander's first experience of

---

[1] I use the outmoded term "instinct" in order to avoid involvement with the position of any one among the several psychological theories now competing for attention.

whole broiled lobster—or no silverware, and a problem has arisen: What should be done? Instincts and habits suggest no ready-made solution, and thought wanders from the conversation to become focused on the problem that confronts us.

Practical problems arise in either of two ways. Sometimes a problem comes about because a situation calls into operation two conflicting instincts, habits or persuasions. For example, a student is settling down in the evening to his homework, when a classmate unexpectedly asks him to go to the movies. His instincts and habits urge him to perform two distinct acts, yet the two are such that performing either of them will inevitably prevent him from performing the other.

Sometimes, however, a problem arises simply because no already developed instinct or habit suggests any specific reaction appropriate to a new or unfamiliar situation, while the situation is such as to demand some response. Such was the difficulty of the dinner guest mentioned a bit earlier in this discussion.

Many practical problems are of a more serious nature than are those used in our illustrations so far. To mention only one: What should I do to meet the threat of warfare involving atomic bombs?

## §1.2 Theoretical Problems

Suppose we were walking in the country and had become very thirsty. Suppose we came upon a brook. Our thirst might urge us to drink some water from the brook. But the many things we have heard and read about polluted streams prompt us not to do so. On the other hand, we may believe that no other source of water than the brook is likely to be found for many miles. What should we do?

The situation just imagined is one suggesting the occurrence of a practical problem) a problem, that is, concerned with the concrete manner in which we shall deal with certain items in the world about us. It is easy to see that we might solve that practical problem if we could find out whether the stream is polluted. Accordingly, we can "translate" that practical problem into this different problem: Is the stream before us polluted?

Now the latter problem is not a practical problem, is not a problem concerning what to do, although solving it may help us solve the practical problem. The latter problem is in fact a question concerning the character or nature of some item in the world about us.

All such nonpractical problems we shall call **theoretical**. Consequently, we may say that human beings are constantly finding themselves confronted with more or less urgent problems; some of these are practical, some are theoretical. Frequently the solution of a theoretical problem will assist us in our efforts to solve practical problems.

As we have just suggested, many theoretical problems arise and are solved in the effort to solve certain practical problems. But it is one of the great good fortunes of our human nature that men are attracted by theoretical problems and actively undertake their solution, even when no practical problems whose solutions would thereby be made easier are in mind. It is just this tremendous intellectual curiosity that has produced the major part of our sciences. The sciences are by and large storehouses of theoretical beliefs. Sometimes the theories developed in a science wait for generations before any practical problems occur to whose solutions those theories are seen to be relevant.[2]

### §1.3 Methods of Problem-solving

We may summarize the discussion so far by saying that both animals and men find themselves frequently confronted with problems, and that they set about trying to solve these problems by various characteristic means. Of these methods, we shall distinguish three, as follows:

**1. The Method of Trial and Error.** The individual makes various random, more or less unpremeditated responses or guesses, actually trying them out one after the other. There is no clear notion that any of these responses or guesses is appropriate to the situation. The best one can say is that the person or animal is doing *something* about the problem. For example, the young child first presented with a set of blocks will try them out, pushing them, biting them, throwing them, perhaps eventually piling them one on the other. These random actions may be largely suggested by the repertory of instinctive and habitual responses that the individual has already learned; but they are being more or less haphazardly applied to a situation unlike any by which these instinctive and habitual responses were formerly evoked.

[2]  The difference between practical and theoretical problems depends not only on the content of the problem, but also on the identity of the problem-solver. If *I* wonder what *you* should do in a given situation, this problem confronting me is a theoretical problem; but if *you* wonder what you should do in that same situation, the problem confronting you is a practical problem. Practical problems are always problems of action-decisions on the part of the problem-solver.

This method of trial and error is undoubtedly the most widespread of the three methods we shall describe. It is used by animals of all types and kinds, from worms, slugs, and even simpler animals all the way up through the higher forms of life to man himself. Under the most favorable circumstances, it produces a genuine solution and may contribute to building up a new habitual type of response. Under less favorable circumstances, it produces no positive harm but leaves the disturbing feature of the individual's surroundings still operative as a disturbance, so that the problem remains unsolved. Under the least fortunate circumstances, an attempted response brings down on the individual a serious injury, or even death itself. The animal which tries out a method for removing bait from a trap and gets caught, well enough illustrates this last situation.

2. **The Method of Imitation.** Many higher animals, including man, learn how to deal with novel situations by imitating the treatment they observe others giving to the same situations. The established procedure of the species, race, or tribe is handed down to the young through their tendency to imitate. Children learn to talk by imitating parents and teachers, the hunting animal learns how to stalk its prey by hunting in the company of older animals in the group.

This method of problem solving is at once more effective, safer, and more intelligent than the method of trial and error. However, it can be used only in situations that are new for the individual but not new for the group to which he belongs. Other members of the group must already have faced the problem and found a solution to it.

3. **The Method of Taking Thought.** Finally, we find man, as also perhaps some of the other higher animals, such as apes, illustrating a yet higher and more effective means for solving problems. He "figures out" a solution. By using his intellectual endowments, he analyzes the problem, develops in imagination various possible solutions, tests these in thought by connecting them with other items of his knowledge, weighs their relative plausibility, selects the more plausible for further testing, and eventually adopts that one which he is persuaded will provide a genuine solution.

By using this method the physical risks involved in the method of trial and error are reduced to a minimum, for most trial takes place here only in imagination and thought, rather than in actual practice.

Likewise, there is an <u>economy</u> in time and effort that marks a clear <u>gain</u> over either of the two more primitive methods. And finally, the method may be applied in completely novel situations, which is an advantage over the method of imitation.

But not all applications of the method of taking thought are equally efficient and equally successful. However, through the ages, men have discovered various <u>guiding principles</u> which, when they are kept in mind and <u>carefully</u> applied, can guide us to a more efficient and more frequently successful use of this method. These guiding principles may be called the *principles of right reason*. We have adopted this phrase ✗ for the title of this book because our entire purpose is to explain these guiding principles (or at least as many as space permits) and how they may be applied to improve the efficiency or the frequency of success of our efforts to use the problem-solving method of taking thought.

The next unit will continue the general discussion of problem-solving and examine more carefully the nature of thought. In terms of that further discussion, we shall see how the principles of right reason are generally divided into three groups: those treated in *logic*, those treated in *methodology*, and those treated in the theory of signs, called *semiotic*. While we shall try there to explain briefly both the differences among those three sciences and the connections among them, the later units of this book will not attempt to keep the three sciences separate. They will instead treat the principles of right reason in a logical order, without assigning them to one or another classification.

## REVIEW QUESTIONS FOR UNIT 1

1. What is meant by a practical problem? How do such problems arise?
2. What is meant by a theoretical problem?
3. Can the solution of theoretical problems ever aid one in the solution of practical problems? Explain and illustrate. (Do *not* use the illustration given in the text.)
4. Name and briefly describe three methods of problem-solving common to animals and to men.
5. What is meant by the principles of right reason?
6. How is the study of these principles related to the three methods of problem-solving?
7. From what three sciences do most principles of right reason come?

# UNIT 2

# *The Act of Thought; Logic, Methodology, and Semiotic*

## §2.1 The Role of Belief

If it is awareness of a problem that starts us on a train of thought, it is the achievement of a problem-solving belief which brings thought to an end. To hold a belief is to be prepared to act in a certain manner under given circumstances. For example, suppose we reach a belief that the brook mentioned in §1.2 is polluted. To hold that belief is to be prepared not to drink from the brook, in spite of our thirst.

Every belief, then, is an adopted plan of action. As such, beliefs supplement our instincts and habits, they are instruments guiding our responses to the world about us. When instincts and habits offer no unchallenged response to a given situation, a problem arises as to what should be done. But this problem is solved as soon as an appropriate belief, dictating a method of response, becomes fixed in the individual's mind.[1]

## §2.2 The Act of Thought

In consequence of the previous discussion, we may affirm that every complete act of thought begins with the recognition of some problem, continues with efforts to resolve that problem, and ends with the attainment of a belief which does solve the problem.

[1] The phrase "adopted plan of action" as one characterizing beliefs was made widely known and was widely accepted as a result of the work on belief done by Charles S. Peirce (1839-1914), famous American mathematician and philosopher.

Strictly speaking, it should be noticed that it applies only to practical beliefs. Theoretical beliefs are rather *matrices*, or *sources*, for adopted plans of action. For example, to believe that this liquid is poisonous is not sufficient *by itself* to produce a plan of action. But it will *combine* with some more general purpose to produce such a plan.

*What* plan of action it produces depends on what general purpose one has with which it may combine: to keep alive and well? then don't drink it; to commit suicide? then drink it; to commit murder? then put it in the person's tea.

However, having noted here this distinction between practical and theoretical beliefs, we can continue in the text to speak of all of them as adopted plans of action.

8

Actually, however, not all thinking shares this perfect structure. This comes about when, for some reason or other, one or more of the three steps involved in a complete act of thought is entirely or almost completely lacking. Hence, we must recognize various types of *incomplete* acts of thought. A large part of any person's thinking consists of just such incomplete acts. We shall list here three types of incomplete act.

**1. Nonproblematic Thought.** In **nonproblematic** thought, a person reaches a belief without first having been confronted by a problem. Thus, his belief is not the solution to an *actual* problem, but only the solution to a possible problem—and he has the solution before the problem ever arose.

Since the belief occurs without there having been any problem, it will occur also without there having been any effort to solve the problem. Thus, in nonproblematic thought there is neither any first, nor any genuine second, stage in the act of thought. Nevertheless, there are experiences which produce the belief.

All nonproblematic thought should be regarded as accidental belief-formation, the accidents that produce the beliefs being fortunate or unfortunate as the case may be. Such accidental beliefs come about in one of two ways. First, we sometimes just notice, without even trying to, that something is true. For example, I may notice, and believe, that some house I pass is made of stone, without ever having been concerned to discover its composition. Second, various more or less competent authorities may *inform* me that something is true without my seeking this information. For example, I may go to the movies to be entertained, and learn from a newsreel that Harvard defeated Yale in a football game.

Sometimes accidental belief-formation occurs as a by-product of genuine problem-solving activity. Frequently these accidental discoveries are of the greatest importance. For example, Roentgen discovered X rays in 1895 when he was conducting experiments on a different, relatively unimportant problem. That part of his thought which terminated in the discovery of X rays must be listed as nonproblematic thought, since the problem Roentgen was dealing with was not the one solved by the discovery of X rays.

**2. Trivial Thought.** An act of thought is called **trivial** when the solution of a presented problem involves no genuine expenditure of effort, so that the second stage in the complete act is almost entirely lacking. The awareness of the problem carries one almost automatically through the phase of effort to solve, so that one reaches belief without conscious deliberation. For example, I may be concerned to know what time it is. A glance at my watch solves the problem. Trivial thought is thought in which the answer to the problem is supplied by a relatively simple process, of observation, memory, interrogation, or the like.

To call this type of thought *trivial* should not be allowed to mislead you. The beliefs reached by trivial thought are often of the greatest importance. It is the thinking, rather than the attained belief, which is trivial. For example, *Is it safe to cross the street now?* is a problem whose correct solution is very important. But the act of solving it, by glancing right and left, is effortless; so that the act of thought consisting of problem, effort, and belief, is listed as trivial.

**3. Unterminated Thought.** Sometimes we recognize a problem but never reach a solving belief. There are many different reasons why acts of thought are so often **unterminated**. Occasionally, when a question or a problem arises, it is not very urgent and it arouses in us too little interest to make us undertake its solution. Sometimes, we begin trying to solve a problem only to give up before a solution is reached, either because interest wanes, other more urgent problems arise, we find we cannot afford the time or money to reach the solution, or we cannot find a solution no matter how hard we try.

For the most part, the study that follows deals with complete acts of thought. What we wish to explain is how to solve problems that do actually arise. But in two respects our study will bear on incomplete acts of thought. First, we may learn to be wary of beliefs which are already a part of our consciousness. Beliefs resulting from nonproblematic and trivial thought are especially in danger of being false. The tests that we shall learn to apply to beliefs will be especially applicable in these cases. And second, our study should make it possible for us more often to carry through our thought to the attainment of a genuine belief. Thus, fewer acts of thought should remain unterminated because of an inability to solve the problems before us.

## §2.3 Successful Thought

There are two levels at which we may distinguish successful from unsuccessful thought. On the one level, any act of thought is successful if it resolves the problem that started it; correspondingly, it is unsuccessful if the problem remains unresolved. This does not mean that thought is successful if the thinker loses interest in the problem. Rather it means that success depends on the thinker's finding a proposition which he recognizes as an answer to his problem and which he can believe. Thought is unsuccessful if the thinker finds no such proposition.

Every complete act of thought is, in the nature of the case, successful at the level just discussed; and every act of thought which is successful at this level must be either trivial or complete. To assure yourself of this, all you need do is look up the definitions of complete and trivial acts of thought given in §2.2. But at another level, many of these complete acts of thought must be regarded as unsuccessful. For the beliefs they produce are false. False beliefs are guides to action all right. But they are unwise and unsafe. What one wants is to achieve beliefs that are true.

Unfortunately, no proposition carries on its sleeve a label "true" or a label "false." The propositions we believe are the ones we accept as true, the ones we disbelieve are those we reject as false. We do, however, make mistakes, accepting some propositions that are in fact false and rejecting others that are in fact true.

Sometimes the errors in judgment just considered are the result of an illogical use of our evidence or of a failure to organize the available evidence in effective ways. The principles of right reason are at once a warning to be cautious and an outline of various positive programs and techniques by whose application this advice of caution may be put into practice.

It must, however, be confessed that not all errors in judgment are due to the thinker's misuse of evidence. Sometimes, what we might call the "perversity of the world" makes the evidence available to us justify a conclusion which is in fact false. This topic will be discussed at greater length in Part V. The only reason for mentioning it now is to remark that what the principles of right reason will ensure for us are beliefs which are justified, not necessarily beliefs that are true. On this second level, then, successful thought is thought which results in justified problem-solving beliefs.

## §2.4 Definition of Logic

Logic may be defined as the science of exact reasoning. This means that the science of logic undertakes to discover and state laws in accordance with which any act of thought may be judged good or bad, that is, correct or incorrect, sound or unsound.

The importance to thought of a science like logic must be apparent to anyone who considers the situation. Nearly every valuable belief, even of the simplest sort, is one which we reach on the basis of thought that involves *reasoning* from evidence. For example, political and moral convictions are not directly seen to be true; but are "argued out" until available evidence is shown to prove a conclusion. Again, no one has seen the roundness of the Earth. But we believe that the Earth is round on the strength of certain evidence, from which we reason to this conclusion. Or again, the chemist does not see, even through a microscope, the atoms that he talks about and believes in. Instead, his experiments provide him with evidence concerning the way in which various substances combine or react. From this evidence he reasons to the conclusion that the substances are composed of atoms with such and such characteristics.

Of course, there are many things that a person believes because someone he trusts has told him they are true. But in such cases, the *original* discoverer must usually have reached *his* belief by reasoning from evidence.

People, however, make many mistakes in their efforts to reason from given evidence to a conclusion. The science of logic teaches us laws or principles by means of which we can test the correctness of any piece of reasoning, either our own or another person's. Armed with such a knowledge, we should be more successful in our attempts at thinking out solutions to problems.

## §2.5 Logic and Methodology

Let us turn our attention for a moment away from problem-solving to a useful analogy, for example to playing tennis or football. As the object of thinking is to win a knowledge of the world, so the object of playing tennis or football is to win a victory over your opponents.

Now the tennis or the football player must, if he would win, attend to *two* different sets of rules. One set of rules simply defines the game. These rules are set up by organizations like the Lawn Tennis Association or the Intercollegiate Athletic Association, and are enforced during games by referees and judges. A player who breaks these rules is simply

n calls for a penalty. These rules are
l

nother set of rules to which a player
rst set of rules tell you how to play,
second set of rules which lays down
ood form, and when applied enables
ing side.

and the Intercollegiate Athletic
this second set of rules. Their dis-
Nor will the judges and referees
es. The "penalty" is exacted by the
o

e like the rules and principles of
m

A person could follow all the rules of logic and still be a very poor and ineffectual thinker, just as he could follow all the rules defining tennis or football and still be a very poor tennis or football player. But the coach's rules, or the rules of methodology, are not *alone* sufficient to make a good player or good thinker: they cannot take the place of the defining rules or the rules of logic. All they do is explain how to play *well* a game that the other set of rules has already described. If you did not know what game you were playing, you could not know how to play it well.

This study of the principles of right reason is a study both of logic and of methodology.

## §2.6 Problem-solving and Language

At least one reason why man has so far outrun the lower animals in his knowledge of the universe rests in his ability to use complicated forms of language. To be sure, the lower animals do communicate with one another by the use of visual and auditory signs. But the capacity to use language is enormously greater in the case of man. He can, and does, learn to use languages of great complexity and subtlety. These more complex languages can much more nearly reproduce the intricacies and fine distinctions in the world he represents by them. To a great extent, he can make his use of language serve as a substitute for thinking, and so leave his actual thought free to deal with and to master the still deeper and more intricate mysteries of the world.

Language thus becomes one of the great tools of thought. It contributes to the possibilities of human truth-seeking in many ways. We shall list here a few of those ways.

1.  Language makes easier and enlarges the possibilities of **communication.** Because of this, the search for truth has been made a genuinely cooperative enterprise. No one need discover all things for himself. The major part of what he knows he can learn from others: parents, teachers, friends and associates, physicians, ministers, and so on.

But the ability to communicate resulting from the use of language does not merely enable us to learn from others what they have already discovered, or to teach others what we have discovered. It also makes possible **collaborative** efforts; two or more people intent on solving the same problem may join efforts, perhaps to succeed when neither one could have done so working alone.

2.  Language makes easier the **preservation** of thoughts and of the discoveries of thought. This contribution of language is perhaps more characteristic of its written forms than of its spoken forms. But even the spoken language is an aid to memory; and with the invention of the phonograph and other sound-recording machines, spoken languages may some day rival written or printed ones as means of preservation.

This preservation value of language enlarges all the possibilities of communication mentioned just above. For example, past generations may speak to those who come after, because language preserves their thought for later reception.

But, in addition, as language preserves thought it makes possible more **long-range, deliberate, leisurely, discontinuous, and critical attacks** upon problems. One may interrupt his thought by a meal, a night's sleep, or other responsibilities without finding his entire train of thought disappeared in thin air. Also he may review, for purposes of further criticism and correction, points he had worked out before. Hence, larger and more complex problems may be attacked and solved because of the preservative value of language.

3.  Finally, language provides us with a **calculus,** with a tool, that is, which can do much of our thinking for us.

Some of us have studied, and all of us have heard of, that branch of mathematics called *calculus*. In a sense, that branch of mathematics deals with only one calculus. By a calculus we should understand any system of signs whose rules for combination and rearrangement reflect legitimate movements of thought. The correct use of any such system of signs thus simplifies and ensures correctness in calculating the solutions of problems that belong to specific types. One simplifies his process of reasoning by recording his data in the language-calculus, rearranging the signs of this record in accordance with learned rules, and reading off the answer.

To illustrate the above, suppose we desired to know for some reason the product of four hundred thirty-eight and five hundred seventy-six. To calculate this result by using the rules of our Arabic number system is immeasurably easier than it would be if we had to use Roman numerals. But using even Roman numerals is easier than doing the problem in our heads without the aid of any language. In effect, we let our manipulation of the number language take the place of, and relieve the strain on, sheer thinking. Every language to some extent, and some languages to a great extent, may be used in similar ways as calculating machines.

## §2.7  Logic, Methodology, and Language

Because human thinking has become so closely tied up with the use of language, some psychologists have even gone so far as to claim that all thinking is nothing but actual or incipient speech. We shall not go that far. But we shall find that the analysis of thought undertaken in logic and methodology will have a much greater practical value if it is carried on largely through an analysis and criticism of the language that people use when they think. Hence, we shall study and criticize the ordinary forms of language that people regularly employ when they express their thoughts. By discovering the meanings, vaguenesses, and defects of this language, as also its merits and strengths, we shall try to reach an understanding and improvement of the thought that it expresses. This study of language will provide the major point of emphasis throughout Part II. In the next section, however, we shall make a beginning on this study of language.

## §2.8  The Uses of Language

We have spoken in §2.6 about the use of language as an aid and tool of thought, and we have outlined some of the features of language that make it useful for this purpose. All such uses of language may be referred to as **cognitive.** It must now be pointed out that human beings use language for a great variety of purposes, so that the cognitive is only one of its uses.

1. By and large, all uses of language may be divided into three great types. Of these three, the cognitive uses described in §2.6 form the first type. The two remaining types are as follows:

2. **Pragmatic Uses of Language.** People frequently use language in order to bring about changes in the world of facts. Suppose, for example, that I desired brighter light in the room where I was sitting. One way of producing this result would be to walk across the room and press the electric-light switch. But another way would be to *say* to a companion, "Please turn on the light." Such a use of language is vastly different from any cognitive use. We say or write something, not in order to communicate a belief or to gain assistance in solving a problem of belief, but solely in order to produce an action. When the use of language is aimed at affecting the action or behavior of people in preconceived ways, the use should be classified as **pragmatic.**

3. **Esthetic Uses of Language.** The author of a poem or novel is often enough not writing in order to affect the action or behavior of his readers. Neither is he trying to communicate items of information. The purpose is instead, like that of music or painting, to express some feeling or attitude and to enable the reader to share this feeling with the author. Sometimes we could classify the purpose as sheer entertainment; sometimes the expression and communication of feeling has a nobler part in the drama of our lives. But however that may be, such uses of language, both by the author and the reader, are different from any we have considered heretofore. The aim is to affect feeling or emotion, and the distinctive use may be spoken of as **esthetic.**

Every use of language, both by author and by reader, will fall under one of the three types listed above. Textbooks, newspaper reports, scientific journals, boards of directors' meetings, sometimes "bull sessions," illustrate mainly a cognitive use of language. Simple commands and requests, advertising, political oratory, lawyers' pleas before juries, propaganda, and the like illustrate primarily pragmatic uses of language. Finally, short stories, novels, poems, plays, and much social conversation illustrate chiefly the esthetic use of language. These different uses of language will be examined in more detail in Units 12 and 13.

## §2.9 Mixed and Deceptive Uses of Language

The three uses of language contrasted in §2.8 are not always distinct. For example, novels often have a moral (pragmatic) and cognitive, as well as an esthetic, purpose. This is true, say, of most of Dickens' novels, or again of Steinbeck's *Grapes of Wrath*. The latter, by way of illustration, is intended to inform (cognitive) its readers of the conditions to which a social group found itself reduced, and to acquaint them (cognitive) with some of the social and economic forces which produced those conditions. But also, by the feeling tone (esthetic) of the report (cognitive), the author hoped so to arouse public opinion that the government would be forced to act (a pragmatic purpose).

Sometimes an esthetic and pragmatic use are combined, sometimes as esthetic and cognitive, sometimes a cognitive and pragmatic, and sometimes, as in the example above, all three uses are intermingled.

There is nothing wrong and no harm, on the contrary there is often a great good, in combinatorial uses of language. But combination becomes harmful, indeed extremely dangerous, when the combination is *deceptive*. Propaganda is a case in point. By and large, propaganda parades as a straightforward cognitive use of language: it purports to *inform* us of certain matters of fact. If it goes so far as to recommend a certain conduct (pragmatic), it recommends it as the intelligent response to the reported *facts*. So far as such communications are sincere, there can be no criticism of them. So far, that is, as their authors sincerely believe that the things they report *are* facts and that these facts do make the recommended action advisable (for example, that no other facts making it ill-advised have been deliberately suppressed), propaganda is a good and worthy use of language. Historically, the word "propaganda" referred to just such sincere and honest uses of language. But in recent years, with a greater knowledge of psychology teaching us how human actions may be influenced, there has appeared such a flood of deceptive and even dishonest propaganda as to give the word itself an evil connotation. The propagandist has often lost all interest in spreading genuine information and focuses all his attention on producing a preconceived type of conduct or activity. Yet he undertakes to achieve this result by the very effective method of *appearing* to provide reliable information. Thus, the sole use is pragmatic, but the pragmatic end is achieved because the propagandist's use of language is *mistakenly* accepted by the reader as a cognitive one. And the propagandist *intends* his use of language to be mistakenly accepted in this way: he is depending on that mistake as the factor which produces the intended pragmatic result. His use of language is deliberately deceptive.

A great deal of advertising exhibits a similar deceptive use of language. To take just one example, one cigarette manufacturer advertises his product as "made of costlier tobaccos," another speaks of his as produced from "just the cream of the crop." Now such advertising must be effective, must exert a tremendous influence on the buying habits of the public, because otherwise advertising agencies and publishers would not continue to find so many customers for their expensive services and space. And this influence on the public habits must be at least partly the result of the reader's believing what he reads. Thus, the intended pragmatic result is produced because the reader accepts the advertiser's statements as being also cognitive.

But consider the situation. *If properly understood*, neither of the illustrative advertising statements given above could be called false. All cigarettes are made of costlier tobaccos, which are the cream of the crop. The cheaper grades and inferior leaves are used for chewing tobacco, snuff, insecticides, and so on. But the advertisements acquire their effectiveness as selling certain brands by being *misunderstood*; the reader mistakenly assumes that the comparison is one with tobaccos used in other brands of cigarettes. If he did not, why should he switch brands of cigarettes? And furthermore, the advertiser is *depending* on the occurrence of this misunderstanding to give his advertisement its appeal. Thus, the advertisement appears to the reader as a cognitive use of language, which it is not because it makes no scrupulously sincere effort to communicate information. Actually the publication of the advertisement constitutes a deceptive pragmatic use of language.[2]

## §2.10 Unintentional Deception

Serious as are the deliberately deceptive uses of language, they do not constitute the only source of danger due to the mistaken interpretation of a language use. Often enough both author and reader, with the greatest sincerity on both their parts, fall victims to the possibilities for confusion present in the language itself. A moving flow of oratory may be mistaken, even by the orator himself, for a straight-

[2]  On advertising in the tobacco industry, see an article by Blake Clark on "Lifting the Cigarette Ad Smoke Screen" appearing in *The Reader's Digest* for July, 1943, pp. 17-21.

forward and honest appraisal of some situation; the esthetic effect on our emotions is conceived to be an enlightenment of our understandings.

This sort of confusion occurs not only in the case of elaborate speech, but also even in the case of single words. To give only a few examples, such words as "patriot," "liberty," "democracy," and "social security" evoke emotions proper to the good things of life. They are, furthermore, familiar words; we have heard them used and used them ourselves, over and over again. Almost invariably what they stand for is held up for praise and admiration as a noble achievement or a worthy ideal. It is not our intention here to suggest that these words do not refer to noble achievements or worthy ideals. What we do wish to point out, however, is that the emotional glow evoked by the words too often combines with their familiarity to produce an illusion of understanding. Perhaps you yourself think you know what these words mean. Then stop for a moment and try to write out a clear *definition* of each word. Now compare your definitions with those in the dictionary. And finally, try to decide what is "wrong" with your own definitions, and also what is "wrong" with the dictionary definitions. Which of the latter, for instance, makes no clear reference to notions intelligible to the understanding?

## §2.11 The Plan of This Book

Because language is so important a tool of thought, no studies of logic or of methodology can get very far without giving some attention to language. To be sure, the major concerns of logic and methodology with language are concerns with its cognitive use, that is, concerns with it as an instrument or tool of problem-solving thought. But in order to understand these features of language, we need to know a good deal about it in general. For example, we need to know more about what language is and in general how it functions. Accordingly, several of the later units of this book will be devoted to a study of those principles of language that may be thought of as bearing specifically on the principles of right reason.

The book is divided into five main parts. The rest of Part I, *General Introduction*, continues the general analysis of a problem-solving act of thought. It will provide in this way a general framework in terms of which to understand the more detailed studies of special topics taken up in the later parts of the book.

Part II, *Language*, discusses that important tool of thought. Starting with the simplest sort of sign situation, it explains the various purposes of language and shows how signs acquire their meanings. This discussion of language belongs to the general science of **semiotic.**

Part III, *The Theory of Terms*, examines those meaningful bits of language, words and phrases, that may be regarded as language's simplest *logical* units. It considers the kinds or types into which they fall and the different aspects of their meaning. This discussion belongs to the science of logic.

Part IV, *Definition*, considers the purposes, uses, and different possible forms of definition. In Part I we shall see how important is definition to any successful use of language as a tool of thought or an instrument of communication. In Part IV we shall discover certain rules which we employ either to criticize the definitions constructed by other people or to guide ourselves in the process of constructing more accurate and effective definitions. Some of the discussions in Part IV belong to the science of logic and some to the science of methodology.

Part V deals with *Inference*. We shall see in Part I that inference is one of the main grounds for justified belief. But many a time we draw incorrect conclusions from the evidence we have available. In Part V, we shall consider what it is one should attend to in order to check on the reliability of an inference. Also, we shall consider what kinds of evidence it is desirable to procure should one wish to draw inferences of certain kinds. We shall examine some of the characteristic procedures of the sciences, bodies of knowledge or belief acquired by the judicious combination of inference with other grounds for belief.

## *REVIEW QUESTIONS FOR UNIT 2*

1. Briefly describe the three stages in a complete act of thought. How is the occurrence of thought related to the existence and disappearance of problems?
2. Name and briefly describe the three kinds of incomplete acts of thought.
3. Under what circumstances may thought be said to be successful or unsuccessful? Describe two levels of success in thought.
4. What connection is there between the principles of right reason and the success or failure of thought?
5. What three sciences contribute most to the principles of right reason? Describe briefly what each of these sciences is about.

6. Explain briefly why language is so useful a tool of thought.
7. Name and briefly describe three kinds of use that people make of language. Which of these uses is the most important to problem-solving?
8. What is meant by a "mixed use" of language?
9. Can uses of language ever be deceptive? How? Illustrate.

# The Recognition of a Problem; Ambiguity and Vagueness

## §3.1 The Purpose of Unit 3

We have seen in Unit 2 that when thought is employed to solve problems, the act of thought characteristically involves three stages or phases:

1. Recognition of the problem
2. Efforts to solve the problem
3. Adoption of a problem-solving belief

We have also noticed that some problems are more easily solved than others, and that sometimes problems are "solved" incorrectly, that is, by the adoption of false, or at least unjustified, beliefs.

The whole study of right reason is based on the assumptions that (1) we can learn to test beliefs and the steps of thought by which we reached those beliefs, and (2) we can learn to go about our problem-solving in ways that are both more efficient and more likely to be successful.

In the present unit and the next, we shall consider only the first step, or stage, in the solution of any given problem.

## §3.2 The Need for Analysis

The first phase in a complete act of thought has been described as the recognition of a problem. One senses some difficulty, practical or theoretical, which he wishes to resolve.

Now the nature of this awareness may vary all the way from a vague sense of discomfort, or disturbance, to a clearly conceived apprehension of the specific difficulty. It stands to reason that the more clearly the problem is conceived, the more appropriately one may select means to solve it, and the greater therefore is the likelihood of reaching a valid solution. The first step in good thinking, then, is to analyze the problem itself.

This process of analysis may be looked at from two points of view. From one side, it is an effort to reach a fuller and more adequate awareness of the problem. As such, it belongs to the first stage in a complete act of thought. But from the other side, it is the beginning of one's effort to solve the problem; to a large extent we solve problems by understanding them. From this latter point of view, analysis of the problem belongs to the second stage of a complete act of thought. We may gather from this duality of viewpoint that the stages in an act of thought are not sharply divided, but rather shade off one into the other. It will even be frequently the case that they are overlapping; we may *return* to the task of analyzing a problem long after we first left it to engage in other efforts at solution.

Simple problems are often grasped and understood without any, or any elaborate, program of analysis. For example, a question as to the length of my desk would not ordinarily require any expenditure of time for its analysis. Instead, I would forthwith proceed to get the yardstick and measure the desk. But other, more intricate, problems suggest in their first occurrence no such program for their solution. In those cases, one must "take time out" to arrive at a clearer understanding of the problem before one tries to go further.

## §3.3 The Formulation of a Problem

It has already been said in Unit 2 that language is one of the great tools of thought. At this juncture we find a first opportunity to help ourselves through the use of language. We may begin our analysis of any problem by formulating it in a question. This interrogative sentence we should phrase in such a manner as to make it the clearest, most precise, and most accurate statement of our problem that we can. This effort to state the problem will serve two ends. First, it will make us realize more precisely what the problem is, and second, it will give us an objective expression of the problem that we can examine and study in detail and at our leisure.

Very likely it will turn out that as we try to state a problem our statement will seem inaccurate or inadequate. What we really wanted to know was something more than, or something slightly different from, what our suggested question asks. Very likely this is true. Hence a new problem arises, which we must do our best to solve before we go further: Does the question accurately formulate our original problem; and if not, should we restate the question, or substitute the problem of the question for our original one?

## §3.4 Vague Problems

The natural presumption is, of course, that we are only trying to state our *original* problem. But the effort to state it may actually suggest that as we first conceived it, the problem was invalid; that there is a valid problem, slightly different from that one, perhaps the one formulated in our question; and that it is this valid problem, rather than the original invalid one, to which we should seek an answer.[1] For example, the problem may have been so vague as to be unanswerable, while the stated question, being more precise and therefore different, is answerable. Surely one objective we have in mind is to get rid of vague perplexities, but we cannot do this if we let our formulated question express that vagueness itself.

On the other hand, we want *really* to be rid of the vague perplexity. It will do no good to find the solution to a clearly stated question unless we are genuinely satisfied that that question is what we want an answer to; it will do no good if the old perplexity still persists. We must be sure that the new, clearly formulated problem is the one we are now interested in, that the transfer of attention to this new problem is progress in understanding our original difficulty rather than a transfer of allegiance to something entirely distinct.

## §3.5 Complex Problems

The problems that confront people are oftener than not complex. Perhaps no single question could adequately represent the problem. Perhaps instead we shall have to make use of a more or less large set of questions. For example, a young man in college might be wondering about his future in such a manner that any single question such as, "What should I do about my future career?" would be entirely inadequate. His problem would be better conceived in terms of a series of related questions:

1. For what profession or business do my talents and aptitudes adapt me?

---

[1] What it means to call a problem or a question "invalid" or "valid" will be explained in greater detail in §4.8.

2.   What profession or business do I wish to enter?

3.   What other considerations than aptitude and desire should I permit to affect the choice of a career?

4.   What career shall I choose?

5.   What kind of academic preparation (such as law school) should I plan to secure?

6.   Where shall I seek that preparation?

7.   What courses ought I therefore to include in my next term of college work?

### §3.6  Vague and Ambiguous Questions

If the language in which we formulate a question is like the language of arithmetic and algebra, clear and precise, a straightforward statement of the question might suffice for this aspect of the analysis of the problem. But the chances are that our question is expressed in some language, like English, in which the various words, and even their modes of combination, are vague and ambiguous. Hence the analyzing question should be carefully examined to make sure that its intent and meaning are absolutely clear. If any vaguenesses or ambiguities are present, these should be removed, either by rephrasing the question or by accompanying it with such definitions, explanations, and illustrations as will help clarify it.

The extent to which our English language suffers from vagueness and ambiguity is oftentimes not fully appreciated. Furthermore, the difference between ambiguity and vagueness is not always understood. We shall accordingly interrupt this discussion of the first step in problem-solving to explain briefly.

What is said about vagueness and ambiguity in the next few sections applies as much to statements and other formulations of information and beliefs as it does to questions and similar formulations of problems. In Unit 4, we shall resume the interrupted study of step 1 in an act of thought.

### §3.7  The Difference between Ambiguity and Vagueness

We come to understand the words and phrases of a language by learning what people customarily mean by them. If every time a word were used it had a different meaning, we could (so to speak) never "catch up" with it and would not know what it meant on *this* or *that* occasion of its use.

Sometimes two or more customary meanings are associated with one word or phrase in such a way that on several occasions it is used in accordance with one of these customs to mean one of these things, while on several other occasions it is used in accordance with another of these customs to mean another of these things. For example, with the word "cardinal" at least three customs are associated. In accordance with one of these, many occurrences of the word are used to refer to a certain kind of bird; in accordance with another, many occurrences refer to a certain color; other occurrences refer to an official in the hierarchy of the Roman Catholic Church; and there are still other customary meanings for this word.

An occurrence of an expression is **ambiguous** if one cannot tell which of two or more customary meanings of the expression was intended by the author of that expression.

Suppose, for example, that a meeting of officials in the Catholic Church was taking place nearby. If, then, you heard someone say, "I saw two cardinals when I was walking across the campus this morning," the occurrence of the word "cardinal" would be ambiguous: you could not tell whether the speaker was referring to birds or to church officials.

Vagueness, on the other hand, is a difficulty involving only one customary meaning for a word or other expression. In this, it differs from ambiguity, which always involves at least two customary meanings. In the case of vagueness, the custom in question has never fixed the exact limits of what is included within the meaning of the term. On some occasions, it is used in a more inclusive sense, on other occasions in a less inclusive sense. Examples of words used with variation in the limits of extension are "thin" (as applied, say, to men), "we" (to include the speaker and a varying number of other people), and such expressions as "greater New York" or "greater Boston," which expressions refer to the named city and an inadequately delimited part of its surroundings.

An occurrence of a word is **vague** when it cannot be determined what limits the speaker intended to put on the inclusiveness of the word in question.

To illustrate, if a person were to ask, "What should we do about the rising frequency of juvenile delinquency?" his use of the word "we" would be vague (unless he added some explanatory comments): one could not tell whether he meant the word "we" to refer simply to himself and the person or persons addressed, or to some larger part of the society; and if the latter, to what larger part. On the other hand, the word "we" in "What shall we do tonight?" as addressed to one's dinner companions, is not vague.

The contrast between ambiguity and vagueness can be visually suggested by these diagrams:

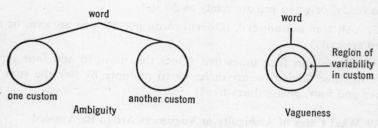

Fig. 1

The opposite of vagueness is **precision,** the opposite of ambiguity is **unambiguity.**

Sometimes an expression is used in such a manner as to be both vague and ambiguous, sometimes it will be one of these but not the other, while sometimes whether an ambiguous word is also vague will depend on how the ambiguity is resolved. To illustrate only the last of these possibilities, unless something in the context or the circumstances made the speaker's intention clear, "George lost a suit," would contain an ambiguous occurrence of the word "suit." If the ambiguity is resolved to reveal that it was a lawsuit which George lost, there is no vagueness. But if the resolution of the ambiguity reveals that what George lost was some clothing, there still remains an element of vagueness: Is the term "suit" to be limited in its application to garments cut from the same kind of material, or is a pair of slacks and a sport jacket, which are worn together, to be considered a suit?

## §3.8 Major Types of Ambiguity

Ambiguities are of two major types, called **simple ambiguities** and **amphibolies.** A simple ambiguity is a case of ambiguity in which the ambiguous expression is a single word or simple phrase. All the illustrations of ambiguity so far considered were simple ambiguities. An amphiboly is an ambiguity of an expression (usually a sentence) arising out of inadequacies in its grammatical structure or its punctuation. Examples of amphiboly are:

1.   The men were all tuckered out. (Does it mean all the men were tuckered out, or the men were completely tuckered out?)

2.   Serve the meat when ready. (Does it mean serve the meat when *it* is ready, or when *you* are ready to do so?)

3.   All men are not evil. (Does it mean not all men are evil, or no men are evil?)

4.   Three plus four times five. (Does this mean to add four times five to three, giving twenty-three, or to multiply by five the sum of three and four, giving thirty-five?)

### §3.9   What Cases of Ambiguity or Vagueness Are to Be Avoided

Ambiguity is not always an evil, neither is vagueness. Sometimes, for example, they produce effects (say, in poetry) that are genuinely desirable, and in fact just what the author was seeking. Also, in everyday conversation vague terms are often useful, when lack of precision will not affect the outcome of the matter in hand. How awkward, if you could not say, "My, but he's a tall man!" and had to say instead, "My, but he's at least six feet one inch tall!"

Yet ambiguity and vagueness can be serious obstacles to problem-solving and to the transmission of information. In the formulation of questions they can cause trouble, because they make it impossible to select an appropriate means for finding the correct answers to the questions. Also, in the statement of basic beliefs they cause trouble, for they make it impossible to determine what can be legitimately inferred from these basic beliefs.

It is partly because of the difficulties arising out of ambiguity and vagueness that serious investigators in special fields of enquiry invent special technical vocabularies. The technical terms in these special fields are more precise and less ambiguous than the general vocabulary of everyday discourse. Hence, a person who explains such words when he uses them is merely extending a courtesy to the reader by saving him the necessity of looking up their meanings in a dictionary or other reference book. But the explanation of common words drawn from everyday discourse is an intellectual necessity, since no dictionary will remove their ambiguity or vagueness.

## §3.10 Some Special Warnings

A word frequently giving rise to ambiguity is the word "should." For example, in "Should I tell the cashier that she gave me too much change when I paid my bill?" the phrase "should I" probably means "is it my duty," that is, "do I have a moral obligation?" In other circumstances, "should I" means "do I have a legal obligation?" and in still others, as in, "Should I buy a French dictionary?" it means, "Would it be advantageous?" Frequently one cannot tell which meaning was intended by a given author.

A popular construction often leading to an amphiboly is the use of the passive voice: "How much should be donated to the Community Fund?" The question is amphibolous because one cannot tell whose donations it is asking about: mine, those of my family, the "average" person, the total of all contributors. This ambiguity will be avoided by using the active voice: "How much should I donate to the Community Fund?"

As you formulate problems in questions, be especially careful to eliminate the ambiguity or vagueness of the simple, common words you use; and give special care to the avoidance of amphibolies. Remember that, as was pointed out in §3.6, vagueness and ambiguity may be removed either by rephrasing the question or by attaching to it accompanying remarks which explain what you meant by the words and phrases in your question.

Sometimes a question may be made still more clear or precise by an indication of the circumstances in which it occurs. Let us take an example. I ask, "How wide is this bookcase?" This certainly appears to be a straightforward question that could be answered simply enough by specifying the number of inches across its front. But when one undertakes to find the answer, several perplexing considerations may arise. What dimension is wanted: the length of the shelf? the outside dimension? at the widest point? or at some other typical point? Again, how accurate a measure is wanted?—for no measurement is entirely accurate; all we can expect is greater or less accuracy. All these questions could be more or less cleared up by indicating the circumstances under which the problem arose. It might be, for example, that I contemplate placing the bookcase against a certain wall and desire to know whether or not it is too wide to fit into the position under consideration. At once I realize that the widest outside dimension is the one required, and that a relatively high degree of accuracy is necessary only if the width of the wall and that of the bookcase are found to be nearly the same.

## EXERCISE

Which of the following sentences are vague, or ambiguous, or both vague and ambiguous, or neither vague nor ambiguous? In each case of vagueness or ambiguity, explain briefly the source of the difficulty; and in cases of ambiguity, indicate whether the ambiguities are simple ambiguities or amphibolies.

1. Is Mr. Smith bald?
2. Would a roll-top desk fit into my living room?
3. Why did Johnnie bat a baseball through my window?
4. Does that suitcase cost ten or fifteen dollars?
5. Are students satisfied with the grades they get?
6. How are lobsters eaten?

## REVIEW QUESTIONS FOR UNIT 3

1. What is meant by a complex problem?
2. Explain briefly the difference between vagueness and ambiguity.
3. Name, explain, and illustrate the two major types of ambiguity.

# The Recognition of a Problem, continued

## §4.1 Classification of Questions; Practical and Theoretical Questions

Once a problem has been accurately stated and explained in the manner discussed in the preceding unit, we may get further light on the methods appropriate for its solution if we classify the question that formulates our problem.

One useful basis for classifying questions has already been discussed in Unit 1, where problems were divided as **practical** and **theoretical**. While there is no fundamental difference between the methods appropriate for solving theoretical problems and those appropriate for solving practical ones, the classification may have a bearing on the choice of methods, as follows: The solution of practical questions generally depends on using various relevant theoretical beliefs. For example, how I solve the practical question suggested in §1.2, *Should I drink water from this brook?* depends on whether I believe that the water in the brook is polluted. Hence, in general, solving practical questions proceeds by amassing relevant theoretical beliefs; and this process will often involve becoming aware of and solving various theoretical problems.

At the same time, however, it is usually some more or less clearly conceived practical belief of a more general order that will determine the relevance of the amassed theoretical beliefs.[1] To use again our former example, it is our general decision to support our life and well-being rather than to do away with ourselves which fixes the relevance of such a theoretical belief as that the water in the brook is polluted. These very general practical beliefs are frequently established by instinct; but they may become the topic of intellectual enquiry in special circumstances. They form in fact a large part of the subject matter investigated in that branch of philosophy called *ethics*.

[1] In this connection, see footnote 1 in §2.1.

31

Also, practical questions usually differ from theoretical ones in that practical ones have to be solved within some more or less definite time span. For example, the question, "Shall I vote for the Republican or the Democratic candidate in the next election?" must be solved by election day. Not to solve it by then, even through the use of some such irrational method as tossing a coin, would entail not voting; but that itself would in effect be a kind of solution: to vote for neither candidate. On the other hand, there is no time limit imposed by the nature of the case on the solution of theoretical problems.[2]

It usually happens that several different methods of solution are conceivable for any one problem, that these methods might differ in the trustworthiness of the solutions they would produce, but that they also differ in the time required to work them out. When the problem is practical, we must choose a method of solution that will provide an answer in the available time, even though that answer is not so trustworthy as the one we might have secured by using a longer and more laborious method of solution.

Of course other factors than the time limits imposed by a practical question will affect the amount of time, energy, and financial outlay we deem prudent to spend on solving a question. Hence, even when the question is theoretical, we may find ourselves obliged to adopt a less demanding and less reliable method of solution. But in these cases we may hedge our belief in the solution reached, accepting it only as tentative and subject to later revision. In such a case, the wise man would be aware of the merely probable character of his solution. But still, through a more or less large area of his life activity, he will have to act *as though* the belief were completely reliable. For example, the basis of his decision to vote for one candidate rather than another may be recognized as not too trustworthy, but still his act of voting will take place in the same manner as would be appropriate if he had complete confidence in the superiority of his chosen candidate.

---

2   While "the nature of the case" imposes no time limit on the solution of theoretical problems, other circumstances often impose a limit on the time during which we shall continue to be interested in solving a theoretical problem. For example, although we have all the time in the world in which to solve the theoretical problem, *Is the water in that brook polluted?* yet when we have finished our walk, reached home and another reliable source of drinking water, we shall in all probability have lost interest in the question.

## §4.2 Direct, Semidirect, and Indirect Questions

There are, however, other, more formal grounds in terms of which questions may be classified. One divides questions into:

1.  **Direct questions**
2.  **Semidirect questions**
3.  **Indirect questions**

A direct question is, so to speak, a straightforward true-false question; it is any question that could be intelligibly answered by "yes" or "no." For example, the question, "Is New York north of Washington, D. C.?" is a direct question. Both "yes" and "no" would be intelligible answers, although the former is correct and the latter incorrect. On the other hand, "What brought about Hitler's rise to power in Germany?" is not a direct question. Anyone who answered "yes" or "no" would be presumed to be making light of the question or not to have understood it.

Put in more technical terms, the direct question puts forward a specific proposition, more or less complex as the case may be, and asks simply whether that proposition is true or is false. The semidirect question puts forward two or more specific propositions and asks *which* of these is true and which is false. Thus the question concerning which of two candidates I should vote for is a semidirect question. Finally, the indirect question does not offer any specific proposition concerning whose truth or falsity it seeks an answer, but rather enquires as to what proposition or propositions would solve an indicated difficulty.

As may be imagined, questions belonging to these three different types would be solved by characteristically different methods. By and large, the indirect questions require for their solution more in the way of imaginative research than do either the direct or the semidirect.

A frequent source of amphiboly is the careless punctuation of semidirect questions that makes them indistinguishable from certain direct questions. Strictly speaking, the question, "Did Bob or Joe go to the post office?" is a direct question; while, "Did Bob, or Joe, go to the post office?" is a semidirect question. The former, direct question is asking whether or not one of these two people went to the post office, while the latter, semidirect question assumes that one of them went and is asking *which* one. But since people are nowadays so careless about punctuation, it is difficult to be certain that a person really meant the question which strictly speaking he may have written. We can avoid this amphiboly by using the correlative conjunction "either" in the direct question, "Did either Bob or Joe go to the post office?" and by repeating the auxiliary verb "did" in the semidirect question, "Did Bob, or did Joe, go to the post office?"

## EXERCISE

Classify each of the following questions as (a) theoretical or practical, and (b) direct, semidirect, or indirect.

1. Did Eisenhower receive more votes in the 1952 election than all other candidates for the presidency put together?
2. Would it be in the best interests of the United States for it to continue its membership in the United Nations?
3. Under what circumstances would it be in the best interests of the United States to discontinue its membership in the United Nations?
4. Will it rain tonight, or will it snow?
5. Does Congress have any constitutional authority to enact a universal fair-employment-practices law?
6. Can I classify this sentence correctly, or should I study the lesson again before I attempt to classify it?

## §4.3 The Presuppositions of a Question

Having classified the question, one may proceed to identify and evaluate its **presuppositions**.

Every problem arises in a context of already formulated beliefs that are to a considerable extent reflected in the question itself. A stock example of this fact is the lawyer's question put to a witness: "Have you stopped beating your wife?" Formally, the question is a direct one; but either answer, "yes" or "no", implies that the witness has in the past practiced wife-beating. We may say, then, that the proposition, *The witness used to beat his wife*, is a presupposition of the direct question asked. In a similar fashion, the proposition, *Jones drove down Main Street last night*, is a presupposition of the indirect question, "How fast did Jones drive down Main Street last night?"[3] A great many questions involve one or more presuppositions.

---

[3] Questions how fast, how long, how far, when, and where in a sense fall between semidirect and indirect questions. No specific alternative propositions are listed for consideration, but the range of propositions in question each time, although indefinitely large, is clearly understood: $x$ miles per hour, $x$ feet, nine o'clock, latitude $x$, longitude $y$, etc. We shall in this book, however, treat such questions as indirect.

The motive for seeking to identify the presuppositions of a question arises from this fact: that unless its presuppositions are all true, the question is not a legitimate one and should not be asked. If Jones were not driving down Main Street last night, it is pointless to ask how fast he was going. Equally, if the witness never did beat his wife, it is illegitimate to ask whether he has stopped doing so.

It is very easy to formulate a question involving various presuppositions without having adequately considered the matter of their truth or falsity. We are frequently almost unaware of what those presuppositions are. Hence we are in danger of not only wasting time trying to answer improper questions, but we even run the risk of becoming seriously distraught by our inability to find an answer. Both in order to remove such disturbances and to avoid futile intellectual activity, we should undertake at some time early in the investigation to identify and judge the truth or falsity of the presuppositions to the question in hand.

## §4.4 Context versus Presuppositions

Care should be taken to distinguish between those beliefs in the *context* of a problem that make the question which formulates the problem vivid or urgent but which are not presuppositions of the questions, and those propositions which are genuine *presuppositions*. The two groups can be distinguished by keeping this definition in mind: A presupposition of a given question is any proposition whose truth is necessary to the validity of the question; that is, any proposition such that if it were false the question would be unintelligible. The difference between the two kinds of proposition may be illustrated as follows. Suppose that we had gone to the furniture store to buy a desk which we intended to place against the wall between two doors. One desk in the company's stock appeals to us very much, but there is some question in our minds as to whether or not it is too wide to fit the intended space. We might then ask: *How wide is that desk?* The little story which has introduced this question contains many statements belonging to the *context* of the question, statements that describe the circumstances which make the question interesting, or urgent, for us. For example, if we had not liked the desk in question we should not have been concerned about its width; if we had available many alternative locations of different sizes, again we need not have worried about its width. But the propositions reported in the story are nevertheless not presuppositions of the question: they could all be false, and the question about the width of the desk would still be intelligible, however uninteresting.

On the other hand, if the desk were *a thing without width*, like honor, or the multiplication table, or a thought, then any question asking how wide it is would be nonsense. Thus, *that the desk in question has a dimension of width*, is a presupposition of the given question: unless this proposition is true, the question does not make sense, is un-intelligible.

## §4.5 Factual versus Formal Presuppositions

It is not always too easy to apply the criterion just explained in an effort to distinguish propositions in the context of a question from genuine presuppositions of the question. This comes about because presuppositions are really of two kinds: *factual* and *formal*. Formal presuppositions are easily distinguished from propositions in the con-text of a question, factual presuppositions are less easily distinguished. We shall explain the difference between these two types of presup-position in terms of two examples.

Consider again two questions already used for purposes of illus-tration:

1.   How fast did Jones drive down Main Street last night?
2.   How wide is that desk?

For each of these questions we have listed a presupposition:

1a.   Jones did drive down Main Street last night.
2a.   That desk has a width.

These two presuppositions differ one from the other with respect to what they demand of you in order that you might determine whether or not they are true: Proposition 1a requires an *observational* check on historical facts, either by yourself or by some other reliable witness. You, or the witness who reports to you, must actually have *seen* Jones driving down Main Street for you to find the presupposition true; or, in order to find the presupposition false, must either (1) have kept an observational check on Main Street and seen that Jones did not drive down it, or (2) have kept an observational check on Jones and seen that he did not drive down Main Street. A presupposition that requires this sort of observational check to determine its truth or falsity, is called a **factual** presupposition.

In contrast, presupposition 2a requires no such observational check. If you know what "desk" means, you know that it means (among other things) a physical object with a front, back, and sides; further, you know that a physical object (among other things) has spatial dimensions, and that "width" simply refers to a spatial dimension identified by reference to the distinction between front and back on the one hand and sides on the other hand. Thus a sheer analysis of meaning reveals the fact that presupposition 2a is true.

If an analysis of meaning will suffice to reveal that a presupposition is true or that it is false, the presupposition is called a **formal presupposition.**[4]

If one or more of the formal presuppositions of a question are false, the question literally makes no sense. It involves a self-contradiction. You cannot imagine how to find an answer to the question. Thus, the question, "How tall is honesty?" makes no sense: a formal presupposition is false.

But if all formal presuppositions of a question are true, then the question itself makes a sort of sense whether or not the factual presuppositions are all true. You at least can conceive how to go about answering the question. Thus question 1 is formally intelligible whether or not Jones drove down Main Street. On the other hand, it is not factually intelligible unless Jones drove down Main Street, because one cannot even begin to find an answer.

Factual presuppositions are more difficult to distinguish from propositions in the context of a question than are formal presuppositions. Yet there is a difference. If a proposition in the context of a question is false, there still remains a way of finding an answer to the question, although there may be no point in doing so. But if a factual presupposition is false, the question has no answer; there is no way of finding an answer to it.

## §4.6 Subtle Presuppositions

Let us consider a somewhat more subtle example than any of the previous ones. "Was George Washington a greater man than Abraham Lincoln?" We might list offhand as a basic presupposition, scarcely open to doubt, that George Washington and Abraham Lincoln are two men who actually lived at certain historical times. But the

---

[4]   The distinction between observation and analysis as grounds for belief is further discussed in Unit 6.

question involves another presupposition, namely that the greatness of one man is comparable to that of another man. Now this is a matter that is frequently taken for granted. Yet sometimes there is, it may be contended, such a difference in the circumstances of two men's lives that we are wholly unable to measure or determine their relative greatness. It might still be held, however, that one *was* greater than the other, however unable we may be to detect this fact.

Nevertheless, the very belief that there exists a relative greatness may be erroneous. It may be that no ground, even no undetected ground, exists for its establishment in fact, let alone for its detection. Thus, to say neither was greater than the other would not necessarily mean that they were equally great. It could mean that only provided the presupposition of comparable greatness were accepted as true. It might instead mean that their qualities of greatness are incomparable, so that the question is invalid since it involves a false presupposition.

The first task, then, is to identify all presuppositions of whatever question confronts us. But once these presuppositions are identified, we must consider their truth or falsity. Three situations may be distinguished:

1. *The presuppositions are all recognized to be true.* In this type of situation the investigator may proceed to attempt the solution of the problem.

2. *The presuppositions are one or more of them recognized to be false.* In this case, the question is invalid and no solution need be sought. On the other hand, one might return to his original problem in an effort either to reformulate it in a different, valid question, or to recognize that the problem, like the question which represented it, is invalid and should no longer disturb us.

3. *No presupposition is recognized as false, but about one or more we are in doubt.* Here the validity of the question must perforce also be in doubt. One procedure would be to abandon temporarily the original question while we attempt to solve these new questions as to whether the doubtful presuppositions are true or are false. On the other hand, it might be that the same investigation that would contribute to solving the original question, in case it turns out valid, will also determine the truth or falsity of the presuppositions. For example, it may be that the way we can discover whether the greatness of Washington is comparable with that of Lincoln is by the same investigation as would

reveal which was greater in case the two are comparable. In such cases, one would proceed *as though* he accepted the original question for a valid one; but he should be prepared to interpret the results of his enquiry as revealing either the invalidity of the question or its solution if valid.

## §4.7 Primary and Secondary Presuppositions

It was said above that we must identify and evaluate *all* presuppositions of whatever question confronts us. This is not strictly true. We shall see in a moment that the presuppositions of a question may be divided into *primary* and *secondary* presuppositions, and that what we must identify and evaluate are all primary presuppositions.

Consider the question, "How fast was John Sprague driving down Main Street last night?" This question has several presuppositions, among which may be listed the following.

1. John Sprague was driving down Main Street last night.
2. There is such a person as John Sprague.
3. There is such a place as Main Street.

If any one of these three propositions were false, then the original question would be an invalid one that should be rejected as having no answer.

But the three propositions are not on an equal footing. For proposition 1 is such that, if it be true, propositions 2 and 3 would also have to be true: John Sprague could not have been driving down Main Street unless he existed and Main Street existed.

Any presupposition of a question such that its truth would follow from the truth of some other presupposition or presuppositions of the same question, is called a **secondary** presupposition. Any presupposition which is not a secondary presupposition is called a **primary** presupposition.

In accordance with the above definitions, proposition 1 is a primary presupposition and propositions 2 and 3 are secondary presuppositions of the original question.

What we must list and test are all *primary* presuppositions of a question. If we find that they are all true, then we automatically know that all the secondary presuppositions are also true and therefore that the question is a valid one. If *any* presuppositions are false (making the question invalid), then at least one primary presupposition will be false. Hence, to test the primary presuppositions will be sufficient.

There is, of course, no real harm done in listing and testing a secondary presupposition along with the primary ones. In fact, it is sometimes easier to test some secondary presuppositions than to test the primary ones. If the test shows that a secondary presupposition is *false*, that is sufficient in itself to prove that the question is invalid. Hence, it is sometimes easier to show that a question is invalid by attending to the secondary presuppositions. But on the other hand, if all secondary presuppositions that you test turn out to be *true*, then you are still not through: the primary presuppositions must still be tested. Consequently, whenever a question looks so "safe" that no false presuppositions immediately attract your attention, it is usually more efficient to concentrate your time and attention on the primary presuppositions. But do not waste too much time worrying over whether or not a certain presupposition is primary or secondary. If you do not readily see how to infer it from other presuppositions on your list, include it as a primary presupposition and test it for truth or falsity. At the worst, you only made the list of presuppositions that you had to test a little longer than necessary. But the chances are that it took less time to test this extra presupposition than it would have taken to find out that it was a secondary presupposition and therefore was an extra.

## EXERCISE

List and evaluate the primary presuppositions of each of the following questions. Say in consequence of your examination of these presuppositions whether or not the question is valid. (If in some case you do not know and cannot readily determine the truth or falsity of a presupposition, explain what you would have to do to find out whether it is true or false, and explain how the settlement of this issue would affect the validity of the original question.)

1. Who is the Chief Justice of the United States Supreme Court?
2. Where did Malenkov and Eisenhower hold their secret meeting during 1952?
3. Why is the delta wing used on all supersonic airplanes?
4. Is an act of Congress sufficient to establish an amendment to the Constitution of the United States?
5. Is an act of Congress necessary in order to establish an amendment to the Constitution of the United States?

## §4.8 Valid and Invalid Questions and Problems

In this and the preceding unit we have examined some of the techniques that could be adopted for a more adequate understanding of whatever problem we might be concerned to resolve by the method of taking thought. Near the beginning of Unit 3 we remarked that any such analysis of a problem could equally well be considered as the first part of the second phase in an act of thought; the first part, that is, of the effort to solve the problem. In the next four units, we shall give our attention to considerations that more especially bear on that second phase. But even there, we shall not be through with everything that bears on this first phase.

What is now important, however, is to notice that sometimes the very techniques we have been already considering suffice in themselves to resolve our original problems. This comes about through the fact that certain problems confronting a thinker are *invalid*. In these cases, the effort to identify the problem will frequently reveal its invalidity and thereby resolve it.

By an **invalid** problem, we mean one which *has no solution* and which, therefore, *ought not to exist*. The occurrence of a problem involves the occurrence of a felt compulsion to find a solution. But if one discovers that there *is* no solution, he at the same time discovers that he ought not to be trying to find a solution. Once he is convinced of this, his problem is evaporated, hence resolved.

In §3.4, we noticed that some problems are vague. Sometimes this vagueness will be so slight, or be involved in the problem in such a manner, that the problem can be solved in spite of its vagueness. But on other occasions the vagueness of the problem is an insuperable barrier to its solution. Such problems are invalid and are, strictly speaking, resolved by noticing their vagueness. However, to notice this invalidity does not always and automatically remove all awareness of *any* problem. It often happens that after we have discerned this type of vagueness there exists in place of the original vague problem a group of one or more rather closely related, precise problems. These are what the original problem was turned into by analysis. While the original problem was, strictly speaking, resolved by analysis, we may consider the effort to solve this new, substitute problem or set of problems as a continuation of the same act of thought. This was the position taken in §§3.3 and 3.4.

Again, a problem with false presuppositions is, in accordance with §4.3, an invalid problem. Hence if we find that some problem confronting us involves false presuppositions, we may use this information gained by analysis of the problem as the means for resolving the problem. But here also, a new, valid problem, not involving those false presuppositions, may arise in place of the original problem; if one does so arise, we may regard the effort to solve the new problem as the continuation of the original act of thought.

As problems may be valid or invalid, so the questions which formulate them may be valid or invalid. We often discover the invalidity of a problem by first discovering the invalidity of the question used to formulate it, or the nonequivalence of the problem to any valid questions suggested for its formulation.

If a problem disappears because on analysis we find it is invalid, the first step in the act of thought produces a resolution of the problem and so swallows up the second and third stages. If no substitute problems remain, the act of thought is complete. But if substitute problems remain, the effort to solve them constitutes the completion of the original act.

To sum up, a question is valid if it is precise and unambiguous and furthermore has no false presuppositions; a question is invalid if it is vague or ambiguous or has one or more false presuppositions.

## EXERCISE

Which of the following questions are valid, which invalid? In each case, briefly explain why you answer as you do.

1. Should I accept the bid of the X fraternity (sorority) to become a member? (Assume that you have received a bid.)
2. What should be done about censorship of the press in the United States?
3. Can the government of a state in the United States send an ambassador or consul to a foreign government?
4. Why are all undergraduate students at X University required to pass certain basic courses before they may be granted a degree?
5. How may a political minority be defined?

## REVIEW QUESTIONS FOR UNIT 4

1. Name, explain, and illustrate the major classifications of questions.
2. What is meant by a presupposition of a question? A *primary* presupposition? A *secondary* presupposition?

3. Explain the difference between a *presupposition* of a question and a proposition belonging to the *context* of a question. Why is this distinction important?

4. Explain the difference between a *factual* and a *formal* presupposition.

5. Must both factual and formal presuppositions be true if a question is to be valid?

6. What does it mean to say that a question is valid? That it is invalid? Explain. Why is this distinction important?

7. Under what circumstances is a question valid? Invalid?

## EXERCISE

Identify and define some problem in the general area suggested by one of the following topics. In your determination of the problem, use the various procedures discussed in this and the preceding unit. Thus, the outline of your report might be as follows:

I. Introduction. Brief description of circumstances giving rise to problem.

II. Formulation of problem in a question (or series of questions, if problem is complex).

III. Explanations that will remove any vagueness or ambiguity from the question. (But try to phrase the question so as to keep this part of your report brief.)

IV. Classification of question as practical or theoretical, and as direct, semidirect, or indirect.

V. List and evaluation of primary presuppositions.

VI. Judgment concerning validity of question.

If possible, select for examination something which is for you a real, live problem, instead of something to which you already know the answer.

A. Fraternities (or sororities).

B. Governmental censorhip of press and literature.

C. Vocational training in liberal arts colleges.

D. Liberal arts courses (English, history, philosophy, etc.) in vocational colleges (agriculture, business, etc.).

E. Local versus federal government.

F. Racial or political minorities.

G. Some problem suggested by a course you are taking.

(Suggestion to the Instructor: This exercise may be assigned as an oral problem, perhaps to be presented for classroom discussion on the day before Unit 5 is prepared. Thereafter, the student could be assigned another topic from this same list, to be worked out in writing and to be submitted by him when he submits a written solution to Exercise 2 on page 86.)

# UNIT 5

## The Nature and Structure of Belief

### §5.1 Conscious and Unconscious Beliefs

In §2.1, we noticed that beliefs exist and function as guides to action, supplementing and correcting the guidance provided by instinct and habit. In §2.2, we noticed that beliefs are the natural product of thought, and that the adoption of a problem-solving belief constitutes the third and final phase in an act of thought. Thus, we were discussing their use and function. In the present unit, we shall try to see something of the *nature* and *structure* of beliefs, what they are as opposed to how they are used. This is important because the principles of right reason, which have to do with the correctness of beliefs we contemplate or have already adopted, can be thoroughly understood only after we analyze this nature and structure.

In the first place, it is natural to think of our beliefs as something of which we are conscious. This natural tendency has perhaps even been reinforced by those remarks in §2.2, which spoke of the adoption of a problem-solving belief as the third and final phase in an act of thought. Nevertheless, we must notice that we do not continually hold in consciousness all our beliefs, and that some beliefs are probably held without our ever being conscious of them.

Let us take these situations one at a time. You and I probably share a belief that two times three equals six. Each of us has probably held this belief ever since he first learned his multiplication table in elementary school. Or again, you and I probably share a belief that the Earth is round. Here too, we have each of us held that belief for many years. And yet we have not been constantly aware of these matters during all the time that we believed them.

 Belief involves a readiness to act as though something were true. As long as the readiness so to act persists, the belief persists; when the readiness so to act has disappeared, the belief has disappeared.

This *readiness* to act persists even when we are not acting on it, that is, when we are not utilizing it. For example, I am not always multiplying two by three, but I am always ready or prepared to get six when I do multiply two by three. Or, to take another example, suppose that this is a hot-water faucet. As long as I believe that, I am ready to act as though it were true: ready to turn it on when I want hot water, to turn on some other faucet rather than it when I want cold water, and in general not to turn it on unless I want hot water. But through a large part of my life, I am not thinking about water, neither desiring it, hot or cold, nor consciously desiring to avoid it. During those large parts of my life I am still ready to act toward the faucet as though it were a hot-water faucet.

Sometimes we give conscious attention to our beliefs, are aware of these states of readiness. Sometimes this happens even when there is no immediate occasion for action, sometimes when there is an occasion for action. At those moments the belief could be said to be conscious.

. Finally, a word about beliefs that are never conscious. In all of us there develop tendencies or readinesses to act in ways that would be appropriate if some proposition were true—that is, to act as though some proposition were true. The development of these tendencies may, or may not, involve a conscious awareness of the proposition and of the readiness to act as though it were true. Sometimes conscious awareness comes only after the readiness so to act is fully developed; sometimes it never occurs to us. A readiness of this sort may still be considered to be a belief, whether or not we ever attain conscious awareness of it.

It would take us too far afield from our main purpose if we were to consider adequately the points of difference between these never conscious beliefs and the instincts and habits noted in Unit 1. The line of separation is surely a thin one. But our primary concerns in this study are with the conscious and deliberate development and testing of beliefs. Let us only say that animals as well as human beings may be properly regarded as acquiring and holding unconscious beliefs.

## §5.2  Major Constituents of Belief

Whether beliefs are conscious or unconscious, they always involve two major components: an *attitude* (conscious or not) and a *content*.

The attitude present in belief is involved in what throughout §5.1 was called *readiness* to act as though true. This attitude of readiness to act as though true we call an attitude of **acceptance.**

However, this readiness to act as though true—this attitude of acceptance—is not sufficient by itself to identify a belief. According as the attitude is taken toward one proposition or toward another, we have different beliefs. For example, to believe that two times three equals six and to believe that this is a hot-water faucet is to have two different beliefs. Yet these two beliefs are not distinguished by any difference in *attitude*: each belief involves the same attitude of acceptance—same readiness to act as though true—as does the other. The two beliefs differ with respect to what is being accepted. This "what" is the content of the belief.

The content of a belief may be called a **proposition.**

 Thus **belief** may be defined as the holding of an attitude of acceptance toward a proposition.

### §5.3  Propositions, Statements, and Facts

The definition of belief, just above, referred to a "proposition." But what is a proposition?

The word "proposition" is one of those words of the sort discussed in §3.7 with which at least two customs have been associated. In accordance with one custom, a very old one, people say that a proposition is a statement or declarative sentence. Thus the sentence, "Washington crossed the Delaware," would be a proposition. According to another custom, a still older one, a proposition is not a sentence but is rather that which a declarative sentence "expresses" or *indicates*.[1] Whenever the word "proposition" is used in this book, we shall be using it in accordance with this *second* custom.

On the other hand, when we wish to refer to a declarative sentence which is indicating or expressing a certain proposition, we shall call that sentence a **statement.**

It is the custom of the sort that we have adopted which people have more or less consciously in mind when they say that two statements, for example an English language sentence and its French translation,

---

[1] In a later section, §14.5, we shall make a distinction between what a sentence *expresses* and what it *indicates*. At that time we shall notice that the sentence *indicates* a proposition but *expresses* the speaker's interest, concern, or attitude toward the proposition. But for the present, we use the words "express" and "indicate" synonymously.

"express the same proposition." Clearly the two sentences are not the same sentence, they cannot *be* the same proposition (in the first explained meaning of the word "proposition"). But they can have the same meaning. The proposition which they both express *is* that meaning.[2]

The explanations given so far, however, will not suffice as a *definition* of the term "proposition." This is true because these explanations suggest that the only propositions there could be are ones toward which people have taken attitudes of acceptance or ones that certain statements express or indicate. The definition must allow that there may be some propositions that have never been the content of a belief and that no language yet devised will express.

By a **proposition** we understand any situation or state of affairs whatsoever.

It makes no difference whether that situation or state of affairs is actual or not, nor whether any person has conceived or thought of it or not, that state of affairs is still a proposition. Thus, Washington's crossing the Delaware is one proposition, two plus two's equaling four is a second proposition, and the Earth's being flat is a third proposition.

Propositions, or states of affairs, are either true or false, actual or not actual. If a proposition is true, it is called a **fact**: if it is false, it is said not to be a fact. Thus, facts are true propositions.[3]

Having explained what is to be understood by the word "proposition," we may re-examine the definition of belief at the end of the preceding section. According to that definition, belief involves *accepting*

---

[2]  It is too complicated to explain at this early stage in just what sense a proposition is the meaning of a statement. The following note may, however, be helpful to those who are reviewing this unit after having read Part III.

A statement is like a singular term; in particular, it is like a definite description (§18.3) in that it purports to refer to one and only one proposition. Now the proposition to which it purports to refer is its meaning in the sense that it is its *referent* (see §21.6). But if the proposition does not exist—is not true or actual, that is, is not a fact—then the statement has no referent but only a purported referent, and in that sense it has no meaning or has a null extension (see §§20.6 and 21.6).

On the other hand, every statement—even one without an actual referent—will have a meaning in the sense of a total strict intension (§23.2). But it will not be worth our while to investigate this sense of meaning at this juncture.

[3]  Some scientists use the word "fact" in a somewhat narrower sense, perhaps to refer to those true propositions whose truth can be *directly* confirmed by observation. But not all scientists are agreed as to how the word "fact" should be used. The definition given in the text is a useful one that is consistent with a wide range of usage for the term.

a proposition. As the proposition is the content of the belief, so acceptance is the attitude involved in belief.

## §5.4  Further Components of Conscious Beliefs

Every belief, when it is present to consciousness, involves a
third component: some sort of pictorial imagery. For example, I say,
and you surely believe, that some horses are gray. As you contemplate
this fact, there undoubtedly arises in your mind some imaginary
picture; perhaps of a fox hunt, with a dozen-odd riders in scarlet coats
spread out across the field, their horses at the gallop, hounds in the lead;
one horse is jumping a stone wall along which alders grow in irregular
clusters. Two horses, those near the middle of the field, are dappled
grays. Or perhaps the picture in your mind is that of a pair of heavy
gray draft horses drawing a beer wagon along a cobbled street beneath
an elevated train track, polished brass ornaments aglitter and red
tassels dancing as the horses walk. This, or something like it, is the
imagery that accompanies your contemplation of the proposition.

Now the interesting and important thing to notice is that this imagery
is *not* the content of your belief. Two people who have the same belief
will "think of" entirely different images as they attend to this belief.
Even one person has different images associated with a given belief at
different times. If we were making a psychological study of belief, we
should find the details and variety of this imagery well worth our time
and attention. But since our study is one of the principles of right
reason, we only mention the imagery in order to dismiss it, as the side
of belief which is of no importance to logical criticism. What does
constitute the important aspect of belief is its content.

## §5.5  Symbolic Expression as a Constituent in Beliefs

In the case of certain beliefs, particularly those of a more
complex, general, or abstract nature, still a fourth element seems to be
indispensably present when the beliefs are conscious. Whether this
element is actually a component of the belief, as are the imagery,
attitude, and content, or whether it is only associated with the belief,
we need not undertake to decide. Neither need we try to decide whether,
if it is a component part of the belief, it should be considered a part
of the imagery or considered an independent fourth ingredient.

The element to which we are referring is the symbolic expression
of the belief. This expression usually takes form in certain sentences of

a natural language (like English) or in certain equations or other formulas of the special symbolism of a relevant science (like algebra or chemistry).

In the case of complex, abstract, or general beliefs, no appropriate imagery such as we suggested for the proposition that some horses are gray occurs to the thinker as a fitting clue to the proposition. In such cases, the imagery called forth is more likely to be that of some sentence or formula expressing the proposition. Even when pictorial imagery is possible, the imagery of expressing sentences can also be evoked.

We have already commented, in earlier units, on the importance of language as a tool of thought. One thing which makes it so important is just the fact here mentioned: that imagery of the language may substitute for imagery of the proposition. It is through this fact that transformations of the language can substitute for experiments on the proposition. All these matters will, however, become the topic for a more detailed study as we go on. For the present, we must return to the study of attitudes and contents.

## §5.6 Cognitive Attitudes toward Propositions

It is important to notice that the attitude of acceptance involved in any belief is only one among many different attitudes which may be taken toward any given proposition. We may, for example, be amused by, interested in, inquisitive about, or doubtful of the proposition, to mention only a few attitudes. All attitudes toward propositions may, however, be divided into two basic groups: *cognitional* attitudes, those that contribute to learning and knowledge, and *noncognitional* attitudes, those that do not so contribute. It is only the cognitional attitudes that need concern us.

Among cognitional attitudes, we may distinguish four fundamental types: attitudes (1) of understanding, (2) of desire to understand, (3) of curiosity, and (4) of credulity. For all these attitudes, contemplated propositions are the objects.

Let us consider, by way of example, the proposition that *The Earth's moon is larger than any moon of Jupiter.*

1. As you contemplate the proposition expressed by the above statement, you will find yourself preoccupied to a greater or less extent with the task of "taking in" what the proposition really is. In some cases (perhaps in *this* case), the meaning of the sentence is entirely clear,

so that the contemplator experiences a sense of confidence that he *knows* what the proposition under consideration is. Thus, for example, in this case you may be entirely confident that you know (a) what is being talked about: the Earth's moon, and the moons of Jupiter. These are well-known satellites of well-known planets. Also, you may be confident that you know (b) what is being said about them: that the *volume* (not weight, mass, density, or other property) of the Earth's moon (counting the volume of its atmosphere if it has any atmosphere) *is* (not was or will be) greater than the volume of *each* moon (not of the sum of all moons) of Jupiter (counting in each case the volume of the moon's atmosphere if it has any).

But in the case of some other proposition, for example that *Horses are more intelligent than dogs*, we may not be so confident that we really understand what the proposition is. For example, is it being affirmed that *every* horse is more intelligent than *any* dog? or that the *average* intelligence of horses is greater than the average intelligence of dogs? And again, what *is* this intelligence, in terms of which the proposition makes a comparison between horses and dogs? Here, as we contemplate the proposition, we have an uneasy feeling that we do not fully understand it.

All these varying feelings of confidence and unease are to be considered together as various attitudes of understanding. What should be noticed is that these attitudes may be arranged in an orderly series, from a high of complete confidence to a low of complete confusion.

2.  If the attitude of understanding held toward a given proposition is one of unease and confusion, it is likely to be accompanied by a felt desire to achieve a greater understanding. This accompanying desire is an attitude belonging to the second type of cognitional attitude mentioned near the beginning of this section.

Attitudes of desire to understand vary among themselves in intensity. Sometimes a person is overwhelmed with a sense of urgency about reaching a fuller understanding of some contemplated proposition. But on another occasion, even though he feels that he does not fully understand the proposition, the desire to understand may be very feeble; the proposition, that is, does not operate for him at that time as a powerful stimulus to intellectual activity. To take an example, you may realize that you do not clearly understand the proposition indicated by the statement, *Horses are more intelligent than dogs.* And yet, you may have so little interest in horses, or dogs, or animal psychology, that you do not feel any particular concern to find out what the proposition might actually be.

On the whole, mankind is blessed with an incurable zeal, so that as understanding is less, the desire to understand is greater. But as we just mentioned, this is not always the case. Furthermore, it is not always true that as confidence in understanding increases, the desire to understand is diminished. In fact, sometimes it works the other way around. This is partly due to our general awareness that we can and do make mistakes; that we sometimes are confident of understanding when in fact we have *mis*understood. Hence, it sometimes happens that increasing confidence brings on an increasing desire *certainly* and *fully* to understand, that is, to avoid the pitfalls of misunderstanding. Increasing confidence sometimes operates to raise one's expectation that *complete* understanding is in fact possible; in a sense, partial success spurs one on to try for a complete victory.

3.   Turn again to the proposition that, *The Earth's moon is larger than any moon of Jupiter.* As we contemplate this proposition, we may be provoked to *wonder* whether or not it is true. This wonder is a mild attitude of curiosity. On the other hand, we may be seriously disturbed by a desire to determine whether it is or is not true. This would be a somewhat stronger attitude of curiosity. And the strength of our curiosity might reach such an intensity as to induce us to forsake all other activities until we can discover the truth or falsity of the proposition. Attitudes of enquiry then, differ like the two previous types of attitude, in *intensity*, varying from an intensity of zero, when we have no interest in determining the truth or falsity, to one that might be described as overwhelming.

4.   Likewise, attitudes of credulity vary in intensity from a high of *complete conviction* or *certainty* (as when a man is ready to risk his life on the truth of the proposition), through a middle range of more or less certainty (I am sure, I am quite sure, I suspect, that the proposition is true), to a low of utter doubt or indecision (I am no more inclined to believe than to disbelieve the proposition, I do not in the least know).

The word "belief" indicates that some attitude from the upper part of this range of attitudes of credulity is taken toward the proposition; the word "doubt" indicates that some attitude from the lower part of this range is taken toward the proposition.[4]

Now it should be noticed that two attitudes from the same range cannot be taken simultaneously toward the same proposition by the same person. I cannot, for example, at one and the same time strongly believe a proposition and also be in doubt about it. Of course, *two* people might take different attitudes, one might believe and the other be in doubt; and it is even possible that one person should take different attitudes at different times, say one day be in doubt and the next day reach a belief, or vice versa.

On the other hand, a person can, and does, simultaneously take four attitudes, one from *each* range, toward one proposition. He may, for example, be confident of his understanding, not desirous of increasing it, in doubt about the truth of the proposition, and anxious to find out about its truth. As already suggested, *any* attitude from any of the four ranges may be accompanied by any attitude from any of the other ranges. This latter fact is not so often recognized. Often it is thought that a high degree of confidence in respect to understanding or a strong conviction in respect to belief must be accompanied by a lack of desire to attain understanding or to attain belief: what I already understand or believe I cannot be anxious to understand or to find out. It is indeed often the case that the attainment of understanding and belief will diminish curiosity; but this is not always so. For example, the early Greek geometers knew and believed many geometrical propositions which they had learned from the Egyptians or their own Greek predecessors, such as that any triangle whose sides have lengths in the proportion 3:4:5 will contain a right angle. But they were consumed with a desire to *prove* these propositions. Or again, various Church Fathers, saints, and theologians have been convinced (as an article of faith) of the existence and goodness of God and yet have sought to establish this proposition. On the other hand, some propositions about which we are in complete doubt do not stir any curiosity at all.

There are four types of ignorance: (1) the ignorance of felt lack of understanding or (2) of doubt; and (3) the ignorance of misunder-

---

[4] For a discussion of disbelief, see the next section.

standing or (4) of error. If I experience confusion or am in doubt, I am ignorant as to what the proposition is or as to whether it is true. Equally if I am confident in my understanding but have misunderstood, I am ignorant; and if I believe the proposition to be true when it is in fact false, I am ignorant. The object or purpose of enquiry is to remove confusion and doubt and to avoid or correct misunderstanding and error. Enquiry proceeds in a rational manner when attention is focused on the proposition. The proposition must be analyzed, related to other propositions, tested by experiments and observations. When non-cognitive attitudes, like emotion, influence credulity, we find an irra-tional determination of belief. It is our aim to discover the principles that determine the meaning and the truth or falsity of propositions, and the methodological techniques that apply those principles in order to reveal or test that meaning or that truth or falsity. Hence, as we get further along in our study, we shall find the discussion to be less and less preoccupied with thinking and more and more preoccupied with propositions. We may go even further: it will eventually be less and less preoccupied with propositions and more and more preoccupied with the sentences and other signs that purport to indicate propositions.

## §5.7 A Note on Disbelief

The thoughtful student may have been disturbed by our account in §5.6 of the attitudes of credulity. You will recall that we set these attitudes in a range, from a maximum of complete confidence down to a minimum of complete doubt or indecision. Where, the student may well ask, does disbelief find a place in this scheme? For surely disbelief is an attitude of credulity. As I accept some propositions as true and am undecided about others, so I reject still others as false. This rejection, or disbelief, is a cognitive attitude that has not been treated.

Were our purpose one of giving a psychological account of disbelief, the suggested criticism would be entirely appropriate. People do assume attitudes of rejection concerning various propositions. Psychologically, perhaps, the attitude of doubt should fall on a scale midway between an attitude of complete acceptance and one of complete rejection. If, for the moment, we represent complete acceptance by $+10$, indecision by 0, and complete rejection by $-10$, we could represent the scale of attitudes of credulity as follows:

10 Complete certainty

9

8 Strong belief

7

6

5 Hesitant belief

4

3

2 Inclination toward belief

1

0 Absolute doubt

−1

−2 Inclination toward disbelief

−3

−4

−5 Hesitant disbelief

−6

−7

−8 Strong disbelief

−9

−10 Complete disbelief

Fig. 2

On the other hand, _every contemplated proposition has a negative or contradictory_. The contradictory of _Washington's crossing the Delaware_, is _Washington's not crossing the Delaware;_ the contradictory of _New York's being farther north than Boston_, is _New York's not being farther north than Boston_, and so on. Now, as we shall later observe, every proposition and its contradictory are opposite in respect of truth and falsity: one of them is true and the other is false. Hence, so far as I am rational or logical in my beliefs and disbeliefs, every degree of acceptance or rejection of one proposition will be accompanied by an equal degree of rejection or acceptance of its contradictory. If we were to represent this on a double scale, one under "_p_" for the proposition and the other under "not _p_" for its contradictory, the results would be as shown in Figure 3.

| $p$ | Not $p$ |
|------|---------|
| 10 | $-10$ |
| 9 | $-9$ |
| 8 | $-8$ |
| 7 | $-7$ |
| 6 | $-6$ |
| 5 | $-5$ |
| 4 | $-4$ |
| 3 | $-3$ |
| 2 | $-2$ |
| 1 | $-1$ |
| 0 | 0 |
| $-1$ | 1 |
| $-2$ | 2 |
| $-3$ | 3 |
| $-4$ | 4 |
| $-5$ | 5 |
| $-6$ | 6 |
| $-7$ | 7 |
| $-8$ | 8 |
| $-9$ | 9 |
| $-10$ | 10 |

**Fig. 3**

Thus, in the rational mind every attitude of rejection is accompanied by a corresponding attitude of acceptance, where the proposition accepted is the contradictory of the one rejected. Of course men are not always or entirely rational and sometimes do reject both a proposition and its contradictory; sometimes they accept both. But the program of logical enquiry is simplified by allowing the column with the positive value to represent both columns, or either one arbitrarily. Hence, in logic we represent rejection of a proposition by acceptance of its contradictory and get a scale of attitudes which in effect covers rejection, but actually uses only indecision and degrees of acceptance.

## REVIEW QUESTIONS FOR UNIT 5

1. Can a person believe something and still not be aware that he has this belief? Explain.

2. What are the major constituents of belief?
3. What is meant by a proposition? A statement? A fact?
4. What attitude toward a proposition is involved in belief?
5. What *other* constituents than the major ones mentioned in answering Question 2 are to be found in conscious belief?
6. Name and briefly describe four types of cognitive attitude that may be taken toward a proposition.
7. To which of the four types named in answer to Question 6 does the attitude involved in belief belong?
8. Does the type of attitude named in answer to Question 7 include any attitudes other than that involved in belief? If so, what are they?
9. Give some examples of noncognitional attitudes that may be taken toward propositions.
10. How may disbelief be treated without introducing a negative attitude of rejection?

UNIT **6**

# *Valid Grounds for Belief*

## §6.1 The Task of Phase Two in an Act of Thought

The foregoing discussion of propositions and cognitive attitudes throws additional light on the second phase in an act of thought. It will be remembered (§2.2) that the second phase consists of efforts to resolve the problem posed in phase one and leads to the attainment, in phase three, of a problem-solving belief.

Suppose that we had just formulated some problem in a question, had analyzed that question, and had classified it as direct, semidirect, or indirect (§4.2). What difference, with respect to the task involved in phase two, would be associated with these differences in the classification of the question?

If our problem has been formulated in a direct or a semidirect question, this means that we have before us for consideration some definite proposition (the direct question) or group of propositions (the semidirect question). Provided our analysis of the question has been adequate, these propositions are clearly and accurately understood. Hence, the remaining problem consists simply and solely in ascertaining for each presented proposition whether it is true or false. Thus the problem is one of deciding whether an attitude of acceptance is appropriate toward the given proposition or toward its contradictory (§5.7). The problem exists because we confront the proposition with a more or less intense attitude of curiosity *and*, perhaps, an attitude of doubt. The problem will be resolved when we find adequate grounds for retaining or changing the attitude of acceptance by another of acceptance (for the contradictory), or for replacing the original attitude of doubt with one of acceptance, either of the proposition or of its contradictory. On the other hand, if the analysis of the question has not been sufficiently thoroughgoing to provide a clear understanding of the proposition in question, efforts to decide on its truth or falsity must be postponed until it is more clearly understood.

Finally, when a problem must be formulated in an indirect question, there is no presented proposition or group of propositions toward which we have only to reach an attitude of acceptance. Instead, our problem is, in part, one of discovering a proposition which at one and the same time:

1.   Provides an intelligible answer to the question, and

2.   Is such that the available evidence justifies our assuming toward it an attitude of acceptance.

It stands to reason that tasks as different in kind as these which we have just considered will be satisfactorily performed only by differing methods. Other differences, even among problems of the same kind, make advisable still other differences in the choice of problem-solving methods. In fact, no hard and fast program can be laid down as the one which must always be followed. Nevertheless, every effective example of problem-solving might be viewed as a *combination* of one sort or another, and more or less complex, of activities that all fall into a fairly small number of types. Each of these types of activity we shall speak of as a **primary,** or as an **auxiliary, valid ground** for belief. In the remainder of this unit, we shall undertake to see what the primary valid grounds may be.

## §6.2  Observation

The first, and probably the most important, primary ground for belief is observation. By **observation** we understand any gathering of information through the more or less unaided or unsupplemented use of any organ of sensation: sight, hearing, smell, taste, touch, or kinesthesia. Many simple problems are solved by the exclusive use of this method. I wonder what color is the desk; I look at it and find that it is brown. I wonder whether it is raining; I look out the window and see that it is. I wonder what the desk is made of; perhaps I look at it and touch it (so as not to be deceived by painted metal) and find that it is wooden. I wonder what type of fabric is used in this garment; I look, feel, and even smell it, and find that it is Harris tweed.

In many other situations, the problems that confront us cannot be so simply solved by a single observation or even by a group of observations. We cannot see the roundness of the Earth, the orbits followed by the planets as they move through the heavens, nor the intricate structure of a molecule. And yet we learn the truth about these matters at least in part by the use of observation. The natural sciences, with their expensive and elaborate laboratories, are monuments to our faith in observation as a source or ground for knowledge. A laboratory is nothing but a place designed to facilitate careful observations under carefully controlled circumstances. But the processes of observation do not *alone* reveal the wonders that our sciences discover. Scientific method depends on combining observation with other types of problem-solving activity.

When observation suffices by itself to solve a problem, we have that kind of incomplete thought previously called *trivial* (§2.2). But when our thought is not trivial, we shall often find that observation takes its place as an indispensable factor in the problem-solving stage of the complete thought.

It should be pointed out here that the background of a person's experience and knowledge enormously affects what he can learn simply by observation. For example, I may be wondering what you have in your hand. A more or less casual glance reveals that it is a pencil. But observation reveals this to me, and so solves my problem, only because of my considerable background of experience with pencils. A primitive savage or a very young child would not "see" a pencil in your hand. The fact is that I have used my past experience in order to form in childhood, gradually and with a considerable intellectual effort, the idea or concept of a pencil. That concept was not reached solely by using observation, although observation contributed a share with other intellectual processes to the formation of the idea. But today, as I look at your hand, I do so in the full possession of this idea. The act of looking so to speak *automatically* calls forth that idea, which I see to be relevant as a solution to my problem.

Also, it should be pointed out that observation, although an indispensable ground of knowledge, is not entirely free from the possibility of error. I may think I see my friend across the campus, but when I run over to him, calling him to wait, I discover that I have halted a total stranger. The stories of eye-witnesses to some event are frequently and notoriously inconsistent with one another. Some people are color-blind, others tone-deaf. And so it goes. But all these risks of mistakes in observation do not deprive this ground or basis of its utility. It still remains an indispensable source. All that can be said is that we must be cautious in accepting the evidence of our senses; that when any reason for doubting this evidence occurs, we must check what the senses reveal by other testimony. But here is the interesting point: by and large this other testimony will include *additional* sensory evidence; we look *again*, more carefully, we taste, touch, listen to, and so on. Frequently, of course, this additional testimony is not purely observational; it might involve asking someone else to look, or reasoning out a confirmatory experiment and then performing it. Yet it will more likely than not involve some reliance on observation at some point or points.

### §6.3 Actualization

Beside observation, we make use of a kind of activity that may be called *actualization*. Suppose I wondered whether heated iron retains its blackish color or whether instead the heated iron exhibits a different color. If I were to depend solely on observation, I might never find out because I am unlikely in the normal course of my daily life to see a piece of heated iron. But I can do something about it: I can take a piece of iron and deliberately heat it. What I am doing is *making actual*,  or **actualizing,** a state of affairs that I may observe what takes place in that state of affairs.

As the illustration may have suggested, actualization is oftentimes more a physical than a mental aspect of our problem-solving activity. But this distinction between physical and mental aspects should not stand in the way of our recognizing the activity as one by which the person, the living, breathing, thinking human, contributes to the solution of his problems. It is the residual of the method of trial and error, described in §1.3. When this residual is combined with other thought processes it becomes a component factor in the general activity of problem-solving by taking thought.

Also we might notice that, unlike observation, actualization can never function as the only factor in the problem-solving stage of thought. Actualization characteristically does nothing more than to *set the stage* for an observation; I heat the iron *and then* I look at it. But this stage-setting activity is frequently an indispensable factor in a problem-solving situation.

In fact, the reliance on actualization as an aspect of method is frequently made the basis of a distinction between true *experiments* and mere observation. An experiment involves the dual activity of actualizing one thing and observing another. Thus, the chemist is experimenting when he combines, heats, chills, refluxes, and so on in order to observe various results. The physicist is experimenting when he sets up balances and levers, alters the inclination of a plane, establishes electric circuits of a preconceived pattern, and so on in order to observe the results of these alterations. In contrast, the astronomer can do little or nothing to affect the condition of affairs on the stars and planets that he would study. His science is less an experimental than an observational science.

Just as we can make mistakes in observation, so also can we do the same in actualization. The doctor in a research hospital, for example, might be experimenting with the use of a newly discovered drug in the treatment of a given disease. He proceeds to administer varying amounts of it, that is, to actualize different conditions of the patient, with respect to the amount of the drug present in the body, and to observe the results. But he *might* get hold some day of the wrong bottle! Or he might administer later doses before earlier ones had been eliminated, so that the activity did not actualize a condition of the patient's system indicated by the size of the administered dose. All such activities could be classed as mistakes in actualization; not because they necessarily harmed the patient, but because they did not bring about the condition they were presumed to have actualized. Such errors may be guarded against in a number of different ways. One is to repeat the experiment. Every new discovery in science sets off a wave of activity in the laboratories; every laboratory undertakes to reproduce the confirming experiments. Sometimes this leads to the discovery that the original experiments did not actualize the conditions they were presumed to have actualized.

Another method of safeguarding against erroneous actualization is the use of independent tests for the presence of the condition sought. The doctor, for example, probably would not rely on the size of his administered dose as the sole ground for presuming that the patient's system contained such and such a quantity of the drug. He would analyze a sample of blood, perhaps, to confirm this fact. All sorts of other analogous procedures may be employed to check the authenticity of an act of actualization.

## §6.4 Analysis

Sometimes we solve a problem by *analysis*. A good example of the *failure* of the analysis, and also of a situation in which it would have sufficed, occurred on the radio program "It Pays To Be Ignorant." The morons were asked, "What river is represented in the famous painting of Washington Crossing the Delaware?" If you have ever listened to this program, you need not be told that the "experts" completely failed to get the answer. The situation, however, is one in which no observation and no previous information is required in order to "see" what the correct answer should be. The answer in fact is already present in the problematic situation. All that is required is to draw it out. This drawing out of the answer is what is meant by **analysis.**

Another, more serious illustration of the effective use of analysis was suggested in §4.5, dealing with factual versus formal presuppositions. There it was explained that the formal presuppositions are ones like *That desk has width*—such that analysis is sufficient to establish their truth or falsity.

If the foregoing examples make the process of analysis appear to be too simple a process to produce significant results, we might remind ourselves that analysis is the principal and distinctive factor in the mathematical sciences, one of the most impressive monuments to intelligence yet achieved by man. In other fields, analysis is prominently represented by the presence of definitions, which are largely the products of analysis. Of course, it figures in other ways as well.

While the method of analysis is occasionally applicable in dealing with indirect questions (compare the first example given above), and is especially appropriate when combined with other methods, its chief value when used alone lies in dealing with direct or semidirect questions. You will remember that in these types of question the problem is to determine the truth or falsity of a *presented* proposition or group of propositions. The second example, above, illustrates this use, the direct question being, *Is such and such a presupposition true?* In analysis, we simply study the meaning of the given proposition to determine whether this meaning is such as to render the truth or falsity "self-evident." To illustrate, the propositions, *All rich men are wealthy,* and, *Triangles (i.e., three-sided plane figures) have three sides,* are self-evidently true. What these propositions say guarantees that they are true. Similarly the proposition, *Either New York is the largest city in the world or it is not,* is a self-evident proposition; while *China is and is not more populous than India* is self-evidently false. In contrast, the proposition that *Boston is farther north than New York* is neither self-evidently true nor self-evidently false. To determine the truth or falsity of the latter, we must make some sort of observational reference, either direct or indirect, to the facts: look at a map, or otherwise determine and compare, the latitudes of the two cities.

Care must be taken to distinguish a reliance on analysis from one on memory or familiarity. Suppose, for example, that I were to ask, "Does butter come from cream?" You might be tempted to reply that of course it does, anybody knows that. But your knowledge of this fact can hardly be said to come from analysis. Rather, you are depending on your memory of a long-familiar fact. Your acceptance of the proposition is so well entrenched that you have difficulty in imagining how you could give it up or even bring yourself seriously to doubt it. But perhaps you can remember, as I can, an experience of your early childhood, when for the first time you saw someone take a bit of cream and churn it into butter. Maybe even before that time you had been told that butter comes from cream and had believed the proposition on the strength of that authority. In that early experience, you *saw* that the proposition was true. Your present acceptance of it rests ultimately on observation (mediated by memory), rather than on analysis.

Analysis is a basic and indispensable source of knowledge. Without it, we should be entirely limited in our knowledge to those meager tidbits that can be gathered solely by observation. In fact, most of our important knowledge arises out of a combined use of observation and analysis, as we shall see later on. Neither ground used alone can give us very much in the way of intrinsically valuable knowledge.

Nevertheless, analysis is a ground of belief that is liable to error and misuse. It is notorious that people disagree with one another over what is self-evident and what is not. For example, the existence of God and the axioms and postulates of geometry have all been taken to be self-evident by some people, while their self-evidence (although not always their truth) has been as vigorously denied by others. The framers of our American Declaration of Independence "hold these truths to be self-evident, that all men are created equal, that they are endowed by their Creator with certain unalienable Rights, that among these are life, liberty and the pursuit of Happiness. . . . That to secure these rights, . . ." and so on. But by some people these same propositions have been regarded as true but not self-evident. Plainly, some criterion for the validity of analysis as a ground for belief is required. It is a major part of the task of logic to formulate such a criterion. We shall return, then, to the discussion of analysis in subsequent units of this book.

## §6.5 Inference

It is important not to confuse analysis with *inference*, the fourth basic ground for problem-solving. Analysis and inference are intimately related and may in fact be grouped together as two modes of *reason*, in this respect being contrasted with the other basic grounds. **Inference** is the passage of the mind from one or more already accepted beliefs to the acceptance of another. The already accepted propositions constitute the evidence for the truth of the inferred propositions. Regarded as evidence, these propositions may be spoken of as the several *premises* in the inference. The proposition whose acceptance is brought about by the inference is called the *conclusion*.

Inference is an activity of thought almost constantly brought into use as a means for establishing a belief or reaching the solution to a problem. But to illustrate its use, consider the following situation. I am wondering how large is a certain section of roof which I wish to reshingle.

To solve this problem, I assemble the following bits of evidence:

1.   The roof area is triangular. (Established by observation.)

2.   The area of a triangle equals one half the product of its base and its height. (Recalled from geometry, where it was established by analysis and inference.)

3.   The base (distance along the eaves) of this triangular roof is 22 feet long. (Established by observation in the form of measurement.)

4.   The height (distance from eaves to peak) is 14 feet. (Established by observation.)

From these four bits of evidence, I infer that the area is 154 square feet.

Or again, the defendant in a criminal trial might undertake to prove his innocence by establishing an alibi. The alibi is that he was in another place than the scene of the crime when the crime occurred. This alibi proves his innocence only inasmuch as its acceptance allows us to *infer* that he was not at the scene of the crime when it occurred; and to *infer* from this intermediate conclusion that he would not have committed the crime. Or, to take another example, the proof of a theorem in geometry is the outline for a series of inferences by which one may pass from the prior acceptance of the axioms and postulates to the present acceptance of the theorem.

It should be noticed that inference differs characteristically from the grounds previously discussed, in that it is a way of building new knowledge on prior knowledge. Observation and analysis do not necessarily presuppose any such prior beliefs as their foundations. Hence, inference cannot function as an entirely independent source of knowledge. To be sure, the premises of one inference may have been originally accepted on the strength of previous inferences; but then those inferences must have had their premises. Where and how could this whole chain of inferences have had its starting point? It is here that observation and analysis come into play. For every rational scheme of knowledge must rest eventually and ultimately on beliefs that are grounded in observation or on analysis. Thus, these two activities must provide the foundation stones for all beliefs that can be said to have rational grounds of any sort.

As observation and analysis are liable to error, so too is inference. We may, and frequently do, draw from presented evidence conclusions that the evidence does not warrant. For example, I might infer from the premise that *Some congressmen are not fools* the conclusion that *Some fools are not congressmen*. Yet acceptance of the latter proposition, no matter how true it may be, is not justified by the presented evidence. To prove it, I should require a different sort of evidence such as is offered in the proposition that *Mr. A. is a fool, but he is not a congressman*. The original inference is then erroneous.

As the example shows, inferences are not to be classed as right or wrong according as their conclusions are true or false. Rather the correctness or incorrectness depends on whether the presented premises justify the conclusion. We shall have more to say about this later (Part V): the criteria for valid inference are a major topic in logic.

## REVIEW QUESTIONS FOR UNIT 6

1. Name and briefly describe each of the four primary valid grounds for belief.
2. Which two of the primary grounds can be used alone, and which two primary grounds must be accompanied by applications of other grounds? Explain.
3. Can any of these four primary valid grounds for belief be erroneously used? If so, which ones? Illustrate.

UNIT 7

# Valid Grounds for Belief, continued

## §7.1 Memory

Two **auxiliary** means are frequently used in our efforts to solve problems. The one is **memory**, the other is reliance on **authority**.

Suppose you were in a dry-goods or department store looking for material to upholster a chair. Among other things, you want the color of the material to harmonize with the other dominant colors in the room. What are these colors? To answer this question, you rely on memory. Perhaps you regard your memory as not sufficiently reliable to justify your immediate purchase of the goods. But at least it will assist you in selecting two or three samples which you may carry home to check by observation.

Or again, I might want to determine the area of my desk top. I *remember* that the area of a rectangle may be determined through multiplying length by width, I observe that the top is (approximately) a rectangle, and I determine (by processes of measurement) the length and the width. I infer the desired answer to my problem. One premise to my inference was the remembered formula: $A = L \times W$. Had I not remembered that formula, or worked it out on the spot, my other data would not have enabled me to get the solution to my problem.

It is to be noticed that, in relying on memory, we do not necessarily recall how the remembered proposition was itself first established. Maybe it was first established by observation, actualization, analysis, inference, or some combination of these. Maybe it came into our own scheme of beliefs on the strength of some other person's telling us that it is true. Or perhaps it arose in our minds through the operation of less rational processes of thought. Of course, we *might* remember how we came to accept the proposition as true. But the plain fact is that most premises we use in inference are simply recalled as things we believe without our recalling the original ground for the belief.

66

The facts just considered make all reliance on memory more liable to introduce errors into our solutions of problems than would otherwise be the case. Even without this, there is a certain risk in trusting memory. For we do misremember things, that is, remember them inaccurately. But if the original proof was possibly faulty so that the original belief was incorrect, then even when our remembrance of the proposition believed is accurate, the evidence supplied by memory may be misleading.

The above considerations do not justify abandoning memory as a source of belief, any more than the possibly faulty character of observation justifies our trying to do without observation. In the first place, we surely could not get along at all without at least some reliance on memory. For example, we must at least remember the solution of our problem long enough to put it into practice. But in the second place, even more than this minimum use of memory is desirable. The more we can trust to memory, the more can we advance to solving new and more intricate problems, instead of having to solve over again problems we have treated before.

At the same time, our reliance on memory should be self-conscious and self-critical. In case anything occurs to cast any doubt, over either the reliability of our remembrance or the truth of the proposition remembered, we should be prepared to make confirmatory tests of that proposition itself. It is only to the extent that we believe such tests would corroborate the truth of the remembered proposition that we are now justified in accepting the testimony of memory.

## §7.2 Authority

As we rely on memory to supply us with data which we do not now test by observation, analysis, or inference, so too we may and must often rely on the word of some *authority*. For example, if we find ourselves ill, we seek the advice of a physician. He tells us what is the nature of our illness and what steps we must take to recover. The physician is our authority. What we do to find an answer to our question is to find out what answer would be given to it by someone whom we trust to answer it correctly.

Human life is from the first full of situations in which we rely on authorities for answers to our questions. At an early age the child is perpetually asking his parents, "What is *this* called?" A little later on, his constant query becomes, "Why?" It makes no difference in either case what answer the parents give him. He is content; someone who *knows* has told him. But the extent of this confidence puts a great weight of responsibility on the parents who must answer these questions.

Yet our dependence on authorities does not come to an end upon reaching maturity. Not only do we seek knowledge from physicians, lawyers, and ministers; our reading of newspapers, magazines, histories, and biographies is largely a dependence on authorities. So too is our use of the dictionary or encyclopedia.

Nor is our reliance on authorities confined to our nonprofessional needs for information. The businessman makes use of stock-market quotations as reported in the paper, of government statistics, and the like as data on which to determine a business policy. The chemist accepts by and large such tables as that of atomic weights, which he finds provided by his predecessors and associates, perhaps checking through one or two cases to be sure that he knows how the values are derived. The lawyer or physician may call in a specialist as consultant in certain specific situations.

It is customary to contrast the methods of modern science with medieval methods of inquiry by saying that the modern scientist does not base his beliefs on authority, while this was a primary source in the Middle Ages. The medieval scholar rested to a great extent on the authority of the Bible, the early Church Fathers, and the Greek philosopher Aristotle (384-322 B.C.). A standard illustration of the changed outlook is the story of Galileo (1564-1642). The story is that for some eighteen centuries scholars had accepted on the authority of Aristotle the view that heavy bodies fall faster than light ones. Galileo was not content to accept so basic a principle simply on the word of that ancient authority. Accordingly he dropped from the famous Leaning Tower of Pisa gun shots of different weights. The proposition was put to an experimental test and found to be false.

This famous experiment is often pointed to as the symbol of a turning point in the history of thought. No longer will scholars rest their beliefs on authority. Instead, the age of science is the age of reliance on observation and experiment.

Such a reading of history and such an understanding of the methods of our modern sciences is incorrect by being oversimple. The modern scientist is constantly using and constantly depending on the reported discoveries of his fellow scientists, both his contemporaries and his predecessors. But his reliance on authority, while fully as frequent as anything occurring in the Middle Ages, is of a different order. For the modern scientist conceives of his authorities as his assistants rather than as his masters. The assistant, or authority, has made observations, performed experiments, and drawn conclusions which the scientist himself *could* have performed, and *could* have drawn if he were able to spend the necessary time and, perhaps, the money. To illustrate, I could diagnose my own illness if I could take time out to go to medical school and learn what to look for and what are the effects of various drugs and treatments. Or the chemist could ascertain for himself the atomic weights of all ninety-six elements if he were to take the time and had at hand the necessary apparatus to perform the needed experiments. Hence, it comes about that our modern reliance on authorities functions as a timesaving substitute for a personal use of observation, analysis, and inference: we simply delegate to someone else the labor of making these observations, analyses, and inferences.[1]

In contrast, the medieval reliance on authority was accepted as a resort to a basis for knowledge quite distinct from any personal use of observation, analysis, and inference. As the prestige of the authority was increased, so too was the unquestionable character of his pronouncements. Sometimes, of course, the ground on which the authority rests was reported: observation, reason, divine revelation. But this was done less to facilitate the learner's checking the accuracy of the judgments emanating from the authority, than to allay or dull any tendencies to skepticism: the authority did not speak as he did because of some idle private whim; on the contrary, he was only the vehicle, by which some cosmic force (reason or God) made known to man its determinations of the nature of things.

To sum up, the medieval attitude toward authority was that it is *unquestionable;* the modern attitude is that though questionable it shall be frequently *unquestioned.*

---

[1] It is quite true that the authorities on whom we rely do draw inferences from their data that would perhaps never have occurred to us had we attempted to solve the problem ourselves. Thus we are indebted to them not only for reaching the conclusions, but even, if we check on their work, for calling our attention to these possibilities of inference. Nevertheless, once the inference is pointed out, we depend on our own ability to analyze in order to settle the correctness or incorrectness of the inference. The authority, as an able and intelligent assistant, calls our attention to something that we might otherwise have overlooked, but we reserve to ourselves the role of judge: is what he proposes correct or incorrect? We presume to be able to settle this by our own use of observation, analysis, and inference.

When put as in the preceding sentence, our reliance on authority can be even more fully understood in its proper context. Oftentimes authorities do not accompany their reports of conclusions with any, or at least any detailed, account of the manner in which they justify these conclusions. When we accept under these circumstances their conclusions for our own, there is a genuine reliance on authority. We do not question the validity of their truth-seeking program. Insofar as this acceptance is *rational* it is so because other considerations (such as that we see on the wall the doctor's diploma from a reputable medical school) lead us to suppose his conclusion to have been reached by a correct application of the basic techniques of observation, analysis, and reason. On the other hand, we do occasionally ask our interrogatee on what he bases his conclusion. Then he must report his observations, analyses, and inferences so that we may consider their validity before we decide whether or not to accept this conclusion. In such a situation, we are not exactly accepting the individual as an authority; rather, his relation to us is that of a collaborator. He points out possible observations, analyses, and inferences that we could make; we undertake to test these and to see whether they lead to the conclusion he suggests. The authority is one whose conclusion we accept without question because (at least in modern times) we believe that he has correctly used a method which (although we have not seen the details of his method) we could ourselves employ to reach the same conclusion. The collaborator is one who suggests for our consideration a conclusion and a problem-solving program for reaching it; we subject this conclusion and suggested evidence to a critical examination. If they pass this test, we accept the conclusion; if not, we reject it and seek another. To illustrate the contrast, it may be pointed out that our study of a geometry book is an example of the use of a collaborator; the author points out in his theorems propositions about the properties of space and spatial figures which might otherwise not have occurred to us, but each theorem is accompanied by a full proof so that we may judge for ourselves the adequacy of the evidence that supports it. On the other hand, our resort to a dictionary and our customary visit to the doctor more nearly illustrate the use of authority. The dictionary does not accompany each entry with a statement of the evidence that supports the conclusion that the spelling, pronunciation, and definition are thus and so. And the doctor seldom explains in more than a cursory fashion how his tests and examination support his diagnosis or why the recommended treatment is appropriate to the indicated malady.

Like reliance on the primary grounds and like the use of memory, trusting to authorities is liable to be misleading. Authorities, after all, are only human and they do make mistakes. Insofar as we accept their conclusions, we too are liable to reach mistaken beliefs. Hence, certain precautions would be appropriate. We can, for example, inquire into the general competence of the authority in the field in which he offers us advice: Where was he trained? How do other experts in his field regard him? Is the proposition he offers us one that has to do with his special field? (It would be foolish, for example, to accept as authoritative someone's word on art or on child care just because he was an acknowledged expert in the field of physics.) And what examples of prior success in dealing with the given type of problem can be provided? Even with all these precautions, the reliance on authorities will sometimes lead us astray.

But despite this risk, the use of authorities is a practice to be recommended. For without it the range of things which we may learn is far too narrow to provide a satisfactory groundwork for a full and healthy life. People must and will find out so much more by extending their own efforts through the intelligent use of authorities that the benefits far outweigh the penalties incurred through acquiring some mistaken beliefs. It cannot, however, be too strongly emphasized that this profitable balance continues only so long as the reliance on authority remains deliberate, self-conscious, and circumspect.

## §7.3 Some Concluding Remarks

In this and the preceding unit we have considered six valid grounds for belief:

| Primary Grounds | Auxiliary Grounds |
|---|---|
| Observation | Memory |
| Actualization | Authority |
| Analysis | |
| Inference | |

*Don't confuse*

It should be kept in mind that these six so-called grounds are in reality six kinds of things that people *do* in order to determine whether or not a certain proposition may justifiably be accepted as true. Thus, by "observation" is meant observ*ing*, and by "actualization," "analysis," "inference," "memory," and "authority" are meant mak*ing* actual, analyz*ing*, inferr*ing*, remember*ing*, and appeal*ing* to an authority.

To call these six grounds valid is to say that these are the six kinds of thing that a person might *properly* do in the second stage of an act of thought, that is, in the effort to reach a *justified* problem-solving belief.

In the next unit we shall consider three *invalid* grounds of belief; that is, three kinds of things that people often do in an effort to reach problem-solving beliefs, but things of such a sort that the beliefs reached by doing them cannot be regarded as justified. And in the latter part of the next unit, we shall consider briefly how the six valid kinds of action are often combined in one problem-solving act of thought.

But to return to the six valid grounds. Throughout this unit, whenever a new valid ground was introduced and explained it was also pointed out that it can be misused: one *mis*observes, improperly actualizes, *mis*analyzes, incorrectly infers, *mis*remembers, and appeals to incompetent authorities. In other words, there are numerous invalid applications, or examples, of these six valid grounds of belief. One major task of the principles of right reason is to provide guidance so as to reduce the frequency with which the valid grounds are misemployed.

One might well ask why, however, if *applications* of the six grounds can be *invalid*, should the grounds themselves be called *valid*. This is because the six grounds are *self-corrective* and *mutually corrective*: The way in which one finds out that he misobserved is, for example, by making other observations. In the same way, new inferences, analyses, remembrances, and the like will correct the judgments or beliefs reached on the basis of earlier applications of these same grounds. Gradually we learn what kinds of precautions to take that beliefs based on applications of these grounds may not so often be overturned by still further study, that is, by still further use of the grounds.

Thus, the continuing use of these six grounds tends to result in a shifting of beliefs into a steadily more stable pattern. It is this increasing stability in the gradually forming pattern of beliefs—a stability in which after a time new observations, analyses, inferences, and the like tend merely to strengthen the beliefs already attained—that justifies our calling the later beliefs corrections of the earlier ones.

Yet, no matter how careful we are and how many precautions we take, it will always remain the case that new uses of these six grounds will on occasion displace and correct beliefs reached through earlier uses of the same six grounds.

A related fact explains why the three invalid grounds discussed in the next unit are called *invalid*. They are invalid in the sense that *no* reuse of them tends to correct earlier uses of them. Reuse of these grounds may *change* one's beliefs; but it is not a change in the direction of a more stable set of beliefs, that is, in the direction of a set that finally ceases to change with still further reuse of these grounds. This noncorrective aspect leads us to maintain that no application of the invalid grounds is valid.

## REVIEW QUESTIONS FOR UNIT 7

1. Name and briefly describe each of the two auxiliary grounds for belief.
2. What is the significance of the distinction between primary and auxiliary grounds?
3. Discuss briefly the difference between the medieval and the modern attitude toward a use of authorities.
4. Can applications of the valid grounds be invalid? Explain.

UNIT **8**

# *Invalid Grounds for Belief;*
# *Methods of Problem-solving*

### §8.1 Emotion as an Invalid Ground for Belief

We have now examined six valid grounds for belief—four primary, two auxiliary. There are, however, other elements that also tend to influence human belief. Any reliance on them must be listed as irrational and invalid. The distinction is this: the six grounds so far treated are such that *some* applications of them are valid and other applications are invalid. One of our tasks through the remainder of this book is to find criteria by which we may test applications for validity and invalidity. But the three grounds discussed in this unit are such that *all* applications of them are invalid and are to be scrupulously avoided.

The first such invalid ground consists in a reliance on *emotion*. Examples of emotional beliefs, that is, of beliefs accepted because of emotional associations, are familiar to us all. The lover is supposed to be blinded by his love to any imperfections in his beloved and to attribute to her all manner of good and endearing qualities which she in no wise actually possesses. Equally true is it that hatred causes people falsely to attribute to the objects of their hatred all sorts of detestable characteristics.

The influence of emotion on belief is particularly noticeable in such periods of national stress as war. You may recall that throughout nearly the whole first year of World War II, from September 1939 to midsummer 1940, the British government and the British people tended to stress a distinction between the German Nazis and the nonparty German citizens. It was often said that the war was not one against the German people, but rather one against the Nazis, a war that would liberate the Germans themselves, as well as the rest of Europe and the world, from the yoke of Nazi domination. But in the summer of 1940 as the losses and the trials of the British people increased, and more especially throughout the next winter when their cities were laid waste

74

by bombing, there grew up a hatred, directed not only at the Nazis but at the whole German nation from within which this terror and desolation came. And with this rising hatred came about a shift in beliefs. No longer were the Germans viewed as subjugated by the Nazi power. Now the rise of Naziism was conceived as a natural expression of the German national character. The German was described as abnormally subservient to dictatorship, devoid of any true feeling or inclination toward the institutions of democracy, one who wished to be ruled, and one who also sought vicarious glory in the military exploits abroad of that same power as ruled himself.

Now it is not our intention here to judge the correctness of this war-fostered appraisal of the German people. A careful and conscientious reading of history, both ancient and recent, would seem to show that it is not entirely wide of the mark. But at the same time, other historical evidence would seem to contradict it. To cite only two items, in the fifteenth century Germany was one of the prime centers of the Protestant Reformation. Surely this movement was, as much as it was anything, a popular demand for religious liberty, a repudiation and valiant struggle against dictatorship. To appreciate the full significance of this evidence, one must not forget that the political power of church and clergy was very much greater in those days than in these. And second, the very late date, only in the time of Bismarck, at which the German nation first achieved genuine political unity, argues strongly for a national popular love of local (that is, self-) government as opposed to dictatorial government from above.

As we said before, our present purpose is not to judge the correctness or the incorrectness of the later British appraisal of the German character. It *may* be true, or at least partly true. Our only purpose is to show how it arose out of the emotional stresses and strains to which the British people were subjected.

Any such emotional ground for a belief is wholly irrational. The belief, you understand, *may* be true. But the emotions which give rise to it do not *show* that it is true. They are a typically misleading ground for the holding of opinions.

The moral we can draw from the above is that emotion has no place as a ground for belief. Its presence actually inhibits the free and reliable operation of those grounds for belief—observation, actualization, analysis, and inference—which we have already discussed. Everything possible should be done by the seeker after truth to free himself during his search from emotional disturbances or distractions.

Let us cite just one precaution, selecting this one rather because it might be overlooked than because it provides so obvious an example. We have already talked a great deal about the use of language as a tool of thought. But we have also called attention to the esthetic use of language. Insofar as language is employed as an aid to the solution of problems, one should be careful to avoid the use of such language as is freighted with emotional significance. For the very contemplation of this language is likely to disturb the emotional balance with which the thinker views his problems. This is why emotional preachers, for example, are better regarded as exhorters of the faithful to action than as guides of the uninformed to truth.

The last paragraph suggests two points that should be briefly mentioned. First, there is a famous saying to the effect that, "The heart has its reasons, of which the reason has no knowledge."[1] The import is clear enough. Some things, so the saying and this type of belief maintain, can never be understood by the cold intellect: sympathy, love, and faith are the means to a "higher understanding."

Now there are several senses in which this claim is correct. If by *sympathy* and *love* we understand no more than the absence of prejudice and antagonism, certainly they are needed. For antagonism and prejudice are as strong deterrents to true discovery as are an excess of sympathy and love. Also if *sympathy*, *love*, and *faith* indicate a constant well of desire to understand, they are necessary: the problems of this world are too complex to be solved by half-hearted efforts. Even if these words suggest a point of view to be tried out, the saying would not be wholly wrong. For this point of view is one which awakens us to possibilities that might not be otherwise conceived. What is required is a "disinterested passion" for the entire truth, as it has sometimes been paradoxically and inadequately described. But if what is meant is that sympathy and love can actually *reveal* truths which rational inquiry cannot grasp, then the saying is mistaken. What they reveal must stand the test of rational inquiry, else it must be recognized as unproved.

On the other hand, and this brings us to the second point, sympathy, love, and faith do have a place in life, even in problem-solving. Life is not all one big attempt to solve problems and problem-solving

[1] *Pensées* by Blaise Pascal (1623-1662), Fragment 277.

involves more than justifying the problem-solving beliefs. In the first place, then, emotion properly operates in a manner to strengthen the sense of urgency with which we recognize a problem at the outset. Without emotion, there might be no awareness of a problem, and without continuing emotion there might not be enough persistence to enable us to solve the problem. The thing to guard against is letting emotional attachment or aversion to a proposed solution stand in the way of a fair judgment of it, based on the six valid grounds for belief.

In the second place, once our belief is settled by rational means it may be fortified as a guide to action if the content of the belief acquires an emotional coloration. Without this emotional corollary, rational beliefs might tend to be true and accurate beacons, but weak and unalluring ones. Emotion has its valid place, then, as the *fortifier* of belief, rather than as its *determiner*.

This becomes particularly evident in practical and theoretical situations in which the rational evidence is not conclusive. What the person *needs* is to get out of his state of doubt into one of belief; better a true belief than a false one, but better any belief than none at all. When the rational evidence is inconclusive and action cannot be safely postponed, then emotions may properly enough balloon a wavering belief into a full-fledged one that can give some genuine, even if faulty, direction to one's action. Let us then remain the masters of our passions (which is not to say remain without passion) rather than their slaves. Let us use them to carry us where *we* will.

## §8.2 Imitation as an Invalid Ground for Belief

The second fallacious source of belief is *indiscriminate imitation*. We spoke, in §1.3, of imitation as one among the three methods of problem-solving open to man and the lower animals. And so it is. It has in fact a valid place in the scheme of life generally. But as the capacity to solve problems by thinking increases, the reliance on sheer imitation should be subjected to curbs and safeguards.

Human beings are inveterate imitators of each other. There seems to be a general dislike for being different. This fact is illustrated in our slavish conformity to fashions of all kinds: fashions in dress, in music, literature, dance styles, furniture, and the like. Even the more enduring customs of a society are only partly imposed by earlier generations on the younger; in part these customs are willingly accepted and adopted. This tendency, to do what our neighbors do, extends even to matters of belief. Beliefs and opinions are taken up by a person simply because he finds his associates holding those beliefs. There is no deliberate consideration of the rational capacity of one's associates, no recognition of them as experts in the field. There is simply the desire to pattern one's ways of thinking after theirs.

In a sense, the reliance on authority is a case of imitation: we adopt as our own the belief which we find held by the chosen authority. But as we have already seen, this reliance on authority is appropriate as an auxiliary method of problem-solving only in case some care has been taken to select a *competent* authority. It is indiscriminate imitation, where no considerations relevant to the imitated person's capacity or expertness are taken into account, that is to be frowned on as fallacious.

### §8.3 Rationalization as an Invalid Ground for Belief

The third fallacious method of belief-formation may be called *ideological thinking* or *rationalization*.[2] This type of thought is very common and extremely difficult to avoid. In essence it consists in adopting whatever belief will justify an *already chosen*, or *already preferred*, line of conduct. As you can see, such a use of intellect is a complete perversion of the natural and proper function of thought. We have already described beliefs as guides to action. The belief, that is, serves us as the instrument by which we *select* the action appropriate in a given situation. But in rationalization the action has *already* been selected, perhaps through the operation of instincts and emotions, and one adopts a belief, almost *any* belief, that will give the appearance of justifying the chosen action.

Let us consider a simple example. A schoolboy is caught whispering and told to remain after school for half an hour. He had, however, intended to go fishing with the gang and has no desire to see his plans thus interfered with. As he broods over the situation, he comes to think how many people were whispering, and how unfair it was to isolate him for solitary punishment. The teacher must have a grudge against him. If he stays after school it will be to satisfy her grudge and not because he was whispering. That would not be right. She would be better treated if he showed her she could not bully him, could not work out her grudges in that way.

---

2   The widespread use of the word "rationalization" to name this process is perhaps unfortunate. We must be careful to observe that a rationalization is an *irrational*, i.e., *unreasonable*, belief which gains acceptance through its *faulty* claim to provide a reason for doing something we want to do. No rational beliefs are rationalizations.

Now it *may* be that the teacher *did* have a grudge against the boy in question. But if his thinking has brought him to a true opinion, it will have been the sheerest accident. The fact is that he did not intend to stay after school, and he proceeded to invent and accept a belief that would justify his not staying after school. He accepts it, not after any consideration of the rational evidence, but because it allows him to do what for other reasons he *wants* to do. His thinking is ideological.

Some of the most unhappy examples of man's ideological thinking are to be found in connection with racial theories and beliefs. Some sociologists even go so far as to say that the very concept of racial subdivisions within humanity is a myth, an ideological idea. However that may be, at least it is true that the traits and natures commonly believed to be characteristic of one race are assigned on ideological rather than rational grounds. One dominant group in a society seeks to justify its continued submergence of another group and sets about this by building up a picture of a "master race," all the while also creating another characterization of the submerged race. The master group may conceive of the submerged group as incapable of education, grasping, devoid of self-control, hence needing to be controlled and managed by an outside power, insensitive. Sometimes endearing qualities are attributed to the submerged race, but they are the endearing qualities of a child, who must be managed "for his own good." Equally the dominant race builds up a picture of itself: alert, responsible, maybe even unselfish: "the white man's burden." In a similar fashion, submerged groups build up pictures of themselves and of their masters, either such as will justify their resigned acceptance of their plight or as will justify perhaps violent revolt against it.

The prevalence of all such ideological thinking makes human progress doubly difficult. For the enlightened reformer must struggle not only against a mode of conduct but even against a mode of disbelief. He must undertake to *re-educate* people who do not want to be re-educated. Yet despite these difficulties such re-education is essential to any improvement either in our individual or our collective human circumstances. What we can do to make this easier and more effective is to realize that we are, each and every one of us, the victims of ideological thinking at some points or other. We can strive to resist these tendencies, which we recognize as pathological; and we can welcome whatever assistance other people can give us in getting rid of our own rationalizations.

### §8.4 Combinations of Valid Grounds. Stage Two in Problem-solving

We have now reviewed six valid and three invalid grounds for belief. A correct use of the valid grounds leads to valid, that is, justified belief. Any reliance on the invalid grounds leads to invalid, or unjustified belief. It makes no difference whether or not the proposition believed happens to be true: if the grounds for believing are invalid, the belief itself is invalid, unjustified; while if the grounds for believing are valid, the belief itself is valid, justified.

It is important at this point also to recall what was said in §7.3 concerning the six valid grounds for belief: there can be *invalid instances of every one of these grounds*. The remaining units of this book will be largely concerned with tests and studies by which we can hope to distinguish more effectively valid from invalid uses of these six types of valid ground.

But before we turn to those more detailed studies, it will be well to pause for a moment, so that we can see in a general way how the various valid grounds for belief might be made to work cooperatively in order to solve a single problem. This general survey will occupy our attention for the rest of the present unit. Furthermore, we shall return to this survey in Part Five.

In the first place, then, if one or two easy applications of the basic grounds lead to a solution of the problem, the problem is a trivial one in the sense described in §2.2. The criteria for correctness studied in the following units will apply as well to trivial thought as to complete acts. But the question confronting us at present is such as not to refer to trivial acts of thought. It is: What to do when full awareness of the problem, attained by such methods as were outlined in Units 3 and 4, does *not* suggest an easy method of solution?

It is possible to distinguish in general two types of approach to the solution of a given problem: the method of **direct inference** and the method of **hypothesis and verification.** In the case of the first method, we cast about among the *already known* facts to discover some from which we may infer a solution to the problem. One might, for example, ask himself whether the problem belongs to a *kind* for which he already knows a *rule* of solution, or whether it can be broken up into a series of problems for which he knows separate rules of solution. To illustrate, suppose that we were concerned to find the area of a given surface;

we could ask: Is the surface a rectangle, for which I know the rule

$$A = L \times W,$$

or a triangle, for which I know the rule

$$A = B \times \frac{H}{2},$$

or a circle, for which I know the rule

$$A = \pi \times r^2;$$

or can the surface be subdivided into figures for which I know rules, so that I can find the areas of the parts by the known rules and then get the area of the whole by the process of adding the discovered areas of the parts? If one discovers that the problem does belong to a kind for which he knows a rule or rules of solution, he may then ask what data are required (such as length or radius) in order to *apply* the known rule or rules; whether he has these data at hand, or whether, if they are not at hand, he can secure them. To ascertain the rule or rules and the data required for their application, one may be likely to make use of any or all methods of observation, actualization, analysis, inference, memory, and authority. But once in possession of the rule and of the data that its use requires, calculating the solution according to the rule from the data will be an act of inference.

Many problems, however, do not belong to recognizable types for which rules of solution have been or can be worked out. In such cases we apply the method of direct inference by amassing whatever data seem to us *might* bear on the solution, and out of these we try to analyze or infer a solution. There is unfortunately no rule that can be laid down to guide the searcher toward a discovery of relevant data. When identifiable types of problem are in hand, rules of calculation can be taught, and these rules do generally specify the possession of certain data. But when the problem belongs to no known type for which rules have been worked out, then the individual can only proceed by considering whatever data seem to him might be relevant. He must examine these items in an effort to discover what, if anything, they do imply relative to the question asked. And from them he must attempt to infer a solution.

The method of *hypothesis and verification* has gained great favor with advances of our natural sciences, which largely illustrate its systematic application. In essence, this method consists in intelligent guessing and testing. One first makes a guess as to what the answer to his problem might be. This guessed at solution is called an *hypothesis*. He then sets about trying to test this hypothesis. The process of testing is called *verification*. If the test shows the hypothesis to be justified, one's problem is solved; if it shows the hypothesis to be invalid, one must make another guess.

It may be observed that the method of hypothesis and verification is really an adaptation of the method of trial and error (§1.3) used so extensively by the lower animals. What distinguishes it and what makes it so valuable is the fact that the hypothesis, or trial, is first entertained only mentally rather than being actually adopted and lived by, and that the subsequent testing is largely an intellectual tying up of the hypothesis with other beliefs; hence, the whole process is safer, quicker, and surer than the primitive technique from which it derives.

Both the method of direct inference and the method of hypothesis and verification have many different variations. They may even be used in combination with one another. For example, the method of direct inference may enable us to identify the *general* character of a correct solution, and we might then apply the other method to set up an hypothesis concerning the *particular* nature of this general type of solution. As we proceed we shall have to examine these two methods in more detail. At the present time it is important only to notice how each of them utilizes all the valid grounds of which we have made mention. To illustrate, the method of hypothesis and verification might proceed by setting up at the outset a number of alternative hypotheses. These may then be *analyzed*, bringing out the fact that one of them *must* be the correct solution. From each in turn certain *inferences* will be drawn, conclusions that would have to be true if that hypothesis were true. The truth or falsity of these conclusions is then ascertained, either by *observation, actualization and observation, memory, or authority*. In case the conclusions are found false, the hypothesis from which they were derived must be *inferred* to be likewise false. This testing of the alternative hypotheses may continue until all but one of them has been eliminated as false. In the light of our previous analysis which had shown that one of them must be true, we may now *infer* that the sole remaining hypothesis is true.

The process just described is often beautifully illustrated in the reasoning of detectives, both in real life and in fiction. The reader should find it profitable to attempt an application of some such descriptive account as ours in the last paragraph to a piece of reasoning like the following by Sherlock Holmes in Chapter IV of *The Valley of Fear:*

"Is it suicide, or is it murder—that is our first question, gentlemen, is it not? If it were suicide, then we have to believe that this man began by taking off his wedding ring and concealing it; that he then came down here in his dressing gown, trampled mud into a corner behind the curtain in order to give the idea that someone had waited for him, opened the window, put blood on the—"

"We can surely dismiss that," said MacDonald.

"So I think. Suicide is out of the question. Then a murder has been done. What we have to determine is, whether it was done by someone outside or inside the house."

Among other things, the reader should observe how the above quotation illustrates the breaking up of a large question, say, "How did this man die?" into a series of subordinate questions.

One important point to be kept in mind is that on many occasions our best efforts at problem-solving will not provide *conclusive* proof that some proposition is a true solution to our problem. More often than not, all we can establish is that the proposed solution is *very probably* true. For example, suppose I am playing bridge and am about to lead. What card shall I play? It may be that my partner has in his hand the ace of spades. Thus, I could formulate a question: "Does my partner now hold the ace of spades?" In the effort to solve this problem, I may recall various bits of useful evidence: what bids my partner and my opponents had made, and so on. If, for instance, I recall or accept these two bits of data:

1. My opponent played the ace of spades on an earlier trick;
2. The deck is a proper one, and so does not contain two aces of spades;

I can infer that my partner does *not* hold the ace of spades. But if the available evidence is of a different sort, I may not be able to infer conclusively either that he does or that he does not hold it; and yet, I could perhaps reasonably infer that he *probably* holds it (or *probably* does not hold it). Oftentimes, we must content ourselves with inference of a probability conclusion.

In all such cases, it is desirable to make the estimate of the probability as accurate as is feasible.

Throughout the entire second stage of a problem-solving act of thought, it is important that we make every effort to have our understanding of relevant data, hypotheses, and whatever else we work with, as clear, precise, and unambiguous as we first made our understanding of the problem. To this end, we shall frequently find it useful to employ much the same methods and techniques as were discussed in Units 3 and 4. Thus, we can:

1.  Formulate data, rules of calculation, and hypotheses in language. (Here we should employ declarative sentences rather than interrogatives.)

2.  Define, explain, and perhaps illustrate any unclear words or phrases occurring in the results of step 1. Reformulate if desirable.

3.  Consider and list at least some of the implications of these rules, data, and hypotheses.

## §8.5 Conclusion of Part One

We have now completed a brief and rapid preview of the fields and topics with which the principles of right reason are concerned. We have seen that these principles consist largely of a combination of principles drawn from the sciences of logic and of methodology. We have also seen that, as reason depends on a use of language, a proper understanding of language is essential to an adequate grasp of these principles of right reason. We have seen, too, what are the six valid grounds of belief, how other invalid grounds are sometimes, unfortunately, allowed to operate in place of these valid grounds, how even the valid are sometimes misused or invalidly applied, and how finally the solution of difficult problems frequently requires the joint use of many or even all of these six valid grounds.

The survey we have made is, nevertheless, only a preview. The thoughtful student may have found it helpful in and for itself. But it should acquire even greater value after we shall have proceeded to fill in some of the details suggested by that over-all survey. For the rest of this book will be an effort to provide a more detailed and adequate understanding of certain items suggested by this preview.

The topic to which we shall now turn is the nature of language. We must understand more fully how languages develop, to what uses they are put, and how their words and phrases acquire the meanings that they have. Armed with that general understanding, we shall be able to turn, in Part III, to the study of topics more specifically belonging to the field of logic.

## REVIEW QUESTIONS FOR UNIT 8

1. Reread §2.11, and indicate how you think the topics for Parts Two to Five, as they are there explained, are connected with the six valid grounds for belief.
2. Name and briefly describe the three invalid grounds for belief discussed in this unit.
3. Sometimes a given grounding of a belief will illustrate simultaneously two or more of the invalid grounds. Can you give an illustration of this sort of situation?
4. Even though emotion is an invalid ground of belief, what legitimate connection does it have with belief?
5. Why is rationalization an invalid ground of belief?
6. What is the difference between authority (a valid ground) and imitation (an invalid ground of belief)?
7. What is the difference between the method of problem-solving called *trial and error* in §1.3 and the one called *hypothesis and verification* in §8.4?
8. Does the method of problem-solving called *direct inference* in §8.4 use any other valid grounds than inference? Explain.

## EXERCISES

1. Indicate which valid grounds for belief might be appropriately employed in seeking correct answers to the following questions, and explain briefly how they might be employed. (Remember that more than one valid ground may be used in finding the answer to a single question, and that in any case, if inference or actualization is employed, then at least one other ground must be employed.)

   a. If both the President and the Vice-President die, who assumes the office of the Presidency?
   b. Which of the following has more angles: an octagon or a nonagon?
   c. Did King Charles II of England suffer a violent death, or a natural death?
   d. Does the presence of fraternities on a college campus affect the scholarship of the student body?
   e. Under present circumstances, would the admission of Communist China to the United Nations reduce or increase the likelihood of another world war?

2.  Look up the definition and analysis of some problem which you worked
    out at the end of Unit 4. Outline the steps which you would recommend
    taking to reach a solution of that problem. Indicate at every step which of
    the valid grounds discussed in Units 6 and 7 you would be employing.
    These indications may be put in the margin of your paper, or in paren-
    theses.

    *Note:*  You are *not* asked to carry out a program of research and to find
    the answer to your problem; you are asked only to *outline* a program of
    research which, *if* carried out, *would* enable you to solve the problem.
    (Note to the Instructor:  See the "Suggestion to the Instructor" made in
    connection with the exercise at the end of Unit 4.)

# LANGUAGE

PART TWO

LANGUAGE

# The Concrete Bases of Language

## §9.1 Productive and Receptive Sign-events

It has been suggested in Part I that language is the great and indispensable tool of human thought and reason: not that every act of thought and reason depends on the use of language, but rather that whenever thought attains even a modest degree of complexity, only a reliance on some kind of symbolism or language can keep the several interweaving lines of thought sufficiently precise, clear, and distinct.

This reliance on language as a tool of thought can be made more effective and more trustworthy if we give some careful attention to the nature of the tool and the manner in which it works. It is for this reason that Part II is devoted to a study of some characteristics of language. The first, and almost the most important, thing to examine is the concrete foundations of language.

It is customary—and proper—to speak of, say, English and French as two languages. It is perhaps less usual—but equally proper—to think of algebra, or at least the symbolism of algebra, as another language, and the formulas of the chemist as belonging to still a fourth language. Yet these languages are each and every one of them, in themselves, extremely abstract things. If we look to the actual, concrete facts from which the languages are abstracted, we must see that these facts consist of people writing and speaking English or French or formulas, and people reading and listening to the noises and signs made by themselves or other people. In short, the concrete facts are things going on, things that we shall call **sign-events**. A sign-event may be roughly defined as any person's making or "reading" a sign.

Let us consider for a moment some of these sign-events. For example, some American traveling in France might say, with a very poor accent, "Avez vous un plume?" We may be tempted to say that he was not *really* speaking *French;* he not only mispronounced the words, but he even made such a grammatical error as to treat "plume" as masculine, saying "un plume," rather than as feminine (which it is), saying "une plume." It is nevertheless likely that the shopkeeper whom he addressed could have understood him and have responded by showing him a tray of pens. We shall call the traveler's speech a sign-event. In short, correctly spoken speeches and misspoken ones, as also correctly understood and misunderstood listenings, are one and all to be considered as sign-events.

Let us consider another example.[1] Suppose that you are traveling a lonely highway in the arid west and the radiator of your car begins to boil. With the water boiling away, you have to stop. As you look around, you see no sign of water anywhere. By lucky chance an old Indian comes down the road riding on a decrepit mule. As he comes abreast of you, you ask him, "Where can I get some water for my car?" His reply is an unintelligible series of grunts and "ool-ah's," and you realize with dismay that there is no common language in which you and the Indian can communicate. Before he can depart, you leap to the front of the car, remove the cap from the radiator, point to the radiator, make pouring motions, and gesture broadly around the landscape. The old Indian's face lights slightly, then he points ahead on the road, dips his hand, holds up two fingers, and finally makes pouring gestures. He prods his mule and moves off in the direction from which you had come.

With some misgivings, you start the car forward at a snail's pace in the direction toward which the Indian had pointed. The lack of water in the radiator prohibits travel faster than a crawl, or for very long without a halt to cool the engine. Yet at just 2 miles from the point where you had queried the Indian, you come to a dip in the road and are overjoyed to find at its bottom a spring, a dipper, and a bucket!

The Indian and you had communicated, and yet for this purpose you had used the signs of no established language. We shall nevertheless speak of your gesturing and of his as *sign-events*. But beyond this, we shall not undertake to decide whether or not the term would apply to an instrumental rendition of *The Star-Spangled Banner*, or to the modeling of a memorial statue; nor, if to these, then whether or not to more purely esthetic art-creations and art-observings. For the concerns of our study are not to be with these borderline cases, so that any question as to whether or not what we shall say about sign-events

---

1 Adapted from an actual incident narrated to me by Professor C. I. Lewis.

truly applies to the borderline cases would be beside the point, however interesting.

There is, nevertheless, a classification of sign-events that must be considered and that the earlier illustrations have somewhat obscured. The account of the communication with the Indian suggested two sign-events: your gesturing, to ask where water might be found, and his answering gestures, that said it would be found in a hollow 2 miles down the road. These two sign-events did in fact take place, but they formed only a half of the entire communicative process. For besides your *making* gestures, the Indian *observed* your gestures; and in addition to his making answering gestures, you observed his answering gestures. In short, people not only speak, but listen; not only write, but read; not only make gestures, but observe gestures; and the listening, reading, and observing of gestures are as truly sign-events as are the speaking, writing, and making of gestures.

We shall speak hereafter of **productive sign-events** and **receptive sign-events**: or for short, of **productive events** and **receptive events**. These terms are useful since they have a "nonpartisan" character that will help us avoid thinking too exclusively in terms of or about only one or two usual modes of communication and neglecting other important types of sign-events. Thus among productive sign-events we must count not only

1.  Speaking the words of some established language, like English;

2.  Writing, typing, or printing the words of such a language or the technical formulas of a branch of mathematics or science;

3.  Making the finger signs of the deaf-mute alphabet;

4.  Making gestures—like those to the Indian—that belong to no established language;

but also such other events as

5.  Painting, or causing to be painted, a yellow stripe on the road over the crest of a hill;

6.  Erecting and turning on, or causing to be erected and turned on, a red and green traffic signal at a road intersection;

7.  Affixing a postage stamp to a letter;

8.  Making a hand signal while driving a car.

Corresponding to each of these and other kinds of productive sign-events, there will be a related kind of receptive event: listening to, reading, or otherwise observing the signs and signals made in the parallel productive event. In fact, it is this matching of productive and receptive events which is involved in every process of communication.

## EXERCISES

1. Explain the sense in which the act of fixing a postage stamp to a letter is a productive sign-event.
2. Give two or three examples of productive sign-events different from the eight examples listed above.

## §9.2 Major Constituents of Sign-events

Despite all the variety to be encountered in sign-events, these events nevertheless have certain definite features more or less in common. In the present section, we shall note certain features of this more or less common structure of sign-events. The entire discussion will be developed by describing and naming the constituents, or parts, of any sign-event.

In general, a typical sign-event may be said to have three parts or constituents: an **interpreter,** a **physical sign-token,** and an **intended second-party.** Let us consider these constituents one after the other.

1. The interpreter of a sign-event is, so to speak, the "figure-outer." In another sense, he is the active, or the responsible, party in the event. In the case of a productive event, this person would be the speaker, or author, or sign-maker. It is he who is responsible for the signs that are being made, he "chooses" them (perhaps largely under the influence of habit and more or less unconsciously) and he in a sense manufactures them: spreads the ink on the paper; makes the noise or the gesture. What he wishes to communicate or express guides him in his choice of the particular signs that he makes. Thus, they are chosen by him out of a consideration of their effectiveness as conveyors of his thought or meaning. On the other hand, when the event in question is a receptive event, the responsible party, who is "figuring things out," is *not* the person who had already made the sounds or other signs being listened to or observed, but is instead the listener or observer himself. He must figure out what the original author meant by producing the signs he did produce.

 We shall frequently refer to the interpreter of a productive event as the **producer,** or the *author;* and to the interpreter of a receptive event as the **receiver,** or the *observer.*

We have spoken as though every sign-event had only one interpreter. Events with only one interpreter are, to be sure, the standard kind, but occasionally an event will have two or more interpreters. In the case of productive events, this happens whenever two or more authors collaborate in the composition of some message. To take an example, a famous old textbook, *Ethics*, New York: 1908, was written collaboratively by John Dewey (1859-1952) and James Tufts (1862-1942). The productive event which constituted the writing of this textbook had two interpreters. In much the same way, when two observers join forces to "figure out" some message, we are confronted with a receptive event that has two interpreters.

Situations of the sort just considered, sign-events with two or more cooperating interpreters, must be distinguished from situations produced by there being several sign-events each with its own single interpreter. For example, when a teacher addresses his class, each student's listening will constitute a separate receptive event with its single interpreter. There would occur a receptive event with two interpreters only if two of the students were helping each other understand what the teacher said.

2. The author in a productive event "manufactures" or produces certain signs, which will in turn usually be observed in correlated receptive events. In some cases, these signs are actual material objects, much as a loaf of bread is a material object made by a baker. For example, as the baker takes flour, yeast, and other ingredients, mixes them and bakes them to make bread, so the author takes ink or chalk or graphite, spreads it out in a certain pattern, and lets it dry (if it is originally a fluid) to make his sign.[2] But in other cases, the sign seems to consist in the physical *behavior* of material objects rather than in the objects themselves. For example, in the case of speech, the signs are noises, which are not themselves material bodies but are the behavioral properties of the atmosphere or other transmitting medium; or again, when gestures succeeded in eliciting from the Indian in §9.1 information concerning the whereabouts of water, the manufactured signs were

---

2 Whether we should consider the paper on which an author spreads ink a part of the sign he manufactures, or whether we should think of the paper as a sort of tray holding the signs, much as a dinner plate is no part of the dinner it holds, is a question we do not need to settle. We shall, however, often find it convenient to speak as though the paper were a part of the sign.

not the arms, hands, torso, and head of the gesturing party, but were instead the very motions of these bodily members.

In any case, however, the producer makes the signs: he either creates the material object out of material ingredients ready at hand, or causes some material body to act or behave in a certain way. In each case, the produced sign is a physical something: either a physical mode of behavior, for example, motion, or a physical object. The productive event consists in the creation of this physical sign.

For reasons which will become clear later on, we shall henceforth avoid speaking of the "physical sign" and shall speak instead of the **physical sign-token** or, for short, of the **sign-token.** Thus a productive event consists of an author's producing a physical sign-token, and the physical sign-token thus produced may be regarded as a constituent of the productive event in which it was produced.

Physical sign-tokens are, however, also constituents of receptive events. In fact, the receptive event actually consists of a receiver's observing a physical sign-token. As often as not, the sign-token observed in a receptive event is identically the sign-token produced in a productive event: I see the chalk marks you put on the blackboard, I hear the noises you make with your voice, I see the gestures you make with your arms. But in other cases, the physical sign-tokens observed in receptive events are only more or less adequate substitutes for the sign-tokens produced in correlated productive events. When I read the news story in the morning paper, I am *not* observing the ink marks "batted out" by the reporter on the office typewriter; instead, I observe *substitutes* for that typescript supplied by the cooperative efforts of the city editor, typesetter, pressman, and all their various assistants and cohorts. When I listen at the telephone or radio, I do not hear the sounds made by the speaker, but instead, I hear other sounds that are more or less reliable reproductions of the original sounds. And when I read the letter sent me by some businessman, I am not observing the sounds he made as he dictated to his secretary, but I observe instead the typescript she made as a substitute for his spoken voice.

Yet in all these cases, both productive and receptive events involve physical sign-tokens as constituents: in productive events, they are manufactured; in receptive events they are observed.

3. When we first think of sign-events, the great majority of those that first come to mind involve someone else besides the interpreter. Who these other people might be is always determined by the inter-

preter. We shall call these other people the **intended second parties** of the sign-events in which they are constituents.

Consider first a productive event. Most authors are addressing their messages to some person or persons. These people are the ones they *intend* to communicate with. They are, so to speak, the intended targets of the message. Whether or not the message actually *reaches* its target makes no difference with respect to the person's having been the target. The person intended by the author as recipient of his message is the intended second party of the productive event.

Let us consider two or three examples. John writes a letter to George. In this productive event, John is the interpreter, the letter he writes is the physical sign-token, and George is the intended second party. That George is the intended second party is in no sense dependent on whether or not George receives the letter. If the letter is destroyed in a railroad accident, or intercepted by some jealous member of George's household, or otherwise prevented from reaching George, it was nevertheless intended for George, so that George is the intended second party for the letter-writing event. Even nonliving or nonexistent individuals may be intended second parties. For example, George may have died unbeknownst to John. In such a case, he will not receive the letter, but he will nevertheless be the intended second party of the letter-writing event. In the case of the child who writes a letter to "Santa Claus, North Pole," the nonexistent Santa Claus is the intended second party.

The examples just considered had this in common, that in each productive event there was one, solitary, intended second party, who was clearly identified by the author. Other productive events differ from these by having either more than one intended second party or by having a less clearly identified intended second party, or by both these facts. For example, when a teacher addresses his class, each member of the class is an intended second party of the speech, so that there are several intended second parties. Again, a person who shouts for help may have no idea as to who, if anyone, might hear him; yet any person able to help who is within earshot is an intended second party. Here the identity of the intended second party is less clearly defined by the author. Finally, the reporter whose story appears in his newspaper intended it for several people (the several readers of the paper), but unlike the teacher who knows the members of his class, the reporter may be entirely unacquainted with the people who buy and read his paper.

We must notice that occasionally a person who receives a message is not the intended second party of the productive event that manufactured the message. For example, the detective from homicide reads the letters found in the desk of the deceased, but unless the letters were written and planted there for him to read, he was not the intended second party of the letter-writing events. Thus, just as failure to receive a message does not make a person fail to be an intended second party to a productive event, so receiving the message does not turn the receiver into an intended second party: everything depends on *what the author intended*.

The intended second party of a productive event will often be referred to as the **intended receiver** of that event.

Like productive events, so also receptive events have their intended second parties. The intended second party of a receptive event is the person *from whom the receiver understands* the message to come. The intended second party may or may not be the person from whom the message actually did come; he is instead the person from whom the message is understood by the receiver to have come. The intended second party of a receptive event will often be referred to as the **presumed author.**

Just as productive events may have one or several intended second parties, and these parties may be clearly or only vaguely identified by the producers, so receptive events may have one or several presumed authors who are clearly or only vaguely identified. For example, a poison-pen letter is usually taken by its recipient to come from some one person, but who that person is, is not clearly conceived. Again, I understand (whether rightly or wrongly makes no difference) that the news stories in *Time* are generally composite efforts. Thus the receptive event which consists of my reading such an article has several presumed authors. If you read the same article but think it to have been written by one person, the receptive event which is your reading of the article will have one presumed author. In the case of the article in *Time*, the identification of the intended second parties in the receptive event which is my reading of the article is only more or less clear: I assume them to include several (but not all, and I do not know which ones) of the staff members listed in the masthead of the magazine, with perhaps a few other contributors in addition. Yet the identity of an intended second party may be even more vague than this. For example, I observe a yellow traffic line in the middle of the road. As I "read" this message, I may understand that "the law" is telling me to keep to the right throughout the stretch of road marked by the yellow line. But who is "the law," the intended second party of my receptive act? I may give much or little attention to this question. It is, however, a kind of question that commands the attention of political scientists and political philosophers.

## EXERCISE

Who is the presumed author of a receptive event which consists in your "reading" a yellow traffic line in the middle of the road? Does it make any difference whether the stretch of road in question is within some city limits, or in the open country? Explain.

## REVIEW QUESTIONS FOR UNIT 9

1. What is meant by a productive sign-event? A receptive sign-event?
2. Must a sign-event involve the making or "reading" of signs that belong to an established language, like English? Explain.
3. Who is referred to when one speaks of the interpreter of a productive sign-event?
4. Who is referred to when one speaks of the interpreter of a receptive sign-event?
5. Under what circumstances would a productive sign-event have more than one interpreter?
6. Under what circumstances would a receptive sign-event have more than one interpreter?
7. Who is referred to when one speaks of the intended second-party of a productive sign-event?
8. Under what circumstances does a productive sign-event have more than one intended second party?
9. Must the interpreter in a productive sign-event have a clear understanding of who is the intended second party? Explain and illustrate.
10. Must the intended second party of a productive sign-event actually exist? Explain and illustrate.
11. Who is referred to when one speaks of the intended second party of a receptive sign-event?
12. Under what circumstances does a receptive sign-event have more than one intended second party?
13. Must the interpreter in a receptive sign-event have a clear understanding of who is the intended second party? Explain and illustrate.

14. Must the intended second party of a receptive sign-event actually exist? Explain and illustrate.

15. What is meant by the physical sign-token of a productive event? Of a receptive event?

16. Under what circumstances is the physical sign-token of a productive event identical with the physical sign-token of a receptive event?

# Communication; Undirected Sign-events

## §10.1 Preliminary Analysis of Communication

In the previous unit, it was noted that the typical sign-event involves three constituents or types of constituent: one or more interpreters, a physical sign-token, and one or more intended second parties. Furthermore, it was noted at the end of §9.1 that the typical act of communication involves two sign-events: the one a productive event, the other a conjoined receptive event. In the simplest forms of communication, the physical sign-tokens of the two conjoined events are identical. Also, the intended second party of each is identical with the interpreter of the other. Let us consider two or three examples.

EXAMPLE 1. George writes a letter to Bill.

| Productive Event George writing the letter | | | Receptive Event Bill reading the letter | | |
|---|---|---|---|---|---|
| Interpreter | Physical sign-token | Intended 2d party | Interpreter | Physical sign-token | Intended 2d party |
| George | The letter | Bill | Bill | The letter | George |

EXAMPLE 2. Mary calls John into the house for dinner.

| Productive Event Mary calling John | | | Receptive Event John listening to Mary's call | | |
|---|---|---|---|---|---|
| Interpreter | Physical sign-token | Intended 2d party | Interpreter | Physical sign-token | Intended 2d party |
| Mary | The sounds that Mary makes | John | John | The sounds that Mary makes | Mary |

EXAMPLE 3. You ask the Indian where water can be secured for your car.

| | Productive Event | | | Receptive Event | |
| --- | --- | --- | --- | --- | --- |
| | You making gestures | | | The Indian observing your gestures | |
| Interpreter | Physical sign-token | Intended 2d party | Interpreter | Physical sign-token | Intended 2d party |
| You | The gestures that you make | The Indian | The Indian | The gestures that you make | You |

In all three examples just given, it was presumed that the communication was successful. In the following examples, communication breaks down in one way or another. Notice how this breakdown might involve nothing more than the fact that the intended second party in one of the conjoined events is not identical with the interpreter of the other.

The telephone has rung in the McClellan household. Mary answers the phone and learns that John is the party wanted. She goes to the back door, sees a man working in the field whom she takes to be John, and calls him to the telephone.

EXAMPLE 4. It *is* John working in the field, but he thinks it is Alice who is calling him to the telephone.

| | Productive Event | | | Receptive Event | |
| --- | --- | --- | --- | --- | --- |
| Interpreter | Physical sign-token | Intended 2d party | Interpreter | Physical sign-token | Intended 2d party |
| Mary | The sounds that Mary makes | John | John | The sounds that Mary makes | Alice |

EXAMPLE 5. It is Bob, instead of John, who is working in the field. Bob, however, recognizes Mary as the caller.

| | Productive Event | | | Receptive Event | |
| --- | --- | --- | --- | --- | --- |
| Interpreter | Physical sign-token | Intended 2d party | Interpreter | Physical sign-token | Intended 2d party |
| Mary | The sounds that Mary makes | John | Bob | The sounds that Mary makes | Mary |

EXAMPLE 6. The same as Example 5, except that Bob mistakes Mary for Alice.

| Productive Event | | | Receptive Event | | |
|---|---|---|---|---|---|
| Interpreter | Physical sign-token | Intended 2d party | Interpreter | Physical sign-token | Intended 2d party |
| Mary | The sounds that Mary makes | John | Bob | The sounds that Mary makes | Alice |

In all six examples just considered, the physical sign-token of the receptive event was identically the same object as the physical sign-token of the conjoined productive event; that is, the observer observed what the producer had produced. However, more complicated processes of communication do take place; and in these cases, the physical sign-tokens in the receptive event are *not identical with*, but are more or less acceptable *substitutes* for, the physical sign-tokens of the conjoined productive event. Let us consider two examples.

EXAMPLE 7. Mr. Jones, president of the Tri-Mutual Company, sends a letter to Mr. Smith.

| Productive Event | | | Receptive Event | | |
|---|---|---|---|---|---|
| Mr. Jones dictating to Miss Tivoli | | | Mr. Smith reading Mr. Jones's letter | | |
| Interpreter | Physical sign-token | Intended 2d party | Interpreter | Physical sign-token | Intended 2d party |
| Mr. Jones | The sounds that Mr. Jones makes | Mr. Smith | Mr. Smith | The letter that Miss Tivoli typed | Mr. Jones |

EXAMPLE 8. Eugene O'Neill writes a play.

| Productive Event | | | Receptive Event | | |
|---|---|---|---|---|---|
| Eugene O'Neill typing the play | | | A member of the audience hearing and watching the play | | |
| Interpreter | Physical sign-token | Intended 2d party | Interpreter | Physical sign-token | Intended 2d party |
| Mr. O'Neill | The original typescript of the play | Member of the theater audience | The member of the audience in question | The voices, gestures, etc., of the cast | E. O'Neill (assuming the member knew who wrote the play) |

## §10.2 Directed and Undirected Sign-events

So far in this and the preceding unit we have considered how sign situations may be analyzed into productive and receptive sign-events and how these productive and receptive events may combine to constitute an act of communication. We have noticed that the typical sign-event, whether it be productive or receptive, involves three constituents: an interpreter, a sign-token, and an intended second party.

In the present section, we shall consider the question whether or not every sign-event *must* have all three of the usual constituents. The explanation of this question will throw more light on the meanings of the terms "sign-event," "interpreter," "physical sign-token," and "intended second party."

Let it be agreed at once that there is no such thing as a sign-event without a physical sign-token and an interpreter. That is to say, every occurrence in the world which is to be regarded as a productive sign-event will involve an author who (or which) *produces* physical sign-tokens, and every occurrence which is to be regarded as a *receptive* sign-event will involve a receiver, who (or which) *observes* physical sign-tokens. Thus, in a sense, the question boils down to this: Do all sign-events have intended second parties? The answer to this question is in the negative.

Sometimes people speak, and perhaps even write, without addressing their message to anyone. Let us take two examples.

1. Bill is not a very good carpenter, but when he realizes one day that his library has outgrown his bookcases, he buys some boards at the lumber mill and proceeds to erect some new shelves. In the course of these operations, he looks at his watch and realizes that within a minute he must leave for his three o'clock class. In his haste to get the last shelf in place before going to class, he hits his thumb a resounding whack with the hammer. "Ouch! damn!" cries Bill.

Now Bill was not talking to anyone, not even to himself. He was just talking. The productive event which consisted of his expostulation had no intended second party.

2. It was a beautiful spring morning in a beautiful suburban town as Wallace kissed his wife good-bye and left to catch the 7:46 for town and business. Unlike many of his fellow passengers on the 7:46, Wallace had allowed plenty of time for the walk to the railroad station. The sweet perfume of springtime was in the air. "Oh to be in England now

that April's there," sighed Wallace as he walked down Maple Lane. He was not talking to anyone. The productive event had no intended second party.

Productive events like the above, which have no intended second party, must be carefully distinguished from ones in which the author is literally talking to himself. If you make a memorandum, or take some lecture notes in class, or write down a column of figures so as to add them up to find the sum, every one of these productive events has an intended second party: you yourself.

So much for productive events: some of them have no intended second party. Is the same sort of thing true of receptive events? That is to say, does an observer ever "read" a message and regard the message as not coming from anyone—as not having an author?

We must be very careful not to confuse the question just asked with another, similar question. The distinction between them can perhaps be brought out by an example. Suppose that I pick up the newspaper some day and read an item that has no by-line. I read the item without once giving any thought to the question, Who is supplying me with this information? In other words, I do not consciously think of the message while I read it as coming from any particular author. Nevertheless, if someone were to ask me later on whether I believed that it did have an author, I should unhesitatingly say, "Of course it did." The situation is like that in which you may be said to believe that six times nine equals fifty-four even at moments when you are not thinking about this matter. The question here to be discussed is not one as to whether or not we always give conscious attention to the authorships of the messages we read; but whether or not, *if* we were to give attention to it, we should sometimes reach the opinion that the messages we read have no authors.

Let us consider another example. Suppose that we are tramping along a country road in the midst of a thunderstorm and we see a bolt of lightning strike a boulder in such a way as to leave on its surface a series of marks which look for all the world like the English word, "HALT!" As we "read" this "message" we may be tempted to say that here is a receptive event with no intended second party. To be sure, the lightning *caused* the marks, but this no more justifies our calling the lightning the author of the message than would the fact that Eugene O'Neill used a typewriter, in Example 8 of §10.1, justify us in calling the typewriter the author of the play. In short, the intended second party of a receptive event is the individual supposed by the observer to be making *deliberate* signs that are either directed to him or overseen by him.

If we had been accompanied on our tramp through the woods by an English-reading primitive savage, his reading of the lightning strokes *might* have involved an intended second party. He could have thought of the message as coming from the presiding genius of the forest or some deity who used the lightning as a pencil to warn us from penetrating farther into the sacred grove. But we, more "enlightened" twentieth-century hikers, would probably insist that no being, neither mortal nor divine, was using the lightning to *tell* us anything. In brief, if the event was considered by us to be a receptive sign-event at all, it would be taken as one without an intended second party.

The last sentence of the preceding paragraph, in fact, raises an important question. Should we properly think at all of our observation of the marks left by the lightning as a receptive sign-event? It is pure coincidence that the marks have the shape of a word in the English language. Had they taken some other form that had no meaning for us, our examination of them would not have been a sign-event. Yet coincidence or not, they did take a form that does have meaning for us, and so long as we look at them with this meaning in mind, our observation of them is a receptive sign-event. It makes no difference whether or not we believe the message we read—we do not believe novels when we read them; it makes no difference whether or not we have taken the message as intended by an author, or if intended, whether or not intended for us; so long as we read a message, we are engaged in a receptive sign-event.

This example of the lightning is helpful and informative; it shows us that receptive events could occur without their having any presumed author. But after all, the supposed behavior of the lightning was just a made-up story, and a highly improbable one at that. Let us now ask whether there is a regularly occurring class of receptive events that have no intended second parties.

Farmer Brown is in the south-east forty mowing hay. As he moves along on the tractor, he glances toward the western sky. "Sure looks like rain," thinks Farmer Brown.

The appearance of the sky, the peculiar heavy stillness of the atmosphere, are natural states of affairs that Farmer Brown has learned to recognize as signs of rain. We shall, in fact, call those states of nature on the observation of which we predict or infer other states of nature natural sign-tokens. Thus the cloud formation is a sign-token of rain, the blush a sign-token of embarrassment, smoke the sign-token of fire. We have to *learn* this "language of nature" just as we learn any "conventional language" like English. The researches of the scientist can be thought of as further studies of the language of nature, its grammar and its vocabulary.

Reading these natural sign-tokens, inferring from their presence something else in nature that they signify, is a receptive sign-event. If we infer nothing from what we see and otherwise observe about us, there is no sign-event; but insofar as we do make inferences, do treat our observed surroundings as signs of other conditions in nature, we are engaged as interpreters in various receptive events.

There are many things that we shall want to consider later on with respect to this language of nature. For the present, however, we shall concern ourselves with just one question: Do the receptive events that constitute our reading of natural sign-tokens have intended second parties?

What does this question mean? We are *not* asking whether the things in nature which we take as signs have causes. Many natural sign-tokens are signs *of* their causes—for example, the smoke is a sign of the fire that causes it, and the blush a sign of the embarrassment causing it. Furthermore, the cause of a sign-token is not necessarily its author in a productive sign-event. To be the author in a productive sign-event is to be the *deliberate* cause of the physical sign-token, a cause that *chooses* to create that sign-token *as* a sign. Hence, when we ask whether the receptive event has an intended second party, we are asking whether the person who reads the signs of nature regards those signs as signs deliberately chosen by causal agents to be signs; that is, whether the reader thinks there was a corresponding productive sign-event that created the natural, physical sign-tokens which he is engaged in reading.

Many people have claimed that the language of nature does have an author—namely, God. Notice that to make this claim is to insist on something more than the belief that God created the world: it is to insist that some features of the world were created by God *as signs;* for example, the wisps of smoke as signs of fire. Perhaps one of the most interesting and impressive forms of this theory was developed by the famous philosopher George Berkeley (1685-1753). An excellent statement of his views on this subject as well as on many others may be found in his *Dialogues between Hylas and Philonous.*

It is not our purpose now to discuss the merits of Berkeley's theory, nor those of other theories akin to that of Berkeley. Our only purpose is to notice that people who hold such theories would, when they are interpreters reading natural sign-tokens, intend (understand) God as the author of those signs. Hence, the receptive events in which *these* people are interpreters would have intended second parties. On the other hand, many people in the world reject every such theory as Berkeley's. For them, natural signs have no authors; for them, these natural signs, like Topsy, "just growed." Thus, when such people are involved in receptive events as interpreters of natural sign-tokens, those receptive events have no intended second parties. That there are many such people in the world is evidence that there are many receptive events without intended second parties.

We have now seen that some sign-events have no intended second parties. All such sign-events will be called **undirected** sign-events. Sign-events with intended second parties will be called **directed** sign-events.

Both our examples of undirected productive events had an interesting and important feature in common. In each case, the author engaged in the productive act as a way of expressing feeling or emotion. It may, in fact, be safely remarked that most, if not all, undirected productive events are more or less deliberately chosen expressions of the interpreter's emotional attitude at the time of the event.

Is every expression of emotion by a person to be regarded as a productive sign-event? For example, an embarrassed person might blush, and the blush would be an expression of the embarrassment. Is the act of blushing to be taken as a productive sign-event, with the blush as its physical sign-token and the blusher as its interpreter? No. To be a sign-event, the cause-effect relation between the cause and physical sign-token must involve some measure of choice or responsibility on the part of the casual agent. The embarrassed blusher cannot help blushing; he does not choose to blush. Hence, his act of blushing is not a productive sign-event.[1]

It must be confessed that, on this score, Bill's swearing when he hammered his thumb may be as involuntary as the embarrassed person's

---

1 While the act of blushing may not be a *productive* sign-event, we have already noticed that the act of *observing* the blush may well be a *receptive* sign-event.

blushing. It is, nevertheless, customary to treat the swearing as a sign-event and the blushing as not one. The ground for this distinction seems to be that the sounds made in swearing are *learned* sounds, belonging to some standard language. People who do not speak English do not say, "Ouch! Damn!" Also, one might swear as a prop to assist one in the avoidance of crying. Insofar as the sounds are learned ones, like the words of a language, or are permitted *in order to* accomplish something else, there is in their occurrence a measure of choice or deliberation, so that the classification as a sign-event is not without some justification. However, there is no sharp dividing line separating productive sign-events from other caused events which are not sign-events. We might say that involuntary swearing is to the distinction between productive sign-events and certain non-sign-events much as a certain color would be to the distinction between red and orange: you may call it either one you like.

While undirected productive sign-events are nearly all responses to their authors' feelings or emotional states, undirected receptive events are on the whole of a quite different kind. The latter consist primarily of those "readings of nature" in which we infer some fact of nature from some observed state of affairs: fire from smoke, embarrassment from a blush, rain from a cloud, and so on.

Most sign-events with which we shall be concerned in remaining units of this book are directed events. We shall, however, have occasion to refer from time to time to these "readings of nature" that are undirected receptive events and to the natural sign-tokens which are constituents of them.

## EXERCISES

1. Classify the sign-events described in each of the following as:
   a. Productive or receptive, and
   b. Directed or undirected.

   Explain briefly why you answer as you do.
   i. The grounds-keeper at a golf course is putting up a sign which reads: REPLACE ALL DIVOTS.
   ii. A golfer, who does not know who ordered or put up the sign mentioned in problem i., is reading that sign.
   iii. A traffic policeman blows his whistle and holds up his hand to stop oncoming traffic.

iv. A fisherman, alone in his boat in the middle of a lake, exclaims, "Good night!" when he catches his first glimpse of the beautiful lake salmon that he is reeling in.

v. A gardener looks at the withered silk on an ear of corn in his garden and decides to pick that ear to cook for his dinner.

2. Give at least one example, in which you were involved as the interpreter, of a productive directed sign-event. Of a productive undirected sign-event. Of a receptive directed sign-event. Of a receptive undirected sign-event.

## §10.3 Meaning

Throughout this and the previous unit we have hardly more than mentioned the meanings of sign-tokens as they occur in sign-events. And yet meaning is the most important aspect of any sign-event. For example, failures of communication like those illustrated in Examples 4 and 5 of §10.1 are relatively uncommon and unimportant when compared with the failures occurring because a receiver does not understand what an author meant by the tokens that he had produced. In fact, it may be fairly claimed that one of the major tasks of this entire book is to assist you toward a clearer grasp of meaning, since nearly all the principles of right reason depend on it.

Many authors actually list the meanings of sign-tokens as constituents in the sign-events containing those tokens. However, we have not done that in this book. The reason why we have not done so is that an adequate understanding of the nature of meaning depends on seeing how its occurrence derives from the *purposes* of interpreters. In Units 12 and 13, we shall take up this question of purpose, and in Unit 14 we shall commence the analysis of meaning.

Thus the units in this Part preceding Unit 14 should be considered as necessary preliminaries to the discussion of meaning.

## REVIEW QUESTIONS FOR UNIT 10

1. Briefly explain how productive and receptive events are involved in communication.

2. What relations (of identity and the like) connect the major constituents of the sign-events involved in successful communication?

3. What failure of the relations mentioned in Question 2 could be responsible for a breakdown of communication?

4. Under what circumstances could all the relations mentioned in Question 2 hold and there still be a breakdown of communication?

5. Can a productive and a receptive event have one and the same sign-token without the two events forming an example of communication? For example, what about "eavesdropping"? Reading someone else's mail?

6. What is meant by a directed sign-event? An undirected sign-event?

7. Give an example of an undirected productive event; of an undirected receptive event.

8. What is meant by a natural sign-token? Illustrate.

9. Does every productive sign-event have at least one interpreter? Explain.

10. Does every productive sign-event have at least one intended second party? Explain.

11. Does every receptive sign-event have at least one interpreter? Explain.

12. Does every receptive sign-event have at least one intended second party? Explain.

# UNIT 11

## Miscellaneous Special Topics*

### §11.1 Reflexive and Irreflexive Sign-events

When we were discussing undirected sign-events (§10.2), we noticed that we must carefully distinguish between undirected events, which have no intended second party at all, and those directed events in which there is an intended second party but who is identical with the interpreter of the event in question. Examples of this latter sort of event occur when one writes a memo to oneself or reads a memo from oneself. Outlining a book as a basis for future review, making the rough draft of a term paper which one intends later to study and revise, taking lecture notes in a class—all these are examples of productive events in which there is an intended second party identical with the interpreter. Likewise, the later reading of these outlines, rough drafts, and lecture notes would be receptive events with an intended second party identical with the interpreter (unless, of course, one had forgotten meanwhile that he had himself been the author of those notes!) None of the above are examples of undirected events.

When a sign-event has an intended second party which is identical with its interpreter, the sign-event is said to be **reflexive**.[1] A sign-event that is not reflexive is called **irreflexive**.

A moment's thought should be sufficient to persuade you that *either* if a sign-event does not have any intended second party, *or* if, in case it has an intended second party, this intended second party is not identical with the interpreter, then the sign-event is irreflexive. Thus, all undirected sign-events are irreflexive and all reflexive events are directed. But *not* all irreflexive events are undirected and not all directed events are reflexive.

Perhaps the greatest number of all *productive* events are directed irreflexive; the next greatest number, directed reflexive; and the smallest number, undirected irreflexive. (The burden of the preceding paragraph was that there is no such thing as an undirected reflexive event.)

---

* This unit is concerned with tying up some loose ends and following a short way some topics suggested by the developments in Units 9 and 10. But this unit may be omitted without disturbing the continuity of the study, since no terms or ideas introduced here will be mentioned later on, except in occasional footnotes.

[1] In general, a thing is called *reflexive* if it involves something's turning back upon itself. Thus, for example, you could speak of suicide as reflexive murder.

When we come to receptive events, the situation is a little different. Since nearly all "readings of nature" or receivings of natural sign-tokens are undirected and therefore irreflexive, perhaps the largest number of receptive events are undirected irreflexive; the next largest group, directed irreflexive; and the smallest group, directed reflexive. (Again, there will be no such thing as an undirected reflexive event.)

Since all productive and receptive events involved in communication with another person are directed irreflexive events, this classification will occupy the greatest part of our attention throughout the next several units of this book.

## §11.2 Personal and Social Sign-events

If a sign-event does not involve as a constituent any person except its interpreter, then it is said to be a **personal** sign-event. If it does involve another person as a constituent, it is called a **social** sign-event.

It is easy to see that all undirected sign-events are personal. Perhaps it is less easy to see that all reflexive sign-events are also personal. Nevertheless, they are. While they do have an intended second party, this person is identically the interpreter. Hence, no person except the interpreter is involved as a constituent. But he is involved in two ways, in two roles: in one way as the interpreter and in another way as the intended second party.

Thus, the class of all social sign-events is the same as the class of all directed irreflexive events, and vice versa. It is, in other words, the class to which we shall be giving the greatest part of our attention throughout the remaining units of Part II.

## §11.3 Actual and Intended Intermediaries

We have seen that every sign-event involves an interpreter and a sign-token as two constituents and that all directed events involve also an intended second party. We wish now to ask whether sign-events ever have any other constituents than these three.

It was noticed in §10.1 that in many cases of communication the physical sign-tokens of the productive and receptive events are identical: I look at the very chalk you spread on the blackboard, and listen to the very sounds that you make as you speak. On the other hand, it was also noticed that the tokens in the receptive event are not always identical with those in the productive event, that quite often they are, instead, acceptable *substitutes* for the tokens originally produced. For example, when I listen at the telephone, I do not hear the sound made by the speaker, but another sound, similar to that one. Other examples were given in Examples 7 and 8 at the end of §10.1.

This use of substitute tokens instead of the original ones usually occurs when the productive and receptive events are widely separated from one another in space or time, or both. In most such cases, the connection of the original productive event and the final receptive event so as to bring about communication is accomplished only with the assistance or cooperation of other people. These people may be called **intermediaries.**

How varied might be the contributions of these intermediaries! In the simplest case, the intermediary merely transports the physical sign-token. Such a role is played by the messenger or letter carrier. Next simplest, he operates machinery which mechanically reproduces the original physical sign-token.[2] Such a task is performed by the telephone or radio engineer or by the engineer who operates a tape recorder or record-producing mechanism, as also by the "disk jockey." Next more complex, the intermediary must observe the sign-tokens that come to him and in turn produce another set of sign-tokens that will be substitutes for the ones he observed. Here a tremendous variety of skills and types of individual responsibility may be called into play. The oral messenger need only resay what he was told. The stenographer and typesetter replace one physical sign (say, a noise) by a standard equivalent (for example, typescript). The translator must replace the signs of one language by equivalent signs of another. The secretary who is given only the gist of a letter and the actor whose script only hints at the gestures, tone of voice, and the like must actually decide on their own initiative important features of the physical sign-tokens that will be presented to the eventual observers.

Whenever such intermediaries are involved, they may be recognized as other constituents in the sign-events in question than the standard three discussed in §9.2. Thus, sign-events may have other constituents than those three.

Strictly speaking, an intermediary is a constituent of a sign-event only if he is an **intended intermediary.** For example, Miss Tivoli is a constituent of the productive event in Example 7 of §10.1, because the interpreter, Mr. Jones, intended her as an intermediary. Suppose, however, that Jim, the office boy, had overheard Mr. Jones dictating and had relayed the substance of the letter to the production manager of Tri-Mutual's chief competitor. Jim would not be a constituent in the productive event that was Mr. Jones dictating to Miss Tivoli, because he was not so intended by the interpreter, Mr. Jones. Jim would be the interpreter in his own receptive act of overhearing and his own productive act of reporting to the competitor's production manager. Also, Jim would be a constituent in the production manager's receptive act of hearing Jim's report: the intended second party of that receptive act.

---

[2] This is next simplest only in the sense that the intermediary need not himself meaningfully observe or produce the physical sign-tokens that are being communicated. The performance of his tasks may nevertheless require great technical skill and elaborate training.

Intermediaries who, like the actor, translator, or stenographer, must observe the tokens produced by the author and in turn produce tokens that will be observed by the intended second party, are themselves engaged in **intermediate receptive events** and **intermediate productive events**. They are, in fact, the interpreters of these intermediate sign-events. Should the need arise, we could distinguish their status in these sign-events by designating them as **intermediate interpreters**. They are intermediate receivers and intermediate producers.

What is their status in the original productive event and final receptive event in such a chain of communication? We shall call them **intended intermediate second parties**. For example, as Mr. Jones dictates to Miss Tivoli in Example 7 of §10.1, Mr. Jones is the interpreter, Miss Tivoli is the intended intermediate second party, and Mr. Smith is the intended **eventual** second party. On the other hand, when Mr. Smith reads the letter that Miss Tivoli typed, Mr. Smith is the interpreter, Miss Tivoli is the intended intermediate second party, and Mr. Jones is the intended **original** second party.

All these problems concerning the nature and the functions of intermediaries and the ways in which they can affect the success of an act of communication are both interesting and important. But to enter into a more detailed consideration of them in this study would draw our attention away from still other issues that will be even more important to us in the later parts of this discussion. From this point on, we shall, therefore, tend to disregard the activities of the intermediaries and to focus attention on the original productive event and the final receptive event involved in the act of communication. It is these two parts of the whole process which exhibit most of the features to which we must attend.

And yet a knowledge of the things we shall discuss can be of value to intermediaries as well. For intermediaries like the actor and the translator are, as we have seen, also interpreters. The more fully they appreciate and understand the essential features of receptive and productive events, the better they can perform their intermediate tasks.

## §11.4 Dramatization of Sign-events

Suppose an actor sat down on the stage and wrote a letter to some character involved in the play. Did a sign-event take place?

To be sure, the actor was communicating with the audience. All his gestures, speeches, and actions are a portrayal of something to the audience. But when he "speaks to another character" on the stage, or when he writes a letter, we should properly say that he is only dramatizing a sign-event or pretending to be involved in one.

To ask whether there really was a sign-event is like asking whether or not there really was a purchase when two children are playing store and one of them "buys" some item. There really was a dramatized purchase, but there was no genuine purchase. Likewise, on the stage there really was a dramatized speech or letter-writing event, but there was no genuine letter-writing or speaking.

Such acted out, but still only pretended, events do not take place merely on the stage or among children at play. In this connection, consider the following example.

George has just received a letter from the circulation manager of *Blah*. The manager asks, where is George's overdue renewal of his subscription? He goes on to remark that it is difficult to understand how a person of even modest intelligence could have read *Blah* for a year and then permitted himself to risk missing even one issue. George's name had already been kept on the mailing list for three months beyond the expiration of his subscription. This was done because the manager was sure that he would eventually remit. But unless the remittance arrived within two weeks, the manager would be obliged reluctantly to remove George's name from his list of intelligent and patriotic Americans, the people who read *Blah*.

The letter, with its suggestions of feeble intelligence and lack of patriotism on George's part, so much provoked poor George that he was, as we sometimes say, practically beside himself, and this feeling became even more acute as he recalled the almost continuous examples of bias and distortion that had characterized the articles of *Blah*. It seemed to George quite pointless to report all this to the circulation manager. He would write, stating that he was *not* renewing his subscription; but before he undertook that letter, he wrote another, destined for the waste basket, but in which he "let himself go" and got these feelings "off his chest."

This first letter, even though addressed to "The Circulation Manager and his Companions in Crime," was really meant for the waste basket. Thus, George's action as he wrote it was an example of dramatized letter-writing. George portrayed a character and dramatized a part, just like the actor on the stage.[3]

It would carry us too far afield to speculate here on the great extent to which adult human life may be viewed as the pretended assumption and dramatization of roles, either temporarily or permanently assumed.

> All the world's a stage,
> And all the men and women merely players . . .[4]

But be that as it may, we do sometimes, like the child at play or the actor or George, assume a pretended role and dramatize the occurrence of a sign-

---

[3] This analysis of George's letter writing activity was suggested to me by Professor John F. A. Taylor.
[4] Shakespeare, *As You Like It*, Act II, Scene 7.

event, productive or receptive. This dramatized sign-event has its pretended interpreter and its pretended intended second party. The dramatization may produce a genuine sign-token, as in the case of George or of the actor speaking on the stage, but the dramatization need not go quite so far. For example, the actor may only pretend to put pencil to paper and thus not actually produce any genuine sign-tokens.

### §11.5 Desirable Physical Features of Physical Sign-tokens

We have already mentioned in §10.1 that communication will fail if a receiver does not understand the physical sign-tokens presented to him by a producer. For example, there would be no point in talking French to a person who does not understand French. This question of understanding is closely related to the question of meaning and will be the main point of many later units.

What, however, may now be noticed is that other factors, physical factors, may have to be attended to as we select the tokens we produce in productive events. Suppose, for example, that you and I were standing on two hilltops separated by a broad valley and that I wished to communicate with you. To ponder whether I should shout in English or in French, and to choose to shout in English because you might not understand French, could all be beside the point: the valley is so broad that you would not hear my shouts no matter what the language in which my shouts are phrased.

The above illustration points to an important consideration which has affected and will continue to affect the development of languages. Physical objects have various physical properties that will make them more and less appropriate as the sign-tokens of productive and receptive events. In this section, we shall briefly consider what some of these characteristics might be.

In general, two kinds of considerations affect the relative merits of one type of sign-token as over against another: ease of control by the producer, and ease of discriminating observation by the receiver. These two kinds of consideration give rise to six determining factors:

1. The physical sign-tokens should be such as are easily produced in variety. Other things being equal, the more easily the sign-tokens are produced, and the more easily produced in variety, the better they are. To illustrate, the human voice is a marvelous instrument over which most human beings are capable of exercising remarkable control, giving rise to an amazing variety of sounds. Furthermore, these sounds can be produced with the expenditure of very little energy as compared, say, to the energy required to produce a similar controlled variety of gestures. This is one reason why a spoken language is preferable to a gesture language. Similar considerations

recommend for many purposes a written language as over against a carved or chiseled language.

2. The physical sign-tokens should be such as are easily eliminated or disposed of when no longer wanted. This is one thing that makes sounds, which die out almost at once, so admirable as physical sign-tokens. The sound of one sentence dies and leaves the atmosphere clean and, so to speak, uncluttered to receive the next sentence. A language of perfumes would be in this respect quite unmanageable: one could not get rid of the already "spoken" odors soon enough to prevent their cluttering and confusing the next odoriferous sentence! It also marks one advantage of blackboards over great blocks of paper and crayon in the classroom, and of paper over clay tablets. Just think how vast would be our city dumps if the daily papers were impressed on indestructible clay instead of on inflammable paper!

3. At the same time, the physical sign-token must be as durable as the demands on it require. Sound, except via tape recordings, is unsuitable as a device for preserving records. Court records are kept in ink, rather than pencil, so that they will not have become smudged and illegible before some interested receiver seeks to read them.

4. The physical sign-tokens should be transportable with as much ease as possible from the producer to the receiver. It is this feature that makes the voice preferable—when the distance is not great—to other types of sign-tokens; it also establishes the superiority of letters written on paper over the heavier letter of the ancient world inscribed on clay. And it finally contributes to the advantage of telephone, telegraph, and radio that transport messages by electric or electronic impulse rather than by the physical transference of material bodies.

5. Physical sign-tokens capable of more rapid transmission are, other things being equal, preferable to those demanding slower transmission. Such considerations of speed would be in part responsible for the Indian's development of smoke signals, the African native's system of signal drums, the system of signal fires arranged for use along the coast of England at the time of the Spanish Armada, and in more recent times, for the development of the telegraph, telephone, and radio. This same consideration of speed also stimulated the development of more rapid means for conveying material sign-tokens such as letters: the pony express, the railroad, the automobile, and the airplane; but here the influence was not on the actual nature of the sign-token itself so much as on the means of conveying an already given type of sign-token.

6. Finally, the physical sign-tokens must be observable by the intended second party, and discriminable by him from their environment. This explains

why one does not *talk* to deaf people (unless they have learned lip reading) or to people in a noisy shop or factory. Under such circumstances, other types of sign-tokens must be employed.

It is easy to see that these six desirable features will sometimes be in conflict one with the other. In such cases one or more of them must in some degree be sacrificed to gain a more important advantage from another of them. Circumstances will dictate which are the more important in any given case.

UNIT **12**

# The Purposes of Discourse: Productive Discourse

### §12.1 What Units 12 and 13 Are All About

The present and the next unit may be best understood as an effort to answer the question, why do people occupy themselves as interpreters in sign-events? Why, that is, do they write, read, talk, listen, and otherwise produce or receive sign-tokens?

When you first consider the question that has just been asked, you may find yourself reacting to it in one or the other of two ways: (1) Perhaps you will recall that in §2.8 there has already occurred a discussion of three uses of language: the cognitive, the pragmatic, and the esthetic. The questions, you may be tempted to say, have already been answered; why bring them up again? (2) On the other hand, you may perhaps have forgotten temporarily the earlier discussion in Unit 2 and will have begun thinking of the tremendous variety of sign-events which fill our lives: chitchat at a dance, quarterbacks calling signals, reading Burma Shave advertisements, writing a weighty tome entitled *Mayan Culture*, making an election campaign speech, reading a barometer, listening to debate in Congress, writing or reading a love sonnet or a short story. The reasons why people do these things are as numerous and varied as the sign-events in which the people find themselves engaged as interpreters. How can you possibly expect to answer a question which has a million different answers, if it has any answer at all!

Both these reactions are in a sense proper; and yet each also in a way suggests the proper antidote to the other. Thus, if your reaction was like the first of those mentioned above, we must notice that the variety of purposes for which people engage in sign-events is so great as to make the brief discussion in §2.8 no more than an introduction to the whole general subject of purposes of discourse. Unless the brief classification of purposes presented in Unit 2 is enlarged and studied, the act

118

of classifying cannot serve a useful purpose, because it does not get us sufficiently into contact with the rich and detailed variety of purposes guiding any single interpreter in a specific sign-event.

On the other hand, if your reaction was like the second of those mentioned above, we may remind you that even though all the detailed mass of purposes in individual sign-events could not be recounted in a single volume, let alone in a single unit of a volume, nevertheless certain broad types or kinds of purpose may be listed and described and individual cases seen to be varied examples of these kinds. Awareness of these facts can help make our reading and listening more intelligent and critical and our reactions to what we read and hear more reasonable and appropriate. Also, it may help us select sign-tokens when we write or speak that are more appropriate to our purposes.

In short, these two units will contain in their first part a descriptive classification of the purposes that actually motivate producers and receivers in sign-events.[1] In their second part, they will contain the outlines for a critique of purposes: both of the purposes themselves and of the propriety of certain sign-tokens as instruments for the fulfillment of those purposes.

## §12.2  Order among Purposes

Probably no one ever does anything with complete singleness of purpose. For example, I eat lunch; but there is no single purpose served by this complex act of eating *that* luncheon, at *that* time, in *that* place, with *that* company. One purpose was undoubtedly to assuage my hunger, but many other relevant purposes might have affected various aspects of this single act: I ate *then* so as to be free to keep an appointment at a later hour, *this* because I preferred it to other things on the menu which I could afford (two purposes), *with him* so as to flavor the food with the pleasure of companionship, *here* so to save the time for dining which would otherwise be spent in travel to an equally attractive but more distant restaurant.

The same sort of thing is generally true of an interpreter's involvement in a sign-event: when he speaks, writes, listens, or reads, his doing this in this manner and at this time may be serving many distinct purposes. This fact has already been noticed in §2.9 on *Mixed Uses of Language*.

---

[1] "The purposes of discourse" are not the purposes of sign-tokens which, being generally inanimate, have no purposes but are instead the purposes for which interpreters produce and receive sign-tokens.

In the next few sections we shall be considering what might be certain ones of those many purposes and how those individual purposes might be classified. But in the present section we shall consider briefly how the different purposes of a single sign-event might be related one to the other.[2] As we proceed to the later sections, we shall note instances of these relations.

A person's purpose may be said to be **primary** or **secondary**: that is, to be one of the *main* things that he wants to accomplish or one of the *minor* things he wants to accomplish.

Also, his purpose may be **immediate or remote**: that is, to be something he wants to accomplish *right away* or *after a while*.

When two purposes are compared, the one may be said to be **subservient** to the other (purposed as a *means* to accomplishing the other); the other subservient to the one; or the two may be said to be **independent** (neither thing which is purposed is purposed as a means, or in order, to accomplish the other).

As we continue, we shall notice that subservient purposes are generally, but not always, secondary and immediate.

### §12.3  The Purposes of Productive Discourse

Let us proceed, then, to consider the purposes of productive discourse, to consider, that is, what producers aim to accomplish by engaging in productive sign-events.

In §2.8 we spoke of three uses of language: the cognitive, the pragmatic, and the esthetic. In the present section we may profitably begin by considering those as major classifications of the purposes for which producers engage in sign-events. Let us then examine each of these in turn, not repeating what was already said in §2.8, but adding further points that can make that earlier discussion more useful.[3] Among other things, we must notice that each of these three types has two principal subdivisions.

**1. Cognitive Purposes.**  Sometimes an author's purpose is to affect or alter in some way or other some person's beliefs or knowledge, or the grounds for those beliefs or knowledge. Any such purpose will be called a **cognitive purpose.**

2    These types of relationship among purposes are illustrated in the purposes of other things than sign-events, but we shall not try in this book to examine their more general application.
3    At this point, it would be advisable to reread §2.8.

Two principal subdivisions of cognitive purposes are to be recognized: **personal** and **social,** according as the author's purpose is to affect *his own* belief or knowledge or to affect someone else's. Examples of a personal cognitive purpose are as follows:

a.  A student takes some notes during a lecture. His purpose is to assure himself that he will know at some future date something which he has just learned today.

b.  A person writes down some algebraic equations and "solves" for *x*. His purpose is to find out how much lumber will be required in order to build a certain bookcase.

c.  A motorist asks directions from a service station attendant. His purpose is to learn the best route to a given destination.[4]

When the cognitive purpose is to communicate to the intended receiver certain items of knowledge or belief already possessed by the author, the purpose may be called **informative.** Example *a*, above, illustrates the personal informative use of language. If we consider, in connection with that same example, the teacher's activity as he lectures, his lecturing illustrates the social informative use of language. In examples *b* and *c*, above, we have noninformative, but nevertheless cognitive, purposes. In each case, the author does not possess knowledge that he is trying to communicate to an intended receiver; he is instead *seeking* information that he does *not* already possess.

### EXERCISES

1.  Describe three productive events the purpose of which would be social cognitive. (Do not use examples given in the textbook.)
2.  Describe three productive events the purpose of which would be personal cognitive.
3.  Which of the events described in your answers to Exercises 1 and 2, above, are examples of informative purposes? Which are examples of noninformative, cognitive purposes?
4.  Social cognitive purposes are only rarely noninformative. Give one or two examples of events with this kind of purpose.

**2.  Pragmatic Purposes.** Sometimes an author's purpose as he speaks or writes is to get someone to do something. Such a purpose may be called **pragmatic.** For examples:

[4]  This last example shows that the sign-event may be social, involving an intended second party who is distinct from the author (§11.2), even though the purpose of the author is personal.

d.  The traffic policeman blows his whistle and holds up his hand. This productive sign-event is undertaken in order to get the oncoming motorist to bring his car to a stop.

e.  Devising the commercial for a radio program is a productive sign-event the purpose of which is to get people in the radio audience to buy the advertised product.

f.  A motorist asks directions from a service station attendant. His purpose is to get the attendant to tell him the best route to a given destination.

You may have noticed that the last example is identical with example *c* under personal cognitive purposes. As this shows, the purposes of a single act may be both cognitive and pragmatic. In this particular case, the cognitive purpose is *primary* and *remote* and the pragmatic purpose is *secondary*, *subservient*, and *immediate*. Sometimes cognitive and pragmatic purposes stand in the opposite relation to one another. To illustrate: the radio commerical in example *e* may be developed around the plan of communicating information to the radio audience on the assumption that if the audience possessed this information, it would buy the advertised product. Such being the case, there would be both a cognitive and a pragmatic purpose, but the pragmatic purpose would be the remote, primary one and the cognitive purpose would be the immediate, secondary, and subservient one.

Like cognitive purposes, pragmatic purposes may be divided into personal pragmatic and social pragmatic purposes, although the division is rather one-sided since most pragmatic purposes are social. But two examples will demonstrate the existence of personal pragmatic purposes:

g.  Little Joe is walking down a country lane on a dark night to post a letter to his sweetheart. Joe is a city boy, born and bred, and this is his first summer in the country. Twig-snaps and rustlings in the brush along the roadside have frightened him almost to the point where he will turn heel and retreat to the safety of his summer camp. To bolster his morale, so as to make sure that he completes his mission, he starts talking to himself. "It's nothing but a squirrel, or at worst a rat. He is frightened and running away from me. . . ." Joe's purpose is pragmatic, to get himself to complete his journey into town; but it is also personal.

h.  William is afraid that he will forget his eleven o'clock appointment with the dentist. He says to his roommate, "Let me know when it is a quarter to eleven." William's purpose is doubly pragmatic: to get his roommate to do something, but that in order to get himself to do something.

**3. Esthetic Purposes.** Like cognitive and pragmatic purposes, esthetic purposes are both personal and social. A productive sign-event has a personal esthetic purpose if it is undertaken in order to affect or express the author's own emotional experience. In example *g*, Joe undertakes to affect his own emotional experience; this undertaking is a secondary purpose subservient to the primary pragmatic purpose already discussed. Quite different instances of personal esthetic purposes were given in §10.2. In contrast with all these, one purpose of many productive events is to affect the emotional experience of persons other than the author. The novelist, poet, orator, and advertiser presume to present us with such sign-tokens as will affect our esthetic sensibilities in chosen ways. Their purpose is a social esthetic purpose.

As the last remarks suggest, esthetic purposes may be primary, or they may be secondary and subservient. Likewise, cognitive and pragmatic purposes may be secondary and subservient to esthetic purposes.

*EXERCISE*

Describe one or more examples of productive events of which:

1. The primary purpose is social pragmatic, the secondary purpose is social esthetic.
2. The primary purpose is social esthetic, the secondary purpose is social pragmatic.
3. The primary purpose is esthetic, the secondary purpose is cognitive.
4. The primary purpose is cognitive, the secondary purpose is esthetic.
5. The primary purpose is pragmatic, the secondary purposes are cognitive and esthetic.

Many people are professional authors, so that one abiding purpose served by their professional productive events is the earning of their livelihoods. Among these professional authors, we should count not only novelists, playwrights, and poets, but historians, scientists, advertising copy writers, newspaper reporters, certified public accountants, physicians, lawyers, ministers, teachers, traffic policemen.

This abiding purpose is a remote, social pragmatic purpose: to get certain people to pay money to the author. The more immediate purposes of the individual sign-events—to slow down that motorist, to educate that student, to cure this patient, and so on—*may* be subservient to the abiding economic pragmatic purpose. But interestingly enough, among the best professional people, either the two purposes are independent or the economic purpose is subservient to the other. Their primary purpose is to teach or to cure, they accept payment for doing it so that they can afford to do it. People who make their teaching, entertaining, or curing purposes secondary and subservient to the remote economic purpose are sometimes called *timeservers* or other even more offensive names.

The disinterested professional author provides an interesting illustration of the unusual fact that a remote purpose (the economic one) can be subservient to an immediate one.

## REVIEW QUESTIONS FOR UNIT 12

1. When we speak of the purposes of a productive sign-event, whose purposes do we have in mind?
2. Can a productive sign-event have more than one purpose? Briefly explain.
3. What is meant by a *primary* purpose? A *secondary* purpose?
4. What is meant by an *immediate* purpose? A *remote* purpose?
5. What is meant by a *subservient* purpose? An *independent* purpose?
6. Discuss briefly, with illustrations, the relations generally holding among the types of purpose mentioned in questions 3 to 5.
7. What is meant by a *personal*, and by a *social*, cognitive purpose?
8. What is meant by an *informative* purpose? Are all cognitive purposes informative? Explain.
9. What is meant by a *personal*, and by a *social*, pragmatic purpose? By a *personal*, and by a *social*, esthetic purpose?

# *The Purposes of Discourse, continued: Receptive Discourse, Communication, and the Critique of Purposes*

## §13.1 The Purposes of Receptive Discourse: Initial and Eventual Purposes

In the preceding unit we found that the account of the purposes of productive discourse could be quite well presented merely by adding a few details to the earlier discussion in §2.8 of the uses of language. The same approach would not be so nearly adequate if we were to use it on receptive discourse. For other factors complicate the situation when we try to understand why (for what purposes) people read, listen, and otherwise busy themselves as interpreters in receptive discourse.

In the first place, we must notice that while a person reads or listens, his purposes in doing so very likely change. For example, suppose that you notice somebody beginning to speak to you, and you listen to him. At the beginning, your act of listening is very likely motivated merely by courtesy and a certain mild curiosity: your purpose is politely to do what he evidently wishes you to do, namely, to listen; and perhaps also to satisfy your own curiosity, to find out what he is about to say. But *as* you listen and discover the kind of thing he is saying, the very content of his speech creates in you new desires, and the satisfaction of these new desires prompts you to keep on listening. Thus new purposes arise to control your listening act. Perhaps you find that the speaker is reporting some occurrence in which you are deeply concerned. Your original purpose, to find out what he will say, disappears and is replaced by this other purpose, to find out what happened. No longer does mere courtesy keep you listening: you find that you cannot tear yourself away from the report that is being made to you.

Something like the shift of purpose just described is characteristic of nearly all receptive events.[1] To be sure, the original and the final purposes may be quite different from those indicated in our illustration. But the situation will be like that in the illustration in that there will be final purposes which are different from the original purposes. This fact of change in purpose is actually so important that we must give special attention to the two classes of purpose. We shall call them **initial purposes** and **eventual purposes**.

A further comment on the terms *initial purpose* and *eventual purpose* will probably be helpful. The manner in which these different purposes have been described and named will perhaps have suggested to you that for any single receptive event there are exactly two, sharply distinguished sets of purposes, the set of initial purposes that guide the first part of the event and then suddenly cease to operate, and the set of eventual purposes that suddenly begin to operate throughout the rest of the event. Nothing could be further from the truth than any such oversimplified notion.

The fact is that, except in the most dramatic situations, change of purpose is a gradual and continuous process. Perhaps the analogy to the fibers in a rope will be helpful. Not all initial purposes (fibers) cease to operate at the same time. Some persist in their influence long after others have died out. Also, eventual purposes usually begin to operate before the initial purposes that they finally replace have ceased to operate. Furthermore, some of these eventual purposes may themselves die out and be replaced by still others.

It should also be noticed that, *unlike* the fibers in a rope, the purposes in a strand of purposes usually begin in a weak and relatively ineffectual way, grow into more prominent guides, and then fade away into weaker members of the whole strand before they finally die. In this sense, the analogy to the members of a family line would be more suggestive than that to the fibers in a rope. The generations overlap, but in infancy and old age the individuals contribute less to responsible guidance of the family's destinies than they do in their middle years.

Yet however oversimplified may be the suggestion contained in the terms *initial purpose* and *eventual purpose*, we shall find this simplified

1 But there are important exceptions to this rule. Many such exceptions occur when a receiver has consulted an authority and is receiving the authoritative information he had sought. Other exceptions occur in cases of receptive sign-events that are reflexive (§11.1).

terminology adequate to our present needs, and consequently more useful for us here and now than a more complex and more generally adequate terminology.

### §13.2 The Purposes of Receptive Discourse, continued

Keeping in mind the distinctions between initial and eventual purposes, we can now see that all the purposes of receptive discourse can be classified as cognitive, pragmatic, or esthetic, and under each heading as personal or social. Let us undertake to suggest this variety in terms of a simple illustration. Remember that what we are considering is the purposes that a listener or reader is undertaking to serve by his act of listening or reading.

Suppose that someone stops you on the street and asks, "Can you please give me directions to the nearest drugstore?" At the moment when you realize that this stranger is about to speak to you, you set yourself to listen, prompted to do so by a certain courtesy. This courteous act serves for you, the listener, both an initial personal esthetic purpose (you "feel" better when being courteous than when being discourteous) and an initial social esthetic purpose (you make the stranger feel more at ease by listening to what he wishes to say than he would if you were to rebuff him). Also, perhaps, you are somewhat curious as to what he does want to say, and you listen in order to find out. This motive or purpose is an initial personal cognitive one. When you realize (about half way through his sentence) that he is asking some directions—instead of, thank goodness, for the price of a cup of coffee—that his immediate purpose is social pragmatic (to get you to say something which you would be quite willing to say, provided you have the desired information) your initial purposes are supplemented, and more or less replaced, by these eventual purposes: a subservient, secondary, personal cognitive purpose—to find out what directions the stranger wishes to receive; and a remote, primary, personal pragmatic purpose—to get yourself to give the stranger the information that he desires. This subsequent action on your part—answering the stranger's question, that is, becoming the interpreter in a productive event—will have for itself a social cognitive purpose (to impart information). And since that will be the purpose of your talking, and since the purpose of your present listening is to do later the talking that will serve this social cognitive purpose, one may say that your present listening has also an eventual, primary, but remote, social cognitive purpose.

We would be carried too far afield if we were to indulge in an attempt to enumerate all the other overtones of purpose that we serve by our listening act. To mention only one such, a social pragmatic purpose: to help the stranger reach his supposed destination without further unnecessary delay. Suffice it to say that in any receptive event the purposes of the interpreter—both initial and eventual—are all classifiable as cognitive, pragmatic, or esthetic, and in each case as personal or social. Some of these purposes are immediate, secondary, and subservient to others which will be primary and generally remote. But others among them will be quite independent.

## EXERCISES

1. Analyze and classify the purposes that motivated the receptive event which consisted of your reading §13.2, above.
2. Suppose a person looks up a word in the dictionary to find out what it means.
   a. Is there likely to be any noticeable difference between his initial purpose and his eventual purpose? Explain.
   b. Classify completely his purpose as indicated in the above phrase, "in order to find out what it means."

## §13.3 Purposes in Communication

We have seen (§10.1) that communication involves the conjunction of a productive and a receptive event; and in the preceding unit and this one, we have seen that these productive and receptive events have their own several and separate purposes. These purposes are the purposes that the interpreters in these events expect or hope will be served or furthered by the component events involved in the communication.

When we compare the producer's purposes in a case of communication with those of the receiver, we must be impressed by their dissimilarity. Occasionally, perhaps even quite often, a producer and receiver share a *common* purpose. For example, the author of a dictionary writes the dictionary in order to inform possible readers about the correct spelling, pronunciation, and meaning (among other things) of words; while readers of the dictionary will read it in order to find out about these very same things. But as often as not, the purposes of author and reader are unshared. The author of an advertisement publishes the advertisement in order to get the reader to buy the advertised product; but the reader does not read the advertisement in order to get himself to buy that product. The advertisement catches his attention or fancy, and he reads it out of curiosity or to be entertained by it. Related to the advertiser's, might be a reader's purpose: to decide whether or not to buy the advertised product. Yet even this, which is not always a purpose of advertisement reading, is not identical with the purpose of advertisement writing. It may well be that reading the advertisement does *cause* the reader to buy the advertised product. In this case, the *author's* purpose was achieved; but it still remains a fact that the eventual buying of the product was not the purpose that prompted the reader in his reading act.

Nevertheless, even when purposes are not shared by author and receiver, they may still be integrated and harmonious. To return to the example of an advertisement, the reader may be fully aware of the advertiser's purpose, but not share it; yet if the reader finds himself induced by the advertisement to buy the advertised product and does not resent this exercise of influence nor subsequently regret having been so influenced, the author's and the reader's purposes in production and reception will be thoroughly integrated and harmonious.

Consider one more example from a quite distinct field. The author of a short story has, one may assume, certain more or less definite social esthetic purposes as he creates his story: plot, situation, and style are all contrived to affect the reader in a certain preconceived way. On the other hand, the reader who picks up this story will usually have no such definite purpose in mind. His initial purpose may be personal esthetic, but it will usually be different from the author's. Perhaps the reader is primarily concerned to distract his mind from pressing cares and worries connected with certain practical problems in his daily life, of which the author was totally unaware. Even as he reads, the receiver may well continue to find himself absorbed and motivated by considerations that were not in the author's mind. Yet the purposes of author and reader can still be harmonious, mutually supporting, even though different. The purposes of each can give rise to actions (writing and reading) that help satisfy the purposes of the other.

On the other hand, the purposes of an author and his reader may easily conflict and thus make their several contributions to the entire act of communication mutually defeating. To cite just one example, suppose an author to write a social problem story, hoping thereby to arouse his readers to take some action that will remedy the social situation. Now suppose a reader to pick up this story hoping to find in it an "escape" from pressing social cares. Here author and reader are acting at cross-purposes. This may be so pronounced as to make the reader discard the story in despair. This done, neither the purposes of the author nor those of the reader are satisfied. The difficulty here was a disharmony of purpose.

Sometimes an author attempts actually to conceal his purposes from the receiver. Occasionally, doing this is the only way in which the author can achieve his purpose. Let us consider a crude example. A student of human nature is interested to discover what proportion of the populace will respond with sympathy and courtesy to innocent requests for assistance. A part of his inquiry might lead him to stop pedestrians on the street and ask them for directions to some such place as the public library. His purpose is merely to find out if they will make a courteous reply. But this he conceals from them, leaving them to believe that his purpose is to find out the location of the public library. If he were to reveal his purpose, his experiment would fail in its purpose.

Sometimes also receivers conceal the purposes of their receptive acts from the persons whose messages they receive.

All such concealment of purpose is, however, akin to a lie. For the identification of one another's purposes is inevitably involved in the process of full and complete understanding. Hence, the deliberate concealment is a deliberate misleading of one's communicant.

Whether any lies, and with them any concealments of purpose by an interpreter, are innocent in the sense of being not blameworthy, is a question we shall not here debate. Our only point now is to note that the receiver who would completely understand an author must identify the author's purposes, and that this understanding of purposes is sometimes made more difficult by the fact that the author has unconsciously or deliberately concealed his purposes. Contrariwise, an author who would successfully communicate with a receiver must be aware of the receiver's purposes in order to adapt his choice of tokens and his own purposes to those of the receiver. This need on the author's part is made more difficult to satisfy when the receiver conceals his purpose.

## EXERCISE

Give one or two examples in which a receiver conceals from an author the purpose of his receptive act.

## §13.4 The Recognition of Purposes

More often than not, one of the best clews to an author's purpose is the sign-tokens that he chooses to produce. For example, if I (who understand English) heard a motorist saying to me, "What is the shortest way to the city hall?" I should recognize his purpose as personal cognitive (to discover the shortest way) and social pragmatic (by getting me to tell it to him.)[2] This discovery of purpose by considering the sign-tokens depends on the receiver's understanding the sign-tokens and, furthermore, on his understanding them in the way that the author intended them.

We shall have more to say about this matter of understanding sign-tokens in the next unit. It is now important to observe, however, that other clews to purpose than the sign-tokens presented are generally available and can often serve to supplement or correct the clews given in the sign-tokens themselves. Among these other clews could be the identity of the producer and the circumstances, time, and place of the production.

For example, a well-known Christmas Carol commences,

> Hark, the herald angels sing,
> Glory to the new-born King.

Were we to attend merely to the words of the carol, the purposes of their production by their author could well seem to be pragmatic and cognitive. The carol begins with a command, to listen; it then proceeds to report what one would hear, that is, what one is to listen to. But when one realizes that the carol was written many centuries after that wondrous first Christmas night, when the angels are reported to have sung hosannahs, and furthermore that the composer was producing the carol for a Christian public, who already knew the Christmas story, one must realize that the purpose is almost entirely an esthetic one, although still mixed and probably both personal and social esthetic. Another kind of example, in a sense a negative example, is found in the desire of publicity experts to "plant" information about their product in news items rather than in paid advertisements. This is because they know that the reader of an advertisement will use the location of the sign-tokens (in an advertisement) as evidence for a remote pragmatic purpose

[2] I might, of course, be mistaken, as was noted in the preceding section. But very probably, the purpose inferred from the consideration of his sign-tokens did guide the motorist's speech.

of the advertiser, that consequently he will be less inclined to take seriously or believe the "information" contained in the advertisement, and therefore will not be so easily influenced by the statements he reads.

Plainly, the more we know about the producers whose sign-tokens we would observe, and about the circumstances under which the production of those tokens takes place, the more clearly we can discern the purposes of the production and thereby the meanings of the messages. It is, for example, this shared background and mutual understanding that enables people who are intimately acquainted—such as the members of a family or intimate business associates—to speak to one another with complete intelligibility in sentences and phrases that are so abbreviated as to be quite or entirely misleading to an outsider. It also justifies the publisher's brief biographical sketch of an author on the jacket of a new book, the time given in courses on literature to the discussion of an author's life and the circumstances under which he produced a given work, even the brief biographical remarks in a scientific textbook that accompany the statement of some scientist's theory.

Somewhat similar comments are appropriate when we turn to the question as to how an author discerns or guesses at the purposes of his intended receiver. But here the importance of knowledge about the receiver and about the time and the circumstances of the receptive event is even more important than in the case already considered. For in the former case, the receiver may *also* use the tokens produced by the author as clews to the author's purpose. But here, since the receiver does not produce tokens, the author has *only* these indirect clews as guides.

## §13.5 The Critique of Purposes

People sometimes do things they ought not to have done, and also leave undone things they ought to have done. Quite often, these cases of misconduct arise out of the unfortunate occurrence of something that was not at all the purpose of the guilty party. For example, a careless driver kills a pedestrian. He killed him, and he ought not to have done it, but he did not purposely kill him. On the other hand, certain cases of misconduct are the direct expressions of blameworthy purposes. Murder, "with malice aforethought," illustrates this situation.

Whenever we criticize a productive event—a speech or a piece of writing—we may consider and criticize the writing at two levels:

(1) What were the author's purposes? Were these purposes in any sense improper or ill-advised? (2) To what extent and in what manner was the productive event suitable or unsuitable as a means for the attainment of the author's purpose?

For example, the Smith Act authorizes the government to bring suit against and to penalize persons who conspire to bring about the violent overthrow of the government. It is this Congressional Act that empowers the government to try the leaders of the Communist Party. Making such conspiracies unlawful expresses the general conviction that these purposes are wrong. Insofar as Communist literature is under criticism, it is criticized as a product of an objectionable, improper, even unlawful, purpose: to bring about the violent overthrow of the government. Here is a pragmatic purpose of productive discourse that is deemed improper; so that both the producer and his sign-tokens are condemned on the ground that the purpose of the productive event is wrong.

Let us consider another example. The city council is conducting open hearings in connection with the contemplated passage of some bill. A citizen makes an impassioned plea for the defeat of the bill. His ultimate pragmatic purpose (to bring about the defeat of the bill) cannot, without further knowledge concerning the details of the bill, be criticized as wrong. But his speech might be found objectionable, nevertheless. The immediate effect of his speech is to incline the councilmen to judge the merits of the bill emotionally rather than rationally. Thus the speaker is contributing to a tendency (to which we are all prone) among the councilmen to rely on that invalid ground of belief, emotion (§8.1), rather than on the valid grounds of belief.

Now it may be that the emotional appeal was very effective, did bring about the hoped for defeat of the bill. It was nevertheless improper, although not illegal. If the speaker's immediate purpose was social esthetic—an effort to condition the council emotionally against the bill—then his immediate purpose was blameworthy even though his remote purpose was not. His speech could be judged an excellent instrument for the achievement of both his blameworthy immediate and his blameless remote purpose. But if the speaker had intended actually to appeal to the reasonableness of the council and to assist them to a rational understanding of the ill-advised character of the proposed bill, then his immediate purpose would have been praiseworthy, but his choice of tokens was most inappropriate. For the tokens, having the emotional effect that has been assumed, will actually make it more difficult for the councilmen to maintain the rational perspective that was intended. Hence, the tokens are an ineffectual instrument for the attainment of the speaker's immediate purpose.

Suppose that we had identified an author's purposes and were about to criticize them. On what kinds of consideration might our criticism be based? In general, any sort of consideration that is relevant to the criticism of *any* purpose will be relevant to the criticism of the purposes of discourse. Thus we could take into account *practical* considerations (for example, what the author is trying to do is impractical, futile, inconsistent with the attainment of other more abiding purposes, and so on), *moral* considerations (what the author is trying to do is improper, deprives others of their rights, does not serve the best interests of the community, and so on), and *artistic* considerations (the aim of the author is trite, lacking in depth or universality, too simple-minded).[3]

To explore in more detail what is involved in the criticism of purposes would lead us away from a general study of the principles of right reason to studies in the special fields of ethics and esthetics. Hence, we shall mention only one other point before leaving this topic: The preceding discussion has been phrased in terms that suggest the criticism by Mr. A of Mr. B's purposes. The possibilities for self-criticism should not be overlooked. Giving careful attention to our own purposes when we write or speak should enable us to improve the level of our own productive discourse.

## §13.6 The Critique of Means

As was suggested at the beginning of the last section, any criticism of a piece of discourse may well include consideration of the question, To what extent and in what manner was the productive event suitable or unsuitable as a means of attaining the author's purposes? This criticism of means can include a great many things: Did the author address his speech to the right people? Did he time his speech effectively so that it was received neither too early nor too late? Were the sign-tokens he chose to produce such as would be most appropriate to the attainment of his ends and purposes?

---

[3]   The illustrative critical comments above were negative in all three cases. Needless to say, practical, moral, and artistic criticism may end in judgments of approval as well as in those of disapproval.

In the next unit, we shall turn our attention to such topics as will help us deal with the last of the questions suggested above. Furthermore, as our investigation proceeds we shall attend less and less to the pragmatic and esthetic purposes of discourse and come consequently to focus our attention on the cognitive purposes and the choice of tokens suitable to the attainment of these cognitive purposes.

## EXERCISES

Consider in turn each of the four passages, *a* to *d*, appearing below (copied from *Logic, An Introduction*, by L. Ruby, New York: 1950, page 82) and answer concerning it these four questions:

1.  Explain briefly what, in your opinion, are to be considered the chief immediate and remote purposes of the productive events in which the quoted statements were first spoken or written.
2.  Classify (personal cognitive, etc.) each of the purposes you listed in answering question 1.
3.  Discuss briefly the propriety of those purposes.
4.  Discuss briefly the appropriateness of the sign-tokens produced as instruments for the achievement of those purposes.
    a.  We will answer their demand for a gold standard by saying to them: You shall not press down upon the brow of labor this crown of thorns, you shall not crucify mankind upon a cross of gold. (W. J. Bryan)
    b.  I warn John L. Lewis and his communistic cohorts that no second carpetbag expedition into the Southland, under the red banner of Soviet Russia and concealed under the slogans of the CIO will be tolerated. If the minions of the CIO attempt to carry through the South their lawless plan of organization, if they attempt to demoralize our industry, to corrupt our colored citizens, to incite race hatred and race warfare, I warn him here and now that they will be met by the flower of Southern manhood, that they will reap the bitter fruits of their folly. (Speech in U. S. House of Representatives, June, 1937)
    c.  All the "best people" from the gentleman's clubs, and all the frantic fascist captains, united in common hatred of socialism and bestial horror of the rising tide of the mass revolutionary movement have turned to acts of provocation, to foul incendiarism, to medieval legends of poisoned wells, to legalize their own destruction of proletarian organizations, and arouse the agitated petty bourgeoisie to chauvinistic terror on behalf of the fight against the revolutionary way out of the crisis. (Communist pamphlet)

d.    The things which will change "the world" are the great discoveries and inventions, the new reactions inside the social organism, and the changes in the earth itself on account of changes in the cosmical forces. These causes will make of it just what, in fidelity to them, it ought to be. The men will be carried along with it and be made by it. The utmost they can do with their cleverness will be to note and record their course as they are carried along, which is what we do now and is that which leads us to the vain fancy that we can make or guide the movement. That is why it is the greatest folly of which a man can be capable, to sit down with a slate and a pencil to plan out a new social world. (William Graham Sumner, "The Absurd Effort to Make the World Over," from the *Essays of William Graham Sumner*, Yale University Press)

## REVIEW QUESTIONS FOR UNIT 13

1.   Explain briefly the distinction between the *initial* and the *eventual* purposes of receptive events.
2.   Do the classifications of purposes explained in the preceding unit apply also to receptive events? Explain and illustrate.
3.   Are the purposes of producer and receiver in communication ever *shared*? *Always* shared? Ever harmonious when not shared? Ever inharmonious?
4.   What would it mean to call these purposes inharmonious?
5.   Why is it important for a receiver to recognize a producer's purposes? For a producer to recognize a receiver's purposes?
6.   What clews to an author's purpose are available to a receiver?
7.   On what two levels relative to purpose may one criticize a productive sign-event? Discuss.

UNIT **14**

# A Preliminary Analysis
# of Meaning

## §14.1 The Arbitrariness of Language

It used to be thought that the words we employ when we write or speak some established language, such as English or French or Latin or Hebrew, have fixed meanings that have been assigned to them by nature, or by Adam, or by God;[1] that when we use a word in order to indicate its natural, or divinely ordained, meaning, we are using the word correctly; and that when we use the word to indicate any other meaning than this natural one, we are using it incorrectly. According to this ancient view, a word might have its proper meaning and maybe *nobody* would know what that proper meaning is, so that *everyone* would use the word incorrectly. The task of a student of language, according to this older view, would be to *discover* the meanings of words that are guaranteed to them, either by divine sanction or by nature.

No such view of language and of the way in which words get their meanings can be seriously maintained today. Yet strangely enough many people reason and argue even today as though that ancient theory were true. In this unit, we shall outline a theory of language which shows that the meanings of words are *arbitrary* (explained shortly below), but that nevertheless an author can use a word incorrectly.

To make a beginning at this task, we must see that when a receiver asks, "What does such and such a sign-token mean?" the form of his question has made no reference to the most important factor involved in every question of meaning. The fundamental task of a receiver is not to find out what the *token* means; but rather to find out what the *author* of the token meant when he employed the token. As has been

---

[1] "And out of the ground the Lord God formed every beast of the field, and every fowl of the air; and brought them unto Adam to see what he would call them: and whatsoever Adam called every living creature, that was the name thereof." *Genesis*, II, 19.

137

said earlier, the author offers the token as a clew to his purpose. Thus, the reader who would understand the message must concern himself with the question: to what purpose on the author's part did the author intend this token to be a clew? Whatever the author intended the token to be a clew to, that is what the token means.

It follows from the above that whatever an author intended his words to mean—for whatever, that is, he intended his tokens to be clews—that is what they *do* mean. In a sense, then, the meaning of any sign-token is whatever its author intended it to be. In this same sense, no author is ever wrong; the tokens do mean what he intended them to mean. In this same sense, furthermore, only the receiver can be mistaken, believe that the author intended the token as a clew to *this*, when as a matter of fact, he intended it as a clew to *that*.

In other words, an author, by *choosing* a token, *gives* it its meaning. *Whatever* token he chooses to produce as a clew to something *has* that thing as its meaning. In this sense, the meaning of every token depends solely upon the will or decision of its author. This is what was meant above when we said that the meanings of words are **arbitrary**; they mean merely what their authors intend them to mean.

On the other hand, a receiver can not bestow meanings on tokens by an act of choice, his task is to *discover*, or to *judge*, what meaning it is that their author has already bestowed upon them. A receiver may be right or wrong in his bestowal of meanings upon tokens.

While an author cannot be wrong in his choice of tokens, he can be very unwise. For according as he chooses one token rather than another to be a clew to something, he makes the receiver's task (to identify that thing) easier or more difficult. We must shortly consider what means are available to an author who would convey a meaning.

## §14.2 Deliberate Sign-tokens and Natural Sign-tokens

In §10.2 we have spoken of "natural sign-tokens," those signs or occurrences in nature that we "read" in undirected receptive sign-events by inferring from them other facts of nature. These natural sign-tokens differ from the sign-tokens discussed in the preceding section with respect to the manner in which they have the meanings that they in fact possess. The tokens discussed just above *acquire* their meanings in productive sign-events, and the meanings that they acquire are those they were chosen to convey, that is, are those bestowed on them by their authors. As was already indicated in §10.2, there is no productive sign-event unless there is an element of deliberation and choice; natural sign-tokens are not produced, they are caused. Hence, their meanings cannot be arbitrary, cannot be bestowed on them by their authors.

Let us use the term **deliberate sign-tokens** to indicate any and all sign-tokens that are not merely natural sign-tokens. Then the intent of the opening section in this unit was to affirm that the meanings of deliberate sign-tokens are arbitrary, are, that is, simply and solely whatever their authors intended them to be.

Every sign-token is either a deliberate token or a natural token. It must, however, not be presumed that no token is both deliberate and natural. On the contrary, it may safely be assumed that every deliberate token is also a natural token (although *not* every natural token is also a deliberate one).

Let us illustrate. Suppose a man to ask me on the street, "Which is the way to the Public Library?" We may regard these noises as a deliberate sign-token, chosen by their author as a means, presumably, to get me to tell him the way to the library. That he chose them for this purpose (if my interpretation is correct) makes that to *be* their meaning.

But from the fact that he spoke these words, I may infer all sorts of other things: The man knows how to speak English. He wants to go to the library. He does not know the way to the library. He believes that I understand English.

All these latter inferences are ones I make when I regard his speech as a natural sign-token. It is a sign of those things, but a natural sign of them. They are not what he deliberately intended to signify by making that speech. Hence, they are not the meanings of his words regarded as deliberate sign-tokens. But they are the meanings of his words regarded as natural sign-tokens.

To sum up: When a sign-token is both deliberate and natural, it has *two* meanings, its meaning as a deliberate token and its meaning as a natural token. These two meanings are different. Every meaning of a token as a deliberate token is arbitrary: simply what its author intended. Every meaning of a token as a natural token is not arbitrary, but is dependent on nondeliberate causes and effects.

In the remainder of this unit, we shall be attending only to deliberate sign-tokens and their meanings as deliberate tokens.

*EXERCISE*

In each of the following sign-situations, identify something meant by the tokens as deliberate tokens and something meant by them as natural tokens.

1.   An instructor says to his class, "Will those who have done the homework please raise their hands!"
2.   A parent to his small child as they drive along the highway: "Look, Jimmie! See the pretty choo-choo!"

## §14.3  Meaning as Purpose: Concern and Topic of Concern

It has now been suggested that what any deliberate sign-token means is whatever its author intends it to mean, and that furthermore what he intends it to mean—what it therefore means—is precisely that purpose of the author for which he intended the token to be a clew. To make this account of meaning in terms of purpose more intelligible and useful, we must first analyze more carefully the general nature of purposes. We can best start by considering an example.

Let us assume that Mr. Author is speaking to Mr. Receiver and that Mr. Author's purpose is primarily cognitive. To identify the purpose as cognitive is, however, merely to catalogue the purpose as belonging to a very large and general type. The author's purpose will actually be much more specific than this and we can hardly know what his purpose is until we know more about its detailed content. In the first place, the purpose will be more specifically to *give* a piece of information, or to *secure* one (by asking a question), or to request the receiver to secure a piece of information, or something else of such a sort. But in the second place, it will be a *specific* piece of information, not just anything at all, that the author will be concerned to give or to receive.

"The first place" and "the second place" mentioned above draw attention to two components that may be found in any purpose: a **concern** and a **topic of concern**. The concern of a purpose is that which the purposer wishes to accomplish; the topic of concern is, roughly, that proposition relative to which he has this concern.[2]

---

[2]   At this point, the student should review §5.3, to remind himself of the sense in which we use the word "proposition."

We say above that the topic of concern is "roughly" a proposition. In general, it *is* a proposition. On the other hand, when a person puts a semidirect or indirect question (see §4.2), his topic of concern may more properly be thought of as a certain propositional form (discussed below) and his concern as one to discover which proposition of that form is true. But the immediate purposes of the present unit will best be served by disregarding these less usual cases and by thinking of topics of concern as propositions.

Fully to understand a person's purpose, we must know both what is his concern and what is his topic of concern.

Let us illustrate by considering again the preceding example. The author's concern will be to *give*, or *receive* (as the case may be), information relative to the truth or falsity of some proposition. The topic of his concern will be the proposition whose truth or falsity he is concerned to communicate or to discover.

While, in the last example, we assumed that the author's purpose was cognitive, one should not infer from that fact that only cognitive purposes have both a concern and a topic of concern. On the contrary, it may be fairly claimed that every purpose whatsoever has a concern and a topic of concern. Thus the cognitive, pragmatic, and esthetic purposes of discourse are each and all of them only so many different illustrations of this general fact about purposes.

Every purpose, then, is analyzable into a concern and a topic of concern. But it must be recognized that the dividing line between these two aspects of a purpose is not absolutely fixed and rigid. The distinction is in this respect something like the distinction between East and West as subdivisions of our country: plainly there are these subdivisions, but there is no fixed line at which you can say, "This is where the West begins." As *your* purposes in drawing the line of separation vary, so will vary the places at which you do draw the line.

The same sort of thing is true with respect to the distinction between concern and topic of concern. Let us illustrate. Suppose that I were to say something to you with the purpose of informing you that the feature picture at the Bijou comes on tonight at eight o'clock. We could analyze my purpose into a concern and topic of concern by drawing the line between concern and topic in at least two places:

| *Concern* | *Topic of Concern* |
|---|---|
| A.  Inform you it is true that | The feature picture at the Bijou comes on tonight at eight o'clock. |
| B.  Inform you | It is true that the feature picture . . . etc. |

In what follows, we shall generally draw the line between concern and topic of concern at a point suggested by Analysis A, above, putting questions of truth and falsity into the concern rather than into the topic of concern. But it is well to remember that this point of separation is not absolutely required. On occasion, we shall find it useful to consider other analyses. In our opinion, some investigators in logic and linguistics have been seriously misled by assuming that there is only one point at which the separation can be made.

## §14.4 Purpose, Meaning, and Language

Broadly speaking, the author in a productive sign-event is producing sign-tokens as clews to his purposes. These tokens are the chosen instruments by whose use he would accomplish his purpose. In general, sign-tokens are employed when an author believes that he can accomplish his purpose by revealing it in this manner.

To the extent that an author uses sign-tokens as a clew to purpose, he should choose them so that the receiver, upon observing them, may identify both his concern and his topic of concern. Let us illustrate. Suppose four speakers made the statements indicated below. We could, by observing the tokens they produced, recognize that the first three speakers all had the same topic of concern, but they had different concerns with this topic. On the other hand, the topic of concern of the fourth speaker was different from that of any of the previous three, but his concern with this topic was the same as the first speaker's concern with his topic. It is only as tokens are clews to *concerns* that we can see differences among the things purposed by the first three speakers. But further, it is only as the tokens are also clews to *topics* of concern that we can see a difference between the purposes of Speaker A and Speaker D.

Speaker A:  Bill's house burned down last night.

Speaker B:  Did Bill's house burn down last night?

Speaker C:  Find out whether or not Bill's house burned down last night.

Speaker D:  The price of butter went up one cent today.

The purposes (concerns and topics of concern) which an author intends his tokens to reveal are what *he* means or intends by the tokens. If we ask, not what *he* means *by* these tokens, but what these *tokens* mean, there can be only one answer: *in themselves*, they mean nothing; but as used by the author they mean what *he* means by them. In short, to speak of the meaning of a sign-token is to speak of the purpose for which its author offered it as a clew.

## §14.5 Expression, Indication, and Signification

When we say that a token means its author's purpose, we must recall that his purpose has its two sides, the concern and the topic of the concern. The token means both these things, but it is generally different aspects of the token that make it an effective clew to each of them. Let us illustrate.

Consider two sentences:
1. It will rain this afternoon.
2. Will it rain this afternoon?

In general, sentence-tokens having either of these forms will be clews that the topic of their author's concern is the fall of rain this afternoon. In other words, the topic of concern is a certain proposition. But tokens of the two forms will in general be clews to different concerns with this common topic: tokens of the first type suggesting that their authors accept this proposition as true and would have the receivers likewise accept it, tokens of the second type suggesting that their authors would have the receivers inform the authors concerning the truth or falsity of the proposition. Thus, the words that appear as grammatical subject, verb, and adverbial phrase ("this afternoon") provide a clew to the topic of the author's concern, while the order of these words is a clew to the author's concern with that topic.

But not every sign-token is a clew both to the author's concern and to the topic of his concern. For example, when we analyze sign-tokens of types 1 or 2, above, we see that these sentence-tokens contain the words "this afternoon" as parts of themselves. These contained tokens are clews to a part of the topic of their authors' concerns, but no clew to their authors' concerns with this topic.

It is often convenient or important to distinguish the revelation of concern from the revelation of a topic of concern. To accomplish this, we shall say that an author **expresses** his concern and **indicates** his topic of concern. Likewise we shall say that, to the extent they are offered as clews, the tokens produced by an author **express** his concerns and **indicate** his topics of concern. Finally, when we wish to refer to the total revelation of purpose, we shall say that an author **signifies** his purpose; and to the extent that his tokens are offered as clews to his purpose, we shall say that his tokens **signify** his purpose.

Thus expression, indication, and signification are three kinds of meaning which an author's sign-tokens have. (The last of these three is, however, nothing more than the combination of the first two.) Sometimes when we ask, What does that mean? or What does he mean? we want to know what is expressed; sometimes we want to know what is indicated, and sometimes we want to know what is signified. For example, if someone were to say to a foreigner at dinner, "Please pass the bread," the foreigner might turn to us and ask, "What does he mean?" We could reply that he wishes you to make it true (concern) that you pass the bread (topic of concern). We have explained the signification of the first speaker's remarks, but in that process we have explained both what his words express (his concern) and what they indicate (topic of concern).

The distinction between expression and indication as two types of meaning helps clear up a confusion that has troubled a good many philosophers. We often find philosophers debating whether the meanings of words are something mental and subjective or something objective. We can now answer that what the words *express* is completely mental, a state of mind, the concern, of the speaker; but that what they *indicate*, the proposition which is the topic of concern, is "in the speaker's mind" in the sense that his concern is directed on it, yet it is equally objective in that its existence or being does not depend on his having it in mind.

### §14.6 Meaning and the Plurality of Purposes

In Unit 12 we have remarked on the multiplicity of purposes for which people perform any act. We noted that this plurality of purposes is characteristic also of productive discourse; a speaker might have in mind several purposes, some immediate, some remote, some independent of one another, some subservient to some others.

Does the discourse signify all these purposes? Undoubtedly not.

To begin, the author does not usually offer his tokens as a clew to all his purposes. In general, an author's tokens are offered as clews only to some of his immediate purposes, the remote purposes to be served by his speech being rather situations that he anticipates will be brought about as consequences, or effects, of his having accomplished his immediate purposes.

Now near the middle of §14.1 we said that "whatever the author intended the token to be a clew to, that is what the token meant." In accordance with that principle, the remote purposes of an author are not usually signified by his tokens. At least, they are no part of the deliberate signification of the tokens, although some or several of them may be signified by those tokens considered as natural sign-tokens.

But let us go on to another point. Each of the author's purposes can be analyzed into a concern and a topic of concern. Some of these purposes will have the same topic of concern and differ one from the other only in their concerns with this topic. But some of these purposes will also differ one from the other with respect to their topics of concern.

For example, suppose that as John was about to leave the house, his wife said to him, "It's going to rain tonight." I can imagine the three following purposes:

| Purpose | Concern | Topic of Concern |
|---|---|---|
| 1. | Express her belief that | It will rain tonight. |
| 2. | Get John to believe that | It will rain tonight. |
| 3. | Get John to make it true that | John takes his raincoat with him. |

The first two, immediate, purposes have the same topic of concern; but the third purpose, a remote pragmatic one, has a quite different topic of concern. Her tokens may be properly regarded as indicating the topic of concern common to the first two purposes, and as not indicating (except perhaps as a natural sign-token) the topic of concern belonging to the third purpose. Also, the tokens express the concern of the first purpose and perhaps also the concern of the second purpose, but not that of the third purpose. Thus, clearly the first purpose is signified, probably the second purpose is signified, but the third purpose is not signified.

In general, if a single speech is to be taken as deliberately signifying several of the speech's different purposes, these should be chosen from among purposes that all have the same topic of concern, and that differ only with respect to their concerns with this topic. All other purposes should be considered as belonging either to the meanings of the tokens as natural signs or to what some writers call the *connotation*, rather than the strict meaning, of the tokens.

## §14.7 Iconic and Conventional Sign-tokens

An author, then, *chooses* what sign-tokens he will produce, and his very act of choosing and producing them gives to them, so to speak, the meaning which was his purpose. Henceforth, they signify that concern and that topic of concern which their author intended to signify by them.

This fact, however, that the chosen tokens *do* signify the author's purpose, will be of little value—either to the author who is attempting to *communicate* his purpose or to the receiver who is trying to discover the author's purpose—unless the receiver is actually aided by the sign-tokens to identify correctly the author's purpose.

Perhaps a diagram of communication will help clarify the situation.

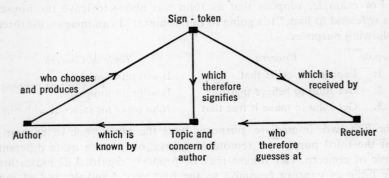

**Fig. 4**

As the diagram in Figure 4 suggests, what the sign-token signifies is completely established by the fact that the author used it to signify that purpose. Furthermore, the receiver's guess at the author's topic and concern is his guess at what the token signifies. The receiver's guess may be right, or it may be wrong. It may even be that the receiver is so puzzled by the sign-token that he is unable to make any guess at all.

A responsible author is going to choose what tokens he will produce in such a manner as to make the receiver's "guessing game" as easy and as safe as he can. Author and receiver are not opponents in a contest, but teammates with the same objective. If the receiver fails to guess at all or, upon making a guess, guesses incorrectly, then both author and receiver have "lost" a round in their game of communication.

In the pursuit of this game, a great deal depends on the author. According as he chooses one token rather than another, he makes the receiver's task easier or more difficult to perform. To illustrate this point, suppose that Mr. A wishes to inform Mr. R that the sun will set this evening at 5:48. *Whatever* Mr. A says will have this meaning, because Mr. A in choosing it for that purpose gives it that meaning. But consider these different things that Mr. A *might* say:

1. Lish'l bog ding nag-bag.
2. The sun will set this evening at five forty-eight.
3. Heute abend geht die Sonne zwölf Minuten vor sechs unter.
4. I ate lamb chops for dinner last night.

Let us agree that if Mr. A were to say sentence 1 or sentence 4 he would be a very foolish man. That is not the point in question at the present time. What is to be remembered is that *if* Mr. A *did* say any one of these four things *in order* to communicate the information mentioned above, then the tokens he produced—the noises he made in saying this sentence —*would* signify that the sun will set this evening at 5:48. Yet only the second of these four things he might say is likely to enable an American receiver correctly to guess at his intention. Sentence 1 looks like a string of nonsense, offers no clew to help any hearer to make any guess at all; sentence 3 would help a hearer who understood German, but otherwise is as useless as sentence 1; and sentence 4 will almost certainly mislead an English-speaking receiver into making a wrong guess as to Mr. A's purpose.

When we consider all the sounds, gestures, writings, and whatever else that a producer *might* produce in order to communicate a certain purpose, and when we recall that whatever sounds or other tokens he produces for that purpose will therefore signify that purpose, we might well ask, How shall he choose his tokens so as to make his receiver's guessing as easy and as likely to be correct as possible? Put in another way our question is, What kinds of tokens that a producer might employ will contribute most to the receiver's successful performance of his task? Tokens that *will* so contribute may be called *appropriate* for the purpose in mind; tokens that will *not* so contribute will be called *inappropriate*. Then our question is, What kinds of sign-tokens is it appropriate for an author to produce?

Broadly speaking, appropriate sign-tokens belong to one or the other (and sometimes to both) of two large classes. These are called *iconic* sign-tokens and *conventional* sign-tokens. What is meant by these two terms is explained immediately below.

An **iconic** sign-token is a token which resembles in some fashion or other the topic of the author's concern. In this class belong the gestures of "gesture-language," the pictures in a "picture-language," and all sorts of diagrams and maps.

An author who uses iconic sign-tokens hopes that the similarity between the token and the topic of his concern will bring that topic of concern into the receiver's mind and thus help the receiver "catch on" to the author's purpose. For example, a person who makes drinking gestures and then looks frantically about himself, depends on the similarity between this "play-looking" and "play-drinking," which are the tokens he produces, and actual discovery of a source of water and actual drinking from it, to enable his receiver to guess that he wants to be shown where he can get some water to drink. Again the lines on a road map cross and join one another in a manner that resembles the intersections and junctions of the roads in a region. It is this similarity that enables the receiver accurately to identify the map maker's purpose, to report that such and such roads do, or do not, intersect or join.

As the example of the map makes clear, an iconic sign-token may be very *unlike* its author's topic of concern in many respects. For example, the color of the map and of the line upon it may be entirely different from the color of the countryside and road upon it. But when some feature of the sign-token is like some feature of the topic of concern, and this similarity is intended to identify the topic of concern, the sign-token is iconic.

Iconic sign-tokens are among the most primitive and the most sophisticated or civilized tokens invented by mankind. Gesture languages and ritual dances are the characteristic iconic tokens of primitive tribes. Maps, graphs, algebraic equations, and chemical formulas are among the most intellectual tokens of civilized men. And yet all these are to a greater or less extent iconic.

A **conventional** sign-token is one that is like other tokens that other people have used when their purposes were similar to those of the user of the token in question. For example, suppose that Mr. A wished to direct the receiver's attention to a certain building. He might say, among other things, "House." Now the particular noise that Mr. A uttered was not an iconic sign-token. That is, it was not similar to the building which he intended to signify by the noise. On the other hand, the noise he uttered *was* like the noises that other people have uttered, when they wished to signify buildings. They also said, "House."

A convention is a "coming together," or an agreement or shared custom. A conventional sign-token is one chosen for production in certain circumstances which is like the tokens other people have chosen to use in similar circumstances. Thus, there is an agreement of wills among all users of those tokens: when the purpose is such and so, then the tokens we make will be of such and such a *kind*.

The use of conventional tokens is the beginning of language in the strict sense of the word. All our regular languages, French, English, Eskimo, Latin, Chinese, arithmetic, came about and are sustained by the fact that their users agree to produce certain *kinds* of tokens in order to signify certain kinds of purposes.

Let us briefly review the sorts of sign-tokens that have been mentioned so far.

1.   Natural sign-tokens (§10.2 and §14.2): causally connected with that which they signify.

2.   Deliberate sign-tokens (§14.2) of two sorts:
    a.   Iconic sign-tokens: similar to that which they signify
    b.   Conventional sign-tokens: similar to other tokens signifying things similar to that which these tokens signify.

Notice how important is the role of similarity, once we leave the field of natural sign-tokens. In fact, we might say that similarity is to deliberate sign-tokens what causal connection is to natural sign-tokens: it is the bond that connects, directly or indirectly, the token with that which it signifies.

Of deliberate sign-tokens, the conventional ones are by far the most important group. As we have already said, all the signs of ordinary language are conventional. With conventional signs, a much greater variety of things can be signified and subtly distinguished one from the other than is at all possible with merely iconic tokens.[3]

## REVIEW QUESTIONS FOR UNIT 14

1.  Explain carefully the difference between a natural sign-token and a deliberate sign-token.
2.  What is intended by the claim that the meanings of deliberate sign-tokens are arbitrary?
3.  Are any deliberate sign-tokens also natural sign-tokens? Explain and illustrate.

[3] We say "merely" iconic because some iconic tokens, such as maps and the equations of algebra, are also partly conventional. These conventional iconic tokens are among the most effective signs that man has created.

4. What is meant by the *concern* of a purpose? By the *topic of concern* of that purpose? Illustrate.

5. Explain the connection between purpose and meaning: Is *every* purpose to which the token is a clew a part of its meaning as a *deliberate* sign-token? If not, which ones are and which are not? Is anything except a purpose, or a part of a purpose, ever a part of the meaning?

6. How do you think that the present theory should deal with the meanings of lies?

7. Explain *expression*, *indication*, and *signification* as three kinds of meaning. Illustrate, by saying what is expressed, what indicated, and what signified by a customer who says to the butcher, "Do you have any lamb chops today?"

8. What is meant by an iconic sign-token? A conventional sign-token? Give examples of each.

9. In what sense is meaning a mental or subjective item, and in what sense is it a nonmental or objective item? How does the distinction between "expression" and "indication" help clear up this problem?

# 15

## *Sign-types and Conventional Signs*

### §15.1 Sign-tokens and Sign-types

How many figures appear in Figure 5, below? It depends on what the word "figures" means. If "figures" means "shapes," the correct answer is: two, a triangular shape and a rectangular shape. But if "figures" means "drawings," the correct answer is: three, the left-hand one, the middle one, and the right-hand one.

The above question illustrates a kind of ambiguity that is liable to attach to all sorts of words used in dealing with language. Among these possibly ambiguous words are "letter," "word," "phrase," "expression," "sentence," and "sign." For example, one might ask, How many words appear in the first paragraph of this section? The correct answer depends on what is meant by "words". If "words" means "dictionary words," then the correct answer is thirty-four.[1] But if "words" means "printings of words," then the correct answer is fifty-four.

That this kind of double meaning is associated with these words about language is readily illustrated by the two following examples: (1) Suppose that your teacher assigns a theme and tells you it "should be about five hundred words long." What he means (and you readily enough interpret his statement in this way) is that your theme should contain about five hundred examples (printings) of dictionary words. He does *not* mean that the theme should contain examples of about five hundred dictionary words. (2) But now suppose that your French teacher tells you that by now you should understand about five hundred words of the French language. What he means is that you should understand examples of five hundred dictionary words.

[1] To get this answer, we count the singular and plural forms as two different words (e.g., "figure" and "figures," "shape" and "shapes"). Had we counted these in each instance as one word, the correct answer would have been thirty-two. This illustrates the presence of still another ambiguity than the one discussed in the text.

The two different kinds of meaning that we have undertaken to distinguish are: (1) one that refers to individual, concrete, particular *specimens* or *examples* of a given kind of thing, and (2) another that refers to *types*, or kinds of specimen of a given kind of thing. Thus,

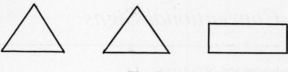

**Fig. 5**

in Figure 5 above, there are three specimens belonging to two types of figure; in paragraph 1 above, there are fifty-four specimens belonging to thirty-four kinds of word. If someone were to tell me that the zoo contains fifty different animals, I might wonder whether he meant fifty specimens of different kinds of animal, or whether he meant specimens of fifty different kinds of animal.

Throughout Units 9 to 14 we have frequently used the expression "sign-token." This expression was used, instead of the simpler expression "sign," in order to avoid any ambiguity of the sort now under consideration. "Sign-token" refers to the individual example of a sign produced by an author or observed by a receiver. It is a concrete physical object, with its definite location in space and time. (See §9.2). Thus, for example, if two people at a dinner party said, "Please pass the bread," there would not only be two productive sign-events, but each of these would have produced a different sign-token. Nevertheless, the two tokens would have been very much alike. We might say that the two people "said the same thing," or "made the same sign." *What* was actually the same in the two tokens was the pattern, or form, or design, or "melody" of the two tokens. This pattern could be, and often is, called the *sign;* it is, after all, the thing to which a receiver must pay attention if he is going to understand the author. But this pattern of noise we shall call the **sign-type.**

The distinction indicated here between a token and a type is a common one, and a kind of distinction that we often make, although we do not so often pay attention to it. If, for example, you hear the band playing, you may recognize the composition and say that they are playing *The Star-Spangled Banner*. When they play the national anthem again next week, you might properly say that they are playing the same thing that they played last week. Yet, in another sense, they cannot play the same thing twice. The second playing is a different concert, with its different date. If we attend to the two, *differently* dated, sets of noises, these two renditions are two song-tokens; but they are two renditions, two song-*tokens*, of the same song-*type*.

As we speak of sign-tokens and sign-types, so we shall usually combine other words dealing with signs and language with the suffixes "token" and "type," thus:

| | |
|---|---|
| Letter-token | Letter-type |
| Word-token | Word-type |
| Phrase-token | Phrase-type |
| Expression-token | Expression-type |
| Sentence-token | Sentence-type |

The tokens are the concrete things, noises or bits of dried ink or gestures, with definite locations in space and time. The types are abstract things, the shapes (visual) or "tunes" (auditory) that we have to recognize in the tokens if we are to understand the tokens. By using the somewhat awkward terms here proposed, we shall avoid ambiguities of the sort that was illustrated at the beginning of this section and hope thereby to escape many confusions in our thought about language.

### §15.2 The Definition of Sign-types

When you receive a letter from a friend, you must look at it in order to find out what he is trying to tell you. In writing the letter, your friend spread ink over a piece of paper. This dried ink is the sign-token that your friend made, and it is this dried ink at which you must look in your receptive event. But it is not enough that you look at the dried ink. There are actually certain characteristics or features of the ink to which you must give special attention. Other features of the ink you may disregard. For example, you need not pay attention to the color of the ink, nor to the thickness of the lines formed by the ink. But you must pay attention to the general shape, pattern, or design formed by the ink. It is that shape or design which makes the ink to be a writing, specimen, example, or *instance* of such and such words; that is, of the very words your friend wished you to read. This general form, or pattern, was deliberately given to the ink by your friend, the author; and you, the receiver, must identify the form or pattern that he gave to the ink.

By a **sign-type** is meant that form or characteristic whose presence in a sign-token determines the meaning of the token.[2] Let us consider a few illustrations of this definition.

1. Suppose that your friend had written, "Then George told James what he thought of him." The ink that your friend spread on the paper is the sign-token. But the pattern, or shape, that the ink traces out, so that it forms just these words rather than some other words, and so that the words it forms are arranged in just this order rather than some other order, is the sign-type. It is this shape which your friend gave to the ink in order to convey this particular message; and it is this shape which you must notice in the ink if you are to understand the message.

2. Little Jimmy says, "Won't you, *please*, come on the picnic, Uncle Bill?" The noise, there and then, is the sign-token made by Jimmy. But the pronunciation, the "tune" that characterizes the noises, is the sign-type which Jimmy gave to the noise and which Uncle Bill must hear in the noise if the communication is to succeed.

3. A dark cloud mass on the western horizon is a sign (natural sign) of rain. The particular cloud is the sign-token. It is the shape, size, color, and position of the cloud that make it mean rain. This shape, size, color, and position are the sign-type.

Sign-tokens, like all other concrete objects, have a great many different characteristics. Two sign-tokens might be alike in respect to one or more characteristics (for example, in respect to color) and dissimilar in respect to other characteristics (for example, in respect to shape). If the characteristic that the two tokens share is one in virtue of which they have the meanings that they do have, then the two tokens belong to the same sign-type; that is, they belong to the sign-type identified by that shared characteristic. No matter how different the two tokens may be in other respects, so long as they share the characteristic defining the sign-type they belong to that type. For example, the word-type "hats" might be spelled out in one token in letters that

2 That the form "determines" the meaning must not blind us to the fact insisted on in the preceding unit, that the meaning is arbitrary, dependent on the will of its author. The author decides what meaning shall be associated with (identified by) that form in this token.

are ten feet high, made of glowing red neon tubes, atop some building. Another token, made of black, dried ink, less than ¼-inch high, could spell out the same word-type. These two sign-tokens would belong to the same sign-type.

## §15.3 Natural Sign-types and Conventional Sign-types

All sign-tokens, both natural ones and deliberate ones (iconic and conventional), have such meanings as they do in virtue of their belonging to some sign-type. In other words, some form or characteristic present in and illustrated by a given token makes it mean what it does mean. If the token did not have that characteristic, it would not have that meaning. Hence, in order to determine the meaning of a sign-token presented to us as interpreters in a receptive event, we must observe in it some one or other of its characteristics.[3] This characteristic defines the sign-type to which the token belongs and thereby determines the meaning of the token.

As has been already suggested (§§10.2 and 14.2) natural sign-tokens are those things or events in nature (including human nature) whose presence or occurrence is causally connected with those things that they signify. The causal connection is not always the same: sometimes, the natural sign-token (for example, smoke or stammering) is an effect of that which it signifies (fire or embarrassment); sometimes, the sign-token (for example, excessive inventories) is a cause of that which it signifies (falling prices); while sometimes, the sign-token (for example, a cloud) is one of two effects of a common cause, the other effect (rain) being that which the sign-token signifies.

Now one fundamental characteristic of nature is sometimes referred to as its *uniformity*. This uniformity of nature bears on our present problem in a manner that may be expressed in the law, *Like causes have like effects*. In other words, learning to read natural sign-tokens involves learning to *classify* under *kinds* or into *types* those things or events in nature in such a manner that *all* things (or *usually*, things) of the kind or type in question are accompanied by things of another kind or type. For example, usually clouds of such and such a character are accompanied by rainstorms. *This* cloud will therefore probably be accompanied by a rainstorm, or *this* cloud is a sign of rain.

---

[3] We must not be led astray at this point. Despite the fact that the identity of the characteristic present in the token determines what the token means, it is still the token, and not the type, that has this determined meaning. The type does not have a meaning, but identifies the meaning which the token has.

Notice that when we say or think "this cloud" we are already thinking of this as belonging to a certain *kind* of thing: the kind, *cloud*. But this is also a beautiful sky. In other words, it belongs to *two* kinds of thing. On the other hand, the kind or type, beautiful sky, is not regularly connected with rain or any other identifiable kind of weather. Hence, to classify this as a beautiful sky is not to pick out the form or characteristic of this thing that determines this to be a sign-token of rain. But to classify this as a cloud of such and such a type *is* to pick out the characteristic which this has and which determines it to be a sign of rain. The cloud-form of such and such a character is, then, the *natural sign-type* of which the given cloud is an instance, and in virtue of its being an instance, the given cloud is a sign-token of rain.[4]

If we think of causal connections as being among the facts of nature, then it is the facts of nature which bring it about that belonging to such and such a sign-type should make a certain token be a sign of such and such another fact. It is this derivation from the facts of nature that justifies our calling such tokens *natural* sign-tokens. The situation is very different when we come to conventional sign-tokens and conventional sign-types.

All clouds that are natural sign-tokens of rain are more or less similar one to the other. The ground of this similarity is a feature regularly connected in nature with the fall of rain. No mere act of human will could bring it about that when that kind of cloud appears, it should *not* rain.

Likewise, all sayings of the sentence, "It will soon rain," are more or less similar to one another. Furthermore, the ground of this similarity is a feature regularly connected in nature (human nature) with the expectation of rain by the speaker. But here the similarity breaks down. For a mere act (or acts) of human will could bring it about that when that kind of sound is made, there should not exist within the speaker an expectation of rain. In fact, sounds of that kind could be signs of anything that their authors chose. (Of course, if they were not signs of the expectation indicated, their authors would not be speaking English.)

We must now notice a somewhat complicated fact. All the sayings of "It will soon rain" are similar in general pronunciation, if not in

[4] Not every cloud is a sign of rain. It is a part of the task of the science called *meteorology* to determine what kinds of clouds are rain-bearing and under what circumstances these rain-bearing clouds will release rain. In other words, meteorology aims at providing a more precise description of the sign-type which makes certain clouds to be sign-tokens of rain.

accent, pitch, or loudness. It is this pronunciation which they all have that makes them all sign-tokens of that same kind of thing: an expectation of rain. This pronunciation is, then, the sign-type to which all those tokens belong. But this sign-type, this pronunciation, does determine the tokens to have that meaning only in virtue of the common will of the several speakers; if they had not *intended* to mean that by their tokens, the tokens *would not* have meant that. Hence, the sign-type is a *conventional sign-type:* a sign-type such that the several tokens of it mean what they mean in virtue of an agreement among the wills of the several producers of those tokens.

## §15.4 Distinguishing Features of Conventional Sign-types

It would be much too complicated a task to try to identify the distinguishing features of the conventional sign-types involved in all languages.[5] Let us rather content ourselves with a discussion of some among the distinguishing features of conventional sign-types in visual English, together with occasional references to oral English.[6]

Written English is generally composed by arranging letters into words and words into sentences and other expressions.[7] As often as not, the sentences thus composed are themselves arranged into still larger units of discourse. Our concern here will be with letter-tokens and letter-types, word-tokens and word-types, and with the yet more inclusive units of discourse which we shall lump together under the headings expression-tokens and expression-types. The comments on these items cannot be considered as an exhaustive study of the entire subject which they treat. But it is hoped that they will be sufficiently detailed and accurate to permit us to make use of them in our later studies.

Written English began, as did most of the visual forms of ordinary languages, as a **secondary language.** That is, the visual forms were only

5   Near the end of §14.7 it was said that the use of conventional sign-tokens was the beginning of language in the strict sense of the term.

6   We consider visual English (written and printed English) as one language, oral English as another, closely related, language.

7   Unless otherwise specified, we shall mean the expression "written English" to refer both to literally written and to typed or printed English, that is, to "visual" English. Furthermore, in this section we are leaving out of account those uses of the English alphabet by which authors occasionally report the non-English noises made by things or characters:

"Awk, glug!"

"Goo-oo-oo," was little Thurber's only comment.

so many instructions telling the reader what noise or sound he was to imagine or to make. For example, the written word "bird" did not refer directly to a feathered creature, but instructed its reader to make a certain sound; it was this sound, the spoken word "bird," that referred to the winged creature. Thus the written language was like a musical score, simply revealing a sequence of sounds that the author wished his reader to imagine that he heard. These sounds were, of course, the sounds of spoken English, and they formed a **primary language,** a language used by their authors to refer directly to things in the world at large.

As time went by, the receivers of written messages, and even their authors, neglected to think, as they wrote, of the particular sounds indicated by the written language, and instead thought directly of the things that those sounds meant. Gradually, there entered the language new visual signs that were not instructions for making certain sounds, which in turn would have a meaning, but were instead direct signs of that intended object. Such, for example, are the Arabic and Roman numbers of our arithmetic. For example, "XX" and "20" are not instructions to stutter while making a clicking noise, nor are they instructions to make the sound indicated by the visual token "twenty." Instead, they refer directly to that same quantity or number as is referred to by the sound of the word "twenty." Thus, gradually, visual English has taken on the character of a primary language, even though it has never entirely lost the character of a secondary language.

In what follows, written English will be treated in general as a primary language.

As was said earlier, written words are formed out of letters. While the words so formed may have meanings, the letters out of which they are formed do not have meaning.[8] But the letters contribute their individual shapes to form the total shape of the entire word.

Every printing or writing of a letter is a letter-token. In the history of the world so far, authors and printers of English have produced millions and millions of letter-tokens. But all these letter-tokens belong

---

[8] This, of course, is true only for written English as a primary language. Considered as a secondary language, the separate letters in a word indicate the separate sounds that are to be made one after the other in pronouncing the word. Also, occasionally, a single letter forms an entire word, for example, "I." In such a case, it is the letter *as a word*, not *as a letter*, which has a meaning.

to one or the other of only twenty-six letter-types, the standard twenty-six letters of the English alphabet.

When we consider the letters of the alphabet, we may notice that it would be next to impossible to give a general geometrical description of a shape that would be possessed by all the tokens of one letter-type and not possessed by any tokens of any other letter-type. For example, there are three alternative shapes associated with the first letter in our alphabet; capital printed "A," lower-case printed "a," and script "*a*." (Capital script *a*'s resemble in shape either capital printed *A*'s or lower-case script *a*'s, depending on the handwriting style of their author.) Each of these three shapes could be described in general geometrical terms such that every token of the letter might be recognized as a logically possible variation on one or the other of these three shapes. But it would be extremely difficult, if not impossible, to give a still more abstract geometrical description which would both apply to all three shapes and yet not apply to any shape associated with any other letter. Instead, we depend on a convention, or agreement, that all tokens, having any one of these three shapes, shall be considered instances of *one* letter-type, the first letter-type in our alphabet.

## EXERCISE

1. How many letter-tokens appear in Figure 6?
2. How many letter-types appear in Figure 6? Explain.

A b M a A B a

**Fig. 6**

Word-tokens are formed by placing, one after the other, letter-tokens belonging to such and such letter-types. The word-type to which a given word-token belongs is simply and solely a matter of its spelling. Thus, "HAT" and "hat" are two word-tokens belonging to one word-type, because they are spelled in the same way. On the other hand, the word-token "hut" is an instance of a different word-type because it is spelled differently.

Notice that what the word-token means has nothing to do with determining what word-type it belongs to. Thus, in the sentence, "Every day, Mr. Day bought a rose," the two word-tokens "day" and "Day" are instances of the same word-type, because they are spelled in the same way, even though the one token refers to a unit of time and the other to a certain man. Similarly, two differently spelled word-tokens, even though they may have the same meaning, belong to different word-types. Thus the two tokens "die" and "perish" in ordinary English mean the same thing, but they belong to two different word-types. Two exceptions to the general rule, that spelling determines the word-type of a given token, must be noticed here. (1) In the case of some words, alternative spellings are generally recognized. For example, the English generally spell "labor" and "honor" with a *u*, "labour" and "honour," while Americans generally omit the *u*. Whenever the dictionary recognizes such variations in spelling as variants of one word, we shall consider tokens of the two forms as instances of one word-type. The identity of word-type despite difference in spelling is similar to the identity of letter-type despite difference in shape. (2) Nouns and verbs take on different "endings" to indicate the difference between singular and plural, or according as the verb is first person, second person, or third person: "one *house*," "two *houses*," "I *go*," "he *goes*." Sometimes, these variations are indicated by a change in the internal spelling of the word: "one *foot*," "two *feet*," "I *am*," "you *are*," "he *is*." Also changes in the tense of a verb change its ending or its internal spelling: "I *look*," "I *looked*," "I *am*," "I *was*." Strictly speaking, we should consider each variation as giving a new word-type. But it will usually be simpler and more practical to treat these as permitted variations in the form of one word-type. If the question whether one should be strict or practical ever becomes important, the decision can be made in a manner that will suit that individual situation.

Finally, still more complex sign-tokens are formed in written English by placing written English word-tokens one after another in horizontal lines and placing the lines so formed one below the other to form columns of lines.[9] Here the *order* of the word-tokens, as well as the

---

[9] We take no account in this brief survey of the variations that are often to be found in advertisements and the like, where the standard arrangement described in the text is discarded for one reason or another:

```
              N
            I
          A
        G   S
      R       A
    A   HELP    L
  B   YOURSELF    E
```

identity of the word-tokens, contributes to a determination of the patterns that are to be distinguished as being different sign-types. For example, the two sentence-tokens,

1. *John kicked George*, and
2. *George kicked John*,

are to be considered as belonging to two *different* sentence-types. In other words, the sign-type of which a complex written English sign-token sentence is an instance, is determined primarily by the word-types to which its component word-tokens belong, *in the order of their occurrence*.

It was said in the last sentence, ". . . determined *primarily* . . . " We must not overlook the important contributions made by punctuation, capitalization of first words in sentences, division into paragraphs, and the use of italics or underlining to indicate emphatic elements or for other purposes. All such variations in manner of presenting the component word-tokens will make a difference in the sign-types to which the complex sign-tokens belong. For example, sentence-tokens 3 and 4 have quite different meanings and must be considered as belonging to different sentence-types, even though the only differences between them are in punctuation.

3. John did not, like Mary, quite like Joan.
4. John did not like Mary—quite like Joan.

Or again, if two sentences are exactly alike except that one is printed entirely in Roman type and the other entirely in italics, then they belong to one sentence-type; but if a third sentence is exactly like the first two, except that it is partly in italics and partly in Roman type, and the difference in type is intended to identify a point of emphasis or otherwise mark a difference in the meaning, then this third sentence belongs to a second sentence-type. Thus, among the following, sentence-tokens 5 and 6 are instances of one sentence-type, while sentence-tokens 7 and 8 are instances of another.

5. George studied the principles of right reason.
6. *George studied the principles of right reason.*
7. George studied *The Principles of Right Reason.*
8. *George studied THE PRINCIPLES OF RIGHT REASON.*

In summary, letter-tokens belong to letter-types. The letter-tokens are not sign-tokens (since they do not have meanings by themselves) but are instead pieces of sign-tokens. By being combined one with the other, they contribute their letter-types to determine the word-types of individual word-tokens. These word-tokens may or may not be sign-tokens; that is, they may have meanings by themselves or have meanings only in combination one with the other. Finally, the word-tokens are combined in a certain order and with such and such punctuation to produce a complex sign-token, a phrase, sentence, paragraph, or larger unit of discourse. The sign-type of this larger unit is determined, primarily, by the word-types of its component word-tokens, in the order in which they appear, and secondarily by the punctuation and other distinguishing marks that are used in presenting these word-tokens.

## EXERCISE

The following "dialogue" pretends to record a scene in which George is testing an "echo." Disregarding the words that identify the speakers, and considering only the passages purporting to quote the dialogue, answer the following questions:

1. How many word-tokens appear in the passage?
2. Strictly speaking, how many word-types appear in the passage?
3. Practically speaking, how many word-types appear in the passage?
4. How many sentence-tokens appear in the passage?
5. How many sentence-types appear in the passage?

George:   The sun is shining.
Echo:      The sun is shining.
George:   Yesterday afternoon, the sun was shining.
Echo:      Yesterday afternoon, the sun was shining.
George:   Where were you yesterday afternoon?
Echo:      I won't tell!

## §15.5 A Minor Practical Problem

A minor, although troublesome, practical problem often arises in cases of poor penmanship, smudged printing, misspelling, and the like, as also in cases of blurred pronunciation or mispronunciation. In all cases, the author has presented to the receiver a sign-token which does *not* have any of the shapes or patterns constituting conventional or accepted variations on accepted and known word-types or sign-types. For example, careless penmanship may make it difficult to determine whether a certain author intended to present a token of the word-type "hat" or one of the word-type "hut."

Strictly speaking, the author's word-token or sign-token is not an instance of any conventional word-type or sign-type. However, if our purpose in reading his token is less to criticize than to understand his message, we use whatever means are at our disposal (for example, context) in order to guess what conventional word-type the author *intended* to present and we then treat the token *as though* it were an instance of that type.

## §15.6 Further Analysis of Conventional Tokens

In §14.7 it was said that a conventional sign-token is a token "that is like other tokens that other people have used when their purposes were similar to those of the user of the token in question." We may now see that for a sign-token to be conventional requires *two* things:

1. It must be an instance of a conventional sign-type.

2. It must be used by its author only when his purposes are like those for which other people used tokens of that same conventional sign-type.

To illustrate, consider the four sentences on page 147 that Mr. A might have used to inform Mr. R that the sun will set tonight at 5:48. Sentence-token 1 does not meet either of the above requirements; sentence-token 4 meets the first requirement, but not the second; sentence-tokens 2 and 3 meet both requirements.

Let us, however, now draw together several further considerations connected with the use of conventional sign-tokens.

a. The use of conventional sign-tokens by an author will have little value unless the receiver is a party to the convention. For example, although both sentence-tokens 2 and 3 (page 147) are conventional, as we have seen, an author who is about to choose between them would be very unwise to use sentence-token 3 if his receiver did not understand the conventions that define German, and equally unwise to use sentence 2 if his receiver did not understand the conventions that define English.

b. The point just made bears not only on the obligation of authors but also on those of receivers. Unless receivers know some conventions they cannot be effectively addressed. Hence, receivers should become aware of conventions and learn to understand them.

c.   Conventions do not fit precisely over the ranges of use of given languages, such as English. Within the broad general uniformity of use defining English, we find more specialized communities with their special conventions. For example, scientists (chemists) agree among themselves as to what they mean when they say "atom" or "compound," and it is likely to be something quite different from what other English-speaking people mean by those words.

d.   Furthermore, conventions change. For example, "It's strictly for the birds," means something nowadays—at least among those who are "hep"—quite different from what it would have meant only a few years ago. And the changes are not only those connected with the rise and fall of slang or the inventions of new technical and scientific vocabulary. Words like "communist," "propaganda," "force," "passion," "formal," and "objective" have come to have quite different meanings than they used to have.

e.   Conventions are not a matter merely of vocabulary. Grammar and punctuation also reflect conventions governing the arrangements of words, and these conventions of arrangement also affect the meanings of the total complex sign-tokens.

f.   Finally, disregard of conventions is an attack upon the most important means available to man for communication. Iconic sign-tokens are nowhere near as adequate for communicating the variety of things we wish to say. And the *only* other means at our disposal is the use of conventional sign-tokens. But every time we violate a convention we are in part destroying it. For the convention is only the agreement to use the tokens in a certain way for a certain purpose. And when we violate the convention, either we are using tokens in that way for *another* purpose (and thus reducing the range of the agreement) or we are making arrangements of words that are unconventional (violating requirement 1 at the beginning of this section) and hence narrowing the dominion of convention.

The above is not to say that no departure from convention is ever justified. Sometimes, no convention is appropriate to our purpose. Furthermore, some conventions are awkward or could otherwise be improved. But violations of conventions should never threaten to destroy the availability of conventions. They should occur only rarely, and against a background of general conformity with other conventions.

They should be *justifiable*, as worthy of becoming new, and better, conventions than the ones that they destroy.

The preservation of civilization depends on the continued ability of man to speak with man. That depends on the preservation of conventional sign-tokens. Here is the reason for courses in English, in communication skills, in foreign languages, and in logic. Here is the reason so many of these courses are required in our public schools and colleges.

## §15.7 Some Applications of the Foregoing Theory of Language

We now have before us various technical terms—sign-token, sign-type, conventional token, conventional type, and so on—together with a theory of language which they are used to explain: What deliberate sign-tokens mean is whatever purpose their author had for which he intended them to be clews; hence, the meanings of tokens are arbitrary. But at the same time, some tokens would be better clews to a given purpose than others, because the receivers of the former would more readily or more correctly identify the author's purpose than would receivers of the latter. By and large, only iconic tokens or conventional tokens will be effective clews to purpose, therefore useful signs. A conventional token belongs to a conventional type and is used by its author only when his purposes are like those of other people when they use tokens of this same type. The development of systems of conventional tokens marks the beginning of true language.

There is an additional technical term which we shall find useful in the future:

1. An author communicates by producing tokens that belong to such and such sign-types. It is sometimes convenient to say that the author **presents** such and such sign-types. All that this means is that he produces tokens belonging to those types.

Furthermore, in terms of the technical terms and the theory of language now at hand, several topics discussed in earlier units can be more precisely or more effectively treated. A few of these may be mentioned here.

2. It is now possible to restate in technical terms the nature of ambiguity and vagueness that were explained in nontechnical terms in §3.7.

*Ambiguity.* An author presents a sign-type with which two or more conventions are associated, and the circumstances are such that it is impossible to determine which of these conventional meanings the author intended by his token. Under these conditions, the author's sign-token is said to be ambiguous.

*Vagueness.* The convention associated with a given sign-type is incomplete in that there has never been established any agreement among people using the sign-type as to where a line is to be drawn between objects to which the sign properly applies and those to which it does not apply. For example, a convention among people who speak English makes the sign "bald" applicable to persons with little or no hair on the crowns of their heads. But the convention is incomplete because it does not include an agreement as to how sparse hair must be before the sign "bald" may be properly applied. Hence tokens of the sign-type "bald" will be vague, unless their authors explain in accompanying remarks what measure of sparseness they use as the dividing line between bald and not bald.

3. The vagueness of tokens is often matched by a corresponding vagueness of thought. This occurs whenever an author not only fails to explain, but even fails to decide, the limits of applicability which he intends when he presents sign-types having incomplete conventions of the sort just discussed. The very familiarity of these sign-types with their partial conventions, and the fact that in many situations the vagueness will cause no difficulty, make it easy for an author presenting them to overlook the fact that his own thought is still vague. The serious consequences of this defect have made scientists particularly sensitive to it, so that they have developed certain standard, or routine, procedures that they almost automatically apply in thier effort to reduce not only vagueness of expression, but also vagueness of thought. This concern accounts for at least some of the standardization, even monotony, of the literary style in much scientific writing, as also for a certain amount of the drudgery that makes up so large a part of scientific study and research.

4. It is also possible, now that the distinction between types and tokens is available, to add something to the discussion of the purposes of discourse contained in Units 12 and 13. In particular, in §13.5 it was suggested that in criticizing an author's choice of means to accomplish the purposes of his productive discourse, we may properly ask, among other things, whether the sign-tokens he chose to produce were such as would be most appropriate to the attainment of his ends

and purposes. More often than not, the identification of the sign-types to which those tokens belong has a great deal to do with the answer to this question.

Many tokens belonging to certain types will tend to arouse more or less directly certain emotions in the receivers of those tokens; tokens of other types will tend to produce certain modes of behavior among the receivers of those tokens; while tokens belonging to still other types will tend on the whole neither to arouse directly certain emotions, nor to evoke directly certain modes of behavior among their receivers.

The sign-types of a language may thus be more or less effectively divided into three fundamental kinds according to the effects on the majority of receivers of tokens belonging to those types: (a) **Emotive sign-types**: sign-types whose tokens tend on receipt to arouse emotions. Example: "democracy." (b) **Directive sign-types** that tend to evoke action. Example: "Please pass the bread." (c) **Neutral sign-types** that are neither emotive or directive.

The above classification of sign-types is made in terms of the probable effects on receivers of tokens belonging to those types. An author will always have chosen his tokens inappropriately if they belong to types contrary to the effects it was the author's purpose to have on his receivers. For example, if an author uses tokens belonging to emotive sign-types when what he wishes is calm consideration of a problem, his choice of tokens was inappropriate.

However, the criticism of the appropriateness of certain tokens in the light of the classification of their sign-types must not be glib or over-hasty. For example, a certain word or phrase may be an emotive sign-type, and yet tokens of it may appear in such a context that their emotional tendencies are completely canceled. And on the other side, simple, neutral words may be put together in such a way as to produce a most moving poem. This classification of sign-types is, then, more suggestive of what must be attended to than effective as a practical instrument for the discharge of these duties by the critic or self-critic.

## REVIEW QUESTIONS FOR UNIT 15

1. What is meant by a sign-type? Explain and illustrate the difference between a sign-token and a sign-type.
2. Are letter-tokens sign-tokens? Explain.
3. Explain the difference between a natural sign-token and a natural sign-type. Illustrate.

4. Discuss briefly the role of science in the identification of natural sign-types.

5. Explain the difference between a *primary* language and a *secondary* language. Do the finger signs of the deaf and dumb form a primary language or a secondary language?

6. What factor or factors determine the word-type to which a word-token of written English belongs? Explain.

7. What factor or factors determine the sentence-type to which a sentence-token of written English belongs? Explain.

8. What is meant by *emotive* sign-types? by *directive* sign-types? by *neutral* sign-types? What responsibilities and obligations of an author or a critic are suggested by these classifications of sign-types?

10. An understanding and working knowledge of the vocabulary and grammar of a language are important to any speaker or writer in making himself understood.

   a. Show why the above statement is true by reference to the iconic and conventional bases of communication discussed in this and the preceding unit.

   b. Describe and explain a similar obligation which rests upon the hearer or reader.

   c. How does disregard of the conventions of vocabulary and grammar constitute a long-range threat to civilization and society?

   d. Under what circumstances may the conventions of grammar and vocabulary be profitably disregarded?

PART THREE

# PART THREE

# THE THEORY OF TERMS

# *Statements and Propositions*

## §16.1 Introduction

It was said in Units 1 and 2 that the principles of right reason come from three sciences: logic, methodology, and semiotic. To a large extent, the study of sign-events and of language occupying Part II of this book belongs to the science of semiotic. We are now to turn to a new topic, the *theory of terms*. This theory is one belonging to the science of logic.

The two sciences, semiotic and logic, are closely related at many points. One of these points of intimate connection is in the theory of terms. You will recall that in the last few units of Part II, we were engaged in a study of meaning. The theory of terms is really only a continuation of that study of meaning, but a continuation with a difference. For here we concentrate on certain topics in the general field of meaning which are of special importance to the conduct of right reason. What we shall have to say will not apply to all sign-events nor to the meanings of all sign-tokens. Rather, we shall be engaged in seeing how one might profitably analyze the meanings of various conventional sign-tokens that would have been produced primarily for cognitive purposes. Certain of those tokens will be said to be tokens of *terms*.

But before we can actually take up the theory of terms, we must consider a preliminary matter: statements and propositions.

## §16.2 Statements and Propositions

In §§5.2 and 5.3 we defined the terms *statement* and *proposition*. Let us repeat those definitions here, only making minor revisions such as the intervening discussions of types and tokens (in Unit 15) and of expression and indication (in Unit 14) make appropriate.

By a **statement** we shall refer to any declarative sentence-type insofar as it is used to indicate a certain proposition.

By a **proposition** we understand any situation or state of affairs whatsoever.

Several points should be noticed in connection with the definition of a statement given just above.

 1. A statement is more like a sign-type than like a sign-token. But it is not a sign-type because sign-types are defined without any references to meanings. (See §15.2.) For example, suppose two authors were to produce tokens of the sign-type: "I saw a cardinal this morning." Suppose, further, that author A was talking about birds and author B was talking about churchmen. Then, although the two authors would have *presented* one and the same *sign-type*, they would *not* have made (or presented) one and the same statement. This follows from the fact that they were using that sign-type to indicate different propositions.

 2. We shall find it useful to speak of tokens of declarative sentence-types as **occurrences of statements,** or sometimes as **statement-occurrences.**

 3. *What* statement occurs in a given sentence-token depends *both* on the sign-type of that token and on the proposition indicated by that token. Thus, if you change the sign-type but keep the meaning the same, you have a different statement. Equally, if you change the meaning but keep the sign-type the same, you have a different statement.

 4. Tokens which belong to sign-types other than declarative sentence-types are also used by authors to indicate certain propositions. For example, "Did Washington cross the Delaware?" and "Washington's crossing the Delaware," could be used to indicate the same proposition as would normally be indicated by "Washington crossed the Delaware." But the two former are not statements because they are not declarative sentence-types; nor would tokens of the two former be statement-occurrences.

 5. Authors frequently produce statement-occurrences in order to express their own acceptance (belief) of the indicated proposition or in order to persuade or inform their receivers that the indicated proposition is true. But these are not the only kinds of concern expressed by the production of statement-occurrences. For example, the novelist writes a series of statements indicating propositions which he neither believes nor wants you to believe. His concern is that you *contemplate* the indicated propositions so that you may enjoy them, not believe them.

 6. On the other hand, grammatical forms which are not declarative sentences are often used to express a belief or to induce a belief in the

receiver. For example, although the concern typically expressed by the direct question is a pragmatic one—to get the receiver to report on the truth or falsity of the indicated proposition—questions are sometimes employed as an emphatic device for getting the receiver consciously and unhesitatingly to accept the indicated proposition (or its contradictory— see §5.7) as true. Questions used for this purpose are called **rhetorical questions.**

7.  To define a statement as a "declarative sentence-type insofar as . . ." is to suggest that what we shall be concerned with is conventional language. We may go further than that. Throughout Part III we shall be studying what it is that is usually indicated, or *conventionally* indicated, by tokens of certain sign-types. It is important to study this matter for two reasons, as already pointed out in §§15.6 and 15.7: (a) knowing the conventions can help us correctly understand the tokens of people who would communicate with us, and (b) knowing these conventions can help us produce tokens that will more readily be understood (because of the fact that we conform to the conventions rather than violate them).

8.  But there is another reason for our present study. We have seen in Part I (Units 1-8) that right reason involves the consideration of propositions and that language is a useful tool facilitating this consideration. A person can make language a more effective tool for many processes of right reason if he gives up using the great variety of language forms actually used by people to indicate propositions in favor of using one form. Then similarities and differences in the language forms used can be relied upon to reflect similarities and differences in the propositions indicated. The language form most commonly used as a tool of thought, and the form most thoroughly studied in logic for this purpose, has been the statement. This is why we turn to it now.

9.  Finally, throughout Part II and the preceding paragraphs of this unit, we have illustrated most of our discussions of languages by references to English. The use of the phrase "declarative sentence-type" in our definition of a statement would probably reinforce a tendency to think in terms of such "natural" languages as English, French, or German. But great advances have been made in science and in other fields by using such "artificial" languages as that of arithmetic and of chemical formulas. We must keep this fact in mind and occasionally illustrate our points by reference to those languages. Mean-

while, we must note that the phrase "declarative sentence-type" as used in the above definition of a statement is intended to refer as well to arithmetic equations like $2x + y = z$ and chemical equations like

$$C_6H_{12}O_6 + 6O_2 \rightarrow 6CO_2 + 6H_2O$$

as to the familiar declarative sentences of English and other natural languages.

## EXERCISES

1. Which of the following sentence-tokens are statement-occurrences, and which are not? (Assume a context that makes production of the token meaningful.)

    a. Did you go to the movies last night?
    b. Yes.
    c. Abraham Lincoln was assassinated in 1865.
    d. Some men are over 12 feet tall.
    e. Fire!
    f. $2(x + 4) = 2x + 8.$
    g. $2(x + 4) = 2x + 4.$

2. Which of the following statement-occurrences are occurrences of the *same* statement and which are not?

    a. That house is built of brick.
    b. The building material used in that house is brick.
    c. (Child, pointing at doll in window display) There is a policeman!
    d. (Same child, a minute later, pointing to man directing traffic) There is a policeman!
    e. (Pedestrian, pointing out to motorist who had asked directions the same man as in d, above) There is a policeman!

## §16.3 The Classification of Propositions

Reason uses language as a tool by representing in statements the propositions with which reason is concerned, and by permitting analyses and comparisons of those statements to simplify and guide the process of analyzing and comparing the indicated propositions. The task before us is one of seeing how this may most effectively be done.

By way of preparing for this task, we must for a while look away from the tools—the statements—to examine briefly the things indicated by those tools—the propositions. Our purpose is to see how we may profitably divide those propositions into different kinds or classes. Hence, the remainder of this unit will be concerned with the classification of propositions.

However, the propositions which we say we are classifying are precisely the propositions that we say are indicated by various statements. Now here is a peculiar fact. An experienced speaker of English—like yourself—might make some statement in English, and yet, if he had never studied logic, he might not regard the proposition which he had indicated as one belonging to one of the types we shall list in our classification. It would appear that we are taking some liberties in the interpretation of his speech.

We may see something of the value, even of the necessity, for taking such liberties if we attend briefly to a sort of parable. Suppose that we could transport ourselves backward in time to ancient Greece, without losing our modern beliefs about the world. And suppose that one day we should meet an ancient Greek who said to us as he looked at the sky, "Is Zeus going to be hurling his thunderbolts this afternoon?" What should we answer, if we believe that there is going to be a thunderstorm?

If we take the Greek's question to be primarily one about the weather, then even though we do not share with him his theology and his beliefs concerning the causes of thunderstorms, we might properly answer his question with, "Yes." But if we suspect that his concern is to test our theology and whether or not we consider Zeus to be instrumental in the production of thunderstorms, then the only honest answer (even though it might oblige us later on to appear before a Congressional Committee!) would be, "No!"

The moral of this puzzle is connected with the propriety of the first alternative, "Yes." People use forms of speech that suggest other of their beliefs than one in the proposition of *immediate* concern. To withhold agreement because we do not accept all these related, and suggested, beliefs would probably make it impossible for any two people ever to agree on anything. Thus, more often than not when we accept the proposition indicated by a colleague, we have taken some liberties in interpreting his statement; that is, in identifying the proposition intended by it. So long as the spheres of difference in interpretation lie beyond the immediate concern of our colleagues and ourselves, this kind of "translation" can be helpful.

The reason for mentioning these matters is that the grammar of any language preserves and reflects peripheral beliefs about the world shared by earlier generations of speakers of that language, or even of still older languages from which that one has been derived. These peripheral beliefs may or may not be shared by the modern users of the language. In fact, the modern users may not even be aware of these peripheral beliefs. What we are about to propose are certain ways of analyzing the propositions that we shall say are indicated by the statements produced by various authors. These forms of analysis are to a large extent suggested by the very grammar of English (and similar languages), and undoubtedly something like these forms of analysis were genuinely intended by the early speakers of our language.

Our study, however, is not a historical one. On the contrary, the forms of propositions that we are about to identify are not recommended for consideration merely because they are plausibly suggested by the sentence-types and phrase-types that are met in languages such as English. Whether our ancestors actually believed that propositions were to be analyzed in these ways is beside the point. Moreover, whether a present-day user of English believes that the propositions he intends to indicate by his sentences are to be analyzed in these ways is beside the point. In each case, both in the case of the ancient user of English and in that of the modern user of English, we claim that we are "translating" his indicated propositions in a manner that will be generally helpful for our understanding of his meaning and of the world. It offers a way of understanding that can help us toward a more effective use of right reason.

But furthermore, the varied types of proposition which we shall identify are not now recommended as of equal *final* value. What we must recognize at this point is a way in which propositions *may* be viewed. Later on, especially in Part V, these types of proposition will be re-examined in more detail, with positive recommendations concerning their relative merits and their relations to one another.

Without further ado, let us turn our attention to some of the various types of proposition that it will be useful to recognize and to distinguish.

### §16.4 Singular Propositions

I-A. First among all the types of proposition that we must recognize is a proposition which imputes some specific character, property, activity, condition, or state to some specific thing. For example:

    i.   John takes logic.

    ii.   George batted a home run.

    iii.   Goliath University offers 2000 courses of study.

In these examples, John, George, and Goliath University are the specific things, respectively, to which the characters or activities of taking logic, batting a home run, and offering 2000 courses of study are respectively imputed.

This kind of proposition could be symbolized by

$$s \text{ is } P,$$

where "$s$" represents the specific object and "$P$" represents the character or activity imputed to $s$.

I-B. Very similar to the above propositions—in fact, so similar that they may be included under this same broad type—are propositions which impute membership in a specific class or group of things to some one specific thing. For example:

iv.   John is a student.

v.   Seven is a prime number.

vi.   My car is a Ford.

Propositions of this kind may be symbolized by

$$s \text{ is a } P,$$

where "$s$" represents the specific object (John, seven, my car) and "$P$" represents the specific group (students, prime numbers, Fords) to which $s$ is said to belong.[1]

II-A. Another type of proposition imputes a specific *relational* character or activity as holding between two specific objects.

vii.   John is taller than George.

viii.   The density of the population in Michigan is greater than that in Arizona.

ix.   Your hat is in the closet.

x.   David slew Goliath.

xi.   Tom approached his employer with misgivings.

---

[1] It will be shown in Part V that the A and B types of proposition distinguished here in §§16.4 and 16.5 are not really different types of *proposition*, but correspond rather to different ways of indicating one type of proposition, that is, correspond to different types of *statement*. It is, however, desirable to distinguish these A and B forms here, because the distinctions are relevant to the classifications of terms discussed in §§18.4, 19.1, and 19.3.

As the examples suggest, any proposition that compares two objects one with the other (vii and viii), or that affirms some physical relationship of two objects (ix), or attitude of one object toward another, or a physical and attitudinal relation of one object to another (xi), or an action of one object on another (x) is affirming some connection or relation of the objects one to the other. Such relationships are often expressed by the use of the comparative forms of adjectives (vii and viii), the use of prepositions (ix), and that of transitive verbs with (xi) or without (x) adverbial modifiers. But any statement that specifically identifies two objects may be viewed as affirming a relationship between these objects. In example vii, the two objects are John and George; in example ix, they are your hat and the closet; in example x, they are David and Goliath; in example xi, they are Tom and his employer.

Example viii is interesting in that it may be analyzed in at least two distinct ways into specific objects and an imputed relation: (a) the two objects (abstract) are the density of the population of Michigan and the density of the population of Arizona, and the imputed relational character is that of *being greater than;* (b) the two objects (concrete) are Michigan and Arizona, and the relational character is that of *having a more dense population than.*

The type of relational proposition here explained may be symbolized by

$$s_1 \text{ is } P \text{ (to) } s_2,$$

where "$s_1$" and "$s_2$" represent the two objects proposed as being so-and-so related, and "$P$" represents the relational property in question.

It must furthermore be mentioned that any proposition of type II-A is automatically a proposition of the type I-A: either of the two specific objects in question may be "absorbed" into the relational property. To illustrate, example vii may be viewed as imputing to John the property of being-taller-than-George, or as imputing to George the property of being-shorter-than-John.

II-B.   Related to type II-A much as I-B is related to I-A, is a type of proposition which imputes to a given individual membership in a class of things so and so related to another individual. Examples: "George is a brother of James," "John is an employee of the Speedy Construction Co."

The type of proposition explained here may be symbolized by

$$s_1 \text{ is a } P \text{ (of) } s_2.$$

In this formula, we have placed the preposition "of" in parentheses after the symbol "*P*," just as we placed "to" in parentheses after "*P*" in the formula for type II-A. It should be noticed, however, that the conventions of English sometimes require no preposition at all (for example, sentence x) and sometimes require a different preposition than the "of" or "to" suggested in the formulas. This remark applies also to the formulas appearing throughout the remainder of this unit.

All propositions of types I and II are called **singular propositions.** Some still more complex forms of singular proposition may be identified, but it would not be worth our while at the present time to investigate them.

## §16.5 General Propositions

Contrasted with singular propositions, discussed in §16.4, are **general propositions.** These latter impute properties (absolute, as in I, or relational, as in II) to some definitely or indefinitely indicated number or proportion of the objects in a specific group. Examples:

xii.　All majors in philosophy take logic.

xiii.　Three players on the team batted a home run.

xiv.　Every Senior is taller than some Freshman.

The properties involved in these examples are the same properties (taking logic, batting a home run, and being taller than) as appeared earlier in examples i, ii, and vii. But instead of imputing these properties to specific objects, the new examples impute them to *all*, or *three*, or *every* and *some*, objects in specific groups of objects.

III-A.　The type of proposition illustrated in examples xii and xiii may be symbolized by

$$x \; S \; \text{is} \; P.$$

"*x*" represents the indicated number or proportion of the objects in the group represented by "*S*" that have the property represented by "*P*."

III-B.　Related to type III-A in the same way in which I-B is related to I-A is a kind of proposition which affirms that a certain number or proportion of the objects in a group *S* are members of another group, *P*. For examples, "Every Freshman is a student," or "One half of the students are women." Propositions of this type may be symbolized by

$$x \; S \; \text{is a} \; P.$$

IV-A.　The type of proposition illustrated in example xiv may be symbolized by

$$x \ S_1 \ \text{is} \ P \ (\text{to}) \ y \ S_2,$$

where "$S_1$" and "$S_2$" represent the specific groups of objects in question, "$P$" represents as before the imputed property, and "$x$" and "$y$" represent the indicated number or proportion of the objects in the groups in question that are related in the manner represented by "$P$."

IV-B.　Again, we find a B type, related in a now familiar way to the corresponding A type. Examples: "Some men are husbands of famous women," "Every person (except Adam and Eve!) is a descendant from some people." Propositions of this type may be symbolized by

$$x \ S_1 \ \text{is a} \ P \ (\text{of}) \ y \ S_2.$$

## §16.6  Mixed General and Singular Propositions

V-A.　Finally, it must be mentioned that some propositions are **mixed general and singular.** These propositions involve always a relational property imputed to hold between a specific object on the one hand and an indicated number of objects in a specific group of objects on the other hand:

xv.　Every fraternity man is taller than George.

xvi.　John met some friends.

The types of proposition here illustrated may be symbolized in an understandable fashion as follows:

$$x \ S \ \text{is} \ P \ (\text{to}) \ s$$
$$s \ \text{is} \ P \ (\text{to}) \ x \ S.$$

V-B.　As before, there is a B type of proposition, related in a now familiar manner to the A type. Examples are: "All Americans are beneficiaries of the Ford Foundation," and "John is an adviser to many people in trouble." Symbolizations of these propositions would be as follows:

$$x \ S \ \text{is a} \ P \ (\text{of}) \ s$$
$$s \ \text{is a} \ P \ (\text{of}) \ x \ S.$$

## §16.7  A Word about the Code Letters

In the formulas proposed in this Unit to represent different types of proposition, there occur several kinds of *code letters*. We shall have much more to say about them in Part V, when we are discussing inference. For the present, it may help to notice that they belong in four groups:

"$s$", "$s_1$", "$s_2$":    represent individual objects.

"$S$", "$S_1$", "$S_2$":    represent groups of objects.

"$P$":    represents the property or characteristic imputed to an object (or to so and so many objects in a specified group), or the relation said to hold between objects.

"$x$", "$y$":    represent *how many* (that is, what *numbers* or *proportions*) of the objects in a group are involved.

When a proposition involves *different* individual objects (or groups of objects or quantities) we must represent these by different code letters, for example, by "$s_1$" and "$s_2$". But if a proposition involves the same object two or more times, we may represent that object by several tokens of the same code letter. Thus, while the formula for example x uses two different code letters, "$s_1$" and "$s_2$", for David and Goliath, the formula for *William killed himself* might contain two tokens of the same code letter, to represent the two involvements (as killer and as killed) of the same individual:

$$s \text{ is } P \text{ (to) } s.$$

Similarly, the formula for example xiv used the two different letters "$x$" and "$y$" to represent the different quantities *every* and *some*. But if the same quantity had been twice involved, as in *Some Freshman is taller than some Junior*, then two tokens of the same letter may occur in the representing formula:

$$x \, S_1 \text{ is } P \text{ (to) } x \, S_2.$$

## EXERCISE

Analyze in turn the propositions indicated by each of the following statements. Symbolize your analysis with "code letters" (for example, $s$ is $P$), tell into which of the ten types of proposition, IA to VB, your analysis puts the given proposition, and classify that type as singular, general, or mixed singular and general.

1. George's I.Q. is higher than Jim's.
2. George is a Frenchman.
3. Jim speaks French fluently.
4. Some American citizens speak French fluently.

5. George is a student under Professor Smith.
6. Few American citizens speak Latin fluently.
7. James is a manufacturer of automobiles. $S$ *is a* $P(of)S$
8. Everybody at the dance snubbed Joe.
9. Caroline danced with every fraternity man.
10. Many who go to college graduate.
11. All salaried employees of the X Co. are contributors to its retirement fund.

## REVIEW QUESTIONS FOR UNIT 16

1. What is the topic of Part III?
2. Is that topic discussed in this unit?
3. Explain briefly the connection between the new topic of Part III and the discussion of meaning in the later units of Part II.
4. What is a *statement*? A *proposition*?
5. Explain briefly the difference between a statement and a sentence-type.
6. What is meant by a *statement-occurrence*?
7. Illustrate and symbolize four types of singular proposition.
8. Illustrate and symbolize four types of general proposition.
9. Illustrate and symbolize two types of proposition called *mixed general and singular*.
10. Can different legitimate methods of analysis result in classifying one and the same proposition under different types, as those types have been explained and symbolized in this unit? Explain and illustrate.

# The Identification of Terms

## §17.1 Propositional and Linguistic Terms

In the preceding unit we have distinguished statements and propositions and have analyzed, symbolized, and classified various types of proposition. The *purpose* of those analyses and symbolizations was to lead us to the theory of terms, which is the major topic of Part III.

Every example of a proposition presented in §§16.4, 16.5, and 16.6 was presented by means of writing a statement which indicated the proposition. The propositions, as analyzed, had parts: the object or objects, or groups of objects, and the imputed property. Correspondingly, the statements that indicated those propositions had parts: their contained words and phrases. Some parts of the statements may be said to represent corresponding parts of the indicated propositions.

Let us call the parts of a proposition represented in the symbolic diagrams of §§16.4 to 16.6 by "$s$", "$s_1$", "$s_2$", "$S$", "$S_1$", "$S_2$", and "$P$", the **terms** of the proposition. Let us call the expressions of language that might be used to identify one or another of these terms also **terms.** (Note that here we fix two conventions for the one word-type "terms": according to the one convention, it refers to a certain kind of part of a proposition; according to the other convention, it means a certain kind of phrase or expression in English or some other language. There will be no ambiguity so long as every token of this type is used under circumstances such that the reader can determine which of these two conventions is intended by that token. But where there might arise some doubt or difficulty, we shall designate terms of the first sort by the phrase **propositional terms** and terms of the second sort by the phrase **linguistic terms.**)

The study of linguistic terms, which is the primary topic of Part III, is carried on for two purposes: (1) It contributes to our understanding of the way in which these expressions contribute to the meanings of statements and of the other more complex signs in which they occur.

In this sense, the study of terms is a continuation of the studies we made in Part II. (2) It provides a basis for any analysis of the propositions or the reasoning about propositions which is the ultimate subject-matter of logic. In this sense, the study of terms has been through many centuries the first topic treated in books on logic.

## §17.2  Definition of Linguistic Terms

It has been suggested that certain words or phrases may be isolated within the sentences in which they occur and be regarded as linguistic terms. But not every word or phrase may be so isolated and so regarded. To make our study most profitable, it will be well to settle more precisely than has yet been done just what words or phrases, or other expressions, are to be treated as terms.

The following definition makes a first step in this direction, but your understanding of this definition will increase as you study the illustrations of its application which are discussed after its statement.

By a **term** is to be understood any expression-type that may be treated for logical purposes as a single unit, insofar as its tokens may be thought of as purporting to refer or apply to an object or objects in the world at large.[1]

To get a clearer understanding of what the above definition means, let us see how it would apply to sentences i to xvi presented in §§16.4 to 16.6, when we were classifying propositions. Several points may be brought out:

1.   A term may consist of one word only or of several words. For example, the analysis of sentence xv, above, suggests that we identify the following three terms, two of which consist of two words each and the last of which consists of one word.

> fraternity man
> taller than
> George

Here the two words "taller than" form one term; they contribute only one logical item to the entire proposition. The two words "fraternity

---

1   It will become clear in the next unit or two, that the word "object" as it is used in this definition must not be understood in too narrow a sense. It is intended here to refer not only to physical, concrete objects—such as a desk, a pebble, and a building—but to events—such as World War II, an election campaign, and a dinner party—and to abstract things—such as honor, triangularity, and weight.

man" are treated as a single term because the expression *may* be treated as a unit, and if we wish to see statement xv illustrating the form

$$x \ S \ \text{is} \ P \ (\text{to}) \ s,$$

we must treat it as a unit. But if we had been influenced by different purposes we could have listed "fraternity" and "man" as two separate terms. Had we wished to bring the analysis of sentence xv under the same form as was used to analyze sentence xii,

$$x \ S \ \text{is} \ P,$$

we would have identified in sentence xv two terms, each consisting of several words:

> fraternity man
> taller than George

2. Words indicating number or quantity, such as "some," "all," "every," "a few," "three," "a," "74%," and so on are not in general to be counted a part of the term that they modify. Instead, they are separately correlated with the **quantifier symbols** "*x*" and "*y*" in the forms suggested in §16.5 above. Thus, for example, in listing the terms for sentence xv, above, it would be wrong to write

> every fraternity man.

Instead, the correct list of terms will include

> fraternity man.

The reason for this rule is not difficult to see. Words like "some," "a few," and so on do not pretend to refer to objects in the world in the sense in which you could meaningfully ask, Which objects in the world are some, and which are not some? as you can ask which objects in the world are blue, or men, and which are not blue, or not men. Nor do these words or phrases, when they modify a noun, pick out a *certain* part of all the things referred to by the noun and thus limit the reference by the noun to just those things. For example, "fraternity men" picks out among all the things that are men those that belong to fraternities, so that the phrase as a whole refers to those things that are in this sub-group, of men that belong to fraternities. But the phrase "three men" does not pick out a *certain* group of three men and refer to the men in *that* group. Hence, "fraternity men" is a term, but "three men" is not a term.

*[handwritten marginalia: "exceptions to rule 2  ③④"]*

3. On the other hand, certain exceptions to the above rule must be noted. (a) If the word indicating quantity appears as part of an expression of some measurement, it may be, and in fact should be, carried along with that expression as part of the term. Examples:

In "That table top is 3 feet long," the terms could be listed as

> That table top
> 3 feet long.

In "The price of my new suit was sixty dollars," we could list the terms as

> The price of my new suit
> sixty dollars.

(b) If the quantifying word must be thought of as modifying only a part of the rest of the term, and cannot be thought of as modifying the whole of the rest of the term, then it should be included in the term. For example, we might analyze sentence xvi, above, using the form provided for sentences i, ii, and iii, in which case we should list two terms as follows:

> John
> met some friends.

Here "some" is included in the second term because it cannot be thought of as modifying the whole "met friends," but must be thought of as modifying only the part "friends."

4. A linguistic term is like a sign-type rather than like a sign-token. Thus, there may be many tokens, or occurrences, of one term. But terms are related to sign-types in a rather complex way which makes the listing of terms both narrower (in one respect) and broader (in another respect) than the listing of sign-types: (a) If two tokens belong to the same sign-type but are obviously used with different meanings, then they are occurrences of two different terms. Thus, the listing of terms takes into account the meanings of expressions, whereas the strict listing of sign-types leaves all consideration of meaning to one side. For example, if someone were to write, "No straw is made of straw," meaning that no tube provided for sipping a beverage is made of the hollow stem of such grains as wheat, rye, and oats, we should list three terms as follows:

> straw (meaning a sipping tube)
> made of
> straw (meaning stem of grain)

But if someone wrote, "George struck George," meaning that George struck himself, we should list only two terms, one of which occurs twice:

George
struck.

(b) On the other hand, minor variations in word formation, such as the difference between singular and plural ("man," "men," "eats," "eat"), are treated as variant occurrences of one and the same term. This practice corresponds to the practical method of identifying word-types described on page 160 rather than to the strict method of identifying them.

The relevance of meaning as a factor identifying and distinguishing terms one from the other makes the concept of a term analogous to that of a statement, as the latter was explained in §16.2. *Both* sign-type *and* meaning must be kept the same if we are to have two occurrences of one term, or of one statement.

### §17.3 The Identification of Terms in Actual Practice

The points made in the preceding section were offered as an aid to your understanding of what is meant by a term. When you come to *applying* that concept, in identifying the terms in a given statement, all those points should be kept in mind. But certain other points will also be helpful. Three such additional ones will be mentioned here.

5.   In discussing point 1 above it was suggested that as your purpose in analyzing a given statement varied, so your classification of the proposition indicated by that statement would vary; and that as your classification of the proposition varied, so would your identification of the terms in the statement vary.

It is seldom the case that we want to see *all* ways in which terms *could* be identified in a given statement. More often, what we want is an identification of the terms involved in *one* mode of analyzing the indicated proposition.

Hence, it is a wise practice *first* to symbolize the type of the proposition indicated by the statement, using for this purpose the code letters and formulas suggested in §§16.4 to 16.6, and *then* to identify the terms which correspond to *that* classification and symbolization of the indicated proposition.

6.   When we come to Part V, on *Inference*, we shall see that what we
want in analyzing a given statement is always the simplest analysis which
suffices for the purpose of testing an inference. This suggests that we use
whenever possible classification I and III (§§16.4 and 16.5). But to test
certain inferences we have to use more complex analyses, like II or IV
or V.

Hence, it would be useful in the meantime to practice using these
more complex analyses in any exercises for which they are appropriate.

7.   It is frequently desirable not only to identify in thought the terms
involved in a given statement, but actually to write these terms in a list.

When terms are thus listed for isolated study, they should not contain
pronouns whose antecedents lie outside the terms as listed. This sometimes requires a slight rephrasing of a part of the given English sentence.
In such cases, we interpret the original tokens of the English sentence
as substitutes for the tokens occurring in the term as separately listed.
For example, in listing the terms in sentence viii, we should write:

> the density of the population in Michigan
> greater than
> the density of the population in Arizona.

Thus, the word "that" appearing in the original sentence is replaced
by its antecedent, "the density of the population."

To make certain that you have not incorrectly transformed a term in
the process of listing it, try substituting the rephrased term back into the
original sentence. If this can be done without altering the meaning
of the original sentence, the rephrasing is legitimate. For example,
were we to substitute the rephrased terms above into sentence viii
giving us

> The density of the population in Michigan is greater than
> the density of the population in Arizona,

we should recognize that this latter has exactly the same meaning as
sentence viii, and that hence the rephrasing of the terms was legitimate.

*EXERCISE*

In connection with each of the following sentences:

1.   Select and symbolize (as in §§16.4 to 16.6 above) some manner of analyzing the sentence.
2.   List the terms that the sentence contains in accordance with your chosen
manner of analysis.

EXAMPLE:   Harold beat William at tennis.

1.  $s_1$ is $P$ (to) $s_2$
2.  $s_1$: Harold
    $P$: beat . . . at tennis.
    $s_2$: William

a.  George is studious.
b.  George is more studious than John.
c.  Most freshmen are more studious than John.
d.  Some wealthy Freshmen are less studious than John.
e.  Every ambitious Freshman is more studious than some indolent Sophomore.

## REVIEW QUESTIONS FOR UNIT 17

1.  What is a propositional term? A linguistic term?
2.  May a term consist of only one word? Of more than one word? Illustrate and explain. (In your explanation, connect your original answer to the question with the definition of a *term* given in §17.2.)
3.  When are words indicating number or quantity to be counted as a part of the terms formed by the words they modify? When are they *not* to be so counted? Illustrate.
4.  Explain the reasoning behind the answers you gave to question 3.
5.  Is a term more like a sign-token, or more like a sign-type? Explain.
6.  What besides sign-type must be attended to in identifying a term? Illustrate.
7.  Why should one symbolize and classify a statement *before* he undertakes to identify the terms that it contains?
8.  What rephrasings, if any, should be made when we list the terms occurring in a given statement?

# The Classification of Terms

## §18.1 Introduction

Terms may be divided into kinds according to many different principles, some of which are grammatical and some of which are based on a consideration of the things that the terms purport to indicate. We say "purport" to indicate, because the mere existence of the term is no guarantee of the existence of the thing it purports to indicate. For example, the term "Santa Claus" purports to indicate a certain jolly man who lives at the North Pole and travels all around the world on Christmas Eve; but there is no such creature, so that the mere existence of the term does not guarantee the existence of the object presumably indicated. Had we said that the term indicates the object, instead of purports to indicate the object, this manner of speaking might have suggested that the object in question had to exist, else it could not have been indicated; therefore, that the existence of the term guaranteed the existence of the object.

In this unit and the next one we shall consider in turn some of the more important classifications that can be applied to terms. By this means we shall prepare ourselves for a fuller understanding of the nature of meaning as it occurs in terms. As we examine these classifications, it will be well to bear in mind that *each* principle of classification studied in the following paragraphs may be applied to *every* term. Thus, we shall be studying five independent ways of classifying terms. The significance of this point is discussed at greater length in §19.4, below.

## §18.2 Simple Terms and Complex Terms

Every term is either simple or complex. A **simple** term is a term such that no analysis of it reveals another term as a component functional part. A **complex** term is one such that analysis does reveal at least one other term as a component functional part.

Let us explain and illustrate. Suppose that we had been analyzing the statement, "Adlai Stevenson was a candidate for the Presidency," and

190

suppose that we decided to treat the statement as one having the form

$$s \text{ is a } P,$$

with two terms as follows:

> s: Adlai Stevenson                    Complex
> P: candidate for the Presidency.

The question to be settled is whether these terms are simple or complex.

Any term that consists of a single word should be classed as a simple term. Hence, the problem of classification becomes more difficult only when the terms to be classified consist, as in the examples before us, of two or more words. In such cases, the problem could be put as follows: Do some of the contained words form by themselves a term with its own meaning such that the meaning of the whole expression is derived from (so to speak, requires a prior understanding of) the meaning of that part of the expression? If such is the case, the original term is complex; if such is not the case, the original term is simple.

Consider in this connection the second of the two terms isolated above: "candidate for the Presidency." Here it is fairly easy to see that the meaning of this entire phrase is "built up" out of the meanings of component expressions. There are several alternative ways in which we could divide the entire term into component functional terms. According to one such analysis, we might list "candidate" and "the Presidency" as two terms each of which is a component functional part of the entire term under consideration. Hence, the original term should be classified as complex.

Let us now consider the first of the two terms isolated above: "Adlai Stevenson." This term is, to be sure, an expression made up of two words, "Adlai" and "Stevenson," and each word may be considered as a term. If these two were considered as terms, each would be treated as a singular term purporting to refer to exactly the same individual as the pair of them together, that is, as the term under analysis. Either of them used alone might be ambiguous: one might not know to which person named "Adlai" or to which person named "Stevenson" the term "Adlai" or the term "Stevenson" purported to refer. But once that ambiguity is resolved, by whatever means, it is easy to see that the meaning of the whole phrase is not "built up" out of the meanings of the separate words. Instead, the meaning of the whole phrase is identically the meaning of the separate words. The entire phrase is merely another term having the same meaning as does each of the words in it. Hence, the term "Adlai Stevenson" is a simple term.[1]

The example just cited fails to be a complex term because the terms contained in it are not functional parts of the entire expression; that is, they are not contributing their meanings as parts of the meaning of the entire expression. .˙. *simple*

Most adjectives or adjective phrases when used in combination with a noun or noun phrase form together with the noun a complex term: the noun will be one component term, the adjective or adjective phrase will be another component term. The combination of the two forms a complex term. For example, in the complex terms "mature crow" and "man who likes raw oysters," "mature" and "crow," and "man" and "who likes raw oysters" are the component terms. (Of these component terms, the last is itself complex, containing the component functional terms "likes" and "raw oysters" which latter itself is again complex.)

Two further comments will complete this section.

1. Strictly speaking, we can sometimes analyze a single word to discern that the syllables in it contribute units to the whole idea. An example is "manslaughter," in which "man" and "slaughter" contribute separate units to the final idea. A less obvious example is "telegraph" in which "tele" (at a distance) and "graph" (writing) contribute separate parts to the entire meaning. But practically, we shall find it useful to end analysis for the purpose of distinguishing simple from complex terms at single words, so that "manslaughter" and even hyphenated words like "word-token" will be counted as simple terms. (Had we been dealing with propositional terms rather than linguistic terms (see above, §17.1) the case might have been different.)

2. Also, strictly speaking, a title used as a part of a name ("Cardinal Mercier," "President Eisenhower," "Dr. Holland," "Mr. Marciano") forms, together with the proper name to which it is prefixed, a complex term. But practically speaking, nothing is gained by treating the pair of words as complex, and we shall accordingly regard such expressions as simple terms.

---

[1] It might be said that the use of the entire phrase is the means by which the possible ambiguity of the individual words is avoided. Hence the meaning of the whole phrase contributes to fixing the meanings of the component words, rather than the meaning of the component words contributing as functional parts to the meaning of the whole expression.

*EXERCISES*

1. For each of the following sentences (1) select and symbolize (as in Unit 16) a method of analysis and list the terms identified by that method of analysis; then (2) classify each listed term as simple or complex. In the case of complex terms, list the component terms.
   a. George is taller than John. Simple - About.
   b. Some automobiles have six cylinders. 6. attlib
   c. Every full-time student pays a student-government tax.
   d. Many Democrats voted for Eisenhower.
2. In each of the following sentences, classify the underlined terms as simple or complex. In the case of complex terms, list the component terms.
   a. All mature crows are bigger than any sparrows. with - did
   b. Each order form in a waitress's order book must be accounted for by the bookkeeper.
   c. Some experiments with heavy hydrogen are of great medical importance.
   d. If the American people keep their heads, there will be no depression.

## §18.3 Singular Terms and General Terms

Every term is either singular or general. A **singular** term is one that purports to refer to exactly one thing, abstract or concrete. A **general** term is one that purports to refer or apply to any of possibly many things.[2]

The difference between singular and general *terms* must be carefully distinguished from that between singular and plural *nouns*. Both "man" and "men" are general terms; in fact, as was explained in §17.2, they are but two spellings of one and the same term. That they can actually be used interchangeably to express the same idea, by making a suitable change in the quantifying sign that accompanies them, is illustrated by comparing sentences 1 and 2:

1. All men are mortal.
2. Every man is mortal.

A better idea of the difference between singular and general terms is to be had by thinking of proper nouns and common nouns. Thus proper nouns ("Abraham Lincoln," "London," "Marshall Field and

[2] Why singular terms purport only "to refer" while general terms purport "to refer or apply" is explained below in §18.4.

Co.") are the names of unique, single, individual objects. Each *purports* to refer to one individual thing and to it alone, whereas most common nouns ("house," "man," "city") purport to refer to any things of a certain kind.

On the other hand, common nouns or noun phrases may be, and often are, used in combination with a "singularizing" word in such a manner as to form a singular term. Thus, "my fountain pen," "the druggist who filled my prescription," "that table," and "this newspaper" are all singular terms, each one purporting to refer to a single individual object. Each was formed by prefixing to a general term ("fountain pen," "druggist who filled my prescription," "table," or "newspaper") a singularizing modifier ("my," "the," "that," "this"). In each case, the entire expression, consisting of modifier and general term, is a singular term.

Singular terms formed in the manner just explained are called **definite descriptions.**

Notice that to form a definite description one must use the general term in its grammatically singular form. If the general term is used in its plural form, the singularizing prefix does not produce a singular term, but produces instead another general term. Thus "my fountain pens," "the druggists who filled my prescription," "those tables," and "these newspapers" are all general terms. It is the use of a singularizing prefix with a singular form of the common noun or noun phrase that produces a singular term.

One cannot be sure that *any* phrase formed in the manner just described will be a singular term. With these phrase-types two conventions are associated, one giving rise to general terms. In order to determine which convention a given author was intending by his tokens, we have to look to the context, usually to the sentence-token in which the term-token appeared, but sometimes even beyond that to the circumstances under which the sentence-token was produced. To illustrate, if we were to read, "The doctor gave him a prescription and told him to stay in bed," we should recognize "the doctor" as a token, or occurrence, of a singular term, purporting to refer to the one and only physician who was attending "him." But if we were to read or hear, "The cow is a commercially valuable animal," we should have to attend to the circumstances under which the sentence was produced before we could decide whether "the cow" was intended as a token for a singular term or as a token for a general term: if the circumstances indicate that what the author meant might otherwise have been expressed by, "Cows are commercially valuable animals," then "the cow" was a token of a general term; but if circumstances reveal that what the author meant might have been expressed by, "The particular cow at which we are looking (or which we have been discussing with a view to her purchase or sale) is a commercially valuable animal," then "the cow" was a token of a singular term. If circumstances will not indicate whether the author intended a singular term or a general term, then his sentence-token is ambiguous.

We shall conclude this section with five comments.

1.   Proper names, such as "London," are often used as names for several distinct objects. To continue with the same example, there are cities called "London" in England and Ontario. Tokens of the word-type "London" are usually tokens of a singular term: on each occasion of its use, this word-type is intended to refer to just one, and a certain one, of the many cities called "London." What we have here is several conventions associated with a single word-type. Each of these conventions fixes one singular term.

2.   When a word-type such as "London" or "John Smith" has associated with it many conventions each of which is a singular term, there frequently arises a tendency to use the word-type also as a general term. For example, one might say, "There is many a London within the British Empire." In such cases, the new tendency is simply a new convention. According to it, some tokens of the word-type "London" are used as meaning what could otherwise be expressed by tokens of the phrase-type "city called 'London'." This new convention identifies a general term, but it does not nullify the older conventions, which continue to identify singular terms.

3.   Definite descriptions are often used in statements affirming an identity. Examples: "John Smith is the doctor who attended me in my last illness;" "Paris is the capital of France;" and "The best student in the class is also the tallest." (Statements of identity may, of course, not contain definite descriptions. Example: "Old Pieface is John L. Bertram.") These statements of identity employ the verb "to be" in accordance with a convention different from that suggested by the formulas for propositions in Unit 16. Here, we must think of "is" as

meaning "is identical with," so that we have in these statements of identity propositions of the form II-A,

$$s_1 \text{ is } P \text{ (to) } s_2,$$

where "$s_1$" and "$s_2$" represent the singular terms in question and "$P$" represents the understood term "identical with."

4.  Definite descriptions should always be classified as complex terms. To understand them, one must always understand the general term out of which they are formed by adding a singularizing prefix. Thus this general term is a component which functions as a term out of which the meaning of the definite description is built up.

5.  Whether or not the singularizing prefix is also another term in the definite description depends on what prefix is used: If its sole function is to singularize (as in "the" and "a certain"), then it is *not* a term. But if it also operates as an adjective indicating *which* one (as in "my," "this," and so on) then it is a second component term in the definite description.

Still other problems, relating to the importance for science of certain types of singular and general terms, will be discussed in §19.2, below.

*EXERCISE*

Classify as singular or general each of the terms in both exercises at the end of §18.2, above.

### §18.4 Denotative Terms and Attributive Terms

Every term is either denotative or attributive. A **denotative** term is one which purports to *refer* to things; or, so to speak, to *name* things. An **attributive** term purports instead to *apply* to things. This distinction is largely a grammatical one, and in fact does not appear in all languages. (For example, the Chinese language does not contain one set of words or phrases for denotative terms and another set for attributive terms.) But the distinction is clear in English and other European languages. In general, nouns and noun phrases are denotative terms; while adjectives, verbs, prepositions, and corresponding phrases are attributive terms. Thus "city," a word that refers to, denotes, or names any of several large communities of people, is a denotative term; while "built of stone," an adjective phrase that may be applied to a great variety of objects but does not purport to name or refer to them, is an attributive term.

Several more or less independent remarks should be made concerning denotative and attributive terms.

1. In the formulas for different types of proposition given in §§16.4 to 16.6, all positions marked by variants of the letter $s$ ($s$, $s_1$, $s_2$, $S$, $S_1$, and $S_2$,) must be occupied by denotative terms. That is, the word or phrase occupying one of these positions will be, considered as a whole, a denotative term, although if it is complex it may contain components which are, when considered apart, attributive terms. On the other hand, terms occupying the positions in those formulas marked by the letter $P$ will be attributive terms in the A types of proposition and be denotative terms in the B types of proposition.

2. All attributive terms are general. Hence, all singular terms are denotative.[3]

3. Attributive terms could be further divided into "terms verbal" (that is, verbs and verb phrases) and "terms adjectival" (that is, adjectives, including prepositions treated as adjectives, and adjective phrases). But having noted that the distinction can be made, it is not really important enough to justify our trying to keep it in mind beyond the limits of this comment.

An example of an attributive term verbal would be "batted a home run" (example ii on page 176) while an example of an attributive term adjectival would be "taller than" (example vii on page 177).

The formulas for types of proposition given in §§16.4 to 16.6 all assume that the attributive term occupying the position marked by the letter $P$ is a term adjectival. This assumption is indicated by the inclusion of the verb "is" in the formula. When supplying a term verbal for the position marked in the formulas by the letter $P$, the word "is" should be removed from the formula, because the term verbal also performs the functions of the verb "is." But the theory of terms is more effectively treated if we mentally disregard the "is" aspect of terms verbal and consider these terms as essentially indistinguishable from terms adjectival.

4. Many denotative terms purport to refer to concrete things or objects: "city," "pebble," "turtle," "my fountain pen," and so on. But

---

[3] This explains why singular terms purport only "to refer" and not also "to apply."

other denotative terms purport to refer to the abstract qualities that various objects do or might possess: "courage," "triangularity," "ugliness."

5. It is often held that attributive terms correctly apply to things if and only if those things possess some property or quality. For example, the attributive term "courageous" is correctly applied only to things that display or have courage. Thus, corresponding to each attributive term there will be theoretically two denotative terms: one denoting the things to which the attributive term correctly applies, the other denoting the quality or property possession of which makes the attributive term applicable:

| Attributive term | First denotative correlate | Second denotative correlate |
|---|---|---|
| courageous | courageous thing | courage |
| ugly | ugly object | ugliness |
| valid | valid thing (e.g., valid question) | validity |
| studies logic | student of logic | study of logic |

6. A further discussion of these first denotative correlates, for a special class of attributive terms called "relative" attributive terms, appears in §19.3, where the distinction between absolute and relative terms is explained.

7. Many word-types have connected with them two or more conventions such that tokens under the one convention are occurrences of an attributive term while tokens under the other conventions are occurrences of one or the other of the denotative correlates. For example, "green" may be used as an attributive term ("My fountain pen is green.") or as the second denotative correlate ("Green is a color.")[4]

## EXERCISES

1. Classify as denotative or attributive each term identified in both exercises at the end of §18.2.
2. In the case of each complex term you classified in exercise 1, list its component terms and classify each of them as:
   a. Denotative or attributive
   b. Singular or general
   c. Simple or complex
   Repeat, until you reach the final, simple components.

4 We shall see in §19.2 that still a third convention is associated with color words like "green."

## REVIEW QUESTIONS FOR UNIT 18

1. What is a denotative term? An attributive term? Give examples of each.
2. Which code letters (*s*, *P*, etc.) in the formulas of Unit 16 correspond to denotative terms? To attributive terms?
3. Do denotative terms ever purport to refer to abstract things? Explain and illustrate.
4. What is meant by the first denotative correlate of an attributive term? Illustrate. The second denotative correlate of an attributive term? Illustrate.
5. Are attributive terms singular or general, or some of them singular and others general?
6. Are the first denotative correlates of attributive terms singular, or general, or some of them singular and others general? Explain.
7. Are the second denotative correlates of attributive terms singular, or general, or some of them singular and others general? Explain.
8. What is meant by a singular term? A general term? Illustrate.
9. What is meant by a definite description? How are definite descriptions formed? Illustrate.
10. Are definite descriptions singular terms, or general terms, or some of them singular and others general?
11. Are definite descriptions denotative terms, or attributive terms, or some of them denotative and others attributive? Explain.
12. What is meant by a statement of identity? To what propositional type listed and symbolized in Unit 16 do statements of identity belong? Explain and illustrate.
13. Explain and illustrate the difference between a simple term and a complex term.
14. Are definite descriptions simple terms, or complex terms, or some of them simple and others complex? Explain.
15. Is a term consisting of a single word always treated as a simple term? Explain and illustrate the points you make.
16. Is a term consisting of two or more words always treated as a complex term? Explain and illustrate the points you make.

**19**

# The Classification of Terms, continued

## §19.1 Concrete Terms and Abstract Terms

Every term is either concrete or abstract. A term is **concrete** if the things to which it purports to refer or apply are concrete; it is **abstract** if the things to which it purports to refer or apply are abstract. These definitions, however, will be of little use until we understand what it means to call a thing (as opposed to a term) concrete or abstract.

A thing is said to be concrete if it occupies a definite location in space and time, while it is called abstract if it does not occupy any such location.[1] Thus such things as the Earth, individual grains of sand, people, atoms, cities, institutions (such as Harvard University or a fraternity), physical fields of force, and individual events or occurrences like the American Revolution, the burning of a log in the fireplace, my eating of breakfast on a certain day—all such things are concrete things, and the terms that purport to refer or apply to them are concrete terms. On the other hand, the qualities or properties that these concrete things, or any things, might have or display, as also the relationships that might obtain between or among these concrete or other things, are abstract things, and the terms that purport to refer or apply to these qualities and relationships are therefore abstract terms.

Some care must be taken not to confuse the distinction between concrete and abstract with the distinction between actual and fictitious or unreal. For example, there is no Santa Claus, or Santa Claus is not an

---

1 The manner adopted in the text of distinguishing between concrete and abstract things may be practically advantageous but is not theoretically sound. For example, according to many faiths, souls have a temporal, but not spatial, location; yet despite the lack of spatial location, they would be considered to be concrete entities. And there are still other difficulties with the proposed criterion. A theoretically preferable basis for the distinction would run somewhat as follows: a concrete entity is a not further determinable thing; an abstract entity is a further determinable thing. But the complications attendant on a careful explanation of "determinable" make the use of this criterion inappropriate in the present book.

actual but only an imaginary, being. Nevertheless, he is conceived as a being with definite location in space and time; that is, he is conceived as a concrete object. Hence the term "Santa Claus" is a concrete term. Similarly "Superman," "Mr. Pickwick," and the names of other famous characters of fiction are all concrete terms.

Careful attention is also necessary in undertaking to classify attributive terms as abstract or concrete. It is worth noting that the *second* denotative correlate of an attributive term (see above, §18.4) is always abstract, but that the *first* denotative correlate of the attributive term is sometimes (often) concrete and sometimes (more rarely) abstract. The attributive term purports to apply to all and exactly those things to which its first denotative correlate purports to refer. Hence, the attributive term is concrete or abstract according as its first denotative correlate is concrete or abstract.[2]

Attention should furthermore be given to the difference between a general term purporting to refer to any thing or object *in* a certain group or class, and a singular term purporting to refer to the group or class *as a whole* in which those objects have their membership. For example, the term "man" purports to refer to any object (Mr. Eisenhower, Abraham Lincoln, Jack the Ripper) which is a member of the human race. On the other hand, the term "the class of all men" is a singular term, purporting to refer to exactly one thing: the class or group in which all and only those things are members that are referred to by the term "man." Or, put in another way, the general term, "man" refers (among other things) to Mr. Eisenhower; but the singular term "class of all men" refers to a certain group or class of things to which Mr. Eisenhower *belongs*. It does not refer to Mr. Eisenhower.

---

[2]  Most writers on the classification of terms consider "abstract" and "concrete" to be classifications of denotative terms. On such a view, terms are divided into three kinds: abstract, concrete, and attributive.

It is difficult for this author to see why the attributive term should be regarded as a thing apart, to which the distinction between abstract and concrete will not apply. *Perhaps* it has been considered in that fashion because it has been conceived as a sort of two-faced grammatical variant both of its first denotative correlate and of its second denotative correlate. Since the one is abstract and the other (often) concrete, the "mongrel" attributive term cannot be classed in either way.

But such an attitude would appear to be a mistaken one. The distinction, in the case of denotative terms, is based on a classification of purported objects in the extension of the term. (On extensions, see Units 20 and 21, below.) And this basis is available for classifying attributive terms. The important thing is not to confuse the attributive term with its denotative correlates. It is a distinct term.

Classes of things (as opposed to the things in them) are abstract. Therefore, terms (both singular and general) purporting to refer to classes of things (as opposed to referring to things in classes) are abstract. A general term purporting to refer to anything in a certain class of things is abstract or concrete according as the class is a class of abstract or concrete things.

Although most terms that are concrete are not abstract, and vice versa, most terms that are abstract are not concrete, a few terms are both concrete and abstract. This can be the case only with general terms, since the thing purportedly referred to by a singular term is definitely concrete or definitely abstract and is not both abstract and concrete. But in the case of a general term, some of the things it purportedly refers to may be concrete and others of those things be abstract. For example, the term "thing" purportedly refers to Mr. Eisenhower, my fountain pen, and courage (among other things). Each of these is a thing. But Mr. Eisenhower and my fountain pen are concrete things, so that the term "thing" is concrete; while courage is an abstract thing, so that the term "thing" is abstract. Hence, the term "thing" is both abstract and concrete.

It is perhaps worth noting that sign-tokens, being physical objects with spatial and temporal locations, are concrete, so that the term "sign-token" is a concrete term; but that sign-types, being the shapes, melodies, or other characteristics of sign-tokens, are abstract so that the term "sign-type" is an abstract term.

## EXERCISES

1. Classify as concrete or abstract each of the terms identified in the Exercises at the end of §18.2.
2. Classify as concrete or abstract each of the following terms:

   House (as in "My house is faced with clapboards.")
   Built of stone
   Ugliness
   City
   Sorority (as in "Do you belong to a sorority?")
   Comfort (as in "He enjoyed a sense of comfort.")
   Comfortable (as in "Is that chair comfortable?")
   Comfortable (as in "Are you comfortable?")

## §19.2 Abstract Singular Terms

In §18.3 we discussed the distinction between general and singular terms. Now that we have also considered the difference between abstract and concrete terms, it will be well to observe how these two modes of classification overlap, for the class of abstract singular terms is a group of terms having considerable importance in the sciences. Certain related abstract general terms are also important in the sciences.

It will be recalled that the things to which terms might purport to refer are sometimes abstract, such as the qualities or properties of concrete things. Thus, the terms "triangularity," "courage," and "green" refer to the shape, virtue, or color that may be possessed by particular concrete objects. Now some abstract terms purport to refer to one specific quality. It makes no difference that the quality in question may be found in many different objects; if it is, then these objects are similar one to the other in that they all have that one quality. On the other hand, some abstract terms purport to refer to any of possibly many different qualities. For example, the word "triangularity" refers to one abstract quality (the quality of being in a plane and bounded by three straight lines), whereas the word "shape" purports to refer to any of possibly many different qualities, two among which are triangularity and circularity.

Abstract terms of the first sort (like "triangularity") are singular terms. Abstract terms of the second sort (like "shape") are general terms.

Whether an abstract term is singular or general can often be determined by considering whether or not the plural form of the word in question "makes sense." If it does, then the original word is a token of a general term; if it does not, then the original word is a token of a singular term. For example: "shapes" makes sense, therefore "shape" is a general term; "triangularities" and "courages" do not make sense, therefore "triangularity" and "courage" are singular terms.[3]

---

[3] The differences noted here are often in part the result of somewhat arbitrary conventions. We often find it desirable to speak of "forms of triangularity" or "types of courage." These complex terms are general abstract terms, purporting to refer to just those qualities which might have been referred to by "triangularities" and "courages" had our linguistic conventions been different from what they are.

All abstract singular terms allow their utilization in the above manner in the construction of complex, abstract general terms.

But this test for singular and general abstract terms must be used with caution because there are some word-types with which two conventions are associated. According to the one convention, the word-type is a singular term; according to the other convention (that is, according to another meaning,) the word-type is a general term. For example, we say, "Green is a color," and here use "green" as a singular term, referring to a certain one of the colors, namely, green. But when we say, "Some greens are less blue than is aquamarine," we use "greens" as a general abstract term, referring to any color that is some shade or form of green.

In the case of such a word-type, the test described above could be misleading. Since there is one convention according to which the word-type is a general term, the plural form of the word will "make sense." This would lead us to say that the original word is a token of a general term. But since, by another convention, the word-type is also used for a singular term, it might well be the case that the original token was a token of this other, singular term.[4]

Definite descriptions (see §18.3), which are singular terms, may be formed out of abstract general terms with the aid of singularizing prefixes. For example "shape" and "shape of my garden" are general terms (my garden could have different shapes in different years); but "the shape of my garden" is an abstract singular term. In fact, abstract singular terms of the sort here mentioned are of great importance, being continually used in the sciences. For example, the law of the balanced lever,

$$W_1 \times L_1 = W_2 \times L_2,$$

is formulated by using symbols for four such abstract singular definite descriptions: "$W_1$" for "the weight of object$_1$," "$L_1$" for "the distance from the fulcrum to object$_1$," "$W_2$" for "the weight of object$_2$," and "$L_2$" for "the distance from the fulcrum to object$_2$."

This law illustrates a fundamental and important kind of use which scientific inquiry makes of abstract terms. Put in the simplest possible

---

[4] It may, in fact, be safely asserted that the majority of those word-types which function as abstract general terms have associated with them a second meaning in accordance with which they function as abstract singular terms. Thus, for example, in "Shape is a geometrical property," the word-type "shape" is functioning as an abstract singular term.

way and without going into details, it is noticed that abstract qualities or properties can be conceived in groups or classes. For example, there are colors, pitches, weights, lengths, and so on. *General* abstract terms will refer to any quality in a certain one of these groups: "color," "pitch," "weight," "length," and so on.

Some of these groups of qualities have very few members. For example, the genes present in a cell of living matter exhibit one or the other of two characteristics, called *dominance* and *recessiveness*.[5]   𝒳

Now the most interesting groups of properties, from the point of view of science, are ones such that: (1) No concrete individual has more than one quality from a given group at any one time. (This is true, for example, of weight, length, I.Q., dominance-recessiveness, shape, and so on. It is not true of pitch or color. An object may be multicolored, and a sound, like a chord, may have many pitches.) (2) The qualities in the group can be represented mathematically and a method of "measurement" can be established to determine which quality or qualities in the group a given object might have. (This is true, for example, of weight, length, I.Q., color, pitch. It is not true of shape in general, but is true of special elements of shape, such as size of angle, curvature, slope, and so on.)

When condition 1 is fulfilled, the scientist may speak of *the* quality from a certain group possessed by a certain object, for example, of "the weight of $x$," "the length of $y$," "the dominance or recessiveness of the color genes of parent $z$," and so on. All such terms are definite descriptions and are singular abstract terms. Then he may seek formulas or laws in accordance with which: (a) the quality from one such group of qualities possessed by a certain object is connected with the quality from another group possessed by that object. For example,

$$33t = v$$

---

[5] Strictly speaking, dominance and recessiveness are *relational* properties, making the propositional forms

$$s_1 \text{ is dominant over } s_2$$

and

$$s_2 \text{ is recessive to } s_1$$

more appropriate to their analysis. But as we pointed out in §16.4, this form of proposition can always also be analyzed under the form

$$s \text{ is } P$$

by "absorbing" one of the subject terms into the predicate. It is in accordance with this kind of consideration that we speak of dominance and recessiveness as simple properties.

(The length of time, in seconds, $t$, that a body has been falling freely toward the earth, multiplied by 33 equals the velocity, $v$, or speed in feet per second, at which that body is moving.) Or for another example,

$$A = \frac{h \times b}{2}.$$

That is, the area of a triangle is equal to one half the product of its height and the length of its base. (b) The quality from one such group of qualities (or the qualities from two or more such groups of qualities) possessed by a certain object is connected with the quality (or qualities) possessed by *another*, related object. For example, the law of the balanced lever, given above. For another example, we find the physicist writing

$$F = \frac{m_1 \times m_2}{d^2},$$

to express the fact that *the-gravitational-force-with-which-two-bodies-attract-one-another* equals the product of *the-mass-of-the-first-body* and *the-mass-of-the-second-body*, divided by the square of *the-distance-between-the-two-bodies*. (Abstract singular terms of the sort under consideration are indicated in the English by italicizing the words connected by hyphens that correspond to each of these terms in the formula.)

*EXERCISE*

Classify each of the following terms as abstract or concrete and as singular or general.

1. Shape
2. The shape of my house lot
3. Horse
4. The horse that I bought yesterday
5. The United States of America
6. Velocity
7. The maximum velocity of The Twentieth Century Limited
8. Man
9. The tallest man on the football squad
10. My man

## §19.3 Absolute Terms and Relative Terms[6]

There are, of course, many other ways than we have studied in which terms might be classified. We shall, however, bring this part of our study to a close by examining only one more type of classification: into *absolute* and *relative* terms.

In §16.4, we saw that many propositions affirm the holding of a relation between two individuals. For examples, "John is taller than William," and "George is a brother of James." Formulas for these two types of proposition were provided as follows:

II-A.   $s_1$ is $P$ (to) $s_2$

II-B.   $s_1$ is a $P$ (of) $s_2$

Terms that could stand in the position occupied by "$P$" in either formula II-A or formula II-B may be called **relative terms.** Relative terms suitable to formula II-A will be relative *attributive* terms— "taller than," "married to," "employed by," "employs," and so on; those suitable for formula II-B will be relative *denotative* terms— "husband," "brother," "employer," "advisor," and so on.

Generally speaking, the question whether or not a given denotative term, $X$, is relative, can be settled by asking yourself whether the phrase "an $X$ of" or "the $X$ of" makes sense, where "of" is not itself an attributive term meaning "possessed by." Thus, the denotative terms listed at the end of the last paragraph are all relative, because "the husband of," "a brother of," "the employer of," "an advisor of" all make sense. But "house" is not a relative term because, although "the house of Mr. Jones" makes sense, the word "of" in this phrase means "possessed by."[7]

In English, if we have a transitive verb, $P$, it may usually be regarded as a relative attributive term appropriate for use in the form II-A. From these transitive verbs—for example, "owns," "murders," "employs"—we regularly form nouns—"owner," "murderer," "employer" —indicating any things (people) that do own, murder, or employ, someone or something. The nouns formed in this way are relative

---

[6] The traditional treatment of the distinction between absolute and relative terms is so vague and the traditional criterion is so broadly applicable as to suggest that all terms are relative. The present account offers a somewhat different criterion which, it is hoped, will make the distinction useful. For an important application of the criterion, see below on Definition, particularly §§29.2 and 29.4.

[7] Occasionally some other preposition than "of" must be used in this test for an absolute term. An example of this situation occurs near the end of §19.5.

denotative terms. They are, in fact, the first denotative correlates (see §18.4) of the relative attributive terms from which they are formed.

On the other hand, the English language contains many relative denotative terms—like "brother," "uncle," "side"—which are not derived from corresponding verbs or adjectives. In these cases, the theoretically possible relative attributive term is lacking in the vocabulary of the English language so that all we have is, so to speak, the first denotative correlate.

Terms that are not relative are called **absolute** terms.

## EXERCISE

Which of the following terms are relative and which are absolute?

1. Shorter than    R – A
2. Teaches (as in "George teaches Latin.")    R
3. Teacher    R – D
4. Athlete    A – D
5. Triangle    A
6. Overcoat    ~ overcoat of (possibly )R
7. Friend    R – D
8. Above    R
9. Table (as in "Put your books on the table.")
10. Replica    R (possessed by

## §19.4 Relations among the Classes of Terms

Every term may be classified on *each* of the five bases that have been explained in this and the preceding unit. With one exception every basis of classification is independent of every other. The one exception is this: Every attributive term is general. Furthermore, again with one exception, the two classes of terms distinguished on any one basis of classification are mutually exclusive (that is, no term belongs to both classes; no term is, for example, both singular and general). The one exception is the case of concrete and abstract: some general terms are both concrete and abstract.

Hence, the five bases of classification identify altogether thirty-two kinds of term, such that every term belongs to one or the other, but to only one, of these thirty-two kinds:

1. Simple, singular, denotative, absolute, concrete, and not abstract.

2. Simple, singular, denotative, absolute, not concrete, and abstract.
3. Simple, singular, denotative, relative, concrete, and not abstract.
4. Etc.
   Etc.
32. Complex, general, attributive, relative, concrete, and abstract.

## EXERCISE

Classify the underlined terms in the following statements. Give a full classification into one or the other of the thirty-two kinds partially listed above.

1. My umbrella is worn out.
2. John Paul Jones is a naval hero.
3. Some guaranteed merchandise is shoddy.
4. The color of her eyes was subtle.
5. Every student has a student number.
6. Blue is my favorite color.
7. Some sign-types are conventional.
8. Many intangible things are nevertheless observable.
9. If one has good vision, sunspots can occasionally be seen by the naked eye.
10. Many a fire is started by carelessness.

## REVIEW QUESTIONS FOR UNIT 19

1. What is meant by a concrete term? A concrete thing? An abstract term? An abstract thing?
2. Are the second denotative correlates of attributive terms in all cases abstract, in all cases concrete, or in some cases abstract and in other cases concrete? The first denotative correlates?
3. Are singular terms purporting to refer to *classes* of things abstract or concrete?
4. Can some terms be both abstract and concrete? Explain and illustrate.
5. Can singular terms be both abstract and concrete? Explain.
6. Classify as abstract or concrete the terms "sign-token," "sign-type," and "sign-event."

7. Discuss briefly the formation and use of definite descriptions which are abstract singular terms in the formulas and laws of science.
   a. Under what circumstances can such definite descriptions be formed?
   b. Under what circumstances can the definite descriptions thus formed be arranged in laws expressed as mathematical equations?
8. Describe briefly the difference between absolute and relative terms.
9. Describe a practical working test for denotative terms by which you can tell whether they are absolute or relative.
10. Are any singular terms attributive?
11. Identify three more kinds of term from among the thirty-two kinds partially listed in §19.4.

### §19.5 Appendix on Relative Terms*

Considerations of right reason require that we keep several points in mind when we are dealing with relative terms. We shall now consider these more or less unrelated points one after the other.

1. Relative terms have basically two different kinds of use: (a) to formulate relational propositions of sorts symbolized as II-A, II-B, IV-A, IV-B, V-A, and V-B of §§16.4 to 16.6, by providing the term "*P*" in these formulas; (b) to provide the basis for a term "*s*" or "*S*" in any of the formulas of Unit 16 for any types of proposition.

2. Let us illustrate and briefly discuss use (b). Sometimes a denotative relative term is used together with "of" and another term so as to form a complex general term which could stand in the place of "*S*" or "*s*" in a propositional formula:

   i.   Every *teacher of George* considers him to be brilliant.
   ii.  Two *sides of figure abc* are more than 5 inches long.
   iii. All of *Barbara's brothers* attended college.

Sometimes complex general terms formed in the above manner are compounded with a singularizing word so as to form a definite description, which is a singular term (§18.3):

   iv. The *father of George* is a banker.
   v.  The *top of the mountain* is flat and grassy.

On the other hand, these relative denotative terms are sometimes used *without* "of" and a following term. In such circumstances, we must usually understand "of someone" or "of something" as the case may be. To illustrate,

*This section may be omitted in part or in whole, without affecting the continuity of the entire book.

there is no difference in meaning between the *a* sentences and the *b* sentences in the following pairs.

vi-*a*.   Will *the fathers* please rise?

vi-*b*.   Will *the fathers of someone* please rise?

vii-*a*.  All *employers* must report to the government wages they have paid.

vii-*b*.  All *employers of someone* must report to the government wages they have paid.

3.   Some relative terms are based on types of relationship that cannot hold both ways around between two objects. For example, if *a* is the father of *b*, then *b* cannot be the father of *a*. Or again, if *a* is taller than *b*, then *b* cannot be taller than *a*. On the other hand, some relative terms are based on types of relationship such that when the relation holds one way around, then it may, or even must, hold the other way around. For example, if *a* is a brother of *b*, then *b* might well be a brother of *a* (on the other hand, *b* could be a sister of *a*). Or again, if *a* is a partner of *b*, then *b* must be a partner of *a*.

Now relative terms of this latter sort (that is, which can hold both ways around) are a frequent source of amphiboly (§3.8). For when they are used as in vi-*a* or vii-*a* above, one often cannot tell whether "of someone" or "of each other" is to be understood.

For examples:

viii.   Will all *the brothers* please rise?

Does the sentence refer to the brothers of each other, or to the brothers of *someone*?

ix.   All *partners* face similar problems.

Does the sentence mean that all partners *of each other* face problems similar to those *of their partners*, or that all partners *of someone* face problems similar to those of all other partners *of anyone*?

4.   We should not close this discussion without noticing a usage which falls half way between the two usages discussed in 2, above. Sometimes a relative term is used with "of" and a *general* term, instead of with "of" and a singular term. In this connection, compare "brother of Martha" with "brother of a college student," or "husband of Caroline" with "husband of an American citizen." For example,

x.   Every husband of an American citizen may claim American citizenship.

5.   And finally, let us consider whether complex terms formed by combining a relative term with "of" and another term are to be classed as relative or absolute. For example, is "brother of Martha" a relative term or an absolute term?

If we use the test indicated in §19.3, we see that this term is an absolute term: the phrase formed by adding "of" to this expression—"brother of Martha of"—does not make sense.[8]

On the other hand, some complex terms formed out of relative terms in the manner suggested *are* relative terms. This comes about in the following way.

Propositional forms II, IV, and V (§§16.4 to 16.6) indicate that certain propositions impute the holding of a relation between some two objects, for example, "John is taller than James." There are, however, other relations, of a higher degree of complexity, the holding of which would involve three, or four, or even more objects. (For the sake of simplicity, we did not symbolize in Unit 16 propositional forms for these more complex relational situations.) For example, "Pennsylvania is situated between Virginia and New York." Here "situated between" indicates a relationship that might obtain among three things. Or again, in "George sold Dobbin to James," the verb "sold" indicates a relation connecting three things one with the other: the seller, the buyer, and the thing sold.

As the last example suggests, transitive verbs, which take not only a direct object but also an indirect object, express regularly relations among three things. Examples are "sell," "give," "teach," "command," and so on. These verbs are then relative attributive terms. Their first denotative correlates will also be relative terms: "seller," "donor," "teacher," "commander." But when we compound these denotative correlates with "of" or "to" and an object of the verb, we *still* have a relative term, because it still makes sense to compound that complex expression with another "of" or "to" and the other object of the verb.

| | |
|---|---|
| Seller of Dobbin | Seller of Dobbin to James |
| Seller to James | Seller to James of Dobbin |
| Donor of fifty dollars | Donor of fifty dollars to the Red Cross |
| Donor to the Red Cross | Donor to the Red Cross of fifty dollars |
| Teacher of Latin | Teacher of Latin to William |
| Teacher of William | Teacher to William of Latin |
| Etc. | Etc. |

[8]  Our classification of this term as absolute distinguishes our treatment of absolute and relative terms from the usual treatment. While the usual treatment is vague, it seems to suggest that any complex term which has a relative term (in our sense of "relative") as a component is a relative term. When that doctrine is coupled with another—that any two terms which are synonyms must be classified in the same way (except that one may be simple and the other complex)—it turns out that nearly all, if not actually all, terms would be relative. This follows from the fact that the adequate definition of nearly every term will involve the use of a relative term (in our sense of "relative").

Thus the traditional distinction between relative and absolute becomes almost useless, because it does not classify, nearly all terms being relative. In this lies the motive for our revised distinction.

Hence, *sometimes*, when a relative term is combined with "of" and an object, the resultant complex expression is also a relative term.

## EXERCISE

Which of the following terms are relative and which are absolute?

1. Business manager of the X Co.
2. Cattle dealer
3. Criminal
4. Auto thief
5. Dispenser

# The Extension of a General Term

## §20.1 Introduction

At the end of this opening section, we shall define the expression "the extension of a term." We shall be using this phrase throughout the remainder of this text, because logical reasoning and scientific procedure cannot be explained without appealing to the concept which it conveys. Hence, it is important to get as clear as possible an understanding of this expression.

Yet the definition at the end of this section will perhaps not be entirely clear when you first read it. Nor will you find immediately after it any further general explanation. In point of fact, the whole of this unit and the next are an explanation of it. But this explanation proceeds piecemeal, first explaining what the expression means as applied to attributive terms, then as applied to general denotative terms, and finally (in the next unit) as applied to singular terms. Do not try too hard completely to understand this definition in this section until you have read the following sections. But as you read them, refer back to this definition and keep this definition in mind, always considering those sections as clarifications of this definition. The definition gives point and unity to the sections that follow; they in turn provide clarification for the definition.

In §20.4, we shall return to the *general* discussion and clarification of this concept of the extension of a term.

By the **extension** of a term is meant the group or class of all those objects to each of which the term refers or applies.

Let us proceed to see what this definition means.

## §20.2 The Extension of an Attributive Term

Let us attend for a moment to some attributive term, for example, "goes to college." Suppose now that we become interested in identifying the things to which this term applies, or in dividing things

214

generally into those to which the term applies and those to which it does not apply. We might begin considering things one after the other, undertaking to decide in each case whether the attributive term does or does not apply to the thing under consideration.

Before we can settle this issue, we must understand what "goes to college" means. That is, we must understand what a producer of the term meant by it. We might assume his meaning to be a conventional one. But even here we find the convention is not entirely free from vagueness. What is meant by "going" and what is to be counted as a "college"? This vagueness must be cleared away before we can decide to what things the term applies.

But suppose now that we have finally made the term sufficiently precise so that given any object, we can discover whether or not the term applies to it. It would, of course, be hopelessly impractical to think that we could consider all the things there are in the world, one by one, to determine whether or not the term applies to them. Nevertheless, we may assume that all the things in the world are divisible into two vast groups, or classes: the class of things to which the term does apply; and the class of things to which it does not apply. And we may furthermore say that about any one thing in the universe we could at least in theory discover into which of those two groups or classes that thing fell.

The class of all those things to each of which an attributive term does apply is called the **extension** of that term.

Several things are to be noted concerning the extensions of attributive terms.

1.  We can discover what does or does not belong to the extension of a term only if we understand the term.

2.  Terms differ one from the other with respect to the numbers of things that do belong to their extensions. For example, an infinity of things (all even numbers) belong to the extension of the term "divisible by two"; a large, but nevertheless finite, number of things belong to the extension of the term "voted for Eisenhower in 1952"; a much smaller number of things belongs to the extension of the term "voted for Washington in 1788"; only two things belong to the extension of the term "served as President of the U.S.A. during a part of 1953"; only one thing belongs to the extension of the term "took office as President of the United States in 1953"; and nothing belongs to the extension of the term "took office as President of the United States in 1954."

3. What objects, and how many objects, belong to the extension of a term depends in part on the meaning of the term. We have seen before that authors decide, or choose, the meanings of their sign-tokens; and if, for example, authors had chosen to mean by the sign-type "divisible by two" what we ordinarily mean by "goes to college," then none of those things that do belong to the extension of the term "divisible by two" with its customary meaning would belong to it; but all those things that in fact belong to the extension of the term "goes to college" would belong also to the extension of the term "divisible by two."

4. In addition to the influence of meaning on extension, noted in point 3, above, we have to recognize that what belongs to the extension of a term is in part a question of facts that are not at all questions of meaning. For example, after the meaning of "goes to college" has been settled, it is still only in part determined what objects belong to the extension of this term. Inflations and depressions, the decisions of draft boards, the quality of performance of students taking courses, even such nonhuman forces as earthquakes, fires, tornadoes, and the like all affect the final historical determination of who does and who does not go to college, that is, of who does and who does not belong to the extension of the term "goes to college." If we lump together all these influences and their consequences and call them the *facts of history*, then we may summarize this point by saying that the extension of an attributive term is in part determined by the facts of history.

The following conclusion may be drawn from the four comments made above. The extension of an attributive term is determined in part by the meaning of the term and in part by the facts of history. Hence, the extension of the term cannot properly be considered to *be* the meaning of the term. It may, on the other hand, be considered a sort of "impure" meaning, or "meaning as in the world." The extension of an attributive term is one aspect of the meaning of that term.

### §20.3 The Extension of a Denotative General Term

It will be recalled from §§18.3 and 18.4 that denotative terms (as opposed to attributive terms) purport to *refer* to objects or things, and that denotative general terms (as opposed to denotative singular terms) purport to refer to *any* of *possibly many* things.

We may distinguish between what a denotative general term purports to refer to and what it actually refers to. This distinction is exactly parallel to the distinction between the meaning of an attributive term and the things to which the attributive term applies. For example, the denotative general term "college student" (which is the first denotative correlate of the attributive term "goes to college") purports to refer to any of possibly many things each of which goes to college. Which things it actually refers to, and how numerous are the things to which it actually refers, are questions whose answers are settled in part by this meaning (purport) of the term and in part by the facts of history. In this manner, the concept of the extension of a term may be profitably applied to denotative general terms as well as to attributive terms.

By the **extension** of a denotative general term is meant the group or class of all (actual) things to each of which the term refers.

(1) Notice that the extension is the class or group of things to each of which the term *refers*, not *purports to refer*. The difference is this: The term purports to refer to anything there might be of such and such a sort; it actually refers only to each thing there is of that sort. For example, "college student" *purports to refer* to any individual who might exist that may have gone to college; it *does* refer to each person who does exist and does go to college. It is this latter group of individuals which constitutes the extension of the term. This first point is reinforced by inclusion of the word "actual" in the definition. But this word is in parentheses and not really needed except as a reminder, because saying "refers" instead of "purports to refer" in fact limits the extension of a denotative term to actual objects.[1]

Certain other comments may be helpful. (2) All the points made in connection with the extension of attributive terms apply in this new situation: (a) Before you can decide whether or not a given object belongs to the extension of a term you must know what the term means;

[1]  The distinction between "purports to refer to" and "refers to" can be the source of some tricky puzzles. For example, one might be tempted to say, on the basis of the above paragraph, that "There are things which a term purports to refer to but does not actually refer to." But this would be mistaken in a rather peculiar way. For the only "things" that a term purports to refer to but does not actually refer to are things that *are not*, that is, things that do not exist. Hence we cannot correctly say that "there are" such things, as was said in the above quotation. Whatever *exists* that a term purports to refer to, it does refer to; whatever a term purports to refer to that does *not* exist, the term does not refer to.

(b) denotative terms differ among themselves with respect to the number of things belonging to their extensions; (c) what objects, and how many objects, belong to the extension of a general denotative term depends in part on the meaning of the term; (d) but it also depends in part on the facts of history. (3) Thus the same conclusion can be drawn, that the extension of a general denotative term is only an "impure" meaning of the term, or an aspect of the meaning of the term.

### §20.4 "Belonging to" the Extension of a Term

The remaining sections of this unit are intended to throw more light on the concept "extension of a term"; it makes no difference whether that term is attributive, general denotative, or singular. (Singular terms are further considered in the next unit.)

Several times we have spoken of "belonging to" or "being in" the extension of a term. When we speak in such a manner, we mean that the term actually refers, or applies, to the thing in question. Notice in this connection that a term might refer or apply to things in which other things exist as parts, and yet not refer to or apply to these parts. For example, fingers are parts of hands, and in fact never exist except as parts of hands. But the term "hand" does not refer to fingers, even though it refers to things of which fingers are parts.

In the case of general denotative terms, the test as to whether or not a given actual object, $x$, is referred to by a certain term, $T$, is the same as the test as to whether or not $x$ is a $T$. For example, is my right index finger referred to by the term "hand"? To test that is the same as to ask, Is my right index finger a hand? Obviously not, it is only a part of a hand. Thus, it is not referred to by the term "hand," but is only a part of a thing referred to by the term "hand." By the same test, my right index finger is not in the extension, and does not belong to the extension, of the term "hand" but is rather a part of a thing in (or belonging to) the extension of the term "hand."

### EXERCISE

Consider each of the general terms in list A and each of the singular terms in list B. Then indicate which terms in list B name things belonging to the extensions of which terms in list A. In any case of doubt, explain briefly what you would have to do to resolve the doubt.

| List A | List B |
|--------|--------|
| City | Boston, Mass. |
| Man | The capital of the State of New York |
| Horse | Dwight D. Eisenhower |
| Animal | Fifth Avenue, New York |
| Alive | The capital of the Kingdom of Oz |
| | Nashua (famous racing horse) |
| | Eisenhower's right arm |
| | The dog who acted as nurse to the children in *Peter Pan* |
| | Sherlock Holmes |

## §20.5 Extensions and the Passage of Time

It has been stressed in previous sections that the extension of a term includes only those actual things—and not fictitious or unreal things—to which the term refers or applies. Differences in human beliefs about what is or is not actual will be reflected in differences among their beliefs about what and how many things are in the extension of a relevant term. To take one example: the general denotative term "god." An ancient Greek, believing in many gods, would have held that many things belong to the extension of the term "god." One of these many things would be Zeus. On the other hand, Christianity is a monotheistic religion, and a devout Christian will hold that the extension of the term "god" contains only one thing, God. According to the Christian view, Zeus does not belong to the extension of the term "god" because Zeus is not an actual thing but merely a product of imaginative religious fancy or superstition. Still a third individual, an atheist, will hold that nothing belongs to the extension of the term "god." Yet however human opinions may vary, there is no change or variation in the things and in the number of things which are in the extension of this or any other term. All actual things to which the term refers or applies are in the extension; no unreal or nonactual things are in the extension.

The above fact must not, however, be misunderstood nor be made the basis for a misunderstanding about the relation of extensions to the passage of time. To say that only actual things are in the extension of a term is *not* to say that only things *now* existing are in its extension. The truth is quite the reverse. For the extension of a term includes all things that ever were, are, or will be actual things referred to by the term. Thus, time of existence is not generally relevant in determining whether an object belongs to the extension of a term. For example, the extension of the term "man" includes not only people now dead, like George Washington, and people now living like Mr. Eisenhower, but people yet to be born.

On the other hand, sometimes a term includes a time stipulation, such as "man living in the eighteenth century" or "man living in the twentieth century." Plainly, George Washington belongs to the extension of the first of these terms and not to that of the second.

The claim made just above has not always been accepted as true. In fact, many people tend to think of the extension of a term as changing through the years; for example, the extension of the term "man" as continually changing according as the facts of death and birth change the identity of the population from one moment to another( Such a view, however, makes the meanings of terms too fluid for serious and systematic study. It is this necessity to fix the meaning which recommends the position taken in this text. )

Nevertheless, the fact that so many people think of the extension of a term as changing in time has the consequence that, for them, time stipulations of the sort mentioned above are unnecessary. This has led to certain conventions for the use of languages such as English, of such a sort that we can correctly grasp the intended meanings of authors only by pretending a tacit (that is, unstated) time stipulation, even though the author himself was not aware of the need for one.[2]

Let us illustrate. Suppose a man to say, "The time will come when every child born in America will receive a college education." What does he mean?

Suppose that we undertake to explain the meaning of his assertion by analyzing it in such a way as to identify as one of its terms, "child born in America." To say that every child born in America will do such

[2]  The omission of time stipulations in a language like English is not entirely due to mistaken views about extensions. It in fact occurs as a consequence of the conjugation of verbs, with their past, present, and future tenses ("was," "is," "will be"). The tense of the verb actually introduces into the sentence a sort of time stipulation. The "verbs" of tenseless languages, like arithmetic, contain no such concealed time stipulations, so that when time stipulations are important, they are explicitly attached to the terms connected by those verbs. Compare for example, the physicist's law

$$v_{t+1} = v_t + 33 \text{ ft/sec}$$

where "$t$" and "$t + 1$" are time stipulations.

But these considerations of differences between tensed and untensed languages are too complicated to be adequately discussed in the present unit. Suffice it to say that the fact that English and other natural languages are tensed languages is probably the cause, rather than the effect, of the mistaken view that the extensions of terms vary with the passage of time.

and such is to say that every object in the extension of the term "child born in America" will do such and such. But according to what has been previously said, Abraham Lincoln belongs to the extension of the term "child born in America." Surely our imaginary author is not trying to tell us that at a certain time in the future, college educations are going to be granted posthumously to people like Abraham Lincoln, and prematurely to people who are at that time still unborn! Of course not.

To make our interpretation logically sound, we must revise our identification of the term involved. A part of this revision involves our providing a time stipulation which was unexpressed (perhaps even considered unnecessary) by our imaginary author. Let us replace the phrase "child born in America" by the phrase "person born in America after date $t$ (who lives in America to maturity)".[3] Now when our author says, "The time will come when . . ." and so on, we may rephrase this as a stipulation that the date, $t$, mentioned in our rephrased term, lies in the future.[4] Hence, the time stipulation, "born after date $t$," restricts the term in such a way as to prevent persons living in earlier ages, like Abraham Lincoln, from belonging to its extension. With this time stipulation, all the objects in the extension of the term will be living after a certain date and our author may quite properly be understood to claim that every object in the extension of the revised term will receive a college education.

## EXERCISE

Below are two lists of terms, A and B. Indicate which terms in list B name things belonging to the extension of which terms in list A. In instances of doubt, what would you have to do to resolve it?

| List A | List B |
|---|---|
| City | Boston, Mass. |
| Man | Pompeii |
| Dog | Franklin D. Roosevelt |
| Having a backbone | Falla (Roosevelt's pet dog) |
| | The white whale in *Moby Dick* |
| | Eisenhower's first-born great grandson |

3  The restrictive clause in parentheses is *another* stipulation not mentioned by our imaginary author, but added by us for other, but equally obvious, reasons.
4  For example, suppose that the remark we are analyzing had been made in 1955. Then the entire remark might be rephrased without using future tenses in the following manner: "There is a date, $t$, which is later than 1955, at which every person born in America after date $t$ (who lives in America to maturity) receives a college education."

## §20.6 Null Extensions and Science

When the extension of a term has nothing in it, that is, when the term does not refer or apply to anything at all, the extension of that term is said to be __null,__ or the term is said to have a **null** extension.

Examples of terms with null extensions are: "elected President of the United States in 1950," "four-sided triangle," and "three-dollar bill."

Terms with null extensions are of special interest and may be recognized as important topics of scientific inquiry. Of course some terms of this sort, such as "centaur," "griffin," "gremlin," and so on are admittedly, and often from the outset of their existence, known as records of imaginative fancy not referring to any actual thing. The ascertainment that the extensions of those terms are null is hardly a serious scientific problem. But discoveries about another class of such terms do constitute real scientific achievements:

It is commonly known that the scientist is interested in discovering and establishing generalizations. A study of things of the sort $S$ may lead to the discovery or theory that

Every $S$ is $P$.

(For example, every mature human is at least 4 feet tall). Corresponding to every such statement there is a complex term constructible by combining the subject term, "$S$," with the negative of the predicate term, "$P$":

$S$ that is not $P$

The original statement is true if and only if nothing belongs to the extension of this correlative complex term. Hence, scientific interest in the truth or falsity of generalizations amounts to an interest in whether or not certain complex terms have null extensions. We shall return to this point in Part V.

## REVIEW QUESTIONS FOR UNIT 20

1. What is meant by the extension of a term? Illustrate what you say by at least one attributive term and at least one general denotative term.
2. What is the smallest number of things that might be in the extension of a term? The largest number?
3. Give examples of terms—some attributive and some general denotative—such that only one thing belongs to the extension of each; such that more than a thousand things belong to the extension of each.

4. Explain briefly how *both* the meaning of the term *and* the facts of history contribute to determining what and how many things belong to its extension.

5. Can nonexistent things belong to the extension of a term? Can not-*now*-existent things belong to the extension of a term? Explain.

6. What does it mean to call the extension of a term *null*?

7. Explain how the scientist's interest in discovering and establishing generalizations may be viewed as an interest in discovering that certain terms have no objects in their extensions.

# The Extension of a Singular Term; Referents of Terms

## §21.1 The Extension of a Proper Name Considered as a Term

In the last unit we noticed how one might attend to a group or class of things only to discover that nothing belonged to the group, or that only one thing belonged to it. For example, only one thing belongs to the extension of the term "elected in 1952 to be President of the United States," and nothing belongs to the extension of the term "elected in 1950 to be President of the United States." Keeping these facts in mind will help us understand what is meant by the extension of a singular term.

Every singular term purports to refer to precisely one object. Whether or not it succeeds in referring depends on whether or not the one and only object purportedly referred to actually exists. If it does, the term does refer to one and only one object; if it does not, the term does not refer to any object. Let us see how this affects the extension of a proper name considered as a term.

In §19.3 it was pointed out that proper names considered as sign-types are often used as the names for several distinct objects. For example, many cities are named "Boston," and at least two men, grandfather and grandson, are named "Adlai Stevenson." But as was said in §18.3, every different convention associated with a proper name —every different intention, now to designate *this* object and then to designate *that* one—identifies a distinct singular term. Thus the one sign-type of a proper name may contribute to the constitution of several singular terms, each purporting to refer to one and only one object. It is this proper name considered as a singular term which we must examine.

In §20.1 the extension of a term was defined as the class of all objects to each of which the term refers. In the case of proper names considered as terms, this class will either be null (nothing in it) when the

224

thing purportedly referred to does not exist, or have exactly one thing in it when the thing purportedly referred to does exist.

For example, the terms "Peter Rabbit," "Santa Claus," "Zeus," "Mr. Pickwick," and "Sherlock Holmes" are terms whose extensions are null. On the other hand, the terms "Abraham Lincoln," "Boston, Massachusetts," "President Eisenhower," and "President Roosevelt" (whether Franklin D. or Theodore makes no difference) are terms whose extensions each have exactly one thing in them.

### EXERCISE

Which of the following terms have null extensions and which do not? For each extension that is not null, indicate how many things are in the extension. If you do not know the correct answers to these questions, what do you have to do to find them?

1. Plato
2. Moses
3. Tito
4. Babbitt

5. Atlantis
6. Washington, D. C.
7. Macy's
8. Ferdinand (the bull)

## §21.2 The Extension of a Simple Abstract Singular Term

Simple abstract singular terms such as "blue," "courage," and "triangularity" are much like proper names in that each purports to refer to one single object, but that object is abstract: a quality, characteristic, or relationship.

Any such term will have a null extension if the quality, character, or relation that it purports to refer to does not exist, or its extension will have exactly one thing in it if this quality, character, or relation does exist.

Two ancient but still vigorous schools of philosophy contend this issue. The one type of philosophy, called *realism*, holds that such abstract entities do in fact exist. Consequently, for realists these singular terms would have extensions each with exactly one thing in it. The other type of philosophy, called *nominalism*, holds that no such abstract entities are actual. Consequently, nominalists would hold that the extensions of these abstract singular terms are null.

It would take us too far afield to explore the arguments pro and con for realism and nominalism. It is the author's opinion that a moderate, intermediate position is the more promising: some of these qualities, characters, or relations are actual and the extensions of the terms purporting to refer to them are therefore not null, while others of these qualities, characters, or relations are not actual, and the extensions of the terms purporting to refer to them are null.[1]

## §21.3 Complete and Incomplete Definite Descriptions

Before we consider the extensions of definite descriptions ("the capital of Massachusetts," "my fountain pen," and so on) we must note that they occur in two distinct kinds.

Every definite description is a singular term formed by "singularizing" some general term, which may be called its **basis**. For example, the general term "resident at 46 Main Street" is the basis of the definite description, "the resident at 46 Main Street."

In the one case, the author of a definite description proposes the general term which provides the basis of the description as sufficient to identify and isolate exactly one thing, to which his definite description purports to refer. "The capital of Massachusetts" would be a good example. I know that the extension of the *general* term "capital of Massachusetts" has only one thing in it. (In this respect it is different from, say, "capital of Australia." Australia has had two capitals, Melbourne and Canberra, so that the extension of "capital of Australia" has two things in it.) But knowing that Massachusetts has only one capital, I can form a definite description, "the capital of Massachusetts," which purports to refer to the one and only thing in the extension of the basic general term.

A definite description is said to be **complete** when it purports to refer to the one and only object presumed to be in the extension of its basis.

On the other hand, people often use the linguistic form called a *definite description* even when they know that the basic general term has more than one object in its extension. For example, a person might say, "The doctor told me to stay in bed for twenty-four hours." Yet he knows that the extension of the term "doctor" contains many more than one person. Or again, I might say, "Use my fountain pen," if the one that you were writing with went dry. And yet I own two fountain pens.

Oftentimes both speaker and hearer recognize some unspecified qualification which, if stated, would have made the general term on

---

1  For a fuller treatment of the author's position, the reader is referred to his article on "The Logic of Existence" in *Philosophical Studies*, Vol. VII, No. 4 (June, 1956).

which the definite description is based have an extension with exactly one thing in it. For example, "the doctor" could have been more unambiguously identified as "the doctor whom I consulted," and "my fountain pen" identified as "the fountain pen of mine which I am handing to you." Sometimes the receiver cannot guess what additional qualification was in the speaker's mind or would be required, but not being interested in the nature of the qualification, accepts the term as sufficient to the purposes in hand.

When a definite description is produced with the intention of referring to exactly one of the presumably many things in the extension of its basis, the definite description is called **incomplete**.

## §21.4 The Extension of a Complete Definite Description

Let "the resident at 46 Main Street" be momentarily considered as a complete definite description. How many things are in the extension of this singular term?

The answer to this question depends on the correct answer to a similar question about the extension of the basic *general* term, "resident at 46 Main Street." Now with respect to it, three sorts of situation are possible: (1) Nobody lives at 46 Main Street, so the extension of the general term is null. In this case, the extension of the definite description is also null. It is just like "Santa Claus." (2) Exactly one person lives at 46 Main Street, so the extension of the general term has exactly one thing in it. In this case the extension of the definite description also has exactly one thing in it: that person who resides at 46 Main Street and is also the sole member of the extension of the general term. (3) More than one person lives at 46 Main Street, so the extension of the basic general term has more than one thing in it. In this case, the extension of the definite description is null! The general term, offered as a sufficient means for picking out one and only one thing, has failed to do the job, and consequently the definite description based on it fails to make a unique reference.

The situation in this latter case is very similar to simple ambiguity (§3.8). There is, however, this difference. Ambiguity is a characteristic of a *token*, making it impossible to tell of what term the token is supposed to be an occurrence. But in the situation now before us, it is the *term*—the complete definite description—which is at fault. What it *purports* to refer to is plain enough, but an erroneous belief about the size of the extension of a general term robs the method of referring of its effectiveness.[2]

## EXERCISES

1. Consider each of the following as a complete definite description and indicate how many things are in its extension. Explain briefly why you answer as you do. If you do not know the correct answer, explain what you would have to do to find it.
   a. The President of the United States in 1955
   b. The President of the United States in 1953
   c. The capital of New York State
   d. The butcher
   e. Adlai Stevenson's son
   f. The Unit of this book which deals with extensions

2. If, in your reading, you happened to come across definite descriptions listed in question 1, which of them would you think were probably intended by their authors as complete definite descriptions and which as incomplete? If in some cases you consider the alternatives equally probable, what additional information—about the author or the context of his writing—would tend to make one or the other alternative the more probable?

## §21.5 The Extension of an Incomplete Definite Description

Strict logic can hardly deal with incomplete descriptions, because it cannot deal with what is only in people's minds and not indicated or expressed by what they say. But you and I must find a way of dealing with them, because we are continually encountering them. The following remarks suggest a generally appropriate approach.

Suppose an author speaks of "the resident at 46 Main Street," and suppose that we are quite certain that the author knows or believes that several people reside at 46 Main Street. We should treat his words as probably intended for an incomplete definite description. In so treating what he said, we are assuming that he had more or less definitely in mind a further characterization of the object to which he intended to refer than the stated one, "resident at 46 Main Street."

---

[2] I am indebted to Mr. Joseph F. Lambert for calling to my attention the difference between simple ambiguity and this difficulty in the case of certain definite descriptions.

Let us call this additional, unstated characterization, involved whenever a person uses an incomplete definite description, **the tacit supplement** of that definite description.

For example, if a person says, "the resident at 46 Main Street," intending to indicate a certain one of several such residents, the tacit supplement might have been, *who is a mutual acquaintance of yours and mine,* or *who is head of the household,* or *of whom we were recently speaking,* or anything else, provided this further characterization is something he had in mind as pinpointing his reference to that certain one of the residents.

Seven points are to be noticed:

1.   Quite often a speaker himself gives little attention to the character of any tacit supplements on which his incomplete definite descriptions depend for effective unique reference. That is, he has only vaguely in mind a sufficient characterization to limit his reference to the one object he intended to refer to.

2.   More often than not, all the purposes of discourse are adequately served without bothering to find out just what the tacit supplement is. But sometimes it is important to know. In such a case, we quite properly ask, "Which one do you mean?" This is a request for the supplement, or some other means by which we can identify the object to which the speaker intended to refer.[3]

3.   Of course sometimes the original speaker is not available to answer such a question. He might, for example, be the deceased author of a book in which we read the definite description, or an orator whose speech we cannot interrupt. Then, if we really want to know what the tacit supplement was, we have to guess at it. Often, however, the circumstances in which the author spoke will make such guessing fairly reliable.

4.   If we guess at, or the author tells us, what his tacit supplement was, then when a statement of this supplement is added to the author's original definite description, that description is turned from an incomplete into a complete definite description.

5.   How many objects were in the extension of the original description is determined by finding the extension of the complete definite

---

[3] It is usually less important to know what the tacit supplement is than to know something such that, if it *had* been the tacit supplement, it would have been effective.

description into which we have turned it. Thus, if the extension of the complex general term consisting of the basis of the original description and the tacit supplement, is null, then the extension of the original definite description is null; if the extension of that complex general term has one object in it, then the extension of the original definite description has one object in it; and if the extension of that complex general term has several objects in it, then the extension of the original definite description is null.

6.  However, a word of caution is necessary in applying the test described just above. Suppose that an application of the test leads to the conclusion that the extension of the original definite description is null. This is more likely than not to be evidence that we made an incorrect guess—or the author improperly reported—the content of the tacit supplement. Rather than insist that the original definite description has a null extension, we had better (in most cases) revise our hypothesis as to what is the content of the tacit supplement.

7.  It has already been remarked—point 2—that we often do not care what the tacit supplement really is. And in point 6, it was shown that even when we do care, if the guess we make gives a null extension to the original incomplete description, we had better assume that we made a wrong guess. What, then, should we say is the extension of an incomplete definite description?

a.  If the general term which is the basis of the original incomplete description (*not* supplemented by the tacit supplement and hence turned into a complex general term) has a null extension, then the extension of the definite description is null. This is because *every* supplement must in this circumstance give a complex general term whose extension is null. For example, there are no such things as dragons. Hence, there can be no such things as friendly dragons, or as fire-breathing dragons, or as armor-plated dragons, or as dragons of any kind.

b.  If the general term which is the basis of the original description has an extension that is not null, then assume that the extension of the definite description contains one object. This is because there is some way of supplementing the general term to get a complex general term with an extension containing just one object. According to point 6, we should not be content with any guess as to what the author's tacit supplement was unless it had just this effect, of giving a complex general term with only one object in its extension.[4]

## EXERCISE

For each of the following incomplete definite descriptions propose a tacit supplement that could well have the effect of giving the definite description an extension containing exactly one object.

1. The speaker
2. The druggist
3. The teacher
4. The coroner
5. The automobile

## §21.6 Referents of Terms

By a **referent** of a term is meant any object to which that term refers or applies. Thus the referents of denotative terms are the things to which those terms refer, while the referents of attributive terms are the things to which those terms apply.

Put in another way, the referents of a term are the objects that belong to, or are in, the extension of that term. Thus a term has as many referents as there are things in its extension. Singular terms will have either one referent or no referent. Some general terms will have no referent, some will have one referent, others will have two, ten, a thousand, or even an infinity of referents.

Since referents belong to extensions and only actual things belong to extensions, only actual things are referents. This does not mean, however, that the referent must be now existing. "George Washington" has a referent, because it refers to an actual, although no longer living, person. Or again, a young married couple might agree that they will name their first son after the father. If eventually they have a son, then

---

4 But this advice cannot always be followed. Sometimes the incomplete description has more the character of a proper name than that of a complete description, and purports to refer to a certain individual who in fact does not exist, no matter how many objects are in the extension of the general term on which the definite description is based. For example, a person might say "the jolly fellow," meaning thereby to refer to Santa Claus. But Santa Claus does not exist. Hence, even though there are many jolly fellows in the world so that the extension of the general term "jolly fellow" is *not* null, the extension of that author's incomplete definite description *is* null.

the term—"John Jones, Jr."—will have had a referent from the time of its first use with this purport.

Referents are more important topics of logical consideration than extensions in the case of *singular* terms, but extensions are more important topics of consideration than referents in the case of *general* terms. The reasons for this will become clearer as we proceed.

Some *singular* terms will have as their referents exactly those things that are the extensions of other, *general* terms. For example, "the class of all men" is a singular term, referring to a certain class. But this class is precisely the extension of the general term "man." In fact, "the extension of the term 'man' " is another singular term, having the same referent as "the class of all men."

But no term has its own extension as one of its referents. Its referents are always *in* its extension, and even when that term has only one referent, so that only one thing is in the extension, still the referent and the extension must be distinguished.

We shall have occasion, when we come to Part V, to consider further the relations of referents and extensions.

## EXERCISE

Which of the following are referents of the terms indicated, and which are not? Briefly explain in each case why you answer as you do.

1. "City"
   a. Washington, D. C.
   b. The capital of Michigan
   c. The capital of the Kingdom of Oz
   d. Arizona
   e. Carthage (destroyed by the Romans in the Punic Wars)
2. "Plays golf"
   a. Julius Caesar
   b. President Eisenhower
   c. Ben Hogan
   d. Santa Claus
   e. King George VI of England
3. "Santa Claus"
   a. Santa Claus
4. "The President of the United States during some part of 1953."
   a. George Washington
   b. President Truman
   c. President Eisenhower

## REVIEW QUESTIONS FOR UNIT 21

1. What is the difference between a proper name considered as a sign-type and a proper name considered as a term?

2. What is the minimum, and what the maximum, number of things that might be in the extension of a proper name considered as a term?

3. Connect the issue between nominalism and realism with an issue concerning the extensions of simple, abstract, singular terms.

4. Explain briefly the difference between complete and incomplete definite descriptions.

5. Explain briefly what determines the number of objects in the extension of a complete definite description.

6. What is meant by the tacit supplement of an incomplete definite description?

7. What is meant by the *basis* of a definite description?

8. Are tacit supplements of incomplete definite descriptions always clearly in the minds of the authors of those descriptions?

9. Discuss briefly how you determine the size of the extension of an incomplete definite description.

10. What is meant by a referent of a term?

11. Must referents be actual things? *Now* existing things? Explain.

12. How many referents might a singular term have? A general term?

13. Can the referent of a singular term ever be identically the extension of a general term? Explain and illustrate.

14. Can the extension of a term ever be also a referent of that same term? Explain.

# *The Intensions of a Term*

## §22.1 Introduction

We have seen in Units 20 and 21 that in order to discover what does and what does not belong to the extension of a term, or in order to discover what is or is not a referent of a term, we have to <u>understand the term</u>; that is, we have to know its meaning. It is, of course, true that we sometimes are <u>helped to understand</u> a term by <u>learning what are at least some of the things in its extension</u>. This is, in fact, the way in which all children learn the first few words of their native language. "Ball," "Papa," "car," "milk," "water," and so on are learned by being heard when objects from the extensions of these terms are presented to the child and are attracting his attention. Gradually, the great miracle of learning takes place and the child <u>associates the word-type with these various objects</u>. The evidence of his understanding is found in his responding to the word in manners appropriate to the thing, and finally in his producing the word to summon the thing, or to secure it.

It is not only a few words first learned by a child, but enormous numbers of words from the vocabulary of everyday discourse, that are learned by all of us in much this same way: <u>by connecting the word-type with certain presented objects belonging to the extension of the term.</u>

But with all this learning via the extension, it is still only a *sample* from the extension that gives us a *hint* at the meaning of the term. A question naturally arises, Does this word or term refer (or apply) also to this, that, and the other thing that were not in the sample from the extension by which we first came dimly or tentatively to understand the word? <u>Only when we fully understand the word can we use it to classify *new* objects and *new* experiences that come into our lives.</u> And only when we can so classify new objects and experiences can we be said fully to understand the term.

The topic of Unit 23 will be that aspect of a term's meaning which, once grasped, will enable us to decide, with respect to objects newly brought to our attention, whether they do or do not belong to the extension of the term. The meaning of a term in that sense is called the *total strict intension* of the term.

There are, however, other related matters that must be discussed first. These preliminary matters are the topic of the present unit.

## §22.2 Common Characteristics and Common Sets of Characteristics

To make a beginning, we note that individual things, of whatever sort, have various definite characteristics. In fact, any true proposition of the form

$$s \text{ is } P$$

isolates and identifies one characteristic of *s*. For example, (1) *This blade of grass is green*, and (2) *That piece of metal is a good conductor of heat*, impute the characteristics greenness and high conductivity of heat to this blade of grass and to that piece of metal, respectively.

It is not always the case that the English language contains simple terms (abstract, singular) that name or refer to the qualities or characteristics possessed by objects, as "greenness" names the characteristic attributed to the grass in statement 1. One can, however, always construct a complex term by using the phrase "the quality of . . .," as in "the quality of being a good conductor of heat."

Every object has many characteristics. Furthermore, many objects will have several of their characteristics in common. For example, not only this blade of grass is green, but so also is that blade of grass, this apple, that leaf, this tablecloth, that emerald.

We must now notice two useful technical expressions, *common* and *peculiar*.

To say that a certain characteristic is **common** to a group of objects is to mean that *every* object in the group has that characteristic.

For example, to say that three-sidedness is common to triangles is to mean that every triangle is three sided.

To say that a certain set (or group, or class) of characteristics is *common* to a group of objects is to mean that *every* object in the group has *every* characteristic in the set.

For example, to say that the set of two characteristics, *having a backbone* and *having lungs*, is common to men, means that every man has each of these characteristics, that is, that every man has a backbone and every man has lungs.

## EXERCISES

1. Is the characteristic *using oxygen* common to all men? Common to all animals? Common to all living organisms?

2. Is the set of characteristics, *using oxygen*, *composed of cells*, and *possessed of a backbone*, common to all men? Common to all horses? Common to all animals? Common to all living organisms?

3. Is the set of characteristics, *having a flat surface*, *having four legs*, and *being made of wood*, common to all tables? Common to all desks? Common to all coffee tables?

### §22.3 Peculiar Characteristics

Not only is it true (as noted in the last section) that certain objects have certain characteristics, but it is also true that certain other objects do *not* have those characteristics. For example, while this blade of grass, that emerald, and so on are green, this blotter, that automobile, this pumpkin, and so on are not green.

If we say that a certain characteristic is **peculiar** to a certain object, we mean that nothing except this object has that characteristic.

If we say that a certain characteristic is **peculiar** to a certain set (or group, or class) of objects, we mean that nothing except all or some of the objects in that group or set has that characteristic; or (what amounts to the same thing) we mean that everything which has that characteristic belongs to that set or group of objects.

## EXERCISES

1. Is being straight sided peculiar to triangles?
2. Is being green peculiar to green things?
3. Is the possession of lungs peculiar to vertebrate animals?
4. Is the possession of eyes peculiar to vertebrate animals?

We may now put to use some of the ideas explained so far in this unit. We have noticed previously (§18.4) that every attributive term has two denotative correlates: the first denoting things to which the attributive term correctly applies, the second denoting the quality or property whose possession makes the attributive term applicable. Now the extension of the attributive term is a set of objects; in fact, it is exactly the same set of objects as is also the extension of the first denotative correlate. The second denotative correlate is an abstract singular term referring to one specific characteristic. This characteristic, denoted by the second denotative correlate, is common *and* peculiar to the set of objects which is the extension of the other two terms (the attributive and its first denotative correlate).

The entire situation may be made perhaps a little clearer with the aid of some further comments and a diagram. Some sets of objects are entirely contained in other sets of objects. (In Figure 7, set C is contained in set E, E is contained in L, and C is contained in L.)

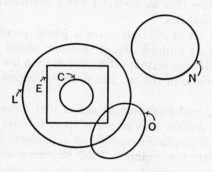

**Fig. 7**

For example, the set of things that are dogs is contained in the set of things that are mammals; again, the set of things that are students is contained in the set of things that are human beings. Other sets of objects overlap one another, without either being contained in the other. (In the diagram, O and E overlap, also O and L overlap.) For example, the set of people less than twenty-five years old and the set of students overlap without either being contained in the other. Finally, some sets (for example, N and E) are such that neither contains the other and that, furthermore, they do not overlap.

Now let E (in Figure 7) represent the extension of some attributive term, say "green," and of its first denotative correlate. Then E and any set of things which is contained (like C) in E will be a set to which the characteristic denoted by the second denotative correlate is common. But sets that are not contained in E (such as L, N, and O) are sets to which this characteristic is not common. Furthermore, E and any set of things (like L) in which E is contained is a set to which the characteristic is peculiar. But sets in which E is not contained (such as C, N, and O) are sets to which the characteristic is not peculiar. When we think for a moment about what has just been said, we see that E is the one and only set of things to which the characteristic is common *and* peculiar.

## §22.4  Jointly Peculiar Sets of Characteristics

In §22.3 we noted that a single characteristic may be peculiar (or common and peculiar) to various sets (or to one particular set) of objects. Suppose now that we consider not a particular characteristic, but a *set* of characteristics.

If we say that a set of characteristics is **jointly peculiar** to a certain object, we mean that nothing except that one object has *all* characteristics in the set. It may be that other objects than the one in question have one characteristic in the set, but no other object has all characteristics.

It may help our understanding to notice that those singular terms which were called *definite descriptions* purport to refer to the one and only object to which a certain suggested set of characteristics is common and jointly peculiar. For example, "the physician who attended me last night" purports to refer to the one and only object to which the suggested pair of characteristics, *being a physician* and *attending me last night*, is common and jointly peculiar: he is a physician, and he attended me last night (common); *only* he is *both* a physician and a person who attended me last night (jointly peculiar). It is *not* claimed that each characteristic in the set is peculiar; that is, it is not claimed that only he is a physician, and it is not claimed that only he attended me last night. What is claimed is that only he has *both* these characteristics.

If we say that a certain set of characteristics is **jointly peculiar** to a certain *set* of objects, we mean that nothing except objects in that set have all the characteristics in the set of characteristics; or (what amounts to the same thing) whatever has all the characteristics in the set of characteristics is an object in the set of objects.

## EXERCISES

1. Is the pair of characteristics, being males and being married, *jointly peculiar* to the set of:

    All husbands?
    All human beings?
    All American citizens?
    All male creatures?
    All married actors?

2.   Is the pair of characteristics mentioned in Exercise 1 *common* to the set of:
All husbands?
All human beings?
All American citizens?
All male creatures?
All married actors?

3.   Is that same pair of characteristics common *and* jointly peculiar to the set of:
All husbands?
All human beings?
All American citizens?
All male creatures?
All married actors?

## §22.5  The Intensions of Terms

Let us glance ahead to see something of the use to be made of these concepts (*common* and *jointly peculiar*) and at the same time to illustrate and thereby clarify them.

When we consider the extension of some general denotative term, it is not always easy to think of a single, simple characteristic which will be common and peculiar to the extension of that term. But it will quite often be possible to think of a set of characteristics that is common and jointly peculiar to the extension of the term. Consider, for example, the term "triangle." It is difficult to think of a single characteristic that is common and peculiar to all triangles except, perhaps, the characteristic triangularity, and thinking of that does not seem to clarify the situation. But we can (as you who have studied geometry know) think profitably of a set of characteristics that is common and jointly peculiar to all triangles:

Lying in a plane
Being bounded
Having straight sides
Having three sides

As we know, this set of four characteristics is common and jointly peculiar to all triangles: every (Euclidean) triangle has all four of these characteristics (common), and only triangles have all four (jointly peculiar). Furthermore, we know that if we took away any one of the four characteristics, the remaining set of three characteristics (although still common) would not be jointly peculiar to the extension of the term "triangle." For example, the first three characteristics are found as well in rectangles and pentagons as they are in triangles.

Our concern throughout the remainder of this unit and the two next is to be with sets of characteristics that are common and jointly peculiar to the extensions of terms. Such sets of characteristics are called the **intensions** of those terms.[1]

### §22.6 The Total Contingent Intension of a Term

Consider any term, for example, "man," and consider now characteristics that are common to all men, common, that is, to the extension of the term selected: *not over 10 feet tall, has a backbone, has a central nervous system, possesses some capacity to reason*, and so on. The number of such characteristics is enormous. In fact, it is infinite, so that we could not possibly hope to consider all these characteristics

---

[1]    Older books in logic regularly speak of "*the* intension of a term" as though each term had one and only one intension. We shall shortly observe, however, that for any one term there are many different sets of characteristics each of which sets is common and jointly peculiar to the extension of that term. Each such set of characteristics is, according to our definition, an intension of that term. Hence each term has many different intensions. The next section and the next two units will discriminate several of these intensions one from the other.

It would be impossible to say which of these many intensions of a term was primarily under consideration in the older logics. The fact is that the different intensions were not discriminated, and this lack of discrimination resulted in such a confusion that some comments in the older logics seem to apply more or less to one of these intensions and some other remarks more generally to another.

Quite different from the above is another distinction raised by certain more modern books on logic: a distinction between what is called the *objective* intension and the *subjective* intension of a term. The distinctions we are about to make relate to this modern distinction in the following manner: Every intension of a term which we shall identify is what these modern authors would call an objective intension. Thus, in a sense, our criticism of the older logics applies equally to these modern logicians: they (the modern logicians) speak of *the* objective intension of a term, as though each term had one and only one objective intension, whereas in fact there are many sets of characteristics *each* of which sets satisfies the definition of an objective intension.

We nowhere discuss the subjective intensions of terms. The phrase "subjective intension" is suggestive but in our opinion also misleading, because the set of characteristics forming the so-called subjective intension seldom if ever has that characteristic "common and jointly peculiar to the extension" which defines an intension. The *general* field of inquiry to which the current discussions of subjective intensions properly belongs is one we have alluded to in a totally different context, under the name "imagery accompanying belief." For that discussion, and the distinction between the imagery and content of a belief, see above, §5.4. Imagery and content are related to belief much as subjective and objective intension are related to a term.

one by one. Nevertheless, we may consider them as a group, and this will be profitable. This group of all such characteristics—that is, of all characteristics common to the extension of the term "man"—is called the *total contingent intension* of the term "man."

More generally, the **total contingent intension** of any term is the set of all characteristics common to the extension of that term.

At the end of the last section it was suggested that any set of characteristics common and jointly peculiar to the extension of a term could be called an *intension* of that term. It will be shown later on (§23.5) that the set of *all* characteristics common to the extension of a term is always jointly peculiar to the extension of that term. (Hence such a set is both common and jointly peculiar.) It is this fact which justifies calling such sets "total contingent *intensions*."

Let us consider now *any* intension of a given term, that is, any set of characteristics common and jointly peculiar to the extension of that term. Obviously, this intension will be either identical with, or contained in, the total contingent intension of that term: for since we chose *any* intension, it *might* be that we chose the total contingent intension; but on the other hand, if we did *not* choose the total contingent intension, then the intension we did choose is contained in the total contingent intension. For every characteristic in the intension we did choose is common to the extension of the term (by the definition of "intension") and is therefore in the total contingent intension (by the definition of "total contingent intension").

Hence we come to this **law:** Every intension of a given term is either contained in, or identical with, the total contingent intension of that term.

It must not, however, be supposed that every set of characteristics contained in the total contingent intension of a term is itself an intension of that term. It is true that every such set is a set of characteristics common to the extension of the term, thereby meeting half of the conditions that define an intension. But not every such set is made up of characteristics that are jointly peculiar to the extension of the term, and hence not every such set is an intension. For example, the set of two characteristics, *having lungs* and *having a backbone*, is a set contained in the total contingent intension of the term "man" since both characteristics are common to all men. But these two characteristics are not jointly peculiar to the extension of the term "man": horses, dogs, cats, chickens, and many other animals have both these characteristics. (Hence this set of two characteristics is not an intension of the term "man.")

It has been at least suggested, however, that *some* sets of characteristics contained in the total contingent intension of a term are intensions of that term. In the next two units, we shall consider what some of these other intensions are.

## REVIEW QUESTIONS FOR UNIT 22

1. What does it mean to say that a certain characteristic or set of characteristics is *common* to a certain set of objects?

2. What does it mean to say that a certain characteristic is *peculiar* to a certain object, or to a certain set of objects?

3. What does it mean to say that a certain set of characteristics is *jointly peculiar* to a certain object or to a certain set of objects?

4. What does it mean to say that a certain set of characteristics is *common and jointly peculiar* to a certain object or a certain set of objects?

5. What is meant by an *intension* of a term?

6. What is meant by the *total contingent intension* of a term?

7. State a law holding between the various intensions of a term and its total contingent intension.

8. Is every set of characteristics contained within the total contingent intension of a term also an intension of that term? Briefly explain and illustrate.

UNIT **23**

# *The Total Strict Intension*
# *of a Term*

## §23.1 Necessary and Merely Contingent Members of the Total Contingent Intension

In the preceding unit we learned what is meant by an intension of a term and by the total contingent intension of a term. In this unit we shall consider another of a term's intensions, called its _total strict intension_. In many ways, this is the most important of a term's intensions, for one can say of it more truthfully than of anything else that it is _the_ meaning of the term.

But how does one identify the total strict intension of a term? What does one mean by this expression? In order to find answers to those questions, let us return our attention for a moment to the total contingent intension of the term "man" (§22.6) and let us consider two characteristics belonging to this set: *having a backbone* and *less than 10 feet tall*. Each of these characteristics belongs to every man. But is there not a difference in the circumstances that bring about the one fact and those that bring about the other? Perhaps we can find an answer to this question if we think for a moment about why we believe the two propositions, that *Every man has a backbone*, and that *Every man is less than 10 feet tall*, and how we would undertake to test their truth.

To take the second of these propositions first, we might think concerning it somewhat as follows.[1] I have seen a good many men here in America. They have some of them been quite short, and some of them quite tall. But none of them have come near to being 10 feet tall. I have heard of "giants." For example, King Frederick the Great of Prussia had a regiment of "giants." But the minimum height for acceptance in his regiment was 7 feet, which is a good deal less than 10 feet. Hence, if there are any men 10 feet tall, they are very unusual. Therefore, if any

[1] The student need not be held responsible for mastering the details of the sample inquiries that follow, only for understanding the point they illustrate.

243

such men are known to exist, I would probably have heard of them. Since I have not heard of them, probably no such men are known to exist. For these reasons, I do not believe there are any such men; that is, I believe all men are less than 10 feet tall.

But if I wish now to give this proposition a more scientific test, I shall have to start collecting statistical data on the variations in height among men. Without going into details, notice merely that what I must be concerned with is the ascertainment of a "typical" height (probably for each race considered separately) and of a rate of decrease in the frequency of instances of men exceeding this typical height by some selected amount. For example (the example is hypothetical), I might find the typical height is 6 feet, and that one third of all men (among those measured by me) were 6 feet plus or minus 2 inches; that when I add an increment of 4 inches so as to consider the group of men 6 feet 4 inches tall, plus or minus 2 inches, that only one ninth of all the men measured fall in this range; and for each additional 4 inches the frequency is the square of the frequency in the previous group.

Of course, there will be a tallest man in the group I actually measured, but I can expect there to be men taller than him. However, if my sample is reliable, I shall expect these men of increased heights to occur less and less frequently:

| Height range | Frequency |
|---|---|
| 5 feet 10 inches — 6 feet 2 inches | 1/3 |
| 6 feet 2 inches — 6 feet 6 inches | 1/9 |
| 6 feet 6 inches — 6 feet 10 inches | 1/81 |
| 6 feet 10 inches — 7 feet 2 inches | 1/6561 |
| 7 feet 2 inches — 7 feet 6 inches | 1/43,046,621 |
| 7 feet 6 inches — 7 feet 10 inches | etc. |
| 7 feet 10 inches — 8 feet 2 inches | etc. |
| etc. | |

It is easy to see that long before I reach the height range 9 feet 10 inches — 10 feet 2 inches, the frequency will have reached so incredibly small a fraction that one might say there is practically no chance at all that any man will be that tall.

Fundamentally, the grounds for the belief considered above, that every man is less that 10 feet tall, are observation and inference. We conceive it logically possible (if not physically possible) for a man to be 10 feet tall, and if such a thing were observed, we should regard

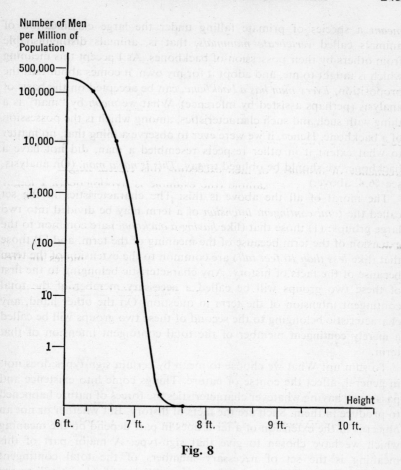

**Fig. 8**

it as an adequate ground for rejecting as false the proposition under consideration.

But now turn to the other proposition, *Every man has a backbone.* Here the approach is entirely different. It is true that I first learned to use this word "man" by being presented with objects from the extension of the term; that only later did I learn about backbones, partly through observation and partly through a reliance on authority. Perhaps still later, I heard, and believed, that every man has a backbone. But when I finally took up the study of biology, I discovered that by "man" is *meant* a species of primate falling under the large classification of animals called *vertebrate mammals*, that is, animals distinguishable from others by their possession of backbones. As I accept this meaning which is taught to me, and adopt it for my own, it comes about that the proposition, *Every man has a backbone*, can be accepted on the basis of analysis (perhaps assisted by inference). What we *mean* by "man" is a thing with such and such characteristics, among which is the possession of a backbone. Hence, if we were ever to observe a thing that, no matter to what extent it in other respects resembled a man, did not have a backbone, we should be obliged to say, *This is not a man*. (On analysis, see §6.4, above.)

The moral of all the above is this: The characteristics in the set called the *total contingent intension* of a term may be divided into two large groups: (1) those that (like *having a backbone*) are common to the extension of the term because of the meaning of the term, and (2) those that (like *less than 10 feet tall*) are common to the extension of the term because of the facts of history. Any characteristic belonging to the first of these two groups will be called a **necessary** member of the total contingent intension of the term in question. On the other hand, any characteristic belonging to the second of these two groups will be called a **merely contingent** member of the total contingent intension of that term.

To sum up: What we choose to mean by certain sign-types does not, in general, affect the course of nature. Things come into existence and pass away having whatever characteristics the forces of nature happened to produce in them. Such are the facts of history. But whether or not an object is in the extension of a term does in part depend on the meaning which we have chosen to give that sign-type. A major part of this meaning is the set of necessary members of the total contingent intension. They constitute, so to speak, a "ticket of admission" to the extension of the term. Nothing in the world is forced by our selection of these characteristics as the meaning of the sign-type to have these characteristics. As already said, the forces of nature give and deprive things of the characteristics that they do or do not have. But whatever comes along and whatever its characteristics might be, it is either admitted or denied admission to the arena of the term's extension according as it has or fails to have all the characteristics which we have chosen to employ as the ticket of admission. Those characteristics are what we understand as constituting the meaning of this term.

Thus the necessary members of the total contingent intension are not characteristics which objects are obliged to have in any absolute sense. Rather, they are necessary only in the sense that objects must have them in order to be admitted to the extension.

This also explains why analysis can reveal which characteristics are necessary characteristics and which are not. In analysis, we are merely "searching our souls" to discover what characteristics we have more or less unconsciously chosen to employ as tickets of admission to the extension.[2]

## EXERCISE

Following each term listed below there is indicated a set of characteristics. Concerning each characteristic in the set indicate whether:

a. It is a *necessary* member of that total contingent intension,

b. It is a *merely contingent* member of that total contingent intension, or

c. It does *not* belong to the total contingent intension of the term it follows.

In doing this exercise, try to understand the listed terms with their conventional meanings. But do not be surprised if you and your classmates disagree about some items. This *may* be because you understand the terms differently due to a vagueness or indeterminacy of the conventions associated with the sign-type. Feel free to use a dictionary in working this problem.

1. "City"
    having a charter
    densely populated
    containing buildings
    containing buildings more than eight stories high
    having paved streets

---

[2] As this explanation of the role of analysis should have suggested, analysis is a sufficient means for revealing necessary members of the total contingent intension only when the analyzer is concerned with the meanings *he* has assigned to terms. If he would know what someone else has chosen to mean by certain sign-types, he must use observation. He could, of course, ask that other person to make an analysis and a report. Then he is using the other person as an authority. Or he may simply observe the speech habits of that other person and try to infer from them what that other person has chosen as necessary members of the total contingent intension.

This explains why the construction of a dictionary is an empirical, observational science rather than an analytical science.

2. "City chicken"
   made of pork
   made of beef
   made of chicken
   made of ground meat
   edible
   made around a wooden stick

3. "Ostrich"
   feathered
   two-footed
   larger than a sparrow
   egg-laying
   having lungs

## §23.2 The Total Strict Intension of a Term

When we were discussing total contingent intensions in §22.6 we noticed that some sets of characteristics contained in the total contingent intension of a term would also be intensions of that term, but that other sets of such characteristics would not be intensions of that term.

Now every term has its total contingent intension and this total contingent intension always contains a set of necessary members.[3] In the light of the preceding paragraph, it becomes natural to ask whether or not the set of necessary members of the total contingent intension of any term is also an intension of that term. As was said in §22.6, sets contained in the total contingent intension are always common to the objects in the extension of the term, but they are not always jointly peculiar to those objects.

We shall see in the next section that this set of necessary members sometimes is and sometimes is not an intension. We shall also see what determines whether or not it is an intension. The only point now to be made is that in a great majority of the cases most important to logic and right reason, the class of necessary members of the total contingent intension of a term is itself an intension of that term.

---

[3] Without necessary members of the total contingent intension, we do not have a term because we do not have a meaning. Instead of a term, all that we would have is a sign-type.

The most troublesome group of terms to deal with under this principle are proper names. They will be discussed shortly below and again in greater detail when we come to Unit 30.

Whenever the set of necessary members of the total contingent intension of a term is an intension of that term, it is called the *total strict intension* of that term.

Hence we may define the **total strict intension** of a term as that intension of the term in question which consists of all and only the necessary members of its total contingent intension.

When the necessary members of the total contingent intension of a term are jointly peculiar to the extension of the term, and thus form its total strict intension, we shall say that the total strict intension of the term **exists**; when they are not jointly peculiar to the extension of the term, so that they do form any intension whatsoever of that term, we shall say that the total strict intension of the term **does not exist.** Thus, to claim that the total strict intension of a term exists is simply to claim that nothing outside of the term's extension has all the necessary characteristics in the term's total contingent intension.

### §23.3　When Does the Total Strict Intension of a Term Exist?

At the beginning of this unit we said of the total strict intension of a term that it is *the* meaning of that term. More properly, that claim should have been made concerning the set of necessary members of the total contingent intension. For whether or not they form an intension and thus constitute the total strict intension, they are the meaning of the term—they are the ticket of admission to the extension of the term.

But in a sense there is another factor in the meaning of a term than the set of necessary members of its total contingent intension. This other factor is closely connected with the classification of terms studied in Units 18 and 19.[4] It has to do with what the term purports to refer to among all the objects, however few or many, that the facts of history bring along bearing their "ticket of admission," that is, having all the necessary characteristics in the total contingent intension. Let us see how this works out.

**1.　General terms.**　A general term purports to refer (or apply) to *any* thing, however few or many such things may be, which has all the necessary characteristics in its total contingent intension. Thus every existent object which the facts of history have produced with those

---

[4] This second factor is closely associated with what medieval logicians studied under the heading of "second intensions." We shall, however, not employ that medieval terminology.

characteristics is a referent of that general term and therefore in the extension of the term, while every existent object that lacks one or more of those characteristics is not a referent and therefore not in the extension. So to speak, the general term says, "I'll let in anything that has a ticket of admission, but nothing get's in on a free pass!"

Thus, in the case of general terms, the necessary characteristics are not only common but jointly peculiar to the extension of the term. Hence they are an intension and may be spoken of as the total strict intension. **The total strict intension of every general term exists.**

**2. Complete definite descriptions.** Each of these terms is a singular term with some general term for its basis (§21.3).

Every complete definite description and its basis have exactly the same set of necessary members in their total contingent intensions. But while the basis, being a general term, purports to refer to any and every thing which the facts of history might produce with this ticket of admission, the complete definite description purports to refer to the one and only thing which the facts of history have produced with this same ticket of admission. So to speak, the definite description says, "I'll let in one thing that has a ticket of admission, and nothing gets in on a free pass. If two or more things show up with tickets of admission, I won't let in anything!"

Now suppose that the facts of history produce nothing at all having all the necessary characteristics, so that the extension of the basis is null, as is also the extension of the definite description. Since nothing whatsoever has all the necessary characteristics, nothing outside the extension of the definite description can have them all. The total strict intension of the definite description will therefore exist, in the sense explained at the end of the last section.

On the other hand, suppose that the facts of history produce exactly one object having all these necessary characteristics. Then this object is in the extension of the definite description and is the only object in the extension of the basis. But the necessary characteristics are jointly peculiar to this object. Once again, they form an intension of the definite description, so that the total strict intension of the definite description exists.

But finally suppose that the facts of history produce two or more objects having all the necessary characteristics. Here is a case in which the necessary characteristics are *not* jointly peculiar to the objects in the extension of the complete definite description: the term accepts none of these objects as referents, its extension is null, and yet objects exist outside its extension which have all the necessary characteristics. These two or more objects are, however, in the extension of the basis.

**The total strict intension of a complete definite description exists if and only if the extension of its basis contains not more than one object.**

**3.   Incomplete definite descriptions and proper names.**   In Unit 30 we shall see why proper names considered as terms should be viewed in a manner much like that appropriate to incomplete definite descriptions. A set of necessary members of a total contingent intension supplies the analytical meaning for each of these terms. But then the proper name and the incomplete definite description, instead of purporting to refer to any thing (like a general term) or the one and only thing (like a complete definite description) having all the necessary characteristics, purport to refer to "a certain" thing having all those characteristics. For example, "Abraham Lincoln" purports to refer to a certain *man;* so does "Mr. Scrooge." So to speak, the term says, "I'll let in a certain thing that has a ticket of admission, but nothing else, whether these others have a ticket of admission or not!"

Now the facts of history may bring the elected individual into existence or they may not. (Usually, proper names are devised with complete knowledge as to what history will do: the thing named already exists and is known to exist when the name is chosen, or the name is chosen as the name of a fictitious character which the facts of history could never bring into existence. But such is not always the case; ships are named before they are built, business firms before they are founded, and so on.) If the facts of history do not bring the thing purportedly named into existence, the extension of the term is null; if they do bring it into existence, the extension has one member.

But whether or not the facts bring *that* thing into existence, they very likely bring other things with the same necessary characteristics into existence. If this likely thing does happen, then the necessary characteristics are not jointly peculiar to the objects in the extension. Otherwise they are jointly peculiar and the necessary characteristics constitute the total strict intension.

**The total strict intension of a proper name or of an incomplete definite description usually does not exist.**

We shall not go on to consider other kinds of term, such as simple singular abstract terms. But let us summarize what has been said above concerning the kinds of term we did consider. General terms always have a total strict intension and the facts of history can in no way affect this situation. On the other hand, singular terms of the three kinds we considered sometimes have a total strict intension and sometimes do not. The facts of history determine whether or not they do: if the facts produce more objects that have all the necessary characteristics than the singular term will admit into its extension, then the term does not have a total strict intension; otherwise it does have a total strict intension.[5]

### §23.4  Total Intensions and the Sciences

By and large, the sciences are more completely concerned with classes and kinds of thing than with individual things belonging to those kinds: with people, rather than with Mr. Jones or Mr. Smith, with trees rather than with this tree or that tree, with metals rather than with this piece of metal or that piece of metal, with numbers, rather than with 3 or with $\sqrt{2}$. Thus general terms rather than singular terms usually indicate the topics of scientific interest. As we have seen, general terms always have a total strict intension.

But the interest of the laboratory or observational scientist is mainly in the merely contingent members of the total contingent intension. For example, the biologist, psychologist, and sociologist are earnestly seeking, by observation and experimentation, to find out more about the nature of man, what he is like, how he lives, how he reacts to situations and conditions in his environment, what limits or stimulates his potentialities for growth and development. All these inquiries may be viewed as efforts to discover what are the merely contingent characteristics in the total contingent intension of the term "man."

However, such observational studies of men can be carried out only by people who know what to observe, who can, in other words, tell the difference between things in the extension and things not in the extension of the term "man." In this sense the development of the laboratory and other empirical sciences depends on and uses the results of prior analysis, that is, of prior studies concerned with the total strict intensions of terms. A laboratory scientist cannot get anywhere until he has

---

5  The author's position on this issue was first developed in connection with the problem of defining proper names and is a consequence of his treatment of that problem. On that problem, see Unit 30.

"defined his terms," and he must continually return to similar problems of analysis. That is, he must continually return to similar concerns with the total strict intensions of his terms.

In mathematics, logic, mathematical physics, and other so-called pure sciences, almost the entire interest of the investigator is taken up with the total strict intensions of the terms treated in his science. Thus, while all branches of science require at least some use of analysis, and some concern with strict intensions, there are some branches in which analysis and the concern with strict intensions make up the whole subject-matter.

## §23.5 Appendix to Unit 23. Why the Total Contingent Intension Is Always an Intension*

In §22.6 it was claimed that although the total contingent intension of a term was defined merely as the set of all characteristics *common* to the extension of that term, it was also jointly peculiar to the objects in that extension, and that therefore it was an intension. It was furthermore promised that this would be shown to be true in a subsequent section. Here we shall consider why this must be true. The proof of this matter is, however, a little complicated.

The proof is divided into three parts, dealing with different kinds of term and different circumstances.

### Part 1: General Terms

Every general term has a total strict intension, as we saw in §23.3. The characteristics in this total strict intension are jointly peculiar to the extension of the term. But these characteristics are also contained in the total contingent intension. Therefore, the total contingent intension is jointly peculiar: If everything that has characteristics A and B (the members of the total strict intension) is in the extension of the term, then everything that has characteristics A and B and C and D (the necessary and merely contingent members) will be in the extension of the term.

### Part 2: Singular Terms with Null Extensions

In §45.6 we shall see that if general term "*S*" has a null extension, then proposition

$$\text{Every } S \text{ is } P$$

is true, *no matter what characteristic "P" may attribute to the things in the extension of "S."* Let *T* be a singular term with a null extension. Then "thing

---

*This section may be omitted by those who wish to move on at once to the next unit.

in the extension of *T*" is a general term with a null extension. Therefore,

> Everything in the extension of *T* is *P*

is a true proposition, no matter what "*P*" may be. Thus both of the following are true:

> Everything in the extension of *T* is round.
> Everything in the extension of *T* is square.

That is, the total contingent intension of *T* contains the contradictory characteristics *round* and *square*. But nothing will have both of these characteristics. Therefore nothing outside the extension of *T* will have them. Therefore, the total contingent intension of *T* is jointly peculiar to the extension of *T*.

### Part 3: Singular Terms with Extensions That Are Not Null

If the extension of a singular term is not null, then it contains exactly one object. Now a famous law stated by the philosopher-mathematician G. W. Leibniz (1646-1716), called the law of *the identity of indiscernibles*, affirms that no two individual objects have all their characteristics in common. But the total set of characteristics belonging to the one object in the extension of the singular term we are considering will be the total contingent intension of that term. According to that law of Leibniz, this set will not belong to any other object, hence will be jointly peculiar to the extension of this singular term.

Since every term is either a general term or a singular term with a null extension or a singular term with a not-null extension, we have proved that the total contingent intension of any term is jointly peculiar to the extension of that term and is therefore an intension of that term.

## REVIEW QUESTIONS FOR UNIT 23

1. What is meant by a *necessary* member of the total contingent intension of a term?

2. What is meant by a *merely contingent* member of the total contingent intension of a term?

3. Is every member of the total contingent intension of a term either a necessary or a merely contingent member, or might some members be neither necessary nor merely contingent?

4. What is meant by the total strict intension of a term?

5. Is the total strict intension of a term a part of (that is, contained in) the total contingent intension?

6. What other kind of factor is there in the meaning of a term besides the necessary characteristics in the total contingent intension?

7. What is this other factor in the meaning of a general term?

8. Do all general terms have total strict intensions? Explain.
9. Do all complete definite descriptions have total strict intensions? Explain.
10. Do all proper names and incomplete definite descriptions have total strict intensions? Explain.
11. Which total intension (contingent or strict) primarily interests the laboratory or observational scientist? Why? The mathematician or logician? Why?
12. Is the total contingent intension of a term always an intension?

# *Definitive and Indexical Intensions*

### §24.1 The Infinite Size of Any Total Strict Intension[1]

The number of characteristics in the total strict intension of a term is very great. In fact, it can be proved that there are an infinity of characteristics in the total strict intension of a term.[2] Because this set of characteristics is so large, nobody could possibly know what all of them are, individually and separately. This is true even of the author of the term, the producer who gives the term its meaning, its total strict intension. It is this fact which lies behind the fact that we can *increase* our understanding of a term which we *already* understand. Even producers, who give terms their meanings, can come to a fuller understanding and appreciation of the meanings that they have given to these terms.

The odd—almost paradoxical—situation described above raises, however, another question. If we can *increase* our understanding in the manner described, there must have been *some* understanding to begin

---

[1] Throughout this unit, we shall speak as though every term had a total strict intension. What is said in it will be true for every term which does have a total strict intension. Near the end of the unit (§24.6), we shall briefly consider how much of what was said holds in the case of terms that do not have total strict intensions.

[2] The proof mentioned in the text depends on considerations that would require explanation before the proof could be persuasive. Hence, it is not reproduced as a part of the text. But to satisfy your possible curiosity, the following outline of the proof is suggested.

Let $C_1$ be a characteristic in the total strict intension of the term $T$.

Let $C_2$ be any characteristic whatsoever.

Then $C_1$-or-$C_2$ is a characteristic in the total strict intension of $T$.

There are an infinity of characteristics to take the place occupied by $C_2$ above.

Therefore, there are an infinity of characteristics of the type $C_1$-or-$C_2$ in the total strict intension of $T$.

Therefore, if there is one characteristic ($C_1$) in the total strict intension of $T$, there is an infinity of characteristics in the total strict intension of $T$.

with. On what was that initial understanding based, and how did we get it in the first place?

This initial understanding is based on another kind of strict intension, called a _definitive_ intension. A definitive intension is a small, finite intension which serves as a clew to the total strict intension. To these definitive intensions we must now turn.

## §24.2  Definitive Intensions

Let us recall from our study of geometry the following definition of a (Euclidean, plane) triangle: A triangle is a plane figure bounded by three straight lines.

This definition, like any good analytical definition, directs our attention to a fairly small number of characteristics all of which are common to the extension of the term being defined and which are furthermore jointly peculiar to that extension. The definition proposes, so to speak, that we understand by the defined term anything with the characteristics enumerated in the definition.

The set of characteristics enumerated in such a definition forms what is called a _definitive intension_ of the term being defined.

We may further recall that the theorems in our geometry book prove that all triangles possess a number of other characteristics not mentioned in the definition. These characteristics are discovered to belong to all triangles by means of analysis (the definitions and postulates in the geometry book) and inference (the proofs of the theorems). The inferences make use of the analyses.

All the characteristics in this manner proved to belong to all triangles are a part of the total strict intension of the term "triangle." Thus the definition of triangle—that is, the definitive intension of "triangle" set forth in the definition—is a clew to the total strict intension of the term.

We may define a **definitive intension** of a term as any smallest intension of the term from which all the characteristics in the total strict intension may be inferred.

What is meant by the above definition of a definitive intension may be made more clear by considering the meaning of "smallest intension," as that expression is intended in that definition. This consideration will also be helped by use of an example. For the purpose of this illustration let us agree that the definition of a triangle at the beginning of this section enumerated a set of three characteristics said to be common and jointly peculiar to triangles:

> being plane figures,
> being bounded by straight lines,
> being bounded by three lines.

This set of three characteristics is then an intension of the term "triangle." Furthermore, it is an intension from which all the characteristics in the total strict intension of "triangle" may be inferred. And finally, it will be a *smallest* intension from which the total strict intension may be inferred if no two of the three characteristics are such that from them alone, without the third characteristic, all the characteristics in the total strict intension may be inferred.

This last point may be put in another way. Suppose a set (for example, the set of three characteristics of triangles given above) such that it is an intension and from it all other characteristics in the total strict intension can be inferred. Then it is a smallest such intension if (1) no one of the characteristics in the set can be inferred from the others in the set, and (2) nothing *not* in the total strict intension can be inferred from it. To illustrate requirement 1, suppose that we added to the set of three characteristics of triangles listed above, the characteristic

> having each interior angle less than a straight angle.

The resulting set of four characteristics would not be a definitive intension, because this fourth characteristic can be inferred to belong to any figure having the first three characteristics. Hence, whatever can be inferred from all four characteristics could equally well be inferred from the first three, so that the set of four is not a smallest intension from which the total strict intension may be inferred.

Or take a different example, for requirement 2. Suppose that to the set of three characteristics listed above, we added the following as a fourth:

> being bounded by green lines.

This fourth characteristic cannot be inferred from the first three, and consequently many things can be inferred from this set of four characteristics which could not be inferred from the original set of three characteristics. But the important point is this: All things inferable from this set of four and not inferable from the set of three are characteristics which do *not* belong to the total strict intension of "triangle."

Of course, all characteristics in the total strict intension are inferable from this set of four: whatever is inferable from the contained set of three is inferable from this containing set of four. But since things *not* in the total strict intension are also inferable from the set of four, this set is not a smallest set from which the total strict intension is inferable.

## §24.3 Further Comments on Definitive Intensions

Let us note a few further facts about definitive intensions.

1. Heretofore, we have studied two kinds of intension: *the* total contingent intension, and *the* total strict intension. The use of the definite article "the" to form definite descriptions suggests that each term has one and only one total contingent intension and one and only one total strict intension. If now you look again at the definition of definitive intensions in the preceding section, you will notice that what is defined is *a* definitive intension instead of *the* definitive intension. The point is that any term may have more than one definitive intension. That is to say, for any term there may be more than one smallest intension from which all the characteristics in the total strict intension of that term may be inferred. Let us see how this could come about.

Perhaps you recall that your geometry book tells you that every regular polygon the sum of whose interior angles equals two right angles is a triangle, and also that every triangle is a regular polygon the sum of whose interior angles is equal to two right angles. These theorems indicate a certain set (pair) of characteristics which are common and jointly peculiar to triangles:

being a regular polygon
having the sum of its interior angles equal to two right angles.

This pair of characteristics is then an intension of the term "triangle." But furthermore, since the methods of the geometry book are analysis and inference, the presence of these theorems means that it can be inferred that whatever has these two properties will also have the three characteristics of triangles listed in the definitive intension given in the preceding section and will therefore have all the characteristics in the total strict intension of the term "triangle." Here, then, is a second definitive intension for the term "triangle."

2. When we compare these two definitive intensions we notice that the one given in §24.2 contains three characteristics and the one given in this section is smaller and contains only two. Does that mean that the

earlier, larger one is not a definitive intension after all, because it is not a smallest intension? Not at all! In the preceding section, we explained how "smallest intension" is to be understood in connection with definitive intensions. If the two characteristics in this later definitive intension had been members of the earlier set, then this set of two would have proved that the original set of three was not a smallest intension from which all characteristics in the total strict intension can be inferred. But since the characteristics in this set of two are *not* members of the earlier set of three, they do *not* prove that the set of three is not a smallest set, that is, that you may take one of the three away and still infer from the remaining two all characteristics in the total strict intension of "triangle."[3]

3.    Any intension of a term which is made up exclusively of necessary members of the total contingent intension, that is, of members of the total strict intension, is called a **strict intension**. Among the many strict intensions of any term will be its total strict intension and each of its definitive intensions.

But a term may have other strict intensions than those just listed. In fact, if we take any class of characteristics which is a definition and add to it any one or more other members of the total strict intension, the resultant class will be a strict intension.

4.    Let us call sets of characteristics formed in the above manner **augmented definitive intensions**. They will have all the characteristics of definitive intensions except the one indicated by the word "smallest": They will be intensions, and from them all the characteristics in the total strict intension can be inferred.

It is indeed not unusual to mistake an augmented definitive intension for a definitive intension. This happens whenever we fail to notice that one of the characteristics in the list under consideration is inferable from the others. Footnote 3 has suggested a case in which this might have happened. On the whole, no great harm will have been done by

---

[3]  On the other hand, the set of three might not be a definitive intension because it might not be a smallest set. For example, from the two characteristics,

> being bounded by straight lines,
> being bounded by three lines,

it is quite possible that one could infer, by solid geometry, the first listed character,

> being a plane figure.

Were this the case, then not the list of three characteristics given in §24.2, but rather this pair of characteristics, would be a definitive intension of the term "triangle."

making such a mistake, the only harm usually being the slight psychological inconvenience of concerning oneself always with a somewhat larger set of characteristics when one might have been concerned only with the smaller definitive intension. (Why no other harm arises will be explained in the next section.)

But when one is dealing systematically with some general subject, it is desirable to check one's definitions to make sure that they are not indicating augmented definitive intensions instead of definitive intensions. Every discovery and removal of such a "blemish" makes a real advance in one's thorough understanding of the total subject.

5.   Definitive intensions and even augmented definitive intensions, once they have been discovered by analysis, provide a sort of "packaged understanding" of the terms that they define. Whatever characteristics are inferable from these definitive intensions belong to the total strict intensions of the terms in question. Hence further study, by inference from the definitive intension to the other characteristics in the total strict intension, is a kind of "unwrapping" of the package: it is useful and instructive, but it does not alter the essential content of the package.

## EXERCISE

Assume that each of the following definitions accurately presents a definitive intension of the term it defines. Indicate which of the characteristics listed below the definition belong to the total contingent intension, which to the total strict intension, which to the given definitive intension, and which to none of those intensions, of the defined term. (Remember that some characteristics may belong to more than one of these intensions.) If in some case you do not know the correct answer, say so and briefly explain what you must do to find the correct answer.

1.   *Fiord:* a comparatively narrow arm of the sea, formed by a deep indentation of the land, and having more or less precipitous slopes or cliffs on each side.

   a.   Formed by a deep indentation of the land
   b.   Filled with water
   c.   Filled with salt water
   d.   At least one-half mile long
   e.   Located where a mountain range borders the sea
   f.   Longer than it is wide
   g.   Site of an amusement park

2. *Pentagon:* a plane figure bounded by five straight lines.

   a. Possessing some color
   b. Bounded by five straight lines
   c. Bounded
   d. Similar in shape to the ground plan of the Department of Defense Building, Washington
   e. Containing five angles

3. *Iceberg:* a large (at least 2-ton) mass of ice floating in the ocean and which has been detached from a glacier.

   a. Floating in the ocean
   b. Floating
   c. Made of fresh (not salt) water
   d. In the northern hemisphere
   e. Weighs at least 2 tons
   f. Weighs at least 1 ton
   g. Blue

## §24.4 Indexical Intensions

    In §23.4 we noted that the empirical scientist is endeavoring by his observational studies to discover various merely contingent members of the total contingent intensions of terms. Not all his endeavors, however, are aimed at this one goal. In this section we may notice another important task which he frequently sets for himself. Careful observational studies will often reveal that a certain small set of characteristics which do not define a term—that is, that are not a definitive intension—are nevertheless a reliable sign that the things having those characteristics belong to the extension of the term. For example, a physician learns to diagnose a patient's ailment by the observation of certain symptoms. These symptoms do not define the disease; but experience (observation) has shown them to be a reliable clew to its presence. They are, then, an *index* to the disease.

    We may define an **index**—or **indexical intension**—as any smallest intension which is not a definitive intension.

    Remarks similar to those made in connection with definitive intensions may be repeated here for indices, thus: (1) By a "smallest intension" is meant an intension (set of characteristics common and jointly peculiar to the extension) such that the removal of any one characteristic from the intension will leave a set of characteristics which is not an intension. (Of course, the set remaining after the removal of this one characteristic will still be common to the extension; hence, since it is not an intension, it will no longer be jointly peculiar.) (2) A term may have more than one index, as it may have more than one definitive intension.

In addition, another point—not like those for definitive intensions—may be noted. While most indices contain merely contingent members of the total contingent intension, a great many also contain one or more necessary members of that intension. Indeed, an index might consist entirely of members of the total strict intension. If such were the case, it would also be a strict intension and would have failed to be a definitive intension merely because not all members of the total strict intension could be inferred from it.

As already suggested, one important project of the empirical sciences is to discover indices for the terms that interest them. One reason for the importance of this task is that frequently the characteristics belonging to the definitive intension will be difficult or impractical to test for. For example, in the days before X rays certain types of disease or malignant growths within the body of an organism could have been directly tested (by the definitive intension) only by impractical exploratory operations. It was a highly important project, then, to discover secondary or indexical clews to these conditions. And the same sort of need is encountered in other scientific fields than that of medicine.

However, this task of discovering indices is more easily undertaken than completed. Oftentimes long and arduous experimental studies will be undertaken without full success. Yet even in the midst of these studies, a kind of partial success is often attained and frequently valuable. For example, the scientist may discover a set of characteristics which are, say, 90 percent reliable. That is, in 90 percent of the cases in which all the characteristics in the discovered set are present, the condition tested for is also present. Perhaps this same set of characteristics is also an 80 percent reliable negative test: in 80 percent of the cases when the test characteristics are *absent*, the condition tested for is also absent.

Unless the set of test characteristics is 100 percent reliable, both as a positive test and as a negative test, then the set of characteristics is not an intension, hence not an index, as that concept has been defined above: To the extent that the set fails to be a positive test, the characteristics in the set fail to be jointly peculiar to the extension of the term;

and to the extent that it fails as a negative test, they are failing to be common to the extension. Nevertheless, near misses of this sort can spur the scientist on to further efforts to close the gap. Often they will suggest the directions which his further inquiries should take. And meanwhile, practical problems may be solved by the cautious use of the "approximate index" which has been discovered.

## §24.5  An Order of Dependence

Throughout these units dealing with extension and intension, the order of our exposition took us from extension to total contingent intension, to total strict intension, to definitive intension, to indexical intension. Furthermore, each succeeding concept was explained partly in terms of the preceding one.

That order of exposition does not, however, represent the order of *discovery* followed by a person who is seeking to understand the conventional meaning of some particular term. His order of discovery is more likely to proceed as follows:

1. Sample of extension
2. Sample of total contingent intension
3. Sample of total strict intension
4. Tentative finite intension
5. Decide whether above (perhaps revised) is an index or a definitive intension
6. Definitive intension (or augmented definitive intension)
7. Further discoveries (with aid of definitive intension) of other members of total strict intension and of other members of extension
8. With aid of above, discoveries of further merely contingent members of total contingent intension
9. Other indexical intensions and additional members of total strict intension

On the other hand, a person might have begun at step 6 by appeal to a dictionary or other authority.

A scientist or other creative thinker who *invents* terms and assigns meanings to them will often begin at step 6 in the above chart. What we must notice is how early and how important to all the rest is the establishment of a definitive intension. In particular, its establishment usually antedates any extensive grasp of the total strict intension.

Indeed, the total strict intension of a term could almost be defined as the set of characteristics inferable from a definitive intension.[4]

## §24.6 Unit 24 and Terms that Have No Total Strict Intensions

If a term (always a singular term) has no total strict intension, then it can have no strict intensions of any sort. Hence, it can have no definitive intension.

But even when a term has no total strict intension, it still has its set of necessary members of the total contingent intension. This set will still be infinite in size, and there still will be finite, smallest "keys" (like definite intensions) from which all those necessary members of the total contingent intension may be inferred. The only difference is that these keys are not jointly peculiar to the extension of the term. In fact, their characteristics will be common to just those objects outside the extension to which the characteristics in the set of all necessary members of the total contingent intension are common.

But all terms, whether or not they have total strict intensions and definitive intensions, will have indexical intensions. In the case of complete definite descriptions, finding one of the "keys" mentioned in the preceding paragraph may be important. But in the case of proper names and incomplete definite descriptions, finding an indexical intension will be much more important.

## §24.7 Conclusion of Part Three

In many places throughout the preceding units it has been suggested that our first understandings of the words and phrases of everyday language are gained through learning to associate a word-type with a sample from its extension. On the basis of this association, a person guesses at certain criteria observed as present throughout the sample and adopts these as a device by appeal to which he may deter-

---

[4] We did *not* define total strict intension in this manner because it seems less faithful to the widespread process of *discovering* definitive intensions for conventional terms. We usually sense what are some of the necessary members of the total contingent intension of a conventional term (step 3) before we discover (step 6) what may be adopted as a definitive intension of that term.

On the other hand, the tendency suggested, to define the total strict intension in terms of the definitive intension, *does* represent an order of derivation closer to practice when we are inventing meanings rather than discovering them. The creative logician or mathematician at least exhibits his subject matter in this order: first a definitive intension, then a willingness to accept anything that follows from it as belonging to the total strict intension.

mine whether or not other objects belong to the extension of the term. Throughout this whole process, the learner is, so to speak, seeking a meaning that he may attach to the word-type so as to convert it into a term.

Two people engaged in this same process may find two sets of criteria which remarkably well isolate the same extension. But do they understand the word-type in the same way? Perhaps so, but perhaps not. The two sets of criteria may be alternative definitive intensions for one and the same total strict intension. In that case, they do understand the word-type in the same way, even if they are not fully aware of this fact. But the two sets may be related as definitive intension to index. In that case, they do not understand the word-type in the same way.

Such a difference in understanding can frequently lead to heated and futile debates. The debaters are using the same word-type, the term each understands by it has the same extension as does the term that the other understands by it, but the terms are not identical—the word-type does not have the same meaning for the two debaters.

It is, of course, of the greatest importance that we come to a common understanding about the meanings of those sign-types that we employ in communication and in debate with one another. But it is equally important that we reach for ourselves a clear understanding of what we mean, or shall mean, when we employ certain sign-types. Only as we attain such clarity and command over our language can we make of it the effective tool of thought that it has already been suggested (§2.6 and elsewhere) it can become.

Now one of the great devices for clarifying and communicating the meanings of terms, is definitions. When, in reading, we meet words that we do not understand, we look up their definitions in a dictionary. When we use words with meanings that we fear will not be understood by our readers, we accompany these uses with definitions and explanations. And when the scientist or other investigator is undertaking to work out some theory, he will usually settle on some terminology and define the chosen terms, both to aid his memory and guide his future trains of reasoning.

The variety of purposes served by definitions results in the fact that they do not all offer the same kinds of explanations of the meanings they indicate. To take one point, by way of illustration. Dictionary definitions usually (but not always) undertake to give either an index or a definitive intension of the words that they define. Yet there is seldom any clew as to which meaning is being indicated. It is unsafe to assume in any given case that the dictionary has given one of these rather than the other.

The making of good definitions is not an easy task. The variety of purposes served by definitions furthermore complicates the situation. Yet the importance of definition and of a proper understanding of its role and correct use obliges us to devote an entire Part of this book to that topic.

As you turn, then, to Part Four, on *Definition*, try to think of it as, in one sense, a new and important topic, but in another sense merely as the practical and natural completion of that study of meaning which has been occupying our attention throughout Part Three.

*EXERCISE*

The second paragraph of §24.7 ends with these remarks: ". . . the two sets may be related as definitive intension to index. In that case, they do not understand the word-type in the same way."

Explain carefully and in detail the meaning of this passage. For example, how are a definitive intension and an index related to one another? How are they related to the total contingent intension and to the total strict intension? Why does the fact that the two intensions are related as definitive intension to index imply that the two people do not understand the word-type in the same way?

*REVIEW QUESTIONS FOR UNIT 24*

1. How many characteristics are included in the total strict intension of a term?
2. What is meant by a definitive intension of a term?
3. What is meant by calling a definitive intension a "smallest intension"?
4. Explain briefly the relation between a definitive intension and the total strict intension of a term.
5. Is a definitive intension a strict intension?
6. Can one and the same term have more than one definitive intension? Explain.
7. Suppose that *T* is a certain *word-type* and that *A* and *B* are two definitive intensions associated with *T*. Under what circumstances would *A* and *B* be definitive intensions of the same *term*, and under what circumstances would they be definitive intensions of *different* terms indicated by the same word-type? (In connection with this question, review also point 4 in §17.2.)

8. What is meant by an augmented definitive intension?
9. What is meant by an indexical intension?
10. May an index (indexical intension) contain necessary members of the total contingent intension of a term? Briefly explain and discuss.
11. Of what importance are indexical intensions?
12. Discuss briefly the ways in which orders of *discovery* (of various intensions and of the extensions of terms) might differ from the order of *exposition* followed in this textbook.
13. If a term does not have a total strict intension, can it have a definitive intension? Explain.
14. What corresponds to a definitive intension in the case of a term without a total strict intension?
15. Do all terms have indexical intensions whether or not they have total strict intensions?
16. Are indexical intensions, or are definitive intensions (or the correspondent "keys" when there are no definitive intensions) the more important in the case of proper names and incomplete definite descriptions?

# PART FOUR

# THE THEORY OF DEFINITION

UNIT **25**

# The Purposes of Definitions

## §25.1 What a Definition Is

Throughout Part III we have been discussing the theory of terms and the different kinds of meaning—extensional and intensional—that every term has. In Part IV, which begins with this unit, we shall turn our attention to a type of activity and a type of statement intended to explain or clarify the distinctive meaning or meanings of one term. This kind of activity or statement is called *definition*. We shall be concerned to examine the purposes of definition, the main types of definition, and rules governing the construction of good definitions.

According to the *Century Dictionary*, a definition is "the act of stating the signification of a word or phrase, . . ." or "a statement of the signification of a word or phrase. . . ."

Like so many word-types ending in "tion," and other words as well, the word-type "definition" has two meanings (among others) conventionally associated with it: in accordance with the one convention, it refers to acts or activities of human beings; in accordance with the other convention, it refers to certain constituents or products of those acts. Other words with this same kind of twofold meaning are "sensation," "observation," "thought," "inference," and the like.

The first meaning for "definition" quoted above makes it refer to a certain kind of productive sign-event, in fact, to any productive sign-event the purpose of which is to state the signification (meaning) of a word or phrase; the second meaning quoted above makes "definition" refer to the physical sign-type or statement that is presented in that productive sign-event. (On the meaning of "statement" review §§5.2 and 16.2.)

In the first units of this part we shall consider definitions as productive sign-events and shall inquire into the variety of purposes that might be served by them. In the later units, we shall consider definitions as sign-types with associated meanings, that is, as statements, shall classify

271

them according to their major forms, and shall correlate these forms
with the purposes discussed in these earlier units.

### §25.2 Personal and Social Purposes of Definition

In Unit 12 there occurred a discussion of the purposes of
productive discourse. As has just been explained, definition is productive
discourse. In discussing its purposes, we shall make free use of the terms
explained in §§12.2 and 12.3.

By and large, an author's immediate purpose in any case of definition
is cognitive: he wishes to affect or alter someone's beliefs or knowledge
concerning the signification of a word or phrase. He may, however,
have remote pragmatic purposes; for example, to influence people to
use certain words or phrases in a manner different from that which they
have employed in the past. For example, I have often found people
using the words "inference" and "implication" as though they meant
the same thing. When I have wanted to break someone of this careless
habit and to get him to use these words more nearly in accordance
with their conventional meanings, I have often defined them for him.
My assumption has been that he did not know precisely what their
conventional meanings were.[1] My act of defining would impart this
knowledge to him, so the act would be directly cognitive. But insofar as
I was imparting this knowledge in order that he might alter his speech
habits, the act of defining would be remotely pragmatic.

As was said in §12.3, cognitive purposes may be either personal or
social. Both types of purpose are illustrated in the case of definition.
Sometimes the author is concerned to explain the meaning of a word or
phrase to someone else. The example in the preceding paragraph
illustrates that situation. In such a case, the purpose is a *social cognitive*
one, that is, an *informative* one.

But on other occasions a person undertakes to define words or phrases
in order to discover for himself what they mean. A prime example of
this kind of purpose is suggested in §3.6. The topic treated in that unit
was the formulation of questions as the first step in an effort to solve a
problem. It was noticed that we might have used vague or ambiguous
words in formulating our problem, and that we ought therefore to
accompany the question with definitions, explanations, and illustrations.
Writing such sentences is actually a case of definition, a case of making

---

[1] Briefly, a sentence or proposition implies; while a person infers. See §6.5 above,
where inference is discussed as a valid ground of belief.

definite to ourselves what we intended, or had better intend, by the words or phrases in the original question which are explained in these sentences. The cognitive purpose is a *personal* one.

Just as the cognitive purposes of definition are sometimes social and sometimes personal, so too are the pragmatic purposes sometimes social and sometimes personal. Social pragmatic purposes have been illustrated above. A personal pragmatic purpose would be illustrated in the case of a person who defines a word or phrase in order to break *himself* of a certain carelessness in his use of that word and to produce in himself a certain consistency in accordance with which his future uses of it will have always the same meaning, perhaps a less vague one than is customary.

It should be noticed that pragmatic purposes of definition are usually more remote than certain other related cognitive purposes which are subservient to the pragmatic purposes. But these pragmatic purposes are themselves often subservient to still more remote cognitive purposes, either personal or social. Nor must it be forgotten that any single definition, like any deliberate act, will probably be made as a means of serving a large number of different purposes.

In the remaining sections of this unit we shall consider the purposes of definition from a variety of other points of view. In almost every case, we shall be able to find that some examples of the purposes there identified could be social, while other examples could be personal. It is well to keep this plurality, of social versus personal purpose, steadily in mind.

## §25.3 Complete and Incomplete Definitions

Sometimes, when a person undertakes to define a word or phrase, his concern is completely to determine or explain the meaning of that word or phrase. On other occasions he is concerned only partially to determine its meaning. In the former case, his definition is said to be complete; in the latter case, it is said to be **incomplete.**

Let us illustrate. Suppose that a child should ask his father, "Daddy, what's an ostrich?" His father might reply, "An ostrich is a great big bird." The father's statement is an incomplete definition: it indicates the kind of thing that is referred to by the word "ostrich" but it does so only in part. Not *every* big bird, in fact or in fancy, is intended when one uses the word "ostrich." On the other hand, what one does mean by an ostrich is always, among other things, a large bird.

The father's definition, despite its incompleteness, may nevertheless have been entirely adequate to the purposes of his child. The child was not concerned, let us assume, to know what kind of *bird*, but only in general what kind of *thing*, is referred to by the word "ostrich." Nevertheless, the incomplete definition could be misleading if it were mistaken for a complete one. That it did mislead the child might be suggested on a visit to the zoo, where the child, pointing to a large eagle, says, "See the ostrich!"

Perhaps the father takes note of his own responsibility for the child's confusion. What he had said in reply to the child's original query *could* have been misunderstood as intending that any great big bird is an ostrich. He resolves that the next time he will not make that kind of mistake. If he were to be asked again, what is an ostrich, he would reply, "An ostrich is a certain kind of great big bird."

Father's new definition is still an incomplete definition. To make his definition complete, he would have to explain *what* kind of great big bird an ostrich is. But at least the new incomplete definition has this advantage over the original, that it will probably be recognized as incomplete and hence not mislead its receiver by his mistaking it for a complete definition.

Sometimes all we can give are incomplete definitions. For we often know *in general* how people use certain words and phrases without knowing *precisely* how they do so. And often we have decided only in general, but not in detail, how we shall ourselves use a word. Hence, we cannot completely explain what we mean.

But frequently all that we *need* to give is an incomplete definition. The child's concern in the example above was probably such as would be satisfied by an incomplete definition. In fact, if the father were to enter into enough details to make the definition complete, it would threaten to become for the child, with his limited knowledge, too complicated, and thus fail to serve the child's immediate purpose.

There is also another, quite different circumstance in which incomplete definitions are satisfactory. When the purpose of the definer is to remove a possible ambiguity, then an incomplete definition of the word-token may be entirely sufficient. "By a 'cardinal' I mean a bird." Here, anyone acquainted with the different meanings conventionally associated with the word-type "cardinal" will find that the above incomplete definition is entirely sufficient to eliminate the threatened ambiguity.

However, there are many circumstances in which a complete definition will be absolutely necessary if the purposes of producer and receiver are to be adequately served. For example, much idle debate could be avoided if people understood their terms in the same manner. Only complete definitions will ensure a thoroughgoing agreement on the meanings of terms. Again, the soundness or unsoundness of a piece of reasoning frequently hinges on the meanings of terms involved in the reasoning. Here complete definitions provide criteria by which to evaluate the validity of the reasoning.

We shall see later on, however, that even complete definitions give us only a starting point for complete understanding. Beyond them lies the need for their systematic organization in *chains*, or sets, of interrelated definitions.

It must be remembered that the above classification of definitions as complete and incomplete is a definition of *acts* of definition according to their purpose. It is not a classification of definitional *statements* according to the completeness of the information they *do* impart. One of the commonest errors to be met in definitions is that of purposing or proposing a complete definition but of imparting only enough information to satisfy the needs of a partial or incomplete definition. In Units 31 and 32 we shall consider rules for correct complete definition. Several of those rules are aimed at helping us avoid this type of error.

## EXERCISE

Which of the following could be regarded as satisfactory complete definitions and which are satisfactory only if regarded as incomplete definitions? Briefly explain why you answer as you do.

1. A horse is a draft animal.
2. A triangle is a plane figure bounded by three straight lines.
3. A polygon is a type of geometrical figure.
4. A blotter is a sheet of absorbent paper intended for use as a means of rapidly drying ink-script by absorbing the excess moisture.
5. A definition is the act of stating the signification of a word or phrase.
6. A table is an article of furniture.

## §25.4  Real and Nominal Definitions

Sometimes when a person reports the meaning of a word or phrase he is merely reporting a decision that he has reached concerning his own productive use of that word or phrase: "When I say — — —, I mean . . ."

Such a purpose will usually motivate the acts of definition which accompany the formulation of problems, as discussed in Unit 3. There, an author has used in his question a word or phrase that is ambiguous or vague. As he used the word, he intended one thing by it rather than another. His accompanying definition simply records this fact, that he had decided to use such and such a word to mean such and such a thing.

A definition put forward by an author to report what he himself means by a certain word or phrase is called a **nominal definition.**

In §15.3 there is a footnote (note 3) reminding the reader that it is sign-*tokens* that have meanings, even though the meanings that they have may be in part determined by the sign-types to which those tokens belong. With this in mind, we note that when a person makes a nominal definition, he is in fact telling the intended second party that the sign-tokens of such and such a sign-type which are produced by *himself* are intended by himself to mean such and such a thing. However, these decisions to use tokens of such and such a type with such and such a meaning may be long standing or short standing, and the nominal definition may be intended correspondingly to apply to only a few of the author's tokens belonging to that type, or to many of them. "In that question, by 'cardinal' I meant a bird." "Throughout this discussion, by 'tall' I shall mean at least 6 feet tall." "Throughout this entire book, by 'Communist' I shall mean an official member of the Soviet Communist Party." So far as the author's nominal definition is concerned, other tokens produced by him belonging to the same type may have quite different meanings than his nominal definition reports.

Nominal definitions are often vague in that they fail to indicate which of an author's tokens belonging to a certain type are the ones he has decided to use in the manner reported.

To be contrasted with nominal definitions are the efforts frequently made by an author to explain what people other than himself intended by certain word-tokens or phrase-tokens which they employed. Such explanations of words or phrases are called **real definitions.**

Examples of real definitions are those you find recorded in a dictionary. The purpose of a lexicographer is to report what people who use the language in question mean by the various tokens they produce of a certain type. He arranges these alphabetically according to type, and under each type reports usually several meanings: some of the tokens have *this* meaning, some of the tokens have *that* meaning, and so on. If he himself uses tokens of the type in question with one of those meanings, this is only because he conforms to conventions that he has discovered. His purpose is not to report his own decision to use tokens in that manner, but to report the intentions of authors other than himself.

However, real definitions occur outside of dictionaries. If George thinks you misunderstood Jim, he might try to explain what Jim *Ex* meant. This act of explanation would be a real definition.

The accounts of nominal and real definitions that have been given above would seem to leave out of account one type of situation. Occasionally an author's purpose in defining some word or phrase is to explain what both he and others mean by it. For example, the author of a textbook in chemistry might begin a chapter with an explanation of the term "compound." What he intends is probably to explain what chemists generally mean by this word *and* that he himself will be meaning this same thing by it throughout his textbook.

Should such definitions be classed as real (reporting what others mean) or as nominal (reporting what their authors mean)? The obvious answer is that they are both nominal and real: nominal to the extent that they report their author's own decision as to how he will use words, and real to the extent that they report how people other than their author use words. Thus we see that these two broad types of definition, nominal and real, are not mutually exclusive: some definings are nominal and not real, some are real and not nominal, while some are both nominal and real.

On the other hand, every definition is either nominal or real.

## §25.5 Hortatory Definitions     *Pragmatic, formerly cognitive*

There is one other interesting and important purpose served by definition that deserves mention here. We have seen (§14.1) that the meanings of sign-tokens are arbitrary; that, in other words, whatever their authors intend them to mean, that is what they *do* mean. It is this very arbitrariness of language which is illustrated in the fact that some authors use familiar sign-types in unconventional ways, with the result that, if they are to be understood, they must frequently offer nominal definitions of their terms.

Why, however, do authors indulge this possibility, of using familiar sign-types in unconventional ways? It has already been stressed (§14.5) that conformity with conventions is perhaps the greatest single resource available to an author who would make himself understood. Why, then, should an author strike out in new directions?

As we consider this question, we must bear in mind that not every case of nominal definition is a case of deviation from conventional uses of language. I *may* tell you that when I say $X$, I mean such and so, when such and so is in fact a conventional meaning for tokens of the sign-type $X$. Two circumstances may lead me to do this: (1) [Avoidance of ambiguity] The sign-type $X$ has two or more conventions associated with it, and I wish to make sure that the receiver interprets my tokens in accordance with the *intended* one of these conventions. (2) I suspect that the receiver is unacquainted with the convention, and I attempt to make sure that he does not misinterpret my tokens by guessing at their meanings instead of going to the dictionary.

On the other hand, nominal definitions are sometimes required because the author's use of a sign-type is not in accord with conventions. Again, there can be two reasons for this. (1) [Avoidance of vagueness] The sign-type he is employing has no sharply focused convention, that is, it is a vague word or phrase. In order to give precision to his own discourse he imposes on this vague word a precision of meaning which it does not conventionally have. Throughout this discussion, by 'tall' I shall mean at least 6 feet tall. (2) The author has in mind some idea or concept that he wishes to designate, but he does not know of any word or simple phrase which conventionally designates just what he has in mind. Here he has two alternatives available to him: he may invent a new (unfamiliar, previously unused) word-type (for example, "radio", "television") and explain in a nominal definition what he will mean by tokens of this type; *or* he may "borrow" an already familiar word-type (preferably one with a conventional meaning analogous to the meaning he has in mind) and explain that when he uses this word-type he will be meaning this new thing by it. (Example: the chemists borrowed the familiar word "atom" to refer specifically to elementary constituents of molecules.)

In both cases just considered (avoidance of vagueness and representation of previously unrepresented meanings) an author departs from conventions because of a genuine inadequacy in the conventions themselves. His departure is not so much a violation of convention (although it may in part be that) as it is a going-beyond convention.

Whenever one goes beyond or violates conventions, nominal definitions are in order.

We can thus answer the question asked near the beginning of this section, Why do people use sign-types in unconventional ways? These tendencies have either of two reasons: inadequate knowledge or understanding of the conventions on the author's part, or a genuine incompleteness or inadequacy of the conventions to the author's purpose. The first of these two reasons is the reason for that disregard of convention deplored in §15.6. It is to be avoided as a threat to the very existence of all conventions, of all possibilities of intelligent discourse. But the second reason must be recognized as a valid reason. The body of conventions that constitute a language are constantly in need of improvement and extension. Their first extension by some individual author necessitates his offering a nominal definition.

Occasionally, an author's use of a word or phrase in an unconventional manner will have no more than a temporary or intermittent value. For example, if I were reporting the results of a study on the relationship between height and scholastic achievement among college men, I might say, "Throughout this report, I shall use the word 'tall' to mean at least 6 feet tall, and the phrase 'very tall' to mean at least 6 feet 3 inches tall." Here is a nominal definition of "tall" and "very tall" which indicates that in my use of them they have a precision of meaning totally lacking in their conventional meaning. But there is no reason to believe that these precise meanings would be desirable as permanent or widely adopted conventions.

On the other hand, there are occasions on which the conventional meanings of words and phrases are vague (incomplete) or awkward and unsatisfactory in such a manner that one might wish the convention to be genuinely altered. It is not merely that the author would find it temporarily advantageous to use the word in an unconventional way. It is rather that he believes society would benefit by adopting a new convention.

Suppose now that he explains this new meaning for the word. As he favors the adoption of this new meaning, it is one which he will be intending in his own use of that word. Thus his definition is nominal. Since the meaning is not a conventional one, his definition is not real. But his defining act is, so to speak, a *recommendation* that other people adopt also in their speech this new meaning for the word; thus, it

is an effort to restructure the language habits or conventions of his
community.)

We shall call such definitions **hortatory definitions.** A hortatory
definition is, then, a definition that has the force of an exhortation to
the community (the intended second parties) that (even if they must
thereby abandon the current conventional meanings or abandon the
current lack of convention) they adopt in their productive discourse
the indicated meaning for the word or phrase.

### §25.6  Other Examples of Hortatory Definition

The discussion of hortatory definition contained in the
preceding section was carried on in terms of an example of nominal
definition, in which the definer has abandoned in his own use of tokens
the conventional meaning for tokens of that sign-type and is furthermore recommending that the intended second party also abandon
these conventions and adopt instead the practice already in use by the
definer. However, hortatory definitions also occur in other circumstances as well as those illustrated above. Let us see what some of
them are.

1.  Sometimes the definer explains a conventional meaning rather
than an unconventional one. Thus his definition is real rather than
nominal, or both real and nominal. If, however, the purpose of the
definition is to persuade the intended second party to conform to that
convention, whereas he previously had not been a party to it, then the
definition is hortatory. The definer is trying to *extend the range* of
people party to a convention that already exists. An example of this
type of hortatory definition is given near the beginning of §25.2, in
definitions of "inference" and "implication."

2.  It is readily seen that hortatory definitions are essentially instances of the pragmatic discourse: they are efforts to mold the speech
habits of the intended second parties. In both example 1, above, and
in the illustrations of the previous section, the hortatory definitions
under consideration had a *social* pragmatic purpose. But occasionally a
hortatory definition has a *personal* pragmatic purpose. This comes about
when the definer is also his own intended second party. For occasionally
a person writes out a definition as a guide to his own future speech and
writing practices. This is likely to happen either (a) when a person
plans to use a term in a more or less unconventional manner and wishes
to fix in his mind the precise meaning he has chosen, or (b) when his

analysis of the word's meaning has shown it to be extremely complex and he wishes in future uses of the word not to overlook the various elements involved in this meaning. In both cases, these personal hortatory definitions have as their purpose ensuring that the definer uses the defined word-type in a consistent manner in the future; in short that his future tokens of the defined word-type will all be tokens of one and the same term.

## §25.7 Informative Definition

*Practically all definitions are*

Definitions which aim at informing their receivers about the meanings intended by authors that they may read or hear are called **informative definitions**. Both real and nominal definitions may be informative. For example, the dictionary tells you what meanings various authors did intend when they said or wrote such and such words; whereas a nominal definition tells you what meanings the definer did or will intend when he did or will write the defined word.

To sum up the difference between hortatory and informative definitions, the former give advice to *producers*, the latter give advice to *receivers*. Hortatory definitions recommend to their receivers that in the future they *produce* tokens of the defined word-type, only when what they wish to communicate is such and such. Informative definitions recommend to their receivers that in the future they *receive* tokens of the defined word-type as having been intended by their authors to mean such and such. This indirect advice in the informative definition, that you should understand such and such when you receive tokens of the defined type, is a consequence of the claim made by the definition, that the authors of those tokens did in fact mean such and such.[2]

Just as a definition may be both real and nominal, so it may be both informative and hortatory. That is to say, a definer may at one and the same time be endeavoring to tell you what other people have meant by a certain word or phrase, and endeavoring to get you to mean that same thing when you produce that word or phrase. This can be the case

---

[2]  There is a curious type of definition of which we shall take note here, but which does not fit into the more important classifications considered in the text itself. Definitions of this type occur when we undertake to read *new* meanings into *old* documents. For example, some expounders of ancient texts—of, say, the Bible or of Plato—ask us to read these ancient texts *as though* their authors had meant such and such, even when we know that their authors did not mean such and such. The motive for this is that we may appreciate, be inspired by, enjoy, or learn from the truths which we find "signified" by these misinterpretations.

because, as we have seen before, the purposes of discourse are usually as complex and plural as those of any other human actions.[3]

On the other hand, the informative and hortatory purposes of definition can get in the way of one another. This is particularly true in the case of real, informative definition. Consider in this connection the task of a dictionary writer. Samuel Johnson (1709-1784) wrote the first famous dictionary of the English language, but it is well known that many of his definitions indicate what he believes people *ought* to mean by certain words rather than what they did in fact mean. Or again, as late as in the *Century Dictionary*, Charles S. Peirce (1839-1914) defines "university" as meaning what he thinks people ought to mean by it rather than as what most reputable authors were meaning by it. Such definitions are primarily hortatory rather than informative. They may inform one as to what the *definer* means when he uses the word, but they do not inform as to what men generally mean. In fact, occurring as they do in the midst of a large set of generally informative real definitions, they can be seriously misleading, because they will be mistaken for informative definitions and consequently lead their readers to misread passages in which the defined words occur.

Considerations like those above have led present-day lexicographers to concentrate upon the production of purely informative definitions. If any hortatory tinge remains, it is only a subordinate hope that readers, by knowing what other people *have* meant by certain words, will tend in their own productive discourse to use those words with those same meanings and thus to preserve the already existing conventions.

Informative definitions may illustrate both personal informative and social informative purposes of discourse (§12.3). A person may address a definition to himself as intended second party. Here the definition is in the nature of a memorandum, in which the definer reminds his future self of the meaning he has established as belonging to such and

---

[3]  It should be noted that the informative and hortatory purposes of a definition are purposes with distinct topics of concern: *Informative:* I (nominal) and/or certain other authors (real) mean such and such by our tokens of the defined word-type. *Hortatory:* You (the receiver) will mean such and such by your tokens of the defined word-type. (In connection with this variety of topics of concern for the different purposes served by a single case of productive discourse, see §14.6, above.) The difference in topic of concern is important in connection with the truth or falsity of definitions. That question will be discussed in §27.8, below.

such tokens of the defined sign-type. The definition is personal informative.

Finally, unlike the classification into real and nominal, the classification into informative and hortatory does *not* present alternatives each of which may fail. Some definitions are not nominal, others are not real. Similarly, some definitions are not hortatory. But in contrast, all definitions, with two slight exceptions, are informative. That is, all definitions undertake to communicate that the authors of such and such tokens of the defined sign-type did (or will) in fact mean so and so by those tokens.

One of the exceptional cases has already been noted in footnote 2, above. The other occurs in what might be called *tentative* definition. Tentative definition occurs when a person is trying to *ascertain* a meaning, either the meaning of other authors when they used tokens of such and such a type or the meaning that the investigator himself might profitably intend when he will use tokens of that type. Under these circumstances a definition might be produced tentatively, so that it may be scrutinized and tested with respect to its truth or advisability. The definition has much the character of an hypothesis proposed in employing the method of hypothesis and verification (§8.4). Subsequent testing of it may result in its abandonment as false or ill-advised. In any case, its first pronouncement was neither informative nor hortatory.

But without further considering the two exceptional cases, we shall claim that all definitions are informative and that some of these informative definitions are also hortatory.

### §25.8 The Use of Hortatory Definitions[4]

Hortatory definitions can be ill-advised. They can, for example, be put forward when the recommended meaning would be less useful to society as a conventional meaning for the word or phrase in question than the current conventional meaning that the recommender would abolish. There are, nevertheless, a great number of circumstances in which the conventions with respect to meaning could be improved. These circumstances have been the occasion for that genuinely enormous

---

[4] Some hortatory definitions are put forward out of a concern for the solution of purely practical problems (§1.1); for example, to eliminate the unhappy effects on conduct of prejudice or emotion many legal definitions belong to this class. We shall in this section, however, concern ourselves only with those put forward to facilitate the treatment of theoretical problems.

number of hortatory definitions which, in the course of history, have shaped our modern language. While we cannot hope to examine in a short section all the circumstances that have made hortatory definitions desirable and effective, we shall nevertheless notice one or two of the more nearly typical features.

Generally speaking, hortatory definitions reflect an advance in human knowledge. A word or phrase came into use at a time when knowledge of the subject-matter roughly indicated by the word or phrase was less reliable or less extensive than at the time when the hortatory definition is proposed. On other occasions, the proposal of the hortatory definition is less a reflection of past gains in human knowledge (less an effort to persuade language conventions to catch up with science) than it is a prediction that the change in conventions will stimulate or facilitate a rapid future extension of human knowledge. But such predictions are usually justified by already achieved gains in human knowledge, so that the two kinds of circumstance cannot be sharply distinguished.

Another typical characteristic is this, that hortatory definitions do not often recommend large changes in the extensions of the terms they redefine: by and large, the change recommended is one in the strict intensions of the terms.

Let us illustrate both of these characteristics.

In ancient times, broad subdivisions of the animal kingdom were made by reference to habitat: animals that live in the sea, on the land, and in the air. Within each broad subdivision, distinct kinds were identified and distinguished from other kinds. One kind among the marine animals was indicated by the term "fish." With advancing biological knowledge, the physiological characteristics of "fish" and other kinds of animal came to be more exactly known and understood. With this came about an awareness that beneath the general anatomical similarity of such "fish" as porpoises and others like, say, mackerel, and beneath their similarity of habitat (in the sea), there were profound differences in physiology. For example, the porpoise is more like land animals than like other fish in that it must rise to the sea's surface to breathe, through a lung system, rather than being able like other "fish" to absorb, through a gill system, the air that is trapped in the water; also the porpoise gives birth to living young rather than being an egg-laying animal. To make a long story short, these and other biological discoveries eventually led to a redefinition of the word "fish." Different characteristics than habitat and anatomy were attended to and given a prominent part in the new definition, that is, in the new definitive intension. With the first redefinition, these newly considered characteristics were largely physiological or morphological, having to do with relation of life processes to structural elements. In much more recent years, still a different basis of definition has been introduced in biology: having to do with the closeness of "family connection" in the evolutionary pattern. But all these redefinitions have only slightly altered the extensions of such words as "fish." Only a few classes of objects, such as porpoises and whales, have been removed from the extension of the term, and few, if any, classes of objects have been added to its extension.

The new definitions of "fish" are examples of hortatory definitions put forward after significant advances have been made in the science of biology. Their authors *recommend* that we, fellow biologists, concern ourselves with *this* definitive intension rather than *that* one when we employ the word "fish." The effect of the changed intension on the extension is slight, but that slight change is a desirable one. For it gives the resulting extension a vastly increased total contingent intension: many, many properties that were not common to the extension of the older term "fish" are in fact common to the extension of the new term "fish." Thus the new definition is systematizing our knowledge. But further, more of these common properties can be seen to be consequences of the properties in the new definitive intension than were consequences of the old definitive intension. Thus the new definitive intension (the new definition) makes a more systematic division of the total contingent intension into merely contingent properties and properties in the total strict intension. And finally, all this reorganization promises to assist in the more rapid and effective acquisition of still further knowledge in the future, not only in a knowledge of those things that remain in the extension of the term "fish" but also in a knowledge of those things that have been *removed* from its extension to the extension of some other term; for example, of porpoises removed to the extension of the term "mammal."

There is, however, another kind of circumstance in which hortatory definitions are desirable. Many words occurring in everyday discourse, rather than in the technical language of a science or a profession, are words that we users have only "picked up" by hearing and reading. Gradually we acquire some grasp of their appropriateness within a limited range of familiar circumstances. Put in technical language, we learn that certain objects belong to the extensions of these terms. In §§22.1 and 24.5 we have already noticed that the first learning of language, and much of the later learning of nontechnical discourse, proceeds by guessing at strict or definitive intensions to match the given samples from the extension.

Probably very few people make persistent efforts to understand the words of everyday discourse in the manner just described. To a great extent, we all permit a feeling of familiarity with the word and of ease in classifying familiar objects as in or not in its extension to substitute for a full grasp of or guess at the word's meaning. But even if two people *did* undertake to guess at its strict intension, it is unlikely that they would come out with identical answers.

Thus the words of ordinary discourse are not quite full-fledged terms: they often do not have a shared or conventional total strict intension. Instead, the convention as to meaning is likely to extend only a little way beyond some agreement about the classification of familiar things as in or out of the extension. Perhaps most people have, in addition to this shared, or conventional, partial understanding of the extension, many attitudes concerning the intension, for example, that this, that, or the other property belongs to the total strict intension. Some of these opinions may be widely shared, or conventional. But not all of them will be so. Furthermore, the scattered list of strictly intensional properties attended to by a given individual will hardly ever satisfy even him as sufficient to constitute a strict intension, let alone a definitive intension.

The situation just described is worse than lack of *agreement* on the strict intensions of words in ordinary discourse: it amounts to a lack of *decision* on any one's part. Into this sea of indecision—which will make impossible anyone's classifying newly discovered objects as in or out of the extension (let alone *agreement* among many people on such classification)—into this sea of indecision steps someone with a proposal: *let* us understand by this word such and such. Here is a hortatory definition, proposing that we reach an agreement by reaching a shared decision.

The example of hortatory definition just proposed differs from the earlier one in this respect: the earlier one recommended replacing one conventional strict intension for a given word-type by another; this one recommends providing a conventional strict intension where none existed before. Our history of the word "fish" was undoubtedly incomplete in that the word was first a word in common discourse without any conventional intension. The first biologists might have offered hortatory definitions of the sort just now described. It would be only their successors, after the persuasive recommendations of the first ones had succeeded in making the word-type into a conventional term—into a word-type with a shared definitive intension—, who could offer hortatory definitions proposing the replacement of one shared intension by another.

### §25.9 A Brief Forward Look

The reader should be advised that the terms "real definition," "nominal definition," "informative definition," and "hortatory definition" have not always been used with the meanings here assigned them. Nor, indeed, are they always used with these meanings even by present-day authors. To this extent, the definitions of these terms provided in the preceding sections of this unit are themselves examples of nominal, hortatory definition and cannot be relied upon to indicate what these same words, as used by other authors, might have been intended to convey.

In Unit 27 we shall interrupt the systematic study of our subject for a brief historical review, accompanied by a consideration of those difficulties in the historical usage which have led the present author to abandon the conventional definitions of these classifications in favor of those definitions given in the unit just completed. Following that historical review, we shall consider the problem of truth and falsity in definition, a problem on which a great deal has been written.

## REVIEW QUESTIONS FOR UNIT 25

1. Briefly explain and illustrate the difference between definition as an *act* and definition as a *statement*.

2. Briefly explain and illustrate the purposes of definition that could be classified as:

     a.  Social cognitive          c.  Social pragmatic
     b.  Personal cognitive        d.  Personal pragmatic

3. Discuss briefly the ways in which the purposes of definition listed in question 2, above, might be related one to the other as more and less immediate or remote, and as subservient or independent one of the other.

4. Explain the difference between complete and incomplete definition.

5. Under what kinds of circumstances will incomplete definitions be appropriately used?

6. Describe two kinds of precaution that must be taken in connection with making complete or making incomplete definitions:

   a. If the purpose is incomplete definition, that the wording be such as not to mislead the receiver into thinking that the purpose was complete definition.

   b. If the purpose is complete definition, that the explanation not be so incomplete as to be appropriate only for incomplete definition.

7. What is meant by a *nominal* definition?

8. What is meant by a *real* definition?

9. Is every definition either real or nominal?

10. Are any definitions both real and nominal?

11. Explain and illustrate what is meant by a *hortatory* definition.

12. Explain and illustrate what is meant by an *informative* definition.

13. Are all hortatory definitions nominal and not real, real and not nominal, real and nominal, or are some of one kind and some of another? Explain briefly why you answer as you do.

14. Discuss the connection between hortatory definition and the pragmatic use of language. Include in your discussion some consideration of the differences between social pragmatic and personal pragmatic uses of language.

15. May definitions be both hortatory and informative, or must they be exclusively the one or the other?

16. How might the informative and hortatory purposes of definition come into conflict?

17. Describe two circumstances under which hortatory definitions would be ill-advised.

18. Discuss and illustrate some of the circumstances under which hortatory definitions have been desirable and effective bits of discourse.

# The Purposes of Definition, continued

## §26.1 Extensional and Intensional Definitions

Let us continue the consideration of the purposes of definition.

We have said that definitions are efforts to explain the meaning of a word or phrase. In general, the word or phrase being defined is to be regarded as a term and the definition indicates the meaning of that term. (Dictionaries, which list several definitions for a given word-type, are in effect treating the word-type as first one term and then another. According to each definition, the word-type is a distinctive term.)

However, in Units 20, 21, and 23 two distinct types of meaning for any term were distinguished and interrelated:

1. Its extension: an "impure" meaning
2. Its total strict intension: a "pure" meaning[1]

Sometimes the purpose of a definition is to explain, that is, to identify (completely or incompletely) only the extension of a term; on the other hand, sometimes it is to explain (completely or incompletely) the total strict intension of a term. In the former case, the definition is called an **extensional definition**; in the latter case it is called an **intensional definition**.

Suppose, for example, that little Johnnie looked up from a book he was reading and said, "What does this mean, 'The first President of the United States?'" If we answer him by saying, "That means George Washington," we have given Johnnie an extensional definition. But if we answer by saying, "That means the first person to be elected to the Presidency of the United States under its Constitution and to take the oath of office," we have given Johnnie an intensional definition.

[1] More accurately, the set of necessary members of its total contingent intension. But these usually are its total strict intension.

Or to take another example, suppose Johnnie asks, "What does it mean when it says 'patriot?'" If we answer, "Why, that means people like George Washington and Abraham Lincoln and the brave soldiers and sailors who fight for their country," we have given Johnnie an incomplete extensional definition. But if we answer, "Why, that means a person who loves his country and works hard *because* he loves it to make it safe, strong, and a good place in which to live," we have given Johnnie an intensional definition.

In general, an extensional definition is an effort to explain the meaning of a term by indicating the things that belong in the extension of the term *without* indicating those essential characteristics from the total strict intension which guarantee inclusion in the extension. In contrast, an intensional definition indicates those characteristics belonging to the total strict intension of the term whose possession by an object is the logical guarantee of inclusion in the extension of the defined term.

It is a little out of place to say here anything about *methods* of definition; this unit is still concerned with purposes. (The systematic discussion of methods begins in Unit 29.) But the difference between extensional and intensional definition may perhaps become more clear if we note that:

1. To indicate an indexical intension (§24.4) of the term being defined would be appropriate and adequate if the purpose of the definition was extensional. (Other appropriate methods of extensional definition are considered later on.) But to indicate an indexical intension is entirely inappropriate and inadequate if the purpose is intensional definition.

2. To indicate a definitive intension (§24.2) of the term being defined is appropriate if the purpose is intensional definition. It *may* be appropriate—but then again may not be appropriate—if the purpose is extensional definition.

### §26.2 Motives for Intensional and Extensional Definition

Extensional definitions, even complete ones—and they are usually incomplete—report both less and more about the meaning of the defined terms than would intensional definitions. They report less than intensional definitions because two or more terms may have identical extensions but different strict intensions. Therefore, merely to give the extension of a term is not to give sufficient information to permit the receiver to identify the strict intension. For example, the terms *featherless biped* and *man* happen to have the same extensions but quite different strict intensions. Now if I were to give you an extensional definition of a term, X, indicating that it has the same extension as "featherless biped" and "man," it would be impossible for you to determine on the basis of this information whether its total strict intension was the same as that of "featherless biped," or the same as that of "man," or even perhaps quite different from either of these.

On the other hand, once one knows a strict intension of a term, say of the term X, one can proceed to an examination of the world in order to *discover* what objects do in fact belong to its extension. All one needs to find out about objects, by observation or by other means, is whether or not they have the characteristics listed in the strict intension. If they do have them, they are in the extension; if they do not, they are not in the extension. Thus, knowing the strict intension does provide a starting point from which to gain a knowledge of the extension. But, as already shown, knowing the extension does *not* provide a sufficient starting point from which to gain a knowledge of the strict intension. It is in this sense that we say that extensional definitions report less about the meanings of terms than do intensional definitions.

Nevertheless, extensional definitions provide information that cannot be gained from intensional definitions except as the knowledge communicated in intensional definitions is brought to bear on further inquiries. As we suggested above, one must observe objects in the world to discover whether or not they have the intensional characteristics that will make them be in the extension of the term. However, extensional definitions directly report that such and such objects are in the extension and hence save the necessity for making these additional observational inquiries. It is in this sense that extensional definitions report more than intensional ones.

Despite the fact that extensional definitions report both less and more than intensional definitions, the extensional definitions are on the whole weaker than intensional definitions. Why then are they ever used? Four kinds of reason for their use may be mentioned:

1. The first of these has to do with the needs and purposes of the receiver. Objects in the extension of the term are often immediately known to the receiver, whereas he may find it more difficult to grasp,

attend to, or understand the abstract qualities that make up its total strict intension. Furthermore, the immediate interest of the receiver may be simply one in the identification of the term's field of application, that is, in its extension. If the first of these circumstances is the case, then an extensional definition is preferable because the receiver will understand it, whereas he might very probably not understand an intensional definition. And if the second of these circumstances is the case, then an extensional definition could still be preferable because it saves the receiver the necessity of making further studies to discover the extension.

2. Second, there remains to be considered the side of the producer. Quite apart from his interested concern for the receiver and the way in which the interests and capacities of the receiver as discussed above may consequently influence the decisions of the producer, there are other considerations that could compel him to utilize an extensional definition. When a producer's defining activity is real definition, it will often be the case that he does not know what these other people *had in mind* as the strict intensions of the terms they used. He may frequently know what are at least many of the things to which the terms refer, but still be in doubt as to *why* the terms refer to these things. This is particularly the case with words and terms that we "pick up" or become familiar with through the ordinary exchanges of everyday conversation and reading.

3. Furthermore, it must be noticed that the terms and words of everyday language are likely to be used by many people with a greater degree of agreement concerning their extensions than exists concerning their strict intensions. The reason for this lies in the fact that these people also "picked up" the word simply through meeting it in use or through receiving extensional definitions of it, and subsequently each person attached to it personally a strict intension which was private to himself. Here, there is no shared strict intension to be reported, so that if the definition is to be a real definition, it must be extensional.

4. Finally, a fourth circumstance may be noted. It is actually a special case of point 3, above, but it is so important that it deserves special mention. It will be argued later on (Unit 30) that those singular terms which are proper names, as opposed to those which are complete definite descriptions, almost never have a total strict intension. Hence for these terms intensional definitions are impossible.

## §26.3 A Historical Comment*

The phrase "extensional definition" will strike some students of logic as almost, if not actually, a contradiction in terms. According to many logicians, all definitions state the (strict) *intensions* of the terms they define. A consequence of that view is that all definitions are statements whose truth or falsity is ascertainable by appeal exclusively to analysis and inference, without ever a need for appeal to observation.

This widely held view has some extraordinary consequences. These come about partly through the fact that holders of the view identify given statements as definitions (that is, as in the extension of the term "definition") not by a scrupulous attention to what this statement about definitions should enjoin, but by thinking about whether or not the authors of those statements called them *definitions*. Then, having acknowledged that a certain statement is a definition, they are compelled to call it *analytic*. A particularly serious case of this difficulty is involved in the treatment of proper names, to be discussed in Unit 30, below.

There are two ways out of the difficulty: (1) Recognize that some (many) definitions are extensional. This is the solution adopted in the present text. Or (2) abandon considering many statements ordinarily listed as definitions as statements falling under the extension of the technical term "definition." This latter solution would, if conscientiously employed, make the extensions of the commonsense term "definition" and the technical term "definition" be so different that the use of the sign-type "definition" for the technical term would seem to have been ill-advised.

## §26.4 Theoretical Definitions

A certain combination of the purposes of definition already discussed is so important as to deserve special consideration. Definitions projected in the interest of this combination of circumstances may be called **theoretical definitions.**[2]

Theoretical definition can occur only when the word-type being defined is already in use by people other than the definer. What the definer undertakes to do is to direct attention to characteristics of things in the extension of the term being defined that are of greater importance in the organization of theory and of our understanding of the world than are the characteristics belonging to the conventional intension of

---

* This section may be omitted without disturbing the continuity of the text.
[2] The name of this type of definition is derived from Irving M. Copi, *Introduction to Logic*, New York: 1953, p. 99. But the account given is somewhat different from Copi's account.

the term. In other circumstances, what the definer attempts to do is to isolate in his definition characteristics of great theoretical importance when the word-type being defined has a widely shared conventional extension but no widely shared conventional strict intension. Many words of ordinary discourse are words of this sort and offer opportunities for theoretical definition.

Thus the theoretical definition is a real, extensional definition. (Sometimes its acceptance involves a slight or minor adjustment in the extension of the term being defined, but practically speaking the definition is a real extensional definition.) Yet at the same time, the definition is also nominal. As nominal, it may be intensional rather than extensional, but this need not be the case. And finally, the definition is hortatory. Again, it may be hortatory intensional but need not be.

Examples of theoretical definitions are the present author's definitions of real and nominal definition (in §25.4) and of theoretical definition (in the present section.)

People's language habits do not remain fixed. If the hortatory purpose of a theoretical definition has its intended effect, after a certain lapse of time people will be attending to the characteristics cited in that definition when they use the defined word. If then, at that later time, the same definition was to be repeated, but repeated as an explanation of the meanings of these *later* tokens, the repetition could well be a real *intensional* definition.

### §26.5 Linguistic and Conceptual Definitions

Sometimes a person defines some word or phrase primarily in order to convey information about the language of which the word is a part. The clearest examples of definitions with this kind of purpose are those in a foreign-language dictionary. For example, a French-English dictionary might contain the entry:

*Cheval:* horse

The author of the dictionary presumes that the reader very well knows what a horse is and that he surely is not looking up *cheval* in order to find out about the nature of a horse. The definition offered by the author of the dictionary only purposes to inform its English-speaking reader that *cheval* is the word French people use in order to indicate a horse, or its French-speaking reader that "horse" is the word that Englishmen and Americans use in order to indicate *un cheval*. The definition does not belong to the science of biology but is instead a minor item in the science of linguistics.

If the purpose of a definer is merely to explain that a certain word or phrase is used to indicate a thing presumably already familiar to the intended second party, then his definition (act of defining) is said to be **linguistic**.[3]

On the other hand, it is often the case that, when a person defines a word or phrase, his major concern is to direct the attention of his hearer or reader *beyond* merely linguistic matters to some fuller or more adequate understanding of the things indicated by the word which is being defined. There can be all sorts of reasons for this concern. For example, when the author of the geometry book defines a *triangle* as a plane figure bounded by three straight sides, he is directing the attention of his reader to characteristics which belong to the total strict intension of the term "triangle" and to which one may refer in proofs that triangles have certain other characteristics. For a different example, when the author of the dictionary defines a *lyre-bird* as an Australian passerine bird of the family Menuridae and genus Menura, he is ranging beyond any list of characteristics belonging to the strict intension of the term. For one thing, that the habitat of the bird is in Australia is not a part of the strict intension. Nevertheless, he is providing useful information about these birds of a kind that a reader of the dictionary might be glad to have.

Both illustrative definitions mentioned above, that of a triangle and that of a lyre-bird, suggest their author's concern to tell us something more than that a certain word is used in a certain way. To be sure, the definitions *do* tell us something about the use of the words they define. But they *also* tell us much about the things or objects indicated by those words.

When the purpose of a definer is at least in part to convey information

---

[3] The definition of "linguistic definition" given in the text is perhaps slightly inaccurate in one respect, yet the effort to eliminate that inaccuracy would complicate the account to too great an extent to be justified in an introductory text.

The inaccuracy occurs in connection with the phrase "presumably already familiar to the intended second party." This presumption is not necessary in order that a definition be linguistic. In its stead, the definer might be unconcerned as to whether or not the receiver is already familiar with the thing indicated by the defined term, but equally unconcerned to provide information about it: *if* the receiver is unfamiliar, then let him look elsewhere for that kind of knowledge.

about the objects indicated by the defined word or phrase, the act of defining is said to be **conceptual.**

As in the case of real and nominal, so here every defining is either linguistic or conceptual. But in contrast with the case of real and nominal, the present classifications are mutually exclusive: no definition is both linguistic and conceptual. This latter fact is not due to any inconsistency between efforts to explain word-usages and to explain simultaneously certain concepts, ideas, or things. Authors frequently try to do both and they very often succeed. The illustrative definition of "lyre-bird" mentioned above illustrates this point. The mutually exclusive character of the two classes of definitions is due instead to the presence of the word "merely" in the definition of "linguistic" and to the presence of the phrase "at least in part" in the definition of "conceptual."

If a definition is linguistic, then it might very properly proceed by the giving of a simple synonym:

Ponderous: heavy

Definition by simple synonym assumes that the reader already has in mind the concept intended by the defined word. But if this cannot be assumed, then a linguistic definition is inappropriate and a conceptual definition should be provided.[4] And furthermore, whenever a conceptual definition is being made, the use of a simple synonym is improper. Simple synonyms will not direct the reader to the intensions of the term defined.

Sometimes, even when the purpose is linguistic, definition by a simple synonym cannot properly occur. This happens when there is no simple synonym for the word being defined, or at least none that the reader can be expected already to understand. In these circumstances, more elaborate, complex phrases must be employed. But since such definitions do give more than merely linguistic information, we can properly class them as conceptual, even though their authors had only, or primarily, linguistic purposes in mind.

It should be kept in mind that both linguistic and conceptual definitions may be either nominal or real (or both). Also, they may be extensional or intensional, complete or incomplete, hortatory or merely informative.

---

4    Except in highly specialized circumstances, such as those prompting an author to write a French-English dictionary. Cf. footnote 3, above.

## EXERCISE

Suppose that a person includes in his examination of some subject one or more definitions for the sake of avoiding ambiguity or vagueness. Will these definitions be linguistic, or conceptual? Or will their classification as the one or the other depend on still other considerations than those mentioned at the beginning of this exercise (that is, than the avoidance of ambiguity or vagueness)? Explain, and if possible illustrate, the points you make.

## REVIEW QUESTIONS FOR UNIT 26

1. What is an extensional definition? An intensional definition?
2. Is stating an indexical intension appropriate if the purpose of the definer is extensional definition? If his purpose is intensional definition?
3. Is stating a definitive intension appropriate if the definer's purpose is extensional definition? If his purpose is intensional definition?
4. In what sense does an extensional definition report *less* than an intensional definition? In what sense does it report *more* than an intensional definition?
5. Indicate two characteristics of the receiver such that if either of these were known by the definer, he would be inclined to provide an extensional definition rather than an intensional definition.
6. What limitation of the definer's knowledge would force him to provide a real extensional definition rather than a real intensional definition?
7. Why is the real definition of everyday words and phrases likely to be extensional rather than intensional?
8. Why is the definition of proper names to be regarded as extensional rather than intensional?
9. What is a theoretical definition? What is the importance of theoretical definitions?
10. What is a linguistic definition? Illustrate.
11. What is a conceptual definition? Illustrate.
12. For what kinds of definition (linguistic or conceptual) are definitions by means of simple synonyms appropriate? For what, inappropriate?
13. When a definition provides a more elaborate account than would be given in a simple synonym, should the definition be classified as linguistic, or as conceptual, or in some cases as the one and in other cases as the other? Explain.

UNIT 27

# A Brief Historical Survey;
# Truth and Falsity in Definitions*

## §27.1 The Content of This Unit

Of the six words introduced in Unit 25 to name various types of definition, two have been long in use as naming kinds of definition, while two others are first introduced for this purpose by the author of the present text. The two words long in use—"nominal" and "real"—have, however, been used to indicate a great variety of things and are used even today in a considerable variety of ways. A brief historical review will perhaps be not amiss. It will both suggest to the reader what some other authors whom he reads might have meant, and provide a review of the confusions which have led the present author not only to abandon old definitions of these terms but also to introduce the two new terms.

The unit will conclude with a discussion of truth and falsity as characteristics of definitions.

Let us begin by noting that the words "nominal" and "real" have usually been used in the past in connection with the word "definition" when the word "definition" intended a statement rather than an act, a sentence said or written in order to define rather than the act of saying or writing such a sentence. (Cf. §25.1) The words were used, then, to indicate the different meanings that such sentences might have.

We have, however, already seen that the meanings which sentences or other sign-tokens have is a consequence of what their authors intended by them; that, in other words, the meanings of tokens are products of the purposes of their authors. For this and other reasons, it has seemed best to refer these distinctions back to the basic purposes of the productive sign-events that determine the meanings of the tokens produced in those events.

## §27.2 Original Meanings of "Real" and "Nominal"

In ancient and medieval times the word "definition" was often used in such a way as to make it possible to speak of defining a *thing* or an

---

* Readers who wish to do so may omit this unit without disturbing the continuity of the text.

*idea*, rather than a *word* or *term*. In all probability, such was the original intension of the word "to define." That usage is still met on occasion even in the present day.

According to this older, original usage, when one is defining he is actively inquiring into, or reporting the results of an inquiry into, the nature of some thing or object; not inquiring or reporting on the meaning of a word. The word which names that object was merely a transparent indicator of the object under consideration. Thus, for example, if one were to speak of defining New York City, he might be speaking of an effort to discover the boundaries (*finis*, as in "define," is the Latin for "end" or "limit") of a certain physical-political *object*, a real *thing*, as opposed to an effort to identify the meaning of a *word*, "New York City." Or again, the definition of a horse (as opposed to the definition of the *word* "horse,") was thought of as an effort to discover or report the essential characteristics of certain *things* or *objects*, not the meaning of a certain *word*.

People who held that certain definitions were concerned (in the manner just suggested) with real things and that others were concerned with words sometimes called definitions of the first sort "real" and definitions of the latter sort "nominal." Under this usage, the phrase "nominal definition" covered both what we have called *nominal* and what we have called *real* definition.

## §27.3  *The Port-Royal Logic*

In the seventeenth century there appeared what is now a famous book on logic entitled *The Port-Royal Logic* (*La Logigue du Port-Royal*). In this book, the author lays great stress on the arbitrariness of language and suggests that science will be greatly advanced if people would not be bound to conformity to the conventional meanings of words, which are often confused, but would instead settle upon a clear and simple meaning which they will intend when they produce tokens of that word-type. These meanings should be carefully and accurately reported. He then proposes to call these reports *nominal definitions*.[1] Thus *The Port-Royal Logic* came very close to defining nominal definition in the manner adopted in the present text. In adopting this proposition, *The Port-Royal Logic* specifically rejected the practice common at that time, of calling reports of the conventional meanings of words *nominal definitions*.[2]

At the same time, however, *The Port-Royal Logic* preserved the old meaning of "real definition" explained in §27.2 above.[3] Thus, that logic recognized three types of definition: nominal definition, conventional definition, and real definition.

[1]  *Port-Royal Logic*, Part I, Chap. 12.
[2]  *Ibid.*, Part I, Chap. 14.
[3]  *Ibid.*, Part I, Chap. 12.

### §27.4 Subsequent Developments

As time went on many philosophers became sceptical of the possibility of any such intellectual activity as was supposedly indicated by the term "real definition." For example, the *thing* New York City is not sharply cut off from its surroundings. Nor can any properties or characteristics of, say, horses be more essentially theirs than any other of their properties. What happens is that men mark off and attend to one segment of the world, New York City, and name this; or attend to one set of characteristics rather than to others, and then name objects with those characteristics "horses."[4] Thus arose the notion that all legitimate definition is an explanation of the meanings of words rather than of the natures or essences of things.

Persons holding to the view just described thus found the traditional phrase "real definition" not naming any process which they regarded as valid. From here it required only a step to borrow the phrase as one naming those definitions of words or phrases in which the definer records what defined words "really," or conventionally, mean. This marks the position represented in the present text.

### §27.5 Real Definition as Analysis of Concepts

The historical transition briefly cited in §27.4 above has not been universal or entirely consistent. It has already been remarked in §27.2 that the original usage of the expression "real definition" is still encountered on occasion. But there is still another theory that has developed and with which this term is sometimes associated.

Even if individual things do not have essences, in the sense that some of their properties are essential and some are accidental, nevertheless our consideration of, or thought about, these things is invariably in terms of their subsumption under kinds or types. We select the kinds or types under which we subsume and think about these things by attending to certain characteristics and disregarding the presence or absence of certain others. Thus, the kind or type is to be identified *conceptually*, and a question might be raised concerning the nature of the concept we are employing as the means or medium of our thought about those individual things.

A real definition may be thought of as the explication of the definer's concept. The word by which this concept is named is not the thing being explained. On the contrary, this word is only the transparent mark directing attention to the concept. The definition will be true or false according as the definition does or does not accurately identify the actual components the definer does in fact "have in mind" when he entertains that concept.[5]

4 In this connection, note again the discussion beginning, "To sum up:" on p. 246.
5 C. I. Lewis prefers to call this kind of definition "explicative definition," thus avoiding the confusions that by this date in the history of logic surround the phrase "real definition." See his *Analysis of Knowledge and Valuation*, Lasalle: 1946, pp. 98ff.

The kind of definition just described represents a legitimate kind of definition, but one we have chosen to designate as conceptual definition (§26.5).

Another facet of the same issue, often confused with the distinction between conceptual and linguistic definition, is the distinction between intensional and extensional definition, (§26.1). Intensional definitions cite necessary characteristics (in older terminology, the *essence*, in our terminology, the *definitive intension*), while extensional definitions cite merely contingent characteristics (in older terminology *inessential* characteristics, in our terminology, an *indexical intension*). If real definition explicates the concept, then, so it was maintained, it must give the essence and not state inessential characteristics.

Thus "real definition" came to represent more or less confusedly what we would call *real, intensional, conceptual definition*. At the same time "nominal definition" came to represent, also more or less confusedly, what we would call *nominal, extensional, linguistic definition*. In this way, the opposites—"real" and "nominal"—came to be not genuine contradictories, but contraries; yet there were no technical terms to designate, nor was there much if any thought given to, six *other* kinds of definition that we can label "real, intensional, linguistic"; "real, extensional, conceptual"; "real, extensional, linguistic"; "nominal, intensional, linguistic"; "nominal, intensional, conceptual"; and "nominal, extensional, conceptual".

But this is not all! In addition to confusing the three bases of classification already mentioned, still another ground for distinction came to be associated with the words "real" and "nominal." Let us see what that was.

### §27.6 Nominal Definition as Stipulation

On many occasions in preceding units of this book we have called attention to the arbitrariness of language, to the fact that an author's words mean whatever he chooses. In this sense, an author can never be in error about what his words mean. The meanings of his tokens are the product of his will.

Logicians who have been mindful of this fact have tended toward the view that nominal definitions—in which an author indicates what his own tokens of the defined sign-type will mean—can therefore not be criticized as either true or false: if the indicated meaning is what the author did intend by his tokens, that is what those tokens do in fact mean. Thus, a sort of double guarantee of the arbitrariness of language is set up: not only do the tokens produced by an author mean what he chooses or wills that they mean, so that one cannot challenge as incorrect his using a certain word with a certain meaning, but also the definition in which he indicates this meaning cannot be challenged as true or false.

To ensure this security of nominal definitions against any possibility of challenge as true or false, it is usual nowadays to speak of nominal definitions as "stipulations,"[6] or as "expressions of volition," rather than as reports or claims.[7] On the other hand, real definitions are said to be reports or claims that such and such tokens (usually produced by other people than the definer) do in fact mean (that is, were in fact intended by their producers to mean) such and such.

The very language in which nominal definitions are sometimes phrased lends credibility to this view of them as stipulations rather than reports. For example, "By X, let us understand Y," is a natural form of speech in the case of nominal definitions, as opposed to the form, "By X is meant Y," in the case of real definitions. It seems altogether inappropriate to call an appeal or a proposal ("Let us do such and so,") or a request either true or false. These are expressions of volition, or contracts, and while there may be a breach of contract or a change of will, the words drawing up the contract or those expressing the will are not usually considered to be true or false. Only such statements as might appropriately express beliefs (that is, report claims) are commonly regarded as true or false.

The view just described—that nominal definitions are stipulations and therefore neither true nor false, while real definitions are on the contrary reports and therefore either true or false—is by far the most widely held view at the present day. Yet the actual cases of definition which are classed as nominal or real do not seem genuinely to possess the characteristics here said to distinguish nominal from real definition.

In the remaining sections of this unit, we shall point out some of the difficulties to be encountered in the popular view just described and explain why we have abandoned it for a different view.

## §27.7 Classification by Concern and Classification by Topic of Concern

It is important to notice that the view just described—namely, that nominal definitions are stipulations and therefore neither true nor false—has shifted the basis of classification away from the topic of the definer's concern to the nature of his concern with that topic. Thus, whereas in §25.4

---

[6] A stipulation is a definite settlement of some matter by specific mention and agreement, a sort of verbal contract or bargain. For example, in a murder trial the defending and prosecuting attorneys might stipulate that the defendant shot the victim with this gun. This stipulation having been made, the prosecuting attorney need not use any part of his time trying to prove this fact, for the defending attorney has agreed that he will accept it as true and will not base his defense on an effort to disprove it.

Logicians who speak of nominal definitions as stipulations seem thus to be thinking of a nominal definition as a sort of contract or promise, rather than as a statement of fact.

[7] See, for examples, Irving M. Copi, *Introduction to Logic*, New York: 1953, pp. 94, 95; or A. N. Whitehead and Bertrand Russell, *Principia Mathematica*, Cambridge, England: 1910, Vol. I, p. 11.

we made the distinction between real and nominal definitions rest on distinctions between their *topics* of concern (that someone *else's*, or the *definer's*, tokens meant such and such), and whereas among logicians prior to the twentieth century it also rested on distinctions between their topics of concern, now among many writers in the twentieth century it is made to rest on distinctions between the concerns with those topics: the real definition reports the truth of its topic of concern, while the nominal definition expresses the will to make its topic of concern true.

Now there is nothing wrong about classifying discourse in accordance with variations in the author's concerns. For example, the major classifications listed in Unit 12—cognitive, pragmatic, and esthetic—are classifications of concerns rather than of topics of concern. Also our own classification of definitions as hortatory and informative (§§25.5 and 25.7) are classifications based on differences in the concern rather than the topic of concern.

But at the same time it must be remembered that the purposes of discourse, like those of all actions, are seldom simple. In Unit 12 we have already noticed how a whole set of interrelated and independent purposes might be associated with a single productive sign-event.

This plurality of purposes is particularly noticeable in connection with concerns, there being expressed in one productive event many different concerns with a single topic of concern. For example, suppose someone says, "The post office closes at five-thirty." A single topic of concern indicated in this speech is easily identified; namely, the post office's closing at five-thirty. But associated with this one topic are expressed at least two concerns; (1) the speaker's acceptance of this topic of concern as a true proposition; (2) his wish that the intended second party accept the topic as true.

Such a multiplicity of concerns is even more apparent in the case of nominal definitions. Suppose, for example, that an author begins some article on changes of human stature with the statement, "Throughout this study, let us use the term 'tall' to mean at least 6 feet tall." The topic of concern is easy to identify, that all tokens of the sign-type "tall" produced by the author in the article he is writing will mean, *at least 6 feet tall*. But what concerns with this topic does his definition express? We could probably list the following: (1) His present volition or determination to make the topic true (that is, his decision so to use the word in the future writing of the article). (2) His confident expectation (or prediction) that when the article is finished, he will so have used the word "tall." (3) His desire that the reader so interpret the word "tall" when he reads the article. (4) His desire that the reader so *use* the word "tall" when he (the reader) produces tokens of it in comment on the article or discussion of the subject it treats.

The fourth concern listed above has a slightly different topic of concern than the preceding three. *Its* topic of concern is the meaning of tokens to be produced by the *reader*. This fourth concern and topic of concern, that is, this fourth purpose, may or may not have been in the author's mind when he wrote his definition. If it was in his mind, then his definition was hortatory as well as informative. But if it was not in his mind, then his definition was not hortatory and was merely informative.

Yet the first three concerns above would suffice, I believe, to lead most logicians to list the definition as nominal. However, of these three concerns, only the first can be said to identify a pragmatic use of language. And this pragmatic use of language is a *personal* pragmatic rather than a *social* pragmatic use. (See §12.3.) The second concern is cognitive, and so also is even the third: To get a person to believe something is listed in §12.3 as an informative, that is, social cognitive, use of language, rather than a pragmatic use of language.

Thus, the so-called stipulative definitions of modern logicians would seem to be proposals for an agreement between definer and reader that the definer will mean such and so by his tokens and the reader will understand such and so when he reads the definer's tokens. If all informative elements (personal and social) and hortatory elements (concerned with the reader's future production of tokens) were removed, and only the definer's expression of a volition so to use the defined word were to remain, few definitions could be listed as nominal.

### §27.8 Truth and Falsity in Relation to Definitions

It is often said that although *real* definitions are true or false (as the case may be), *nominal* definitions are neither true nor false, but only wise or unwise. Let us see what is the truth about this matter.

As we analyze a definer's purpose into concerns and topics of concern a little care is necessary. Insofar as his definition is *informative* (§25.7), it may be said to have *one* topic of concern: that such and such tokens produced or to be produced by the definer (nominal) or by others (real) have such and such a meaning. But insofar as his definition is *hortatory* (§25.5), it may well have another topic of concern: that such and such tokens to be produced by the *receiver* of the definition have such and such a meaning.[8] The concerns with the topic of an informative definition may be the will to make its topic true (nominal definition), a belief in its truth (both nominal and real definition), and a concern that the receiver accept it as true (both nominal and real definition). The concern expressed in hortatory definition is a pragmatic concern that the receiver so act in future productive discourse as to make true the distinctive topic of concern of the definition as hortatory. We must

---

[8] Informative definitions may predict a receiver's future meanings; hortatory definitions try to *shape* those meanings.

remember that all definitions are informative and that some definitions are in addition hortatory.

Let us momentarily leave the hortatory element present in some definitions and concentrate on the informative element present in all definitions. As informative, the definition has one single topic of concern. This topic of concern is a proposition to the effect that such and such tokens have such and such a meaning. Respecting this topic, the definer may have several concerns, as previously explained. But this proposition which is the topic of concern is, like all propositions, either true or false. Insofar as the topic of concern is the meanings of tokens yet to be produced, the truth or falsity of the topic will be determined only by future events. The topic is nevertheless either true or false, as the case may be.

On the other hand, the definer's concern, or concerns, with his topic of concern, being what they are, are all of them facts, hence *true* propositions. (To be sure, we may not always *know* what those concerns are; in fact, we can seriously misinterpret an author's concern, just as he may inadequately express it.)

Still one other point should be noted: the language practices constituting the topic of concern may be wise or unwise practices. For example, if they are unconventional, they may lead to misunderstanding and confusion; on the other hand, even if they are conventional, they may be unwise insofar as the conventions are inadequate or otherwise unsatisfactory.

Hence, any definition offers an opportunity for two points of inquiry and three points of criticism. (Needless to say, the definer himself may, and often should, engage in self-criticism along these same lines in an effort to find the most appropriate form for his definition.)

I.   Points of inquiry:

1.   What is the definer's topic of concern? That is, what tokens of what sign-type are being affirmed to have what meaning?

2.   What is the definer's concern with this topic? Is he merely expressing his own belief in the truth of the topic of concern, trying to get me to believe it, expressing his resolve to make it true, or trying to make me resolve to make it true?

II.   Points of criticism:

1.   Is the definer's topic of concern a true, or a false, proposition?

2.   Is the definer's concern with this topic a wise or an unwise concern?

3.   Are (or would) the language habits indicated in the topic of concern (be) wise or unwise habits?

Suppose now that we are examining some *real, informative* definition. And suppose that examination has cleared up the two points of inquiry. What about the points of criticism? By and large, if the topic of concern is true, the definer's concern with it is wise; if the topic of concern is false, the definer's concern with it is unwise. That is, he does well to believe and to try to make me believe what is true, and he acts unwisely when he believes or tries to make me believe what is false. Furthermore, since in a real definition the definer and the people whose tokens are being defined are distinct, any criticism on the third point, of *them* for meaning such and such by their tokens, is no criticism of the definer. Hence, the major criticism of a real informative definition will be one concerning the truth or falsity of its topic of concern.

But now consider a *nominal* informative definition. In it, the topic of concern is the meaning the definer did intend by certain tokens in the past, or the meaning he will intend by certain tokens in the future. Here the question of truth or falsity in the topic of concern is a relatively minor point. Presumably the author is in a better position than we are to know what he did or will mean by certain tokens, so that by and large we may take his topic of concern to be true (except in such cases as are discussed below).[9] Nor can we seriously criticize his concern with this topic insofar as it is to report what he did or will mean by such and such tokens.

On the other hand, when we come to the third topic of criticism—the wisdom of the language habit indicated in the topic of concern—we are criticizing the definer, if not his definition: he would do (or would have done) better *not* to use tokens in the manner indicated. Insofar as he is indicating his past practice, our criticism is one of his past behavior and not one of his present definition. Insofar as he is indicating his future intentions, he is expressing a present resolve, and our criticism is one both of those future intentions and that present resolve.

If our criticism is negative and we persuade the definer, it may well be that the effect of our criticism is so to change his resolves that he abandons them and hence makes the topic of his concern a false proposition.

To sum up, in the case of real informative definitions the question concerning the truth or falsity of the definer's topic of concern is a first point of criticism. It would, furthermore, be a criticism of his definition and any further criticism of *him* would be a consequence of what we found concerning the truth or falsity of his topic of concern. On the other hand, in the case of nominal informative definition, whether the topic of concern is true or is false largely depends on our judgment concerning the wisdom of the language habits that it indicates: If we find those habits unwise, we may strive to make the topic of concern false; if we find them wise, we may strive to make the topic of concern true. In every case, our judgment of the wisdom of these

---

[9]  But not always so. Often, in criticizing a piece of discourse, e.g., an article or book, we find internal evidence which shows that the author did not use tokens with the meanings he assigned to them in his definitions.

language habits is a criticism of the definer: of his past habits if he is reporting the meaning of his past tokens, of his present concern if he is reporting his future intentions. Hence, the question of truth or falsity is likely to be a minor, secondary matter in a nominal definition, even though its topic of concern is genuinely true or false.

Let us turn now to hortatory definitions. Here the same points of inquiry and points of criticism may be considered. The topic of concern will be that such tokens to be produced by the receivers of the definition have such and such a meaning. The definer's concern is to bring about the truth of this topic of concern.

Suppose now that we have established the points of inquiry and turn to the points of criticism. Here, as in the case of nominal informative definition, any question about the truth or falsity of the topic of concern is not the place to start. First consider whether the language habit constituting the topic of concern would be wise or unwise. Should we deem it wise, we can approve the definer for encouraging us to adopt it, and by adopting it, we can make the topic of concern true. But should we deem the language habit unwise, we can disapprove the definer's effort to make us adopt it, and by refusing to follow his advice we can make the topic of concern false.

Remembering finally that all definitions are informative, we must notice that hortatory definitions have in effect two topics of concern: their informative topic of concern and their hortatory topic of concern. (See §25.7, footnote 3, above.) These differ only as to which tokens of the defined sign-type are under consideration as having such and such a meaning. But these two topics of concern may be one true and the other false (although in many cases they would be both true, or both false). When the two topics of concern are the one true and the other false, what do we say of the definition: is it true or is it false?

In §14.6 we noted that not every purpose motivating an author is signified by his tokens. In particular, the tokens generally signify only the immediate, subservient purposes which the author would accomplish by his productive sign-event. Now it is usually the case in hortatory definition that the informative purpose is more immediate than the hortatory. This imparting of information concerning the way in which the author and other people use, or resolve to use, certain words is counted on as a device which will influence the receiver to adopt the same practice. Hence, while the meaning which the receiver will give to his tokens of the defined word-type is the topic of concern of one of the purposes served by hortatory definition, it will generally not be the topic of concern indicated by the tokens produced in the act of definition. Instead, those tokens will generally indicate that *other* topic of concern—the informative purpose.

The conclusion that we draw from the above is this. Sentence-tokens produced in an act of definition are to be considered true or false according as the topic of concern of the informative purpose of the definition is true or is false. That the topic of concern of the hortatory purpose of the definition might have an opposite quality of truth or of falsity should not persuade us to alter the evaluation—as true or as false—which we assign to the definition itself.

Since every definition has an informative purpose, every definition may be adjudged to be either true or false.

## REVIEW QUESTIONS FOR UNIT 27

1. What was the *original* meaning of the terms "real definition" and "nominal definition"?
2. Briefly describe the popular view in terms of which real definitions *report* meanings while nominal definitions express resolves or stipulate meanings.
3. Briefly explain two reasons why the present author rejects the popular distinction between real and nominal definitions referred to in question 2.
4. Outline two points of inquiry and three points of criticism appropriate to any definition.
5. How does the criticism of real definitions differ from that of nominal definitions on the points outlined in answer to question 4?
6. How does your answer to question 5 show that questions of truth and falsity are major points of criticism for real definitions but relatively minor points of criticism for nominal definitions?

UNIT **28**

# *Review and Preview*

## §28.1 A Review of the Ten Types of Definition Already Discussed

Through the preceding units of this Part of our text we have been considering definition as an "act of explaining the signification of a word or phrase." In the above dictionary definition of "definition" occurs a doubly ambiguous expression: "the signification of a word or phrase." A large part of our inquiry through the preceding units may be regarded as an effort to disentangle the various things that might be meant by that expression. According as an author's act is an effort to explain one of these things or another, his act of definition belongs to one or another of the kinds of definition which we have described. Let us see how this may be.

1. The dictionary definition speaks of "the signification of a *word* or *phrase*." But it does not tell us whether it is word-*tokens* or word-*types* whose signification is explained.

Now we know from §§15.2 and 15.3 that it is word-tokens which have meanings. But we also know that many tokens of a certain word-type may have one meaning while other tokens of that word-type have another. Thus, there often are many meanings, or significations, associated with a single word-type. This makes the use of the definite description (§18.3), "*the* signification . . ." ambiguous if by "word" is meant word-type.

Our previous discussion resolved this ambiguity by taking the expression to mean what would be more awkwardly expressed by saying, "the signification common to some group of word-tokens or phrase-tokens all belonging to the same word-type or phrase-type." Each definition clearly identifies the word-type or phrase-type involved and, more often than not, only less clearly identifies which tokens of that type are being explained. This identification of the tokens in question is usually in terms of their authorship. If they are all produced by the definer, the definition is nominal, not real; if all are produced by other people, the definition is real, not nominal; if some are produced by the

309

definer and some by other people, the definition is both nominal and real.

2.　But the awkward substitute expression proposed in the preceding paragraph is still ambiguous. (This is why we called the original expression *doubly* ambiguous.) For we have seen (Units 20, 21 and 23) that terms have actually two kinds of meaning:

　a.　An extension
　b.　A total strict intension[1]

Which of these meanings does a definition seek to explain when it explains "*the* signification"?

Many definers will attempt to explain one only of these significations, some will undertake to explain both. Thus, according as the purpose of the definer resolves this second ambiguity in one or the other of these three ways, the definition is classified as:

> Extensional, not intensional
> Intensional, not extensional
> Intensional and extensional.

Other types of definition discussed in the preceding units were not distinguished in consequence of the double ambiguity already mentioned. Instead, they follow from the fact that the dictionary definition of "definition" describes a broad and general type of activity, so that several distinct kinds of activity would be special cases of this general sort of thing. Thus:

3.　The dictionary spoke of an "act of explaining . . . ." The effort of the definer—the explainer—may be to explain *in whole* (complete definition) or to explain *in part* (incomplete definition).

4.　It is the signification common to tokens of a certain word-type which a definition seeks to explain. If the definer presumes that the intended receiver is already acquainted with the extension, or the total strict intension, signified by the term in question, he may limit his act of explanation to one of connecting that term with that extension or total strict intension (extensional *linguistic* and intensional *linguistic*

---

1　We may neglect here the other types of intension. Contingent intensions, including indexical intensions, are all dependent on the extension, and other strict intensions, including definitive intensions, are all defined in terms of the total strict intension.

Also, we speak of "the total strict intension" rather than use the more accurate, but more awkward expression "set of necessary members of the total contingent intension."

definition). But on the other hand, he may conceive his task as one of getting the receiver to contemplate, perhaps for the first time, the extension or intension in question and only then to connect the defined term with that extension or intension. In such cases, the definition is an extensional (or intensional) *conceptual* definition.

5.   Finally, a definer may attempt not only to explain what certain producers (either himself or others) did, do, will, or propose to mean by certain tokens, thus to explain how a receiver of those tokens should understand them (informative definition); but he may *additionally*, as a *second* purpose, be urging the receivers of his definition also to mean this same thing when they produce tokens of the same word-type (hortatory definition).

## §28.2 Seventy-two Types of Definition!

In the preceding section we have reviewed the ten types of definition described and named in the preceding units of this Part:

1.   Complete—incomplete
2.   Nominal—real
3.   Informative—hortatory
4.   Linguistic—conceptual
5.   Extensional—intensional

The ten types of definition were described and named in pairs, as the table above may remind you. Two of these pairs (1 and 4), it was pointed out, are mutually exclusive: no definition can be both complete and incomplete, or both linguistic and conceptual. On the other hand, this mutually exclusive character does not apply in the case of the other three pairs: some definitions are nominal and not real, others real and not nominal, and still others both real and nominal; *all* definitions are informative, some of these are also hortatory, the rest of them are not also hortatory. Finally, some definitions are extensional and not intensional, others intensional and not extensional, and others both extensional and intensional.[2]

While the five bases differ in the manner just described—some supplying mutually exclusive pairs of types and others overlapping pairs of types—all five bases are alike in that each provides a jointly

---

[2]  E.g., many theoretical definitions are nominal-intensional and real-extensional. See §26.4, above.

exhaustive pair of types. Thus, for example, every definition is either complete or incomplete, every definition is either nominal or real, and so on.

Keeping in mind what has been remarked in the two preceding paragraphs, we see that the ten types of definition discussed in the preceding units suffice actually to identify 72 different kinds of definition![3]

1. Complete, nominal, not real, informative, not hortatory, linguistic, extensional, not intensional definitions.

2. Complete, nominal, not real, informative, not hortatory, linguistic, extensional, intensional definitions.

3. Complete, nominal, not real, informative, not hortatory, linguistic, not extensional, intensional definitions.

4. Complete, nominal, not real, informative, not hortatory, conceptual, extensional, etc., etc.

It is well to notice how many (72) kinds of definition have been identified. But it would be a foolish waste of time to list the 72 kinds. All that *is* needful in this connection is to keep in mind what has been said above about the exclusive or nonexclusive character of the five pairs of types, and the fact that each of the five pairs is an exhaustive pair. Then, given any definition we can undertake a complete classification of it into precisely *one* of the 72 kinds.

[3] To get the number, 72, first consider each of the five bases of classification separately to determine how many kinds of definition that basis, considered alone, will identify:

| Basis (as numbered in text) | Types of Definition Identified |
| --- | --- |
| 1 | 2 |
| 2 | 3 |
| 3 | 2 |
| 4 | 2 |
| 5 | 3 |

(If the pair of types *listed* on one basis is mutually exclusive, the answer is 2, if not mutually exclusive, the answer is 3. Had any of these pairs not been jointly exhaustive, the answer would have been greater by one than the answers actually given in the above table.)

Next multiply together the five answers found in the preceding step:

$$2 \times 3 \times 2 \times 2 \times 3 = 72.$$

Do this because each successive basis divides *each* type of definition *already* found into two or three subtypes, as the case may be.

*EXERCISES*

1.  Is theoretical definition (§26.4) one of the 72 kinds of definition sug-
    gested in the partial list just above?
2.  If so, which of the 72 kinds is it? Describe it in the manner of the
    descriptions given in the partial list, above.
    If not, is it a kind which could be said to be a combination of several of
    these kinds? Which kinds would belong to this combination?

It might be thought that 72 kinds of definition identified in terms of
purpose would be enough. But in this connection it should be remembered that the 72 kinds are a simple consequence of combining the
results of considering the definer's purpose from only five different
points of view, the five bases in terms of which the original ten types
of definition were identified. There are, to be sure, still other purposes of
definition than those we can catch in this five-based net. Some of these
are often important. But they are usually remote purposes, thus usually
not signified by the definition itself. We shall deal with a few of them
later on under the heading, "The Uses of Definition."

Meanwhile we shall find it more profitable to turn our attention away
from the *purposes* of definition and to examine some of the various
means or *methods* employed in order to achieve these purposes. Here
again we cannot notice every detail in the varied techniques employed
by definers. Rather, we shall examine certain broad, general techniques
of definition and shall consider more or less critically how these techniques are related to the purposes mentioned in the preceding unit.

## §28.3 Ostensive and Indicative Definitions

It has been suggested (§25.1) that a definition (an act of
explaining) is a sign-event. This is, indeed, generally and largely true.
In fact, it may be said that every act of definition *includes* a sign-event.

Yet quite often the definitional act includes something over and above
the sign-event. In particular, it frequently includes the actual *presentation* to the receiver of the thing (or a sample of the thing) meant by the
term being defined. For example, the young child first learns the meanings of words by being confronted with the things they refer to at the
same moment that he hears the words, "Papa," "ball," "baby." Again,
the sign over a cage at the zoo confronts the passer-by with a sample
from the extension of the term printed on the sign. Or yet again, a paint
manufacturer gives color cards to his prospective customers; these

consist of names for the colors of the paints he manufactures together with actual examples of the colors so named, the names and the examples being so displayed on the card as to associate each name with a certain example.

All such definitions ("This is a polar bear.") which depend on actually confronting the receiver with the extension or some sample from the extension of the term in question are called **ostensive definitions.** Definitions that are not ostensive are called **indicative definitions.**

The borderline between ostensive and indicative definitions is not sharp. For example, the pictures of birds in a bird guide, or the stuffed skins of animals in a museum, make the attached signs or labels operate very much like ostensive definitions, the only difference being that the receiver is confronted not with an actual object, but with a likeness to an object, from the extension of the term in question.

As has been suggested above, the technique of ostensive definition is to confront the receiver with a sample from the extension of the term being defined while at the same time he is confronted with a sample of the word-type tokens of which are being defined. Since it is the extension of the term that is being exhibited, this type of definition is primarily useful as a form of extensional definition and will hardly serve the purposes of intensional definition.

While ostensive definitions are undoubtedly indispensable, at least in the child's earliest experience with language, they also have their limitations, many of which are those of extensional definitions in general. Chief among these is a kind of inevitable vagueness. (1) When I point (and ostensive definition involves a kind of pointing) just what is pointed at? Is it a *region* ("This is Boston.") and, if so, how large or small a region? Is it a *physical object* ("This is an adult polar bear.") and if so, throughout how much of its life span (usually more than the time during which my finger is pointing)? Is it a *quality* ("This is indigo blue.") and if so, what and how much variation from the quality-as-presented-in-the-instance will still leave the ostensively defined name appropriate? (2) What *other* things than those presented in the ostensive definition also belong to the extension of the defined term? Put in another way, how can you tell, concerning a thing not presented in the ostensive definition, whether it does or does not belong to the extension of the term defined?

All the above doubts and queries indicate that ostensive definitions will never be sufficient in themselves, and unsupplemented, to function as complete definitions. They may, however, be very effective incomplete definitions and could perhaps often be used to increase the effectiveness of other defining activities.

From this point on we shall be concerned with indicative definitions.

## §28.4  The Core of an Indicative Definition

The indicative definitions, to which we now turn, are sign-events. As such, they consist in the production of certain sign-tokens. The tokens thus produced may form in their entirety several sentences; on the other hand, they may form no more than a single sentence, or even possess a nonsentential form (as do the definitions given in a dictionary).

In all complete, indicative definitions, however, there are produced sign-tokens the meaning of which is that such-and-such tokens of such-and-such a type signify such-and-such a thing.

EXAMPLES:

1. Horse: a hoofed quadruped used for draught or the saddle.
2. An extensional definition is one aimed at explaining what belongs in the extension of a term.
3. Let us use the word *referent* to indicate any actual object to which a term purports to refer.
4. When Father says, "We'll see," he means, All right!
5. You should use the word "fish" to refer only to objects in the biological family *pisces*.

As may be seen, these examples are quite varied in their form. Furthermore, as we consider the various purposes of definition discussed in the preceding units, we must notice that the samples given above are ambiguous or vague (or both) in the sense that we cannot always tell merely from the above what kind of explanation the author was intending. In each case in which one of the above occurred, the total act of defining should have taken place in such circumstances, or included such other remarks, as would have made the purpose or meaning of the above tokens clear, precise, and unambiguous.

Nevertheless, in each of the above cases it might be said that the listed tokens did present the **core** of a definition. They presented a certain *proposition* for consideration: that tokens of such and such a type have such and such a meaning. *What* proposition they presented (that is, *which* tokens they refer to) would, it is hoped, have been made clear by *other* remarks produced in the defining act. Whether the indicated meaning was merely the extension or was the strict intension should also have been made clear. And whether the definer's concern is merely informative or also hortatory could or should also be revealed, perhaps elsewhere, in the total act of definition.

We shall, however, find it useful to give separate attention to the tokens that form the core of a definer's definition. They form this core in virtue of the fact that they themselves belong to, and hence present, a sign-type which conventionally determines in large part the meaning that the definer would convey. Hence these tokens are tokens not merely of a certain sign-type but also of a certain *statement*.[4]

In §25.1 we quoted two definitions of "definition": "the act of stating the signification . . ." and "the statement of the signification . . . ." What we would now notice is that the tokens which form the core of an act of definition are also a statement occurrence of the statement which is the definition in the second sense defined in §25.1. Thus a definition considered as a statement is not everything said in an act of definition. Many accompanying remarks may, and often should, be made as a part of the total act of definition. The definition considered as a statement is simply the statement presented in the core of an act of definition.

From this point on we shall be concerned to examine different forms of definition in this new sense; that is, the different statements that may be offered as the cores of acts of definition.

## §28.5 Definiens and Definiendum

As has been said, people present definitions in all sorts of ways. For example, at the end of §24.3 are three exercises each of which starts with what we said was a definition. One of these is:

1. *Pentagon:* a plane figure bounded by five straight lines.

Here we see the term to be defined given first, next a colon, and that in turn followed by the expression which states the meaning of "pentagon." But the normal conventions of English usage would have allowed any of the following sign-types (as well as others) to be employed by a producer whose purpose was to define the word "pentagon."

2. By a *pentagon* is meant a plane figure . . .

4 On "statements" see §§5.2 and 16.2.

3.  A pentagon is a plane figure . . .
4.  One uses the word "pentagon" to refer to any plane figure . . .
5.  A plane figure bounded by five straight lines is called a *pentagon*.
6.  Let us understand by the term "pentagon" any plane figure . . .

All these definitions have this in common: They present the expression to be defined and they present the expression chosen by their producer as the means of definition. They differ one from the other in their manner of presenting these items, that is, in their linguistic context.

Our future discussions will be helped by the introduction of a standard form for the presentation of definitions (in §28.6) and, prior to that, of six technical terms for the discussion of definitions.

a.  By the **definiendum** (plural: *definienda*) of a definition is meant the term whose meaning is explained in that definition. For example, all six alternative definitions given above have the same definiendum: "pentagon."

b.  By the **definiens** (plural: *definientia*) of a definition is meant the expression that explains the meaning of the definiendum of that definition. For example, all six definitions above have the same definiens: "a (or "any") plane figure bounded by five straight lines."

[The words *definiendum* and *definiens*, like many other technical terms in the sciences, come from Latin. In Latin, the word *definiendum* means "the thing to be defined," while *definiens* means "the defining (thing or expression)."]

Two things are to be noticed in connection with these technical terms. First, they are *relative* terms rather than *absolute* terms. (See §19.3) That is to say, a word like "pentagon" is not *always* a definiendum, as it *is* always a noun, but is a definiendum in this, that, or the other definition; just as grammatically it is not always a subject (for example, not a subject in definitions 4, 5, or 6, above), but is a subject in this, that, or the other sentence (for example, in definition 3, above).

Second, English usage allows the sign-type "definition" to be employed so as to refer *either* to an entire statement of the sort illustrated in 1 to 6, above, *or* to that part only of such a statement as we have called its definiens. Thus, in accordance with *one* conventional meaning of the word-type "definition," "definiens" and "definition" mean the same thing; but in accordance with *another* conventional meaning of the word "definition," a definition contains a definiens but also contains other parts: a definiendum and an indication that definiendum and definiens have the same meaning. It is in accordance with this second convention that we use the word "definition."

Let us, however, turn to another matter. Just a bit above this paragraph there appear definitions of "definiendum" and "definiens." Suppose I were to ask, what is the definiendum of the second of these definitions? From one point of view, we could say that it is the term "definiens"; that is, after all, the word whose meaning is being explained. Yet when we examine the definition as a whole, and in particular when we examine its definiens, we see that, strictly speaking, the definition does not explain the meaning of the single word "definiens." Rather, it explains the meaning of the *phrase* "The definiens of a definition." The explanation of the phrase may have been *for the sake* of explaining this word in the phrase; but the explanation is still an explanation of the phrase.

The distinction just explained—between an entire phrase or other expression whose meaning as a whole is explained in the definiens, and the word or other part of that phrase for the sake of whose explanation the definition is proposed—brings to mind a similar distinction in grammar: between the *simple* subject and the *complete* subject of a sentence, or between the *simple* predicate and the *complete* predicate of a sentence. Accordingly, we shall define as follows:

c.  By the **simple** definiendum of a definition is meant that word or phrase in the definiendum for the sake of explaining which the definition occurs.

d.  By the **complete** definiendum of a definition is meant the entire expression the meaning of which is said to be equivalent to that of the definiens.

Looking over all the definitions given so far in this section, we may distinguish their simple and complete definienda as follows:

| Definition | Simple Definiendum | Complete Definiendum |
|---|---|---|
| 1, 4, 6 | Pentagon | Pentagon |
| 2, 3, 5 | Pentagon | A pentagon |
| a | Definiendum | The definiendum of a definition |
| b | Definiens | The definiens of a definition |
| c | Simple | The simple definiendum of a definition |
| d | Complete | The complete definiendum of a definition |

Several points may be noticed in connection with this distinction between simple and complete definienda.

i. Sometimes the simple definiendum is identical with the complete definiendum. (See top row of above table.)

ii. Sometimes the difference between simple and complete definiendum consists merely in the inclusion or exclusion of the definite or indefinite article, "the" or "a". (See second row of above table.)

iii. Words appearing in the complete definiendum but not a part of the simple definiendum often appear also in the definiens; but in well-constructed definitions the simple definiendum does not appear in the definiens. (See any of the definitions given above.) In fact, we shall discover later on rules for correct definition that will *require* the repetition in the definiens of certain words or other expressions appearing in the complete definiendum.

iv. As point iii suggests, a definition assumes that the meanings of words or phrases in the complete definiendum which are not a part of the simple definiendum are already clear and may be assumed by the producer to be already understood by the intended receiver.

v. When tokens of the phrase-type of the simple definiendum will have different meanings in different contexts, a complete definiendum can isolate one context in which the meaning is defined without affecting the meaning of the definiendum in other cases. For example, it could be quite inappropriate to try to eliminate the vagueness of the word "large" by giving it one and the same meaning in all contexts. But a report of some study made on mice could contain the following definition. "By a large mouse is meant a mouse weighing at least 6 ounces." Here the simple definiendum "large" is given a precise meaning in certain contexts. What meaning is to be assigned to tokens of this same type in *other* contexts, that is, as applied to other things than mice, is in no way affected by this definition.

## EXERCISE

Identify the simple definiendum, the complete definiendum, and the definiens in each of the following definitions.

1. A modern chemistry book is a chemistry book written later than 1930.
2. By a parallelogram is meant a quadrilateral whose opposite sides are parallel.

3.  Let us understand by an "educated man" any person who is a college graduate.

4.  $x$ is between $y$ and $z$ means that either $x$ is to the left of $y$, and $z$ is to the left of $x$; or $x$ is to the left of $z$, and $y$ is to the left of $x$.

We come finally to the last pair of technical terms:

e.  A definition is said to be **absolute** if either its simple definiendum and its complete definiendum are identical or its complete definiendum contains in addition to its simple definiendum only the definite or indefinite article ("the" or "a").

f.  A definition is said to be **contextual** if it is not absolute.

To illustrate, all six definitions of "pentagon" at the beginning of this section are absolute, but the definitions given of "definiens," "definiendum," "simple," "absolute," and "contextual" are all contextual. The definitions given in a dictionary are almost always absolute.

Absolute definitions have a certain appeal: they seem so clean-cut and definite. But contextual definitions also have their advantages. Some of these are suggested above in points iii, iv, and v, in the discussion following the definitions of simple and complete definienda. Still other values of contextual definitions will be discussed as we continue.

*EXERCISE*

Classify as absolute or contextual each of the four definitions given in the preceding exercise.

## §28.6  A Standard Form for Definitions

In addition to its complete definiendum and its definiens, a definition contains words or other signs (perhaps merely a colon) to indicate that the definiens is an explanation of the definiendum. We have seen how great may be the variety of these other signs. Also the order of presentation of definiendum and definiens varies: sometimes, the definiendum is given first; sometimes, the definiens is given first.

We shall, however, find it useful to adopt and use throughout the remainder of this discussion only one standard form for definitions. By "putting definitions into" this form, we can more readily compare them, note their relative merits, and discover whether or not they conform to the rules for sound definition.

Let $X$ stand temporarily for the complete definiendum and $Y$ for the definiens. Then a definition in standard form will be written,

$$X =_{Df} Y.$$

A few remarks on the standard form of a definition will help relate it to the discussions that have preceded this section.

1. The standard form is a standard form for no more than the core (§28.4) of a defining act. Standing alone, it would very likely be ambiguous: one could not tell merely by inspecting the standard form whether the author was recommending (hortatory) or reporting; nor could one tell which tokens of the type of the definiendum he was explaining, nor whether his explanation was extensional or intensional, linguistic or conceptual.

2. Hence, unless circumstances provide answers to all these questions, the definition, as act of explaining, should include more than the mere presentation of a standard form. Those additional remarks should be adequate to remove the just-mentioned risks of ambiguity in the standard form. These accompanying remarks will turn the token of a sign-type in standard form from a token of a type into a token of a statement since they will associate a definite meaning with that type.

Of course, the *different* accompanying remarks in different definitions will associate *different* meanings with one and the same type.

3. The standard form presented here is most appropriate for complete definitions. Incomplete definitions may sometimes be expressed in this form, but more often they cannot. Incomplete definitions will be given separate consideration at a later stage. Meanwhile, occasional remarks concerning them will appear from time to time.

4. Despite the fact that accompanying remarks will make different tokens of the standard form have different meanings, there will still be certain points of similarity in meaning. It is these points of similarity that make attention to the standard form worthwhile. For it permits us to discuss once and for all important factors distinguishing good definitions from bad, no matter whether those definitions are real or nominal, extensional or intensional, hortatory or not hortatory. It is these points to which we shall be giving our attention in the next unit.

5. When a definition is not given in standard form (and the demands of good literary style frequently require the use of other forms), it is often desirable for the critic to "put the given definition into standard

form." This amounts to nothing more than rewriting the given definition in standard form. The result in standard form should have the same meaning as the original statement, except that the original statement may have included some suggestions that should *accompany, but not be a part of,* the standard form.

For examples: (a) All six definitions of "pentagon" at the beginning of §28.5 would be put into the same standard form:

A pentagon $=_{Df}$ a plane figure bounded by five straight lines.

(b) Example 4 in §28.4 would be put into the following standard form:

We'll see $=_{Df}$ All right.

## EXERCISES

1. Put into standard form the illustrative definitions given in §28.4.
2. Put into standard form the definitions in the Exercise near the end of §28.5.

## REVIEW QUESTIONS FOR UNIT 28

1. Explain carefully two elements of ambiguity in the phrase "the signification of a word or phrase."
2. How are different types of definition discussed in the preceding units connected with the resolution of the double ambiguity explained in answer to question 1?
3. List the five pairs of types of definitions discussed in the preceding units.
4. In which of the five pairs of types of definition listed in answer to question 3 are the two types of definition mutually exclusive?
5. Which pair is such that *all* definitions belong to one type in the pair? To which type in that pair do all definitions belong?
6. What does it mean to call a pair of types of definition jointly exhaustive?
7. Which of the five pairs listed in answer to question 3 are jointly exhaustive pairs?
8. How many distinct kinds of definition can be identified in terms of the ten types already discussed? Briefly explain. Illustrate by citing one or two kinds not mentioned in the partial list given in the text.
9. Are there other purposes of definition than those referred to in question 8? If so, under what heading or headings have they, or will they, be treated in this book?
10. What is an ostensive definition? An indicative definition? Illustrate each type.

11. Are ostensive definitions generally more appropriate for extensional definition or for intensional definition? Explain briefly why you answer as you do.

12. What is the chief weakness, or limitation, of ostensive definition?

13. Does the weakness pointed out in answering question 12 suggest that all ostensive definitions are to be avoided? Why do you answer as you do?

14. What is meant by the core of an indicative definition?

15. Does the core of an indicative definition always include everything which is said in the act of definition? Explain.

16. How are definitions, considered as "statements of the signification . . .," related to the cores of acts of indicative definition? Explain.

17. Define (in your own words, if need be) and illustrate what is meant by each of the following technical terms.

   a. Definiendum           d. Complete definiendum
   b. Definiens             e. Absolute definition
   c. Simple definiendum      f. Contextual definition

18. What is meant by "a definition in standard form"? By "putting a definition into standard form"?

# Techniques of Definition and the Classification of Terms: General Terms

## §29.1 The Purpose of Units 29 and 30

In this unit and the next we shall be concerned with a problem of a definer: how to construct a good indicative definition.

To a considerable extent, the discussions in the preceding units should be directly helpful to a person who wishes to define certain expressions. They suggest that he should be thoroughly clear about his purposes and should give adequate attention to making those purposes clear to the receiver. Also, he can often separate to advantage the core of his definition from the accompanying remarks, so that attention may be focused, both by himself and his receiver, upon that core when the accompanying relevant issues are clear.

Finally, the definer should keep in mind the capacities and limitations of his receiver. This is especially important in respect to the linguistic capacity and general educational background of the receiver. There is no point in using words or appealing to ideas and experiences with which the receiver is totally unacquainted.

But leaving all those matters aside, we shall be concerned in these units with the general techniques of definition in standard form that are most appropriate in different circumstances. We have already distinguished two such techniques of definition: absolute definition and contextual definition (§28.5). What remains to be done is to note still other techniques, also to note certain special forms that contextual definition may take, and finally to consider under what different circumstances using one of these forms of definition rather than another is likely to prove the more effective or appropriate.

The "different circumstances" twice referred to in the preceding paragraph will be identified through two kinds of consideration:

1.   What kind of expression is the simple definiendum? In particular, is the simple definiendum a term? Or is it instead some expression (like "all," "a few," "the") which is not a term? And if it is a term, what kind of term is it? For example, is it a singular term or a general term, abstract or concrete, attributive or denotative?

2.   What kind of definition is sought? In particular, is the definition which is being constructed to be offered as a complete or an incomplete definition? An extensional or an intensional definition? A linguistic or a conceptual definition? (The techniques of definition we shall discuss here work equally well whether the definition is supposed to be nominal or real, also whether or not it is supposed to be hortatory. Hence, those classifications of definitions need not be kept so much in mind during the following discussions.)

Thus we see that the "different circumstances" are to be identified by bringing together two sets of considerations which we have previously studied: the classification of terms and the classification of definitions.

Our procedure throughout these two units will be as follows: We shall first identify some kind of term (singular, general, and so on) to be defined, then we shall describe various techniques of definition appropriate for defining terms of this kind, and finally we shall consider which of these techniques is the more or the less appropriate according as the purpose of the definition is extensional or intensional, complete or incomplete, and so on. Techniques for defining expressions which are *not* terms will be briefly considered only at a later time, in §34.1.

The suggestions to be made in these two units should be helpful to the definer whether his act of definition is a reflexive sign-event (entered into only so as to help him "figure out" for himself the meaning of an expression) or a social sign-event (in which he is undertaking to impart information or advice (hortatory) to another person).[1] Even in the latter case, a period of "figuring out" usually precedes the process of imparting. They should also prove helpful to the receiver of a definition. In part, they may help him identify the purpose of the definition he receives: Insofar as he can trust the skill of the definer, the definer's purpose is likely to be the one best served by the technique of definition that was employed. And in part, these suggestions will provide the receiver with tools to criticize the definition: Where other remarks or

[1]   On reflexive and social sign-events, see §§11.1 and 11.2.

circumstances reveal that the definer's purpose was such and such, the definition may be criticized in terms of the appropriateness to that purpose of the technique of definition chosen by the definer.

The remainder of this unit will be devoted to a discussion of techniques for defining general terms; Unit 30 will take up techniques for the definition of singular terms.

### §29.2 The Definition of Attributive Terms

It has already been suggested (§28.5) that contextual definitions are useful when the simple definiendum belongs to a word-type or phrase-type that will have different meanings in different verbal contexts. The complete definiendum isolates and identifies one of those contexts and permits the definition to be made in terms of that context. Such definitions are particularly useful in the case of adjectives and adjective phrases, which often have different meanings according as they modify one noun or another. For example, the word "good" has quite different meanings when it occurs with different nouns in such phrases as "a good book," "a good woman," "a good soldier," "a good try," "a good dinner." While these different meanings may be more or less vaguely related to one another, the sign-user's immediate purposes will often be better served by a precise definition of this word in one context (the context in which the word is to occur throughout a given discourse) than by a vaguer indication of its general or pervasive sense.

As the illustration of the preceding paragraph may have suggested, it is particularly in connection with the definition of attributive terms that contextual definition can be valuable. For words expressing attributive terms, more generally than any others, take on meaning from their contexts, hence become tokens of distinct terms in diverse contexts.

But contextual definition, of a somewhat different sort, can be helpful in still another way in the definition of attributive terms. Let us see what this other sort of contextual definition may be and how it might be used.

The analysis of propositions outlined in Unit 16 suggests a fundamental role of attributive terms in statements. In those analyses, the attributive term was represented by "$P$".

The definition of an attributive term, $P$, can be made most effective if the complete definiendum has the form of a singular proposition. For example, instead of trying to give an absolute definition of "perpendicular," give a contextual definition of "line $a$ is perpendicular to line $b$"; instead of trying to give an absolute definition of "equal," give a contextual definition of "person *a* is equal to person *b*" (for example, in an effort to determine the meaning of "All men are created free and equal.").

When the complete definiendum in a contextual definition has the form of a sentence, the definition will be called a **sentential contextual definition.**

For example, a definition of "perpendicular" with "line *a* is perpendicular to line *b*" as its complete definiendum will be a sentential contextual definition. So also would be a definition of "equal" with "person *a* is equal to person *b*" as its complete definiendum. On the other hand, a definition of "good" with "a good book" for its complete definiendum would be a contextual definition, but not a sentential contextual definition.

In connection with sentential contextual definitions, note particularly that it is the *singular* proposition forms (I-A and II-A in §16.4) which must occur as the context in the contextual definition. The meanings of attributive terms in general propositions (§§16.5 and 16.6) follow from, or can be explained in terms of, their meanings in singular propositions. But the opposite is not always true, as is explained below.

Two motives for the sentential contextual definition of attributive terms may be cited. First, as in any contextual definition, the context provides a concrete setting for the term and hence makes it easier to grasp or understand its meaning. Second, and more important, the provision of a context often forces us to notice that the term we are defining is a relative term (§19.3) when we had carelessly taken it to be absolute. This relational character will be brought out by the fact that the complete definiendum will contain two or more subject terms (*a, b*, and so on) instead of only one. In fact, the *discovery* of the relational character of an attributive term, and of the number and identity of the things involved in the relationship, can be one of the greatest contributions to clear and effective thinking made by definitions.

This relational character of a term is especially easy to lose sight of when terms are used in statements of general propositions or similarly with plural subjects. To illustrate this difficulty let us compare the two sentences,

1. All the people in this room are English,

and

2. All the people in this room are acquainted.

To simplify the comparison, let us assume that George, Bill, and Jim are the only people in the room. Then statement 1 above says, in effect, that

  1′  George is English, and Bill is English, and Jim is English.

But statement 2—even though its grammatical structure is just like that of statement 1—makes a totally different kind of assertion. This becomes apparent when we try to interpret statement 2 in terms of George, Bill, and Jim—that is, with the aid of singular propositions— as we interpreted statement 1 in statement 1′. Were we to use precisely the same form and write,

  2′  George is acquainted, and Bill is acquainted, and Jim is acquainted,

we should be writing nonsense. Instead of 2′, we must write,

  2″  George is acquainted with Bill and with Jim, and Bill is acquainted with George and with Jim, and Jim is acquainted with George and with Bill.

In a word, the singular statement forms used as clauses in 1′ and 2″ bring out the fact that "English" is an *absolute* attributive term, whereas "acquainted" is a *relative* attributive term. This difference between the two attributives is concealed by the grammatical similarities of the forms for the general statements 1 and 2.

Now the main points brought out so far in this section may be summarized as follows: (1) Attributive terms are usually best defined in contextual definitions. (2) The best type of contextual definition is likely to be a sentential contextual definition. This type is especially appropriate when there is any likelihood that the attributive term being defined is a relative term. (3) The complete definiendum in a sentential contextual definition should have the form of a singular proposition.[2]

Two further points about sentential contextual definitions should be noted here: (4) In the complete definiendum of such a definition, do not

---

[2] This is true whenever a *term* is being defined. When we define signs of quantity, like "all," "a few," "75%," we might use contextual definitions, but then we would have to employ the forms of the general propositions which these signs of quantity identify:

$$\text{All } S \text{ is } P =_{\text{Df}} \text{---}$$
$$75\% \text{ of } S \text{ is } P =_{\text{Df}} \text{---}$$
$$\text{Etc.}$$

(On signs of quantity and on definitions of expressions which are not terms, see §§16.5 and 34.1, respectively.)

write the several subject terms all as *grammatical* subjects. Let only one be a grammatical subject and put the others in the grammatical predicate. For example, do not write, "Line $a$ and line $b$ are perpendicular $=_{Df} \ldots$ ." Write instead, "Line $a$ is perpendicular to line $b =_{Df} \ldots$ ." Failure to observe this precaution can be as misleading as is using general statements instead of singular statements for the complete definienda.

(5) The subject positions in the sentential definiendum should be occupied by letters or by arbitrary names like "John Doe" which are not the names of specific individuals but rather specify any individuals. For example, if we are defining what it means for two people to be equal we should not write, "President Eisenhower is equal to Benson Ford $=_{Df} \ldots$ ." Rather we should write, "Person $a$ is equal to person $b =_{Df} \ldots$ ," or "John Doe is equal to George Coe $=_{Df} \ldots$ ." The definition should be applicable no matter who the people are.[3] This is the reason why we must not mention specific individuals.

The methods of definition suggested in this section for attributive terms are equally appropriate whether the definition is to be extensional or intensional. On the other hand, they are not completely suitable for incomplete definitions, but work best for complete definitions.

## EXERCISES

1. For each of the following adjectives, list two or three nouns such that the conventional meaning of the adjective will be different according as it modifies one or the other noun. Briefly indicate what the difference in meaning would be.

   a. Sharp            b. Crude            c. Fiery
   d. Extended         e. Cooperative      f. Visual

2. For each of the following, write a complete definiendum appropriate for use in a sentential contextual definition of the expression involved:

   a. Taller           b. Friendly (toward)   c. Severe
   d. Opposed          e. Related             f. Transient

---

[3] To say that the definition is applicable no matter who the people are does not mean that in that application the singular proposition corresponding to the definiendum is necessarily true. It does mean that the definition will explain the meaning of the singular proposition, no matter who the people are and no matter whether the singular proposition is true or is false.

## §29.3  Conditional and Operational Definitions

There is one problem that frequently concerns the definer and it arises as often in connection with the definition of attributive terms as it does anywhere. We shall accordingly discuss it here. But the problem treated also arises in connection with the definition of general denotative terms, so the discussion in this section is as appropriate to the sections following as it is to the preceding section.

Sometimes a general term may be "formally" understood and "formally" defined in the sense that we know how its meaning connects with the meanings of a great many other terms, but we may still be unable to determine when any object in the real world belongs or does not belong to the extension of this term. It is as though, for example, we were studying three terms, $A$, $B$, and $C$, and we knew, let us say, that

1. All $A$'s are $B$'s.
2. All $B$'s that are also $C$ are $A$.
3. No $B$'s except those that are $C$ are $A$.

We could summarize this knowledge in the contextual definition:

4. $x$ is $A =_{Df} x$ is $B$ and $x$ is $C$.

But our difficulties lie in the fact that we do not know any means by which to tell of any given $x$ whether or not it is $A$, whether or not it is $B$, and whether or not it is $C$.

What we need is an *experimental test* which we may apply to different $x$'s to determine whether or not they have one or the other of the attributes $A$, $B$, or $C$. The application of such a test would involve the actualizing (§6.3) of some prescribed test condition and the observation (§6.2) of the outcome in order to determine whether or not a certain test criterion is exhibited. Let $D$ represent the test condition to be actualized, and $E$ the criterion to be looked for. Then the relevance of this experimental test could be recorded in the following **conditional definition:**

5. $x$ is $A =_{Df}$ if $x$ were $D$, then $x$ would be $E$.

EXAMPLES:

6. $x$ is soluble (in water) $=_{Df}$ if $x$ were put in water, then $x$ would dissolve.

7.   Angle *abc* is a right angle $=_{Df}$ if line *ab* were extended through point *b* to some point, *d*, then angle *abc* = angle *cbd*   *intensive*

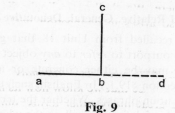

**Fig. 9**

When its definiens has this "if . . . then . . ." form, a definition is said to be **conditional.** When, furthermore, the "if" clause describes a performable (actualizable) experiment, and the "then" clause describes an observable outcome of the experiment, then the conditional definition is called an **operational definition.**

It should be noted that not every term in a "system" need have an operational definition in order to determine empirically whether or not a given object belongs to its extension. For example, in our little system of concepts *A*, *B*, and *C*, if we had operational definitions of *B* and of *C* we should not need a separate one for *A*: Definition 4 would show us how to make use of the experiments defining *B* and *C* in order to determine which objects are in the extension of *A* and which ones are not.

Operational definitions may be either extensional or intensional. For example, definition 6, above, could with reasonable plausibility be offered as a real, intensional definition. But to define gold as in definition 8, below, would seem to be reasonable only in the sense of extensional definition.

8.   *x* is gold $=_{Df}$ if *x* were placed in aqua regia, then *x* would dissolve.

Conditional and operational definitions are usually also written as sentential contextual definitions.

Operational definitions are of great importance in the experimental sciences. They provide the bridges by which the elaborate schemes or systems of ideas developed in the sciences are systematically connected with experience or observation. Hence, to a great extent they make possible the systematic testing of scientific theories in the laboratory.

Without them, it could not be fairly claimed that the laboratory experiments had anything to do with the truth or falsity of the scientific theories in question.[4]

## §29.4 The Definition of Relative, General, Denotative Terms

It will be recalled from Unit 18 that general denotative terms are terms which purport to *refer* to *any* object of a certain kind, and that these terms may be either concrete or abstract, or both. (See in this latter connection §19.1.) In English, such terms are regularly expressed by nouns or noun phrases. Whether the terms are abstract or concrete, the same kinds of definition will on the whole be appropriate. Hence, we may discuss the definition of this kind of term in general, without further regard to whether or not the terms are abstract or concrete.

We have already noticed, in the two preceding sections, that the problems of definition for attributive terms and for general denotative terms are much the same. We should expect, therefore, to find that contextual and operational definitions would frequently be desirable in the case of the denotative terms now under consideration. This is particularly true when the denotative term to be defined is a relative term (§19.3) or when the definition is to be an operational one. Hence little more need be said here than that all the suggested techniques of the two preceding sections may be applied when one wishes to define a relative denotative term. Only one or two special comments need be added.

Relative denotative terms have in general two kinds of use: to denote objects standing in a certain relation to a *specified* individual, and to denote objects standing in that same relation to some individual that is not specified. For example, we might use the relative denotative term "brother" in such sentences as "John is a brother of Roberta," "Some of Roberta's brothers are lawyers," or "John and James are brothers of one another." On the other hand, we find statements of the following

---

4 Many logicians and others theorizing about the methods of the sciences have believed that all these operational definitions are intensional. A careful examination of the actual structure of scientific literature suggests that such a view must be in error. Operational definitions in practice *supplement* other, nonoperational, definitions of the same terms. The view here criticized has undoubtedly come to be so widely held as a consequence of the widespread assumption that all definitions are intensional. On this problem, see above, §§26.1, 26.2, and 26.3.

kinds where no specified individual is referred to: "John is a brother," "All brothers of lawyers are fortunate," and so on.[5]

In defining a denotative relative term, we should use that kind of complete definiendum in which letters represent specified individuals. Thus we should define "*a* is a brother of *b*" rather than "*a* is a brother."[6]

When we are concerned with the meaning of some noun, adjective, or verb, we should pay special attention to the question, Does it have a relational meaning that I (perhaps) have overlooked, so that I should define the word as a relative term? Careful attention to this question can often mark the beginning of a new understanding and insight into the things we read and a new forcefulness and clarity in the things we write.

## EXERCISE

Write appropriate definienda for definitions of each of the following relative denotative terms. (If you do not know what some of these words mean, look them up in a dictionary before doing this exercise.)

1. Nephew    2. Teacher    3. Friend    4. Tangent
5. Emulsion    6. Senate    7. Advisor    8. Senator

## §29.5 The Definition of Absolute, General, Denotative Terms

Oftentimes absolute, general, denotative terms will be effectively defined in conditional definitions. Such definitions will be contextual and usually also operational. (See §29.3, above.) Such definitions may be either extensional or intensional.

When, however, terms of the sort here under consideration are not given a conditional definition, they are usually defined by one or the other of two techniques of absolute definition (§28.5). These two

---

[5] Strict mathematical logic classifies the complex terms having "brother" as a constituent as terms denoting the *referents*, the *domain*, and the *limited domain* of the relation of brotherhood. In this introductory text, we shall not discuss those classifications of the complex terms, but merely note the corresponding kinds of use which the constituent term "brother" might have.

[6] It should be noted that attributive terms are also used in these two ways. For example, not only do we say, "Sara is affianced to John," but, "Sara is affianced." Or again, "George murdered William," and, "George murdered." The same precaution applies in defining these attributives as is made here in the text for relative denotatives.

techniques of absolute definition are distinguished one from the other by the character of the definiens:

1.  **Enumerative definitions.**  The definiens simply lists, one by one or group by group, or partly in one way and partly in the other, the objects falling in the extension of the term being defined. For example, a club secretary's membership list would make a good definiens for a one-by-one enumerative definition of the term "member of the club." Another example of definition by enumeration, which would be group by group, would be the definition of a domestic animal as a cow, horse, sheep, pig, goat, cat, or dog.

Many enumerative definitions are incomplete (§25.3), either purposely so or accidentally so. Such definitions will be discussed later, in connection with the general problem of incomplete definition.

Definition by enumeration will usually be extensional, or at least more appropriately extensional than intensional. This is especially the case with concrete denotative terms. Enumerative definitions of abstract general terms may, on occasion, be genuinely intensional. For example, the logician defines the term "truth-value" as the quality of truth or falsity attaching to a proposition.[7] This is an intensional enumerative definition: the term "truth-value" was invented *in order* to refer to either one of these two qualities.

2.  **Classificatory Definition, or Definition by Classification.**  Some definitions will proceed by indicating in the definiens several classes (or properties) to all of which objects in the extension of the defined term belong (or all of which objects in the extension of the defined term have). (Compare in this connection the discussion of *common sets of characteristics*, in §22.2.) For example, the definition of man as a featherless biped is an extensional definition by classification: every man is featherless (but so also are some other things) and every man is a biped (but so also are some other things); on the other hand, *only* men are *both* featherless *and* bipeds.

As the example above shows, some of the classifications in this (and other types of) definition may be indicated by attributive terms. (The attributive term used above is "featherless.") And as this fact suggests, correct extensional definitions of this sort, *when complete,* state an index

---

7   Rewritten as a sentential contextual definition, this is:
$a$ is the truth-value of proposition $b$ = $_{\text{Df}}$, $b$ is true and $a$ is the property *truth*, or, $b$ is false and $a$ is the property *falsity*.

of the term being defined. (See §24.4.) When incomplete, such definitions indicate groups of characteristics that are *approximately* indices of the terms being defined. On the other hand, correct intensional definitions of this sort when complete state a definitive intension of the term being defined. (See §24.2.) When incomplete, they contribute to the statement of a definitive intension.

Definition by classification may be thought of as first indicating some large general class that includes the extension of the term being defined but that includes other things as well; and then narrowing the *part* of this class to be attended to, by reference to other classes or characteristics, until attention is focused on just that part of the original class which is the extension of the term in question. For example, the definition of "man" discussed above first indicates the class of all bipeds (or all featherless things) and then narrows attention to the things in this class that are featherless (or are bipeds). If the process of narrowing attention does not go far enough, we have a definition which is incomplete; not in the sense that the definition does not apply to everything in the extension, but in the sense that the definition *does* apply to things *not* in the extension. Thus, we see that definitions may be incomplete either by being too broad or too narrow.

Definitions by classification form the traditional pattern of intensional definitions:

"A house = Df a building used as a shelter for animals of any kind."
"A tyro = Df a person imperfectly acquainted with a subject."

This type of definition is especially appropriate for general denotative terms, either concrete or abstract. Traditionally, it has been called *definition by genus and difference*, or, in the Latin, *per genus et differentiam*.

As applied to the definition of denotative terms, the definiens consists of a denotative term ("building" or "person" in the two examples) modified by one or more attributive terms ("used as a shelter for animals of any kind" and "imperfectly acquainted with a subject"). The denotative term states the genus. The extension of the definiendum is entirely contained within the extension of the term stating the genus. But if this were all that could be said concerning these two terms, the definition would be an *extensional* definition by classification. In the case of *intensional* definitions every characteristic in the total strict intension of the term stating the genus is a characteristic in the total strict intension of the definiendum. It is this relation between their intensions that guarantees the previously described relation between their extensions.

Each attributive term that modifies the denotative term stating the genus is said to state a difference. The relation of definiendum to difference is like that of definiendum to genus: extension of definiendum contained in extension of term stating difference, and total strict intension of term stating difference contained in total strict intension of definiendum.

Only one more relationship is to be noted: every object in the extension *both* of the genus *and of each* difference is in the extension of the definiendum; and every characteristic in the total strict intension of the definiendum is in the total strict intension *either* of the genus *or* of *at least one* listed difference. If only the indicated relation of extensions holds, the definition is extensional; if also the indicated relation of total strict intensions holds, and thereby guarantees the relation of extensions, the definition is intensional.

## EXERCISE

Turn at random to some page in a dictionary and consider a single column of entries.

1. How many word-types are listed for definition?
2. How many terms are defined? (Note that some word-types like "all" will not be terms and must therefore not be counted, while other word-types like "table," will be different terms for each different definition and must therefore be counted several times.)
3. How many definitions of terms are *per genus et differentiam*.
4. Select one of these definitions *per genus et differentiam* and put it in standard form.

## REVIEW QUESTIONS FOR UNIT 29

1. What is the general purpose of this unit and the next? Illustrate by discussing the manner in which some particular topic outlined in the present unit contributes to the attainment of that purpose.
2. Describe briefly three circumstances that make contextual definition especially appropriate for the definition of attributive terms.
3. What is meant by a "sentential contextual definition"? Why is this form of contextual definition particularly useful in the definition of attributive terms?

4.  Explain briefly two precautions that should be taken in forming the complete definiendum in a sentential contextual definition.

5.  Explain and illustrate what is meant by a conditional definition; an operational definition.

6.  Are operational definitions usually extensional, or usually intensional, or frequently of the one kind and frequently of the other? Explain.

7.  Discuss briefly the importance of operational definitions to the development of the sciences.

8.  What technique of definition is recommended for the definition of relative denotative terms?

9.  What kind of precaution must be taken in writing the definienda of definitions for relative denotative terms?

10.  Name and briefly describe two techniques of absolute definition suitable for the definition of absolute denotative terms.

11.  Immediately below appears a list of all the techniques of definition treated thus far in this book. Following the list is a series of questions.

### Techniques of Definition

a.  Absolute definition *specific*
b.  Ostensive definition (§28.3) *actual sample*
c.  Indicative definition (§28.3) *signs*
d.  Contextual definition *not that*
e.  Sentential contextual definition *sentence form*
f.  Conditional definition *if then*
g.  Operational definition *adjectival concludes*
h.  Enumerative definition *group*
i.  Classificatory definition *ex - in*
j.  Definition *per genus et differentiam* *broad - narrow*

i.  Which (if any) of the eleven terms listed above name one and the same technique of definition?

ii.  Which of the techniques of definition listed above are special forms of which other techniques of definition, also listed above?

iii.  Which of the above techniques of definition are identified by the nature of the complete definiendum?

iv.  Which are identified by the nature of the definiens?

v.  Which (if any) are identified by still another means?

# UNIT 30

# *Techniques of Definition and the Classification of Terms: Singular Terms*

In this unit we turn our attention to singular terms and to the techniques of definition appropriate to them. It will be recalled (page 197, point 2) that all singular terms are denotative. Nevertheless, there are several kinds of singular terms: concrete singular, abstract singular, simple singular, complex singular. The kind of definition that is appropriate to a singular term varies quite regularly with the kind of singular term that is to be defined. We shall, therefore, consider these classes of singular terms one after the other.

## §30.1 The Definition of Simple, Concrete, Singular Terms

Terms of the sort here under consideration include all proper names: "London," "Ike Eisenhower," "Harvard University," and the like. If one of these terms is to be defined, it would occur as the definiendum of the definition in standard form:

Ike Eisenhower = Df . . .

The question to be considered is, what form could the definiens appropriately take?

To use another simple concrete singular term as the definiens—as in

Ike Eisenhower = Df Dwight David Eisenhower—

could not further the purposes of conceptual definition (§26.5). Such a definition might be very useful for purposes of identification, but it would be appropriate only in linguistic definition. For this definition presumes that the receiver has already identified the object referred to by the definiens.

If conceptual definitions of simple, concrete, singular terms cannot properly take simple, concrete singulars for their definientia, what can they take? Obviously, the definiens in such a definition must be a con-

338

crete singular term; if it were not, the definiens and definiendum would not have the same meaning, with the result that the definiens would not have *explained* the meaning of the definiendum. Therefore, the definiens should be a *complex*, concrete singular term.[1]

The type of complex, concrete singular term most useful for this purpose is the type called a *definite description* (§18.3). In fact, this is the only type of complex concrete singular term which will be considered throughout this unit.

What we should expect then as the standard form of definition for a simple concrete singular term would be one in which the definiens is a definite description.

EXAMPLE:

Ike Eisenhower = $_{Df}$ the President (in 1954) of the United States.

Such a definiens offers to the receiver a *criterion* (being President of the United States in 1954) that he may employ in order to determine whether or not any given object is the referent of the definiendum.

A question arises, however, as to whether or not any such definition should appropriately be offered as an intensional definition or as an extensional definition. Put in other words, and applied to the example given above, should being President of the United States in 1954 be considered as a definitive intension (§24.2) or as an index (§24.4) of the term "Ike Eisenhower"?

The following argument is intended to show that by and large the definitions of simple concrete singular terms used in normal discourse should be offered as extensional definitions. To see how this argument runs, we must see what would be the consequences of treating a definition like the above example as an intensional definition:

It has been pointed out in connection with the arbitrariness of language (§14.1) that an author may mean or intend whatever he wishes by the sign-tokens that he produces. Thus a person could decide that he will intend by sign-tokens of the type "Ike Eisenhower," the President (in 1954) of the United States. If he made such a decision, he could report the decision in the definition given above, and in that case the

---

[1]   Unless one is content with an incomplete definition, e.g.,

Ike Eisenhower = $_{Df}$ a certain man.

On such incomplete definitions, cf. below, §30.2.

definition would be an intensional definition. After making this decision, that author might remark some day, "Ike Eisenhower was President of the United States in 1954." If someone asked him how he knew that this was true, he should properly reply, "Why, by analysis! (See §6.4.) I do not have to read the papers, or make personal observations. What I *mean* by 'Ike Eisenhower' is the President of the United States in 1954."

But now suppose that this same person had been around, and talking, in 1946. Very likely he would have mentioned "Ike Eisenhower" back in those days. What could he have meant by tokens of that word-type produced back in 1946?

Let it be granted that in 1946 no one knew that the man then known as "Ike Eisenhower" was going to be President in 1954. To be sure, some people may have *hoped* he would run for election, may even have *predicted* that, provided he was living and in good health, he would run for election, even predicted that if he ran he would be elected, and that if elected in 1952, he would survive in office until 1954. But they could not have known this with a certainty in 1946. In other words, as they used the sign-type "Ike Eisenhower" in 1946 they could not have been using it to intend, with the definitive intension, President of the United States in 1954.

Our supposed author would have been in no different a position in 1946 than any of his friends. By whatever right he *now* assigns "President in 1954 of the United States" as a definitive intension to "Ike Eisenhower," he must *then* have been assigning a different definitive intension, say "the president (in 1946) of Columbia University."

But what is the consequence? That tokens of the type "Ike Eisenhower" produced by our supposed author in 1946 and similar tokens produced by him in 1954 must be tokens of two *different* terms. For they have different definitive intensions: being President in 1954 (1946) of the United States (Columbia University). And no amount of analysis and inference, unassisted by observation, will enable us to prove that the president of one of those institutions in the one year was the president of the other in the other year.

As a result, sentences like

$$\text{Ike Eisenhower} = \text{Ike Eisenhower}$$

become thoroughly ambiguous. Do they mean:

1.  The president of Columbia (in '46) = the president of Columbia (in '46),

2. The president of Columbia (in '46) = the President of the United States (in '54), or

3. The President of the United States (in '54) = the President of the United States (in '54)?

If they mean sentence 1 or 3, they are analytic (may be accepted as true on the basis of analysis). But if they mean sentence 2 they are not analytic (must be judged true or false partly on the basis of observation). It is unwise to permit sentences which *look* <u>analytic</u> (like the given *Ex* one) to turn out *not* to be so, as in example 2.

All the above suggests that it would be unwise to decide on the meanings of proper names in such a way as to make the original definition of "Ike Eisenhower" to be intensional. That definition should be offered as an *extensional* definition. This would not only have the advantage of permitting all tokens of that type produced by *us* to be tokens of the same term (so long as they referred to the same man), but it would have the further advantage of permitting our tokens of that type to be tokens of the same term as are the tokens of that type produced by *other* people, even when they use a different criterion, or indexical intension, for the term than we do.

When we put this conclusion with our earlier one, it turns out that all complete definitions of proper names, both those by other proper names and those by definite descriptions, are best regarded as extensional definitions.

## §30.2 Strict Intensions and Proper Names

Does the above mean that simple, concrete, singular terms have no definitive intension and no total strict intension? If they have such intensions, why can they not be given in the definien's of an intensional definition?

The correct answer to these questions must probably run somewhat as follows: <u>The conventional use of these names by a society all of whose producers identify one and the same object when they use a given name far exceeds the conventional sharing of any criterion for the use of that name.</u> Undoubtedly, many of these names are "picked up," made a part of one's working vocabulary by his having heard them in connection with a presentation of the named object. This first association of name and named individual works for the bearer much as would the receptive act of attending to an ostensive definition (§28.3).

But the circumstances of our various learnings of the name are almost certain to have the effect that we do not have the same criterion in all our minds as we all use the name. It is in fact more than likely the case that many of us have in mind no clearly apprehended criterion at all! Probably for most of us there is little more than a vaguely felt willingness to mean—that is, to accept as the strict intension—whatever the first assigners of the name intended by it. In the case of people's names, this would generally be to accept as the intension whatever the parents who named the child meant by the name, such as, "the child born to x and y on such and such a date."

In the case of the names of cities, many business firms, and the like, as well as the names of people belonging to by-gone generations, the first namers are no longer here to be consulted as to just what they did have in mind. But even if the first assigners of a name were available, it is unlikely that they could recall having in mind a specific definite description of the object to which they assigned the name. Indeed, it is quite likely that they did not even formulate their thoughts in terms of definite descriptions.

Thus, we had best conclude that simple concrete singular terms have in general no definitive intensions and no strict intensions, but only indices.

On the other hand, it would be unwise to assume that there are no necessary members of their total contingent intensions.[2] That Ike Eisenhower is a human being, London is a city, and Harvard is a university are propositions which could properly be regarded as analytic. Given an understanding of the terms involved in these propositions, the method of analysis is sufficient to justify the acceptance of these propositions as true.

What kind of properties can be necessary members of the total contingent intensions of proper names? Probably we would be safe in saying that they are:

1. Invariant properties of the thing purportedly named. For example, Eisenhower is a human being at every moment of his existence, so that being a human being is an invariant property; but he is not President of the United States at every moment of his existence, so that being President is not an invariant property.

[2]  These necessary members will not form a total strict intension because they will not be jointly peculiar to the individual who is the referent of the singular term. On this point, see §23.3, above.

2. Other properties (deductively) inferable from the necessary invariant properties in the total contingent intension. For example, if Eisenhower is a human being, then it is inferable that he was born at some time or other. Hence, although he is not always being born, so that being born is not an invariant property, still being born at some time or other could be a necessary property in the total contingent intension of the term "Eisenhower." But on the other hand, being born on such and such a date, of such and such parents, or graduating from West Point, are *not* properties inferable from being a man. Hence, they are not necessary members of the total contingent intension of the term "Ike Eisenhower."

The above considerations are not intended to suggest that *every* invariant property of Ike Eisenhower necessarily belongs to the total contingent intension of "Ike Eisenhower." What they are intended to suggest is that nothing except invariant properties (and others inferable therefrom) would advisedly be included among the necessary members of the total contingent intension of a proper name. Some one or two, or other small number, of these invariant properties might well be thought of as what the proper name primarily means and all other properties—both variant and invariant—inferable from this original small number of properties would also necessarily belong to the total contingent intension of the term.

This small number of invariant properties, conceived as necessary members of the total contingent intension of the term, might well provide the basis for an *incomplete* intensional definition. For example, the following could appropriately be offered as an incomplete intensional definition of "Ike Eisenhower."

Ike Eisenhower = <sub>Df</sub> a certain human being.

Thus intensional definitions of proper names might have general terms in their definientia, but these terms should be introduced by "a certain", making the definientia to be *incomplete* definite descriptions (§21.3). To get a general term for the definiens which would have in its extension only one object—namely, the presumed referent of the definiendum—so that the general term could be introduced by the definite article "the" and be made into a complete definite description, will probably require the use of merely contingent members of the total contingent intension of the proper name. Hence, the definitions produced in this manner would preferably be considered as extensional definitions, giving only an index and not a definitive intension.[3]

In a sense, we have dealt with the hardest case first! The rest of this unit should be relatively simple.

## EXERCISE

For what kind of real definition (intensional or extensional, linguistic or conceptual, complete or incomplete) would the following be appropriate? Briefly explain why you answer as you do.

E  1.  London = Df a certain city in England.  *Conceptual, Incomplete*
   2.  London = Df the capital of Great Britain.
   3.  London = Df the largest city in the British Empire.
   4.  Beethoven = Df a famous composer of the late eighteenth and early nineteenth centuries.
   5.  Beethoven = Df the composer of the *Eroica Symphony*.
I  6.  John Stuart Mill = Df the son of James Mill.
   7.  George Washington = Df the first President of the United States.
   8.  Macy's = Df a certain department store in New York City.
I  9.  Satchmo = Df Louis Armstrong.  *Linguistic, Complete*

## §30.3 The Definition of Simple Abstract Singular Terms

The terms here under consideration are those that name (or purport to name) individual qualities, characteristics, modes of

[3] Many modern logicians and philosophers tend to speak of all proper names as "definitional abbreviations" for complete definite descriptions. (On definitional abbreviations see §34.2, below.) This view might be acceptable were it not for the fact that these same people seem to regard every definition as an instance of what we have called *intensional* definition. To speak of definitional abbreviation connotes having two terms (one short and one long, the definiendum and the definiens) with the same meaning: the same strict intension. Hence it suggests treating these definitions of proper names as intensional.

Treating them so is what we have been arguing against throughout this and the preceding section. If *extensional* definition were recognized and definitions of proper names in terms of complete definite descriptions acknowledged as extensional definitions, we should all be in complete agreement. But then the proper name could hardly be regarded merely as a definitional abbreviation for the definiens.

What has just been said cannot, however, deprive those logicians of their right to mean by the tokens they produce whatever they will. Hence they *may*, if they wish, treat all the proper names they pronounce as definitional abbreviations (intensional) for complete definite descriptions. But then those definitions must be regarded as nominal. They will not correctly report what other people mean when they utter tokens of the same proper-name sign-type. Nominal definitions of this type are permissible. But the point of our argument in the text is that they would be unwise.

relationship and the like; such as "courage," "azure," "marriage," "friendship," "symmetry." (See §§18.2, 18.3, 19.1, and 19.2.)

Every such term may be thought of as the second denotative correlate of some attributive term: "courageous," "azure," "married," and so on. (See §18.4.) On the whole, one would do much better to put his major effort into "figuring out" and defining these attributive terms, and then define quite simply the abstract singulars by definite descriptions that make use of these attributives, as for example:

Courage = $_{Df}$ the quality attaching to an individual who is courageous.

Marriage = $_{Df}$ the relationship of two people one to the other who are married one to the other.

It must be noted, however, that the task of defining the abstract singular term is not really complete, when one follows this procedure, until the cognate attributive appearing in the definiens has also been defined. This problem of defining attributives has already been discussed in §29.2.

The immediate definition of the abstract singular term may be regarded as intensional. But the remoter definition of the attributive term may be extensional or intensional; and since this immediate definition in a sense delegates the task of definition, we might say that the *pair* of definitions gives an intensional or extensional definition of the abstract singular according as the definition of the cognate attributive is intensional or extensional.

This advice, to define attributives rather than their second denotative correlates, is not given because the attributives are easier to define. They possibly are not. But attending to the attributives does get thought down to a concrete level and probably makes *good* definition easier.

## EXERCISE

For each of the following terms, state a definition in terms of a cognate attributive term.

1. Friendship
2. Peace
3. Parenthood
4. Freedom
5. Justice

6. Equilibrium   *Balance*
7. Poise
8. Knowledge
9. Virtue
10. Quiescence

## §30.4 The Definition of Complex Singular Terms

Complex singular terms are abstract (for example, "manly courage"), or they belong to the class of terms called *definite descriptions* (§18.3): "the title of your textbook," "my fountain pen," "the author of *Tom Jones*," "that apple," "the size of your contribution." The definition of complex abstract singular terms presents no specifically new problems and will not be discussed in this text. But the definition of definite descriptions deserves a little of our time.

As was previously remarked, every definite description consists of a general term to which has been added a "singularizing prefix." The general term may itself be simple or complex. Also it may be concrete (second, third, and fourth examples above) or abstract (first and fifth examples). According as the general term is concrete or abstract, the singular term constructed from it will be concrete or abstract.

We should furthermore note that the singularizing prefix may also serve a second purpose, being in addition an attributive term: "my," "that." In fact, the only singularizing prefix which is not also an attributive term is the definite article "the."

Finally, we must notice that to construct a complex singular term, the general term out of which it is constructed must be expressed in its grammatically singular form: "My fountain pens," "those apples," and "the sizes of your contributions" are general terms, not singular terms.

Suppose now that we were concerned to provide an *extensional* definition of a complex singular term. As we express that definition in standard form the complex singular term to be defined would be the definiendum. For definiens we could put *any* singular term, simple or complex, that has the same referent. Examples:

The first President of the United States = <sub>Df</sub> George Washington.

The first President of the United States = <sub>Df</sub> the Commander-in-Chief of the Continental Army during the American Revolution.

The size of your contribution = <sub>Df</sub> $25.00.

The size of your contribution = <sub>Df</sub> your bank balance!

Notice that the formulation of these extensional definitions requires— if we are to be confident of their truth—a certain knowledge of the "facts of history." But in this respect, they are no different from any other extensional definitions.

In contrast, intensional definitions require for their confident development no knowledge of the facts of history other than (particularly in the case of real definition) the history of language. The primary grounds of belief in these cases are analysis and inference (§§6.4 and 6.5). How, then, do we proceed to produce an intensional definition of a complex singular term?

1.   Suppose that the singular term to be defined has been constructed by prefixing the definite article "the" to a general term. Then that general term will be denotative. In effect, the task before us is to find a good intensional definition of that general term (Unit 29) and to use here the definiens of that definition, replacing the indefinite article "a" in that definition by the definite article "the."

EXAMPLE:

To define:

"the first book of the Bible."

(Note that an extensional definition would be:

The first book of the Bible $=$ $_{Df}$ *Genesis*.)

Corresponding general term:

"(a) first book of the Bible."

Intensional definition of corresponding general term:

A first book of the Bible $=$ $_{Df}$ a major subdivision of the Old or New Testament such that, when the entire contents of these testaments is printed and bound in its normal or customary order, this subdivision precedes every other subdivision.[4]

Required intensional definition:

The first book of the Bible $=$ $_{Df}$ the major subdivision of . . .

Notice that the method of solving the problem of definition just stated makes this assumption: that it is not the meaning of the definite article "the" which is to be explained. If, however, the meaning of the definite article requires explanation, that should be done in a *separate*

---

[4]  If we had considered the given definite description and resulting general term to be complete definienda containing "first" as a simple definiendum—i.e., if we had considered our task to be one of defining "first" as applied to books of the Bible—the definientia could have included the phrase "book of the Bible" instead of defining it. Taking the entire expression as simple definiendum requires us to define *both* "first" and "book of the Bible." See above, §28.5, and below, §32.3.

definition. Here we must use the definite article in the definiens and hence cannot explain it.

The definite article is not a term; therefore, any definition of it would be a definition of an expression which is not a term. On the definition of such expressions, see below, §34.1.

*EXERCISE*

      Define in the manner just explained each of the following definite descriptions:

1. The President's personal physician.
2. The 1954 winner of the Boston Marathon.
3. The house that Jack built.

There is, however, still another method of accomplishing the definition of a complex singular term, and this other method often serves all purposes of the definer. Instead of giving one definition of the complex term, give *separate* definitions of various terms contained within it. This *set* of definitions serves as a definition of the complex term.

To continue with the same example as before, we could give two definitions: a contextual definition of "first" as appearing in the term "the first book of the Bible" and a separate definition of the general term "book of the Bible." Anyone who understood the logic of English grammar could, if he wished, then put these two definitions together to get the one definition given above. But sometimes it is desirable to give a definition which puts these pieces together. This is especially the case when grammatical and other elements of organization serve to conceal constituent ideas. For example, the apostrophe in "the President's personal physician" makes unnecessary any explicit reference to *attending on* the President, both in sickness *and* in health. But this idea would not be derived merely from separate definitions of "the President," "personal," and "physician."

*EXERCISES*

1. What constituent terms contained in the definite descriptions of the preceding exercise might be *separately* defined as an aid to the definitions of those definite descriptions?
2. Which of the three definite descriptions in the preceding exercise would be adequately defined by defining the constituent terms you listed in answer to question 1, and which would not?

2.   Suppose the singular term to be defined is not of the sort considered under point 1. Then the problem of definition may profitably be divided into two parts:

a.  Treat the given definite description as a complete definiendum containing the singularizing prefix as simple definiendum (§28.5), and provide as definiens a definite description of the sort just discussed in point 1.

EXAMPLE:

To define:

"my fountain pen."

Step a:   My fountain pen = Df the fountain pen that belongs to me.

b.  Either produce a second, absolute definition (§28.5) which has for its definiendum the definiens of the definition produced in step a. (This involves an application of the first of the two methods explained in point 1, above.) Or produce separate definitions of various terms contained in the definiens provided in step a. (This is to apply the second method explained in point 1, above.) To continue with the same example, in accordance with the first alternative, we should define in step b "the fountain pen that belongs to me"; but if we adopt the second alternative, we should define *separately* the general denotative term "fountain pen," the attributive term "belongs to," and the singular term "me."[5]

## EXERCISE

Make a "step a" definition of each of the following definite descriptions and report what expressions you would then recommend defining in step b.

1. New York's mayor
2. Our automobile
3. My train (As in, "My train is due at 3:45.")
4. My wife's umbrella

---

[5] To consider pronouns as terms raises certain serious problems that cannot be treated here. Strictly, they are not terms, but substitutes for terms. Their general definition is strictly a case of defining an expression that is not a term (§34.1). But the specific *occurrences* of them may be given extensional definition by appeal to the term that they replace. Following this method in the above example, "me" would have only an extensional definition: "Mr. Leonard," or whatever was the proper name of the speaker.

# REVIEW QUESTIONS FOR UNIT 30

1. What difficulties are encountered if one undertakes to give a complete intensional definition of a proper name?
2. What two kinds of characteristics may appropriately be regarded as necessary members of the total contingent intensions of proper names?
3. Why do the necessary members of the total contingent intensions of proper names not constitute total strict intensions of those proper names? (Review in connection with this question also §23.3.)
4. Can proper names be given incomplete intensional definitions? Explain and illustrate.
5. Explain and illustrate the technique of definition recommended for simple abstract singular terms.
6. Why is the technique of definition you explained just above recommended for abstract singular terms?
7. Under what circumstances should the definitions produced by that technique (question 5) be regarded as intensional definitions? As extensional definitions?
8. How may complex singular terms be extensionally defined?
9. In giving an intensional definition of a complex singular term:
   a. What consideration must be given to the kind of singularizing prefix occurring in the term to be defined?
   b. How can defining the general term (simple or complex) out of which the definite description is formed serve to define the definite description?
   c. What other method than that described in answer to question b, above, can be used in the definition of definite descriptions?

# UNIT 31
# *Rules for Complete Definition*

## §31.1 Introduction

Most logic books include in their treatment of definition a list of rules for definition. These rules propose certain criteria in terms of which one may criticize definitions that he reads and may guide the construction of those he makes. When we consider the wide range of purposes served by definitions and the variety of forms they may take, we must suspect that no rules will be applicable as guides to criticism in all cases of definition. Nevertheless, the consideration of some rules and of their propriety to certain types of definition can be helpful.

Many of the rules we are about to consider have been stated and explained in books on logic throughout many generations. In these cases, we shall phrase the rule in a more or less traditional fashion and undertake to explain in supplementary comments how the rule applies to the process and formulation of definition as we have explained it.

There are, however, a few preliminary comments that will help relate the present discussion to the general topic of definition as we have treated it. First, the rules of definition that are traditionally set down apply mainly to what we have called *complete definition* (§25.3). In a later unit, we shall consider briefly certain varieties of incomplete definition and we shall point out at that time which of the present rules are still applicable.

Second, the rules apply primarily to that statement which we have called the *core of a definition* (§28.4) and more often than not only when that core has been put into standard form (§28.6). Thus, they describe features that should be illustrated in the core in standard form and such that, if the core fails to illustrate them, the whole act of definition may be rejected as having failed of its purpose.

Third, not every rule can be applied to every kind of definition. For example, some rules are applicable only to (the cores of) conceptual definitions (§26.5), some only to (the cores of) intensional definitions (§26.1). Limitations of applicability will be pointed out as we proceed.

351

Fourth, the rules stated here offer no limitation on the right of any individual to mean by the tokens he produces whatever he may choose to mean. (See §14.1 on the arbitrariness of language.) Thus these rules still apply even in the case of nominal definition: in such cases, they restrict only the definer's manner of explaining what he has chosen to mean by the simple definiendum, not the meaning that he is undertaking to explain (If he does not explain the meaning in accordance with these rules it will not have been explained.)

Fifth, these rules do not repeat or summarize the general advice given in Units 29 and 30, in which certain techniques of definition are recommended as appropriate under certain identified circumstances. Rather, these rules are supplemental: the definition, however appropriate in technique as discussed in Units 29 and 30, will fail of its purpose unless it satisfies the requirements set down in these rules.

But let us turn without further delay to the rules themselves. They may be divided into three groups: rules stating *literary* requirements, those stating *factual* requirements, and those stating *formal* requirements. The first two groups of rules will be discussed in this unit, the third group will be discussed in Unit 32.

## §31.2 Rules for Definition Stating Literary Requirements

### Rule 1: A definition should be as clear as possible.

This requirement is, of course, true of all discourse. That being the case, the only reason for setting it down here as a specific rule of definition is that certain particular points may be cited as especially meriting attention if we are to secure clarity in the case of a definition. Several of these will be enumerated here. They may be thought of as subrules falling under the general Rule 1.

a.   In §28.4 it was noted that the core of a definition is not usually sufficient in itself to indicate what kind of definition (real, nominal; linguistic, conceptual; complete, incomplete; extensional, intensional; informative, hortatory) its author is proposing. Unless the context or the circumstances clear this up, the definition will not be so clear as possible. Hence, Rule 1 requires the definer to *accompany* the core of his definition with such further remarks as will make entirely clear the kind of definition he is proposing.

b.   The demand for clarity has, however, also another significance. It suggests that the definition is the sign-token produced in a directed sign-event (§10.2) and the rule enjoins the definer (the producer) to consider the cultural attainments of the intended second-party: the definiens must be expressed in language that the intended second party can be expected to understand. This does not mean, of course, that the producer cannot reasonably expect the receiver to make any effort to understand the definiens. (He may have to study it, even use a dictionary or reference book.) But it does mean that within those limits of endeavor, the definiens should be so phrased that the intended second party can understand it.

A consequence may well be that the definer would have to abandon some ideal of scientific thoroughness in the interest of clarity. Suppose, for example, that the definition is to be offered in response to an inquiry from the intended second party, and that the term in question is a highly technical term belonging to a science with which the intended receiver is unfamiliar. Perhaps the term is "magnetic reluctivity." An intensional definition would have to use in its definiens other technical terms from general and special branches of physics, and would therefore be, under the supposed circumstances, unintelligible to the intended receiver. The requirement formulated in Rule 1 may therefore require the author to content himself with an extensional definition rather than an intensional one, or an incomplete definition rather than a complete one. In such cases, however, the definition should be so phrased, or accompanied by such remarks, as will make its extensional character or incompleteness known to the intended second party.

c.   On the other hand, the demand for clarity may frequently require than an intensional definition, rather than an extensional one, be provided. In fact, one might say that whenever possible, that is, whenever other considerations or circumstances do not dictate a contrary procedure, Rule 1 recommends the giving of complete, intensional definitions. These are the fullest, therefore the clearest, definitions. They settle the propriety of the term in all *possible*, not merely in all known *actual*, circumstances.[1]

---

[1]   An amusing murder story ("You Shall Know Them" by Vercors) has a plot hinging on this issue: living specimens of a "missing link" are discovered and one of them is killed. Is this killing a punishable crime, murder, the killing of a man; or is it only the perhaps deplorable, but unpunishable, killing of a nonhuman animal? The courts demand an applicable *intensional* definition of man in order to adjudicate the case.

**Rule 2: A definition should avoid figurative and metaphorical language.**

a.  Definitions are properly to be considered as bits of technical discourse, even when they occur in the midst of nontechnical discourse. As such they should contain nothing tending toward vagueness and imprecision. Figurative and metaphorical language is notoriously vague and imprecise, and hence has no place in any technical discourse, unless it be occasionally in an "aside" to lend color and psychological appeal to the technical discourse which it interrupts. A definition, however, is no interruption of the technical discourse, but a fundamental part of it. Hence, its definiens must not employ vague or figurative language.

For example, to define "the devil" as "the prince of darkness" or "a college" as "a gateway to opportunity" would be inadmissible, involving a violation of Rule 2.

b.  Strictly speaking, this rule only isolates for special attention a particular way in which one may violate Rule 1. From the systematic point of view, it could quite properly have been presented as commentd under Rule 1. But custom has tended to accord it the more prominent status of a coordinate rule. No serious harm is done if we follow custom in this respect, provided the connection between the two rules is clearly understood.

To sum up this point: A violation of Rule 2 automatically constitutes a violation of Rule 1. But the converse of the preceding statement is not true: there are *other* ways of violating Rule 1 than by violating Rule 2.

*EXERCISE*

Which of the following definitions does and which does not violate Rule 1? Which does and which does not violate Rule 2? (Assume in every case that accompanying remarks or circumstances have indicated whether the definition is offered as complete or incomplete, extensional or intensional, and so on.) Briefly explain in what consists each violation that you claim to have found.

1.  *Money* is the root of all evil.
2.  (Addressed to a six-year-old) A set, S, of characteristics is said to be *jointly peculiar to* a class, C, of objects when and only when every object which possesses every characteristic in S is a member of C.
3.  (Addressed to a college Freshman) Same as preceding example.
4.  To be wealthy is to have quite a little money.

5. By a sign-event is meant any act of deliberately producing or of interpretatively observing a sign-token. *(clear-non-figurative)*

6. Necessity is the mother of invention. *(figurative)*

## §31.3 Rules for Definition Stating Factual Requirements

### Rule 3: The definiendum and its definiens should be coextensive.

a. <u>This rule applies only to complete definitions.</u> The complete
definiendum consists of a term to which is prefixed or not, as the case
may be, <u>the definite or indefinite article</u> ("the" or "a"). In the same
circumstances, the definiens also consists of a term, with or without the
definite or indefinite article. Needless to say, these terms, particularly
the definientia, are usually complex terms.

Being terms, the definiendum and definiens both have extensions.
What this rule demands is that the extensions of these two terms be
identical. *Nothing* must be in the extension of either term which is not
in the extension of the other.

A violation of the rule may come in any one of three ways:

(i.) The definiens is too broad: its extension includes objects that are
not in the extension of the definiendum.

EXAMPLE:

A house = $_{Df}$ a building.

(ii.) The definiens is too narrow: its extension excludes objects that
are in the extension of the definiendum.

EXAMPLE:

A house = $_{Df}$ a brick building used as a human habitation.

iii. The definiens is both too broad and too narrow.

EXAMPLE:

A house = $_{Df}$ a brick building.

c. In the case of some contextual definitions, the definiendum and
definiens will not be terms in themselves but will instead be models,
or patterns, for the construction of terms. This occurs when the defini-

endum and definiens contain letters (*"a," "b," "x,"*) called *variables*.[2] Every sentential contextual definition contains one or more such variables in its definiendum and again in its definiens. But contextual definitions that are not sentential may contain such variables. For example, I might define "a large *x*" (instead of "a large mouse," as on page 319) as "an *x* which is larger by at least 10 percent than the *mode* of all *x*'s."

All such definienda and definientia become statements or terms as soon as terms are substituted for the variables actually occurring in them. In all such cases, the demand made by Rule 3 amounts to the appropriate one of the following:

i. Nonsentential definitions: Whatever substitution of terms for variables may be made in the definiendum and definiens, the extensions of the terms thereby produced from the definiendum and definiens must be identical.

ii. Sentential contextual definitions: Whatever substitution of terms for variables may be made in the definiendum and definiens, the propositions thereby indicated by the definiendum and by the definiens are either both true or both false.

The key words in both these interpretations are the phrase *"whatever substitutions."* Let us illustrate by considering some examples of sentential contextual definitions.

$$x \text{ is taller than } y =_{Df} x \text{ is not shorter than } y.$$

This definition violates the demands made in ii, above, that is, violates Rule 3: Some substitutions may be made for "*x*" and "*y*" such that the propositions resulting from the definiendum and the definiens will be both true or both false. For instance, if we were to substitute "The Empire State Building" for "*x*" and "The White House" for "*y*", the definiendum ("The Empire State Building is taller than The White House") and the definiens ("The Empire State Building is not shorter than The White House") are both true. Or again, if we substitute "Bunker Hill" for "*x*" and "Mount Everest" for "*y*", the definiendum and definiens are both false. So far, so good. But ii demands that

---

[2] We have met variables before, particularly in Unit 16 ("*s*," "*P*," etc.), where they were employed in order to represent various types or forms of proposition: "*s* is *P*," "*xS* is *P*," etc. References to them will be made in several of the remaining rules for definition. But a detailed study of them as a special kind of sign will have to be postponed until we reach Unit 38.

*whatever* substitutions be made, definiendum and definiens will either be both true or be both false. And this is not the case for the above example, because if we substitute for "*x*" and "*y*" names of two objects that are in fact the *same* height—for example, "Mr. Leonard's Ford" and "Mr. Packard's Ford"—then the definiendum ("Mr. Leonard's Ford is taller than Mr. Packard's Ford") will be false while the definiens ("Mr. Leonard's Ford is not shorter than Mr. Packard's Ford") will be *true*. Thus, the above definition violates Rule 3.

On the other hand,

$x$ is taller than $y$ = $_{Df}$ $y$ is shorter than $x$,

does *not* violate Rule 3. Whatever substitutions for "*x*" and "*y*" make the definiendum true, those same substitutions make the definiens true; and whatever substitutions make the definiendum false, those same substitutions will make the definiens false.[3]

d.  Rule 3 is the fundamental rule for extensional definitions. In fact, all other rules may be considered as only precautionary rules aimed at securing the achievement of Rule 3 or effective communication with the intended receiver. For example, Rule 2 not only serves to secure conformity with Rule 1, but is indispensable to the testing of a definition by Rule 3. If the definiens contains figurative or metaphorical language, it is a phrase-type without a fixed meaning, vague, hence without a fixed extension. Therefore, its extension cannot be compared with that of the definiendum to determine whether or not they are identical.

e.  But Rule 3 is not the fundamental rule for intensional definitions. That place is fulfilled for those definitions by Rule 4. Nevertheless, Rule 3 can be of some value in criticizing intensional definitions, a matter that will be discussed below in connection with Rule 4.

## EXERCISE

Which of the following definitions violate Rule 3, and which do not? (Assume that the definitions are offered as real definitions, proposing to explain the conventional meanings of their definienda.) Briefly explain the character of each violation which you cite.

1.  An automobile = $_{Df}$ a four-wheeled vehicle.  *Not co-ex (too broad)*
2.  A square = $_{Df}$ a four-sided figure.  *too broad*

---

[3]  There is an exception which must be made to the phrase "whatever substitution" as that occurs in i and ii, above. This exception is discussed in connection with Rule 10, in §32.6.

3.  A pet = Df a cat or a dog. *Narrow*
4.  x is worthless = Df if the owner of x tried to sell x, he could not find a purchaser for x.
5.  An inexpensive x = Df an x, the price of which is at least 15 percent less than the average price of all x's offered for sale. (Note: In testing definition 5, only concrete, general denotative terms may be substituted for "x".)
6.  Green = Df the prevalent color of leaves and grass during the growing season.
7.  A house lot = Df any parcel of land reserved primarily for use as the site of a private dwelling.

**Rule 4: An intensional definition must give the essential characteristics of the term being defined.**

a.  Rule 4 does not apply to extensional definitions. It is, however, the fundamental rule of intensional definitions.

b.  Furthermore, Rule 4 applies only to complete definitions.

c.  Roughly speaking, what it affirms is that the total strict intensions of the complete definiendum and the definiens must be identical. But this explanation of the rule is called "roughly speaking" because the same types of case must be distinguished as were distinguished under Rule 3. If the complete definiendum and definiens are terms, to which may or may not be prefixed the definite or the indefinite article, then the explanation given applies to these terms. But if the complete definiendum contains variables (see discussion under Rule 3), then:

i.  If the contextual definition is nonsentential: the explanation given must apply to every pair of terms producible by substituting terms for the variables.

ii.  If the contextual definition is sentential: the explanation given applies to every pair of statements producible by substituting terms for the variables.

d.  Without further considering at this point the special cases i and ii under c, above, let us try to become quite clear about the principal claim made in paragraph c, which is the same thing as becoming clear about the meaning of Rule 4.

An intensional definition has been defined (§26.1) as a definition whose purpose is to explain (completely or incompletely) the total strict intension of a term. We may say that "essential characteristics" of a term, as that phrase is used in Rule 4, are characteristics belonging to the total strict intension of the term. When Rule 4 affirms that the definition must give "*the* essential characteristics," it is demanding that it give *all* essential characteristics, and *only* essential characteristics: if it did not give *all* it would be an *incomplete* definition; if it did not give *only* essential characteristics, it would *not* be *intensional*.

How can *all* the essential characteristics be given? They cannot be separately listed, since (as was noticed in §24.1) the number of these essential characteristics is infinite. What one can do, and in fact does, is to give directly, as definiens, another term with the same total strict intension as the definiendum. The component parts of this definiens direct immediate attention to certain characteristics which together must form (when Rule 4 is satisfied) a definitive intension for the definiendum. By directing immediate attention to all the characteristics in some definitive intension, one "gives" implicitly the total strict intension.

e.   As said before, Rule 4 is the fundamental rule for intensional definitions. Furthermore, a definition that satisfies Rule 4 will automatically satisfy Rule 3. It is, in truth, this connection between Rules 4 and 3 that accounts for the importance of correct intensional definitions: *they guarantee coextensiveness*.

f.   But this connection between the two rules may be stated in reverse: a definition that violates Rule 3 automatically violates Rule 4. Thus, Rule 3 may have a negative value in the testing of intensional definitions. Suppose an intensional definition is shown to violate Rule 3, then without further quibble it must be rejected as an unsatisfactory definition because it will have violated Rule 4.

g.   On the other hand, suppose that a proposed definition has already been found to satisfy Rule 3. This is no guarantee that it also satisfies Rule 4. To determine that it does satisfy Rule 4, it must be *further* tested. This further testing is aimed at finding out whether or not: (i) the characteristics "given" in the definiens are *necessary* members of the total contingent intension of the definiendum, and (ii) that set of characteristics is *necessarily* jointly peculiar to the extension of the definiendum. The problem is like that discussed earlier, in §§23.2 and 23.3.

h.   Nominal definition, one is tempted to say, almost cannot fail to satisfy Rule 4 except by deliberate resolve on the part of the definer: he *decides*, subsequent to his act of definition, to use the definiendum with a different meaning from that which he had indicated in the act of definition.[4] Such deliberate shifts in meaning are likely to be announced, so that a critic of the nominal definition may place considerable confidence in it, as satisfying Rule 4, in the absence of any such renunciations of the definition by the definer.[5]

i.   On the other hand, it is often said that a man is his own worst critic. If he would understand his own purposes, motives and behavior, he would wisely consult keen observers and students of human nature who are acquainted with him, rather than attempt to analyze himself. This general fact has its bearing on the criticism of nominal definitions. Sometimes the outside observer, by observing the language habits of the definer, will discern that he is not using the definiendum in accordance with the meaning indicated in the nominal definition, and that the nominal definition is thus violating Rule 4 and therefore false; this can be the case even when the nominal definer is unaware of it.

j.   In sum, then, to test definitions by Rule 4 involves making a comparison of the actual language practices of people using the definiendum and the proposals for its use embodied in the definiens. This comparison may be more or less cursory or more or less extended and detailed. Comparisons of this sort are appropriate both in the case of nominal definitions and in the case of real definitions. Other things being equal, one can have greater confidence that a nominal definition satisfies Rule 4 than that a real definition does so.

k.   The discussion of proper names in §§30.1 and 30.2 indicated that they have no total strict intensions, hence that no complete intensional definitions of them are possible, therefore that Rule 4 never applies to their definitions.[6]

4   One might be "tempted to say," as indicated above, that all violation of Rule 4 by nominal definitions is deliberate. But that, of course, would be false. When an author, subsequent to his act of definition, uses a token, he is then and there deciding what it shall mean. This decision might be inconsistent with his earlier resolve or prediction, as expressed in the earlier nominal definition, without his noticing the inconsistency. Such a failure to notice would probably occur because the earlier definition is momentarily out of mind. In such a case, his later decision is not to use the sign-type with a different meaning, but to use it with such and such a meaning; and the *additional* fact is that such and such a meaning *is* a different meaning than that previously announced in the definition.
5   In connection with this entire problem, review §27.8.
6   But something *approximating* complete intensional definition is possible for proper

## EXERCISE

Assume that each of the following is offered as a real intensional definition, explaining the conventional meaning of its definiendum. Which of them involve violations of Rule 4, and which do not? In each case, briefly explain why you answer as you do. (Words may be looked up in the dictionary, but do not thoughtlessly assume that the dictionary definitions are intensional rather than extensional.)

1. House = Df a building used as a sheltered place of habitation for animals or people.
2. Rectangle = Df a parallelogram all of whose interior angles are right angles.
3. Politician = Df a person who makes a business of seeking and holding public governmental office. *No*
4. Freshman = Df a student in the first-year class in a secondary or collegiate institution of learning.
5. Giraffe = Df a mammal with extremely long front legs and an extremely long neck.
6. Thesaurus = Df a dictionary of synonyms and antonyms.

## REVIEW QUESTIONS FOR UNIT 31

1. Name three groups of rules which may be applied to guide the formulation and criticism of definitions.
2. Will the rules referred to in question 1 apply equally well to complete and to incomplete definitions? Explain.
3. State (in your own words, if need be) two rules for definition expressing literary requirements.
4. What connection is there between the two rules stated in answer to question 3?
5. When would these rules require a definer to give an extensional definition rather than an intensional definition? An intensional definition rather than an extensional definition?

---

names: an incomplete intensional definition which gives all the essential characteristics of the definiendum:

George Washington = Df a certain man.

This incomplete definition may be called a *full* intensional definition if the necessary members of the total contingent intension of "George Washington" form a set identical with the total strict intension of "man." It would not be full, or not be intensional, if that identity of sets of characteristics did not hold. Thus, Rule 4 could have a so-called application to full, incomplete, definitions of proper names. But extensional definitions are more important than intensional ones when we are dealing with proper names.

6. State the fundamental rule governing complete extensional definitions. Briefly explain what the rule means.

7. How does the presence of variables in a definition affect the application of the rule stated in answer to question 6?

8. State the fundamental rule for intensional definitions. Briefly explain what the rule means.

9. Discuss briefly the relation between the fundamental rule for extensional definitions and the fundamental rule for intensional definitions. In this connection, show how the former rule provides a negative check on conformity with the latter rule.

10. Discuss briefly differences between the problem of applying the fundamental rule for intensional definitions to nominal definitions and that of applying it to real definition.

11. Does the fundamental rule for intensional definitions ever apply to proper names? Explain why you answer as you do.

**32**

# *Rules for Complete Definition, continued*

---

## §32.1 Rules For Definition Stating Formal Requirements

The rules for definition to be studied in this unit are all said to state "formal" requirements. By this it is meant that a mere examination and consideration of the sign-types appearing in the core of the definition (put in standard form) will be sufficient to determine whether these rules are satisfied or violated. So to speak, in order to test definitions on the preceding rules, you had to know something about the *world;* for example, the degree of the intended receiver's education (Rule 1), whether a given object is or is not in the extension of a term (Rule 3), or whether a certain person would refuse to apply a certain term to anything that failed to have a certain characteristic (Rule 4). But to test definitions by the rules now to be stated you need know little more than the grammar of the language in which the definition is formulated.

These rules are, nevertheless, not arbitrary rules. They pick out certain formal characteristics of such a nature that whenever one of these formal rules is violated, one or more of the preceding rules will also automatically be violated. Hence, they direct attention to certain technical features upon which one may immediately check whenever he wishes to evaluate a given or suggested definition.

## §32.2 Circularity and Word-substitution

Rule 5: The simple definiendum of a definition must not appear in the definiens.

Examples of definitions violating this rule are:

A house = ₒf a house.

A desk = ₒf any piece of furniture used as a desk.

A complete inventory = ₒf an inventory that is complete.

a.   Definitions which violate this rule are said to be **circular.** Such definitions, considered merely as statements of sameness of meaning, are true enough. But they must be rejected as definitions because they do not explain the meaning of the definiendum: a person who did not already understand the definiendum could not understand the definiens. Hence, a violation of this rule involves automatically a violation of Rule 1, that a definition should be "as clear as possible."

b.   However, a word of caution is necessary with respect to the application of this rule. In §30.3 it was recommended that in defining a simple abstract singular term (for example, "courage") one might employ in the definiens the attributive term ("courageous") of which the definiendum is the second denotative correlate. Now some logicians would hold that any definition is circular in which the simple definiendum and a term in the definiens are cognates, related as an attributive term and its first or second denotative correlate. Thus, for example, if the term "circle," "circular," or "circularity" is the simple definiendum, then if any one of these appears in the definiens, the definition violates Rule 5.

It is quite true that anyone failing to understand one of two or more cognate terms will almost inevitably not understand any of them. Hence, a definition of the sort under consideration will, *by itself*, not illuminate the intended second party and hence will violate Rule 1.

But the advice in §30.3 did *not* propose that the definition which employed the attributive correlated with the abstract singular would stand by itself. In fact, it was specifically pointed out that to complete the definition of the abstract term one must *proceed* to a definition of the attributive term. This *pair* of definitions, of the abstract denotative and the corresponding attributive, form a small "definitional chain." Definitional chains will be further considered in Unit 33. For the present, we may adopt the following as a practical criterion to be employed in the application of Rule 5:

If the definition employs in its definiens a cognate of the simple definiendum, then it is to be regarded as circular *except* when accompanied by another definition that has that cognate as its simple definiendum.

c.   But we must note still another precaution with respect to the application of Rule 5. Rule 5 is concerned with the repetition of the *simple* definiendum in the definiens. Now it has been pointed out in

§28.5 that one purpose of contextual definition is to explain the meaning of the simple definiendum as that term appears in certain types of context. In other contexts, the simple definiendum might have quite a different meaning. Hence, if the *sign-type* of the simple definiendum is repeated in the definiens, but occurs there in a context so different from that of its context in the complete definiendum that its repetition may be regarded as the presentation of a *different term,* or as no term at all, then no circularity may be presumed to have occurred and the definition should not be considered to violate Rule 5.

An interesting example of this situation occurred in connection with a famous definition of the number "one," devised by the British mathematician-philosopher Bertrand Russell (1872-    ). Russell was defining the cardinal number one:

One = Df the class of all classes each of which has exactly one member.

Here "one" is the simple definiendum and also is repeated in the definiens. But in the simple definiendum it appears as an abstract denotative term; in the definiens it appears as a sign of quantity and not as a term at all (§16.5). Furthermore, an earlier definition by Bertrand Russell has already explained what it means to say that a class "has exactly one member." Hence, although the sign-type "one" appears both as simple definiendum and in the definiens, the definition does not violate Rule 5.

## EXERCISE

Which of the following do, and which do not, violate Rule 5. In each case, briefly explain why you answer as you do.

1. Round = Df circular or elliptical.
2. A table of contents = Df a list, enumerating in the order of their appearance the titles of all chapters, or other divisions, in a book, magazine, or pamphlet.
3. Snake = Df the offspring of a snake.
4. Beauty = Df that quality in virtue of possessing which any object is beautiful.
5. Virtue = Df the virtue of honesty, courage, temperance, wisdom, and so on.

**Rule 6: The definiens of a definition should avoid the use of simple synonyms of the simple definiendum.**

Definitions which violate this demand are said to involve the <u>fallacy of word substitution.</u> Where the purpose of the definer is linguistic definition rather than conceptual definition (§26.5), this rule does not apply. This explains why so many dictionary definitions, both foreign language-English and English-English, will violate this rule: the purposes of the author of the dictionary are largely linguistic definition. But in all cases of conceptual definition the rule has some force and value. However, it is a vague rule and cannot be enforced too rigorously. After all, the definiens as a whole must be a synonym for the complete definiendum. But is it a "simple" synonym?

Conformity to this rule is the motive for definition by enumeration or by classification (§29.5).

Conceptual definitions that violate this rule automatically violate Rule 1.[1]

## EXERCISES

1.  How do definitions by enumeration and by classification ensure conformity to Rule 6?
2.  Which of the following definitions satisfy Rule 6 and which violate it?
    a.  Awkward = $_{Df}$ clumsy.
    b.  An awkward situation = $_{Df}$ an embarrassing situation.
    c.  A wagon = $_{Df}$ a cart.
    d.  A wagon = $_{Df}$ a wheeled vehicle designed to be drawn by an independent (detachable) source of power.

## §32.3  The Rule on Repetition of "Parts"

**Rule 7: Every "part" of the complete definiendum that is not a part of the simple definiendum must occur also in the definiens.**

a.  This rule should be contrasted with Rule 5. According to Rule 5, *no* "part" of the *simple* definiendum *may* appear in the definiens; according to the present rule *every* "part" of the *complete* definiendum which is not in the simple definiendum *must* so appear.

---

[1] It may be questioned whether or not Rule 6 should be listed with the "formal" rules. Perhaps it belongs in group I, with the "literary" rules.

b.  The word "part," as used in this rule, is intended to apply to three kinds of word or expression:

i.  The definite or indefinite article, if it modifies the rest of the complete definiendum considered as a whole. That is, if the complete definiendum has the form "the such and such," then the definiens must have the form "the so and so"; and if the complete definiendum has the form "a such and such," then the definiens must have the form "a so and so."

EXAMPLES: "*The* father of a person = $_{Df}$ *the* male parent of that person." "*A* large mouse = $_{Df}$ *a* mouse which . . . ." "*A* person's uncle = $_{Df}$ *a* brother of one of that person's parents."

ii.  Each simple term that is contained in the complete definiendum (but not in the simple definiendum).

EXAMPLES: "person" and "mouse" in the definitions just above.

iii.  Each variable (see discussion under Rule 3, §31.3).

EXAMPLES: "$x$ is a grandfather of $z$ = $_{Df}$ $x$ is the father of a parent of $z$."

c.  A *moderate* relaxation of this rule is perhaps permissible in practice, if not in theory:

The definiens may contain another word, or other words, in place of the part omitted, but such that an unambiguous paraphrase of the given definiens would restore the omitted parts. For example, in

"a person's uncle = $_{Df}$ a brother of one of his parents,"

we have a definition of "uncle"; hence "person" is a part of the complete definiendum that should, according to the rule before us, appear in the definiens. But instead of it, we find the pronoun "his." This pronoun stands in place of the expression "that person's," and when the substitution is made the rule is completely satisfied. To object to the above definition because it, strictly speaking, breaks the rule, would be needlessly pedantic.

However, such relaxations of the rule should be extremely cautious. For example, there must be no ambiguity concerning the legitimacy of the paraphrase that will permit a strict application of the rule.

d. It is sometimes difficult to say whether a given definition which repeats some word that appears in its complete definiendum is violating Rule 5 or conforming to Rule 7, or whether some other definition which does not repeat such a word is violating Rule 7 or conforming to Rule 5. Such difficulties arise when it is not clear how much of the complete definiendum is to be considered as belonging to the simple definiendum. If, however, one has confidence in the logical competence of the definer, these two rules may be applied, so to speak, "in reverse":

i. Whatever terms *were* repeated in the definiens, belonged to the complete definiendum and not to the simple definiendum, and whatever terms were *not* repeated belonged to the simple definiens.

ii. If no terms in the complete definiendum were repeated in the definiens, the definition was an absolute definition; if some terms thus appearing were repeated in the definiens, the definition was contextual. (See §28.5.)

e. Definitions which violate Rule 7 will automatically violate either Rule 3 or Rule 4 (§31.3) or both.

*EXERCISE*

In connection with each of the following definitions explain whether or not it violates Rule 7. (The simple definiens is printed in italics.) If it does violate Rule 7, indicate in what consists the violation that you claim and in what sense Rules 3 or 4 are consequently also broken.

1. A *tall* man = Df *over 6 feet tall.*
2. x *speaks* to y = Df *an audible sign-token is addressed to y.*
3. A *right* triangle = Df *one containing a right angle.*

## §32.4 The Rule of Similar Structure

**Rule 8: The complete definiendum and the definiens must have the same logical structure.**

Rule 8, as formulated above, is commendably short, and therefore more easily remembered. But it contains a certain inaccuracy, the price paid for brevity. When Rule 8 refers to "the same logical structure," only three features of logical structure need be attended to, and other features may be disregarded. Hence, a more accurate, if longer, formulation of Rule 8 would be as follows:

i. **If the complete definiendum has the form of a statement, then the definiens must have the form of a statement;**

ii.   If the complete definiendum has the form of a singular, or a general, or a denotative, or an attributive, or a concrete, or an abstract term then the definiens must have the same one of these forms;

iii.   If the complete definiendum consists of a general term introduced by the definite or indefinite article ("the" or "a"), then the definiens, if it consists of a general term must be introduced by the same article, or a synonym for it.

a.   Part iii of this rule is really unnecessary, since what it demands is actually covered by part ii and by Rule 7. But the fact that part ii does cover this point might not be too easy to see, and this is a very important point. It does no harm to isolate it for special attention. When we come to Rule 9, we shall see how important the point is.

b.   To a considerable extent, the present rule recommends a literary merit rather than a strictly logical one. It is the basis for your English teacher's objection if you write, for example, "Beauty is when a person likes something." Here the definiens has the form of a dependent clause, or (if we omit the word "when") the form of a statement; but the definiendum has the form of an (abstract) singular, denotative term.

But the rule cannot be completely dismissed as merely recommending a good literary style. Violations of it reflect sloppy, unclear thought. Unless we conform to its demands, we shall be confusing concrete things with abstract things, individuals with classes, objects possessing a quality with the quality they possess. These confusions are difficult to avoid in any case. There is no need to complicate the difficulty by admitting definitions which reflect avoidable confusions of this sort.

c.   It will be noticed that in clause ii no mention was made of the classifications of terms as simple or complex. These are characteristically the *one* form in which definiendum and definiens may differ. More often than not, the definiendum is a simple term and the definiens a complex one. In fact, this will always happen when we seek a conceptual definition (§26.5) of a simple term and use for this purpose an absolute rather than a contextual definition.

## EXERCISE

Which of the following definitions involve violations of Rule 8 and which do not? Explain briefly the source of each violation that you cite.

1.   A turtle  $=$  Df the shell-covered amphibian.
2.   Courageous  $=$  Df the virtue of bravery.

3.  Wisdom = $_{Df}$ when a person knows many things.
4.  $x$ contributed to $y$ = $_{Df}$ a gift of money made by $x$ to $y$.

## §32.5 The Rule of Unambiguous Reference*

**Rule 9: Except when Rule 8 dictates otherwise, every simple denotative general term in the complete definiendum which is repeated in the definiens in accordance with Rule 7 must be modified wherever it occurs in the definiens by "that," "the aforementioned," or some such synonym, so as to produce in its occurrence there a definite description.**

For examples, see the definitions under Rule 7 and also the definitions of "definiendum" and "definiens" in §28.5.

a.  If the application of Rule 7 has been somewhat relaxed, as allowed in clause c under Rule 7, the pronoun appearing in the definiens in place of the general term must be in the grammatical singular rather than in the plural. This is true because the pronoun is really taking the place of the entire definite description. Thus, the illustrative definition of "a person's uncle" in clause c above says, "a brother of one of *his* parents," *not* ". . . of *their* parents."

b.  As suggested in the formulation of this rule, the demand that it makes is occasionally overridden by a demand made by Rule 8. This happens when the simple definiendum is an attributive term and the complete definiendum is a general term modified by this attributive. Example: "a large mouse," in which "large" is the simple definiendum. In the case of this example, Rule 8, clause iii, requires that the definiens read, "a mouse which . . .," whereas Rule 9, if considered alone, would require us to write, "the aforesaid mouse which . . . ." Here the opening phrase of Rule 9 affirms that the demand made by Rule 8 is to take precedence.

c.  The reason for Rule 9 may be explained as follows: In a great many definitions, the *simple* definiendum is a *relative* term (§19.3). In such a case, the rest of the complete definiendum indicates the thing *to* which an object might stand in the relation being defined. This thing may be individually identified by a variable, or only generally classified by a general term: "an uncle of $y$," or "an uncle of a person"; "the hypotenuse of triangle *abc*," or "the hypotenuse of a right triangle"; "an employer of $y$," or "an employer of a person." If a variable is used in the definiendum, Rule 7 will demand the repetition of that variable in the definiens, so that the definiens will refer to *that same individual thing*. But even when a variable is not used, the definiens must refer to *the same individual things* as are only generally indicated in the definiendum.

---

*   This section and the next one may be omitted without disturbing the continuity of the text.

To illustrate, were one to write, "a person's wife = $_{Df}$ any woman to whom a (*not* 'that') person is married," it would follow that every married woman is every person's wife!

d.   Under very unusual circumstances, other exceptions to Rule 9 than the one specifically allowed (by saying that Rule 8 takes precedence) may occur. However, these circumstances are so unusual and rare that Rule 9 is best left standing in its present form. If you ever find (or are tempted to write) a definition that breaks Rule 9, the violation should be specifically justified: *this* occurrence of the same general term in the definiens is, so to speak, accidental, in the sense that no reference to the individual involved in the definiendum is intended; furthermore, the definition is entirely free of ambiguity in this respect.

e.   Definitions which violate Rule 9 will also violate Rule 3 or Rule 4, or both.

## EXERCISE

Which of the following definitions violate Rule 9 and which do not. In each case of a violation of Rule 9, explain the nature of the violation and also show how Rule 3 is likewise violated.

1.   A person's uncle = $_{Df}$ a brother of one of a person's parents.
2.   The hypotenuse of a right triangle = $_{Df}$ the side of a right triangle opposite its right angle.

## §32.6  The Rule for Signs of Quantity

**Rule 10: Every simple denotative general term appearing in the definiens which was not in the complete definiendum, and every variable in the definiens which was not in the complete definiendum, must be accompanied by "a," "some," "every," "five," or some other sign of quantity, or by the definite article, "the," so as to form with it a singular term.**

For examples, see above under Rule 7; also compare: "$x$ is a grandfather of $z$ = $_{Df}$ there is some $y$ such that $x$ is the father of $y$ and $y$ is a parent of $z$.

a.   Violations of this rule will violate Rule 3 or Rule 4, or both. For example, suppose that instead of the illustrative definition of grandfather, just above, we had written: $x$ is a grandfather of $z$ = $_{Df}$ $x$ is the father of $y$ and $y$ is a parent of $z$. Here, the rule is violated, since the variable $y$ appears in the definiens without any accompanying sign of quantity. Now under Rule 3, clause c explains that when a definition contains variables and is sentential, Rule 3 is satisfied if and only if, whatever terms are substituted for the variables, the propositions then indicated by the definiendum and definiens are either both true or both false.

Suppose now that we substitute terms for the variables "*x*," "*y*," and "*z*" in the above definition, as follows:

For "*x*" substitute "Henry Ford,"
For "*y*" substitute "Abraham Lincoln,"
For "*z*" substitute "Benson Ford."

Then the definition becomes:

Henry Ford is a grandfather of Benson Ford = Df Henry Ford is the father of Abraham Lincoln and Abraham Lincoln is a parent of Benson Ford.

Here, the definiendum is true and the definiens false. Hence Rule 3 is violated. This violation of Rule 3 is an automatic consequence of violating Rule 10.

The effect of accompanying variables by quantifying signs as required in this rule is to *remove* the variables so accompanied from the set of variables for which substitutions *may* be made as indicated under Rules 3 and 4. In the above example, not *any* substitution of a term, for example, "Abraham Lincoln" for "*y*" will make definiendum and definiens both true or both false. Quantifying "*y*" with the word "some," as in the definition just following the statement of the rule, makes the definiens *say*, in effect: You must pick your substitution for "*y*" with care, or definiens and definiendum will not be the same with respect to truth and falsity; but there is nevertheless at least one way to pick it that will make them both true or both false. (If the accompanying sign of quantity were "all," or something else than "some," it would carry a *different* meaning but would still remove the variable from the principle of substitution discussed under Rules 3 and 4.)[2]

Similar considerations apply when the item which must be modified by a sign of quantity is a general term rather than a variable.

*EXERCISE*

Which of the following definitions violate Rule 10 and which do not? Explain any violations that you cite. What sign of quantity would you supply to "correct" the definition?

    a.  *x* is the tallest *y* = Df *x* is a *y*, and if *z* is a *y* other than *x*, then *x* is taller than *z*.

    b.  Long division = Df method of finding ratios between numbers.

## §32.7 Concluding Remarks

There are other rules applicable to complete definitions which could be stated here. Indeed, some others (such as that the definiens should, whenever possible, be expressed in affirmative, rather

---

[2] This whole matter will become clearer when we study inference, in Part V.

than in negative, terms) have been formulated in most of the traditional logic books. And still others, of a highly technical nature, are only in recent years coming to be recognized.

But we shall stop at the ten rules already formulated. The traditional rules we have omitted call for so many exceptions in their conscientious application that they seem not to be deserving of retention. And the newer technical rules which we have omitted would increase to too great a degree the technical details of this introductory text.[3] After all, even rules 7, 8, 9, and 10 make the discussion highly technical!

Instead, let us turn our attention to other problems relating to definition.

## REVIEW QUESTIONS FOR UNIT 32

1.  What is meant by calling a definition "circular"? State a rule of definition having to do with circularity.

2.  Discuss briefly the connection between the rule about circular definitions and the advice in §30.3 concerning the definition of abstract singular terms.

3.  Under what circumstances might there occur "apparent" violations of the rule about circularity which should not be treated as actual violations of this rule.

4.  State a rule of definition having to do with the fallacy of word substitution.

5.  Does violation of this rule constitute a fallacy in the case of linguistic definition? In the case of conceptual definition? Explain.

6.  State the rule governing repetition of "parts" of the complete definiendum.

7.  Compare the rule stated in answer to question 6 with the rule against circularity (stated in answer to question 1).

8.  What is meant by a "part" of the complete definiendum, as that word "part" is used in the rule on repetition of parts (stated in answer to question 6)?

9.  Is a moderate relaxation of the rule on repetition of parts ever permissible? If so, under what circumstances?

10. How can the rules against circularity and for repetition of parts be used to discriminate between the simple definiendum and the complete definiendum? Between absolute definition and contextual definition?

---

[3]  For example: No more than one token of any one variable should occur in the definiendum.

11. State and explain the rule of similar structure for definiendum and definiens. Why is this rule important?

If §§32.5 and 32.6 were omitted, omit questions 12 and 13.

12. State the rule for signs of quantity that should occur in the definiens of a definition.

13. State the rule of unambiguous reference.

# *Definitional Chains*

## §33.1 Introduction

Twice in the preceding units we have had occasion to notice circumstances in which a single definition does not give adequate information about the meaning of some term. On both occasions, the definitions in question were, nevertheless, complete definitions.

The first of these occasions appeared in §30.3, in which we were discussing techniques appropriate for the definition of abstract terms: "friendship," "freedom," "triangularity," and so on. It was recommended that these terms be defined, so to speak, in two steps: (1) Define the abstract singular in terms of the attributive term of which it is the second denotative correlate. (For example, "Friendship = $_{Df}$ the relationship obtaining between two people in virtue of which one is a friend of the other.") (2) Define the attributive term (or its first denotative correlate) in a contextual definition. (For example, "*a* is a friend of *b* = $_{Df}$ . . . .")

The second of these occasions appeared in §30.4, where we were considering the definition of definite descriptions. On page 349, it was proposed that if the singularizing prefix serves also as an attributive term, then the definite description may be defined via the use of two definitions: a first one which treats the singularizing prefix as simple definiendum and the entire definite description as complete definiendum, and a second one which has the definiens of the first one as both its simple and its complete definiendum.

But there are also other circumstances in which a definition does not seem to give adequate information concerning the meaning of its definiendum. For example, I am sure that we have all had the experience of looking up some word in the dictionary only to find that the definiens contained another word that we did not understand and that we had to look that up also.

375

These needs for two or more definitions to explain the meaning of a single term arise even when each definition in the group is itself a complete definition. It would have been natural enough to have relied on several definitions of a single term if each had been an incomplete definition. But what we are considering here are groups of complete definitions. Furthermore, only one of the definitions has as its definiendum the term that all in the group help explain: the others have for their definienda terms appearing in the *definientia* of some definitions already given. And yet these others are thought of as contributing to the explanation of the original definiendum.

How this may be is suggested in §31.3 under the discussion of Rule 4 for intensional definitions: An intensional definition must give the essential characteristics of the term being defined. It is pointed out that the definition cannot *enumerate* all the essential characteristics, that is, all the characteristics in the total strict intension of the term being defined. It "gives" them, however, by enumerating the characteristics in a definitive intension of that term. But more light can be thrown on the meaning of the original term if certain other characteristics in its total strict intension are specifically enumerated, not merely "given." This is accomplished by defining one or more of the terms used in the original definiens as signs indicating characteristics in the original definitive intension.

The point to be noticed is that these second and third definitions, even though they do not contain the term which was the definiendum of that first definition, nevertheless contribute to the explanation of that definiendum. They form, together with the first definition, a *definitional chain* for the original definiendum.

## §33.2  A Definition of "Definitional Chain"

The expression "definitional chain" appearing at the end of the last section may be slightly misleading. Perhaps "definitional tree," or some other phrase that suggested the "branching" character of the chain, would have been preferable. However, "definitional chain" is the expression regularly employed in books about logic, and we shall accordingly use it also. But let us see what is intended. And for this purpose, a diagram may help.

Suppose a term, $A$, is defined, and suppose that its definiens contains two terms: $B_1$ and $B_2$. We may diagram this definition in standard form as follows:

(1) $$A =_{Df} B_1, B_2.$$

The diagram does not suggest *how* $B_1$ and $B_2$ were used in the definition. They may, for example, have been contained in a conditional definition (§29.3):

$$x \text{ is } A =_{Df} \text{if } x \text{ is } B_1, \text{ then } x \text{ is } B_2.$$

Or they may have been contained in an enumerative definition or a classificatory definition (§29.5):

$$\text{An } A =_{Df} \text{anything which is either } B_1 \text{ or } B_2.$$
$$\text{An } A =_{Df} \text{any } B_1 \text{ which is also } B_2.$$

And there are still other conceivable ways of involving $B_1$ and $B_2$ in the definiens, for example:

$$\text{An } A =_{Df} \text{any } B_1 \text{ provided it is not } B_2.$$

All that the diagram records is the identity of the simple definiendum, $A$, and the identity of the terms appearing in the definiens, $B_1$ and $B_2$.

Now the fact we are presently concerned with is this, that the terms $B_1$ and $B_2$ may themselves have been or be defined:

(2) $$B_1 =_{Df} C_1, C_2.$$
(3) $$B_2 =_{Df} D_1, D_2.$$

And the terms appearing in the definientia of these definitions may some or all of them be defined.

(4) $$C_1 =_{Df} E_1, E_2.$$
(5) $$D_2 =_{Df} E_2, F.$$

And so on.

For reasons which will be made clear in a moment, let us add one more diagrammatic definition to the set of five already given. This will be a *second* definition of $B_1$:[1]

(6) $$B_1 =_{Df} E_1, E_3, E_4.$$

But now for a definition of definitional chains.

By a **definitional chain** for a given term is meant any series (that is,

---

[1] It is quite possible to have two or more true complete definitions for one and the same term: one could be intensional and one extensional, both extensional, or both intensional. In the latter case, they would present two different definitive intensions for that term.

arranged set[2]) of complete definitions, the first of which is a definition of the term in question, and each later member of which is a definition of some term appearing in the definiens of a definition standing earlier in the series, and no two of which are definitions of the same term.

One or two words of further explanation and a few illustrative applications of this definition should suffice to make its meaning quite clear.

*First*, the definition explains that a definitional chain is a series of definitions, and the attached footnote explains what is meant by a series, or arranged set. In the case of a series (of the sort here under consideration) one can always find which member of the set is *first* in the series, which is *next*, which is *next after that*, and so on.

The term "series," however, is used in everyday conversation in such a way as to imply that a series must have at least two members. If it had exactly two members, the member next after its first would be its last. But in technical discussions one often uses the word-type "series" for a term that differs slightly from the everyday term, in this respect: that a thing or set may have only one member but may still be a series. In such a series, the first member would also be the last.

We shall find it useful to think of series in this more technical sense. Hence, any definition standing by itself *is* a definitional chain, for the term which is its simple definiendum. For example, diagrammatic definition (1), all by itself, is a definitional chain for $A$; definition (2) is a definitional chain for $B_1$, definition 6 is *another* definitional chain for $B_1$, and so on.

*Second*, the definitional chains in which we are most often interested

---

2　A series differs from a set, or group, of things in that the members of a series are arranged in an order, so that you can speak of earlier and later members of the series, sometimes of the first member, the next member after a given one, etc. Any one set of things may be arranged in many different ways, each distinct arrangement constituting a distinct series. For example, the householders living on a certain street form a set that may be "arranged" into any of many different series: (a) according to their ages, from youngest to oldest; (b) according to the alphabetical arrangements of their names, as in the telephone directory; (c) according to the numbers assigned to their houses, as in a city directory; etc.

A definition of a series must not only explain what is in the series, but how these things are arranged. The definition of "definitional chain" does just that, except that it does not *completely* settle the arrangement: *any* arrangement that conforms to the requirements of arrangement stated will be a definitional chain. See the illustrations in the text that are given following the definition.

are, nevertheless, chains with more than one member, and furthermore, chains all of whose members come from some given set of definitions.

*Third,* suppose now that we are interested in definitional chains for $A$ such that all the definitions in the chains come from the set of six definitions given above. Surprisingly enough, that set of six definitions suffices to provide twenty-five different definitional chains for $A$! Let us see how this may be. (At this point, the reader will find it helpful to copy the six definitions onto a sheet of paper so that he may refer to them easily as he reads on without having continually to turn back to the pages on which they are printed.)

i.   As noted above, definition (1) is, all by itself, a definitional chain for $A$.

ii.   A further examination of the definition of definitional chains shows that *every* definitional chain for $A$ (drawn from our set of six definitions) must start with definition (1). Furthermore, its *next* definition, if there is to be more than the one definition in the chain, must be a definition of a term already appearing in the definiens of (1), that is, a definition of $B_1$ or of $B_2$. But there is no further requirement. Hence, we may choose whichever of these we wish, and thus get three chains with two members for term $A$:

(a)                              (1), (2).
(b)                              (1), (3).
(c)                              (1), (6).

iii.   A still further examination of the definition of definitional chains reveals that in a fashion similar to the point already made, every chain having three (or four, or five, and so on) members is simply a chain of two (or three, or four, and so on) members with one more definition added to the end. Thus, to get, from our set of six definitions three-membered definitional chains for $A$, we must take one (*any* one) of the two-membered chains already constructed and add one definition to it. Each two-membered chain that we take, and each definition we add to it, gives us a distinct three-membered chain.

There are, however, certain restrictions as to what definition we may add to a given chain. These restrictions are imposed by the definition of a definitional chain:

(i).   The added definition must not be another definition of a term already defined. Thus, if definition (2) is already in the chain, definition (6) must not be added to the chain; and if (6) is in the chain, definition (2) must not be added.

(ii).   The added definition must be a definition of some term already used in a preceding definiens. Thus, if we are adding a definition to one of the two-membered chains, (a) or (b) or (c), above, we must not add definition (5) to chain

$$(1), (2),$$

although we may add it to chain

$$(1), (3);$$

and we must not add (4) to chain

$$(1), (3),$$

although we may add it to chain

$$(1), (2).$$

Hence we get the following three-membered chains:

(d)                    (1), (2), (3).
(e)                    (1), (2), (4).
(f)                    (1), (3), (2).
(g)                    (1), (3), (5).
(h)                    (1), (6), (3).

iv.   So far, we have found and listed nine chains for $A$. Reasoning similar to that in iii, above, shows how the three-membered chains listed there may be added to so as to produce four-membered chains, and how those in turn may some of them be added to so as to produce five-membered chains. But our original set of six definitions will not produce any chains for $A$ that have more than five members.

## EXERCISES

1.  Why cannot the original set of six definitions be arranged into a six-membered definitional chain for $A$?
2.  On the basis of the three-membered chains for $A$, (d) to (h), given above, construct out of the original set of six definitions all the possible four-membered chains for $A$.
3.  Which, if any, four-membered chains for $A$ constructed in answer to question 2, cannot be expanded into five-membered chains?
4.  Out of the six definitions given above, construct a two-membered chain for $B_1$.

## §33.3 Equivalent and Covered Definitional Chains

The preceding discussion of definitional chains must have suggested that any two chains for one and the same term must be related to each other in exactly one of the three following ways:

1. Every definition in either chain is a definition in the other chain.

2. Every definition in one of the chains is a definition in the other chain, but not vice-versa.

3. Each chain contains at least one definition which is not in the other chain.

These possibilities for relationship are conveniently referred to by using attributive terms that may be defined as follows:

Two definitional chains for one and the same term are said to be **equivalent** (that is, each of the two chains is equivalent to the other) if every definition in either chain is a definition in the other chain.

One definitional chain for a given term is said to be **covered by** another definitional chain for that term if every definition in the one chain is a definition in the other, but not vice-versa.

Then the three ways described above in which two chains for one and the same term might be related could be stated as follows.

a. The two chains are equivalent.

b. One of the two chains is covered by the other.

c. The two chains are not equivalent and neither is covered by the other.

When two definitional chains are equivalent, each of them really conveys exactly the same information as the other. The only difference is in the *order* in which the bits of information are reported. When one chain is covered by another, the covered chain reports nothing not reported by the covering chain, but on the other hand, the covering chain gives additional information not given by the covered chain. Finally, when two chains are not equivalent and neither is covered by the other, then each chain reports some information not reported by the other.

## EXERCISES

1. Consider the eight definitional chains for $A$, (a) to (h), listed in the preceding section and answer the following questions concerning them.

   a. Which pairs of these chains are equivalent?

  b.   Which pairs of them are such that one covers the other?

  c.   Which pairs are such that they are not equivalent and neither covers the other?

2.   Suppose that you had three definitional chains, $X$, $Y$, and $Z$, for one and the same term. Answer the following questions.

  a.   Suppose that $X$ was equivalent to $Y$. Would $Y$ be equivalent to $X$? Explain.

  b.   Suppose that $X$ was equivalent to $Y$ and that $Y$ was equivalent to $Z$. Would $X$ be equivalent to $Z$? Explain.

  c.   Suppose that $X$ was equivalent to $Y$ and $Y$ was covered by $Z$. Would $X$ be covered by $Z$? Explain.

  d.   Suppose that $X$ was covered by $Y$ and $Y$ was covered by $Z$. Would $X$ be covered by $Z$? Explain.

  e.   Suppose that $Y$ was covered by $Z$. Would $Y$ be equivalent to $Z$? Explain.

  f.   Suppose that $X$ was covered by $Y$. Would $Y$ be covered by $X$? Explain.

A set of equivalent definitional chains are so many different pictures of one and the same explanation of their first definiendum. Since it is really this explanation that is of value, there is no need to collect more and more equivalent chains. We can attend to any one of the equivalent chains and let it represent all the chains equivalent to itself.

The twenty-five chains for term $A$, constructible out of the six definitions given above, may be divided into twelve *sets* of chains such that all the chains in one set are equivalent to each other and all the chains equivalent to each other are in one set. Representing each set by a chain belonging to the set, we may display these sets as follows.

(1)
(1), (2)
(1), (3)
(1), (6)
(1), (2), (3)
(1), (2), (4)
(1), (3), (5)
(1), (3), (6)
(1), (2), (3), (4)
(1), (2), (3), (5)
(1), (3), (5), (6)
(1), (2), (3), (4), (5)

## §33.4 Circular Definitional Chains

If a term in the definiens of some definition belonging to a definitional chain is also the simple definiendum of a definition appearing earlier in that same chain, then that definitional chain is said to be circular.

For example, suppose that to the set of six diagrammatic definitions given in §33.2, we add a seventh,

(7)                    $E_1 =_{\text{Df}} F, A.$

Now consider the following definitional chain for $A$:

Chain I                    (1), (2), (3), (4), (5), (7).

This chain is circular, since its last definition contains in its definiens a term, $A$, that is also the simple definiendum of an earlier definition.

In the example just given, the chain contains, so to speak, one "big" circle. Chains may be circular by containing instead certain "little" circles. For example, add still another definition,

(8)                    $F =_{\text{Df}} B_1, G,$

and the following chain will be circular.

Chain II                    (1), (2), (3), (4), (5), (8).

It is often maintained that circularity is as scrupulously to be avoided in the construction of definitional chains as it is in the construction of individual definitions. (See Rule 5 in §32.2.) In many circumstances, it is true that the construction of circular chains would defeat the purposes of the definer. But there are other, legitimate, circumstances in which the construction of circular chains is unavoidable.

Consider, for example, the task of a dictionary maker. Ideally, his objective is to define every word in the language.[3] If every word is defined, the words in the definientia will all be defined. But the arrangement of these definitions into chains will show that the chains must eventually be circular. Thus the dictionary maker's goal—the definition of every word—is attainable only by the admission of circular chains.[4]

---

[3]  This ideal is, of course, impossible of attainment, and the dictionary maker generally sets for himself a more practical, limited, goal. But even then, the words he uses in his definientia should be defined in his dictionary. Hence, the circular chains noticed above are bound to occur.

[4]  Strictly speaking, the dictionary maker does not produce chains, but only sets of definitions. That is, he does not arrange these sets of definitions into chains.

On the other hand, the reader who is carried from one definition to another by looking up the definitions of terms used in the definientia of previously read defi-

The circularity of chains in the dictionary can, then, not be avoided; but at the same time it need not be a serious handicap to the reader; provided the circles are not too small. Readers will generally "get on" one of these circles at one point—different for different readers—and "get off" at another point. So long as that part of the chain over which the reader "traveled" was not circular, no harm has been done. So to speak, the "received" chain was not circular. If the "received" chain is not circular, then it can be genuinely illuminating.

However, when definitions occur as part of a systematic treatment of a subject matter, where the subject matter treated includes the objects in the extensions of the terms defined—for example, when definitions appear in a book on physics, geometry, chemistry, biology, logic, and so on—then the order of presentation of these definitions should not be such as to constitute circular chains.[5] It is presumed that the book will be read in its entirety, from front to back. If the order of presentation constitutes circular chains, then the reader receives circular chains, and to that extent the subject matter is not illuminated.

Thus every systematic treatment of a subject involves the use of words, or terms, which are not defined. These undefined terms make possible the construction of noncircular definitional chains for the other technical terms appearing in the treatise.

Actually, this avoidance of circular chains in a systematic treatment of some subject is usually achieved by the author partly through his decision to report some statements as definitions and to report others as not being definitions. For example, in §24.3 we noticed that a single term might have two or more definitive intensions. An author might wish to report several of these. But if he did, he would list only one of these reports as a definition of the term. The other reports would be listed as theorems or axioms or laws, whatever the case might be.

But are not these "undefined" terms explained? And are not explanations definitions? (Cf. §25.1) To be sure, most of them are. But most

---

nitions is arranging the dictionary maker's set of definitions into a definitional chain. If the reader persists long enough, he is bound to have arranged a set of those definitions into a circular chain.

5   Actually, the order used to define a chain in §33.2, above, is the *reverse* of the order of presentation in a well-constructed treatise: Every noncircular chain uses some terms in its definientia which are not defined in that chain. In a well-constructed treatise, if terms are going to be defined they are not used until they have been defined. Hence, the undefined terms precede the defined terms. But in the definition of a definitional chain in §33.2, what words are left undefined is discovered only after having read through to the end of the chain.

of the explanations are given either in extensional definitions or in incomplete definitions. Incomplete definitions do not appear in chains. And extensional definitions may be listed as statements of fact rather than as definitions, and by this means excluded from the chains.

## REVIEW QUESTIONS FOR UNIT 33

1. How is it possible that a definition should be complete (give the essence of its definiendum, as Rule 4 says) and there yet be a place for further illumination, such as would be given by a second definition?
2. Explain briefly the difference between a series and a class.
3. What is meant by a definitional chain for a given term?
4. May a single definition be regarded as a definitional chain? Explain.
5. May a definitional chain contain two definitions of the same term?
6. When are two definitional chains said to be equivalent?
7. When is one definitional chain said to be covered by another?
8. What is the importance of noting that one chain is equivalent to another, or that one is covered by another?
9. Under what circumstances would a definitional chain be said to be circular?
10. Is the construction of circular chains *always* to be avoided? *Ever* to be avoided? Explain.

# UNIT 34

## Miscellaneous Topics Relating to Definition

### §34.1 The Definition of Expressions That Are Not Terms

In discussing definition, we must not overlook the fact that not all words or expressions may be counted as terms. In Unit 17 we considered the problem of identifying the terms involved in a given statement. Throughout that discussion, we found that words or phrases indicating quantity—"some," "all," "every," "ten," "a few," "75 percent of the," and so on—are not to be considered either as attributive terms or (except in certain cases) as parts of terms formed by them and the noun phrases that they modify. Yet these words or expressions do mean something and any explanation of their meaning would amount to a definition of them. How may they best be defined?

To begin, we must notice that when it is said they mean something, this assertion cannot be treated as a claim that they purport to refer to something, or to apply to something. So to treat the assertion would be to claim that these expressions were terms, because a term is precisely any expression that purports so to refer or apply. (See the definition of "a term" in §17.2.) What must be intended is that these words affect or alter in identifiable ways the identity of the *propositions* indicated by the *sentences* in which the words occur. For example, there is a vast difference in meaning between, "Every man is a mouse," and "No man is a mouse," yet the only difference in the *sentence* lies in the choice of quantifier "every" or "no."

To sum up, we may say that to claim that these quantifiers *have* a meaning merely claims that their presence in sentences *affects* the meanings of the sentences in explicable ways.

The last remarks, above, suggest that the clearest explanation of the meanings of quantifiers will be provided in contextual definitions—more specifically, in contextual definitions of such a kind that the complete definiendum has the form of a statement.

386

This context should not characterize the rest of the sentence any more narrowly than is necessary to show the effect of the quantifying word. It must, however, indicate (without further specifying) what word or expression is modified by the quantifier. Let us see how all this might be done, illustrating the point with a definition of the quantifier "no."

The only terms to which quantifiers may be attached are general denotative terms. Propositions involving these general denotative terms were analyzed above (§16.5) as general propositions. In the presentations of those propositions, the capital letters "$S$," "$S_1$," and "$S_2$" were used to represent the general denotative terms that could be modified by quantifiers.

We may borrow the symbolism of that earlier section to write in standard form contextual definitions of the quantifier "no." Notice that in the complete definienda of these definitions, "no" and other quantifiers replace the quantifier-signs "$x$" and "$y$" used in §16.5.

1.   No $S$ is $P$ = $_{Df}$ For every individual, $s$, if $s$ is an $S$, then $s$ is not $P$.

For example, "No house is made of gold" means the same thing as, "For every individual thing, $s$, if $s$ is a house, then $s$ is not made of gold."

2.   $s_1$ is $P$ (to) no $S$ = $_{Df}$ For every individual, $s$, if $s$ is an $S$, then $s_1$ is not $P$ (to) $s$.

For example, "John is acquainted with no senior," means the same thing as, "For every individual, $s$, if $s$ is a senior, then John is not acquainted with $s$."

We could continue with still other definitions, each explaining the meaning of "no" in still another context. But for reasons which it would not be profitable to enlarge on here, other explanations of other quantifiers will suffice to get practically every occurrence of "no" into one of the above contexts. Hence, an extended set of further contextual definitions of "no" would seem to be unnecessary.[1]

The problem of defining (explaining) in the manner illustrated above, the quantifiers and other widely used expressions, such as "is", "if",

---

[1] The *only* other *necessary* contextual definition of "no" appears to be:

3.   For no individual, $s$, is it true that . . . = $_{Df}$ For every individual, $s$, it is false that . . .

But in this definition, the forms considered are so remote from those discussed in Unit 16 that we shall not further examine it here.

"not", etc., is the business of logic. To the extent that you undertake to explain such expressions, you are in fact becoming a logician. It should be noticed that in defining one quantifier, "no", we made use of another, "every." All quantifiers could be defined, but always the definition of one will involve the use of another. Hence, if they *were* all defined and these definitions were gathered into a definitional chain, that chain would be circular.

## EXERCISE

On the basis of definitions 1 and 2, above, write for each of the following a statement that has the same meaning but does not contain the word "no."

1. No neckties are made of wood.
2. George owns no automobile.
3. James gave no money to the Red Cross.
4. No potatoes are for sale in the market.
5. Willard gave no thought to the consequences of his act.

[#5 requires more drastic rearrangement than a simple application of the definitions might suggest.]

### §34.2 The Uses of Definition

In Units 25 and 27 we were engaged in an extensive study of the purposes of definition. That study resulted in a classification of definitions under five bases: extensional, intensional; nominal, real; and so on. The purposes identified in those ten classes are the *immediate* purposes of definition, those purposes in terms of which the meaning of the produced sign-tokens may be identified.

After definitions have once been made, the statements which are the definitions thus produced can be appealed to as instruments to serve still other purposes, the appeals and purposes being either those of the author or those of the receiver. Indeed, the serving of these other purposes might well have been in the author's mind even when or before he first framed the definition. In that case, they would have been among the remote purposes of the original defining activity.

However that may be, other occasions for appealing to the definition, once it is available, will readily occur to both author and receiver. In this section, we shall list and briefly consider the major kinds of ulterior use to which definitions may be put. What we shall say here applies generally to complete definitions, and only occasionally to incomplete ones. Also, we are assuming the definitions to be true, which is, after all, the assumption of a person who uses the definition.

**1. Abbreviation.** Almost invariably, a definiendum is a more compact, shorter expression than its definiens. Thus statements and discussions that contain the definiendum are shorter and simpler than otherwise similar ones that contain the definiens. Yet the two sets of statements would have the same meaning (intensional or extensional according as the definition is intensional or extensional). Hence, introducing the shorter term (in a nominal definition) or noting the identity of meaning (in a real definition) enables one to abbreviate his discourse by establishing the availability of the shorter terms as substitutes for the longer ones. For example, the mathematician's definition of powers enables us to replace long expressions, like "a × a × a × a" or "10,000,000," by short ones, like "$a^4$" or "$10^7$."

Scientific discourse makes a great deal of abbreviative use of definitions. For example, this book has been much shorter than it otherwise would have been because we had short terms like "sign-token," "sign-type," "intensional definition," and so on, available for use in place of longer expressions with the same meanings. But we could not have used these terms in successful communication unless we had previously explained their meanings, that is, defined them.

**2. Elaboration.** In an opposite sense, we may often use a defined term and then replace it by its definiens. This act of replacement serves to direct attention to detailed items involved in the meaning of the defined term. The replacement of the one term by the other does not change the meaning of the statement in which the replacement occurs. But it does call the reader's attention to *components* in the meaning that he might otherwise momentarily overlook.

**3. Evidence.** Extensional definitions may be used as factual premises from which we can infer other matters of fact.

**4. Validation.** Intensional definitions may be appealed to as statements of the principles in accordance with which we infer certain facts from certain other facts. This use of definitions is illustrated in the geometry book, where the proofs of theorems from postulates are shown to be valid (legitimate) by citing various already stated definitions.

All the above uses of definition, but in particular the last two, will be discussed further in connection with *inference*, which is the topic of the next and final part of this book.

## §34.3 Incomplete Definitions

In §25.3 we distinguished complete and incomplete definition as two different purposes of definition. We must now say a little more about this distinction, and then give a little attention to possible techniques for incomplete definition.

You will recall that complete definition was described as an effort completely to explain the meaning of the definiendum, while incomplete definition is an effort partially to explain this meaning. Now from one point of view, it would have to be admitted that every definition would be incomplete. Nobody tries to call attention to every one individually of the infinity of characteristics making up the total strict intension, or pure meaning, of the definiendum. Nor does anyone try to point out for each individual object whether or not it is in the extension, or impure meaning, and just when and where it existed. That point of view, then, which would make all definitions incomplete, cannot be a worth-while point of view from which to think of this classification.

There are also other things that a person might do or omit to do in making a definition and which it would be worth while to disregard:

1. Disregard the psychological question, whether he tried to make the meaning perfectly clear *to the receiver.* If he gave up trying before the receiver understood, that does not make his definition incomplete. The fault might quite possibly lie with the receiver. Perhaps the definition was complete but the receiver not sufficiently acquainted with the entire field to permit him to understand the definiens, and hence to understand the definiendum. In fact, it has even been suggested in an earlier unit that an incomplete definition may sometimes be psychologically clearer than a complete one: for example, it may not confuse the receiver's thought by forcing him to attend to complicated characteristics in a definitive intension which he will not understand.

2. Disregard the question whether or not the definer accompanied his definitional core with a definitional chain, thus defining certain terms in the original definiens. From a practical point of view, perhaps he should have done so, and his receivers are not fully enlightened unless he does. But this is really a variation on the psychological issue. Assume the improbable, that the receiver completely and thoroughly understands the definiens, and *then* ask whether giving that definiens provided a complete definition of the definiendum.

3. Disregard whether or not the definer accompanied his definitional core with such remarks as make clear which tokens of the sign-type of the definiendum he is explaining. Of course he ought to do this, and we can call his definition imperfect unless he does so. But his failure to do so only makes it difficult or impossible to know whether or not some token of the sign-type in question is a token or occurrence of the term he defined; it does not affect the adequacy or thoroughness with which he explained what the meaning of that term is.

4. Disregard the question whether he gives only an extensional, or only an intensional, definition and not also the other. Perhaps it would be well to give both. But we may think of those as two definitions, two acts of definition, and we may ask about each whether or not it is, in itself, a complete definition.

What, then, is there left that we should *not* disregard, when we try to distinguish complete from incomplete definitions? Actually there are just two things, and in the case of intensional definitions, a third thing. A definer who does not try to make all these things logically clear (that is, understandable by that ideal receiver mentioned in paragraph 2, above) is engaged in incomplete definition, while a definer who is trying to make all of them fully clear is engaged in complete definition. (Of course, he may fail in his attempt and give an unsatisfactory complete definition.) Let us see what these things are.

a. Does he undertake to indicate whether the mode of purported reference is general or singular? In §23.3 we noted that there is another factor in the meaning of a term in addition to the necessary members of its total contingent intension. This other factor has to do with whether the term purports to refer to *any* (general term) object of a certain kind, or purports to refer to *precisely one* (singular term) object. If the definer does not try to clear up this point, he is engaged in incomplete definition. But if he does try to clear up this point, then (provided he also tries completely to clear up point b, below) he is engaged in complete definition. The importance of this point for complete definition is suggested by Rule 7 for complete definition, on the repetition of "parts" (§32.3).

b. Does he undertake to provide a definiens such that the ideal receiver (who thoroughly understands the definiens) by discovering the extension of the definiens, and having been enlightened on point a, will thereby be able to discover precisely the extension of the defini-

_endum_? If not, then he is attempting an incomplete definition. If so, then (provided he also satisfies requirement a, above) he is attempting a complete definition. This is the reason for Rule 3, in §31.3.

c. Persons who are engaged in intensional definition are trying to do one more thing as well: to cite in the definiens nothing but necessary characteristics of the total contingent intension of the definiendum. If the effort is toward complete intensional definition it also is the case that the definer is trying to cite such necessary characteristics that all the other necessary characteristics are inferable. This is the reason for Rule 4, in §31.3.

We have seen (§30.1) that although a person may undertake it, thence be engaged in it, he can never achieve a satisfactory complete intensional definition of a proper name or of an incomplete definite description. The lack of total strict (and therefore of definitive) intensions for these terms makes the achievement of goal b above incompatible with the attainment of goal c. One or the other may be achieved, but not both.

The upshot of what has been said so far in this section is that the difference between complete and incomplete definition depends on what the definer is attempting in the core of his act of definition. All the other statements which he makes or leaves unmade may affect the final value or usefulness of his act of definition, but they will not affect its completeness or incompleteness.

## §34.4 A Second Meaning of Complete and Incomplete Definition

Any definer, like anyone else, might succeed or fail to accomplish what he is undertaking. For example, a definer would have failed if his attempt or purpose was complete definition and yet the definiens that he offered only partially explained the meaning of the definiendum. That definitional core would have been satisfactory if his effort had been incomplete definition. Or again he might fail even when his aim is limited to incomplete definition: when his definitional core is completely "off the beam." For example, a person who said,

A bird = _Df_ a certain kind of underwater animal,

would not have given a satisfactory incomplete definition.

Hence we are led to a secondary meaning of complete and incomplete definitions. Instead of using these terms to classify acts of definition, let us now use them to classify definitional cores, statements: A **complete definition** (definitional core) correctly and entirely explains (to that ideal receiver) the meaning (extensional or intensional) of its definiendum. An **incomplete definition** (definitional core) correctly, but only partially or approximately, explains (to that ideal receiver) the meaning (extensional or intensional) of its definiendum. The same three considerations, a, b, and c, are to be kept in mind, but the question now is not what the definer is trying to do, but what his definitional core actually accomplishes.

Throughout the rest of this unit and the next, we shall be concerned with complete and incomplete definitions in this secondary sense.

## §34.5 Incomplete Contextual Definitions*

Throughout the preceding units we have conceived of the definitional core as consisting of a single statement, which could be put in the standard form

$$X = \text{Df } Y.$$

This form is particularly appropriate for complete definitions. But we must now note that a single statement of this form could be a complete definition of its *complete* definiendum and yet at the same time be only an incomplete definition of its *simple* definiendum. (On complete and simple definienda, see §28.5, definitions c and d.) This can happen in contextual definition. The context may be much narrower than the whole range of contexts in which the simple definiendum[2] may occur.

An example of this situation occurs in §34.1. There we gave *two* definitions in standard form, each for the simple definiendum "no." Each defined it in a different context than did the other. Each was a complete definition of its complete definiendum but an incomplete definition of its simple definiendum.

When may a single contextual definition in standard form be regarded as a complete definition of its simple definiendum? Two things must be true:

1. It must be a complete definition of its complete definiendum.

2. Any other contexts in which its simple definiendum might appear must be capable of being put into the standard form of the context appearing in the contextual definition. For example, if the definiendum has the form "$x \times (y + 1)$" (where the simple definiens is "$\times$"), then other contexts might still be put into this standard form:

| Other Contexts | In standard form |
|---|---|
| $x \times 3$ | $x \times (2 + 1)$ |
| $x \times (24 + 5)$ | $x \times [(24 + 4) + 1]$ |
| $x \times z$ | $x \times [(z - 1) + 1]$ |

---

* This section may be omitted without disturbing the continuity of the text.
[2] By the simple definiendum, we do *not* mean merely the sign-type, which may have several conventions associated with it, but the *term*, or other expression like "no" so long as it is used to convey one and the same meaning.

On the other hand, even when a *single* definitional statement in standard form happens to be an incomplete definition of its simple definiendum, it may well be true that a *group* of two or more such statements will provide a complete definition of their common simple definiendum. When would this happen?

a.   Each statement in the group must be a complete definition of its complete definiendum.

b.   Any other contexts in which the simple definiendum might appear must be capable of being put into the standard form of at least one of the contexts for the simple definiendum provided by the group of contextual definitions.

Certain special circumstances in which such groups of individually incomplete definitions can form collectively what practically amounts to a complete definition will be considered in the next unit.

## REVIEW QUESTIONS FOR UNIT 34

1.   In what sense can it be said that an expression which is not a term (because it does not purport to refer) has a meaning?

2.   What technique is recommended for the definition of expressions that are not terms?

3.   Name and briefly describe each of four kinds of use which may be made of definitions.

4.   In deciding whether a given act of definition should be classified as complete or incomplete definition, should you take into account whether or not the definer:

   a.   Accompanied his statement of the definitional core with a definitional chain?

   b.   Tried to indicate whether the definiendum was a singular or a general term?

   c.   Tried to make the meaning perfectly clear *to the receiver?*

   d.   Tried to provide a definiens with exactly the same extension as the definiendum?

   e.   Tried to make sure that he had explained which tokens of the sign-type of the definiendum are tokens (or occurrences) of the term being defined?

   f.   Tried to make sure that all necessary characteristics in the total contingent intension of the definiendum are inferable from the definiens?

   g.   Tried to give only an extensional (or only an intensional) definition rather than trying to give both?

In each case, briefly explain why you answer as you do.

5. Briefly explain secondary meanings for "complete" and "incomplete" definition, and contrast these secondary meanings with the primary meanings hitherto considered.

   (If §34.5 was omitted, then omit questions 6, 7 and 8.)

6. How might a contextual definition in standard form be a complete definition of its complete definiendum and only an incomplete definition of its simple definiendum?

7. What two requirements must be met by a contextual definition in standard form if it is to be a complete definition of its simple definiendum?

8. What two requirements must be met by a group of incomplete contextual definitions of the same simple definiendum if the group as a whole is to be a complete definition of that simple definiendum?

**35**

# *Recursive and Implicit Definitions**

---

## §35.1 Recursive Definitions

In §34.5 we were considering incomplete contextual definitions, and we noticed that under certain conditions a group of such definitional statements might collectively form a complete definition of their common simple definiendum:

1. Each statement in the group is a complete definition of its complete definiendum.

2. Any other contexts in which the simple definiendum might appear can be put into the standard form of at least one of the contexts for the simple definiendum provided by the group of contextual definitions.

In this unit we shall consider a very important type of situation in which a pair of separately incomplete contextual definitions can be constructed in such a manner that they have, when considered together, most of the important characteristics of a complete definition of their simple definiendum.[1] Pairs of statements of the sort we are going to consider are called "recursive definitions."

However, before we can understand just what a recursive definition is, we must understand what a series is.

## §35.2 The General Nature of Series

In §33.2, in connection with definitional chains, we came across the idea of a series. A series is nothing more than a set or class of objects arranged in a definite order, in accordance with some principle.

One set of things can be arranged in many different orders or series by using different principles as the basis for the arrangement. For example, a set of sample screws (no two alike in length or weight) could be arranged in a hardware display either in accordance with their lengths, from shortest to longest,

---

* This unit may be omitted without disturbing the continuity of the text.
[1] That they do not actually constitute a complete definition will be explained in §35.5.

or in accordance with their weights, from lightest to heaviest, or in any number of other ways in which no two were alike.

Different ordering principles would very likely arrange the screws in different orders. For example, screw *A* might be shorter but also heavier than screw *B*. Hence if the screws were arranged in order of length, screw *A* would come before screw *B*, but if they were arranged in order of weight, screw B would come before *A*.

Now many series are similar to one another in certain important respects, but then still other series will be different from any of those former ones in just these same respects. For example, if you arrange a *finite* set of objects (say, the screws in that hardware display) into a series, that series will always have a first member (for example, the shortest screw) and also every member except that first one will come next after a certain other member. Finally, the set will have a last member.

On the other hand, if the set of things that you are arranging is *infinitely* large, then one, or two, or even all three of those characteristics of finite series will not hold of that infinite series. For example, the set of positive whole numbers, together with the number zero, will, when arranged in order of size, form a series that has a first member (zero) and every member comes next after a certain member (1 next after 0, 2 next after 1, and so on), but there is no last member. If you arranged all the negative whole numbers and zero according to size, there would be a last member (0) but no first member, and yet every member would come next after a certain other member. If you arranged all the whole numbers, positive and negative according to size, there would be no first member and no last member, but every member would come next after a certain other member. While if you arranged all proper fractions according to size, there would be no first member and no last member (no fraction is the smallest and none the largest), and furthermore no member would come next after any other.[2]

Now series that have a first member, and every member except the first coming next after another member, are a very important kind of series. Series having these two characteristics are called **discrete series with first members.**

---

[2] Let $\frac{1}{x}$ be any proper fraction, as small as you please. Then $\frac{1}{x+1}$ will be smaller. Let $\frac{x}{x+1}$ be any proper fraction, as large as you please. Then $\frac{x+1}{x+2}$ will be larger. Finally, let $\frac{a}{b}$ be any proper fraction and $\frac{c}{d}$ any other fraction which is larger than $\frac{a}{b}$. Then $\frac{c}{d}$ is not next larger than $\frac{a}{b}$, because $\frac{(b \times c) + (a \times d)}{2(b \times d)}$ will be a proper fraction larger than $\frac{a}{b}$ but smaller than $\frac{c}{d}$.

If a series of this type is also finite, it is called a **finite discrete series.** If such series is infinite, it is called a **progression.**

Discrete series with first members are important because nearly every s of things can be arranged into such a series.[3] For example, a definitional chai is a series of this sort. It is in connection with discrete series with first membe that recursive definitions occur.

### §35.3 Fundamental Ideas Connected With Discrete Series Having Fir Members

Suppose we have arranged a set of objects into a discrete serie with a first member. We need now some symbols by means of which we ca refer to those objects by reference to their position in the series.

Let us use $i$ to represent the first member of the series. Thus, for example if the objects we have arranged are those sample screws, arranged accordin to length, then $i$ will be the shortest screw; but if what we have arrange are the positive whole numbers and 0, according to size, then $i$ will be th number 0.

Let us use $x$ and $y$ to represent any members of the series. And finally let us use n$x$, n$y$, and so on to represent the member of the series which come next after $x$, next after $y$, and so on. For example, n$i$ would represent th member next after the first member. If it were the series of screws, n$i$ woul be next to the shortest; if it were the series of numbers,

$$n i = n 0 = 1.$$
$$n 4 = 5.$$
$$\text{Etc.}$$

Since the series we are considering is a discrete series with a first membe we may be sure that if $x$ is any member of the series whatsoever, then eithe

$$x = i$$

or there is exactly one member of the series, $y$, such that

$$x = n y.$$

### §35.4 The General Pattern of Recursive Definitions

Suppose now that we wished to define some characteristic belonging to the members of our series but differing among them in accord ance with their position in the series. For example, suppose that we wishec to define the length of a screw. We could do this as follows.

(a)   The length of $i$ = $_{Df}$ ¼ inch
(b)   The length of n$x$ = $_{Df}$ the length of $x$ + ⅛ inch.

This pair of definitional statements constitutes a recursive definition for th

[3]   The only sets of things that cannot be so arranged are sets that can be arranged into "continuous" series, such as the points on a line.

ngth of a screw in the arranged sample. Needless to say, in this example e have an extensional definition: we must have measured the first screw determine that it was ¼ inch long and the others to discover that they creased in length at a rate of ⅛ inch per screw. Some recursive definitions e extensional and some are intensional.

By using the illustration just given, let us see what are the important atures in a recursive definition.

1.   The complete definiendum in each of the two definitional statements a definite description.

2.   The simple definiendum is a simple or complex relative denotative term: ing standing in such and such a relation to (so and so), or thing of such a nd standing in such and such a relation to (so and so).

3.   What is important is that each object in the series of objects has one ad only one thing standing in that given relation to it: *the* length illustrated object $x$. Definitional statement (a) says in its definiens what this thing is hich stands in the given relation to object $i$: the length illustrated in object $i$ ¼ inch.

4.   But equally important is the fact that *the* thing standing in such and ach a relation to a given object in the series must itself stand in a describable lation to the thing that stands in that same relation to the *just preceding* bject in the series. This describable relation must not vary from one place the series to another. For example, the length of any given screw (except e first) is everywhere exactly ⅛-inch greater than the length of the just receding screw. Definitional statement (b) identifies in its definiens the ngth of n$x$ as the thing standing in such and such a relation to the length of $x$.

5.   Thus, the pair of definitional statements enables you to figure out for ny object in the series what is the thing that stands in such and such a lation to that object, *provided* that you know where that object stands in the ries. Let us illustrate. Suppose that I must know the length of the third crew in the series. By definitional statement (b), this equals the length of the econd screw plus ⅛ inch. But again by definitional statement (b), the length f the second screw equals the length of the first screw plus ⅛ inch. Now by efinitional statement (a), the length of the first screw equals ¼ inch. There- ore the length of the third screw equals

$$[(¼ + ⅛) + ⅛] = ½ \text{ inch.}$$

We may now formulate a general pattern or diagram for **recursive defi- itions**. Let "D" represent the simple definiendum, that denotative relative arm mentioned in 2, above. And let "the D of $x$" represent the definite escription based on D. Then definitional statement (a) always has the general orm,

a)                              the D of $i$ = Df $Y$.

This definitional statement must conform to all the rules of definition give in Units 31 and 32, with one exception. Rule 7, on the repetition of "parts (§32.3), would require that the definiens, $Y$, contain a token of sign-type "$i$, since "$i$" is a part of the complete definiendum but not a part of the simp definiendum. However, in the case of a recursive definition, $Y$ may repeat "$i$ but need not.

Let "$R(m)$" represent the thing standing in the relation R to thing $m$ Then the second definitional statement in a recursive definition has the gener form,

(b)                     the D of n$x$ = $_{Df}$ R (the D of $x$).

This statement always violates the rule of circularity (§32.2): It repeats th simple definiendum, D. It also violates the rule on repetition of parts: it doe not repeat "n," or "n$x$," although it does repeat "$x$."

In spite of the violations of rules, recursive definitions are effective an powerful instruments. They constitute one of the keys to the constructio of computing machines.

### §35.5  Are Recursive Definitions Complete Definitions?

Are recursive definitions complete definitions? In this section we shall show why that question must be answered in the negative. But als we shall try to show why recursive definitions are "*almost* as good as" com plete definitions.

Each of the two definitional statements in a recursive definition is a complet definition of its complete definiendum. Hence, recursive definitions meet th first of the two requirements for complete definition specified above in §35. The reason why they are not complete definitions is that they do not meet th second of those two requirements.

This second requirement demands that every context in which the simpl definiendum might appear may be transformed into one or the other of th two contexts represented by the two definienda. Now recursive definition generally fail to meet this requirement in two respects:

1.   Usually the idea represented by the simple definiendum can be applie to things other than those objects lying in the ordered series to which th recursive definition does apply it. For example, we regularly inquire abou the lengths of things that are not screws in that hardware display. Thus, th expression "the D of $x$" might be meaningful even when "$x$" was not referrin to an object in the series. In such a case "D" would be occurring in a contex that cannot be transformed into one of the contexts appearing in the defini enda of the recursive definition.

This first objection is, however, not so serious as one might suppose Recursive definitions are usually developed with limited purposes in mind for use during consideration of the objects in that series. It is like the investi

gator who says, "By a tall man I shall mean a man over 6 feet in height."
Over 6 feet in height is a meaning for "tall" that conforms very well with the
conventional *general* meaning of tall so long as that general meaning is
applied to men. But it would be entirely unsatisfactory as a meaning for
"tall" as applied to mountains. We might say that the definition of "tall" is
complete within a specified range of application, and that range of application
is all that immediately concerns the definer. Furthermore, the meaning
assigned within that range is consonant with the general meaning: It is what
the general meaning would amount to when the general meaning is applied
to things within that range.

In the same way, the recursive definition of length, while it does not explain
what is meant by length in general, does nevertheless explain what that
general idea amounts to when it is applied to things within the given series.
Thus we might claim that the recursive definition is complete within a range
of application.

2.   But can we even say that much? We saw in the preceding section that
if you know where in the series a given object lies, you can use the definition
to calculate its length. But the simple definiendum can occur in contexts such
that the context does not reveal the location in the series of the object referred
to. For example, "the length of the blue screw" is such a context. No amount
of *logic* will enable one to transform "the blue screw" into "$i$" or into some
expression of the form n.x. Of course, other considerations than logic may
permit one to make the transformation. But these considerations may or
may not be available.

Hence we have to conclude that not every context in which the simple
definiendum might occur, even when those contexts are expressions referring
to objects in the series, can be transformed into one of the contexts appearing
in the two definitional statements, and that therefore the definition is incomplete.

Nevertheless, it is "almost as good as" a complete definition. Because,
while we cannot always make the transformation, there is always a way to
make it. The recursive definition defines the length of every *object* in the series
in terms of its position in the series. And every object in the series *has* a position in the series. The only difficulty is that an object in the series might be
referred to by an expression which does not itself indicate, directly or indirectly, what is the position in the series occupied by the object referred to.

## §35.6 Extended Recursive Definitions

Many of the most useful applications of the idea of recursive
definition involve a simple definiendum that identifies things standing in a
given relation to a *pair* of objects, rather than in a given relation to a single
object. Arithmetical operations, for example, addition or multiplication,

require two things to be added or multiplied, their sum or their produ
being the thing that stands in the relation of sum or product to the pai

We shall not make here a detailed analysis of the way in which the notio
of recursive definition may be extended to such cases. Let it suffice if w
diagram the pattern for such extended recursive definition, with one or tw
explanatory comments, and give a few illustrations from the field of arithmeti

(a)                    the D of $x$ and $i$ $=$ $_{Df}$ $Y$

The complete definiendum must make reference to *both* objects, $x$ and
But only one of them is identified in terms of its being first in the series,
The definiens, $Y$, may or may not repeat "$x$," and as before, may or may no
repeat "$i$."

To illustrate, let us consider three first definitional statements, for additio
multiplication, and raising to a power. In all cases, the class of numbers is th
class of positive integers together with 0, and they are arranged in order o
size. Thus $i = 0$, $1 = n0$, $2 = n1$, and so on.

(a)                    $x + 0 = _{Df} x$.
(a)                    $x \times 0 = _{Df} 0$.
(a)                    $x^0 = _{Df} 1$.

The second definitional statement will take the following form:

(b)          the D of $x$ and $ny$ $=$ $_{Df}$ R (the D of $x$ and $y$).

In the case of addition, multiplication, and raising to a power, these become

(b)                    $x + ny = _{Df} n (x + y)$.
(b)                    $x \times ny = _{Df} (x \times y) + x$.
(b)                    $x^{ny} = _{Df} x^y \times x$.

### §35.7 Incomplete Absolute Definitions

Much of our attention to incomplete definitions through Unit 3
and the first six sections of this unit has been concentrated on incomplete
contextual definitions. Absolute definitions also are on occasion incomplete

In earlier units, it has been suggested that the standard form for a definition
may sometimes be used for incomplete absolute definitions. In such cases
instead of writing,

An $X = _{Df}$ a $Y$,

we write,

An $X = _{Df}$ a certain kind of $Y$;

and instead of writing (in definitions of singular terms),

$X = _{Df} Y$,

we write,

$$X = _{\text{Df}} \text{ a certain } Y.$$

If we had a complete definition,

$$\text{An } X = _{\text{Df}} \text{ a } Y,$$

it would follow that every $X$ is a $Y$ and every $Y$ is an $X$. In contrast, from the incomplete definition,

$$\text{An } X = _{\text{Df}} \text{ a certain kind of } Y,$$

it follows that every $X$ is a $Y$ but it does not follow that every $Y$ is an $X$. In fact, the incomplete definition specifically suggests that it is false that every $Y$ is an $X$. Thus we see that the suggested technique for using the standard form as a device for incomplete definition is appropriate only when the definiens is too broad, but not too narrow, to be the definiens of a complete definition.

But also we see that the same incomplete definition could have been put in the nonstandard form,

$$\text{Every } X \text{ is a } Y.$$

And this suggests other ways of expressing incomplete definitions. When, for example, the proposed definiens is too narrow, one might express this situation by,

$$\text{Every } Y \text{ is an } X.$$

($Y$ still represents the definiens and $X$ the definiendum.) Or one could express this by,

$$\text{Most } X\text{'s are } Y.$$

In fact, *any* form of statement might be employed in the presentation of an incomplete definition. As is suggested in one of the examples above, the definiendum need not be the grammatical subject of the defining statement. If the statements are offered as justifiable by analysis, then they are contributing to an incomplete intensional definition. Otherwise, they are contributing to an incomplete extensional definition.

## §35.8  Implicit Definitions

When we were discussing circular definitional chains (§33.4), we noticed that circular chains do not occur in systematic works in the sciences, with the consequence that a certain number of the technical terms in a science remain undefined. These undefined terms nevertheless appear in, and are in fact even explained by, a series of laws, postulates, or axioms. It has sometimes been said that these laws, postulates, and axioms form an *implicit* definition of the otherwise undefined terms. We are now in a position to see what that means.

In effect each postulate or axiom is an incomplete definition of each other
wise undefined term contained in it. Oddly enough, there is no sharp dis
tinction between definiendum and definiens: *Each* otherwise undefined term
may *in turn* be regarded as definiendum, and the rest of the postulate a
definiens. Hence, there is a kind of circularity. But the postulate does never
theless illuminate the connections between the terms it contains, even if i
(partially) explains them in terms of each other.

Usually postulates and axioms do not come singly, but in groups. If eacl
postulate is an incomplete definition, might not the entire group be a complet
definition, much as the pair of statements in a recursive definition is a com
plete definition? The question raised is one of the most difficult questions to
answer under investigation by logicians of the present day. In some cases, th
answer would be, Yes. In others, No. The problem of the modern logician
may be put this way: How can we tell whether a set of postulates is a complet
(implicit) definition of the terms it contains, and under what circumstance
can we hope, by adding more postulates to a set that is an incomplete defi
nition, to get a complete definition?[4]

But this problem is too difficult to be investigated in this text and any
further consideration of postulates, their uses and the sense in which they may
be regarded as incomplete definitions, would raise too many complicated
issues to be justified here. Suffice it to say that *any* analytic statement (that is
any statement establishable by analysis—see §6.4) explains in part the mean
ings of the terms that it contains; hence any such statement may be regarded
as an incomplete intensional definition of any term contained within it
Postulates are usually analytic statements of this kind.

---

[4] More properly, what logicians are investigating under the heading of "com
pleteness" is not quite what we have called completeness in §34.3. They are usually
dealing with intensional definitions. What they demand is that requirements a and c
(§34.3), but not usually b, are met: That is, for the postulates to be a complet
implicit definition, they require that every *analytic* statement containing the implicitly
defined terms be inferable from the postulates.

# INFERENCE

# Inference and Proof

## §36.1 The Major Problems of Part Five

We now commence the fifth, and final, part of this study of the principles of right reason. The title of this part is "Inference". As you read it, you will discover that we discuss a good many things in addition to inference, although most of these other topics are closely related to it. On the other hand, many of these discussions of related topics also are valuable in themselves, quite apart from the manner in which they contribute to the study of inference.

In the present section we shall briefly call to mind some things that have already been said about inference and, in the light of that review, suggest some of the main features of the study that lies before us.

Inference was first mentioned in §6.5, where it was referred to as one of the four primary valid grounds for belief. (The other primary grounds were observation, actualization, and analysis.) In that section, it was described as "the passage of the mind from one or more already accepted beliefs to the acceptance of another." Those already accepted propositions constituted evidence persuading the thinker also to accept this other proposition.

It was, however, pointed out that inferences can be faulty or invalid: we may, and in fact often do, draw from evidence conclusions that we are not justified in drawing. One major task of Part V will be to describe some procedures and some principles of right reason that one may follow and apply to determine whether or not a given inference was justified.

There are two things to examine for weakness or for strength when one is examining a given inference to determine whether or not it is justified. One is the reliability of the evidence itself. Perhaps those propositions which had been previously accepted are not themselves true; if not, they do not provide good reasons for accepting the now inferred proposition. Thus our study of inference will eventually require a consideration of those other valid grounds for belief and of the way in which their use might provide a test, or check, upon the evidence used for an inference. The other thing to examine when checking the reliability of an inference is the _connection between_ the previously accepted evidence and the now-inferred conclusion. Are the propositions accepted as evidence and the proposition inferred as conclusion related to one another in such a manner that the truth of the evidence is genuinely relevant to the truth of the conclusion? If so, we call the inference **valid;** otherwise, it is **invalid.**

The first units of Part V will be concerned with outlining some principles of right reason that may be employed to determine whether or not an inference is valid.

However, it is very difficult to apply a principle to so fleeting a thing as a thought, a passage of the mind from one belief to another. Much better, let this thought be recorded in language or other signs, and state the principles in terms of what they tell us about these linguistic records. That, in any case, is the procedure which will be followed.

### §36.2 Inferences and Proofs

The words "proof" and "prove" come from the Latin, _probare_, which means _to try_ and _to test_. We get our English words "probation" and "probationary" from the same source. Thus originally to prove something meant to test it, and a proof of something meant a test of it. It made no difference whether the outcome of the test was positive or negative, favorable or unfavorable; to test was still to prove, and the testing was still a proof. This original meaning still persists in certain usages. For example, in printing, a proof is a sheet printed for trial or testing purposes from the type that has been set up. It makes no difference whether the sheet printed for testing purposes shows that the type was properly set, or whether it reveals errors that must be corrected; in either case, the printed sheet is still called a _proof_.

But as time went on, the meanings of "proof" and "to prove" underwent a change as they were applied to beliefs or propositions. A proof of a proposition came to mean not merely a test of that proposition, but rather a _favorable_ test, one which showed that believing the proposition would be justified. If the test were unfavorable and showed that the proposition was false and belief would be unjustified, the test came to be called a _disproof_.

Other changes followed. (1) While originally _any_ test, using _any_ of the valid grounds of belief might be called a proof (for example, looking in the closet and seeing my hat there would be a proof that my hat is in the closet), gradually the word "proof" became limited in its application—at least, by some people using this sign-type—to favorable tests that involved the use of inference. Thus, direct tests using merely observation or analysis, and even experimental tests that used actualization and observation, came to be regarded as not falling within the extension of the term "proof." This implied no discredit of those tests. They might be excellent tests. But they were not the kind of test that was intended when one spoke of "proof." If a test were to be called a *proof*, these direct methods of observation and analysis would do no more than supply the evidence from which the proved proposition could be inferred.

2. Finally, people report their testings to one another; they communicate. Thus, in the course of time, many people who used the word "proof" came to be thinking of the report of a testing procedure rather than of the testing procedure itself. For example, in geometry, the proof of a theorem is not the actual testing of the theorem, but the *report* of the test for the theorem. Thus the proof actually lies in the geometry book; that is where the report is.

Through the balance of this text we shall use the word "proof" as a technical term with a meaning slightly different from, but suggested by, the outcome of this entire historical development. By the term **proof** we shall mean a certain kind of linguistic structure with an associated conventional meaning, which *could* be used as the record or report of an inference.

## §36.3  Analysis of the Definition of "Proof"

Let us look at an example of proof and by applying to it the definition given at the end of the last section try to get a more adequate understanding of what the term "proof" means.

**Sample Proof I**

John Smith's car is two years older than George Jones's car. Jones's car is three years old. Therefore, John Smith's car is five years old.

1. The linguistic structure presented above is what somebody might have written if he were recording or reporting an inference. This linguistic structure is a proof.

Notice two things. First, it is not necessary that anybody actually write these very sign-types (with their conventional meanings). Nor, second, is it necessary that anybody who did write them was actually intending to record or report an inference. For example, I, the author of this book, just wrote them, but I was not trying to report or record an inference. The first two sentences do not express my belief in, or acceptance of, the propositions that they indicate. Yet the declarative sentence form is appropriate for doing just this. Thus, they *could* have been used for this purpose. Neither does the third sentence express my belief in the proposition it indicates. Nevertheless, the three sentence-types form together a structure that I (or anyone else) *could* have written in order to record an inference. Hence, they *are* a proof.

2. A proof was defined as a "linguistic *structure* . . . ." Thus, a proof is not a sign-*token*, but rather it is a complex sign-*type*. It is a sign-type with which existing conventions have associated a meaning. Furthermore, the meaning that those conventions have associated with that sign-type is such that if one presented the sign-type, that is, produced tokens belonging to that sign-type, he could very well be reporting an inference. (But—to insist on the first point—he *need* not be reporting an inference.)

3. If we look again at Sample Proof I and think what it would mean if it were used to report an inference, we might notice the following things: (a) The first two sentences indicate certain propositions and would signify that those propositions were accepted by the speaker. (b) The third sentence indicates a certain other proposition and would signify that the author also accepted this proposition. (c) The word "therefore" which appears at the beginning of the third sentence would signify the fact of inference, of passage *from* the acceptance of the first two propositions *to* the consequent acceptance of the third proposition. A proof always indicates what proposition or propositions would have been operating as evidence (if the proof were used to report an inference) and what proposition would have been accepted on the basis of that evidence, would have been inferred from that evidence.

The definition of a proof given at the end of the last section does not specify the point just made. For example, the sentence, "Yesterday I made an inference," is a linguistic structure that could be used to report an inference. Thus, this sentence is in the extension of the definiens. But this sentence is not a proof because it does not report what propo sitions were the evidence and what proposition was the inferred conclusion in the inference which it would report. Every proof does just that. Hence, the definition at the end of the last section is incomplete since it is too broad. But any linguistic structure which satisfies that definiens and also has the characteristics specified in this comment will be a proof.

4.    Let us look again at Sample Proof I, and suppose it to be reporting an inference. We might ask, Was the reporter justified in making that inference? As pointed out in §36.1, two things will affect the correctness of our answer to that question: (a) the reliability of the evidence from which he made the inference, and  (b) the manner in which the proposition which was inferred is related to the propositions used as evidence.

What it is important now to notice is that essentially these same questions can be asked about the proof itself as were formerly asked about the inference: (a) To what extent would one (*anyone*) be justified in accepting as true the propositions indicated as evidence? (b) Is the proposition indicated as conclusion so related to the propositions indicated as evidence that being justified in accepting them one would be justified also in accepting it? Thus we can think about proofs in much the same manner as we think about inferences. If the answers to both the above questions about a proof are favorable, then any inference which it faithfully reports will have been a *justified inference*.

5.    When we examine these two questions still further, we notice that question b can be considered and answered quite independently of any consideration of question a.

For example, in connection with Sample Proof I, we can see that this proof satisfies requirement b: the conclusion *is* so related to the evidence that *if* one were justified in accepting the evidence, then he *would* be justified in accepting the conclusion. On the other hand, suppose that the conclusion had been, "Therefore John Smith's car is six years old." You and I do not have to be very keen mathematicians to see that if one were justified in accepting the evidence in Sample Proof I, he would be so far from justified in accepting this conclusion that he would even be justified in rejecting it as false.

Thus, a proof may be *evaluated* relative to requirement b without knowing *either* whether or not a given speaker is using it to report an inference *or*, in case he is so using it, whether or not it satisfies requirement a.

The principles of logic are by and large concerned with questions that bear on making this sort of evaluation of proofs with respect to whether or not they satisfy requirement b.

6.    Proofs that fail to satisfy requirement b are just as genuinely proofs as are those that satisfy this requirement. The only thing is, they are not good proofs, and one would hate to see somebody using such a proof to report an inference.

7.    A proof that satisfies requirement b is said to be **valid.** One that does not satisfy requirement b is said to be **invalid.** Thus whether or not a proof would, if used to report an inference, satisfy requirement a in no way affects the validity or invalidity of the proof. Furthermore, we can test a proof for validity without considering whether or not it ever was, is, or will be used to report an inference. The principles of logic equip us with procedures by which we may perform such tests.

The facts considered in this section naturally lead us to the question, What else would one use a proof for than to report an inference? The next section will be concerned with that very question.

## §36.4  On the Uses of Proofs

1.    **Record of an Inference.**  Proofs can be, and are, used for a great variety of purposes. Of course, one might use a proof as a record and report of an inference actually made. Here, the proof reports a belief reached by the author of the proof and also the evidence which led him to that belief.

2.    **A Device for Testing the Wisdom of an Inference.**  But frequently a person writes out and studies a proof *prior* to any act of inference and as an aid in testing the wisdom of making a contemplated inference. By stabilizing in a linguistic structure what might be a record of the fleeting thought process, one can examine at greater length the possible act of inference, subject the validity of the proof to a thorough scrutiny, determine whether or not the proposed evidence would be sufficient to warrant the conclusion and whether the proposed evidence is itself justifiable. One can even solicit the assistance of one's friends and associates in evaluating the proof and thus benefit from their judgment. If the proof stands up under this criticism, one might then go on actually to make the inference indicated by the proof. But if the proof does not stand up, one has been saved by this opportunity to examine the proof

from actually making the ill-advised inference that the proof might have been used to record.

3. **A Tool of Inference.** We spoke in §2.6 of the use of language as a calculus. The construction of proofs often illustrates this use. In this use, the proof neither records an inference already made nor a possibility of inference already clearly conceived and awaiting a test. Rather, one writes down the premises and by comparing them one with another, noting their specific structure and content, discovers what could be inferred from them (provided that they can be accepted as true). For example, in writing the premises of Sample Proof I, above, we discover that by adding two to three, we shall ascertain the age of John Smith's car. Here a proof is used as a tool for the performance of an inference, not merely as a record or report of an actual or contemplated inference.

4. **An Instrument of Persuasion.** Here the proof is used by its author as an invitation to inference on the part of the receiver. This is the typical use made of proofs in debate, even in advertising, but also in scientific treatises. At least in the latter cases, and in many of the former as well, the author of the proof does actually believe the proposition indicated as the conclusion of the proof. But he might well have reached that belief in any number of ways rather than by an inference from the evidence indicated in the proof. The author's purpose is not to report what *he* has done, but to develop in the receiver a belief in the conclusion. The evidence proposed in the proof is of such a kind or offered in such a manner that the receiver is likely to accept it. The proof exhibits the relevance of the evidence to the conclusion and hence encourages the receiver to infer the conclusion.

5. **Exhibition of an Implication.** Frequently a proof is written out and examined when the author has no intention of accepting the indicated evidence or of inferring from it the indicated conclusion. Rather, the sole purpose of the author is to exhibit or discover that *if* the propositions indicated as evidence *were* true, *then* the proposition indicated as conclusion *would* be true. There is a great difference between on the one hand believing *A* and inferring *B* from it, and on the other hand believing that *if A, then B*. But a proof with *A* for evidence and *B* for conclusion will be valid (§36.3, comment 7) if and only if it is true that if *A*, then *B*. Thus a proof is an effective instrument in terms of which to

examine and exhibit such if . . ., then . . . connections between propositions.

Indeed it is often said today that the geometer is not concerned to assert his postulates and axioms and to assert inferentially his theorems. Instead of that, it is held that the proofs of his theorems are given *only* as a means of showing that *if* the postulates were true, *then* the theorems would be also true.

**6. A Component in the Method of Hypothesis and Verification.** The preceding use has an important application in employing the problem-solving method of hypothesis and verification. This method of problem-solving was explained in §8.4. It consists essentially in guessing at the solution to a problem and then proceeding to test that hypothesis or guess.

A part of the testing procedure consists in developing valid proofs that have the hypothesis for one of the indicated bits of evidence. If all the other indicated bits of evidence cited in the proof are reliable, then the proof is evidence (in the manner of point 4 above) that if the hypothesis were true, then the conclusion of the proof would be true. Of course one should not *infer* along the lines of the proof, because the hypothesis is a questionable bit of evidence. Instead, what one does is to seek *independently* of the proof to determine the truth or falsity of the indicated conclusion.

Now if this independent investigation of the conclusion, perhaps by observation, memory, or authority, convinces us that the conclusion is false, then we must reject the hypothesis as also false. For the proof has shown that if the hypothesis were true, the conclusion would be true.

On the other hand, if the independent testing of the conclusion shows it to be true, then the hypothesis is shown, not to be true, but to be plausible. A sufficient collection of several proofs, all having the hypothesis as an indicated bit of evidence and all with their conclusions independently known to be true, can provide a test for the hypothesis that will show it to be highly probable.

### §36.5 The Core of a Proof

When we were studying definition we noticed that a person frequently says a great deal more than the core of his definition. Many of those accompanying remarks are not only useful, but even necessary, to the proper understanding of the definitional core. And yet in order to criticize definitions intelligently and to guide our own efforts at definition, we found it necessary to distinguish the definitional core from the remarks that accompanied it.

Much the same situation holds with respect to proofs. People who formulate or state proofs frequently accompany their statement of the proof's core with all sorts of additional remarks. Many of these accompanying remarks are genuinely helpful to a receiver who would understand the proof itself—the core of the proof. But even these should be discriminated from the core. With an even greater urgency, one must discriminate from the core various "side remarks" such as comments on the strength of the author's conviction or belief, the difficulty in or importance of discerning the truth of some item in the core of the proof, and so on.

What, then belongs to **the core of a proof**? There are three kinds of element. These can be discerned if we think of the proof in terms of its possible use as the record of an inference. (1) Every indication or statement of a bit of evidence from which the inference is made belongs to the core. (2) The indication or statement of any conclusion which is inferred from the indicated evidence belongs to the core. (3) Some sign that the conclusion is inferred—instead of being just another claim made by the author—must be included in the core.

If we look back at Sample Proof I on page 409 we see that that proof contains nothing but a core. There were no accompanying remarks. Nothing was said which was not a statement of the two bits of evidence, a statement of the conclusion, or an indication (by the word "therefore") that the conclusion was inferred. Yet a proof with identically the same core might have been presented with all sorts of accompanying remarks. Sample Proof II is an example of such a proof:

**Sample Proof II**

Now you know as well as I do that John Smith's car is two years older than George Jones's. Well let me tell you, I have it straight from Jones himself—that Jones's car is three years old. Don't you see, then, that Smith's car *must* be five years old?

What kind of accompanying remarks, which do not belong to the core, are illustrated in Sample Proof II? (1) A remark concerning the equality of the high strengths of belief with which author and receiver accept one of the bits of evidence: "Now you know as well as I do." (2) An indication of the valid ground (authority) for believing another bit of evidence: "Well let me tell you, I have it straight from Jones himself." (3) A vehement style in expressing the claim that the conclusion is inferable from the evidence: "Don't you see, then, . . . *must* . . . ."

## §36.6 Premises and Conclusion

All future discussions of proof are simplified by our having available certain technical terms that can be used in referring to the various parts of the core of a proof.

By a <u>premise</u> is meant that statement, or other indication, in the core of a proof, of a bit of evidence from which the conclusion is inferred.

Every proof has at least one premise and many proofs have two, three, or even four premises.[1] Sample Proofs I and II each had two premises. There is no logical reason why a proof could not have a tremendous number of premises: a hundred or a thousand. But *psychological* considerations tend to prevent human beings from contemplating such proofs: They simply cannot hold so many facts simultaneously in mind in order to discern what might be inferred from them.[2]

By a **conclusion** is meant that statement, or other indication, in the core of a proof, of a proposition which it is claimed can be or has been inferred from the premise or premises.

Every proof has at least one conclusion and every **simple** proof has *only* one conclusion. However, **complex** proofs have more than one conclusion. In these latter cases, from some of the premises an **intermediate** conclusion is inferred and then this intermediate conclusion is in turn used as a premise from which to infer a **final** conclusion. An example of this kind of situation is given in Sample Proof III:

### Sample Proof III

Now every employee of The X Company lives in the suburbs. Ralph is employed by The X Company. Hence, Ralph lives in the suburbs. But no one living in the suburbs can vote in the city election. Therefore, Ralph cannot vote in the city election.

Every proof has only one final conclusion.

---

1　There is an esoteric sense in which we can speak of some proofs as having no premises at all! (Cf. R. Carnap, *The Logical Syntax of Language*, New York: 1937, §10.) We shall consider that type of situation only at a later stage. For the present, it is well to think of every proof as having at least one premise.

2　This is one reason for the invention and construction of computing machines. They can be so constructed that they will point out valid conclusions based on larger numbers of premises than human beings can cope with.

In listing the premises of a complex proof, do not list the intermediate conclusions, even though they are used *as* premises at some stage in the proof.

## EXERCISES

1. List the premises in Sample Proof II, in Sample Proof III.
2. What is the final conclusion of Sample Proof II? of Sample Proof III?
3. Does Sample Proof II contain any intermediate conclusions? Does Sample Proof III? In each case, if the answer is affirmative, list the intermediate conclusion or intermediate conclusions.

By a **sign of inferential connection** is meant any word, phrase, or other sign appearing in the core of a proof that serves to indicate (a) that the entire structure is a proof, and (b) which items are premises, which are conclusions.

"Then," "therefore," "hence," and "thus" often serve as signs of inferential connection.[3] They are regularly *attached to the conclusion* which they identify. On the other hand, the words "since" and "because" are often used as signs of inferential connection, but when they are used, they are *attached to a premise.* Their use usually (but not always) occurs when the conclusion has been stated before the premises. The words "therefore" and "hence" can be used only when the conclusion is stated after the statement of at least one of the premises. Thus when the conclusion is stated first, some other sign of inferential connection must be employed. In these cases, "since" or "because" is attached to the premise stated immediately after the conclusion.

Sometimes both "therefore" or "hence" and "since" or "because" are used. This occurs most frequently when the statement of the conclusion comes *between* the statement of one premise and that of another. In such cases, the premise following the conclusion is introduced by "since" or "because."

**Sample Proof IV**

William is the top man in his class, because he got all A's and no one else got all A's.

**Sample Proof V**

Everybody in Upper Brackets owns a Cadillac. Therefore Ted owns a Cadillac, since he lives in Upper Brackets.

---

[3] The sign-types "hence" and "thus" have also other uses, so that the mere presence of tokens belonging to these types is no sure sign that the entire structure is a proof.

### §36.7 Putting Proofs into Gross Standard Form

We found it helpful to discuss definition in terms of a standard form, and to criticize definitions after they had been put into standard form. The same advantages will be gained by putting proofs into standard forms. All rules dealing with validity are directly and most readily applied only to proofs in standard form.

We conclude this unit with some suggestions as to how to put a proof into **gross standard form.**[4]

1. Place each premise and each conclusion on a separate line.
2. Express each premise and each conclusion in an unambiguous declarative sentence or other unambiguous symbolic structure (for example, $s = j + 2$) appropriate for use in affirming the premise or conclusion which is indicated.

3. Arrange these lines in such an order that every premise or intermediate conclusion from which a given conclusion is inferred comes on some line *above* the line on which that conclusion is presented.

4. Number the lines from top to bottom: (1), (2), (3), (4), . . . .
5. Precede the number of any line which represents a conclusion (final or intermediate) with the sign " ∴ ".

6. Make sure that everything in the original which does *not* belong to its core has been omitted as you put it into standard form.

By way of illustrating the application of these six rules, we shall put Sample Proof II from §36.5 into gross standard form:

(1) John Smith's car is two years older than George Jones's car.
(2) George Jones's car is three years old.
∴ (3) John Smith's car is five years old.

Gross standard form differs from **detailed standard form** in only one matter: detailed standard form requires that certain special sentence structures, rather than any unambiguous declarative one, be used in stating the premises and the conclusions. We shall commence the study of detailed standard form in Unit 38.

In addition to putting a proof into standard form (gross or detailed), it is frequently desirable to "annotate" the core in standard form. This involves placing explanatory comments opposite each line of the proof in standard form. Many remarks contained in the original proof,

---

[4] The meaning of *gross* standard form is explained shortly below.

but omitted when it was put into standard form, will find a place in this annotation. Other comments, not appearing in the original will also be placed here. We shall commence the study of annotation in Unit 37.

## EXERCISES

1. Put Sample Proofs III, IV, and V (from §36.6) into gross standard form.
2. Put each of the following proofs into gross standard form.
   a. George is taller than Jim. Jim is taller than Bill. Therefore, George is taller than Bill.
   b. This body has been falling freely for three seconds, with no initial force other than gravity. Therefore, it is falling at a rate of 96 feet per second. Because a freely falling body accelerates at a rate of 32 feet per second per second.
   c. Since no one on the committee can change his demands without first getting permission from the people he represents, and since that permission cannot be gotten during a committee meeting, the committee cannot reconcile its opposing demands during this committee meeting.
   d. I infer that the sun will rise tomorrow at 5:21 from the fact that it rose today at 5:20 and the fact that at this season of the year it is rising every day a minute later than on the day before.
   e. George has hair the same color as his brother's. George's brother has red hair. Therefore George has red hair. I conclude that George will not be hired by the X combo, because they hire only black-haired musicians.

## REVIEW QUESTIONS FOR UNIT 36

1. What two things would you examine for their reliability, if you were concerned to discover whether a given inference was justified? Briefly explain each.
2. What is meant when we call an inference *valid? Invalid?*
3. Why is the study of valid inference conducted in terms of the linguistic records of inferences?
4. What was the original meaning of the word "proof" and through what phases did this meaning gradually change in the course of history?
5. How is the term "proof" defined for use as a technical term in this book?
   a. Explain and illustrate what this definition means.
   b. Is this definition complete or incomplete? Explain.
6. May questions similar to those concerning the reliability of inferences be asked concerning proofs? Can they be asked even though we do not regard the proof as the report of an inference? If so, what would these questions about proofs be?

7. Can the two questions about proofs reported in answer to question 6 be considered and answered independently of one another? Explain and illustrate.

8. Under what circumstances is a proof said to be *valid*? Said to be *invalid*?

9. Briefly describe five types of use to which a proof may be put other than as a record or report of an inference.

10. What components in a proof belong to the core of the proof? What kind of components are to be considered as remarks accompanying the core?

11. What is meant by a premise?

12. Do all proofs have the same number of premises? Explain.

13. What is meant by a conclusion? An intermediate conclusion? A final conclusion?

14. Do all proofs have intermediate conclusions? Final conclusions?

15. How many final conclusions might a proof have?

16. What is meant by a *sign of inferential connection*?

17. What words are regularly used in English as signs of inferential connection? Where do they usually occur in the proof, and under what circumstances is one used rather than another?

18. What is involved when one puts a proof into gross standard form?

19. What is the difference between the gross standard form and the detailed standard form of a proof?

UNIT **37**

# The Annotation of Proofs; Deductive versus Inductive Proofs

## §37.1 The Annotation of Proofs

It was said in the preceding unit that some of the miscellaneous remarks made in the course of a proof not in standard form might be preserved when the proof is put into standard form. These remarks should be separated from the core of the proof, as already explained. But they may then be attached to that core in a series of comments called, technically, the **annotation** of the proof.

Each numbered line of the core of the proof in standard form may be accompanied by one or more comments or remarks. When these annotations are themselves in standard form, they will appear in brackets, to the right of the column of statements which form the proof's core. An illustration appears below.

The annotation to the right of each line serves only to indicate briefly the justification for accepting that line. Thus, by and large, the annotation will indicate how one or the other of the six valid grounds of belief discussed in Units 6 and 7 justifies the line in question. In general, the indication is kept as brief as possible.[1]

By way of illustration, let us preserve the remarks accompanying Sample Proof II appearing in §36.5, transforming the remarks as we put the proof into standard form.

(1)  John Smith's car is two years older     [According to your memory
      than George Jones's car.                and mine.]

---

[1] These indications are kept as brief as possible because the main consideration when the proof is in standard form is *how* the premises justify the conclusion. That is, the main consideration is to exhibit the *validity* of the proof. If, however, extended comments seem to be called for, then the brief annotation might contain some such statement as "See note 1," and the extended remarks be put into note 1. Examples of this sort of thing appear later on in this section.

421

*It presupposes*

(2)   Jones's car is three years old.          [On the authority of Jones.]

∴ (3)   John Smith's car is five years old.          [From (1) and (2).]

## §37.2 Further Comments on Annotating Proofs

In subsequent units, we shall notice various special items that might be placed in the annotation of a proof. In the meantime, a few further comments may be helpful.

1.   A **fully annotated** proof will have an annotation opposite each line. This annotation will be either:

a.   A sufficient clew in itself to what the author considers an adequate justification for accepting the annotated line; or

b.   A clew to a source for further information on the grounds for accepting the annotated line; or

c.   A clew that the author is not asking that the line be accepted, but is developing the proof for other reasons; or

d.   A clew that the author is not at the moment interested in considering the grounds for accepting the annotated line. We shall briefly discuss each of these four items.

2.   In the example of an annotated proof given above, each annotation is of sort a, under 1: It briefly indicates why the author thinks the statement made in the given line may be accepted. The annotations show that the first line is, the author believes, to be accepted on the basis of memory; the second line, on the basis of a named authority; and the third, on the basis of an inference from indicated premises.

3.   It might have been thought that the sign " ∴ ", which *precedes* the third line, was a sufficient indication that the line was to be accepted on the basis of an inference. So it is. But the annotation indicates in addition precisely *what* premises are used in that inference. When a proof is complex, containing intermediate conclusions, not every conclusion depends directly on every preceding line as a premise. For example, the final conclusion will not usually depend directly on the premises used to reach an intermediate conclusion. But on the other hand, it does depend on that intermediate conclusion and will use it as a premise.

To illustrate, let us put Sample Proof III (from §36.6) into standard form and annotate.

(1)    Every employee of The X Company lives in     [Premise.]
       the suburbs.

(2)    Ralph is employed by The X Company.     [Premise.]

∴ (3)   Ralph lives in the suburbs.     [From (1) and (2).]

(4)    No one living in the suburbs can vote in the     [Premise.]
       city election.

∴ (5)   Ralph cannot vote in the city election.     [From (3) and (4).]

4. Sample Proof III, which we just put into standard form, contained no comments on its premises. Nevertheless, we annotated each one, simply with the word "Premise." We shall often do that in the future. It is sometimes even advisable to annotate premises by this word even when they will be accompanied by other comments. Thus, for example, line (1) of the proof given in §37.1 could be annotated:

[According to your memory and mine.   Premise.]

5. As all the remarks so far made must have suggested, the annotation of a proof involves not merely preserving comments made in the original proof, but adding further comments that will throw more light on the proof. However, all these newly added comments are aimed merely at exhibiting the logical structure of the proof. They are such things as "Premise," "From (1) and (2)," and so on. They are not an effort to discover and report, for example, *additional* justification for a premise. (This remark is, of course, true only in case our *sole* endeavor is to put the proof into standard form. If we are trying simultaneously to *strengthen* the proof, as an author might do if he were putting into standard form a proof he had himself constructed, then we could add further justifications. But in that case, the proof in standard form is not really equivalent to the original. It may be very similar to it, but it is presumably a better proof.)

6. Sometimes the establishment of a given item in a proof is more complicated than can have been indicated in the annotation of a proof. Under such circumstances, the establishment of that item may well have been undertaken in another section of an author's writings. Now he wants to use the item there established. His present annotation will simply refer to the earlier or other affirmation of that proposition.

Examples appear in the proofs of theorems in geometry. A person might quote a previously proved theorem or a previously stated definition. Under these circumstances his present annotation might be:

[by Theorem 6]

or

[by Definition 2].

In different circumstances, he might write:

[see Chapter 4]

or something to that effect.

Essentially all such annotations are groundings of the assertion by authority: the authority of the author himself. But they also invite us to review exactly how he came to hold the position that he affirms.

7.   The proper attitude to assume when you are putting a proof into standard form is that of the original author of that proof. You are simply putting yourself in his place and trying to rewrite his proof for him in a form that will better reveal its strength or weakness. You are not trying to strengthen the proof (unless you were the author of the original proof); you are trying only to improve its manner of presentation.

8.   The annotation of some proofs is so simple that it is pointless to complicate matters by supplying it.

*EXERCISES*

Put each of the following proofs into standard form and annotate.
1.   According to §23.3, every general term has a total strict intension. But according to the definition of "total strict intension" in §23.2, no term has more than one total strict intension. From these two facts, I infer that every general term has one and only one total strict intension.
2.   If a term has any strict intensions, it will have a total strict intension. A definitive intension is a strict intension. Therefore, if a term has a definitive intension, it has a total strict intension. Consequently, if a term has no total strict intension, it will have no definitive intension.

### §37.3 Deductive versus Inductive Proofs

Most people are familiar with the words "deduction" and "induction" and understand more or less vaguely that they refer to different kinds of proof, inference, or reasoning. Through the years several different notions have come to be associated with these words.

In the following sections, we shall review a few of these ideas. Perhaps among them you will find your own ideas more or less represented. Finally, in §37.7 we shall explain what the terms deduction and induction will mean throughout this text.

## §37.4 Reasoning to or from the General

Probably the oldest and still the most widely held view is that deduction is reasoning from the general to the particular, while induction is reasoning from the particular to the general.

These contrasted modes of reasoning could be illustrated in the two following proofs:

**Proof I**

(1)  Every man requires protein in his diet.
(2)  John is a man.
∴ (3)  John requires protein in his diet.

**Proof II[2]**

(1)  These tomato plants were killed by frost at a temperature of 32 degrees.
(2)  Those tomato plants were killed by frost at a temperature of 32 degrees.
(3)  These other tomato plants were killed by frost at a temperature of 32 degrees.
∴ (4)  Tomato plants (that is, all tomato plants) will be killed by frost at any freezing temperature.

Proof I is the model for deduction, or deductive proof. One of its premises cites a general principle, the second premise notes that a particular object is of the sort treated in the general principle, and the conclusion affirms that this particular object has the characteristic which the general principle affirms of all objects belonging to that sort.

A certain amount of variation from the model in Proof I is allowed under this notion of deduction and the proof would still be regarded as

---

2  This and other models of inductive proof appearing in this unit are not valid as they stand. Later models will exhibit progressively more of the features of valid inductive proofs. But the full quota of these features will not be considered until Unit 48, when we take up the study of induction. Meanwhile, these models do bring out and illustrate the features which have been regarded as characteristic of induction. To make them more complicated for the sake of validity would not affect the points that are to be made in this unit and would only obscure the issue.

deductive. For example, the general principle might be negative in form, as in Proof III:

**Proof III**

    (1)   No man is over 10 feet tall.
    (2)   John is a man.
∴ (3)   John is not over 10 feet tall.

Or, the particular, instead of being a particular individual, could be a particular kind, as in Proof IV:

**Proof IV**

    (1)   Every man requires protein in his diet.
    (2)   Every American citizen is a man.
∴ (3)   Every American citizen requires protein in his diet.

Or, both of these variations might occur in one proof:

**Proof V**

    (1)   No man is over 10 feet tall.
    (2)   Every American citizen is a man.
∴ (3)   No American citizen is over 10 feet tall.

Proof II is the model for induction, or inductive proof. Here the premises direct attention to several particular objects of a certain kind that exhibit a particular characteristic, while the conclusion is to the effect that objects generally, or all objects, of that kind have that characteristic.

As with the deductive, so here with inductive proofs, a certain range of variation from the model in Proof II is permitted and still the proof is considered to be inductive. Thus, the premises could note groups or classes of things of a certain sort or they could direct attention to individual objects of that sort. Also the premises and conclusion could be negative in form:

**Proof VI**

    (1)   This dog with an amputated leg did not grow a new leg.
    (2)   This cat with an amputated leg did not grow a new leg.
    (3)   This monkey with an amputated leg did not grow a new leg.
∴ (4)   No mammal with an amputated leg will grow a new leg.[3]

---

[3] Some simpler forms of animal do reproduce lost parts or members instead of merely healing the wounded surface with a growth of new skin.

## §37.5  Necessary versus Probable Conclusions

If we look again at Proof I and Proof II, we may notice still another difference between them than that the one reasons from a general premise to a particular conclusion while the other reasons from particular premises to a general conclusion. This other point of difference could be described as follows. In the case of the so-called deductive proof (Proof I), granting the truth of the premises necessitates granting the truth of the conclusion. Put in another way, one might say the conclusion is *necessary* on the assumption that the premises are true. If all men, without exception, do truly require protein in their diets and if John is a man, then it would have to be true that John requires protein in his diet.

On the other hand, the premises of the inductive argument (Proof II) in no way make the conclusion necessary. There is nothing inconsistent with those premises in the possibility of there being *other* things of the sort (tomato plants) reported on in the premises which do not have the character reported in the premises. For example, there may be an especially hardy strain of tomato plant that will not be killed by frost at any temperature above 26 degrees. Thus, in the case of the inductive argument, the premises might all be true and the conclusion might nevertheless be false. The most that one can say is that the truth of the premises renders the conclusion *probable*.

## §37.6  Revisions of Proof I and Proof II

The outcome of §37.5 seems to suggest that Proof II is not correctly formulated. In fact, it has been proposed that inductive generalizations of the sort illustrated in Proof II are not valid if their conclusions are absolute affirmations, as in Proof II, and that instead of this the conclusion ought to be one affirming a probability. Thus, it has been proposed to revise the model for inductive proofs from the form illustrated in Proof II, to the following:

**Proof VII**

(1)  As in Proof II
(2)  As in Proof II
(3)  As in Proof II
∴ (4)  It is probable that all tomato plants will be killed by frost at any freezing temperature.

Proof VII records many of the features that are supposed to be typical of scientific reasoning. Of course, many precautions must be taken in the selection and control of particular objects from which an inductive generalization will be made, or the generalization will not be valid. We shall see what some of these are when we reach Unit 48. At this point, we need only note that Proof VII does not record the fact of any such precautions having been taken and is therefore an invalid proof.

Yet aside from that, Proof VII does record much of what goes into scientific reasoning. For example, the experimental and observational sciences gather data from the laboratory or the field of observation. These data are always to the effect that such and such particular objects of a specific sort or kind have such and such a characteristic. On the basis of these observed cases, the scientist draws a general conclusion that all objects of that sort have that characteristic.[4] But the key point is that the conclusion is always held to be only probable. It is regularly affirmed that scientific knowledge is only probable knowledge. The observed data do not guarantee the *truth*, but establish only the *probability*, of some generalization. Proof VII recognizes this fact by making its conclusion to be a claim of probability.

But before we rest content with Proof VII as the model for inductive generalization, let us see whether or not a similar revision might not be made in the model for deductive proof. We noted in the preceding section that the premises of the deductive model, Proof I, made their conclusion necessary. Could not this necessity be recorded as a part of the conclusion, as in the following:

**Proof VIII**

    (1)   As in Proof I

    (2)   As in Proof I

∴ (3)   It is necessarily true that John requires protein in his diet.

Here, however, we run into a difficulty. The difficulty is really an instance of that form of ambiguity called *amphiboly* (§3.8). This must be avoided.

---

4 The account here is oversimple. Frequently among the observed cases only a certain percentage less than all are seen to have the characteristic in question. The conclusion in that case is that among all cases of the sort in question, roughly the same percentage will have the characteristic under consideration. For example, observed litters of newborn cats contained 46.5 percent females and 53.5 percent males. Therefore among all newborn cats 46.5 percent are females and 53.5 percent are males. But this matter will be taken up in Unit 48.

Generally speaking, to call a certain proposition necessary or necessarily true is to claim that analysis (or analysis aided by inference) will suffice to establish the truth of the proposition. A proposition which is necessarily true is always one whose negative involves a self-contradiction. For example, *Every man has a backbone* is a necessary proposition. The very term "man" means (has in its total strict intension) among other things having a backbone.[5] This being the case, the proposition, *Some men (that is, things with backbones) do not have a backbone*, is self-contradictory and the proposition it negates is necessarily true.

But surely the conclusion of Proof VIII is not an affirmation that analysis would show the proposition, *John requires protein in his diet,* to be true and its negative, *John does not require protein in his diet*, to be self-contradictory. No. The necessity does not lie in the proposition which *is* the conclusion, but lies rather in the *connection between* the premises and the conclusion: *Granting the premises*, there is no escaping the conclusion; but the conclusion is not *in itself* necessary. It could be escaped by rejecting the premises.

In point of fact, no valid deductive argument proves that a conclusion is in itself necessary unless all the premises are in themselves necessary. Proof IX is an illustration.

**Proof IX**

   (1)   Triangles necessarily have three sides.
   (2)   Quadrangles necessarily have four sides.
∴ (3)   Quadrangles necessarily have one more side than do triangles.

Since Proof VIII looks as though it were claiming in its conclusion the *necessity* of a proposition, whereas all that can be validly claimed is the *truth* of that proposition, with the phrase "It is necessary that" really modifying " ∴ " instead of modifying the statement that follows it, this amphibolous form of speech should be abandoned and we should return to the original Proof I as the model for deduction. Proof I is valid, Proof VIII is invalid (unless the phrase "It is necessary that" is *not* counted as a part of the conclusion).

All of this discussion of Proof I and Proof VIII raises a question as to whether or not Proof VII is an improvement on Proof II. Is it not possibly the case that the expression "It is probable that," which appears as a part of the conclusion in Proof VII, should really be

5  Compare in this connection §23.1.

thought of as, so to speak, modifying " ∴ " instead of modifying the statement which follows it?

We shall see in a later unit that probability, like necessity, can be used in both ways, hence that Proof VII is, like Proof VIII, amphibolous. But the interpretation for Proof VII which has just been suggested raises an opportunity for us to discern another difference between the deductive model, Proof I, and the inductive model, Proof II. We shall examine that difference in the next section.

### §37.7 Conclusive versus Inconclusive Proofs

As life goes on, you and I are continually gaining new experience, continually learning things that we did not previously know.

Sometimes this new experience brings with it a sad realization that some proposition in which we had previously placed the greatest confidence has after all turned out to be false.

Suppose, however, that we shared two very unlikely pieces of good fortune: first that we never used as a premise from which to infer a conclusion any proposition that later experience showed to be false, and second that the proofs in accordance with which we made our inferences were always valid. What could our new experience as life goes on do to the inferences we had made and the proofs in accordance with which we had inferred?

One thing, it could provide us with additional premises from which to draw conclusions. But since, in accordance with the supposition of the preceding paragraph, the new experience never shows any previously used premise to be false, the old premises are still available and can actually be combined with new premises available because of new experience, so as to permit us to infer new conclusions which could not be validly inferred before.

Will these new conclusions ever contradict the former conclusions? Put in another way our question is, Will the addition of premises to a proof (always keeping the old premises) ever make a proof which was valid into one which is invalid?

Here we find a big difference between Proof I and Proof II, the models for deduction and induction. Let us look again at those two proofs.

**Proof I**

   (1)   Every man requires protein in his diet.
   (2)   John is a man.
∴ (3)   John requires protein in his diet.

This is a valid proof. The assumption that no additional experience will show premises (1) and (2) false means that they can still be used as premises. Now the interesting and important fact is that no matter how many *other* propositions we might *add* as third, fourth, fifth, and so on, premises, and no matter what those other propositions might be, if the original conclusion is kept as the conclusion in the new proof, this new proof will be valid:

**Proof X**

- (1)   Every man requires protein in his diet.
- (2)   John is a man.
- (3)   John is in good health.
- (4)   John is an Eskimo.
- ∴ (5)   John requires protein in his diet.

The proof is still a valid proof.

But the situation is quite different in the case of Proof II:

**Proof II**

- (1)   These tomato plants were killed by frost at a temperature of 32 degrees.
- (2)   Those tomato plants were killed by frost at a temperature of 32 degrees.
- (3)   These other tomato plants were killed by frost at a temperature of 32 degrees.
- ∴ (4)   All tomato plants will be killed by frost at any freezing temperature.

It is not too difficult to see that our new experience *could* bring us new evidence which, when added to the three premises already on hand, would make the conclusion to Proof II invalid. Not any and every additional premise would do it. But there are some that would do it. For example, Proof XI is such. It is invalid.

**Proof XI**

- (1)   These tomato plants were killed by frost at a temperature of 32 degrees.
- (2)   Those tomato plants were killed by frost at a temperature of 32 degrees.
- (3)   These other tomato plants were killed by frost at a temperature of 32 degrees.
- (4)   This fourth set of tomato plants were exposed to a temperature of 30 degrees and were not killed by frost.
- ∴ (5)   All tomato plants will be killed by frost at any freezing temperature.

Plainly the conclusion is no longer valid. The new evidence, reported i
premise (4), makes it invalid. And yet this new evidence is not such a
makes any of the original premises false. Still, it makes what wa
presumably a valid conclusion from them *alone* not valid when they ar
retained but added to.

The situation would not have been saved if we had adopted th
pattern of Proof VII, instead of keeping that of Proof II, and ha
concluded:

∴ (5)   It is probable that all tomato plants will be killed by frost at an
freezing temperature.

For the new evidence, the fourth set of tomato plants makes it highl
*improbable*, in fact invalid to conclude it is probable, that all tomat
plants will be killed by frost at any freezing temperature.

The point that has been illustrated in this section may be put in th
form of a **general principle:** Valid deductive proofs can never be mad
invalid merely by adding more premises; valid inductive proofs can b
made invalid merely by adding more premises. In fact, we shall use thi
principle as the criterion or mark by which deductive proofs ar
distinguished from inductive proofs. Hence the following nominal
intensional **definitions:**

A valid proof is **deductive** = Df there is no statement which, i
added to that valid proof as a further premise, will turn that proo
into an invalid proof.

A valid proof is **inductive** = Df there is at least one statemen
which, if added to that valid proof as a further premise, will turi
that proof into an invalid proof.

In the next section, we shall briefly examine these definitions and se
how they compare with ideas concerning deduction and inductio
considered in earlier sections.

## §37.8  Comments on the Definitions of Deduction and Induction

1.   The first thing to notice about the two definitions o
deduction and induction is that they are contextual definitions, applying
only to *valid* proofs. What about invalid proofs? Are they not deductive
or inductive, and what principles may be used to classify them? Surel
we are in the habit of saying such things as, "That is an invalid deduc
tion." What would such a remark mean?

On the whole, there is not much point in trying to classify invalid arguments as deductive or inductive: they are invalid, and that should usually be an end of the matter. But occasionally, when we are confronted with an invalid proof, we are concerned to discover how it "went wrong," or what changes made in it could "patch it up" into a valid proof. Thinking of it in these terms, we are comparing and contrasting it with other more or less similar proofs which are nevertheless valid. These valid proofs to which we compare the invalid one are deductions or inductions. Thus, without attempting to be too technical or precise, we might propose that when a person says, "That is an invalid deduction," he means, "That is an invalid proof, but it is quite similar in form or structure to a valid deduction." Similar remarks may be made concerning, "That is an invalid induction."

2.   The difference between deductions and inductions used in the preceding section as a definitive difference has for a long time been noted by logicians as a difference. But even while it was noted and often remarked on and discussed, it was not taken to be the definitive difference. These characteristics were, so to speak, noticed as belonging to the total contingent intensions of "deduction" and "induction." But they were not thought of as forming definitive intensions. It is this difference in the *status* of the characteristics which makes the definitions nominal.

3.   Yet the present definitions are not merely nominal. They come very close to being theoretical definitions (§27.4). For while the extensions of the terms so defined may be somewhat different from the extensions of the terms "deduction" and "induction" as used by many authors, it may nevertheless be claimed that these definitive intensions do in fact pick out extensions that more nearly conform to general usage than do many definitive intensions previously cited. Furthermore, it is maintained that the characteristics cited in the definitions (that a deductive proof is conclusive and cannot be invalidated by additional premises, while an inductive proof is inconclusive) are of greater theoretical importance than the characteristics noted in the other definitions of deduction and induction that we considered and rejected. Let us, however, give our attention to the extensions of these terms.

4.   A review of the two definitions will show that every valid proof is either deductive or inductive. Either there is *no* statement (in which case the proof is deductive), or there is *some* statement (in which case the

proof is inductive), that, added as a premise to the original proof, will make that proof invalid.

Some earlier authors have thought of deduction and induction as only two among many types of proof so that making them jointly exhaustive of valid proofs does enlarge the extensions of the terms. But other authors have used the terms in just such a jointly exhaustive sense.

5.   The criteria first suggested, reasoning to or from the general (§37.4), do not make the two classes of proof jointly exhaustive. For example, Proofs XII and XIII, below, reason from the particular to the particular, so that *according to the criteria of §37.4*, they would be neither deductive nor inductive.

**Proof XII**

  (1)   George is either the president or the vice-president of the Senior class.
  (2)   George is not the president of the Senior class.
∴ (3)   George is the vice-president of the Senior class.

**Proof XIII**

  (1)   John and James are Freshmen at X University.
  (2)   They graduated from the same high school.
  (3)   They plan to enter the same profession.
  (4)   They enjoy the same sports.
  (5)   They are taking the same courses.
  (6)   John joined the Glee Club.
∴ (7)   Probably James joined the Glee Club.

Most logicians would list Proof XII as a deductive proof, even though it does not reason from the general. According to our definition it is a deductive proof. On the other hand, many logicians would claim that Proof XIII is neither deductive nor inductive, but rather belongs to a third kind of proof called *proof by analogy*. At the same time, many logicians have noted the similarity between proof by analogy and inductive generalization. In fact, some logicians have tried to justify proof by analogy in terms of inductive generalization. Such efforts are ill-advised. Yet according to our definitions, Proof XIII is an inductive proof.

6.   The familiar criteria of §37.4 (reasoning to and from the general) would make Proof XIV an inductive proof:

**Proof XIV**

   (1)   John is in the room and he is an American citizen.

   (2)   James is in the room and he is an American citizen.

   (3)   William is in the room and he is an American citizen.

   (4)   John, James, and William are the only people in the room.

∴ (5)   Everyone in the room is an American citizen.

In fact, this sort of proof, in which the premises individually, but exhaustively, report on the extension of the term generalized on in the conclusion has been called *perfect induction.* Yet many logicians insist that perfect induction is a form of deduction.

Our definitions will list Proof XIV as a deductive proof. It is not an induction, according to our definitions, because no further evidence added as a premise can make the conclusion invalid.

It is much more important to notice the above fact about Proof XIV than to notice that it draws a general conclusion from particular premises. Proofs like Proof II (or Proof VII) are still inductions and may in fact be distinguished from inductions like Proof XIII by being called **inductive generalizations.** Inductions like Proof XIII may be called **analogical inductions.**

Hence we arrive at the two following principles: (1) Not every valid proof leading from particulars to a general conclusion is an induction. (2) Not every induction is a proof leading from particulars to a general conclusion.

7.   In §37.6 we took note of a tendency to associate proofs in which the conclusions affirm probabilities with induction and those in which the conclusions make absolute affirmations with deduction. This association, however, is not reliable.

If the premises in a valid proof affirm probabilities, it is very likely that the affirmation of a probability can be *deduced* from the premises. One entire branch of mathematics, called *probability theory*, is concerned with deductive proofs of this sort. By way of example, consider deductive Proof XV.

**Proof XV**

   (1)   The probability that my partner has the ace of spades is $1/2$.

   (2)   The probability that he has the ace of hearts is $1/3$.

(3)   His having the ace of spades and his having the ace of hearts are independent events (that is, there is no causal connection between these two events).

∴ (4)   The probability of his having both the ace of spades and the ace of hearts is $1/6$ ($= 1/2 \times 1/3$).

On the other hand a great many proofs leading to probability conclusions are inductive, and the vast majority of inductive proofs do have as their conclusions statements affirming a probability.

In the next few units we shall be concentrating on deduction. Finally, in Unit 48, we shall take up briefly the study of inductive generalization.

## REVIEW QUESTIONS FOR UNIT 37

1. What is meant by the annotation of a proof?
2. What kind of comments or remarks should be included in the annotation of a proof? That is, what kinds of things should the annotation attempt to record?
3. When is a proof said to be fully annotated?
4. When a given proof is being put into standard form and annotated, must the annotator limit himself to preserving the comments and remarks appearing in the original proof? Or may he add comments which did not appear in the original proof? If the latter, what sort of comments may be added?
5. Explain briefly the original meanings of the words "deduction" and "induction." Are those meanings still in use today?
6. Why is it generally amphibolous to use the expression "it is necessary that" as part of the conclusion in a deduction?
7. Explain the fundamental difference between deductive and inductive proofs in terms of which *deduction* and *induction* are defined in this text.
8. What could it mean to say that a certain proof is an invalid deduction? An invalid induction? Explain.
9. As the terms *deduction* and *induction* have been defined in this text, is it true that:
  a. Every valid proof is either deductive or inductive?
  b. Every valid proof leading from particulars to a general conclusion is an induction?
  c. Every induction is a proof from particulars to a general conclusion?
  d. Every valid proof affirming a probability in its conclusion is an induction?
  In each case, briefly explain why you answer as you do.
10. What is meant by inductive generalization?
11. What is meant by analogical induction?

# Variables and the Representation of Forms

---

### §38.1 The Problem of the Next Few Units

During the next few units, we shall be concerned with deductive proofs and, in particular, with the question of how you can tell whether a given proof is a valid deduction.

Efforts to answer this question will not always be successful. There are no mechanical rules that can be laid down, like the rules for multiplication or long division, such that you can always apply the rules and when you have applied them you will always have found the answer. Rather, we have to depend on two things: a knowledge of the principles of deductive logic and a general skill or know-how in the matter of applying these principles. Sometimes, this matter of application is quite simple and direct. On other occasions it is more complicated and difficult. In the next three units we shall see what some of the principles of deductive logic are and how they may be applied in direct and simple cases. Then, in Unit 42 we shall consider a few somewhat more difficult problems of application.

What has just been said might suggest that nobody could distinguish a valid argument from an invalid one until he had studied the principles of logic. Of course, nothing could be further from the truth. You and I have been trying—and often quite successfully—to do just that for as long as we can remember. Indeed, it is this very fact—that people do distinguish between valid and invalid proofs—that caused the science of logic to get started in the first place. The situation is like our attention to animals. Long before we studied biology, we were noticing animals, their differences and similarities, and their characteristic modes of behavior. Biology is only a more systematic, thorough, and careful assembling, correction, and extension of these same observings and of the judgments based on them. Unless people had been able to notice such things without biology, there would not have been anything to systematize. And the same sort of thing is true in logic. Unless "pre-logicians" could have been aware of a difference between valid and invalid, there would have been nothing for logic to have undertaken to systematize.

## §38.2 Principles of Logic and What They Are Concerned With

We shall not try to suggest here everything which might be of interest to the logician. Let us limit ourselves to his concerns insofar as they bear on the validity of proofs.

To speak of "the validity of proofs" is at once to think of the logician's task in terms of language. Because, as we have seen, a proof is a linguistic structure. But this does not mean that the logician is limited to a concern with English, or French, or any other specific language. Indeed, we even find him *inventing* language of his own in order more clearly and effectively to formulate those principles that bear on the validity of proofs. We shall ourselves borrow a few signs from some of his languages.

Nevertheless our interest here continues to be in the application of his principles to English, the language that most of us use as our tool of thought. Hence, we shall first state in general terms what it is that the principles of logic are concerned with. Then we shall illustrate in terms of English.

Logic may be said to be the study of the effect on the meanings of statements—and consequently on the validity of proofs that might contain those statements—of all parts and aspects of those statements *except* the intensions of their terms. Thus it studies the effect of a term's being singular or general, the effect of the signs of quantity, like "all," "some," "four," and so on, that modify general terms (see §§16.5 and 17.3), the effect of the verb "to be" that connects terms (see §§16.4, 16.5, and 16.6), the effect of the sign of negation "not," the effect of conjunctions, like "if," "or," "and," that combine statements into more complex statements, even the effect of having several tokens of the same term occurring in a certain pattern. The only thing it does not study is the effect of the specific intensions which the terms occurring in the statements and the proofs might have. Studies of the specific intensions of specific terms belong to the various special sciences: of "George Washington" to history, of "animal" to biology, and so on.[1]

## §38.3 Variables

How does the logician go about isolating just those items that were mentioned and studying their effects? The key to his approach lies in his use of a special kind of sign, called a *variable*. We have already used variables in this text. For example, when we were classifying propositions in Unit 16, we used the letters "*s*" and "*P*," and those were variables. And again in Part IV, when we were studying sentential contextual definitions and the rules for definition, we used such letters as "*x*" and "*y*." They were variables. Even the pronouns of English, "I," "he," "it," and so on, are variables. It is important to *understand* them.

To make a beginning, it may be said that a **variable** is a sign-type insofar as tokens of that sign-type are regularly used as *abstractive substitutes* for other tokens.

Regarded as a definition, the statement just made will probably not be very illuminating until it has itself been explained. In the next two sections, we shall undertake to explain what it means. One point, however, may be noticed here before we go on to those explanations. The definition defines a variable as a sign-type insofar as tokens of it are used in a certain way. This is similar to the definitions of terms and statements, given earlier in this book. They were sign-types with associated meanings. Thus not all tokens of a given sign-type are tokens of one term: they are tokens of one term only insofar as they (the tokens) have the same meaning. Similarly, a variable is a sign-type with an associated *use*. Not all tokens of that sign-type will be tokens of that variable. For example, not all tokens of "he" or of the letter "*x*" are tokens of the variables "he" and "*x*." They will be tokens of a variable only when they are being used as abstractive substitutes for other tokens.

## §38.4 Variables and Simple Substitution

Our languages usually contain a special set of sign-types, tokens of which are regularly used in two *different* kinds of substitution.

---

[1]  Logic is concerned with more effects than those on validity of the items suggested. For example, it is also concerned with their effect on the self-contradictoriness of a statement and on the mutual inconsistency of groups of statements. But since our concern now is with validity, we shall not attempt to formulate a more nearly adequate definition of logic.

One of these we shall call **simple substitution,** the other **abstractive substitution.** When a token of one of these sign-types is used as a simple substitute, it is not a token of a variable, but when it is used as an abstractive substitute, it is a token of a variable. The logic of our languages would be much easier to understand if we did not use tokens of one and the same sign-type for both kinds of substitution. But in most languages we do just that. Thus it becomes necessary to understand the two kinds of substitution so that we can tell them apart. In this section, we shall discuss simple substitution.

Perhaps the most familiar examples of simple substitution are those cases in which we use a pronoun in place of an available term. For example, instead of saying, "Please give Mr. Black Mr. Black's hat," we say "Please give Mr. Black his hat." Similarly, if Mr. Black had asked Mr. Green how to reach the library, Mr. Green might reply, "I am going there. Let me show you the way." This is much less awkward than if he had said, "Mr. Green is going there. Let Mr. Green show Mr. Black the way."

A different sort of example of simple substitution occurs when we undertake the solution of certain mathematical problems. To illustrate, suppose that we had information to the effect that Joe owned twice as many sheep as he did cows. Maybe we have other information at hand and we wish to discover the number of Joe's sheep. We might begin by deciding to let "$S$" represent the number of Joe's sheep and "$C$" the number of his cows. With these decisions made, we formulate the information already given in the form of an arithmetic equation:

$$S = 2C.$$

Here the use of "$S$" and "$C$" is a case of simple substitution. They are, so to speak, the pronouns of algebra, substitutes for the definite descriptions "the number of Joe's sheep" and "the number of Joe's cows." Mathematicians speak of them as representing "unknowns," not because we do not know definite descriptions that would refer to the same things, but because we do not know which "proper name"— "2," "3," "4," and so on—would refer to that same thing.

Tokens of one sign-type are used as simple substitutes for tokens of another for at least two different kinds of reason: (1) to avoid monotonous repetition of the sign-types they are substituted for, (2) for abbreviative purposes. ("$S$" is much simpler than "the number of Joe's sheep" and "you" is much simpler than "the person whom the present speaker is addressing.")

But what is most important to notice is that every token of a sign-type used as a simple substitute for a token of another sign-type is a token of a **constant,** that is, of an expression that is *not* a variable. Usually—and this is true of all the above examples—it is a token of a *term*. The token has its purported referent, Mr. Brown, or the number of Joe's sheep, or whatever. (Occasionally, as in tokens of plural pronouns—"we", "they," and so on—the token will be a token of a *general* term.)

What is peculiar about terms created by this kind of simple substitution is their temporariness and one might almost say the constant "flicker" with which tokens of the sign-type in question alternate from being tokens of one term to being tokens of another term. For example, all the tokens of the pronoun "I" produced by Mr. Brown will be tokens of one term, purporting to refer to Mr. Brown, while all the tokens of "I" produced by Mr. Green will be tokens of another term purporting to refer to a different individual, Mr. Green. Or again, all tokens of "$S$" produced while we let "$S$" stand for the number of Joe's sheep will be tokens of one term; while as soon as we start work on the next problem, about slot machines and cash registers, the tokens of "$S$" and "$C$" will be tokens of other terms.

To sum up, *simple* substitution gives rise to a token of a constant; *abstractive* substitution (to which we turn in the next section) gives rise to a token of a variable.

## §38.5 Variables and Abstractive Substitution

Suppose we were watching a "race" between a bicycle and an automobile, and suppose that the automobile traveled always twice as fast as the bicycle: when the bicycle was going 5 miles an hour, the automobile was going 10 miles an hour; when the bicycle speeded up to 10 miles an hour, the automobile speeded up to 20 miles an hour, and so on.

Now all the time the race is going on, the distance that each vehicle has traveled over is increasing. But in spite of this fact, there remains a constant *relation* between the distances over which the two vehicles have moved. If we let "$d$" represent the distance over which the bicycle has traveled, and "$D$" represent the distance over which the automobile has traveled, then no matter at what time during the race we compute these distances (so long as we compute them both for the same moment), it will be true that

$$D = 2d.$$

This equation represents something that remains constant even while the values of "$D$" and "$d$" vary according as we take the measurement at one time in the race or at another.

In the above equation, "$D$" and "$d$" are tokens of variables. Their use is entirely different from that of pronouns and signs for unknowns considered in the preceding section. In the earlier section, each token represented one individual thing: it was *different* tokens, or *different* problems, that gave you tokens of the same sign-type representing a different individual. But here, the one token "$D$" is supposed to vary over a whole lot of individuals: the individual distances that the automobile will have traveled at different moments during the race.

The systematic use of tokens in the manner just described marks one of the distinctive features of modern science, beginning in the seventeenth century. Nearly all the laws of physics are expressed in just such equations, which are supposed to hold even while the values of the tokens change. For example, Boyle's Law of Gases describes a constant relation between the varying volumes ($V$) and pressures ($P$) of a gas when its temperature is kept constant:

$$\frac{V_1}{V_2} = \frac{P_2}{P_1}.$$

That is, no matter at what points in its varying volumes and pressures you choose to measure these quantities, for a given amount of gas, as the volume gets bigger the pressure gets smaller, and vice versa. Here the equation is supposed to hold through all variations of the volume and the pressure.[2]

Other sciences as well use tokens in much the same manner. For example, if you have studied algebra, you will remember the equation

$$(x + y)^2 = x^2 + 2xy + y^2,$$

which holds true no matter how the numbers represented by "$x$" and "$y$" might vary. Or again, if you have studied geometry, you will recall the formula for the area of a triangle:

$$A = \frac{B \times H}{2}.$$

---

[2] As you probably know, this law does not hold at extremely high pressures.

This equation holds for all variations in shape and size of the triangle. Thus the tokens "*A*," "*B*," and "*H*" may take on all sorts of values, and yet the equation will remain true.

Much the same sort of use of tokens occurs in many of our uses of simple pronouns. For example, consider the statement, "If a man marries, he is responsible for debts incurred by his wife." The main clause of this statement is much like the equations we have just been looking at. It contains two tokens of the pronoun "he." But the whole intent of the statement is to affirm that no matter how you vary the thing referred to by "he," so long as you limit its range of variation to married men, the statement, "he is responsible for debts incurred by his wife," will be true. How different this is from the meaning of precisely the same clause in this other context: "Mr. Brown is married. Therefore, he is responsible for debts incurred by his wife." In this latter occurrence of the clause, we have a case of simple substitution; "he" purports to have a unique referent, namely, Mr. Brown; "he" is a token of a singular term. But in the former occurrence of the clause, "he" does not purport to have a unique referent, neither Mr. Brown nor Mr. Green nor anyone else. As some logicians might say, its referent varies over the range of all married men.

How are we to understand these uses of sign-types? We shall speak of them as cases of **abstractive substitution.** In a clause, sentence, equation, or other expression, there have been placed tokens of the sign-type in question. Usually, the places these tokens occupy in these large expressions are places that *might* have been occupied by terms.[3] But the tokens occupying those positions are *not* terms, for it cannot be determined what they purport to refer to. In fact, it can be determined that they do not purport to have any identifiable referents. So to speak, they are deliberately ambiguous tokens, and therefore not tokens of terms. They are tokens of variables.

But what is the point? By putting these tokens of variables in those positions, one can represent in the total expression à whole class of propositions, equations, or whatever: all of these that you *would* get by having terms where the variables occur. Thus the variables permit us to represent a *form*, or kind, of expression by presenting what

---

[3]  But this is not *always* so. For example, in §§16.5 and 16.6 we placed *x*'s and *y*'s in positions that might have been occupied by signs of quantity rather than by terms.

amounts to a token or specimen of that expression, except that in the specimen we have substituted tokens of variables for tokens of terms.[4]

There are all sorts of reasons why we might wish to attend to such forms. One kind of reason is that frequently we can affirm that every statement having one of those forms will be true, provided that the tokens occurring in these statements where the variables occur in this representation of the form meet some specifiable condition. For example, every statement of the form, "he is responsible for debts incurred by his wife," is true, provided that the term occurring in that statement in the places occupied by "he" in this representation of the form is a singular term whose referent is a married man. Or again, every equation of the form

$$A = \frac{B + H}{2}$$

is true, provided that the term having the position occupied by "$A$" is a singular term referring to the area of some triangle, and so on.

### §38.6 Variables, Abstractive Substitution, and Logic

One is tempted to say that the use of variables and abstractive substitution is as old as the hills. One can safely guess, however, that it is *nearly* as old as pronouns. But its tremendous value as an instrument of scientific thought is much less old. The ancient Greeks had a dim grasp of the device, which they used to great advantage in the development of geometry. When, for example, a proof begins, "Let figure *abc* be a right-angled triangle with angle *abc* a right angle . . .," the Greeks were using abstractive substitution. "*a*," "*b*," and "*c*" were being used as variables. They did not purport to name specific points in space, but rather *any* points provided that the lines

---

[4]  These representations of forms through the use of variables are a kind of iconic sign, like a map or diagram, since they are expressions having the forms they represent. (On iconic signs, see §14.7.)

It should now be clear that the variable *in itself* has no meaning or purported referent. It contributes to the meaning of the expression in which it occurs. It contributes to making that expression represent a class, or form, of expression. This being so, certain remarks made on the last page or so must be seen to be not literally true. For example, it is false that "Its referent varies over the range of all married men," and also false that variables are "deliberately ambiguous." These remarks are false because variables neither have nor purport to have referents. They have no meaning. But perhaps that metaphorical manner of speaking helped us achieve the recognition of what has been claimed in the present paragraph: that variables have a use, as substitutes for terms so that one can represent forms.

connecting those points would form a right angle at point *b*. And other uses of abstractive substitution occurred among the Greeks.

But a great impetus to the systematic use of abstractive substitution and thus of variables came with the introduction of algebra.[5] Here was another field, not points (as in geometry) but numbers, over which variables might be allowed to range. And effective results could be achieved by allowing them to do so.

The use of variables and abstractive substitution provides precisely the instrument needed by the logician to enter upon the task that was described in the first two sections of this unit. For, by substituting variables for the terms in a statement, one can attend to the form of that statement and to the manner in which every part and aspect of it except the intensions of its terms affects its meaning.

Going on from there, we might substitute variables for the terms in a proof to represent the form of the proof. Certain forms of proof are such that all proofs having that form will be valid. An example is the following.

> (1)   Every *M* is a *P*.
> (2)   *s* is an *M*.
> ∴ (3)   *s* is a *P*.

This is one type of syllogism.

Logic is developed largely by representing through the use of variables certain forms of proof such that all proofs having that form will be valid. Other parts of the science are developed by setting up rules for abstracting a form from a proof by the use of variables and determining from the character of the abstracted form whether the original proof was valid.

As the last example may suggest, to represent a form of proof generally involves representing the forms of its constituent premises and conclusion. In the next unit, we shall commence this inquiry by considering the forms of statements representing singular propositions.

## EXERCISES

1.  In §38.4, we have Mr. Brown and Mr. Green talking to one another. Are the tokens of the sign-types "Mr. Green" and "Mr. Brown" which

---

[5] Algebra is a very old branch of mathematics. The earliest Western work in this field is that of Diophantus in the fourth century. But it became a subject of more general study in the West only in the sixteenth century. It was this later cultivation of algebra which brought efforts to apply systematically the same techniques of abstractive substitution in other fields.

appear in that section tokens of variables? Are some of them tokens of variables and some of them not? Does it make any difference whether the token you are considering occurred inside quotation marks (as a part of what somebody said) or was not in quotation marks?

2. When the police know that a crime has been committed but do not know the name of the person who committed it, they sometimes secure a "John Doe warrant" for the arrest of the criminal. This warrant authorizes them to arrest "John Doe." Where the criminal's name would appear if they knew what his name was, the warrant has the name "John Doe." Is the use of that token of the sign-type "John Doe" a use of <u>simple substitution</u> or a use of abstractive substitution? Explain.

*one spec. person*

3. A manual on police procedures might contain a specimen warrant for arrest, so that police students may study it and learn the correct form in which to draw up such warrants. In that specimen warrant appears a token of the sign-type "John Doe," where the police officer should write in the name of the person to be arrested. Is the use of this token of the sign-type "John Doe" in the specimen warrant a use of simple substitution or a use of <u>abstractive substitution</u>? Explain. *take place of anyone or class*

## REVIEW QUESTIONS FOR UNIT 38

1. Must people have studied logic before they can ever tell the difference between a valid and an invalid proof? Discuss briefly why you answer as you do.

2. How could you describe which features of a proof are attended to by the logician when he develops principles in accordance with which one might classify proofs as valid or invalid? What feature is it that he does *not* attend to?

3. What linguistic tool does the logician find most useful in the formulation of his principles? Discuss briefly the manner in which this tool is used.

4. Describe and illustrate what is meant by simple substitution. By abstractive substitution.

5. What is a variable?

6. What is a constant?

7. Do other sciences than logic use variables? Give one or two examples.

# *Singular Statements*

---

## §39.1 A Review

In this unit, we shall consider how to represent the form of a singular statement. This will pave the way to representing the forms of valid proofs that contain singular statements.

In §16.4 there occur formulas said to represent four types of singular proposition:

| | |
|---|---|
| I-A. | $s$ is $P$. |
| I-B. | $s$ is a $P$. |
| II-A. | $s_1$ is $P$ (to) $s_2$. |
| II-B. | $s_1$ is a $P$ (of) $s_2$. |

In a footnote to that section, it was pointed out that these four formulas actually represent the forms of statements *indicating* singular propositions rather than the forms of the propositions themselves. Thus they provide us with a good point of departure for the work of this unit.

As this unit proceeds we shall frequently need to refer back to points made in Units 16 through 19. It might be as well to recall some of them now. If these reminders are not sufficient, you might find it advisable to review the units.

1. In §16.4 it was said that any statement having form II-A also had form I-A, and any statement having form II-B also had form I-B. This point was further discussed in §17.3. If we analyze any such statement by the simpler form, I-A or I-B, then we are counting as a complex term an expression which the more detailed analyses represented by formulas II-A and II-B break up into two terms. For example, "John is a brother of William," could be analyzed in either way. Analyzed by form I-B, the term corresponding to "*P*" is "brother of William." But when the same statement is analyzed according to II-B, the expression "brother of William" is broken up to reveal and isolate the constituent terms "brother" and "William."

Thus forms II-A and II-B are special cases of the more widely illustrated forms I-A and I-B.

2. In formulas II-A and II-B, the prepositions "to" and "of" appear in parentheses to indicate that sometimes the conventions of good English do not require any word in these positions (for example: "John is hammering the nail.") and that sometimes these conventions require a different word than "to" or "of." (For example, "John is taller than James," or "John is a refugee from Poland.")

3. In statements having any of these forms, the terms occupying the positions taken by "$s$," "$s_1$," or "$s_2$" are singular terms (abstract or concrete) while those occupying the positions taken by "$P$" are general terms. If the form is either I-A or II-A, that general term is attributive; whereas if the form is I-B or II-B that general term is denotative. In forms I-A and I-B, the general term is absolute, whereas in forms II-A and II-B it is relative. "$P$" (pg 08) of (passed by)

4. In statements of form I-A or II-A, the attributive term occupying the position taken by "$P$" could be a verb or verbal phrase. For example, "John laughs," or "John hammered the nail." In such cases, the connecting verb "is" is omitted.

## §39.2 Subjects and Predicates

It is very helpful to be able to refer to the terms in statements in some less complicated fashion than by saying, for example, "the term occupying the position taken by '$s$'." Furthermore, we do not always use just the four formulas printed at the beginning of this unit. We might, for example, find it desirable to represent some statements by "$s_3$ is a $Q$" instead of by "$s$ is a $P$."

We can nevertheless supply names for those terms by reference to just these four formulas.

A logical subject of a singular statement on a given analysis is any term occupying a place which would be taken by "$s$," "$s_1$," or "$s_2$" if one of the formulas appearing at the beginning of this unit were used to represent that analysis.

The logical predicate of a singular statement on a given analysis is the term occupying the position taken by "$P$" if one of the formulas appearing at the beginning of this unit were used to represent that analysis.

For example, in "John is a brother of George," "John" is the subject and "brother of George" is the predicate on an analysis according to I-B; but "John" and "George" are the first and second subjects and "brother" is the predicate on an analysis according to II-B.

The words "subject" and "predicate" are used as terms in grammatical analysis, but there they have slightly different meanings from those they have in logic. First, what constitutes the logical predicate is often only a part of the grammatical predicate, which will also include the words "is" or "is a" and the second logical subject (if the analysis chosen supplies one). Second, what is the grammatical predicate cannot be changed by choosing first one method of analysis and then another. Put in more technical terms, what are the grammatical subject and grammatical predicate is relative only to the sentence; whereas what are the logical subject(s) and the logical predicate is relative both to the statement and to the method of analysis.

In the future, when we say "subject" or "predicate," we shall mean the logical subject or logical predicate. If we wish to refer to the grammatical subject or grammatical predicate, we shall use the word "grammatical." We may sum up the points made in the preceding section as follows: On any analysis, a singular statement has one predicate and one or more subjects. The subjects are always singular terms (either abstract or concrete) and the predicate always a general term. If the form in question is I-A or I-B, the predicate is an absolute term; if it is II-A or II-B, the predicate is a relative term. If the form is I-A or II-A, the predicate is an attributive term; if the form is I-B or II-B, the predicate is a denotative term.

## §39.3 Standard Formula I

Let us compare the two statements in each of the following pairs.

(1a)         Figure *abc* is triangular.
(1b)         Figure *abc* is a triangle.
(2a)         That watch is made of gold.
(2b)         That watch is a thing made of gold.

In each pair, the first statement is of form I-A and the second is of form I-B. Yet the two statements in each pair have exactly the same meaning; that is, each purports to indicate exactly the same proposition as does the other.

The reason for this identity of meaning lies in the relation between their two predicates. The first statement in each pair has an attributive

$$S \text{ is } P \text{ to } S_2 \quad - \quad S \text{ is a } P \text{ of } S_2$$

term for its predicate, while the second statement has as its predicate the first denotative correlate of that attributive term. Any attributive term and its first denotative correlate have the same extension and the same total strict intension. Now each statement in the pair amounts to an affirmation that the purported referent of the subject term has all the characteristics in the total strict intension—thus is in the extension—of the predicate. But since the total strict intensions of the predicates are identical, as are also their extensions, the affirmations are identical.

What is more important than that those two pairs of statements were pairs with identical meanings, is the fact that every statement of form I-A has such a matching statement of form I-B. For every statement of form I-A has an attributive term for its predicate and every attributive term has a first denotative correlate. If the vocabulary of English does not provide it, we can always invent it by using the word "thing" or some other word, as in statement (2b) above.

Thus every statement of form I-A could be transformed into an equivalent statement of form I-B. We shall not always bother actually to make that transformation. But the fact that it can be made permits us to use the formula for form I-B as the standard formula to represent the form of any statement *either* of form I-A *or* of form I-B. Since we shall use it both for statements of form I-A and of form I-B, we shall call it simply **standard formula I.**

When we represent the form of some given statement by a standard formula, we should say what the terms are in that statement which the variables "$s$," "$P$," and so on, replace. For example, if we were to represent the form of "John is a student," we should write:

Let: "$s$" replace "John."[1]

"$P$" replace "student."

Then the form of the given statement is represented by

$$s \text{ is a } P.$$

In accordance with the decision to use "$s$ is a $P$" for both I-A and I-B, when we in fact have a statement of form I-A, we should put in our "dictionary" opposite "$P$" the first denotative correlate of the predicate

---

[1] In these "dictionaries" that accompany representations of forms, we say "replace" rather than "represent" to suggest that the substitution of the variable for the term is abstractive substitution (§38.5) rather than simple substitution (§38.4).

actually appearing in the statement. For example, if we were to represent the form of "John is angry," we should write:

Let: "*s*" replace "John."

"*P*" replace "angry person."

Then the form of the given statement is represented by

*s* is a *P*.

Strictly speaking, we should in the last example let "*P*" replace "angry thing" rather than "angry person." But practically speaking, no great harm is done if on occasion we "narrow" the extensions of the first denotative correlates in some such appropriate way as this. And in fact sometimes we *must* do so. For sometimes a statement in form I-A assigns a characteristic to the purported referent of the subject term on the basis of a comparison (often understood but unexpressed) and the field of the comparison need not be the field of all things generally. For example, "John is tall" does not mean that he is tall in comparison with things generally, including the Washington Monument and Mount Everest, but that he is tall in comparison with people or with children of his age, or whatever. To transform such a statement by writing, "John is a tall thing," would be incorrect because this suggests that the basis of comparison is things generally. Hence, for this statement we *should* write:

Let: "*s*" replace "John."

"*P*" replace "tall person."

## EXERCISE

Represent the forms of the following statements. In each case, write your "dictionary."

1. George Washington is a famous American.
2. That house is made of wood. *S is a P*
3. My dog is highly educated. *S is a P* (*My dog is a highly educated animal*)
4. This piece of candy is sweet.
5. John is lucky at cards.

## §39.4 Standard Formula II

In dealing with form II-A and II-B [$s_1$ is $P$ (to) $s_2$, and $s_1$ is a $P$ (of) $s_2$] the situation is not essentially different: There always is, or we can always invent, a first denotative correlate for the attributive predicate of a statement in form II-A; hence we can always transform that statement into form II-B. Thus, we shall use the formula for form II-B to represent the forms of all statements that we wish to analyze by forms II-A or II-B. We shall speak of this as **standard formula II.**

EXAMPLE: John is taller than James.

Let: "$s_1$" replace "John."

"$s_2$" replace "James."

"$P$" replace "taller thing."

Then the form of the given statement is represented by

$$s_1 \text{ is a } P \text{ of } s_2.$$

Note two things about the above. First, we have removed the word "of" from parentheses. Second, we have used the standard preposition "of" in representing the form even though the particular statement we were analyzing would use the word "than."

## EXERCISE

Represent the forms of the following statements *twice*, first using "$s$ is a $P$" and second using "$s_1$ is a $P$ of $s_2$." Give each "dictionary."

1. Frederick is an employee of The X Company.
2. Frederick is employed by The X Company.
3. The bat struck the ball.
4. His house is located at 78 Green Street.
5. Red is more exciting than blue.
6. William recited *Thanatopsis*. will is a reciter of the

## §39.5 "To Be" as an Affirmation of Existence

Certain statements present special difficulties with respect to their logical analysis. In this section and the next we shall consider two types of situation in which we must be especially careful.

A famous philosopher, René Descartes (1596-1650), once wrote what has since become a famous statement: "I think, therefore I am."[2] Our present concern is not with the truth or falsity of his statement, but with the form of its main clause, "I am." On the surface, this looks quite different from forms I and II. Apparently it contains a subject

[2] See, for example, his *Meditations*, Part II. But the statement is repeated in many of his other writings.

term, "I," and the verb "to be," but no predicate. Thus, instead of "*s* is a *P*" we seem to have the form "*s* is."

The solution to this riddle has two parts. First, we have seen that many sign-types have several meanings associated with them. The verb "to be" is no exception to this general fact. Tokens of "is" in statements of the form "*s* is" have a different meaning from tokens of "is" in statements of the form "*s* is a *P*." What Descartes is affirming he could as well have affirmed by saying, "I exist."

Second, once we notice the above fact, it is easy to see that in statements of the form "*s* is," the verb "is" is the predicate. Rather than that the predicate has disappeared, the *connective* verb "is" has disappeared, just as it does in any statement (like "John laughs") in which the predicate is a verb.

In order to avoid this source of confusion when one is making logical analyses, it is wise not to regard a sentence of the form "*s* is" as in standard form. In general, replace "is" by "exists."

The term "to exist" is one of the few terms which must be treated in logic. Hence we shall treat "*s* exists" as **standard formula III,** by the use of which we can represent the forms of certain statements. Thus, for example, we could represent the form of Descartes' statement "I am" as follows.

Let: "*s*" replace "Descartes."

Then the form of the given statement is represented by

*s* exists.

On the other hand, "exists" is a predicate, so that "*s* exists" represents a special case of form I, just as II represents a special case of form I. Hence, if we were not concerned to record the details of the special case, we could represent the form of Descartes' statement as follows:

Let: "*s*" replace "Descartes."
"*P*" replace "existing thing."

Then the form of the given statement is represented by

*s* is a *P*.

Before leaving this topic, we should notice that not every sentence-token of the form "*s* is" has a meaning and logical form that can be represented by "*s* exists." For example, suppose that you and I over-heard the following quarrel:

Mr. A: You're not even honest!
Mr. B: I am!

Plainly, Mr. B. means "I am honest," rather than "I exist." In repre-senting the form of his statement, we must supply the missing, but understood, term:

Let: "*s*" replace "Mr. B."
"*P*" replace "honest person."

Then the form of Mr. B.'s statement is represented by

$$s \text{ is a } P.$$

### §39.6 "To Be" as an Affirmation of Identity

Statements such as "Ike is Dwight David Eisenhower," and "George Washington is the first President of the United States," require a treatment of "is" somewhat similar to that given it in the preceding section.

The *apparent* form of these statements could be represented by

$$s_1 \text{ is } s_2.$$

But again, the sign-token "is" has the meaning of a relative attributive term and the "is" of connection has been omitted as in any sentence using a verb for its predicate term.

The meaning of "$s_1$ is $s_2$" is plainly given in "$s_1$ is identical with $s_2$," a statement of form II.

Since "identical with" is another of the few terms that must be analyzed in logic, we shall use "$s_1$ is identical with $s_2$" as **standard formula IV,** and with it represent the form of certain singular state-ments. Thus we could represent the form of the first illustrative state-ment at the beginning of this section as follows:

Let: "$s_1$" replace "Ike."
"$s_2$" replace "Dwight David Eisenhower."

Then the form of the given statement is represented by

$$s_1 \text{ is identical with } s_2.$$

On the other hand, "$s_1$ is identical with $s_2$" is a special case of form II and if we had no wish to preserve the record of this special case, we could have represented the form as follows.

Let: "$s_1$" represent "Ike."
  "$s_2$" represent "Dwight David Eisenhower."
  "$P$" represent "identical thing."

Then the form of the given statement is represented by

$$s_1 \text{ is a } P \text{ of } s_2.$$

## EXERCISE

Represent the form of each of the following statements, using always the forms for special cases where they will apply.

1.  George kicked the ball.  *$s_1$ is a P of $s_2$*
2.  George is the person who kicked the ball.  *s is a P*
3.  John is a voter.  *$s_1$ is identical with $s_2$*
4.  John voted in the last election.  *$s_1$ is a P of $s_2$*

## §39.7 Affirmative and Negative Statements

We have now distinguished and represented four forms of singular statement to which attention is given in logic:

I.       $s$ is a $P$.
II.      $s_1$ is a $P$ of $s_2$.
III.     $s$ exists.
IV.      $s_1$ is identical with $s_2$.

Of these four forms we have noticed that the last three represent directly or indirectly special cases of the first. We must now take note of the fact that these four forms will cover, so to speak, only half of the singular statements that we run across. For these statement forms are appropriate only when an author's concern is to *affirm* that $s$ is a $P$, or a $P$ of $s_2$, or an existent, or identical with $s_2$. Suppose that he was concerned to *deny* one or another of these things. Then, instead of writing a statement that has one of these four forms, he would write such a statement *except* that he would introduce a **sign of denial:**

(1)  John is *not* a student.
(2)  George *fails* to be a voter.
(3)  *It is false that* James is taller than William.
(4)  The President of the United States is *not* the President of the United States Senate.

Hence we must recognize four standard statement forms that differ from the original four merely by their inclusion of a sign of denial.

Singular statements that in standard form contain no sign of denial are said to be **affirmative** statements, those that in standard form contain one sign of denial are said to be **negative** statements. The standard sign of denial for singular statements will be the word "not" and its standard position will be immediately after the verb "is." Hence, we get finally a table of eight standard representations of forms for singular statements:

| Type | Affirmative | Negative |
|------|-------------|----------|
| I. | $s$ is a $P$. | $s$ is not a $P$. |
| II. | $s_1$ is a $P$ of $s_2$. | $s_1$ is not a $P$ of $s_2$. |
| III. | $s$ exists. | $s$ does not exist. |
| IV. | $s_1$ is identical with $s_2$. | $s_1$ is not identical with $s_2$. |

*EXERCISE*

Represent the form of each of the four statements listed earlier in this section. Use the most detailed representations available.

### §39.8 Interpretations of Affirmative and Negative Statements*

In the preceding section, we spoke of a "sign of denial." Also we spoke of the affirmative statement as "suitable" when the author's concern is to affirm that $s$ is a $P$ and the negative statement as "suitable" when the author's concern is to deny that $s$ is a $P$. All this talk about concerns and suitability is true enough, yet we must reconsider those interpretations for a moment so as to reach a more adequate view.

In Unit 14 we saw that in every piece of productive discourse, the produced tokens expressed their author's concern and indicated the topic of their author's concern. This topic of concern is usually a proposition. In this expression of concern and indication of topic consists the meaning, or signification, of the sign-tokens that are produced.

Let us now consider some pair of affirmative and negative statements with identical subjects and predicates, for example, "John is a voter," and "John is not a voter." Now the account in the preceding section (summarized two paragraphs above) seems to suggest that these two statements, considered as tokens produced by an author, indicate one and the same topic of concern but express different concerns with it. Both the affirmative and the negative statement indicate, on this view, as their topic of concern that proposition or state of affairs which consists in John's being a voter. The two statements differ in that the affirmative statement expresses the author's *acceptance* of

---

* This section may be omitted without disturbing the continuity of the text.

this proposition as true, or a fact; while the negative statement expresses the author's rejection of that proposition as false, or not a fact. On this interpretation, the entire signification of the sign of denial (the only feature that distinguishes the token of the negative from that of the affirmative) is referred to expression of the author's concern.

Actually, the preceding section did not claim that this is what affirmative and negative statements *do* signify. It only claimed that this is what they are *suitable* or *appropriate* to signify. To be sure, they are appropriate for these purposes and are often used to serve them. But also declarative sentences are frequently used to serve other purposes, so that their utterance does not always express acceptance or rejection of some indicated proposition. We saw, for example, in §36.4 on the uses of proofs, many uses which did not involve either acceptance or rejection of propositions indicated by the statements which are the premises and conclusion of a proof.

Therefore, it seems desirable to explain the signification of signs of denial in some manner that does not connect them with the changing concerns that statements express.

This can be done by claiming that affirmative and negative statements with identical subjects and predicates do not indicate one and the same proposition. Rather, let it be claimed, they indicate **mutually contradictory** propositions. For example, "John is a voter" indicates that proposition or state of affairs which consists in John's being a voter, while "John is not a voter" indicates that proposition or state of affairs which consists in John's not being a voter. The two indicated propositions are mutually contradictory; that is, each of them is a state of affairs which consists in the falsity or nonexistence of that state of affairs in which the other consists. Under these circumstances, one and only one of the two indicated propositions will exist, or be a fact.

Under this interpretation, the sign of denial has its signification exhausted by its contribution to identifying what proposition is indicated by the entire statement of which it is a part. The statement with that sign of denial omitted indicates one proposition, the statement with that sign of denial included indicates another, the mutually contradictory, proposition.

But how does the business of affirmation and denial fare under this interpretation? *When statements are uttered in order to express acceptance or rejection,* we say that they invariably express acceptance of the indicated proposition. But in the rational man to accept one proposition is to reject its mutual contradictory. Hence to affirm the negative statement—that is, to express acceptance of the proposition indicated by the negative statement—is tantamount to denying the corresponding affirmative statement—that is, to expressing rejection of the proposition indicated by the corresponding affirmative statement. But equally, to affirm the affirmative statement is to deny the negative statement.

The reader who looks back to §5.5, "A Note on Disbelief," will see how closely this interpretation of affirmative and negative statements coincides with the account presented in that section.

There is only one further comment to be made. Throughout this discussion, and indeed at many places in earlier units, we have spoken of "the proposition indicated by a statement." This expression is in fact slightly inaccurate. Throughout all those passages we should have said "the proposition purportedly indicated by the statement." But the more accurate phrasing was avoided so as not to cloud the issue by an added complication.

Why would the latter phrase be more correct? When we attend merely to what a statement *indicates* and disregard what it *expresses*, we can see that a statement is very much like a definite description, with the indicated proposition or state of affairs as the thing it purports to refer to.[3] But suppose that this proposition or state of affairs is false, is not a fact, that is, does not exist. In such a case, the purported referent of the statement does not exist, so that the statement has no referent, does not refer, but only purports to refer. Equally we should say that it does not indicate, but only purports to indicate.

Nevertheless, we understand such statements, just as we understand definite descriptions, even when their purported referents do not exist. We understand them through their strict intensions; that is, through the characterizations by consideration of which they are proposing, or purporting, to isolate for attention one unique event, state of affairs, or proposition. It is *because* we understand them that we can discover whether or not they are true, whether or not their purported referents exist. For example, by understanding the statement, "John voted in the last election," grasping its strict intension, we know how to go about making investigations that will settle whether or not its purported referent, a certain purported event, exists and is a fact.

---

[3] In connection with definite descriptions, their referents, and their strict intensions, see §§21.4 to 21.6 and 23.3.

That statements may be compared to descriptions, hence treated as terms, becomes evident when we consider complex statements, containing other statements as constituents. For example the statement, "If John voted, then he voted the straight Republican ticket," may be thought of as illustrating the form

$$s_1 \text{ is a } P \text{ of } s_2,$$

where "$s_1$" replaces "John voted," "$s_2$" replaces "John voted the straight Republican ticket," and "$P$" replaces "if . . ., then . . . ." (On the logic of complex statements, see Units 43 and 44, below.) Here the *constituent* statements (replaced by $s_1$ and $s_2$) *only* indicate; it is the entire complex statement that expresses a belief: the speaker has not expressed any belief concerning the truth or falsity of the propositions indicated by the constituent statements, only a belief that those propositions are *related* in a certain way.

## §39.9 Restructuring Statements before Representing Their Forms

In the earlier sections of this unit we have discussed questions concerning how to represent the form of a given statement. One type of situation involved a mental restructuring of a given statement: statements that actually had form I-A or II-A were represented as though they had first been rewritten, by using the first denotative correlates of their attributive predicates, in form I-B or II-B. In this section we shall consider some other restructurings or rewritings which it is often useful to perform, either actually or mentally, before one represents the form of a given statement.

1.  People often use what we may call a *sign of affirmation* more or less parallel to the signs of denial considered in §39.7: "*It is true that* George went to Boston." "That sunset is *truly* magnificent."

From one point of view, it may fairly be claimed that such signs of affirmation add nothing to the meanings of statements which contain them.[4] Hence, they may simply be dropped from consideration when we represent the form of the given statement. Thus, in the case of the illustrative examples, we should represent their forms as though they had been written, "George went to Boston," and "That sunset is magnificent."

2.  Many statements contain two, or even more, signs of denial: "It is false that George did not try to telephone his wife." To claim that some negative statement is false has exactly the same force as to claim that the corresponding affirmative statement is true: "George did try to telephone his wife." This is the **law of double negation.** Hence, the two signs of denial may be "canceled" and the form of the given statement represented as though neither sign of denial had been included in it.

3.  We must, however, be cautious about applying this law of double negation: the one sign of denial must indicate negation of precisely the negative statement produced by the other. Statements can contain signs of denial that are not in just this relation to each other, as in

---

4  Strictly speaking, there is a difference in what is purportedly indicated. But it is like the difference between "Boston, Mass." and "the existing Boston, Mass." If either has a referent, the other does. If either purportedly indicated proposition is true (exists), the other is true.

"John is not well or he is not happy." In cases like this latter one, the two signs do not cancel and must both be retained:

$$s \text{ is not a } P \text{ or } s \text{ is not a } Q.$$

Also, sometimes a "sign of negation" occurs as part of a term rather than as a sign of denial: "John is not a nonvoter." Such signs of negation should not be counted as signs of denial justifying cancellation. The form of the given statement is

$$s \text{ is not a } P,$$

where "$P$" replaces "nonvoter." Later we shall see under what special circumstances signs of negation as parts of terms may cancel signs of denial.

## EXERCISE

       Represent the forms of the following statements. Do not forget to give your "dictionary."

1. It is not true that John weighs 310 pounds.
2. It is false that John does not like that piece of chocolate cream pie.
3. It is true that John weighs 265 pounds.

\*4.   Frequently a statement contains both a concrete singular term and an abstract term: "Peacefulness suffused the landscape." "Intelligence informed George's action." "Honesty characterizes John's business." "That picture has great beauty."

As a first step toward treating any such statements, we notice that they each in a different way affirm that a certain concrete object is characterized by a certain quality or attribute. Hence we could literally or mentally restructure each one into the form "$s_1$ is characterized by $s_2$," where $s_1$ denotes the concrete object and $s_2$ denotes the abstract object: "The landscape is characterized by peacefulness." "George's action is characterized by intelligence." And so on.

Restructured in this manner, each has a form that could be represented by

$$s_1 \text{ is a } P \text{ of } s_2,$$

where "$P$" replaces "thing characterized by."

But this is not a very profitable form in which to leave the statements, nor a very profitable way in which to represent their forms. One or the other of two *further* transformations is desirable. One of these makes all the terms

---

\* The remainder of this section may be omitted without disturbing the continuity of the text.

oncrete, the other makes all the terms abstract. We shall briefly describe
each process.

5.  The first of these processes depends on noting that the abstract term
represented by "$s_2$"—"peacefulness," "intelligence," "honesty," and so on—
is the second denotative correlate of an attributive term. To say that a thing is
characterized by beauty is to say that it is beautiful. Hence we again transform
the given statements, this time using the attributive term of which the given
abstract term is the second denotative correlate: "The landscape is peaceful."
"George's action is intelligent." "John's business is honestly run." "That
picture is beautiful." Each of these statements is such that its form may be
represented by "$s_1$ is a $P$," where "$P$" represents the first denotative correlate
of the given attributive term. Here the terms represented by "$s_1$" and by "$P$"
are both concrete.

All these transformations may be mentally, instead of literally, made and
"$s$ is a $P$" be said to represent the form of the original statement *provided*
that one gives his "dictionary." But "$s$ is a $P$" fits the original statements so
indirectly that if one is being casual and not giving his dictionary, he had
better literally rewrite the original statement so as to present the statement
whose form is directly represented by "$s$ is a $P$."

6.  When it can be done, there is often a great advantage in transforming
such statements as we have been considering so that all terms involved are
abstract. To see how this is done and when it is advantageous, let us go back
to the middle stage, where we had the form

$$s_1 \text{ is characterized by } s_2.$$

The problem in this case is to find some abstract, general denotative term,
"$P$," such that two things are true:

1.  $s_2$ is a $P$.
2.  $s_1$ has one and only one quality in the extension of "$P$."

The second of these things being true, we may form a definite description:
"the $P$ of $s_1$." Thus the concrete term, $s_1$, gets "buried" in a definite description
which is an abstract singular term. We then transform the statement "$s_1$ is
characterized by $s_2$" into the statement "The $P$ of $s_1$ is identical with $s_2$."
The form of this statement is represented by

$$s_3 \text{ is identical with } s_2,$$

where "$s_3$" replaces "the $P$ of $s_1$." Both terms in this statement of an identity
are abstract.

The illustrative statements at the beginning of paragraph 4 do not easily
lend themselves to this form of treatment. This is because it is difficult to find
a suitable term "$P$." Most things that readily occur as possible terms do not
satisfy requirement 2, above. For example, if we tried to transform "Honesty

characterizes John's business," into "The virtue of John's business is identi
with honesty," we should probably have failed, because John's business v
likely has more than one virtue: it may very well also be prosperous or so
other virtuous thing. Perhaps a case could be made out for transforming
first example into "The emotive effect of the landscape is peacefulnes

But even that is hardly profitable and all these examples are undoubte
best handled by the method described in paragraph 5. The cases in wh
this method is most strikingly useful are those where "$P$" has in its extens
a set of qualities that can be ascertained by measurement: weight, leng
temperature, and so on. Here the advantages of this form of statement
so great that we frequently transform statements already in the usual form w
two concrete terms into this form with two abstract terms. For examp
before dealing with "John weighs 125 pounds," which has the form ".
a $P$," where "$s$" and "$P$" replace concrete terms, the physicist will transfo
it into "The weight of John is identical with 125 pounds" which has the fo
"$s_1$ is identical with $s_2$," with "$s_1$" and "$s_2$" as abstract terms. Of cou
after having mentally transformed, the physicist will probably "transla
into the language of arithmetic:

$$W = 125 \text{ lb.}$$

But this arithmetic statement still has the form "$s_1$ is identical with $s_2$" a
its terms are still abstract.[5]

## REVIEW QUESTIONS FOR UNIT 39

1. What is a logical subject of a singular statement? The logical predica
   Illustrate.
2. Can a singular statement have more than one subject? Illustrate. M
   than one predicate? Explain.
3. Does the method of analysis affect what is identified as subject and
   predicate? If so, how? Illustrate.
4. List the eight standard representations for the forms of singular sta
   ments.
5. Which of the eight standard representations of forms listed in answer
   question 4 represent special cases of others among these eight form
   Of which among these others are they special cases? Explain a
   illustrate.

[5] In connection with this use of abstract terms in the sciences, the reader is refer
to §19.2.

# Sets of Singular Statements; Valid Statements and Valid Proofs

## §40.1 The Form of a Set of Singular Statements

Suppose that we wished to represent *comparatively* the forms of *two* singular statements. Let us take the following pair for purposes of illustration.

(1)   George is taller than James.

(2)   George is not taller than William.

The process is very simple. We represent the form of each statement separately. However, we do not necessarily use the variables, "*s*," "*s₁*," "*s₂*," and "*P*," used in the formulas of the preceding unit. Instead, we select which variables we shall use in accordance with the following **rules:**

1.  Use small letters "*r*," "*s*," "*s₁*," "*s₂*," and so on, to represent singular terms.

2.  Use capital letters, "*P*," "*Q*," "*M*," and so on, to represent general terms.

3.  Throughout all the statements we would compare, replace all the tokens of one term by tokens of one and the same variable.

4.  Replace tokens of *different* terms by tokens of *different* variables.

Applying these rules to the pair of statements given above, we could proceed as follows. Notice that we give only one "dictionary" for the pair of statements.

Let:   "*s*" replace "George."
       "*s₁*" replace "James."
       "*s₂*" replace "William."
       "*P*" replace "taller thing."

Then the form of the given pair of statements is represented by:
(1)   $s$ is a $P$ of $s_1$.
(2)   $s$ is not a $P$ of $s_2$.

We may not be interested in quite so detailed a representation of the form of the pair of statements. In particular, we may not be interested in noticing just when and where different tokens of one term appear. This would give a more general representation of the form, a form that would be shared by pairs of statements that did not repeat terms in just the same manner.

To accomplish this we disregard Rule 3 and "enrich" our dictionary by providing several variables to replace various tokens of one term. For example, we could treat the sample pair of statements as follows.

Let: "$s_1$" or "$s_2$" replace "George."
      "$s_3$" replace "James."
      "$s_4$" replace "William."
      "$P$" or "$Q$" replace "taller thing."

Then the form of the given pair of statements is represented by:
(1)   $s_1$ is a $P$ of $s_3$.
(2)   $s_2$ is not a $Q$ of $s_4$.

This representation of the form of the pair notes merely that each statement is an affirmative statement of type II. It in no way indicates which terms, if any, are repeated or where those repetitions take place.

Although Rule 3 may be disregarded in the manner just explained, under no circumstances may Rule 4 be disregarded or violated.[1]

The same procedures may be used when there are more than two statements in the group.

Still another way in which less detailed representations of a form may be brought about has already been suggested in the preceding unit: Treat larger "chunks" of the given statements as terms. For example, in the case of our illustrative pair of statements, we could proceed as follows.

Let: "$s$" replace "George."
      "$P$" replace "taller than James."
      "$Q$" replace "taller than William."

[1]   Some logicians permit a violation of Rule 4. But the consequence is that their representations of forms cannot be used for the same comparative purposes as our more conventional ones. For an example of the less usual method, see R. Carnap's *Logical Syntax of Language*, New York: 1937, §4.

Then the form of the given pair of statements is represented by:

(1)  *s* is a *P*.

(2)  *s* is not a *Q*.

Notice that in this situation we *must* use different variables, "*P*" and "*Q*," because "taller than James" and "taller than William" are different terms, not tokens of the same term, even though they contain a common part.

### EXERCISE

Represent in the greatest possible detail (with the means so far available) the forms of each of the following sets of statements.

1.   a.   George is the president of the Senior class. *S₁ is identical with S₂*
     b.   George is taller than Albert. *S₁ is a P of S₂*
     c.   The president of the Senior class is taller than Albert. *S₂ is a P of S₃*

2.   a.   This color is attractive. *S is a P*
     b.   This color is complementary to that color. *S₁ is a Q of S₂*
     c.   That color is attractive. *S₂ is a P*

*if us m in place of Q in © you disregard rule 3*

## §40.2 Illustrations of a Form

Through the preceding unit and the first section of this unit, we have been dealing with a problem that could be put as follows: Given, a statement or set of statements, to represent its form. Now we must think briefly about a reverse problem. Given, a representation of the form of a statement or set of statements, to find a statement or set of statements that has that form.

Since the problem as it was set does not require us to find true statements, it is not a difficult one. You and I know lots of terms, both singular and general, and all that we have to do is to replace the variables in the representation of the form by appropriate terms: singular terms in place of "*s*," "*s₁*," and so on; absolute general terms in place of "*P*," "*Q*," and so on, if these appear in form I, "*s* is a *P*"; and relative general terms in place of "*P*," "*Q*," and so on, if these appear in form II, "*s₁* is a *P* of *s₂*." Thus, if there is only one formula, say "*s* is a *P*," the problem is easy.

There is only one **rule** that we must follow: If the representation of the form contains several tokens of one variable, these must all be replaced by tokens of one and the same term.

So far we have not met any formulas for statement forms that contained more than one token of any one variable. But such a formula is entirely possible. Indeed, if we were applying Rule 3 of the preceding section to "John is talking to himself," we would get such a formula: "*s* is a *P* of *s*." When the problem is reversed, the present rule applies as much to two tokens of one variable in a single formula as it does to two tokens in different formulas.

When we are constructing an illustration of a form, the variables in the representation of the form need not be replaced in order, say from left to right and top to bottom, as one would read. We may start *anywhere*. And no problem arises except keeping the above rule in mind. To follow this rule, all we have to do is this: Check each variable-token as we replace it, to see whether or not it is a token of some variable we have already replaced elsewhere. If it is, we must use here a token of the same term as we used there. If it is not, we are free to use a token of any appropriate term we wish.

Let us look at one or two examples.

*Example I.*     (1)   *s* is a *P*.
               (2)   *s* is a *Q* of $s_1$.
               (3)   $s_1$ is an *R*.

   *First Solution:*
               (1)   John is a college graduate.
               (2)   John is married to Sylvia.
               (3)   Sylvia is an American citizen.

In Example I, only "*s*" and "$s_1$" appear more than once. All tokens of each are replaced in this solution (as required by the rule) by tokens of one and the same term: tokens of "*s*" by tokens of "John" and tokens of "$s_1$" by tokens of "Sylvia." But no tokens of *different* variables are replaced by tokens of the *same* term.

   *Second Solution:*
               (1)   Fido is a dog.
               (2)   Fido bit Rover.
               (3)   Rover is a dog.

In this solution, the rule is followed. But furthermore, the tokens of two distinct variables, "*P*" and "*R*," are replaced by tokens of one and the same term. The rule does not prohibit this. On the other hand, the solution thus produced not only illustrates the form represented in Example I, but also illustrates a form which is a special case of the form represented in Example I:

(1)   $s$ is a $P$.
✗ (2)   $s$ is a $Q$ of $s_1$.
(3)   $s_1$ is a $P$.

Had our problem been the reverse problem, given the set of statements in the second solution, to represent its form, then we would have reached the above solution if we had followed all four rules of §40.1. But we would have found Example 1 as the solution if we had disregarded Rule 3 in the manner described near the end of §40.1.

*Third Solution:*

(1)   Sylvia's husband is an American citizen.
(2)   Sylvia's husband is married to Mrs. Jones.
(3)   Mrs. Jones is an American citizen.

This solution raises all sorts of interesting questions. In the first place, "$s$" has been replaced by a definite description rather than by a proper name. Second, the definition of "husband" ($x$ is a husband of $y = _{Df} x$ is a man and $x$ is married to $y$) permits us to assert as analytic

(4)   Sylvia's husband is married to Sylvia.

Thus, third, we are tempted to infer from the given statements that

(5)   Sylvia is identical with Mrs. Jones.

But, fourth, this would be a mistake, because to make an inference from statements (1) to (3) is to have accepted them as true, and it was specifically said near the beginning of this section that we are not required to supply true statements in solving problems of the kind here under consideration.

In spite of this, it is quite possible that statement (5) still interests us as somehow or other logically connected with the earlier statements. Perhaps we misspoke when we said we could *infer* it from them. Perhaps what we should have said is that a proof which had them for premises and it for conclusion would be valid.

But even this would be wrong. The conclusion tempts us as a valid one because we are so accustomed to taking it for granted that every husband has only one wife, is married to only one person. But this is true only in monogamous societies, like America or Europe. Furthermore, even in those countries, its being true is not analytic, as the truth of (4) is analytic. In other words, (5) is not a valid conclusion

in a proof with statements (1), (2), and (3) as its sole premises. Nevertheless, we know another statement (about monogamy in America) which
both is true (even if not analytic) and is such that, if added as a fourth
premise to statements (1), (2), and (3), would turn the proof into a
valid one. (Of course, we are even then assuming still another thing,
that Sylvia's husband abides by the marriage laws of the country in
which he holds citizenship.)

### §40.3  Corresponding Statements

Let us briefly review the form represented in Example
and the illustrative sets of statements having that form given in the
preceding section. The point now to notice is this: We can pick many
statements to illustrate various ones of the different statement forms.
For example, we can pick (as we did) "John is a college graduate" to
illustrate the first statement form and "Fido bit Rover" to illustrate
the second statement form. But we can*not* put both of these choices
into *one* solution, illustrating the form of the set. We cannot do this
because they replace tokens of "$s$" by different terms.

If we can use two statements together, in one solution of the kind of
problem treated in the preceding section, those statements are said
to be **corresponding** illustrations of the formulas for statement forms
that they separately illustrate. Thus "John is a college graduate" and
"John is married to Sylvia" are corresponding illustrations of "$s$ is a $P$"
and "$s$ is a $Q$ of $s_1$." But "John is a college graduate" and "Fido bit
Rover" are *not* corresponding illustrations of "$s$ is a $P$" and "$s$ is a $Q$ of
$s_1$." They are illustrations, but they are not corresponding illustrations.

Sometimes a set of formulas for statement forms is such that when
we have chosen illustrations for one or two of the formulas in the set
there will be only one corresponding illustration of the remaining
formulas. This happens whenever the remaining formulas contain no
variables except ones that also occurred in the other formulas. It is
not true of Example I, but it is true of Examples II and III:

*Example II.*          (1)  $s_1$ is a $P$ of $s_2$.

                        (2)  $s_2$ is a $P$ of $s_3$.

                        (3)  $s_1$ is a $P$ of $s_3$.

*Example III.*          (1)  $s$ is a $P$.

                        (2)  $s$ is not a $P$.

In Example II, if you find corresponding statements to illustrate any two of the formulas, only one statement will be a corresponding illustration of the third formula. And in Example III, for any statement that illustrates either of the forms, there is only one corresponding statement that illustrates the other.

In the next section, we shall examine some of the logic of corresponding affirmative and negative statements, that is, of corresponding statements that illustrate the formulas in Example III.

## §40.4 The Law of Contradiction

Two famous laws of logic are known as the law of contradiction and the law of excluded middle. There is no single manner in which each of these laws is formulated. We shall consider various ways in which to conceive each of them.

**The law of contradiction** could be stated as follows: No statement is both true and false.

At first glance, the claim made in this law appears so obvious that there would seem to be nothing more that need be said. And in a sense that is the case. Any statement purports to refer to a certain proposition or state of affairs. For the statement to be true is for the state of affairs to be a fact; for it to be false is for the state of affairs not to be a fact. But the state of affairs or proposition cannot both be and not be a fact. That is, the statement cannot be both true and false.

Yet how often have you heard someone answer a question with the remark, "Well, yes and no"? Is he not saying that the statement about the truth of which the question inquires is both true and false? And is not this a denial of the law of contradiction?

The answer is that the *sentence* offered *as* a statement is vague, ambiguous, or incomplete. From one point of view or with one interpretation, it is one statement, and that statement is true; but from another point of view or with another interpretation, the sentence is a token of a different statement, and this different statement is false. For example, a person might ask, "Do you like tea?" And the answer might be, "Well, yes and no." If you mean to ask whether I drink tea with some regularity and enjoy doing so, the answer is Yes. But if you mean to ask whether I prefer tea to other beverages, the answer is No. Or finally, if you mean to ask whether I should *now* enjoy some tea, the answer is still No.

Or, to consider another problem, "John is a young man" might seem to be true in the days of John's youth but false in his old age. Does this not violate the law of contradiction?

Not at all! The law of contradiction does not deny the fact of change. What statement is affirmed by uttering the words "John is a young man" changes with time. Uttered in John's youth, the statement affirmed is true. The statement affirms that on such and such a date, say January, 1925, John is a young man, and this remains true: even in 1960 it is true that in January, 1925, John is a young man. However, to utter in 1960 the words, "John is a young man" will not mean that in January, 1925, John is a young man. What the words uttered in 1960 mean is something different. Hence they are tokens of a different statement. This *latter* statement is false, but the *former* one has not become false.

Finally, it is sometimes maintained that a statement might be true for some people or at one time but false for other people or at another time.[2] For example, consider the statement that "The Earth is flat." It has been maintained that this statement could be true for some people and at some times but false for other people and at other times. The proponents of this view do not mean merely that one group of people believes the statement and the other group disbelieves it. Rather, they mean that the statement is an effective guide to action for the one group but not for the other group. The group which finds it an effective guide to action is, presumably, a stable society not given to travel nor concerned with problems of astronomy and physics beyond what is necessary to the keeping of their calendars and the operation of their primitive agriculture.

It might be agreed that "The Earth is flat" is an effective guide to action for those people *for all the actions they care to undertake*. Thus, they might be excused, so to speak, for believing it and acting on it. But limiting the range of actions they care to undertake is limiting the extent to which they care to test the statement. Can we afford to say that untested statements are true simply because they are untested? I think not. And I think that the notion of relative truth—true *for him*—must be abandoned, and the law of contradiction reaffirmed.

What does the law mean so far as the eight forms of singular state-

---

[2]  For an example of this position, see William James. He expounds this position in *Pragmatism*, New York: 1907, as well as in other places.

ment are concerned? It means that no pair of corresponding affirmative and negative statements are both true. Thus evidence that one of such a pair is true is evidence that the other is false. The following would, then, be **validating** forms of proof, that is, forms of proof such that every proof having one of these forms would be valid.

(1)   *s* is a *P*.
∴ (2)   It is false that *s* is not a *P*.

(1)   *s* is not a *P*.
∴ (2)   It is false that *s* is a *P*.

It is interesting to notice that the conclusions in these two proofs are not in standard form. In the first proof, if the conclusion were put in standard form it would be "*s* is a *P*," which is identically the premise of that proof. (See §39.9, point 2.) In the second proof, the conclusion would become "*s* is not a *P*," which is identically the premise of *that* proof. (See §39.7.) Thus, in a way, the law of contradiction affirms that it is valid to put statements out of standard form in either of the two ways here indicated. But is that not what we should expect *if* a statement in standard form and out of standard form have the same meaning? And are not rules for putting statements into standard form based on an assumption of an identity of meaning? The law of contradiction turns out to be a partial demonstration of the identity of meaning implicit in our rules for putting statements into standard form.

## §40.5 The Law of Excluded Middle

**The law of excluded middle** may be stated as follows: Any statement is either true or false.

The law of excluded middle derives its somewhat picturesque name from the thought that there might be a "middle ground" between truth and falsity, but the law excludes this possibility. There is a middle ground between belief and disbelief, namely an attitude of doubt. I believe some statements, disbelieve others, and am in doubt concerning still others. But according to the law of excluded middle, all these statements, no matter what my cognitive attitudes, are either true or false.

The law of excluded middle could be put in the following manner so far as our eight singular statement forms are concerned: Either *s* is a *P* or it is false that *s* is a *P*. When the latter alternative is put in standard form, the **law** becomes:

> Either *s* is a *P* or *s* is not a *P*.
> Either *s* is a *P* of $s_1$ or *s* is not a *P* of $s_1$.
> Either *s* exists or *s* does not exist.
> Either *s* is identical with $s_1$, or *s* is not identical with $s_1$.

We could write all of these. They are all analytic. But we do not need to, because each of them is a special case of the first. Hence, to claim that the first holds, no matter what terms "*s*" and "*P*" might be, is to claim that all the others hold.

But let us see what the law means in terms of validating forms of proof. As the above law affirms, in any corresponding pair of affirmative and negative singular statements, *at least one is true*. That is, evidence to the effect that one of them is false, is evidence to the effect that the other is true. The following are therefore **validating** forms of proof.

> (1)   It is false that *s* is a *P*.
> ∴ (2)   *s* is not a *P*.

> (1)   It is false that *s* is not a *P*.
> ∴ (2)   *s* is a *P*.

These two validating forms have premises that are not in standard form. But if the premises were put in standard form, they would be precisely the statements that appear here as the conclusions. Furthermore, we have exactly the same statement forms as we did in the two validating proof forms for the law of contradiction, only what were the premises there are the conclusions here and what were the conclusions there are the premises here. So to speak, these validating forms say that it is valid to put statements of such and such forms into standard form. This in a way gives the other half of the proof that the nonstandard form and the standard form have the same meaning.

## §40.6 Symmetry

When mathematicians or logicians speak of "commuting" an expression, they mean reversing the order of its terms. Thus to commute "$x + y$" is to write "$y + x$," to commute "$x \div y$" is to write "$y \div x$," to commute "$s_1$ is identical with $s_2$" is to write "$s_2$ is identical with $s_1$."

The three examples in the preceding paragraph illustrate this fact: some expressions are such that the result of commuting them is another expression *with the same meaning* as the original, but some other expressions are not of this sort. For example, "$x + y$" and "$y + x$" indicate exactly the same number, so that the meaning of "$x + y$" has not been altered by commuting it.[3] On the other hand, "$x \div y$" and "$y \div x$" do not in general indicate the same quantity.[4] As with "$x + y$," so with "$s_1$ is identical with $s_2$," statements (expressions) having this form may be commuted without altering their meaning.

When expressions are built up by supplying terms for a sign of an "operation" ("$+$" is a sign for the operation of addition) or "relation" ("identical with" is a sign for the relation of identity), and when such expressions may be commuted without changing the meaning of the total expression, no matter what terms have been supplied to build up the expression, then the operation or relation is said to be **symmetrical.** Thus the mathematician says that addition is symmetrical, and the logician says that identity is symmetrical.

A claim that an operation or relation is symmetrical can be expressed in many ways. One very effective way is in an expression for the form of a statement of identity. Thus the mathematician writes

$$x + y = y + x.$$

And the logician could write

($s_1$ is identical with $s_2$) is identical with ($s_2$ is identical with $s_1$).[5]

[3]  The phrasing here, and frequently throughout these units, is somewhat abbreviated for the sake of simplicity. But the abbreviation makes the statement inaccurate if read literally. Literally, "$x + y$" and "$y + x$" do not indicate numbers, since "$x$" and "$y$" are variables. What they do indicate, or represent, are forms of expression each of which indicates a number. To be literally accurate, the statement in the text should read: "For example, corresponding instances of $x + y$ and of $y + x$. . . ." But the phrase "corresponding instances of" so complicates statements that are already complicated that it will often be omitted. The next statement in the text also omits this technically essential phrase.
[4]  When $x$ is identical with $y$ then $x \div y$ is identical with $y \div x$; otherwise (therefore, "in general") it is not.
[5]  Actually, he does not write this formula because most of his work is conducted in special languages for logic, like the special languages for arithmetic. What he does write is

$$(x = y) \equiv (y = x),$$

or

$$(x = y) = (y = x),$$

or some other such expression, depending on what language for logic he is using.

His languages for logic, like the mathematician's algebra, are extremely subtle and powerful tools. We do not study those languages in this book. That would constitute a study in logic. Our study is one in *applied* logic. For this latter purpose, the present author has transferred to considerations of English some of the findings now usually formulated in the logician's special languages.

But what does the fact that identity is symmetrical imply with respect to validating forms of proof? It gives us two **validating** forms:

*Analytic strictly speaking valid* ⎰ (1)  $s_1$ is identical with $s_2$. ⎱ *Justifying Rule is If $s_1$ then $s_2$*

      (1)  $s_1$ is not identical with $s_2$.
∴ (2)  $s_2$ is not identical with $s_1$.

One of these forms deals with affirmative statements of identity and the other with negative statements of identity. The fact that both forms are validating must not lead you to an ill-advised conclusion that whenever a form of proof is validating, you may change all affirmative formulas into negatives and all the negatives into affirmatives and the result will be a validating form. We shall see many situations (for example, in the next section) in which this is not true. So to speak, it just *happens* to be true in the above case.[6]

We have seen that affirmations and denials of identity are symmetrical, and this has provided the basis for two validating forms of proof involving standard forms for singular statements. What about the other standard forms for singular statements?

1.   To commute "*s* is a *P*" into "*P* is an *s*" is to change a formula representing a statement form into a formula such that expressions having the represented form are nonsense expressions: It is not a question of their being true or false, they are not even statements. For example, "Fido is a dog" is a statement, true or false as the case may be; but "Dog is a Fido" is nonsense. For it to be meaningful, "dog" would have to be a singular term and "Fido" a general term. But this they were not, or the original expression, "Fido is a dog," would not have been a meaningful statement.[7]

[6]  Of course, there is a reason why this "just happens." If

               (1) A
     ∴ (2) B

is a validating form of proof, then

               (1) It is false that B
     ∴ (2) It is false that A

is also a validating form of proof. In the case examined in the text, to negate both premise and conclusion represents the same form of proof as is represented by negating the premise and conclusion and reversing their roles.

[7]  Sometimes it looks as though some such statement had been successfully commuted. For example, people often use the sign-type of a general denotative term also as a singular term. Many dogs are named "Rover," perhaps others are named "Hunter." This being so, we might have a statement "Rover is a hunter" and

2.  The same holds for "*s* is not a *P*," "*s* exists," and "*s* does not exist." To commute any of these is to produce nonsense.

3.  When we come to "$s_1$ is a *P* of $s_2$" and the negative form "$s_1$ is not a *P* of $s_2$," the situation is different. Here the formulas, when commuted, represent meaningful forms: "$s_2$ is a *P* of $s_1$" and "$s_2$ is not a *P* of $s_1$." Furthermore, there are some terms that might replace "*P*" and the resulting formulas would be symmetrical. "Identical with" is an example, as we saw earlier in this section. But other predicates also produce symmetrical statement forms: "$s_1$ is married to $s_2$," "$s_1$ is a cousin of $s_2$," "$s_1$ is equal in price to $s_2$," and so on. In these cases validating forms of proof may be set up:

> (1)   $s_1$ is married to $s_2$.
> ∴ (2)   $s_2$ is married to $s_1$.

> (1)   $s_1$ is not married to $s_2$.
> ∴ (2)   $s_2$ is not married to $s_1$.

> And so on.

On the other hand, some predicates are such that if they replaced "*P*" in "$s_1$ is a *P* of $s_2$," the result would not be a symmetrical formula. We shall consider such cases in the next section.

## §40.7  Asymmetry and Nonsymmetry

Suppose that in "$s_1$ is a *P* of $s_2$," we replace "*P*" by "father" to give "$s_1$ is a father of $s_2$." When any statement of this form is true, the corresponding statement in the commuted form is *false*. Other predicates with this same effect are "taller than," "husband," "hotter than." Relations of this sort are said to be **asymmetrical.** Each of them gives rise to a validating form:

> (1)   $s_1$ is taller than $s_2$.
> ∴ (2)   $s_2$ is not taller than $s_1$.

> (1)   $s_1$ is a husband of $s_2$.
> ∴ (2)   $s_2$ is not a husband of $s_1$.

(Here we have examples of something claimed in the last section: validating proof forms such that changing all the affirmatives into

---

"commute" it into "Hunter is a rover." But this is not commuting because, although we interchanged the *sign-types*, we did not interchange the *terms*. Were the *terms* identical in both sentence-tokens, one of the sentence-tokens would be nonsense and not a token of a statement.

negatives and the negatives into affirmatives will change the proof form into one which is not validating. For example,

$$(1) \quad s_1 \text{ is not husband of } s_2.$$
$$\therefore (2) \quad s_2 \text{ is husband of } s_1.$$

is not a validating form: the premise could be true and the conclusion false. Validating proof forms resting on *symmetry*, however, always have the corresponding negative forms also validating.)

Still other predicates are such that the commuted form "makes sense"—is a statement—but the predicates are neither symmetrical nor asymmetrical. This is to say that corresponding instances of the original formula and the commuted formula will sometimes be both true, sometimes be one true and the other false, and sometimes be both false. For example, "$s_1$ is a brother of $s_2$" is insufficient evidence on which to determine whether or not "$s_2$ is a brother of $s_1$." ($s_2$ may be brother, or may be sister, of $s_1$.)

Predicates of the sort just discussed are said to be **nonsymmetrical.** Examples of nonsymmetrical predicates are "brother," "talks to," "learns from," "votes for," and so on. Nonsymmetrical predicates do not give rise to any validating forms comparable with those we have been considering.

Finally, some predicates are such that the commuted form does not even make sense. An example is "is characterized by." If "$s_1$ is characterized by $s_2$" is meaningful, then "$s_2$ is characterized by $s_1$" is nonsense. For the first subject-term in this statement form must be concrete and the second subject-term abstract. [8]

*EXERCISE*

Classify each of the following predicates as symmetrical, asymmetrical, nonsymmetrical, or one such that the commuted form makes nonsense.

1. Exchanges guns with
2. Grandfather
3. Likes
4. Identical with
5. Kills       nonsym.
6. In the extension of       asym

---

[8] This claim is slightly inaccurate. The first subject-term may be abstract. But then the second subject-term must be on a higher level (logical-type) than the first. Hence, in any case, the commuted formula is nonsense.

## §40.8 Pure Logic and Applied Logic

Much of the discussion in the last two sections (and the exercise at the end of the last section) is not a part of the science of pure logic. Rather it belongs to applied logic.

The explanation of what it means to be symmetrical, asymmetrical, or nonsymmetrical is a part of the subject of logic. But finding examples of these kinds of relation, or finding out whether a given relation is the one or the other (symmetrical, asymmetrical, or nonsymmetrical) is generally not a part of logic. Rather, those inquiries belong to applied logic. For example, finding that "grandfather" is asymmetrical is an exercise in the logic of biology (albeit a part of biology which is in the realm of common knowledge). It is a part of what is involved in the organization of any science as it defines its terms. Only a few examples of symmetrical or other kinds of relation will be established *as* such in the science of logic. An example was the establishment that identity is symmetrical. "Identical with" is one of the few predicates studied in logic. Thus the establishment of its symmetry is a problem in logic.

In the last two sections and in the exercise familiar relative terms were chosen in order to illustrate the logical concepts of symmetry, asymmetry, and nonsymmetry. Thus we were depending on a shared understanding of those terms that you might "see" the difference between symmetrical and other types of relation. But in "seeing" this difference, you have also to "see" that a certain relation, for example, "converses with," is symmetrical. How, though, could one *establish* a claim that it is symmetrical?

Here is the point at which applied logic begins and at which intensional definitions of terms could come into use. We might appeal, for example, to the following definition:

1.   $x$ converses with $y$ = Df $x$ talks to $y$ and $y$ talks to $x$.

Now we start with the original premise form and with the aid of the definition reach the final conclusion:

| | | |
|---|---|---|
| (1) | $s_1$ converses with $s_2$. | [Premise] |
| ∴ (2) | $s_1$ talks to $s_2$ and $s_2$ talks to $s_1$. | [From (1) by definition 1] |
| ∴ (3) | $s_2$ talks to $s_1$ and $s_1$ talks to $s_2$. | [From (2)] |
| ∴ (4) | $s_2$ converses with $s_1$. | [From (3) by definition 1] |

Complete definitions permit one to replace in a proof the definiendum by the definiens (or an expression in the form of the definiendum by a corresponding expression in the form of the definiens) or vice versa. This is why the appeal to Definition 1 justifies lines (2) and (4). Line (3) is justified by appeal to the following validating proof form, where "$p$" and "$q$" are variables taking the place of statements.

(1)   $p$ and $q$.
∴ (2)   $q$ and $p$.

(That is, "and" is a symmetrical connective of statements.)

In the above indirect proof we have a proof that "converses with" is symmetrical, that is, that

(1)   $s_1$ converses with $s_2$.
∴ (2)   $s_2$ converses with $s_1$.

is a validating form. The indirect proof has no premise except this premise and its final conclusion is this conclusion. Every step in the indirect proof is vouchsafed as a legitimate logical procedure. But, in addition to what you might learn from logic, you have to use a definition of "converses with." Now it is not the business of logic to define "converses with." Logic gives you rules to use in constructing and testing definitions. But it does not give you the definitions. You get the definition by applying logic to a term of ordinary discourse. Hence, the claims that "converses with" is symmetrical and that

(1)   $s_1$ converses with $s_2$.
∴ (2)   $s_2$ converses with $s_1$.

is a validating form, are *not* claims of pure logic.

Pure logic is applied in this same manner to every field of scientific inquiry and to the field of ordinary discourse. These applications of logic include, among other things, the definitions of terms and the demonstration that certain forms of proof are validating. The results of such inquiries, that is, the definitions thus produced, are often spoken of as the logics of those fields. Thus one hears people speak of the logic of physics or the logic of biology. But the logic of some such science is a branch of applied logic rather than a branch of pure logic. Furthermore, it is a part of the science of which it is "the logic." Thus, the logic of biology is a part of the science of biology. It is that part of the science which consists in applying logic to the terms and other expressions in biology. It will result in definitions of those terms, and demonstrations that certain forms of proof involving those terms are validating. It includes that entire half of the science of biology which rests merely on analysis and inference, a half without which the other half, resting on observation, could not proceed.

### §40.9 Summary and Exercise

In this unit the following validating forms have been listed as established *within* the science of pure logic:

I.          (1)   $s$ is a $P$.
       ∴ (2)   It is false that $s$ is not a $P$.

·II.        (1)   $s$ is not a $P$.
       ∴ (2)   It is false that $s$ is a $P$.

III.        (1)   It is false that $s$ is a $P$.
       ∴ (2)   $s$ is not a $P$.

IV.        (1)   It is false that $s$ is not a $P$.
       ∴ (2)   $s$ is a $P$.

V.          (1)   $s_1$ is identical with $s_2$.
       ∴ (2)   $s_2$ is identical with $s_1$.

VI.        (1)   $s_i$ is not identical with $s_2$.
       ∴ (2)   $s_2$ is not identical with $s_1$.

## EXERCISES

1.  List at least two other validating forms of proof presented in this unit than the six forms listed just above.

2.  Why does the author claim that these other validating forms of proof are not established *within* the science of pure logic? On what besides logic does their establishment depend?

3.  Listed below are six proofs. Some of them are valid and some are not. Some are illustrations of one of the six validating forms listed above, and some are not.

   a.  Will *all* those that illustrate *any* of the six validating forms be valid?

   b.  Could some of those that do not illustrate any of the six validating forms be valid? Why or why not?

   c.  Indicate for each proof whether or not it illustrates one of the six validating forms listed above. If it *does*, say which one it illustrates and say which terms in the proof replace which variables in that validating form. If it does *not*, first say whether or not you consider the proof to be valid, and then represent its form in as much detail as possible.

A.     (1)    Mr. Jones is the president of The X Company.

∴ (2)    It is false that Mr. Jones is not the president of The X Company.

B.     (1)    Mr. Jones is older than Mr. Smith.

∴ (2)    Mr. Smith is younger than Mr. Jones.

C.     (1)    That automobile is not the car in which Joe won the race.

∴ (2)    The car in which Joe won the race is not that automobile.

D.     (1)    Joe is at least as tall as George.

∴ (2)    George is at least as tall as Joe.

E.     (1)    Joe is an American citizen.

∴ (2)    Joe is a human being.

F.     (1)    Jack is a classmate of Bill.

∴ (2)    Bill is a classmate of Jack.

## REVIEW QUESTIONS FOR UNIT 40

1. What four rules govern the *comparative* representation of the forms of a *set* of singular statements? (The rules may be stated in your own words.)

2. Which of those rules, if any, may be disregarded in order to give a less detailed representation of comparative forms? In what manner may it be disregarded?

3. What rule governs finding a set of statements to illustrate a formula for the form of a set?

4. What is meant by corresponding illustrations of a set of formulas for statement forms?

5. What is meant by a validating form of proof?

6. What is the law of contradiction, and what validating forms of proofs have been presented in consequence of it?

7. What is the law of excluded middle, and what validating forms of proof have been presented in consequence of it?

8. What is meant by symmetry? By asymmetry? By nonsymmetry?

9. Explain and briefly discuss the distinction made between pure logic and applied logic.

# *Reflexive and Transitive Terms*

### §41.1 Reflexive and Irreflexive Terms

The relationship of identity, affirmed in statements of the form, "$s_1$ is identical with $s_2$," has an important property called *reflexiveness*. This means that any and every statement of the form "$s$ is identical with $s$" is true.

More generally, a relative term, "$P$," is **reflexive,** means that every statement of the form, "$s$ is a $P$ of $s$" is true.

The fact that identity is reflexive has been called the **law of identity.** In the older logic books, it is often formulated in the expression,

$$a \text{ is } a.$$

That the reflexive character of identity should be recognized in a law suggests two things: First, that not every relative term is reflexive; and second, that when a relative term is reflexive, this fact is of considerable importance. Let us consider these matters, one after the other.

It is easy to think of many relative terms which are not reflexive: "father," "shoots," and "taller than." But here, as with symmetry, we can distinguish two types of case: the one in which "$s$ is a $P$ of $s$" is *always false*, and the one in which "$s$ is a $P$ of $s$" is sometimes true and sometimes false. For example, no one is his own father, and no one is taller than himself. Hence "$s$ is a father of $s$" and "$s$ is taller than $s$" are forms such that all statements having either of these forms are false. In other words, the corresponding negates are true:

$s$ is not a father of $s$.
$s$ is not taller than $s$.

On the other hand, some statements of the form "$s$ shoots $s$" are true while other statements of this form are false.

A relative term, "$P$," is said to be **irreflexive** if every statement of the form

$s$ is not a $P$ of $s$

is true.

481

A relative term, *"P,"* is said to be **nonreflexive** if some statements of the form

$$s \text{ is a } P \text{ of } s$$

are true and some are false.

The second point, the importance of reflexiveness, is discussed in the next sections.

## EXERCISE

Which of the following relative terms are reflexive, which are irreflexive, and which nonreflexive?

1. Heavier than
2. As heavy as
3. Votes for
4. Brother of
5. Marries
6. Proud of

## §41.2 Reflexiveness and Analysis

Suppose for a moment that we use the form "$s_1$ talks to $s_2$" to mean that at some time in his life, $s_1$ is the producer in a productive sign-event which has $s_2$ for its intended second party, and suppose that we were asked to determine whether "talking to" with this meaning is reflexive, irreflexive, or nonreflexive.

It is easy to rule out the classification as irreflexive: I talk to myself (write memos, and so on) and I suspect that you, as a college student, must have talked to yourself (for example, taken lecture or reading notes that you intended your future self to read). But to decide between reflexive and nonreflexive is to decide whether or not *everybody* talks to himself.

Knowing human nature as we do, and knowing how useful signs can be as an aid to thought, I am prepared to believe that everybody at some time or other has talked to himself. Surely, everyone who ever learned a civilized language has talked to himself. But even primitive and uneducated people must have made a mark or some other simple sign at some time in their lives in order to remind themselves of something or to help themselves figure something out. Possibly people who die at a very early age—one month old or so—never talked to themselves. But they would very likely be the only people who never did.

The point of this inquiry, whether "talking" is a reflexive or nonreflexive term, is to notice that finding the answer requires an investigation of empirical matters of fact of the sort that might be investigated in psychology or biology. It is true that we have to know the meaning of the term we are investigating, "talking," but if we limited our attention to that, we would never find the answer. Some direct or indirect use of observation, of the ways in which human beings behave, is essential.

How different this is from the situation that faces us if we try to answer a similar question about the term "identical with." In this case, to understand the term is to apprehend that it is reflexive. The statement "$s_1$ is identical with $s_2$" affirms that the purported referents of "$s_1$" and "$s_2$" are one and the same object, that although there are in fact two *tokens* of "$s_1$" and of "$s_2$" in the statement, there is only one purported referent. Now *if* the two tokens were tokens of one and the same term, this result would be assured. For tokens of the same term are, by definition, tokens of the same sign-type with the same meaning (intension), hence with the same purported referent. Hence, analysis assures us that every statement of the form "$s$ is identical with $s$" is true. That is to say, these propositions are analytic.

## §41.3  Analytic Propositions and Valid Proofs

Suppose that we were considering some proof, which can temporarily be represented by:

(I)                              (1)    *A*.
                              ∴ (2)    *B*.

Let us assume that "(1) *A*" represents temporarily any series of one or several premises, so that the above representation does not restrict our attention to proofs that have a single premise. Thus, for example, one proof form, among others, which we have under consideration would be a proof with two premises:

                              (1a)   *C*.
                              (1b)   *D*.
                              ∴ (2)   *B*.

Another would have three premises, and so on.

To make the following discussion easier to grasp, let us have in mind a concrete illustration:

(I′)          (1)   *A*:   Everything which is identical with *s*, is a *P*.
          ∴ (2)   *B*:   *s* is a *P*.

What would it mean to say that this proof, (I) or (I′), is valid? A review of §36.3 reveals that for the proof to be valid is for the truth of the premises (if they are true) to be a sufficient guarantee of the truth of the conclusion. That is, the proof is valid if *analysis* suffices to reveal that accepting the premises as true would justify one in accepting the conclusion as true.

Suppose now that we had *another* proof with the same premises, "*A*," as Proof (I) above, the same conclusion, "*B*," but an additional premise, "*C*":

(II)                                    (1)    *A*.
                                         (2)    *C*.
                                   ∴ (3)    *B*.

To carry on with the same concrete illustration, (II) might in particular be the proof (II'):

(II')          (1)    *A*:   Everything which is identical with *s*, is a *P*.
                (2)    *C*:   *s* is identical with *s*.
          ∴ (3)    *B*:   *s* is a *P*.

And suppose, furthermore, that we knew Proof (II) to be valid, that is to say, that analysis had convinced us that if we were justified in accepting the premises, "*A*" and "*C*," then we would be justified in accepting the conclusion "*B*." (Proof (II'), for example is valid.)

Proof (II) could be a great help in showing us that Proof (I) is valid. For suppose that premise "*C*" be analytic, could be accepted on the basis of analysis, as it is in the illustrative example, (II'). Then Proof (I) would be valid: Analysis would reveal that accepting premise "*A*" as true would justify us in accepting the conclusion as valid. The analysis would have two "parts." In one part, it would justify adding "*C*" to our list of premises. In the other part, it would reveal that then we could reach conclusion "*B*." But since only analysis was used in order to justify adding "*C*" to the list of premises, only analysis was used in getting us from the original premise, "*A*," to the conclusion.

It is oftentimes easier to "see" that a certain proof is valid if we break up the analysis by means of which we see this into parts along the lines suggested above: Add one or more premises each guaranteed by analysis, and by a further analysis see that the resulting proof is valid. Conversely, premises that are justified by analysis may be dropped from a valid proof and the resulting proof will still be valid. But it is not always easy to "see" that this resulting proof is valid by any *other* means than that the dropped premises were analytic and that the original proof was valid.

Here, then, is the great value of analytic statement forms such as "*s* is identical with *s*." They (or statements having these forms) may be added to or dropped from the list of premises in a given proof without altering the validity of the proof. Dropping them, in the case of proof *forms*, reveals a new proof form that may subsequently be accepted and used as a validating form. Adding them, in the case of *proofs*, represents a part of the analysis which shows the original proof to be valid.

But now let us return to Proof (II) and consider a different supposition, that analysis is *not* sufficient to justify the acceptance of "*C*." Suppose, however, that *observation* will show this premise to be true. Then the fact that Proof (II) is valid will not prove that Proof (I) is valid. It does prove that the only *other* bit of evidence required that we may be justified in accepting the conclusion "*B*" is the evidence contained in premise "*A*." But "*A*" does not necessarily suffice *alone* validly to prove "*B*"; rather, it suffices *with* "*C*" validly to prove "*B*."

Let us illustrate. Suppose that Proof (I) and Proof (II) had been the following:

(I'')                    (1)   *A*:   Every *Q* of *s*, is a *P*.
               ∴ (2)   *B*:   *s* is a *P*.

(II'')                   (1)   *A*:   Every *Q* of *s*, is a *P*.
                         (2)   *C*:   *s* is a *Q* of *s*.
               ∴ (3)   *B*:   *s* is a *P*.

Then *if* premise (2) in Proof (II'') is analytic, then Proof (I'') is valid. But if premise (2) is not analytic, yet observation has justified its acceptance as true, then Proof (I'') may not be valid, and yet all we need *further* to establish in order to be justified in accepting its conclusion, "*B*," is the truth of its premise, "*A*."

The above discussion should explain why it is important to distinguish between statements that are analytic and other possibly true statements, thus, for example, between relative terms for which reflexiveness is guaranteed by analysis and those for which reflexiveness is established only by observation.

## §41.4 Some Useful Technical Terms

In the preceding section, we spoke of certain statements and statement forms as "analytic." It will be useful to define "analytic" as well as certain other terms with which we can discuss various proofs and proof forms. You will notice that we give two contextual definitions for each defined term: one for its meaning as it applies to statements, another for its meaning as it applies to statement forms. For the most part, illustrations and comments will be put in footnotes.

(1a)　A statement is **analytic** means that analysis, or analysis combined with inference, suffices to reveal that the statement is true.[1]

(1b)　A statement form is **analytic** means that analysis, or analysis combined with inference, suffices to reveal that every statement having the given statement form is true.[2]

(2a)　A statement is **analytically false** means that analysis, or analysis combined with inference, suffices to reveal that the statement is false.[3]

(2b)　A statement form is **analytically false** means that analysis, or analysis and inference, suffices to reveal that every statement having the given statement form is false.[4]

(3a)　A statement is **synthetically true** means that it is not analytic or analytically false, but that observation, perhaps combined with other valid grounds, suffices to reveal that it is true.[5]

(3b)　A statement form is **synthetically true** means that it is not analytic or analytically false, but that observation, perhaps combined with other valid grounds, suffices to reveal that every statement having the form is true.[6]

(4a)　A statement is **synthetically false** means that it is not analytic or analytically false, but that observation, perhaps along with other grounds, suffices to reveal that it is false.[7]

[1]　Examples: "John is identical with John," "Either John is a voter or John is not a voter." "Every house is a building."
To say that "analysis combined with inference suffices" implies that establishing the premises of any inference used did not require a reliance on observation.
Also, this expression does not mean that the analyses *have* been made, but that circumstances are such that they *could* be made. Thus a statement could be analytic without our knowing that it is analytic. Analysis involves attending to the *strict* intensions of terms.

[2]　Examples: "*s* is identical with *s*," "*s* is *P* or *s* is not *P*."

[3]　Examples: "John is taller than John," "John is a voter and John is not a voter."

[4]　Examples: "*s* is taller than *s*," "*s* is a *P* and *s* is not a *P*."

[5]　Example: "New York City has a larger population than Boston, Mass."
To say that "observation . . . suffices" does not mean that the observations have been made, but that the world is such that, at least in principle, they could be made and would reveal the indicated outcome.

[6]　Example: "If *s* is a man, then *s* is less than 10 feet tall."

[7]　Example: "New York City has a smaller population than Boston, Mass."

(4b)   A statement form is **synthetically false** means that it is not analytic or analytically false, but that observation, perhaps with other grounds, suffices to reveal that every statement having the form is false.[8]

(5)   A statement form is **indeterminant** means that it is not analytic or analytically false, or synthetically true or synthetically false.[9]

A few comments are in order.

i.   Every statement that is analytic or synthetically true, is true. Also, every true statement is either analytic or else synthetically true.

ii.   Every statement that is analytically false or synthetically false is false. Also, every statement that is false is either analytically false or synthetically false.

iii.   Every statement is either analytic, analytically false, synthetically true, or synthetically false. This explains why we do not define "indeterminant" above in a contextual definition that applies it to statements.

iv.   No statement has two of the characteristics defined in (1a), (2a), (3a), and (4a), above.

v.   Every statement form has one and only one of the characteristics defined in (1b), (2b), (3b), (4b), and (5), above.

vi.   The main point of the preceding section may be summarized as follows.

Suppose

(I)                          (1)  $A$.
                        ∴ (2)  $B$.

to be a proof (or a proof form). And suppose that we can find a statement (or statement form), "$C$," such that (a)

(II)                         (1)  $A$.
                             (2)  $C$.
                        ∴ (3)  $B$.

is valid (or validating), and (b) "$C$" is analytic. Then (I) is valid (or validating). But suppose there is no statement (or statement form), "$C$," such that (a) and (b) are true. Then (I) is not valid (or validating). On the other hand, there may yet be a statement (or statement form) such that (a) is true and (c) we know "$C$" to be synthetically true. Then

---

8   Example: "$s$ is a man over 10 feet tall."
9   Examples: "$s$ is a $P$," "$s$ is a $P$ of $s$."

even though (I) is not valid (or validating), yet all we need do in order validly to infer "*B*" is to establish the truth of "*A*"; since (II) is valid (or validating) and we already know the truth of "*C*." To establish that certain relative terms are reflexive or irreflexive can thus be useful, either as a step in proving that (I) is valid (or validating)—when the reflexiveness or irreflexiveness is analytic—or in providing a tested premise for (II), when the reflexiveness or irreflexiveness is synthetically true.

## §41.5 Analytic versus Synthetic Symmetry and Asymmetry

Considerations much like those of the two preceding sections apply in the case of symmetry, asymmetry, and all other bases for valid proofs and validating proof forms. Let us state the general principle, first for proofs and then for proof forms, and finally let us illustrate by applying it to symmetry and asymmetry.

Corresponding to every proof, there is a complex "if . . ., then . . ." statement, in which the "if" clause is identical with the premise (or a combination of all the premises connected by "and") and the "then" clause is identical with the conclusion:

(1)        (1)   *A*.

∴ (2)   *B*.

            If *A*, then *B*.

(2)        (1)   *A*.

         (2)   *C*.

∴ (3)   *D*.

            If *A* and *C*, then *D*.

(3)        (1)   $s_1$ is taller than $s_2$.

∴ (2)   $s_2$ is not taller than $s_1$.

            If $s_1$ is taller than $s_2$, then $s_2$ is not taller than $s_1$.

Let us call this corresponding "if . . ., then . . ." statement the **justifying principle** of the original proof. We shall call it the justifying principle whether or not the original proof was valid. It *purports* to justify, and if it is true, it *does* justify, the conclusion.

Now there are two important things to notice. *First*, if the justifying principle of a proof is added as a further premise to that proof, then the resulting proof is valid. It makes no difference whether the original proof was valid or not. The resulting proof will be valid. And it makes no difference whether the justifying principle is true or not. The resulting proof is valid. If the justifying principle is false, the valid proof will have a false premise, but it will nevertheless be valid.

For example, from case (1), above, we get the following valid proof.

(4)     (1)  $A$.
        (2)  If $A$, then $B$.
   ∴ (3)  $B$.

And from cases (2) and (3) we get the following valid proofs. *always true prop*

(5)     (1)  $A$.
        (2)  $C$.
        (3)  If $A$ and $C$, then $D$.
   ∴ (4)  $D$.

(6)     (1)  $s_1$ is taller than $s_2$.
        (2)  If $s_1$ is taller than $s_2$, then $s_2$ is not taller than $s_1$.
   ∴ (3)  $s_2$ is not taller than $s_1$.

On the whole, when the justifying principle is false, to get a valid proof in the manner just described is not of much use because it will have a false premise and therefore cannot reflect a sound inference. Also, the original proof will have been invalid. But when the justifying principle is true, the matter is quite different. Let us consider those cases in which the justifying principle is true.

If the justifying principle is analytic, then the original proof is valid. This is just another illustration of the point made in the last two sections. But if we know that the justifying principle is synthetically true, then, although the original proof will not be valid, we know another valid proof with the same premises and only the justifying principle as an added premise. But this added premise is already tested and found true. Hence all that *remains* to do before we accept the conclusion of the original proof is to test the premises of that original proof.

A very similar line of reasoning may be applied to proof forms. Corresponding to every proof form, is an "if . . ., then . . ." statement form, in which the "if" clause is identical with the premise formula (or a combination of all the premise formulas connected by "and") and the "then" clause is identical with the conclusion formula. [See examples (1), (2), and (3), above.]

Let us call this "if . . ., then . . ." statement form the **justifying principle** of the original proof form.

If the justifying principle is added as a further premise to the original proof form, the result is a validating proof form. [See examples (4), (5), and (6), above.]

If the justifying principle is analytic, then the original proof form is a validating proof form. On the other hand, if the justifying principle is synthetically true, the original proof form is not validating, but we have a validating form [(4), (5), or (6)] with one of its premises already known to be true. All that remains to do before we may accept as true a statement having the form of the conclusion is to find true corresponding statements in the forms of the original premises.

In Unit 40 we talked *as though* symmetry and asymmetry were always established (when true) by analysis. In §40.8, we even illustrated this possibility by appeal to the definition of "converses with." But the fact is that some symmetrical and asymmetrical terms are such that their symmetry or asymmetry can be established only by observation, so that the justifying principle for a proof by symmetry or asymmetry is only synthetically true. For example, "$s_1$ succeeds $s_2$ as president of Harvard University" is asymmetrical: none has "split" a term of office, so that he was president just before and just after someone else. But definitions and analysis will not establish this fact. One has to see what are the facts of history.

Thus

(I)      (1)   $s_1$ succeeds $s_2$ as president of Harvard University.
        ∴ (2)   $s_2$ does not succeed $s_1$ as president of Harvard University.

is not a validating form. Yet its justifying principle is synthetically true.

Let us say that a proof (or proof form) like (I) above, in which the justifying principle is not analytic but is, however, synthetically true, is **loosely speaking** valid (or validating). A proof (or proof form) is **strictly speaking** valid (or validating) when and only when its justifying principle is analytic.

*EXERCISE*

In §§40.6 and 40.7 are listed six forms of proof which were said to be validating. Which of those (if any) do you consider strictly speaking validating, and which (if any) only loosely speaking validating? Could a difference in the choice of definitions make a difference in your answer? Discuss.

## §41.6 Transitivity and Intransitivity

Consider the proof form

I.
    (1)   $s_1$ is identical with $s_2$.
    (2)   $s_2$ is identical with $s_3$.
   ∴ (3)   $s_1$ is identical with $s_3$.

An understanding of the predicate "identical with" should suffice to persuade you that this is a **validating** form: every proof having this form will be valid.

The above proof-form may remind you of the axiom in geometry that "Things equal to the same thing are equal to each other." That axiom holds also for identity: things identical with the same thing are identical with each other. Put as a claim about validating forms of proof, this latter amounts to a claim that

II.
    (1)   $s_1$ is identical with $s_2$.
    (2)   $s_3$ is identical with $s_2$.
   ∴ (3)   $s_1$ is identical with $s_3$.

is **validating.** This claim is in fact correct, so we do have two validating forms here for "identical with." Furthermore, since "identical with" is symmetrical (§40.6), knowing that either of these forms is validating would be sufficient to prove that the other is validating. To illustrate, suppose that we knew that form II was validating. We could prove that form I is validating by taking the premises of form I and proceeding as follows:

III.
    (1)   $s_1$ is identical with $s_2$.    [Premise.]
    (2)   $s_2$ is identical with $s_3$.    [Premise.]
  ∴ (3)   $s_3$ is identical with $s_2$.    [From (2) by symmetry of "identical with".]
  ∴ (4)   $s_1$ is identical with $s_3$.    [From (1) and (3) by form II.]

But let us return to form I.

Form I represents a special case of form IV, in which "identical with" has replaced "$P$":

IV.
    (1)   $s_1$ is a $P$ of $s_2$.
    (2)   $s_2$ is a $P$ of $s_3$.
   ∴ (3)   $s_1$ is a $P$ of $s_3$.

Form IV is *not* a validating form of proof. But there are many special cases of this form which are validating forms. Form I is only one of several such cases. Other validating special cases would be represented if we replaced "$P$" in form IV by "taller (than)," "ancestor (of)," "hotter (than)," "equals in price," and so on. All such predicates are said to be _transitive._

A relative general term, "$Q$," is called **transitive** if upon replacing "$P$" by "$Q$" in form IV, proof form IV is converted into a validating form.

In accordance with this definition, all the predicates mentioned in the paragraph before the definition are transitive.

Among all the relative terms which are not transitive two types may be distinguished. **Intransitive** terms make form V validating.

V.  (1)  $s_1$ is a $P$ of $s_2$.
    (2)  $s_2$ is a $P$ of $s_3$.
  $\therefore$ (3)  $s_1$ is not a $P$ of $s_3$.

(Examples are "father," "grandfather," "child," "next after" (as numbers in a series), and so on). **Nontransitive** terms do not make form IV validating and do not make form V validating. (Examples are "friend," "cousin," "within 10 miles (of)," and so on.)

## EXERCISES

1.  Which of the following relative terms are transitive, which intransitive, and which nontransitive?
    a.  Talks (to)
    b.  North (of) _ye intra_
    c.  Brother (of) _yes_
    d.  Married (to) _untrans_
    e.  Next in line after . . . as President of the United States. _intrans._

2.  a.  Give an example of a relative term which, when replacing "$P$" in form IV, makes that form _strictly_ speaking validating.
    b.  An example which makes that form _loosely_ speaking validating.
    c.  An example which makes form V _strictly_ speaking validating.
    d.  An example which makes form V _loosely_ speaking validating.

### §41.7  Logical Relations between Symmetry, Transitivity, and Reflexiveness*

In this unit and the preceding one we have studied three important characteristics of certain relative terms: symmetry, reflexiveness, and transitivity. We have noticed that the relative term "identical (with)" has all three of these characteristics. But also we have noticed that other relative terms do not have all these characteristics. Some terms are symmetrical and others not, some are reflexive and others not, and some are transitive and others not.[10]

---

\* This section may be omitted without disturbing the continuity of the text.
[10]  Throughout this section we shall not be concerned to distinguish between the

One might now raise a *further* question about these three characteristics: is there any *connection* between them such that having or not having one or two of these characteristics implies having or not having a second or third? For example, are all symmetrical relative terms also transitive?

It is fairly easy to find examples of relative terms which have or do not have *one* of these characteristics and at the same time do not have or do have another. That is to say, examples will show that the three characteristics are independent one of the other when considered two at a time:

1. Symmetrical, transitive: "identical (with)"
2. Symmetrical, not transitive: "married (to)"
3. Symmetrical, reflexive: "identical (with)"
4. Symmetrical, not reflexive: "married (to)"
5. Not symmetrical, transitive: "taller (than)"
6. Not symmetrical, not transitive: "shoots" (as in, "Mr. A shoots Mr. B," *not* as in "Mr. A shoots this pistol.")
7. Not symmetrical, reflexive: "at least as tall (as)"
8. Not symmetrical, not reflexive: "taller (than)"
9. Transitive, reflexive: "identical (with)"
10. Transitive, not reflexive: "taller (than)"
11. Not transitive, reflexive: "acquainted (with)" (as a relation between people)
12. Not transitive, not reflexive: "married (to)"

However, when we begin looking for examples of terms that have two of the three characteristics and have or fail to have the third, the task becomes more difficult. A part of the way, it is relatively easy:

13. Symmetrical, reflexive, transitive: "identical (with)"
14. Symmetrical, reflexive, not transitive: "acquainted (with)" (as a relation between people)
15. Reflexive, transitive, not symmetrical: "at least as tall (as)"

But to find an example of the last remaining such combination—symmetrical, transitive, not reflexive—is almost impossible.

The reason that this is almost impossible is that one can almost prove that a relation which is symmetrical and transitive will be reflexive. To see how this is done, we can proceed as follows.

Let "$P$" represent a relative term and "$s_1$" and "$s_2$" represent singular terms such that:

a. "$P$" is transitive.
b. "$P$" is symmetrical.
c. $s_1$ is a $P$ of $s_2$.

---

two *ways* of failing to have one of the three characteristics: asymmetry and non-symmetry, irreflexiveness and nonreflexiveness, intransitivity and nontransitivity.

Then the following valid proof has for its conclusion the statement that is $P$ of $s_1$, that is, that "$P$" is reflexive.

(1)   $s_1$ is a $P$ of $s_2$.        [Premise.   By assumption c.]
∴ (2)   $s_2$ is a $P$ of $s_1$.        [From 1.   By assumption b.]
∴ (3)   $s_1$ is a $P$ of $s_1$.        [From 1 and 2.   By assumption a.]

We said above that one can "almost prove" that a term which is symmetric and transitive is also reflexive. Why is the above *almost* a proof of that point and in what way does it fail to be a complete proof of it?

To be a *complete* proof that "$P$" is reflexive, the conclusion "$s_1$ is a $P$ of $s_1$" would have to be a statement form that was true *no matter what* singular term "$s_1$" might be. But in order to get the proof started, we had to assume that "$s_1$" (and "$s_2$") were carefully chosen so that the premise, (1), would be true. Hence, the conclusion does not have the generality that is required for a proof that "$P$" is reflexive.

Nevertheless, the above proof pattern does show that *whatever* object, $s$, stands in the relation $P$ to something or other, $s_2$, will stand in the relation to itself (provided that $P$ is symmetrical and transitive). From this it follows that if everything stands in the relation $P$ to something, then everything stands in the relation $P$ to itself. Now this is *almost* a proof that $P$ is reflexive, because there are very few symmetrical, transitive relations in which people are interested (hence, for which they have invented relative terms) which do no connect everything with something. These relations are in general relations of equality (in some respect or other): equality in height, in weight, in price, in education, in intelligence, or whatever. And in general everything will be equal to something or other, in any respect that can be meaningfully considered. Hence, everything will be equal to itself in any respect that can be meaningfully considered.[11]

We have said that "there are very few symmetrical, transitive relations in which people are interested . . . which do not connect everything with something" and which are not therefore also reflexive. There are, nevertheless, few such relations. Examples appear in such phrases as "fellow American," "fellow teacher," "fellow student," and the like. Let us define "fellow American" as follows: $x$ is a fellow American of $y$ = Df $x$ is an American citizen and $y$ is an American citizen. From this definition, it follows that *fellow American* is a symmetrical and transitive relation, but that it is not reflexive, it being in fact nonreflexive: if $s$ is an American citizen, then $s$ is a fellow American of $s$; but if $s$ is not an American citizen, then $s$ is not a fellow American of $s$.

11   For example, it is not meaningful to ask whether triangularity is equal in price to circularity. "Equal in price" is a concrete term, "triangularity" and "circularity" are abstract terms. Hence, "Triangularity is equal in price to $s_2$" is not meaningful, hence not a statement, hence neither true nor false.

To complete this study of symmetry, transitivity, and reflexiveness, it need only be noted that there are relative terms having *exactly one* of these characteristics, and also relative terms that have *none* of them:

16.  Symmetrical, not transitive, not reflexive: "married (to)"
17.  Transitive, not symmetrical, not reflexive: "taller (than)"
18.  Reflexive, not symmetrical, not transitive: "addresses a sign-token (to)" (as a relation among adults)
19.  Not symmetrical, not transitive, not reflexive: "shoots"

## REVIEW QUESTIONS FOR UNIT 41

1.  What is meant by a *reflexive* relative term? An *irreflexive* term? A *nonreflexive* term? Give examples of each.
2.  What is the law of identity?
3.  Explain what important uses can be made of analytic statement forms, such as "*s* is identical with *s*."
4.  What does it mean to call a statement *analytic?* To call a statement form *analytic?* Illustrate.
5.  What does it mean to call a statement *analytically false?* To call a statement form *analytically false?* Illustrate.
6.  What does it mean to call a statement *synthetically true?* To call a statement form *synthetically true?* Illustrate.
7.  What does it mean to call a statement *synthetically false?* To call a statement form *synthetically false?* Illustrate.
8.  What does it mean to call a statement form *indeterminant?* Illustrate.
9.  Discuss the relation between truth and falsity and the concepts explained in answer to questions 5 to 8, above.
10.  What is meant by the *justifying principle* of a proof or proof form?
11.  Suppose that the justifying principle of a proof or proof form were added as a further premise to that proof or proof form. Would the resulting proof or proof form be: (a) always valid or validating, (b) always invalid or invalidating, or (c) in some cases valid (or validating) and in other cases invalid (or invalidating)?
12.  What can be said about the validity or invalidity of a proof according as its justifying principle is false, analytic, or synthetically true?
13.  What does it mean to call a proof or proof form *loosely speaking* valid or validating? *Strictly speaking* valid or validating?
14.  What does it mean to call a term *transitive? Intransitive? Nontransitive?* Illustrate each.

# The Logic of Complex Terms

## §42.1 Negative Terms

So far, we have been considering various characteristics, such as symmetry, that might or might not belong to a general term. Throughout the present unit, we shall consider ways in which the structure of a complex term may provide the basis for an analytic statement form or a validating proof form.

In §39.9, we observed that in addition to signs of denial, we often encounter **signs of negation** which are constituent parts of the terms in a statement. The more usual signs of negation of this sort in English are "not," "non-," and the prefixes "un-" or "in-": "George is a non-voter," "William was undismayed," "Tom is ineligible for election to the presidency," "That counter contains merchandise not returnable for refund or exchange."

Certain other signs occur in English that are a good deal like the above signs of negation but that must be carefully distinguished from them. An example is the prefix "dis-," as in "John dislikes coffee," or "Tom is disinclined to vote for Smith." These signs might be called **signs of contrariety**. We shall not study them in this text except to observe the difference between them and signs of negation. Prefixes of this sort indicate, so to speak, an extreme opposite of such a sort that there exists a genuine middle ground between the affirmative and the contrary terms. For example, there is a middle ground—of indifference—between liking and disliking coffee, and a middle ground—of lacking inclination—between being inclined and being disinclined (that is, being inclined not) to vote for Smith.

Another such contrary, as opposed to negative, prefix is "a-" as in "asymmetrical." But even the prefixes that *usually* indicate negatives are sometimes used to indicate contraries. Thus "in-" serves to indicate a contrary in the terms "intransitive" and "irreflexive." And as a result of that, even the prefix "non-" has come to denote a *different* contrary in the terms "nonsymmetrical," "nonreflexive," and "nontransitive."[1]

In short, there are a variety of conventions associated with prefixes whereby some tokens of a prefix denote a contrary and other tokens of that same prefix denote a negative. Because of this, we shall abandon the use of standard English prefixes in dealing with negative terms. We shall instead employ a prime suffix as follows: When we are putting an English statement into standard form, we shall enclose the affirmative basis of a negative term in parentheses and suffix a prime sign, thus:

(1)    John is a nonvoter.
(2)    John is a (voter)'.

And when we are representing the form of a statement, we shall suffix a prime sign to the variable which replaces the term that is the affirmative basis of the negative term. Thus the form of either statement (1) or statement (2) above is represented by

(3)    $s$ is a $P'$.

(It should be noted in passing that the form of statements (1) and (2) could have been represented by

(4)    $s$ is a $P$,

in which case our dictionary would have said

Let "$P$" replace "(voter)'."

Thus, the forms we are representing here are merely representations of special cases of form I, in which attention is specifically drawn to the fact that the predicate is a negative term.)

Not only absolute terms, but also relative terms, may be negated. Thus, if we represent "Tom is eligible for election to the presidency," by "$s_1$ is a $P$ of $s_2$," (where "$s_2$" represents the abstract singular term "election to the presidency"), we could represent "Tom is ineligible for election to the presidency" by "$s_1$ is a $P'$ of $s_2$."

On the other hand, it must never be forgotten that singular terms do not in general have corresponding negative terms. Thus it makes no sense to speak of "non-George" or "non-the President of the United States."

---

[1] As this text suggests, a term may have more than one contrary. There are many directions in which one may move to get to an extreme opposite to some term.

*EXERCISE*

Represent in as much detail as possible the forms of the following statements. Give your dictionary in each case. But if you are going to use "*P'*" or "*Q'*," let your dictionary say what "*P*" or "*Q*" replaces, not what "*P'*" or "*Q'*" replaces.

1. George is a nonpartisan.
2. George is not a partisan.
3. This watch is unreliable. *s is a P'*
4. That chair is unsafe.
5. James was undeceived by Tom's action. *s, is a P' of s₂*
6. That beam is unequal to the strain you propose to put on it.
   (Note: Treat "the strain you propose to put on that beam" as a singular term.)

## §42.2 Validating Forms of Inference Involving Negative Terms

The existence of affirmative and corresponding negative terms gives rise to many possibilities for valid inference. In this section, we shall note three kinds of valid inference that may occur.

**1. Obversion.** From any statement, one may validly infer a corresponding statement which is like the original in all respects save that:

a. It is opposite in quality (that is, if the premise is affirmative, the conclusion is negative; if the premise is negative, the conclusion is affirmative), *and*

b. The predicate of the conclusion is the same as the predicate of the premise save it is opposite in quality (that is, if the premise has an affirmative (or negative) predicate, the conclusion has as predicate the corresponding negative (or affirmative) term).

The above rule of obversion makes all the following **validating** forms of inference.

I.         (1)   *s* is a *P*.
           ∴ (2)   *s* is not a *P'*.

II.       (1)   *s* is not a *P*.
           ∴ (2)   *s* is a *P'*.

III.      (1)   *s* is a *P'*.
           ∴ (2)   *s* is not a *P*.

IV.      (1)   *s* is not a *P'*.
           ∴ (2)   *s* is a *P*.

V.            (1)  $s_1$ is a $P$ of $s_2$.
          ∴ (2)  $s_1$ is not a $P'$ of $s_2$.
VI.           (1)  $s_1$ is not a $P$ of $s_2$.
          ∴ (2)  $s_1$ is a $P'$ of $s_2$.

It may be noted that obversion is valid even when the premise and conclusion are general, rather than singular, statements. For example, the following is a <u>validating form of proof</u>:

VII.          (1)  No $S$ is $P$.
          ∴ (2)  Every $S$ is $P'$.

## EXERCISES

1.  Obvert each of the following statements:
    a.  John is unhappy.    *S is not P*
    b.  That beam is not horizontal.
    c.  Alex is not a nonpartisan.
    d.  This section of town is nonresidential.

2.  Suppose the four statements in question 1 to be premises in four proofs and the four statements you wrote in answer to question 1 to be the conclusions of those proofs. Would the proofs be valid?

3.  Which of the following are examples of obversion and which are not? In each case explain why you answer as you do.
    a.  (1)  John dislikes coffee        *obversion*
       ∴ (2)  John does not like coffee.
    b.  (1)  John is not unmarried    *obversion ( not*
       ∴ (2)  John is married.
    c.  (1)  Twenty-one percent of the male population over twenty-five years of age is unmarried      *obversion ( no middle quid*
       ∴ (2)  Twenty-one percent of the male population over twenty-five years of age is not married.
    d.  (1)  Some unmarried people are wealthy      *quality proper pred change there*
       ∴ (2)  Some married people are not wealthy.      * *not obvers*

**2. <u>Double Negation</u>.** As with statements and signs of denial, *not obvers* so with terms and signs of negation: two signs of negation on a single term cancel one another and may be dropped. Equally, two signs of negation may be added to a term. The point is that $P$ and $P''$ not only have, but purport to have, the same extension. For example, "a non-ineligible person" purports to refer to exactly the same people as does "an eligible person."

Thus proofs that have the following and similar forms are **valid**:

VIII.
  (1)  $s$ is a $P$.
  $\therefore$ (2)  $s$ is a $P''$.

This law of double negation applies to general terms even when they are not predicates, as in general propositions. Thus the following is a **validating** form of proof:

IX.
  (1)  Every $S$ is $P$.
  $\therefore$ (2)  Every $S''$ is $P$.

In this, it differs from obversion. Obversion is valid only for predicates. The following, for example, is *not* valid.

  (1)  Every student is a human being.
  $\therefore$ (2)  No nonstudent is a human being.

Instead of (2), the valid obverse of (1) is "No student is a nonhuman being;" and the valid conclusion by double negation of the subject is "Everything that is not a nonstudent is a human being."

**3. Repositioning.** We have seen that statements containing a relative predicate may be regarded as special cases of the general form, $s$ is a $P$. In order to treat "$s$ is a $Q$ of $s_1$" in this manner, we must treat "$Q$ of $s_1$" as representing a complex general term which is replaced by "$P$" in "$s$ is a $P$."

Suppose now that we were concerned with a singular statement having a negative relative predicate: $s$ is a $Q'$ of $s_1$. We could in the same manner treat "$Q'$ of $s_1$" as a complex absolute term. But notice that this complex absolute term is positive, even though it has a negative component, "$Q'$."

On the other hand, this sign of negation may be "repositioned" so as to apply to the entire complex expression and this repositioning will not alter the purported extension of the term. Thus "$Q'$ of $s_1$" and "$(Q$ of $s_1)'$ " are different terms but they purport to refer to exactly the same things. Hence, repositioning a sign of negation in the above manner will constitute a **validating** form of proof:

X.
  (1)  $s$ is a $Q'$ of $s_1$.
  $\therefore$ (2)  $s$ is a $(Q$ of $s_1)'$.

XI.
  (1)  $s$ is a $(Q$ of $s_1)'$.
  $\therefore$ (2)  $s$ is a $Q'$ of $s_1$.

In ordinary English, there often appears an element of ambiguity as to whether a complex term is to be regarded as an instance of "$Q'$ of $s$" or an instance of "$(Q$ of $s)'$." When the sign of negation is actually combined with the relative term, as in "ineligible for election to the presidency," perhaps the more natural interpretation is as an instance of "$Q'$ of $s$." And when the complex term has the form of a clause beginning with the expression "<u>who is not,</u>" as in "person who is not eligible for election to the presidency," perhaps the more natural interpretation is as an instance of "$(Q$ of $s)'$." But the very point of repositioning as a valid form of proof is that the two interpretations give terms with the same purported extensions, so that this ambiguity in English can never give rise to any logical errors. In fact, you may *think of* such English expressions as having whichever of these forms, "$Q'$ of $s$" or "$(Q$ of $s)'$," you prefer.

*EXERCISE*

      Which of the following proofs are valid and which are not? In the case of valid proofs, state which, if any, of the three types of valid proof discussed in this section it illustrates.

1.     (1)   John is not unacquainted with George.    DN
    ∴ (2)   John is acquainted with George.

2.     (1)   Every person not unacquainted with George is lucky.   DN
    ∴ (2)   Every person acquainted with George is lucky.

3.     (1)   Some people unacquainted with George are happy.
    ∴ (2)   Some people acquainted with George are not happy.   R

4.     (1)   Some people unacquainted with George are wealthy.
    ∴ (2)   Some people who are not acquainted with George are wealthy.   O

## §42.3 The Utility of Obversion, Double Negation, and Repositioning

      Obversion changes the quality of a statement (from affirmative to negative, or vice versa). It also changes the identity of its terms. Double negation and repositioning also change the identity of the terms involved in a statement.

    The changes brought about by these modes of proof are particularly useful when one wishes to prove something from two premises in combination with one another by some *other* principle of logic. Let us illustrate this point.

When a proof rests on the transitivity of some relative term, "$P$," it contains two premises and there is a certain pattern to the recurrences of terms:

$$(1) \quad s_1 \text{ is a } P \text{ of } s_2.$$
$$(2) \quad s_2 \text{ is a } P \text{ of } s_3.$$
$$\therefore (3) \quad s_1 \text{ is a } P \text{ of } s_3.$$

Both premises and the conclusion have the same predicate, "$P$"; furthermore, the singular terms which are subjects reappear in a certain pattern. Finally all three statements are affirmative.

Suppose that we were concerned to prove, "$s_1$ is not a $P'$ of $s_3$," from "$s_1$ is a $P$ of $s_2$" and "$s_2$ is not a $P'$ of $s_3$," when "$P$" is a transitive term. *As they stand*, the two premises are not in appropriate form to capitalize on the transitivity of "$P$." But they can be put into appropriate form by obversion. And finally, the resulting conclusion can then be put into the form of the desired conclusion by another obversion. Thus we get an *indirect* proof: The first step gets data into a form appropriate for the second step, and the third step gets the result of that second step into the form desired in the conclusion:

|  |  |  |
|---|---|---|
| (1) | $s_1$ is a $P$ of $s_2$. | [Premise.] |
| (2) | $s_2$ is not a $P'$ of $s_3$. | [Premise.] |
| $\therefore$ (3) | $s_2$ is a $P$ of $s_3$. | [From (2) by obversion.] |
| $\therefore$ (4) | $s_1$ is a $P$ of $s_3$. | [From (1) and (3) by transitivity of "$P$".] |
| $\therefore$ (5) | $s_1$ is not a $P'$ of $s_3$. | [From (4) by obversion.] |

The indirect proof above illustrates in a small way the "rhythm" of most proofs. Except for the simplest cases, a proof has its "key" step (in the above case, transitivity); but the material (premises) must first be "rearranged" into a form so that the key step can be applied, and the results of applying it must again be rearranged into the form of the desired conclusion.

Sometimes several key steps must be taken one after the other before one can get from the given premises to the desired conclusion. Then the rhythm of proofs really becomes apparent: rearrange, step, rearrange, step, rearrange, step.

Sometimes, of course, the given material is already in such a form that a key step may be taken at once, without any prior rearrangement. And then again, the rearrangements that are needed are sometimes so extensive that several lines of a proof must be given over to them before a key step may be taken.

Principles that contribute to the possibilities of rearrangement include not only ones like obversion, double negation, and repositioning, but also replacement in accordance with definitions and many others as well. The use of definitions for this purpose is illustrated in §40.8, in the proof that "converses (with)" is symmetrical.

## §42.4 <u>Converse Relative Terms</u>

Consider the following pairs of statements.

| | |
|---|---|
| (1a) | George strikes John. |
| (1b) | John is struck by George. |
| (2a) | New York is east of Chicago. |
| (2b) | Chicago is west of New York. |
| (3a) | William's office is above George's. |
| (3b) | George's office is below William's. |

Statements in each pair are related as (4a) and (4b):

| | |
|---|---|
| (4a) | $s_1$ is a $P$ of $s_2$. |
| (4b) | $s_2$ is a $Q$ of $s_1$. |

Yet they make identical claims because the relative predicates, replaced by "$P$" and "$Q$," are *interrelated* so as to compensate for reversing the order of the subjects, "$s_1$" and "$s_2$." In the first case, the two predicates are the active and passive voice of the same verb; in the other two cases they are derived by using first one and then the other of a set of paired prepositions.

Terms related as these predicates in the pairs of statements are said to be **converses** of one another. Thus "struck by" is the converse of "strikes," and "strikes" is the converse of "struck by"; "above" is the converse of "below," and "below" is the converse of "above"; "taller than" is the converse of "shorter than," and "shorter than" is the converse of "taller than."[2]

To represent the converse of "$P$," let us write "$\breve{P}$." Thus we get two **validating** forms of proof, as follows.

| | | |
|---|---|---|
| XII. | (1) | $s_1$ is a $P$ of $s_2$. |
| | ∴ (2) | $s_2$ is a $\breve{P}$ of $s_1$. |
| XIII. | (1) | $s_1$ is a $\breve{P}$ of $s_2$. |
| | ∴ (2) | $s_2$ is a $P$ of $s_1$. |

---

[2] Grammar establishes the fact that the active and passive voices of a verb indicate converse relations. But it takes a definition to exhibit the fact that different prepositions or different comparative adjectives indicate converse relations. Hence, that "shorter" is the converse of "taller" is a matter of applied logic.

In accordance with these validating forms, either statement in any of the pairs at the beginning of this section would be a valid conclusion from the other statement in that pair taken as a premise.

Three comments will close this section.

1. If any relative term is reflexive, symmetrical, or transitive, then the relative term which is its converse is also reflexive, symmetrical, or transitive. The same holds for irreflexive, nonreflexive, asymmetrical, nonsymmetrical, intransitive, and nontransitive terms: the term and its converse will be alike in all these characteristics. Thus, for example, since "taller than" is irreflexive, asymmetrical, and transitive, its converse, "shorter than," is also irreflexive, asymmetrical, and transitive.

2. If a term is symmetrical, it is its own converse. Thus "marries," "equals," and "is identical with" are their own converses. That is, you may reverse the order of the subject terms *without* changing the predicate, and the meaning of the statement is not altered.

3. The value of converse terms lies in their permitting one to reverse the order of the subject terms even when the relative predicate is not symmetrical. Thus *either* subject term may be absorbed into a complex predicate under an analysis using the general form "*s* is *P*." For an example, consider the following proof:

| | | |
|---|---|---|
| (1) | $s_1$ is taller than $s_2$. | [Premise.] |
| (2) | Anyone shorter than $s_1$ is $Q$. | [Premise.] |
| ∴ (3) | $s_2$ is shorter than $s_1$. | [From (1) by converse predicate.] |
| ∴ (4) | $s_2$ is $Q$. | [From (2) and (3) by syllogism.][3] |

## *EXERCISE*

For each statement below, write another, equivalent statement which uses the converse of the predicate used in the given statement.

1. John read the letter.
2. Chicago is north of St. Louis.
3. That rock is heavier than this one.
4. Fourteen is twice seven.
5. Yellow is a more intense color than gray.

## §42.5 Definite Descriptions

Definite descriptions, like "that rock," "the President," and so on, offer an opportunity for formulating certain analytic statements which can be useful in proofs.

[3] On syllogism, see Units 46 and 47, below.

Heretofore, we have represented definite descriptions by the small letter variables, "$s$," "$s_1$," and so on, that we regularly employ to replace singular terms. This has been sufficient for all our purposes to date. But now we need a symbolism which reveals the *general* term—"rock," "President," and so on—on which the definite description is based.

Let us use "**c**" and "**i**," prefixed to a variable for a general term— "$P$," "$Q$," "$S$," and so on—to represent a complete, "**c**," or incomplete, "**i**," definite description based on the general term represented by the variable. Thus "$c(P)$" will represent "the $P$," where a complete description is intended, while "$i(P)$" will represent "a certain $P$," or "the $P$," when an incomplete description is intended.

Now statements like "That rock is a rock," and "The President is a President," would seem to be <u>true by analysis</u>. The analytic character of these statements may be acknowledged by noting that they are special instances of one or the other of the following **analytic** statement forms:

XIV.  $\quad\quad\quad\quad$ $c(P)$ is a $P$.

XV.  $\quad\quad\quad\quad$ $i(P)$ is a $P$.[4]

---

[4] These statement-forms are, to be sure, analytic, but the given statements are not *strictly* speaking examples of these forms. To take the first example, "That rock is a rock," fails to have the form "$c(P)$ is a $P$" because in the given statement "that rock" does not mean "the rock" but rather "the rock at which I am pointing," or some such thing. Thus, to get an instance of "$c(P)$ is a $P$" we should have to write "That rock is a rock at which I am pointing," or some such thing.

It would complicate the present illustrative survey too seriously to show in detail just how the actual form of the illustrative statement is itself analytic. Certain related considerations will be mentioned in Unit 43. But just to hint at the solution, **complex conjunctive terms** like "iron ring" and "rock at which I am pointing" offer an opportunity for a valid inference. If we represent such a conjunctive term by "$P \frown Q$" where "$P$" replaces "iron" or "rock," "$Q$" replaces "ring" or "at which I am pointing," and "$\frown$" represents the conjoining of these factors into one term, then the validating form of inference is represented by

$$(1)\ \ s \text{ is a } P \frown Q.$$
$$\therefore\ (2)\ \ s \text{ is a } P.$$

For example, "That is an iron ring; therefore, that is iron." Or, "That is a rock at which I am pointing; therefore, that is a rock."

Now, to represent "that rock" we should write "$c(P \frown Q)$." Then form XIV in the text allows us to assert as analytic

$$c(P \frown Q) \text{ is a } P \frown Q.$$

From this, by the validating form of inference given in this footnote, we infer

$$c(P \frown Q) \text{ is a } P.$$

Strictly speaking, "That rock is a rock," and "The President is a President," are instances of the analytic form just written. But no great harm will be done if we

While pure logic offers forms XIV and XV as analytic, *applied* logic will permit us frequently to replace the definite description which is the subject term by a proper name. For an intensional definition of the proper name will show it to be synonymous with a certain incomplete definite description. Thus, for example, applied logic might propose "Mr. Eisenhower is a man" and "Mr. Pickwick is a man" as special cases of form XV. In fact, whenever $P$ is a necessary member of the total contingent intension of "$s$," then "$s$ is a $P$" is analytic and either strictly or loosely speaking an instance of form XIV or form XV.

## §42.6 Existence Statements

The proposals of the preceding section raise a problem that we cannot afford to overlook any longer. This problem has to do with the relation between "$s$ is a $P$" and "$s$ exists."

Near the beginning of §39.3 it was suggested that any statement of the form "$s$ is a $P$" amounts to "an affirmation that the purported referent of the subject term has all the characteristics in the total strict intension—thus, is in the extension—of the predicate." But to say that a thing is in the extension of a term implies that the thing exists or is actual, an important point repeatedly stressed in Unit 20. Putting all these facts together suggests that the following should be regarded as a validating form of proof:

(A)                              (1)   $s$ is a $P$.
                              ∴ (2)   $s$ exists.

Many logicians do in fact propose that the above is a validating form of proof. But to accept it as validating demands a reconsideration of statement forms, like XIV and XV, which have been listed as analytic.[5] As we explained in §41.4, if a statement form is analytic, then every statement having that form is true. Thus, if statement form XIV,

$$c(P) \text{ is a } P,$$

is analytic, then statement (1), below, is true.

---

regard them as, loosely speaking, instances of form XIV and thus avoid for our present purposes the need to complicate the account by introducing the formula "$P \frown Q$" in order to represent the formulas mentioned in this footnote.

5   Other statement forms which would have to be reconsidered in the same manner are "$s$ is identical with $s$," and all other analytic statements of reflexiveness. We have listed these as analytic in §41.1. In the text, however, we shall focus attention on form XIV, which will sufficiently illustrate the problem involved.

(1)          The president of England is a president of England.

But if statement (1) is true, then by the validating form of proof (A) given just above, statement (2) is also true:

(2)                    The president of England exists.

Now we know that statement (2) is false: England is a monarchy and does not have a president. Hence *something* is wrong among the assumptions we made which enabled us to prove that (2) is true. A fairly complete list of these assumptions would be as follows.[6]

i.   Statement (1) does have the form represented in formula XIV.

ii.  Statements (1) and (2) are corresponding illustrations of the forms represented as premise and conclusion in proof form (A).

iii. Statement form XIV is analytic.

iv.  Proof form (A) is validating.

It is difficult to question the legitimacy of assumptions i and ii. It is true that statement (1) has only loosely speaking the form of formula XIV: The subject term would ordinarily be understood as purporting to refer to the person who is *now* president of England, while the predicate would be taken as purporting to refer to any person who ever was, is, or will be president of England. But this difference cannot affect the point under consideration.

Thus we are left with assumptions iii and iv. These cannot both be correct, for if they were both correct, we could prove certain statements, such as (2), to be true that we in fact know are false. Yet both these assumptions are very plausible.

The solution to this problem would seem to lie in finding that one or the other (or maybe both) of these two assumptions is, so to speak, *generally* reliable but not *always* so. When, furthermore, the factors that limit its reliability can be listed, the problem will be completely solved.

Many logicians have approached this problem by accepting assumption iv—that form (A) is validating—and rejecting assumption iii. In place of form XIV they put a claim that statement form (B) is analytic.

(B)                    If **c**(P) exists, then **c**(P) is a P.

That solution has much to recommend it. Among other things, it

6  We call the list "fairly complete." It actually includes *all* the assumptions which the author can discern that could in any way bear on the problem.

lets us regard statements of the form "*s* is a *P*" as always affirming *s* to be in the extension of "*P*." But it also has serious drawbacks. Among these, it is continually forcing us to attend to questions of existence before we can apply principles of logic.

In this text an alternative solution to this problem will be adopted. We shall regard formula XIV as analytic, but we shall hold that proof form (A) is not always validating. In particular, it is not validating whenever its premise is analytic. In other words, it is validating only when its premise is synthetic.[7] The effect of this rule is that forms XIV and XV can never supply premises for proofs that will be valid examples of form (A), because premises thus supplied would be analytic.

In a larger sense, what is the effect of this rule on the meaning of the form "*s* is a *P*"? In the second paragraph of this section is a quotation from §39.3. That quotation proposes to say what "*s* is a *P*" means. In the middle of the quotation is the parenthetical clause "thus, is in the extension." That parenthetical clause must be recognized as not universally valid. What "*s* is a *P*" affirms is a connection between *intensions*, as explained in the main clause of the quotation. When that connection between intensions holds, "*s* is a *P*" is true. But if that connection between intensions holds *analytically*, nothing about extensions can be inferred, hence nothing about extensions is affirmed in "*s* is a *P*." On the other hand, if the connection between intensions is synthetically true, then the *historic* fact of its being true is equivalent to the purported referent of "*s*" being in the extension of "*P*."

## REVIEW QUESTIONS FOR UNIT 42

1. Explain the difference between signs of negation and signs of contrariety as constituent parts of a term. Illustrate.

2. Can some tokens of a sign-type be signs of negation and other tokens of that same sign-type be signs of contrariety? Explain and illustrate.

3. Can signs of negation be meaningfully attached to singular terms? To general terms? To absolute terms? To relative terms?

---

[7] A further limitation on the circumstances under which form (A) is validating is required, but it is of relatively little *practical* importance and is too complicated to enter into here. It has to do with getting a synthetic premise for form (A) by obversion. Generally, "*s* is not a *P*; therefore *s* exists," is not validating. But if obversion is allowed, the above premise can be turned into "*s* is a *P'*," which might be synthetic and could allow an inference that *s* exists. A way of avoiding this difficulty is explained in the author's article on "The Logic of Existence" in *Philosophical Studies*, Vol. VII, No. 4 (June, 1956).

4. What is meant by *obversion*. Is obversion always valid?

5. Describe and illustrate proof by the double negation of terms. Can double negation apply to other terms than the predicates of statements?

6. What is meant by *repositioning* a sign of negation? Does this process give rise to valid proofs?

7. Discuss briefly the general utility of valid processes like obversion, double negation, repositioning, and replacement in accordance with definitions.

8. What does it mean to say that two terms are *converses* one of the other?

9. Do all relative terms have converses? Do any absolute terms have converses?

10. Discuss briefly the connection between the fact of two terms being converses of one another and of their being reflexive, symmetrical, transitive, and the like.

11. What distinguishes symmetrical terms from others with respect to their converses?

12. What is one of the major uses of converse relations?

13. Symbolize two analytic statement forms involving definite descriptions. Explain what the symbols that you used represent.

14. How may the statement forms written in answer to question 13 be used in *applied* logic to justify as analytic statements containing proper names instead of definite descriptions?

15. Explain briefly why some restriction must be put on the assumption that "c(*P*) is a *P*" is analytic, or on the assumption that

$$(1) \quad s \text{ is a } P.$$
$$\therefore (2) \quad s \text{ exists.}$$

is validating. Describe two alternative solutions to this problem.

# UNIT 43

## Molecular Logic and Truth Functions

### §43.1 Molecular Logic

We have now devoted four units to the study of singular statements and their logic. It is time we moved on to examine the logic of other types of statements. In this present unit and the next we shall look briefly at some principles of "molecular logic." Throughout this study, we shall find the use of variables and the consideration of statement forms and proof forms still the major key to the study of logic.

**Molecular logic** is that branch of logic which deals with complex statements, that is, with statements that contain other statements as constituent parts of themselves.

Let us illustrate. The English language contains many words belonging to a part of speech called *conjunctions*: "or," "and," "but," "although," "if," "neither," and so on. These conjunctions frequently serve to combine several statements (called *clauses* by the grammarian when they are so combined) into one complex statement.[1]

EXAMPLES:

1. *If* it rains, I shall stay at home.
2. *Either* that man is a Frenchman *or* he is an Italian.
3. *Although* China has many natural resources, it is not highly developed.

Other linguistic means than conjunctions, however, may be used to produce complex statements. Among these other devices, we have already studied signs of denial, "not" and "it is false that." Every

---

[1] In grammar, one distinguishes between a *compound* sentence (containing two or more *main* clauses) and a *complex* sentence (containing one *main* clause and one or more dependent clauses). In logic, we lump all these together and call them *complex* statements.

negative statement is really a complex statement containing its corresponding affirmative statement as a constituent part of itself:

4. *It is false that* two plus three equals six.
5. John is *not* an American citizen.

But in addition to these signs of denial, other expressions or phrases might serve to introduce statements as constituent parts of other statements, and thus make the larger, containing statements complex:

6. *George told me that* North Carolina is larger than Tennessee.
7. *The fact that* John is twenty-one *implies that* he is eligible to vote.

One interesting and important feature in the forms of complex statements may be represented by replacing their constituent statements by **statement variables,** "*p*," "*q*," "*r*," and so on. When such an analysis is made, we do not concern ourselves with the forms or constituent terms appearing *in* the constituent statements. Our only concern is that some statement or other appears in such and such a context in a complex statement. According to this method of analysis, the seven illustrative complex statements given above might be said to have the following forms:

1'. If *p*, then *q*.
2'. Either *p* or *q*.
3'. Although *p*, *q*.
4'. It is false that *p*.
5'. Not *p*.
6'. George told me that *p*.
7'. The fact that *p* implies that *q*.

Any analysis of statements or proofs which represents their forms with the aid of statement variables, as above, and without the aid of other types of variable (such as term variables "*s*" and "*P*") may be called a *molecular* analysis. Any principles of logic that can be formulated in terms of molecular analysis may be said to belong to molecular logic.[2]

---

[2]   Molecular logic gets its name from a certain analogy to chemistry. In this branch of logic, the component clauses in a complex statement may be thought of as molecules, having their subjects and predicates as constituent atoms. Thus in molecular logic we are studying the manner in which these molecules combine with one another to form larger, more complex logical structures. But we are studying this matter only insofar as no *internal* analysis of the constituent molecules into their atoms is needed in the study. When such internal analysis is required, we are involved in the logic of singular statements, or general statements, or statements of whatever sort the internal analysis reveals.

It will be quite impossible even to mention in two units all the topics that have been investigated in molecular logic. Rather than try to do so, we shall single out a few important and illustrative topics for more careful consideration.

### EXERCISE

Represent the molecular form of each of the following statements. In each case give your dictionary. By way of illustration, the solutions to the first three statements are given, with some explanatory comments.

1.  To say that John is a liar is to insult him.
    Let "*p*" replace "John is a liar."
    Then the form of the given statement is represented by
    To say that *p* is to insult John.

*Comment:* When the given statement contains a pronoun and its antecedent, but the antecedent will have disappeared in the representation of the form, then replace the pronoun by its antecedent when you represent the form. (In the above, we replaced "him" by "John.")

2.  Either that triangle is isosceles or it is equilateral.
    Let "*p*" replace "that triangle is isosceles."
    "*q*" replace "that triangle is equilateral."
    Then the form of the given statement is represented by
    Either *p* or *q*.

*Comment:* When you give your dictionary replace pronouns by their antecedents when those antecedents are not in the clause being represented. (We replaced "it" by "that triangle.")

3.  Either Tom or George will report the accident.
    Let "*p*" replace "Tom will report the accident."
    "*q*" replace "George will report the accident."
    Then the form of the given statement is represented by
    Either *p* or *q*.

*Comment:* English, like other common languages, is abbreviative: When two clauses have the same grammatical predicate but different subjects (as above), or the same subject but different grammatical predicates (as in "George is either forgetful or stupid"), the identical part is not repeated and the conjunctions which would ordinarily come between the clauses are put between the two stated subjects or stated predicates. When we represent the logical form, however, we should indicate the complete clause that is replaced by each variable and represent the conjunctions as though they appeared between the complete clauses.

4.  It will not rain this afternoon.

5. George and Harry left the meeting early.

6. Although that coat is expensive, I shall buy it.

7. Either the citizens are not aware of corruption or Mr. X will lose the election.

## §43.2  Truth Functions

We have already seen an example of the kind of situation studied in molecular logic. In §40.8, in connection with the proof that "converses with" is symmetrical, we had occasion to make use of the validating form

$$(1) \quad p \text{ and } q.$$
$$\therefore (2) \quad q \text{ and } p.$$

The fact that this form is validating is a minor principle of molecular logic.

Also, we have given some attention to other principles studied in molecular logic. We did this when we noticed how signs of denial might occur in singular statements. The laws of double negation, of contradiction, and of excluded middle are really laws of molecular logic rather than of the logic of singular statements. This is true because it actually makes no difference whether the negated statements are singular statements, general statements, or mixed singular and general statements. Thus our study of those laws in the preceding units was really a study of molecular logic as it applies to singular statements.

Now, however, we are concerned with molecular logic in itself. This is attested by the fact that we do not concern ourselves with any question as to whether or not the statements replaced by "$p$" and "$q$" are singular, general, or mixed. *All* we are interested in is the way in which those statements are combined into various complex statements.

Let us call any representation of a statement form a **statement function** if the only variables which it contains are statement variables. Thus, all the representations of statement forms studied in molecular logic are statement functions. All the representations of statement forms given in the preceding section are statement functions.

Statement functions belong to many types and kinds. One important kind of statement function is called a *truth function*. We can learn to distinguish functions of this kind from others by comparing the two following statement functions.

(1)  Brubacher believes that *p*.

(2)  It is false that *p*.

In many ways these two functions are similar one to the other. For example, each contains only one occurrence (token) of only one statement variable. And again, each is such that some statements illustrating the form it represents will be true and others will be false.

But on the other hand, there is one very great and important difference between them. Mr. Brubacher, like all human beings, is limited in the extent of his knowledge. We all have mistaken beliefs, as well as correct ones. Thus, there are bound to be *true* statements—say, *A* and *B*— such that Mr. Brubacher believes *A* but does not believe *B*, while there will be *false* statements—say, *C* and *D*—such that Mr. Brubacher believes *C* but does not believe *D*. Suppose now that you consider some statement, for example,

(3)  Brubacher believes that all hydrogen atoms have the same atomic weight,

which has form (1) and is derivable from (1) through replacing "*p*" by

(4)  All hydrogen atoms have the same atomic weight.

For us to know whether or not (4) is true will not give us sufficient evidence to enable us to determine whether or not (3) is true. Yet how different is statement function (2). Were we to replace "*p*" in it by (4), giving

(5)  It is false that all hydrogen atoms have the same atomic weight,

the mere truth or falsity of (4) is sufficient in itself to determine the truth or falsity of (5): If (4) is true, then (5) is false, while if (4) is false, then (5) is true.

This difference between statement functions (1) and (2) holds quite generally. It is no consequence of our choice of (4) as a statement to replace "*p*." *Whatever* statement, *X*, we may choose as a replacement of "*p*," so as to give

(6)  Brubacher believes that *X*,

and

(7)  It is false that *X*,

the mere truth or falsity of *X* will *not* suffice *in itself* to determine the truth or falsity of (6), but it *will* suffice to determine the truth or falsity of (7). This latter fact is precisely what is affirmed in the laws of excluded middle and of contradiction.

Statement functions (1) and (2) illustrate the difference between those functions that are truth functions, such as (2), and those that are not, such as (1). In fact, we may define a truth function as follows:

A **truth function** is a statement function such that the mere truth or falsity of the statements that replace its variables, in giving illustrations of the form it represents, always suffices to determine the truth or falsity of those illustrations.[3]

Not all truth functions contain only one token of only one variable, as was the case with (2). For example,

(8)   p and q

is a truth function containing one occurrence of each of two variables, "*p*," and "*q*." It is a truth function for reasons that the following table shows.[4]

| If *p* is | and if *q* is | then (*p* and *q*) is |
|-----------|---------------|------------------------|
| True | True | True |
| True | False | False |
| False | True | False |
| False | False | False |

Truth Table for Conjunction

Consider, by way of illustration,

(9)   I looked in the closet and saw my hat.

---

[3] The word "always" is an important feature of this definition. For example,

p is analytic

is not a truth function because, although the truth or falsity of statements replacing "*p*" is *sometimes* sufficient to determine the truth or falsity of the corresponding illustration of the function—if the statement replacing "*p*" is false, then the corresponding illustration of "*p* is analytic" is false (on "analytic," see §41.4)—this is not *always* so: *Sometimes*, when a *true* statement replaces "*p*," the corresponding illustration of "*p* is analytic" is *true*, sometimes the corresponding illustration is *false*. EXAMPLES: "Eisenhower is Eisenhower," and "Eisenhower was elected President in 1952."

[4] In the table, we say "If *p* is True," "If *q* is True" and "then (*p* and *q*) is True," etc. Strictly speaking, the table should read, "If, in a statement of the form '*p* and *q*,' the statement replacing '*p*' is True, and the statement replacing '*q*' is True, then the statement in question with the form '*p* and *q*' is True," etc. Yet the simpler structure of the table as presented is perhaps psychologically clearer than the more complex, but more accurate, formulation here presented.

If "I looked in the closet," and "I saw my hat," are both true, then (9) is true, but if either or both of them are false, then (9) is false.

Some branches of molecular logic deal with certain statement functions which are not truth functions. However, the remainder of our study will illustrate molecular logic only in terms of its treatment of truth functions.

### §43.3 Standard Forms and Tables for Truth Functions: Negation and Conjunction

English, like all natural languages, offers a wide variety of ways in which to "say the same thing." As we have so often seen in earlier units, logic makes its progress by selecting one of these ways as a standard form and by expecting other statements to be put into this standard form.

In the present section and the next, we shall consider standard forms for certain truth functions and also some other English expressions that may be put into these standard forms.

We have already noted that signs of denial, "it is false that" and "not," are truth functions. When "not" is employed, it usually occurs in the midst of the statement which replaces "$p$": "John is not an American citizen." But sometimes it precedes that statement: "Not every American citizen is patriotic." On the other hand, "it is false that" regularly precedes such a statement: "It is false that every American citizen is patriotic."

We shall call any truth function constituted by a sign of denial a **negation.** Throughout our study of molecular logic, we shall consider "**not**" as the standard expression and its standard position as preceding the statement which replaces "$p$." Thus,

$$\textbf{not } p$$

will be the standard representation of negation. Finally, whenever "$p$" is replaced by a complex sign, for example, by a statement, standard form shall require that the complex expression replacing "$p$" be enclosed in parentheses. Thus, the three examples of negation should be put in one or the other of these standard forms:

(1)    **Not** (John is an American citizen).

(2)    **Not** (Every American citizen is patriotic).

In the preceding section, there is a table showing how the values (truth and falsity) of "$p$" and of "$q$" affect the value of "$p$ **and** $q$." We can give here a similar table for negation. But in this and future tables, we shall use the initial letters "T" and "F" instead of the words "True" and "False."

| If $p$ is | then **not** $p$ is |
|:---:|:---:|
| T | F |
| F | T |

Truth Table for Negation

*EXERCISES*

1. Put each of the following into standard molecular form:
   a. It is false that Congress abolished income taxes in 1955.
   b. George is not taller than James.
   c. The king of America does not exist.
   d. New York City is not the capital of New York State.

2. In each of the above, suppose that the *constituent* is true; what would be the value (true or false) of the given statement? Suppose that the constituent statement was false; what then would be the value of the given statement?

The truth table for "and," given in the preceding section, is the truth table for **conjunction.** We shall regard "$p$ **and** $q$" as the standard form for representing conjunction. But many other words are available in English as representations of the same truth functional meaning. Thus, "but," "although," "though," and "even though" mean the same thing as "and," and when we put expressions containing them into standard form, they should be replaced by "and."[5]

It was said above that "but," "although," and so on have the same truth functional meaning as "and." Thus they are alternative expressions indicating the truth function called *conjunction*. English usage, however, suggests different circumstances under which "and" is appropriately used and under which they are appropriately used. When the truth of one clause makes the truth of the other one mildly or extremely surprising, then the first mentioned clause is often introduced by "although," "though," and so on.

[5] "And" always comes between the statements or clauses that it connects, while "although," "though," and "even though" are frequently put at the beginning of the first clause. When they are replaced by "and" it must naturally be put between the clauses even when the word it replaces was at the beginning of the first clause.

EXAMPLES: "She wore a coat even though the day was quite warm." "Although the problem is a simple one, you had better use paper and pencil to solve it."

On the other hand, "but" is used when one clause is affirmative and the other negative, or when the truth of either clause makes the truth of the other surprising.

EXAMPLES: "The box was large, but not heavy." "The box was large, but of light weight." "That statement is true, but unimportant."

As with negation, so here, when complex expressions replace "*p*" and "*q*," standard form requires that they be put in parentheses.

## EXERCISES

1. Put the following statements into standard form. (Note that you may have to use both the standard forms for conjunction and for negation in one problem.)

   a. The umpire's decision was fair, even though he reached it quickly.

   b. John is heavy, but not fat.

   c. I went to the committee meeting although I did not want to go.

   d. Every chair in the room is sturdy, though it is false that they all look so.

2. By consulting the truth tables for conjunction and negation given in this and the preceding section, determine which of the following are validating forms of proof and which are not. In each case, explain briefly why you answer as you do.

   a.  (1)  *p*
       (2)  *q*
       ∴ (3)  *p* **and** *q*

   b.  (1)  *p*
       (2)  **not** *q*
       ∴ (3)  **not** (*p* **and** *q*)

   c.  (1)  *p*
       ∴ (2)  *p* **and** *q*

   d.  (1)  **not** *p*
       ∴ (2)  **not** (*p* **and** *q*)

   e.  (1)  *p* **and** *q*
       ∴ (2)  *q*

   f.  (1)  **not** (*p* **and** *q*)
       ∴ (2)  **not** *p*

## §43.4 Alternation

Still another truth function is expressed by the word "or" as in the weather prediction, "Rain or snow," (that is, "Either it will rain or it will snow.") The truth function so expressed is called **alternation.**

When statements are connected by "or," the usual intention is a claim that *at least one* of the connected statements is true. It is *not* usually intended to claim that *only*, or *precisely*, one of the connected statements is true, even though the character of the connected statements is such that they could not both be true. For example, "John is an American citizen or he is not an American citizen," is an affirmation that at least one of the connected statements, "John is an American citizen," and "John is not an American citizen," is true. The law of contradiction (§40.4) further assures us that one of them is false, hence that *exactly* one of them is true. But the above statement is not *affirming* this additional fact: it is affirming merely that at least one of them is true.[6] Thus, to go back to our first example, we should say that the weather prediction turned out correct if it rained and did not snow, snowed but did not rain, or both rained and snowed; it would have turned out incorrect only in the event that it neither rained nor snowed.[7]

Hence we get the following table of truth values for alternation.

| If $p$ is | and $q$ is, | then ($p$ **or** $q$) is |
|:---:|:---:|:---:|
| T | T | T |
| T | F | T |
| F | T | T |
| F | F | F |

Truth Table for Alternation

[6] *Occasionally* people use "or" to claim that *exactly* one of the two alternatives is true. But to do so is an unwise convention, since it increases the risk of ambiguity. Some languages contain separate conjunctions to express these two different meanings. Thus in Latin, *vel* means at least one, while *aut* means exactly one, is true. English does not contain two such conjunctions. Thus both Latin conjunctions are usually translated by "or." But they do have different meanings.

When you wish to affirm that exactly one of two statements is true, it is well to add, "but not both," as in "$p$ or $q$, but not both."

[7] As always, standard form will require that complex replacements of "$p$" and "$q$" be placed in parentheses.

### §43.5 "Multiplication Tables" for Truth Functions

Let us briefly review some of the main points in this unit. Suppose that we are examining a statement which illustrates some truth function—say, negation, or conjunction, or alternation. In order to "calculate" the truth or falsity of this illustration, it is not necessary that we know what are the statements, or even the meanings of the statements, which appear as constituents in this illustration: all we need know is whether these statements are true or whether they are false. Of course, unless we are relying on authority or memory, we could hardly find out whether they are true or false without knowing what they mean. But once we have found out whether they are true or false, we can, so to speak, forget what they mean and still calculate the truth or falsity of the statement in which they occur as constituents.

We shall find it helpful to think of these calculations as made in accordance with "multiplication tables" for the various truth functions. These multiplication tables really report just what has been recorded in the truth tables given above. But they report it in a convenient compact fashion that omits all reference to anything except the crucial truth or falsity of the constituent statements:

| *Negation* | *Conjunction* | *Alternation* |
|---|---|---|
| (not T) = F | (T and T) = T | (T or T) = T |
| (not F) = T | (T and F) = F | (T or F) = T |
| | (F and T) = F | (F or T) = T |
| | (F and F) = F | (F or F) = F |

"Multiplication Tables"

### §43.6 Complex Truth Functions

We have already seen that statements illustrating one truth function may contain statements illustrating another. For example, "It is false that John is both stupid and dishonest." is a negation, but the negated statement is a conjunction. Such statements may be called **complex truth functions.** [8]

In sentences that indicate complex truth functions, you often find *correlative* conjunctions: "*both* . . . and," "*either* . . . or," "*neither* . . . nor," and so on. These correlative conjunctions serve much the same

---

[8]   More accurately, the given statement *illustrates* a complex truth function, while the formula representing its form *is* a complex truth function. However, it is often convenient to call statements *functions* that have forms represented by functions.

purpose as parentheses, to show which is the main function and which the subordinate one. For example, "John is tall and he is handsome or he is lucky," is amphibolous. Either it illustrates the form

$$(p \text{ and } q) \text{ or } r,$$

in which case it should have been written, "Either John is tall and he is handsome, or he is lucky." Or it illustrates the form

$$p \text{ and } (q \text{ or } r),$$

in which case it should have been written, "Both John is tall and either he is handsome or he is lucky."

When we put complex truth functions into standard form, and thus insert parentheses, we can omit the correlative conjunctions ("both," "either," "neither," and so on) in such pairs.

## EXERCISE

Represent the molecular forms of the following complex truth functions. Make the representation as detailed as possible; that is, let "$p$," "$q$," and so on replace the simplest of the contained statements.

1. Either New York is farther north than Chicago, or it is not.
2. You can fool all of the people some of the time and you can fool some of the people all of the time, but you cannot fool all of the people all of the time.
3. Either that figure is a triangle and its largest angle is a right angle, or it is a quadrilateral and its largest angle is greater than a right angle.
4. That figure is a triangle and either its largest angle is a right angle or its largest angle is greater than a right angle.

## §43.7  Truth Calculations for Truth Functions

As already pointed out, if you know the truth values (truth or falsity) of the statements appearing in a truth function, you can easily calculate the truth or falsity of the function itself. In the case of simple truth functions, this could be done in accordance with the multiplication tables already given (assuming that the function is a negation, conjunction, or alternation). But the same may be done even in the case of complex truth functions. In this latter case, however, you will have to take several steps in order to complete your calculations.

I.    Represent the molecular form of the given statement, but instead of replacing the constituent statements by "$p$," "$q$," and so on, replace them by "T" if they are true and by "F" if they are false.

To illustrate, suppose we had a statement of the form

(1)                    **(not** *p*) **or** (*q* **and** *r*)

and suppose that we knew that:

> The statement replaced by "*p*," above, is true.
> The statement replaced by "*q*," above, is false.
> The statement replaced by "*r*," above, is false.

Then, instead of writing the above formula, we should write

(2)                    **(not** T) **or** (F **and** F).

II.   Using the multiplication tables given above, replace the simplest functions by the values they would have, do the same on the result, and so continue until you write a value for the entire function given by Rule I.

To continue with the same illustration:  It contains the two simplest functions "**not** T" and "F **and** F." According to the multiplication tables, these equal "F" and "F," respectively. Hence, in accordance with the present rule we write.

(3)                    [**(not** T) **or** (F **and** F)] = (F **or** F)
(4)                                     = F

That is, under the indicated circumstances, the given complex statement function was false.

## E X E R C I S E S

1. Suppose that *p* is false, *q* is false, and *r* is false. Calculate the value of the formula given in (1), above.
2. Suppose *p* and *q* to have the values assigned in Exercise 1, above. Calculate the value of

> **(not** *p*) **and** [*p* **or** (**not** *q*)]

3. Suppose that New York is not farther north than Chicago, that Pittsburgh is not farther north than Chicago, and that I shall not eat my hat. Calculate the value of

> Both New York and Pittsburgh are farther north
> than Chicago, or I shall eat my hat.

## R E V I E W   Q U E S T I O N S   F O R   U N I T   4 3

1. What is a complex statement? Give some examples of statements that are complex and others of statements that are not complex.
2. Explain briefly what is meant by molecular logic.

3. What is a statement variable? Illustrate the use of statement variables to represent the forms of complex statements.

4. When may the representation of a statement form be called a statement function? Illustrate, giving examples that are statement functions and other examples that are not statement functions.

5. What is a truth function? Give examples, and also examples of statement functions that are not truth functions.

6. Give the standard molecular form and the truth table of values for negation.

7. Give the standard molecular form and the truth table of values for conjunction.

8. Give the standard molecular form and the truth table of values for alternation.

9. Give the multiplication tables for negation, conjunction, and alternation.

10. Review the method by which one may calculate the value of a complex truth function, given the values of its simplest constituents.

# *Some Uses of Molecular Logic*

### §44.1 Analytic and Other Molecular Forms

Truth functions frequently lie behind the fact that certain statements are analytic. For example analysis confirms the law of excluded middle, that any statement of the form

(1)                                  *p* or (not *p*)

is true.

Truth tables not unlike those of the preceding unit can be very helpful in exhibiting an analysis in order to discover whether or not analysis suffices to establish the truth or falsity of statements having a given molecular form. Let us see how this may be done and, for first illustrations, let us consider formula (1) above and formula (2):

(2)                                  *p* and [*q* or (not *p*)]

What we wish is a truth table, like those of the preceding unit, that has the formula we would test as one heading and each statement variable contained in the formula we would test as another heading. Thus, we must first construct the table. Thereafter, we may inspect the table to see what we can learn from it about the statement form in question. Four rules will suffice to guide the table construction and inspection. After stating and illustrating these rules separately, we shall briefly comment on them as a whole.

**Rule 1**   Write a row of headings for a truth table by first listing each statement variable in the truth function you would test and then listing that formula itself.

In the case of formula (1), since it contains only one variable (although it contains two tokens of that variable), Rule 1 produces a row of two headings:

(1.1)                        *p*         *p* or (not *p*)

On the other hand, formula (2) contains two variables. Hence the rule produces a row of three headings:

(2.1)                    *p*   *q*       *p* and [*q* or (not *p*)]

Notice that, for the sake of simplicity, we omit from the row of headings such additional words as appeared in the tables of the preceding unit:

If *p* is        then [*p* **or** (**not** *p*)] is

**Rule 2.** Beneath the headings that consist of single statement variables write rows of T's (for "True") and F's (for "False") until every arrangement of these letters is listed.

In the case of row (1.1), since there is only one variable, there will be only two "rows," each only one letter long:

(1.2)                    *p*        *p* **or** (**not** *p*)
                         T
                         F

Since row (2.1) contains two variables there will be four rows of T's and F's:

(2.2)            *p*   *q*        *p* **and** [*q* **or** (**not** *p*)]
                 T     T
                 T     F
                 F     T
                 F     F

If there had been three variables there would have been eight rows:

                 *p*   *q*   *r*  . . . .
                 T     T     T
                 T     T     F
                 T     F     T
                 T     F     F
                 F     T     T
                 F     T     F
                 F     F     T
                 F     F     F

And in general, if there are *n* variables, there will be $2^n$ rows of T's and F's.[1]

**Rule 3.** Extend each row of T's and F's under the formula to be tested by calculating the value (truth or falsity) of the function if the

[1] When there are only two or three variables, it is quite easy to write down all possible rows of T's and F's. But when there are more variables, and therefore a great many more rows of T's and F's, it becomes difficult to be sure that you have not overlooked and omitted some rows and perhaps without noticing it repeated some other rows.

These difficulties can be avoided by supplying the rows in accordance with the statements replacing its variables had the values indicated in the row being extended.

Here we use the methods of calculation explained in §43.7. In accordance with the rule, we must make a separate set of calculations for each row of values in the table we are constructing. To extend any one row, we copy on scratch paper the formula in which we are interested, except that as we do so we replace the variables by the values (T and F) assigned to them in the row we are extending. Thus, to extend the top row of table (1.2), we write:

$$\text{T or (not T)}$$

Then we calculate the value as in §43.7, using as there explained the multiplication tables given at the end of §43.5:

$$\text{T or (not T)} = \text{T or F}$$
$$= \text{T}$$

We place the calculated value in the top row under the formula in question and proceed to the next row.

In accordance with this rule, table (1.2) would be completed as follows:

(1.3)

| $p$ | $p$ or (not $p$) |
|-----|------------------|
| T   | T                |
| F   | T                |

When we come to completing table (2.2), the procedure is exactly the same, although the separate calculations are slightly more complicated. For example, to discover with what value (T or F) to extend the top row of table (2.2), we calculate on scratch paper as follows:

$$\text{T and [T or (not T)]} = \text{T and [T or F]}$$
$$= \text{T and T}$$
$$= \text{T}$$

And to discover with what value to extend the second row of table (2.2), we calculate as follows:

$$\text{T and [F or (not T)]} = \text{T and [F or F]}$$
$$= \text{T and F}$$
$$= \text{F}$$

following rules. The three illustrative tables in the text above have had their rows of T's and F's arranged in accordance with these rules.

(a) Write a row that consists entirely of T's.

(b) Copy the last row written, up to its right-hand T, replace that with an F, and complete the row (if it is not already complete) with T's.

(c) Repeat rule (b) as often as possible, i.e., until you have written a row that consists entirely of F's.

By calculating in a similar way values for the third and fourth rows, we finally complete table (2.2) in the following manner:

| (2.3) | p | q | p and [q or (not p)] |
|---|---|---|---|
| | T | T | T |
| | T | F | F |
| | F | T | F |
| | F | F | F |

**Rule 4.** Inspect the *column* of values beneath the formula being tested:

a.   If the column consists entirely of T's, every statement having the form represented by the formula is *analytic*, therefore true.

b.   If the column consists entirely of F's, every such statement is *analytically false*.

c.   If the column contains at least one T and at least one F, analysis of the form is insufficient to establish the truth or falsity of statements having the form; that is, the form is *indeterminant*. (On "indeterminant," see §41.4.)

According to this rule, table (1.3) shows that statements having the form represented by "p or (not p)" are analytic, while table (2.3) shows that having the form "p and [q or (not p)]" will guarantee neither the truth nor the falsity of statements illustrating it and is therefore indeterminant.

A little thought should make plain why these table tests will work: No matter what statements replace "p," "q," and so on in an illustration of a form being tested, those statements are bound to have one or another of the combinations of values listed in the table. If the form is such that—as in (1.3)—every combination forces the illustration of the form to be true, then the form guarantees the truth of its illustrations. Otherwise, it either guarantees the falsity of its illustrations (clause b in Rule 4) or makes no guarantee either way.

*EXERCISE*

Construct tables and make table tests for each of the following truth functions:

. p and (not p)

. (p and q) or [(not p) and (not q)]

. {not [(p or q) and (not p)]} or q

### §44.2 Truth Tables and Validating Forms of Proof

At the end of §43.3 there occurred an exercise in whic
you were asked to determine by consulting certain truth tables whethe
or not certain given forms of proof are validating. Whenever proo
forms are based on truth functions, such table tests can be very helpful
The rules governing such tests are very similar to those explained in th
preceding section. We shall illustrate them by considering the tw
following proof forms:

A.                         (1)  **not** (*p* **and** *q*).
                      ∴ (2)  (**not** *p*) **or** (**not** *q*).

B.                         (1)  (**not** *p*) **or** *q*.
                            (2)  *p*.
                      ∴ (3)  *q*.

**Rule 1.** Write a row of headings by first listing each statemer
variable in the proof form you would test and then listing each premis
and the conclusion of that proof form (insofar as they were not liste
n listing the statement variables). Above each premise and the conclu
sion, put its "annotation number."

Rule 1 gives us the following row of headings for proof form A

|  | | (1) | ∴ (2) |
|---|---|---|---|
| (A.1) | *p*  *q* | **not** (*p* **and** *q*) | (**not** *p*) **or** (**not** *q*) |

It gives us the following row of headings for proof form B:

|  | (2) | ∴ (3) | (1) |
|---|---|---|---|
| (B.1) | *p* | *q* | (**not** *p*) **or** *q* |

**Rule 2.** (Same as Rule 2 of the preceding section.) Beneath th
headings that consist of single statement variables, write rows of T'
(for "True") and F's (for "False") until every arrangement of thes
letters is listed.

2 Similar procedures can frequently be used even for statement functions tha
are not truth functions. It would, however, take us too far afield to go into the specia
precautions that must then be employed. But in connection with them, the reade
may consult this author's article on "Two-Valued Tables for Modal Functions" i
*Structure, Method and Meaning*, edited by Paul Henle *et al.*, New York: 1951. A
example of such a table occurs later on in §44.5.

By applying this rule to (A.1) and (B.1), we get the following results.

|  |  |  | (1) | ∴ (2) |
|---|---|---|---|---|
| (A.2) | $p$ | $q$ | not ($p$ and $q$) | (not $p$) or (not $q$) |
|  | T | T |  |  |
|  | T | F |  |  |
|  | F | T |  |  |
|  | F | F |  |  |

|  |  | (2) | ∴ (3) | (1) |
|---|---|---|---|---|
| (B.2) |  | $p$ | $q$ | (not $p$) or $q$ |
|  |  | T | T |  |
|  |  | T | F |  |
|  |  | F | T |  |
|  |  | F | F |  |

**Rule 3.** (Practically the same as Rule 3 of the preceding section.) Extend each row of T's and F's under each remaining heading by calculating the value (truth or falsity) of that formula if the statements replacing its variables had the values indicated in the row being extended.

By applying Rule 3 to (A.2) and (B.2), we get the following results:

|  |  |  | (1) | ∴ (2) |
|---|---|---|---|---|
| (A.3) | $p$ | $q$ | not ($p$ and $q$) | (not $p$) or (not $q$) |
|  | T | T | F | F |
|  | T | F | T | T |
|  | F | T | T | T |
|  | F | F | T | T |

|  |  | (2) | ∴ (3) | (1) |
|---|---|---|---|---|
| (B.3) |  | $p$ | $q$ | (not $p$) or $q$ |
|  |  | T | T | T |
|  |  | T | F | F |
|  |  | F | T | T |
|  |  | F | F | T |

**Rule 4.** Cross out every row of T's and F's in which any *premise* is listed as F, and inspect the remaining values in the column beneath the conclusion:

   a.  If these remaining values are all T's, the proof form is validating.

b.   If one or more of these remaining values are F's, the proof form is not validating.

Applying Rule 4 to table (A.3), we must cross out every row that contains an F in column (1). That is, we must cross out the first row:

|  |  | (1) | ∴ (2) |
|---|---|---|---|
| (A.4)   *p* | *q* | **not (*p* and *q*)** | **(not *p*) or (not *q*)** |
| ~~T~~ | ~~T~~ | ~~F~~ | ~~F~~ |
| T | F | T | T |
| F | T | T | T |
| F | F | T | T |

We then inspect the *remaining* values in the column under " ∴ (2)." Since we find that these are all T's, we conclude that the proof form is validating.

Applying Rule 4 to table (B.3) gives a similar result. First, we cross out all rows containing an F in column (1) or in column (2), and then we inspect the remaining values in column ∴ (3):

|  | (2) | ∴ (3) | (1) |
|---|---|---|---|
| (B.4) | *p* | *q* | **(not *p*) or *q*** |
|  | T | T | T |
|  | ~~T~~ | ~~F~~ | ~~F~~ |
|  | ~~F~~ | ~~T~~ | ~~T~~ |
|  | ~~F~~ | ~~F~~ | ~~F~~ |

The reason for crossing out certain rows is this: In testing a proof form, we are not interested in whether or not the conclusion is true of and by itself; our interest is in whether or not, *if the premises were true,* the conclusion would then be true. Hence we do not wish to concern ourselves with the truth or falsity of the conclusion in rows that make one or more of the premises false.[3]

3   Two special cases may be briefly mentioned:

a.  Suppose that in applying Rule 4 you have to cross out every row of the table, because in every row one or more of the premise columns contains an F. This shows that the premises are mutually contradictory, hence that they could not all have been true. For reasons we shall not go into here, logicians list all such proof forms (i.e., all proof forms with mutually contradictory premises) as validating. But this is not to say that they recommend such proof forms as good. Remember that for an inference to be sound, it must be valid *and* have true premises (see §36.1). No proof with any of these forms will have all its premises true. Hence, it will not correspond to sound inferences.

b.  Suppose, on the other hand, that in applying Rule 4, you find that there are no rows to be crossed out. This would be because every premise column consists

## EXERCISE

For each of the following proof forms, construct a truth table and test thereby whether or not the form is validating.

1.  (1) **not** ($p$ **and** $q$).          *Intallogry*
    (2) $q$.
    ∴ (3) **not** $p$.
2.  (1) **not** ($p$ **and** $q$).
    (2) **not** $q$.
    ∴ (3) $p$.
3.  (1) $p$.
    ∴ (2) $p$ **or** $q$.
4.  (1) $p$ **or** $q$.
    (2) (**not** $q$) **or** $r$.
    ∴ (3) $p$ **or** $r$.

## §44.3 Conditional Statements

Throughout the preceding unit we have no more than briefly mentioned one of the most widely used and important expressions in our English language for the indication of statement functions: the pair of correlative conjunctions "if . . ., then . . . ." Synonyms for this pair of words are: "provided" and "on condition that." Thus, "I shall pay the plumber if I receive an itemized bill," means the same thing as, "I shall pay . . . provided that I receive . . .," and as, "I shall pay . . . on condition that I receive . . . ." We shall treat "if . . ., then . . ." as the standard form for the expression of all these statement functions.

Statements which have the standard form "**if** $p$, **then** $q$" are called <u>conditional statements.</u>

"If" and "then" behave rather differently from such statement functions as "or" and "and," which we have studied heretofore. In the case of statements formed by *any* of these, we may reverse the order of the constituent statements *without* altering the meaning or truth value of the complex statement. Thus "$p$ **or** $q$" means the same thing as "$q$ **or** $p$," "$p$ **and** $q$" means the same thing as "$q$ **and** $p$," and

---

entirely of T's. Thus every premise would be analytic (see §44.1). In such a case, proceed as usual to examine the column for the conclusion. If it also consists entirely of T's, the proof form is validating; if it contains one or more F's, the proof form is not validating. But if the proof form was validating, the conclusion was also analytic and hence could have been known to be true by analysis without any reliance on inference in accordance with the tested proof form.

"**if** $p$ **then** $q$" means the same thing as "$q$ **if** $p$." But notice the difference in the case of "if," the conjunction "if" was *carried along* with the constituent it introduced when the order of these constituents was changed. (The word "then" is omitted in good English when the clause it introduces precedes the "if" clause.) But to carry "or" or "and" along with the clauses they introduce when you reverse their order and thus to write "**or** $q$, $p$" or "**and** $q$, $p$," is to write nonsense.

On the other hand, the word "if" need not be carried along with the clause it introduces. Thus "**if** $q$, **then** $p$" makes just as much sense as "**if** $p$, **then** $q$." But while both expressions *make* sense, they do not make the *same* sense. For example, there is a great difference between the meaning of, "If any animal is a dog, then it has four legs," and "If any animal has four legs, then it is a dog."

Thus in the analysis of conditional statements, it is less important to discover which constituent statement is first and which second than it is to discover which is introduced by "if" and which by "then." The grammarian calls the "if" clause the *dependent* clause and the "then" clause the *main* clause. In logic, the statement introduced by "if" (or its synonyms "provided," "on condition") is called the **antecedent**, and the constituent introduced by "then" ("then" may be presented or understood) is called the **consequent.** These constituent statements are called *antecedent* and *consequent* even when the "if" clause is written or said last and the "then" clause first. Thus in "That animal is warm-blooded if it is a dog," the antecedent is "that animal is a dog," and the consequent is "that animal is warm-blooded."

When conditional statements are put into standard form, the antecedent is always written *first*. Thus, to put the last illustration into standard form, we must rewrite it in the form, "If that animal is a dog, then it is warm-blooded." To represent its form, we should write:

Let "$p$" replace "That animal is a dog."
    "$q$" replace "That animal is warm-blooded."

Then the form of the given statement is represented by

**If** $p$, **then** $q$.

## EXERCISE

Represent in as much detail as possible the molecular forms of the following statements.

1.  I shall go on the picnic if it does not rain.

2.  You will receive an "A" provided you have done all the exercises correctly.
3.  If that figure is a rectangle and all of its sides are equal, then it is a square.
4.  Tom cannot read that book if it is written in Latin or in Greek.

## §44.4 The Ambiguity of Conditional Statements*

People make conditional assertions under a great variety of circumstances, and as these circumstances vary, so does what the speaker intends by his conditional statement vary. Thus arises a certain ambiguity about the words "if" and "then." In this section, we shall distinguish and symbolize three meanings of "if . . ., then . . ." statements.

The problem before us, however, is not so simple as the preceding paragraph might suggest. Three things complicate the problem. (1) At least one of the three conventional meanings we shall distinguish is quite vague, and the studies of various scholars, both scientists and philosophers, have not resulted in any precise meanings that all have agreed would be desirable substitutes for this vague meaning. (2) There are probably still other meanings sometimes associated with "if" and "then" than the three we shall list. Thus the words "if" and "then" are regularly employed to indicate one or another of a considerable "family" of relations, and the three relations we shall explain are really only representatives of this larger family of relations. (3) People who use English are often unaware of this variety of meanings and hence make "if . . ., then . . ." statements without any awareness of an ambiguity in what they affirm.

**1.  Analytic Conditionals.**  Sometimes a conditional statement is used to affirm that the antecedent would be a sufficient premise from which to `infer` deductively the consequent. With this meaning, "If $p$, then $q$" has the same meaning as " '$p$, therefore $q$' is a valid proof." It does *not* declare that the antecedent, $p$, is true. Rather it declares that anyone who accepted the antecedent as true could validly infer the consequent. Thus, it does not mean the same thing as "$p$, therefore $q$," but rather, as was said before, " '$p$, therefore $q$' is valid."

For example, were I to say, "If that figure is a triangle, then it has three sides," I might well be meaning to affirm that "From 'that figure is a triangle,' taken as a premise one may validly infer 'that figure has three sides.' "

When we wish unambiguously to symbolize an analytic conditional, let us replace "**if** $p$ **then** $q$" by the formula "$p \rightarrow q$."

**2.  Causal Conditional.**  Sometimes a conditional is used in order to claim some sort of causal connection between antecedent and consequent. For example, were I to say, "If you tease that dog, he will bite you," I should

---

* This section and the next may be omitted without disturbing the continuity of the text.

hardly be intending to claim that, "You tease that dog," would be a sufficient premise from which one could *deductively* infer, "That dog will bite you." Thus I should hardly be intending to claim an analytic conditional. (Had I intended an analytic conditional, my statement would have been false.) Rather, I am claiming that teasing the dog will cause him to bite you.

The idea of causal connection is an extremely vague one, and it will hardly be wise for us to interrupt the present discussion in order to investigate it. Hence, without being satisfied by the above account, let us nevertheless pass on to the third meaning.[4]

When we wish unambiguously to symbolize a causal conditional, we shall write "*p* **C** *q*."

**3. Truth Functional Conditionals.** Finally, we must note that people frequently use "**if** *p*, **then** *q*" with a meaning which makes it synonymous with "(**not** *p*) **or** *q*." For example, "If it rains, I shall stay home," means the same thing as, "Either it does not rain or I shall stay home." With this meaning, the conditional statement indicates a truth function and is therefore called a **truth functional conditional.** We may symbolize it by "*p* $\supset$ *q*." Via "(**not** *p*) **or** *q*," we can see what its truth table must be:

| *p* | *q* | *p* $\supset$ *q* i.e., (**not** *p*) **or** *q* |
|-----|-----|-----|
| T | T | T |
| T | F | F |
| F | T | T |
| F | F | T |

## §44.5 Relations among the Three Types of Conditional Statement

The three types of conditional statement analyzed in the preceding section have certain logical connections which deserve notice here.

These connections can perhaps be most compactly represented by listing in a truth table all the logically possible combinations of truth and falsity for five statements that are corresponding illustrations of the forms *p*, *q*, *p* $\rightarrow$ *q*, *p* **C** *q*, and *p* $\supset$ *q*. While five statements *not* logically related one to the other might be characterized by any one of thirty-two (= 2⁵) combinations of truth and falsity, statements that are corresponding illustrations of the five

---

4 A tentative suggestion for the analysis of causal conditionals might run as follows: There are characteristics in the total contingent intensions of the terms occurring in antecedent and consequent ("you," "tease," "that dog," and "bite," in our example), and there are laws of nature such that a proof containing the antecedent of the causal conditional as one premise and statements of these characteristics and these laws of nature as other premises, and containing the consequent of the causal conditional as conclusion, would be deductively valid.

listed forms invariably have one or the other of only ten combinations of truth and falsity:

| $p$ | $q$ | $p \rightarrow q$ | $p \mathbf{C} q$ | $p \supset q$ |
|---|---|---|---|---|
| T | T | T | T | T |
| T | T | F | T | T |
| T | T | F | F | T |
| T | F | F | F | F |
| F | T | T | T | T |
| F | T | F | T | T |
| F | T | F | F | T |
| F | F | T | T | T |
| F | F | F | T | T |
| F | F | F | F | T |

Truth Table for Three Types of Conditional Statement

A closer examination of just what rows are present in the above table will reveal the following facts:

1. Whenever the antecedent is true and the consequent is false, all three types of conditional statement are false.

2. Whenever an analytic conditional ($p \rightarrow q$) is true, the corresponding causal conditional ($p \mathbf{C} q$) and truth functional conditional ($p \supset q$) are both also true.

3. Whenever a causal conditional ($p \mathbf{C} q$) is true, the corresponding truth functional conditional ($p \supset q$) is true.

On the other hand, a causal conditional might be true and the corresponding analytic conditional false; likewise a truth functional conditional might be true and the corresponding causal conditional false.

The three facts listed above could be put in another way: By applying Rule 4 of §44.2 to the above table, we could see that each of the following is a **validating** form of proof:

| | I | | II | | III |
|---|---|---|---|---|---|
| (1) | $p$ | (1) | $p$ | (1) | $p$ |
| (2) | **not** $q$ | (2) | **not** $q$ | (2) | **not** $q$ |
| ∴ (3) | **not** $(p \rightarrow q)$ | ∴ (3) | **not** $(p \mathbf{C} q)$ | ∴ (3) | **not** $(p \supset q)$ |

| | IV | | V | | VI |
|---|---|---|---|---|---|
| (1) | $p \rightarrow q$ | (1) | $p \rightarrow q$ | (1) | $p \mathbf{C} q$ |
| ∴ (2) | $p \mathbf{C} q$ | ∴ (2) | $p \supset q$ | ∴ (2) | $p \supset q$ |

One **validating** form which the table does not reveal, but which lies at the basis of the choice of names for these types of conditional, is the following:

VII

(1)   $(p \supset q)$ is analytic.

∴ (2)   $p \rightarrow q$.

This, together with form IV, suffices to establish the following as also **validating**:

VIII

(1)   $(p \supset q)$ is analytic.

∴ (2)   $p \; C \; q$.

In the next section, we shall list several quite commonly used validating forms of proof that involve one or more conditional premises and a conditional conclusion. The forms of proof we shall list are validating no matter what kind of conditional statement is involved, *provided* that in any one instance all conditional statements are of the same sort. For example, if the premise is a truth functional conditional, then the conclusion must also be truth functional rather than analytic or causal.[5]

### §44.6  Some Validating Forms of Conditional Proof

Four forms of conditional proof will be met over and over again. All four are **validating.** In fact, they have been recognized as validating for so many centuries that they long ago received Latin names. It will be helpful to learn to recognize these forms and to identify examples of them by name.

**Modus ponens.**

(1)   **If** $p$, **then** $q$.

(2)   $p$.

∴ (3)   $q$.

[5]   Do not make a rash inference from what is said above to the effect that all forms of proof which are validating for one kind of conditional are validating for all. The forms presented in the next section have been carefully selected to conform to this principle. But there are forms for which this is not the case. For example,

(1) $q$

∴ (2) $p \supset q$

is validating, as a truth table would show. Yet the two following forms, analogous to it, are not validating.

(1) $q$                    (1) $q$

∴ (2) $p \rightarrow q$          ∴ (2) $p \; C \; q$

EXAMPLE:

    (1)   If that man is a United States citizen, then he speaks English.
    (2)   He is a United States citizen.
∴ (3)   He speaks English.

The name *modus ponens* means "the affirming type" of proof. Notice that one premise affirms the *antecedent* of the conditional premise, and the conclusion affirms the *consequent* of that conditional premise.

**Modus tollens.**

    (1)   **If *p* then *q*.**
    (2)   **not *q*.**
∴ (3)   **not *p*.**

EXAMPLE:

    (1)   If George misses the train, he will telephone.
    (2)   George did not telephone.
∴ (3)   George did not miss the train.

The name *modus tollens* means "the denying type" of proof. Notice that the second premise denies the *consequent* of the conditional premise, and that the conclusion denies its *antecedent*.

**Transposition.**

    (1)   **If *p*, then *q*.**
∴ (2)   **If (not *q*), then (not *p*).**

EXAMPLE:

    (1)   If George speaks in favor of the motion, then John will speak against it.
∴ (2)   If John does not speak against the motion, then George did not speak in favor of it.

Transposition is quite similar to *modus tollens*, except that instead of claiming in a second premise that the consequent *is* false and inferring that the antecedent is false, one infers that *if* the consequent is false *then* the antecedent will be false.

**Hypothetical Syllogism.**

    (1)   **If *p*, then *q*.**
    (2)   **If *q*, then *r*.**
∴ (3)   **If *p*, then *r*.**

EXAMPLE:

    (1)   If the weather is fair, I shall go on the picnic.

    (2)   If I go on the picnic, I shall see Mary.

∴ (3)   If the weather is fair, I shall see Mary.

In Unit 46, we shall see another kind of syllogism, called *categorical*. Notice in the hypothetical syllogism that both premises are conditional, that the consequent of one is the antecedent of the other, and that the conclusion brings together in yet a third conditional the other antecedent and consequent appearing in the premises.

Hypothetical syllogisms are valid because the relation (between propositions) represented by "if . . ., then . . ." is transitive. (On transitivity, see §41.5.) This relation is, furthermore, reflexive (§41.1), so that the following statement form is analytic.

**If *p*, then *p*.**

### §44.7 Four Common Fallacies

In presenting the four validating forms of proof given in the last section, we called special attention to the *location*, as antecedent or consequent, of various statements involved in the proofs. Proofs which are quite similar in form to those listed above, but that differ from them in this matter of location, are often accepted as valid, whereas in point of fact they are invalid. To use any such invalid forms is to commit a fallacy—an error in reasoning. The fallacies just mentioned are so commonly committed that they have been given names. We shall point out these fallacious forms here and illustrate them. Notice that in many of these illustrations, the premises are true, but the conclusions false. This is a sure sign that the forms which these examples illustrate are not validating.

**Fallacy of Denying the Antecedent.**

    (1)   **If *p*, then *q*.**

    (2)   **not *p*.**

∴ (3)   **not *q*.**

EXAMPLE:

    (1)   If Detroit is larger than New York, then it is larger than Buffalo.

    (2)   Detroit is not larger than New York.

∴ (3)   Detroit is not larger than Buffalo.

**Fallacy of Affirming the Consequent**.

      (1)  **If *p*, then *q*.**
      (2)  *q*.
   ∴ (3)  *p*.

EXAMPLE:

    (1)   If Detroit is in New York State, then it is east of Chicago.
    (2)   Detroit is east of Chicago.
 ∴ (3)   Detroit is in New York State.

**Fallacy of Illicit Conversion**.

      (1)  **If *p*, then *q*.**
   ∴ (2)  **If *q*, then *p*.**

EXAMPLE:

     (1)   If that figure is a triangle, then it has straight sides.
  ∴ (2)   If that figure has straight sides, then it is a triangle.

    The fallacy of illicit conversion is related to the fallacy of affirming the consequent in much the same manner in which the validating form of proof called *transposition* is related to *modus tollens*.

    Illicit conversion is a fallacy because the relation (between propositions) represented by "if . . ., then . . ." is not symmetrical (§40.6). This relation is in fact nonsymmetrical, rather than asymmetrical (§40.7).

**Fallacies of Hypothetical Syllogism**.

     (1)  **If *p*, then *q*.**        (1)  **If *p*, then *q*.**
     (2)  **If *p*, then *r*.**        (2)  **If *r*, then *q*.**
  ∴ (3)  **If *q*, then *r*.**     ∴ (3)  **If *p*, then *r*.**

EXAMPLES:

    (1)   If Chicago is in New York State, then it is east of Denver, Colorado.
    (2)   If Chicago is in New York State, then it is east of Detroit.
 ∴ (3)   If Chicago is east of Denver, Colorado, then it is east of Detroit.

    (1)   If that animal is a cat, then it has a backbone.
    (2)   If that animal is a dog, then it has a backbone.
 ∴ (3)   If that animal is a cat, then it is a dog.

## EXERCISE

Each of the following proofs illustrates one of the four validating forms of proof or four types of fallacy explained in this and the preceding section. In the case of each, first represent its form, next state whether or not it is valid, and finally name the validating form of proof or the type of fallacy that it illustrates.

1. If the Dodgers beat the Braves, they will win the pennant. If the Dodgers win the pennant, the World Series will be played in New York. Therefore, if the Dodgers beat the Braves, the World Series will be played in New York.

2. If John gets an A, he will win a scholarship. He won a scholarship. Therefore he got an A.

3. If John does not get an A, he will not win a scholarship. John did not get an A. Therefore he did not win a scholarship.

4. If the circus comes to town, I can get a job working for it. If I can get a job working for the circus, I can pay my debts. Therefore if the circus comes to town, I can pay my debts.

5. If you do not have a driver's license, then you should not drive a car. You should not drive a car. Therefore, you do not have a driver's license.

6. If that grain contains warfarin, it is poisonous. Therefore, if that grain is not poisonous, it does not contain warfarin.

7. If that figure is not a parallelogram, then it is not a square. Therefore if that figure is not a square, it is not a parallelogram.

8. If William invests his money wisely, he will put some of it into government savings bonds. If William is patriotic, he will put some of his money into government savings bonds. Therefore, if William invests his money wisely, he will be patriotic.

9. If Jim is conscientious about his work, his employer will not fire him. Jim's employer did fire him. Therefore, Jim was not conscientious about his work.

10. If Clara prefers turkey to chicken, the annual dinner will consist of turkey. Clara does not prefer turkey to chicken. Therefore the annual dinner will not consist of turkey.

## REVIEW QUESTIONS FOR UNIT 44

1. Explain how to construct a truth table in order to test a given truth function.

2. Explain what inspection of a truth table for a truth function can reveal concerning the truth or falsity of statements illustrating the form represented by that function. Why are these table tests reliable?

3. Explain how a table may be constructed in order to test whether or not a truth functional proof form is validating.

4. What is a conditional statement? What is the standard form for a conditional statment?

[5.⁶ Briefly distinguish three meanings conventionally associated with the conditional form, "**If** *p*, **then** *q*."]

[6. Discuss briefly the logical relations between the three meanings of conditional statements distinguished in answer to question 5.]

7. Represent the forms of proof named by each of the following and state whether or not it is a validating form of proof.
   a. *Modus ponens*
   b. *Modus tollens*
   c. Transposition
   d. Hypothetical syllogism

8. Represent the forms of proof named by each of the following and state whether or not proofs having these forms would be valid.
   a. Denying the antecedent
   b. Affirming the consequent
   c. Illicit conversion
   d. Fallacies of hypothetical syllogism

⁶ If §§44.4 and 44.5 were omitted, then questions 5 and 6 should be omitted from the questions for review.

UNIT **45**

# *General Statements;*
# *The Square of Opposition*

## §45.1 The Topic of This Unit

In the last several units we have considered some aspects of the logic of singular statements and of the logic of complex statements. Now we shall turn our attention to a few topics in the logic of general statements.

General statements were identified in §16.5 under the heading of *general propositions*. At that time, we distinguished one from the other several types of general statement. Also, in §16.6, we distinguished several types of mixed, singular and general statement. In this unit and the next, we shall consider various ways of dealing both with general statements and with mixed, singular and general statements.

We shall, however, be obliged to leave many interesting and important types of problem unconsidered. For we shall be able to treat only a few of the forms of general statement that have been, or can be, distinguished. Yet even so, what we do discuss can be made to apply to general statements of all sorts and types, so that while it will not show the *whole* of the logic of any type, it will show a part of the logic of every type.

A clew to how this result comes about may be found in review of the logic of singular statements, particularly that part which was developed in Unit 39. In §39.7 of that unit we listed four types of singular statement and under each we put a standard affirmative and a standard negative form:

| Type | Affirmative | Negative |
|------|-------------|----------|
| I. | $s$ is a $P$. | $s$ is not a $P$. |
| II. | $s_1$ is a $P$ of $s_2$. | $s_1$ is not a $P$ of $s_2$. |
| III. | $s$ exists. | $s$ does not exist. |
| IV. | $s_1$ is identical with $s_2$. | $s_1$ is not identical with $s_2$. |

But what is more to the present point, we went on to notice that the

542

last three types represented special cases of the first type, so that every singular statement which illustrated any one of the last three types *also* illustrated the first type. In order to "see" such a statement as an illustration of Type I, all we had to do was to identify its predicate as complex, "$P$ of $s_2$" or "identical with $s_2$," or as being specifically the predicate "exists."

The same sort of thing can be done in the case of general statements. Of all the forms of general statement recognized in §§16.5 and 16.6, we shall separate out for special consideration only the one

$$x\ S\ \text{is a}\ P,$$

and shall notice that every other type of general statement, or of mixed, singular and general statement is just a special case of this type. Thus, while the special cases have their own special logic, we shall be dealing with the logic of all general statements only insofar as their logic is the logic of this one general type.

## EXERCISE

Represent each of the following statements by the form

$$x\ S\ \text{is a}\ P.$$

(The important part of this exercise is making your dictionary:

Let "$x$" replace . . .
    "$S$" replace . . .
    "$P$" replace . . .

Sometimes, you may have to "twist the given statement around" before it will fit the required form. For example, to treat, "Tom talked to some Republicans," we would have to write:

Let "$x$" replace "some"
    "$S$" replace "Republican"
    "$P$" replace "person Tom talked to"

Then the form of the given statement is represented by

$$x\ S\ \text{is a}\ P.$$

We think of the given statement *as though* it had been, "Some Republicans were people Tom talked to," which means the same thing as the *actually* given statement.)

1. Fifteen club members are Republicans.
2. Every club member is a voter.
3. Some club members voted for Eisenhower.

4.  George is acquainted with every club member.
5.  No club member is a Communist.
6.  Every club member sat at the banquet table beside some nonclub-member.

## §45.2  Signs of Quantity

In the exercise at the end of the last section we found several different signs of quantity: "fifteen," "every," "some," "no." The different signs of quantity that might be used in general statements are actually infinite in number. But in §16.5 we noticed that these numberless signs of quantity may be classified into two main kinds: those that indicate *how many*, and those that indicate *what proportion.* For example, in "*Five* men were riding in the automobile," or in "160 million people reside in the United States," the signs of quantity, "five" and "160 million," indicate *how many* men or people were doing so and so. On the other hand, in "Every child in the school has had polio shots," or in "60 percent of the voters favored the bill," the signs of quantity, "every" and "60 percent," indicate *what proportion* of the children or voters did so and so. We cannot translate this indication of a proportion into an indication of how many without knowing how many children or voters there are, but given that additional information, we could do so. For example, 60 percent of 200 = 120. Also, we cannot translate an indication of how many into an indication of a proportion without knowing how many objects are in the extension of the subject term; but given that additional information, we could do so. For example, 10 = 20 percent of 50.

Let us call signs of quantity that indicate how many, **absolute** signs of quantity. Let us furthermore call signs of quantity that indicate what proportion, **proportional** signs of quantity. Then signs of quantity may be said to be absolute or proportional.

It was furthermore said in §16.5 that these signs of quantity indicate "definitely or indefinitely" the number or proportion of objects in question. Thus we can distinguish four fundamentally different kinds of signs of quantity:

### Definite Signs of Quantity

| *Absolute* | *Proportional* |
|---|---|
| One | 50 percent of |
| Five | three-fourths of |
| Fifty million | Every |
| | All |

### Indefinite Signs of Quantity

| Absolute | Proportional |
|---|---|
| From ten to twelve | Between 30 and 35 percent of |
| Eight or nine | More than half of |
| At least twenty | Less than a third of |
| At most sixteen | |

Not every sign of quantity can be put clearly into one of the four classes indicated above. There are certain *vague* signs of quantity, such as "several," "few," "quite a few," "nearly all," and so on. Generally, these can be thought of as indefinite signs of quantity which are either absolute or proportional, as the case may be. But the vagueness permits that the limits, within which the quantity indefinitely falls, might have been conceived proportionally when the quantity is absolute or absolutely when the quantity is proportional. For example, "Several people got into the automobile," and "several people came to the stadium," suggest quite different numbers of people, inasmuch as the *capacities* of an automobile or a stadium are so different. But let us not worry further about vague signs of quantity.

Finally, there is one important sign of quantity that properly belongs in *two* of the classes which we have distinguished. This is the word "no," as in "No senator is a Communist." The word "no" may be regarded both as a definite absolute sign of quantity and as a definite proportional sign of quantity. 0 and 0 percent are the only absolute and proportional quantities that can be translated into each other without knowing in addition how many objects are in the extension of the subject term. We may regard "no" as indicating either the absolute quantity 0 or the proportional quantity 0 percent.

### EXERCISE

Classify the following signs of quantity. In the case of vague signs, indicate that they are vague, but then put them in the most appropriate of the classes.

1. Between 80 and 90 of
2. No more than 70 percent of
3. A majority of
4. 432
5. Many
6. None of
7. Virtually all

## §45.3 Three Important Signs of Quantity

Among all the different signs of quantity which might be replaced by "$x$" in the statement form

$$x\ S \text{ is a } P,$$

we shall concentrate our attention on three: "some," "every," and "no." These three have in fact provided the ground work for almost all the logic of general statements which is not more effectively treated by the special methods of mathematics: arithmetic, algebra, or statistics.[1]

Logic is a science with a very long history, stretching back even to ancient Greece in the fourth century B.C. But during the last one hundred years studies in logic have revealed the fundamental importance of the signs of quantity "every" and "some." In fact, these studies have shown that all the logic of other signs of quantity, such as those studied in mathematics, depends ultimately on the logic of these two signs of quantity. We shall not attempt in this book to show the manner of that dependence. But the fact of the dependence provides a further justification for our concentrating attention on these signs.

## §45.4 The Square of Opposition

"Every" is a definite, proportional sign of quantity. We shall take

$$\text{Every } S \text{ is a } P$$

as a standard form illustrated in many general statements. What any statement having this form affirms is that 100 percent of the $S$'s are $P$'s. Notice that the objects in question are the objects in the *extension* of the term "$S$." Thus "Every man is less than 10 feet tall," affirms that every object in the extension of the term "man" is in the extension of

---

[1] Throughout most of the history of logic, the sign of quantity "all" has been treated (along with "some" and "no") rather than the sign "every." We have chosen to use "every" rather than "all" in our standard forms because it gives a standard structure more directly comparable with the standard form for singular statements:

$$s \text{ is a } P.$$
$$\text{Every } S \text{ is a } P.$$

The forms "All $S$ is $P$" (where $P$ must for good English be an attributive term) or "All $S$'s are $P$'s" (where both subject and predicate must be in the grammatically plural form) indicate the same state of affairs as "Every $S$ is a $P$." Hence the different choice of standard form does not alter the logic, but only the expression of the logic, treated throughout the history of the subject.

the term "less than 10 feet tall." It does *not* affirm that every "possible" man, but only that every "actual" man is less than 10 feet tall.

For it to be true that, Every *S* is a *P*, it will, however, not only be the case that the extension of "*S*" is contained in the extension of "*P*"; it will also be true that the total contingent intension of "*P*" is contained in the total contingent intension of "*S*." In fact, these relations of extensions and of total contingent intensions are simply two facets or aspects of one and the same proposition.

This relation of total *contingent* intensions *might* have been a consequence of a similar relation of total *strict* intensions. In fact, if the total strict intension of "*P*" is contained in the total strict intension of "*S*," then the total contingent intensions will be similarly related. In such a circumstance,

Every S is a P

will be analytic. But if this relation of total strict intensions does not hold, and the relation of total contingent intensions and extensions does hold, then

Every S is a P

will be true, but not analytic.

"Some" is an indefinite absolute sign of quantity. When used with a grammatically singular noun, as in "Some man walked into the office," it means the same thing as "at least one." It *allows* that more than one, but insists that at least one, walked into the office. On the other hand, when "some" is used with a plural noun, as in "Some men walked into the office," it suggests the same thing as "at least two." However, we shall take its meaning as it modifies a grammatically singular noun for a standard form. Thus,

Some S is a P

is a standard form by which to affirm that at least one *S* is also a *P*; that is, that at least one object in the extension of "*S*" is in the extension of "*P*."

When we were discussing the logic of singular statements, we found it necessary to add standard forms for negative statements to those for affirmative statements. Thus, in addition to "*s* is a *P*," we also considered "*s* is not a *P*." We furthermore noted two signs of denial and two standard forms for the negative: "not" as in "*s* is not a *P*," and "It is false that" as in "It is false that *s* is a *P*." In the logic of singular statements, these two forms of negative statement were equivalent, had the same meaning. But this is not the case in the logic of general statements. For example, "It is false that some $S$ is a $P$" has quite a different meaning from "Some $S$ is not a $P$." We must briefly examine this situation.

"It is false that," written before a general statement, indicates the *contradictory* or *negative* of that statement. Thus, "It is false that every $S$ is a $P$" is the negative of "Every $S$ is a $P$," and "It is false that some $S$ is a $P$" is the negative of "Some $S$ is a $P$." In the symbolism of molecular logic, we could rewrite these standard forms for denial as

$$\textbf{not} \text{ (Every } S \text{ is a } P)$$

and

$$\textbf{not} \text{ (Some } S \text{ is a } P).$$

For it to be true that **not** (Every $S$ is a $P$), it has to be the case that *at least one $S$ is not a $P$*; that is, that Some $S$ is not a $P$. Thus "**not** (Every $S$ is a $P$)" and "Some $S$ is not a $P$" have the same meaning. Also, for it to be true that **not** (Some $S$ is a $P$), that is, that **not** (At least one $S$ is a $P$), there must be *less than one $S$* which is a $P$; that is, it must be true that *no $S$ is a $P$*. Thus "**not** (Some $S$ is a $P$)" and "No $S$ is a $P$" are statement forms with identical meanings.

Thus, we are led to four standard forms for general statements to which we shall give special attention. These four forms have been given names and are often arranged for purposes of comparison in what is called **the square of opposition.** The four types have played so important a part in the history of logic that they long ago received code letters to distinguish them. Thus, for example, one often speaks or reads about an "**A** proposition." This means a statement of the form "Every $S$ is a $P$."

The names, code letters, and statement forms constituting the square of opposition are often displayed in the following pattern.

Notice that when a statement illustrates one of the forms in the square of opposition, it contains *two* terms. (Either of these terms might be complex.) Both terms are general terms. One is modified by a sign of quantity, the other is not. The term which is modified by a sign of quantity is called the **logical subject** of the statement. The term which is not modified by a sign of quantity is called the **logical predicate** of the statement.

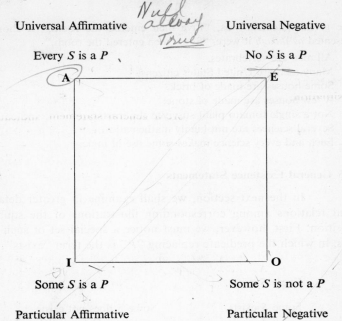

Universal Affirmative    *Not always True*    Universal Negative

Every *S* is a *P*                    No *S* is a *P*

**A**                                  **E**

**I**                                  **O**

Some *S* is a *P*                    Some *S* is not a *P*

Particular Affirmative              Particular Negative

SQUARE OF OPPOSITION

## *EXERCISES*

1. Represent the form of each of the following statements by the appropriate formula from the square of opposition. Always give your dictionary.

   a. Each student recited. *A*
   b. Some student did not recite well. *O*
   c. None of the students was unprepared. *A or E*
   d. All of the students were less than twenty years old. *A*
   e. Some people in the room were not students. *O*
   f. Any person in the room who was not a student was a parent of a student. *A*

2. Represent the form of each of the following statements by the most appropriate formula from the square of opposition. In this exercise, the signs of quantity do *not* always mean what the signs of quantity in the square mean. Thus the problem is to "throw away" a part of the meaning and to keep only as much as can be represented in the square of opposition. For example,

if the given statement was, "Five men entered the room," it should be represented *as though* it were, "Some men entered the room."

a. All men are vertebrates.
b. Many men are United States citizens.
c. Some houses are made of brick.
d. A few houses are made of stone.
e. Not a single tomato plant survived the frost.
f. Several sciences are not highly mathematical.
g. Each and every science makes some use of logic.

## §45.5 General Existence Statements

In the next section, we shall examine in greater detail the logical relations among corresponding illustrations of the square of opposition. First, however, we must notice a special set of such statements, in which the predicate replacing "$P$" is the term "exists":

| A | E |
|---|---|
| Every $S$ exists. | No $S$ exists. |
| Some $S$ exists. | Some $S$ does not exist. |
| I | O |

As we noted in the last section, general statements are concerned to affirm or deny something, $P$, of some number or proportion of the objects *in the extension* of the subject term. In Units 20 and 21, it was brought out that the extension of a term is the class of actual, or existing, things to which the term refers or applies. With this in mind, we can see that, no matter what general term "$S$" might be, the statement, "Every $S$ exists" must be true. For it is affirming that 100 percent of those things which are in the extension of "$S$" exist. But as said just above, in order to be in the extension, a thing must exist. Thus "Every $S$ exists" is analytic. (On "analytic," see §41.4.) And by the same token, the denial of "Every $S$ exists," namely, "Some $S$ does not exist," must be analytically false.

The situation is radically different, however, with the other two statement forms in this square: "Some $S$ exists" and "No $S$ exists." In §20.6 we discussed briefly the fact that some terms have null extensions, that is, are such that they refer or apply to no actual or existing thing. On the other hand, other terms refer or apply to one, many, or even an infinity of actual things, that is, do not have null extensions.

Suppose that "*S*" has a not-null extension; in other words, suppose that "*S*" refers or applies to at least one thing. Then the statement, "Some *S* exists," will be true, and its denial, "No *S* exists," will be false. Suppose, on the other hand, that "*S*" has a null extension, thus does not refer or apply to any actual thing. Then the statement, "No *S* exists," will be true and its denial, "Some *S* exists," will be false.

Thus the statement forms in *this* square of opposition provide us with forms with which to affirm that the extension of a term is null or is not null, as the case may be. On the whole, the **A** and **O** forms in this square are relatively useless, being invariably true and false, respectively. But the **E** and **I** forms are extremely valuable, since determining which is true and which false is determining in each case something important about the world.

## EXERCISE

For each of the following terms replaceable by "*S*" in the square of opposition at the beginning of this section, state which of the four statements will be true and which false. EXAMPLE: "*S*" replaces "United States citizen." Then **A** is true, **E** is false, **I** is true, and **O** is false. (That is, "Every United States citizen exists" is true, "No United States citizen exists" is false, and so on.) Note that to do this exercise you must draw on your general knowledge: for example, there are some United States citizens.

1. Speedometer
2. Ghost
3. Million-year-old tree
4. Child
5. Citizen of the kingdom of Oz

One further point: Suppose that for a certain pair of terms, "*S*" and "*P*," "Some *S* is a *P*" is true, we may combine these terms into a complex term, "*S* that is a *P*," and the statement "Some *S* that is a *P* exists" will be true. On the other hand, suppose that "Some *S* is a *P*" is false, that is, that "No *S* is a *P*" is true. Then the existence statement "No *S* that is a *P* exists" is also true.

In a similar fashion, "Every *S* is a *P*" means the same thing as "No *S* that is not a *P* exists," and "Some *S* is not a *P*" means the same thing as "Some *S* that is not a *P* exists."

This possibility of changing all statements in any square of opposition into "existence statements" was already suggested in §20.6. It has, in fact, been used also as the basis for a very effective and powerful systematic treatment of logic. However, we shall not often make reference to it or use of it in the future. Once in a while, it will be useful. That is why we mention it here.

## EXERCISE

Translate each of the following into an equivalent "existence statement."

1. Some men are courageous.
2. No men are 10 feet tall.
3. Some men are not honest.
4. Every man is a vertebrate animal.

## §45.6 Relations among Statements in the Square of Opposition

Let us now consider four corresponding illustrations of the four statement forms making up the square of opposition. (On corresponding illustrations, see §40.3.) These corresponding illustrations will be four statements all having the same subject, "S," and also having the same predicate, "P." For example, they might be the four statements.

A. Every cow is a domestic animal.
E. No cow is a domestic animal.
I. Some cow is a domestic animal.
O. Some cow is not a domestic animal.

What can be known in general about the truth or falsity of any such set of corresponding illustrations of the square of opposition?

1. We saw in §45.4 that the four statements in the square consist actually of two sets of mutually contradictory statements: the **O** statement contradicts the **A** statement, and the **E** statement contradicts the **I** statement. The laws of contradiction and excluded middle tell us that in any pair of contradictory statements, one will be true and the other false. Since the square contains two such pairs, we know that two statements in the square will be true and two will be false. Furthermore, we know that these true and false statements will be at opposite ends of the diagonals across the square. (See the arrangement of the statements in the diagram on page 549.)

All the above allows us to recognize certain proof forms as **validating**. For example:

(1)   Every *S* is a *P*.
∴ (2)   **Not** (Some *S* is not a *P*).

(1)   **Not** (Every *S* is a *P*).
∴ (2)   Some *S* is not a *P*.

(1)   Some *S* is a *P*.
∴ (2)   **Not** (No *S* is a *P*).

## EXERCISE

Write five more validating forms of proof, like the three given above, which depend on the fact that diagonally opposite statements in the square of opposition are mutually contradictory.

2.   What *other* logical relations exist among the statements in the square of opposition? What these other relations are depends upon whether or not the subject term has a null extension. Suppose, first, that it does have a null extension, so that

No *S* exists.

In that case, the two particular statements, **I** and **O**, must both be false: Since there are no *S*'s at all, it must be false that at least one of them is a *P*, and also false that at least one of them is not a *P*. But if the two particulars are false, then their contradictories, the two universals, **A** and **E**, must both be true. All these considerations justify the following four **validating** forms:

(1)   No *S* exists.              (1)   No *S* exists.
∴ (2)   Every *S* is a *P*.       ∴ (2)   No *S* is a *P*.

(1)   No *S* exists.              (1)   No *S* exists.
∴ (2)   **Not** (Some *S* is a *P*).   ∴ (2)   **Not** (Some *S* is not a *P*).

3.   Suppose, on the other hand, that the extension of the subject term is not null, that is, that

Some *S* exists.

This in itself will not be sufficient to determine the truth or falsity of any one statement in the square of opposition. But it will give us further information about the relations among those statements. In this case, at least *one* of the two particular statements will be true, and therefore also, at least one of the two universal statements will be false.[2] This is quite different from situation 2, above.

3a. When, in addition to knowing that "Some $S$ exists," we know also the truth or falsity of one statement in the square, we can often validly infer the truth or falsity of every other statement in the square. For example, suppose we knew that:

| | | |
|---|---|---|
| (1) | Some $S$ exists. | [Premise.] |
| (2) | Every $S$ is a $P$. | [Premise.] |

Then we could infer that:

| | | |
|---|---|---|
| ∴ (3) | **Not** (Some $S$ is not a $P$). | [From (2), as in situation 1, above.] |
| ∴ (4) | (Some $S$ is a $P$) **or** (Some $S$ is not a $P$). | [From (1), as in situation 3, above.] |
| ∴ (5) | Some $S$ is a $P$. | [From (3) and (4) by molecular logic.[3]] |
| ∴ (6) | **Not** (No $S$ is a $P$). | [From (5), as in situation 1, above.] |

As the above proof shows, given that "Some $S$ exists" and that **A** is true, we can validly infer that **E** is false, **I** is true, and **O** is false. On the other hand, given that "Some $S$ exists" and that **A** is false we can validly infer only that **O** is true: nothing can be inferred concerning the truth or falsity of **E** or of **I**.

## EXERCISES

1. Given that "Some $S$ exists" and that "No $S$ is a $P$." What can be validly inferred concerning the truth or falsity of:

[2] This can be established in the following manner. From the assumption that some $S$ exists, we can infer that at least one thing is an $S$, and by the logic of singular statements, either that thing is a $P$ or it is not a $P$. In the former case, some $S$ is a $P$, while in the latter case, some $S$ is not a $P$. Hence at least one of the particular statements is true, and therefore at least one of the universal statements is false.

[3] Lines (3), (4), and (5) have the following molecular form, where "$p$" replaces "Some $S$ is a $P$" and "$q$" replaces "Some $S$ is not a $P$":

| | |
|---|---|
| (3) | **Not** $q$ |
| (4) | $p$ **or** $q$ |
| ∴ (5) | $p$ |

A truth table would show that this is validating.

    a.  Every $S$ is a $P$.
    b.  Some $S$ is a $P$.
    c.  Some $S$ is not a $P$.[4]

2.  Given that "Some $S$ exists" and that "**Not** (No $S$ is a $P$)." What can be validly inferred concerning the truth or falsity of a, b, and c in question 1, above?

3.  Given that "Some $S$ is a $P$." What can be validly inferred concerning the truth or falsity of:

    a.  Some $S$ exists.
    b.  Every $S$ is a $P$.
    c.  No $S$ is a $P$.
    d.  Some $S$ is not a $P$.

4.  Given that "Some $S$ exists" and that "**Not** (Some $S$ is a $P$)." What can be validly inferred concerning the truth or falsity of b, c, and d in question 3, above?

5.  Given that "Some $S$ is not a $P$." What can be validly inferred concerning the truth or falsity of:

    a.  Some $S$ exists.
    b.  Every $S$ is a $P$.
    c.  No $S$ is a $P$.
    d.  Some $S$ is a $P$. *Indeterminate*

6.  Given that "Some $S$ exists" and that "**Not** (Some $S$ is not a $P$)." What can be validly inferred concerning the truth or falsity of b, c, and d in question 5, above?


## REVIEW QUESTIONS FOR UNIT 45

1.  Why can any general statement, or mixed, singular and general statement be said to have the form

$$x \, S \text{ is a } P?$$

2.  What is meant by:

    An absolute sign of quantity?
    A definite absolute sign of quantity?
    An indefinite absolute sign of quantity?
    A proportional sign of quantity?
    A definite proportional sign of quantity?
    An indefinite proportional sign of quantity?

---

[4] Hint: Work out in much the same way in which a similar case was worked out in the text in situation 3a, above.

3. Write the names, code letters, and statement forms constituting the square of opposition.

4. Briefly discuss the conditions that affect the truth or falsity of statements in the following square of opposition:

| A | E |
|---|---|
| Every S exists. | No S exists. |
| Some S exists. | Some S does not exist. |
| I | O |

5. How may statements from an "ordinary" square of opposition be translated into "existence statements"?

6. How many of the four statements in a square of opposition will be true, and how many will be false? Briefly explain.

7. Suppose "S" to be the subject term in four statements belonging to a square of opposition and that no S exists. Which of those four statements will be true and which false? Briefly explain.

8. As in question 7, but suppose that some S exists. Which of the four statements will be true and which false? Briefly explain.

# UNIT 46

## Conversion, Obversion, and Syllogism

### §46.1 Conversion

Statements belonging to the square of opposition in effect affirm or deny certain relations between the extensions of their terms:

**A.**   Every $S$ is a $P$:   The extension of "$S$" *is contained in* the extension of "$P$."

**O.**   Some $S$ is not a $P$:   The extension of "$S$" *is not contained* in the extension of "$P$."

**I.**   Some $S$ is a $P$:   The extension of "$S$" *overlaps* the extension of "$P$."

**E.**   No $S$ is a $P$:   The extension of "$S$" *does not overlap* the extension of "$P$."[1]

Notice that "the extension of '$S$' " and "the extension of '$P$' " are singular terms. Thus, the four translations given above of statements in the square of opposition change those statements into statements having one or the other of the forms,

$$s_1 \text{ is a } Q \text{ of } s_2.$$
$$s_1 \text{ is not a } Q \text{ of } s_2.$$

[1] The translations given in the text are not the only ones possible for statements in the square. In particular, much light has been thrown on the logic of general statements by keeping the indicated translations for **A** and **O** and by translating **E** and **I** as follows:

**E.**   No $S$ is a $P$: The extension of $S$ is contained in the extension of $P'$.
**I.**   Some $S$ is a $P$: The extension of $S$ is not contained in the extension of $P'$.
These translations have the advantage of treating all four statements in the square of opposition in terms of the same relation, "contained in."
The two sets of translations show that "overlaps the extension of $P$" means the same thing as "is not contained in the extension of $P'$."
The translations used in the text have the advantage of translating *as* negative the statements in the square that are *called* negative: **E** and **O**. They also retain throughout the predicate $P$ rather than replacing it by $P'$ in the translations of the statement forms. These advantages are slight, but they are nevertheless real, especially in the present context.

The relational predicates involved and replaced by "$Q$" are "contained in" and "overlaps." (We have considered these relations, "contained in" and "overlaps," in another context, in §22.3.)

Having noticed these translations, one naturally raises a question whether or not these relational predicates are symmetrical, reflexive, or transitive, and so on. (On symmetry, reflexiveness and transitivity see §§40.6, 40.7, 41.1, and 41.6.) Without beating around the bush we can answer those questions as follows:

> *Contained in* is: Nonsymmetrical, reflexive, and transitive.
> *Overlapping* is: Symmetrical, nonreflexive, and nontransitive.

What does this mean?

That *contained in* is nonsymmetrical means that the truth of "Every $S$ is a $P$" provides no conclusive evidence either for or against the statement "Every $P$ is an $S$." In the case of *some* terms replacing "$S$" and "$P$"—for example, "husband" and "married man"—both of these universal affirmatives will be true: Every husband is a married man, and every married man is a husband. But in the case of other terms replacing "$S$" and "$P$"—for example, "husband" and "man"—the first statement will be true and the second false. Hence, both following proof forms are **nonvalidating:**

>     (1)   Every $S$ is a $P$.          (1)   Every $S$ is a $P$.
> ∴ (2)   Every $P$ is an $S$.      ∴ (2)   Some $P$ is not an $S$.

On the other hand, *overlapping* is symmetrical: if $s_1$ overlaps $s_2$, then $s_2$ overlaps $s_1$. Thus the following proof form is **validating:**

>     (1)   Some $S$ is a $P$.
> ∴ (2)   Some $P$ is an $S$.

Principles of molecular logic would show that if any relational term, "$Q$," is symmetrical, then the negate of that term, "$Q'$," is likewise symmetrical.[2] From this it follows that if "$Q$" is not symmet-

---

[2]  It would take us too far afield to explain in detail how molecular logic proves this principle. The following sketch must suffice.
Suppose that $Q$ is symmetrical. This means that

I.                           (1)  $s_1$ is a $Q$ of $s_2$.
                        ∴ (2)  $s_2$ is a $Q$ of $s_1$.

is validating. Since I is validating, its justifying principle (see §41.5 for justifying principles) is analytic:

II.  **If** ($s_1$ is a $Q$ of $s_2$), **then** ($s_2$ is a $Q$ of $s_1$).
From II, by transposition (§44.6), the following is analytic:

rical, then its negate, "$Q'$," will also not be symmetrical (although one of the two may be nonsymmetrical and the other asymmetrical.) All this implies that since overlapping is symmetrical, its negate, nonoverlapping, is also symmetrical. Thus the following form is also **validating:**

$$(1) \quad \text{No } S \text{ is a } P.$$
$$\therefore (2) \quad \text{No } P \text{ is an } S.$$

It also implies that noncontainment is not symmetrical. It is, as a matter of fact, nonsymmetrical. Thus both of the following forms are **nonvalidating:**

| | |
|---|---|
| (1)   Some $S$ is not a $P$. | (1)   Some $S$ is not a $P$. |
| $\therefore$ (2)   Some $P$ is not an $S$. | $\therefore$ (2)   Every $P$ is an $S$. |

*EXERCISE*

Which of the following are valid, which are not? Explain—that is, show which of the six forms given above is illustrated in each case, and state whether or not the illustrated form is validating.

1. Some animals are cows; therefore some cows are animals. *V*
2. Every vegetable is a turnip; therefore every turnip is a vegetable. *N u (?)*
3. Some vegetable is not a turnip; therefore some turnip is not a vegetable. *N v*
4. Some college students are Freshmen; therefore, some Freshmen are college students. *V*
5. No good hockey players are track stars. Therefore no track stars are good hockey players. *V*
6. Some jewels are not expensive; therefore, some expensive things are not jewels. *N v*

To reverse the order of the terms in a statement belonging to the square of opposition is called **conversion.**

The point made in this section may be summarized as follows: The conversion of **E** and **I** statements is a valid form of inference, but the conversion of **A** and **O** statements is not valid.

---

III.   If [not ($s_2$ is a $Q$ of $s_1$)], then [not ($s_1$ is a $Q$ of $s_2$)].
Therefore, by obversion (§42.4), the following is analytic:

IV.   If ($s_2$ is a $Q'$ of $s_1$), then ($s_1$ is a $Q'$ of $s_2$).
But IV is the justifying principle of

V.
$$(1) \quad s_2 \text{ is a } Q' \text{ of } s_1.$$
$$\therefore (2) \quad s_1 \text{ is a } Q' \text{ of } s_2.$$

Since IV is analytic, V must be validating (see §41.5). But if V is validating then $Q'$ is symmetrical.

## §46.2 Identical Subjects and Predicates

It was said in the preceding section that containment is a reflexive relation, but that overlapping is nonreflexive. What does this mean?

Every statement of the form

Every *S* is an *S*

is analytic, therefore true. (On "analytic," see §41.4.) For examples, "Every house is a house," and "Every doormat is a doormat," are true.

On the other hand, not every statement of the form

Some *S* is an *S*

is true: some statements of this form are true and some are false. For example, "Some chair is a chair," is true, but "Some centaur is a centaur," is false. This is to say, overlapping is nonreflexive.

This latter fact, that overlapping is nonreflexive, so that some statements of the form

Some *S* is an *S*

are false, may at first glance seem surprising and even incorrect. But a little further thought will show why it must be correct.

In the preceding unit, we saw that "Some *S* is a *P*" affirms that at least one *S* is a *P*, and that this form will be false if no *S* exists. (See §45.6.) Now "Some *S* is an *S*" is just a special case of "Some *S* is a *P*," and it is false if no *S* exists. This is why it is false that some centaur is centaur: no centaur exists.

On the other hand, if some *S* exists, then some *S* is an *S*. This can be proved as follows.

(1)    Some *S* exists.           [Assumption.]
(2)    Every *S* is an *S*.       [Containment is reflexive.]
∴ (3)  Some *S* is an *S*.        [From (1) and (2) by Square of Opposition. See §45.6.]

Since "Every *S* is an *S*," is analytic, its contradictory, "Some *S* is not an *S*," is analytically false. That is, noncontainment is irreflexive.[3] Likewise, since "Some *S* is an *S*," is sometimes true and sometimes false, its contradictory, "No *S* is an *S*," is sometimes true and sometimes false: true whenever no *S* exists, and false whenever some *S* exists.

---

[3] This situation illustrates a general law: if any relational term, *Q*, is reflexive, then its negate, *Q'*, is irreflexive, and vice versa.

## §46.3 Obversion

In §42.2, we studied a validating form of inference, called **obversion**. While our major interest at that time was with singular statements, we noted that obversion is also valid in the case of general statements.

Here we need merely recall and apply what was said before, noting that obversion makes each of the following a **validating** form of inference:[4]

| I | II |
|---|---|
| (1)  Every $S$ is a $P$. | (1)  No $S$ is a $P$. |
| ∴ (2)  No $S$ is a $P'$. | ∴ (2)  Every $S$ is a $P'$. |

| III | IV |
|---|---|
| (1)  Every $S$ is a $P'$. | (1)  No $S$ is a $P'$. |
| ∴ (2)  No $S$ is a $P$. | ∴ (2)  Every $S$ is a $P$. |

| V | VI |
|---|---|
| (1)  Some $S$ is a $P$. | (1)  Some $S$ is not a $P$. |
| ∴ (2)  Some $S$ is not a $P'$. | ∴ (2)  Some $S$ is a $P'$. |

| VII | VIII |
|---|---|
| (1)  Some $S$ is a $P'$. | (1)  Some $S$ is not a $P'$. |
| ∴ (2)  Some $S$ is not a $P$. | ∴ (2)  Some $S$ is a $P$. |

## EXERCISES

1.  Which of the following are true and which are false? Explain.
    a.  Every truck driver is a truck driver.  T
    b.  Every four-sided triangle is a four-sided triangle. T
    c.  No four-sided triangle is a four-sided triangle.  F

---

[4] All the validating forms for obversion of general statements given here in the text can be proved to follow from the validating forms of obversion for singular statements studied in §42.2. But the proof involves considerations which it would take too long to investigate here.

On the other hand, the obversion of universal statements (forms I to IV in the text above) may be seen to be special cases of a more general form of inference available for proportional quantifiers:

(1)  $x$ percent of the $S$'s are $P$.
∴ (2)  $(100 - x)$ percent of the $S$'s are $P'$.

Notice that "every" is the same as "100 percent" and "no" is the same as "0 percent."

The alternative translations for **E** and **I** statements suggested in footnote 1, above, make obversion automatic, for that same translation would be used for the obverse, "Every $S$ is a $P'$."

   d.   Some ostrich is an ostrich. $T$

   e.   Some ostrich is not an ostrich. $F$

   f.   Some people who live on the Moon are people who live on the Moon. $F$

2.   Which of the following are valid and which are not? Explain.

   a.   Every student was prepared; therefore, no student was unprepared. $T$

   b.   Some gardens are untidy; therefore, some gardens are not tidy. $T$

   e.   Some employers are not inconsiderate; therefore, some employers are considerate. $F$

   d.   Some nontaxpayers are wealthy; therefore, some taxpayers are not wealthy. $F$

## §46.4 Immediate Inference

We have now studied three types of valid inference appropriate to general statements: those dependent on the square of opposition, conversion, and obversion. Inferences and proofs that rest merely on these three bases are called **immediate inferences.**[5] Thus, any case of conversion or of obversion is a case of immediate inference, so also is any inference based on the square of opposition.

These three types of immediate inference may be combined one with the other to form complex proofs which will reach final conclusions different from any that can be reached by one of these processes all alone. (On complex proofs, see §36.6.) For example, from the two premises, "Every $S$ is a $P$" and "Some $S$ exists," we may validly reach the conclusion that "Some $P$ is an $S$":

   (1)   Every $S$ is a $P$.    [Premise.]

   (2)   Some $S$ exists.    [Premise.]

∴ (3)   Some $S$ is a $P$.    [From (1) and (2) by square of opposition.]

∴ (4)   Some $P$ is an $S$.    [From (3) by conversion.]

Any conclusion that can be reached by such a combination of immediate

---

5  The name "immediate inference" is an old one used in logic books for many years. It would perhaps be better were we to say "immediate proof" rather than "immediate inference", since what we are discussing is primarily proofs rather than inferences. But we shall not tamper with the traditional name and shall continue to speak of "immediate *inference*."

What the name means is inference from a single premise, which, that is, does not need to be "mediated" by, or helped by, a second premise. When this term was first invented, logicians had not noticed that some of the inferences we have studied *do* need to be helped by a second premise, that Some $S$ exists. Hence they were all called *immediate*. We shall continue to use this term, even in cases where the existence premise is necessary.

inferences will also be called an *immediate inference* from the original premise or premises.

It might be thought that one could keep on forever drawing immediate inferences, simply by making longer and longer complex proofs. But such is not the case. Two facts inevitably bring such chains of proof sooner or later to an end: *First*, it does no good to convert or to obvert twice in succession, without some other step intervening, because the second conversion or obversion brings you right back to your original premise. For example,

|       |                   |                             |
|-------|-------------------|-----------------------------|
| (1)   | Some *S* is a *P*. | [Premise.]                  |
| ∴ (2) | Some *P* is an *S*. | [From (1) by conversion.]   |
| ∴ (3) | Some *S* is a *P*. | [From (2) by conversion.]   |

Or for another example,

|       |                   |                            |
|-------|-------------------|----------------------------|
| (1)   | Every *S* is a *P*. | [Premise.]               |
| ∴ (2) | No *S* is a *P'*.   | [From (1) by obversion.] |
| ∴ (3) | Every *S* is a *P*. | [From (2) by obversion.] |

*Second*, **A** and **O** statements cannot be validly converted. Hence, if you reach an **A** or an **O** by obversion and the square of opposition will not offer a means to another conclusion, your chain of reasoning is at an end. For example, we might have extended the chain of inference on page 562 by one more step:

|       |                       |                          |
|-------|-----------------------|--------------------------|
| ∴ (5) | Some *P* is not an *S'*. | [From (4) by obversion.] |

But that is as far as we could go, since the conclusion reached in (5) is an **O** statement and cannot be validly converted.[6]

On the other hand, whether one starts his chain of inferences with a conversion or with an obversion will make a difference: conclusions reached by starting in one way will not be reached by starting in the other. For example, compare the two following complex proofs:

|        |                   |                    |
|--------|-------------------|--------------------|
| (1)    | No *S* is *P*.    | [Premise]          |
| (2)    | Some *S* exists.  | [Premise]          |
| (3)    | Some *P* exists.  | [Premise]          |
| ∴ (4)  | Every *S* is a *P'*. | [(1), obversion] |
| ∴ (4') | No *P* is an *S*. | [(1), conversion]  |

---

6 We could, of course, draw the conclusion "**not** (Every *P* is an *S'*)" by square of opposition. But let us leave out of this discussion all conclusions of the form "**not** *p*" that might be inferred by the square of opposition.

∴ (5)  Some $S$ is a $P'$.          [(2), (4), square]
∴ (5′)  Every $P$ is an $S'$.          [(4′), obversion]
∴ (6)  Some $P'$ is an $S$.          [(5), conversion]
∴ (6′)  Some $P$ is an $S'$.          [(3), (5′), square]
∴ (7)  Some $P'$ is not an $S'$.          [(6), obversion]
∴ (7′)  Some $S'$ is a $P$.          [(6′), conversion]
"End of the line"
∴ (8′)  Some $S'$ is not a $P'$.          [(7′), obversion]
"End of the line"

No conclusion reached anywhere in either of these complex proofs appears anywhere in the other proof.[7]

## EXERCISES

1.  Given, that some apples are inedible. Which of the following can, and which cannot, be inferred by immediate inference?
    a.  Some edible things are apples.
    b.  Some inedible things are nonapples.
    c.  Some apples exist.
    d.  Some apples are edible.

2.  Given, that every student in the room has a scholarship, and that there are some students in the room. Which of the following can, and which cannot, be validly inferred by immediate inference?
    a.  None that does not have a scholarship is a student in the room.
    b.  Someone that does not have a scholarship is not a student in the room.
    c.  Someone that has a scholarship is a student in the room.

---

[7]  In each complex proof there were two points at which we exercised a choice:
I.  In getting line (6) from line (5), we converted, whereas we might have obverted. Also, in reaching line (7′) from line (6′) we converted whereas we might have obverted. Had we obverted at these two points, the left and right chains would have continued as follows.

∴ (6″)  Some $S$ is not a $P$. [ (5), obversion]
"End of the line"
∴ (7‴)  Some $P$ is an $S$. [ (6′), obversion]
"End of the line"

II.  In getting (4) and in getting (5′) we could have appealed to the square:
∴ (4″)  Some $S$ is not a $P$. [ (1), (3), square]
∴ (5‴)  Some $P$ is not an $S$ [ (4′), (3), square]
∴ (5″)  Some $S$ is a $P'$. [ (4″), obversion]
∴ (6‴)  Some $P$ is an $S'$ [ (5‴), obversion]
    etc.
       etc.

All these other choices introduce only two new conclusions, (6″) and (7‴). Every other conclusion has already been reached in some other complex proof.

## §46.5 Syllogism

Nearly everybody has heard of syllogisms. But not so many people know just what they are. Many people seem to think that almost any kind of deductive proof is a syllogism. Yet the term "syllogism" refers to a very special kind of proof.

We may define a **syllogism** as any simple proof which contains two premises and a conclusion of the following sorts:

1. Each premise and the conclusion is a statement belonging to a square of opposition.

2. The two premises have a common term; that is, they have the same subject, or they have the same predicate, or the subject of one premise is the predicate of the other premise. (This common term is called the **middle term** of the syllogism.)

3. The conclusion has for its subject and predicate the two other terms appearing in the premises.[8]

An example of a syllogism could be given as follows:

(1)   Every resident of Golden Green voted.
(2)   Some resident of Golden Green was ineligible to vote.
∴ (3)   Someone who was ineligible to vote voted.

The following is an example of a proof which is not a syllogism, although it looks considerably like one.

(1)   Every man is a mammal.
(2)   Every man is two-legged.
∴ (3)   Every man is a two-legged mammal.

This latter proof is valid but not a syllogism, because it violates the third requirement in the definition of a syllogism: that the subject and predicate of the conclusion be the two other terms in the premises. In this proof, the two other terms are combined to form a complex term which is the predicate of the conclusion, while what looks like the middle term, "man," is repeated as the subject of the conclusion.

Some syllogisms are valid. For example, the illustrative syllogism given above is valid. But other syllogisms are invalid. An example of an invalid syllogism is the following:

---

[8] What has been defined here is more precisely a *categorical* syllogism. In §44.6 we studied *hypothetical* syllogisms.

On "simple proof" as opposed to "complex proof," see §36.6.

> (1) Some member of the team is a Senior.
> (2) Some member of the team is a fraternity man.
> ∴ (3) Some fraternity man is a Senior.

In the remainder of this unit, we shall consider certain rules by the use of which one may test a syllogism in order to determine whether or not it is valid[9].

## EXERCISE

Which of the following are syllogisms (or forms for syllogisms) and which are not?

1. Every cat is an animal. Every cat is a living thing. Therefore, some living thing is an animal.

2. Either some camper brings a tent or we sleep under the stars. We do not sleep under the stars. Therefore, some camper brings a tent.

3. No hotel is completely fireproof. Every building constructed by The X Company is completely fireproof. Hence, no building constructed by The X Company is a hotel.

---

[9] Syllogism was named and first extensively studied by the great Greek philosopher Aristotle (384-322 B.C.). Since his time, it has been the object of a great deal of study. The most important change in the theory of the syllogism is that represented in the discussions in §47.1, below. No adequate recognition of the problems discussed in that section occurred until fairly recent times, i.e., since 1850.

Extended studies of the syllogism through the centuries resulted in a whole vocabulary of technical terms (many of which go back to Aristotle) and in the formulation of various special rules for special types of syllogism. In the next section, we shall define two technical terms necessary for stating the general rules for valid syllogism. However, the text omits all the other technical terms that have grown up around the doctrine of the syllogism.

These other technical terms do, however, have a certain historical interest. Furthermore, since they are so often encountered in the world's great literature, in all fields from politics and sociology to physics and religion, knowing what they mean can frequently illuminate a passage that would otherwise be vague or unintelligible. For that reason, some of the more important of these terms are defined here.

**Minor term:** The subject of the conclusion.

**Major term:** The predicate of the conclusion.

Notice that a syllogism contains three terms: the middle term, the minor term, and the major term. But the syllogism contains two tokens, or occurrences, of each of these three terms: the middle term appears once in each premise, the minor term once in the conclusion and once in a premise, and the major term once in the conclusion and once in the other premise.

**Minor premise:** The premise which has the minor term for its subject or its predicate.

**Major premise:** The premise which has the major term for its subject or its predicate.

It has been traditional to consider that a syllogism was not in standard form unless its major premise was written first, its minor premise second, and its conclusion third. (In this text we do not insist on that order for the two premises.)

4. Some *A* is a *B*. Some *B* is a *C*. Therefore, Some *A* is a *C*.   *y*
5. No *X* is a *Y*. Every *Y'* is a *Z*. Therefore, no *Z* is an *X'*.   *N*

## §46.6 Distributed and Undistributed Terms

The rules that are usually given in order to distinguish valid from invalid syllogisms are stated with the aid of certain technical terms which must be understood and kept in mind if the rules are to be correctly applied. Most of these terms have already been mentioned and explained. They will be briefly reviewed and two additional terms then explained.

---

**First figure:** The middle term is the subject of the major premise and the predicate of the minor premise:

$$M \quad P$$
$$S \quad M$$
$$\therefore \ S \quad P$$

**Second figure:** The middle term is the predicate of each premise:

$$P \quad M$$
$$S \quad M$$
$$\therefore \ S \quad P$$

**Third figure:** The middle term is the subject of each premise:

$$M \quad P$$
$$M \quad S$$
$$\therefore \ S \quad P$$

**Fourth figure:** The middle term is the predicate of the major premise and the subject of the minor premise:

$$P \quad M$$
$$M \quad S$$
$$\therefore \ S \quad P$$

**Mood:** The characterization (as an **A** statement, **E** statement, **I** statement, or **O** statement) of each premise and of the conclusion in a given figure. Thus, for example, "**AII** in the first figure" means "a syllogism in which the major premise is an **A** statement, the minor premise is an **I** statement, and the conclusion is an **I** statement, while the figure is first figure." Specifically, the syllogism would have this form:

(1) Every *M* is a *P*.
(2) Some *S* is an *M*.
∴ (3) Some *S* is a *P*.

Not every mood in every figure is valid (or validating). The validating moods, however, received names. For example, "Barbara" means "**A A A** in the first figure," "Darii" means "**A I I** in the first figure." (In these names, the first three vowels indicate the statement types of the major and minor premise and the conclusion, respectively. What *figure* is indicated by a given name had simply to be memorized.)

Statements belonging to a square of opposition are said to be **universal** (when the subject is modified by the sign of quantity "every" or "no") or **particular** (when the subject term is modified by "some"). Also they are said to be **affirmative** ("Every *S* is a *P*" and "Some *S* is a *P*") or **negative** ("No *S* is a *P*" and "Some *S* is not a *P*").

A term is said to be **distributed** in a statement containing it if *either* (1) it is the subject of that statement and the statement is universal, *or* (2) it is the predicate of that statement and the statement is negative.

According to the above definitions, the terms marked with a **D** are distributed in the statements in which they occur.

| Universal Affirmative | Universal Negative |
|---|---|
| **D** | **D** **D** |
| Every *S* is a *P*. | No *S* is a *P*. |
| | **D** |
| Some *S* is a *P*. | Some *S* is not a *P*. |
| Particular Affirmative | Particular Negative |

A term is said to be **undistributed** in a statement if it is not distributed in that statement.

The point presumably in mind when the theory of distribution was conceived would seem to be something like this: When a term is distributed in a statement, that statement makes a claim covering every object in the extension of the term. Thus, plainly, the subjects of universal statements would be distributed and the subjects of particular statements not distributed. One can also see that the predicates of affirmative statements would be undistributed: there might well be other objects in the extension of "*P*" than those *S*'s which are affirmed to be *P*'s; about these other *P*'s nothing has been settled. *Some* of the *P*'s are *S*'s (by conversion, and assuming in the case of the **A** statement, that Some *S* exists). But nothing is said about the *rest* of the *P*'s. It is, however, harder to see that in a sense a negative statement makes a claim about every object in the extension of its predicate. Yet it could be made plausible as follows: To make sure that No *S* is a *P* (or Some *S* is not a *P*), we must consider each (or some) *S* and make sure that it is not *this P*, nor *that P*, nor *this other P*, nor in fact any *P* at all.

There are, however, so many ways of thinking about what a statement affirms that it is both safer and wiser to define and think of *distributed* in the purely structural manner proposed in the definition given above:

subjects of universal statements and predicates of negative statements are distributed in those statements; no other terms are distributed in any statement.

## *EXERCISE*

Classify each of the following statements as universal or particular and as affirmative or negative. Then state concerning each of its terms whether it is distributed or undistributed in that statement.

1. Every cat is an animal.
2. No person who has gone to college is unable to read.
3. Some person who has gone to college is able to read six languages.
4. Some person who is able to read is unable to read six languages.
5. Every American citizen has traveled in at least two states.
6. Some people who have traveled in at least two states are not American citizens.

## §46.7 Rules for Valid Syllogism

A syllogism will be a valid proof if and only if it satisfies all the requirements indicated in the six rules which will be given below. We shall list and briefly comment on five of the rules in this section and shall list and discuss the sixth rule in the next unit. The five rules presented in this section fall into two groups, depending on the characteristic which they treat.

## I.  Rules of Quality

**Rule 1.**   No more than one premise may be a negative statement.

*Comment.*   The effect of this rule is to affirm that any syllogism which has two negative premises will be invalid. Of course, many validating proof forms will have two or more negative premises, but they will not be syllogisms. For example, the following is a validating form:

(1)   No *M* is a *P*.
(2)   No *S* is an *M'*.
∴ (3)   No *S* is a *P*.

This has two negative premises, but it is not a syllogism: it has no middle term; its premises contain instead two different, but related terms, "*M*" and "*M'*." By obversion, the second premise above could be made affirmative and the conclusion then drawn by syllogism. But then the syllogism would not violate this rule:

(1)    No *M* is a *P*.
(2)    No *S* is an *M'*.
∴ (3)    Every *S* is an *M*.    [From (2) by obversion]
∴ (4)    No *S* is a *P*.    [From (1), (3) by syllogism]

Suppose, for example, that we had two premises of the following form:

(1)    No *M* is a *P*.
(2)    Some *S* is not an *M*.

These are both negative. The terms, furthermore, are appropriate for a syllogism: there is a middle term. The rule then informs us that no conclusion inferred from these premises which has "*S*" and "*P*" for its two terms will be valid. This means even that no statement with *other* terms—such as "Some *P'* is not *S'*"—from which a statement with "*S*" and "*P*" for terms could be validly inferred, would be a valid conclusion from those premises. (There are, of course, valid conclusions which may be inferred from those premises. For example, "**Either** (No *S* is a *P*) **or** (Some *P* is not an *M*)." But this molecular conclusion is not a *syllogistic* conclusion.)

**Rule 2.**    If either premise is negative, the conclusion must be negative.

*Comment.*    As before, the rule is dealing with *syllogisms*. Affirmative conclusions may be validly drawn from negative premises, but they will not be *syllogistic* conclusions. Furthermore, they will not have as valid consequences any affirmative statements which could have been contemplated as syllogistic conclusions from the given premises.

Neither Rule 1 nor Rule 2 demands that a valid syllogism have any negative premises. Many valid syllogisms have two affirmative premises and no negative premise. All that Rule 1 demands is that at least one of the two premises be affirmative (they might both be affirmative) and all that Rule 2 requires is that *if* one of the premises is negative, then the conclusion be negative.

**Rule 3.**    If both premises are affirmative, then the conclusion must be affirmative.

*Comment.*    Remarks similar to those made above could be made here.

## II.  Rules of Distribution

**Rule 4.**   The middle term must be distributed in at least one premise.

*Comment.*   This is perhaps the rule which is most frequently violated by careless thinkers, who think they see a connection between two terms when the middle term, by not being distributed in either premise, does not provide a connecting link. Three invalid forms that break this rule are especially to be guarded against:

| | | |
|---|---|---|
| (1)  Some *M* is a *P*. | (1)  Every *P* is an *M*. | (1)  Some *M* is a *P*. |
| (2)  Some *M* is an *S*. | (2)  Every *S* is an *M*. | (2)  Every *S* is an *M*. |
| ∴ (3)  Some *S* is a *P*. | ∴ (3)  Some *S* is a *P*. | ∴ (3)  Some *S* is a *P*. |

EXAMPLE:

| | |
|---|---|
| (1)  Every dog is an animal. | (1)  Every college course is difficult. |
| (2)  Every cat is an animal. | (2)  Some difficult things are worth while. |
| ∴ (3)  Some cat is a dog. | ∴ (3)  Some college course is worth while. |

Syllogisms which violate this rule are said to involve the **fallacy of undistributed middle**.

**Rule 5.**   Any term that is distributed in the conclusion must be also distributed in the premise containing it.

*Comment.*   Notice that the rule does *not* require that if a term is distributed in the premise it must be distributed in the conclusion: the requirement goes in only one direction: *if* distributed in conclusion, *then* distributed in premise. Thus when you are checking a syllogism for violation of this rule, look first at the conclusion: if no term is distributed in the conclusion, the rule is satisfied. If a term is undistributed, forget about it, for it cannot produce a violation of this rule. But when (if at all) you find a term distributed in the conclusion, then look at the premise which contains this term: if that term is distributed in this premise, the rule is satisfied, but if the term is undistributed in this premise, the rule is broken and the syllogism is invalid.

Many more rules for valid syllogism have been formulated in the course of history. For example, "At least one premise must be universal," and "If either premise is particular, then the conclusion must

be particular." These rules are correct, and often convenient; but there
is no need to add them to the list of five rules given above, because
every syllogism which violates either of these two rules will *also* violate
one of those five rules. Hence the five rules that we have listed will
suffice to rule out such syllogisms as invalid.

Most syllogisms that satisfy the five rules already stated will be valid,
either completely valid or as good as valid. There is, however, one
circumstance that can still give trouble. The kind of trouble it can give,
and a rule to deal with it, will be discussed in the next unit.

One point should be noticed before we leave this unit. In §46.1, it
was stated that *contained in* is a transitive relation, but that *overlaps* is
nontransitive. To say that *contained in* is transitive amounts to claiming
that the following proof form is **validating**:

> (1)   Every *S* is an *M*.
> (2)   Every *M* is a *P*.
> ∴ (3)   Every *S* is a *P*.

A moment's consideration of this form will reveal that it is a form of
syllogism which satisfies all five rules formulated above. It furthermore
satisfies the sixth rule, to be stated in the next unit, and is indeed valid.

To say that *overlaps* is nontransitive is to claim that both of the
following are **nonvalidating**:

|               A               |               B               |
| (1)   Some *S* is an *M*.      | (1)   Some *S* is an *M*.      |
| (2)   Some *M* is a *P*.       | (2)   Some *M* is a *P*.       |
| ∴ (3)   Some *S* is a *P*.     | ∴ (3)   No *S* is a *P*.       |

Again we have two forms of syllogism, but in this case each form is
invalid; form A violates Rule 4 (undistributed middle) and form B
violates Rules 3 (negative conclusion from affirmative premises),
4 (undistributed middle), and 5 (twice: both terms distributed in
conclusion but neither of them distributed in its premise).

*EXERCISE*

State which of the following proofs are syllogisms and which are
not. In case a proof is a syllogism, state whether or not it violates any of the
five rules of syllogism given above, indicating every rule (if any) that it breaks.

1.   No completely protein-free diet is healthful. No diet that includes meat is
a completely protein-free diet. Therefore every diet that includes meat is
healthful.

2. Every course in philosophy at X University is a course carrying less than 7 credits. No course in philosophy at X University is a course carrying less than 3 credits. Therefore, some course carrying less than 7 credits is not a course carrying less than 3 credits.

3. Some people coming to the dance do not belong to fraternities or sororities. Every person coming to the dance is a student at X University. Therefore, some students at X University do not belong to fraternities or sororities.

4. Anyone who drives faster than 60 miles an hour on this street is a law-breaker. Someone drives faster than 60 miles an hour on this street. Therefore, someone is a lawbreaker.

5. No metal except magnesium is inflammable. No metal except magnesium is less dense than ice. Therefore something not less dense than ice is not inflammable.

6.   Every $M$ is a $P$ of $s$.
   Every $S$ is an $M$.
   ∴ Every $S$ is a $P$ of $s$.

7. Every learned profession is an economically sound vocation. Some economically sound vocation is undermanned. Therefore, some learned profession is undermanned.

8. Some ways of making a dollar are not honest types of behavior. Some honest types of behavior are approved by society. Therefore, some ways of making a dollar are not approved by society.

## REVIEW QUESTIONS FOR UNIT 46

1. How may statements belonging to a square of opposition be interpreted as illustrating the singular statement forms

$$s_1 \text{ is a } Q \text{ of } s_2,$$
$$s_1 \text{ is not a } Q \text{ of } s_2?$$

2. Which, if any, of the four statement forms in the square of opposition indicate symmetrical relations between their subjects and predicates? Which (if any) indicate asymmetrical relations? Which (if any) indicate nonsymmetrical relations?

3. What is meant by the *conversion* of a general statement? Under what circumstances is it valid? What connection is there between the answer to this question and your answer to question 2?

4. Under what circumstances is a statement in a square of opposition, with the same term for subject and for predicate (for example, "Some $S$ is an $S$"), true? Under what circumstances false?

5. What is meant by the obversion of a statement belonging to the square of opposition? Illustrate. Is the obversion of such statements *always* valid? Sometimes valid and sometimes not? Never valid?

6. What is meant by immediate inference?
7. Is there any limit to the number of conclusions that may be drawn by immediate inference from a given premise? Explain.
8. Will an additional "existence premise" increase the number of conclusions that may be drawn from a given premise by immediate inference? Always? Sometimes? Never? (Hint: does it make a difference whether or not the given premise is universal or particular? Explain.)
9. What is a (categorical) syllogism?
10. Are any proofs that are not syllogisms valid?
11. Are any syllogisms invalid?
12. Under what circumstances is a term said to be distributed in a given statement? Said to be undistributed in that statement?
13. State (in your own words if you wish) three rules of quality that may be used to determine whether or not a syllogism is valid. Using capital letters (for example, S, M, and P) to represent terms, construct for each rule a syllogism which conforms to the rule, and another that violates it.
14. State two rules for distribution that govern the distinction between valid and invalid syllogisms. Using capital letters to represent terms, construct for each rule a syllogism that conforms to it and another that violates it.
15. Are there any valid syllogisms that break one or more of the five rules stated in answer to questions 13 and 14?
16. Will every syllogism which conforms with the five rules stated in answer to questions 13 and 14 be valid?

# *Syllogism, continued*

## §47.1 Rule 6 For Valid Syllogism

In the last unit we studied five rules that might be applied to distinguish between valid and invalid syllogisms. It was said there that any syllogism which violated any one or more of those rules would be invalid, but that most syllogisms that conformed to all five rules would be valid. We must now consider what syllogisms conforming with those five rules could still be invalid and what additional rule must be invoked.

Let it be said at once that any syllogism conforming to those five rules which has a particular premise, and any such syllogism which has a universal conclusion, will be valid. The difficulty comes when both premises are universal and the conclusion is particular.

In Unit 45, when we were studying the square of opposition, we saw that in case no $S$ exists, then any **A** or **E** statement that has "$S$" for its subject term will be true. Also we saw that if an **I** or an **O** statement is true, then the extension of its subject term must contain at least one object. (See especially §45.6.) In other words, the truth of a universal statement does not guarantee that there is any object in the extension of its subject term, nor in the extension of its predicate term. On the other hand, the truth of "Some $S$ is a $P$" implies that some $S$ exists and also that some $P$ exists, while the truth of "Some $S$ is not a $P$" implies that some $S$ exists and also that some $P'$ exists.[1] Thus when both premises

---

1   Let us grant that

|   |   |   |   |
|---|---|---|---|
| (1) Some $S$ is a $P$. | | (1) Some $S$ is not a $P$. | |
| ∴ (2) Some $S$ exists. | | ∴ (2) Some $S$ exists. | |

are validating forms by the square of opposition. Then the other existence conclusions mentioned in the text can be shown valid as follows:

     (1) Some $S$ is a $P$. [Premise]
∴  (2) Some $P$ is an $S$. [From (1) by conversion]
∴  (3) Some $P$ exists. [From (2) by square]
     (1) Some $S$ is not a $P$. [Premise]
∴  (2) Some $S$ is a $P'$. [From (1) by obversion]
∴  (3) Some $P'$ is an $S$. [From (2) by conversion]
∴  (4) Some $P'$ exists. [From (3) by square]

in a syllogism are universal and its conclusion is particular, the premises do not guarantee the existence of objects in certain classes while the conclusion assumes or implies their existence, and the syllogism is therefore invalid.

These invalid syllogisms may be avoided by the addition of one additional rule:

**Rule 6.** If the conclusion is particular, then one of the premises must be particular.

Let us look at a typical syllogism which violates this rule.

(1) Every woodworking course at X Academy carries a $20 laboratory fee.

(2) Every woodworking course at X Academy (is a course that) meets in Shaler Hall.

∴ (3) Some course that meets in Shaler Hall carries a $20 laboratory fee.

This syllogism satisfies all five rules given in §46.7, but it violates Rule 6. And we ought not to trust it. It is possible there are no woodworking courses at X Academy. In that case, the premises would both be true.[2] But in that case, their truth would be no assurance that the conclusion was true: maybe no course meets in Shaler Hall, or maybe there are courses meeting there but none of them charge $20 laboratory fees.

## EXERCISE

Which of the syllogisms, if any, in the exercise at the end of Unit 46 violate Rule 6 and are therefore invalid?

## §47.2 Augmented Syllogisms

Let us look again at the invalid syllogism, near the middle of this page, about woodworking courses at X Academy. But suppose this time that we have information to the effect that there are some woodworking courses at X Academy and that this additional information is formulated in a third premise:

(1) Every woodworking course at X Academy carries a $20 laboratory fee.

[2] In fact, the premises might have been *established* as true by the governing board of X Academy, in anticipation of starting some woodworking courses, but the courses might never have been started.

(2)   Every woodworking course at X Academy (is a course that) meets in Shaler Hall.

(3)   Some woodworking course at X Academy exists.

∴ (4)   Some course that meets in Shaler Hall carries a $20 laboratory fee.

This new proof is valid. (We shall see why shortly.) But it is not a syllogism, because it contains three premises rather than only two, as required by the definition of a syllogism.

Let us call proofs like the new one given above *augmented syllogisms*.[3] To see just what is the important point, we define an augmented syllogism as follows:

An **augmented syllogism** is any proof which could have been produced by adding to a syllogism a third premise of the form "Some *S* exists," where the term "*S*" is one of the three terms appearing in the original syllogism.

A re-examination of the sample given above will reveal that it satisfies the requirements of this definition and is therefore an augmented syllogism.

## EXERCISE

Which of the following represent forms of augmented syllogisms and which do not?

1.  (1)   No *A* is a *B*.
    (2)   Some *C* is a *B*.
    (3)   Some *C* exists.
    ∴ (4)   Some *C* is not a *P*.

2.  (1)   Every *M'* is a *P*.
    (2)   No *S* is an *M'*.
    (3)   Some *S* exists.
    ∴ (4)   No *S* is a *P*.

3.  (1)   Some *M* is an *S*.
    (2)   No *S'* is a *P*.
    (3)   Some *P* exists.
    ∴ (4)   Some *P* is an *M*.

---

[3] Notice that an augmented syllogism is not really a syllogism at all, any more than, for example, a mashed banana is a banana. It is something *made out of* a syllogism (or a banana) but in the course of making the new thing (augmented syllogism or crushed banana) we destroy the form which in part defines the original material (banana or syllogism). In the same way, a house is not a pile of lumber, although we might describe it as a sawed up, rearranged, and nailed together pile of lumber.

**4.**     (1)   Every $W$ is a $T$.
          (2)   Every $W$ is an $S$.
          (3)   Some $S$ exists.
    ∴ (4)   Some $S$ is a $T$.

**5.**     (1)   Every $W$ is a $T$.
          (2)   Every $W$ is an $S$.
          (3)   Some $W$ exists.
    ∴ (4)   Some $S$ is a $T$.

## §47.3 Valid Augmented Syllogisms

We saw in the last unit that some syllogisms are valid and some are invalid. In much the same manner, some augmented syllogisms are valid and some invalid. For example, the sample augmented syllogism at the beginning of the last section is valid. For contrary examples, any proof having the form of Exercise 4, above, will be an augmented syllogism but will be invalid.

How can we tell the difference between valid and invalid augmented syllogisms? Here we must distinguish three types of situation. The first two are not so interesting in themselves, but must nevertheless be taken into account. In describing all these situations, we shall speak of the "original syllogism," meaning by that the syllogism out of which we can imagine the augmented syllogism to have been constructed by adding a third premise.

**1.   First Situation:**   The original syllogism is valid. In this situation, the augmented syllogism is also valid. This is true because valid syllogism is a form of *deductive* proof. In §37.7 we observed that a valid deduction cannot be made invalid merely by adding more premises. Hence, if the original syllogism is valid, the augmented syllogism will be valid.

Augmented syllogisms of the sort here described—ones that contain a valid original syllogism—are not usually of much interest from a practical point of view: the added premise is, so to speak, a fifth wheel. It is not contributing to the proof of the conclusion, which can be validly reached without it. But despite this uninteresting character, these augmented syllogisms are valid.

**2.   Second Situation:**   The original syllogism violates one or more of Rules 1 to 5. In this situation, the original syllogism is invalid. But so also is the augmented syllogism. The third, added, premise does not contribute the kind of additional information needed in order to justify accepting the conclusion. Hence when a syllogism violates one or more of Rules 1 to 5, there is no point in determining whether objects exist in the extensions of its terms: this sort of additional information will not help you validly to infer the original conclusion. If you are interested in establishing the truth or falsity of that conclusion, look elsewhere, for another kind of evidence, that will have some bearing on the matter.

**3. Third Situation:** The original syllogism satisfies Rules 1 to 5, but violates Rule 6. Here is a situation in which the additional premise may have turned an invalid proof into a valid proof: it may have provided just the additional information needed to justify inferring the original conclusion. But then again, it may *not* have done so, and the augmented syllogism may itself be invalid. It all depends on whether or not the added premise gives information about the *appropriate* term from the original syllogism. One of them will always be appropriate and make a valid augmented syllogism, two of them will always be inappropriate and make invalid augmented syllogisms.

How can we tell whether the added premise in an augmented syllogism has talked about the appropriate term and thus has produced a valid proof? We shall explain this matter in the next section.

## §47.4 Appropriate and Inappropriate Existence Premises

Suppose that we are considering an augmented syllogism of the sort described in the third situation above. To be such, the original syllogism must have satisfied Rules 1 to 5 for valid syllogism, but violated Rule 6. To violate Rule 6, its two premises must have been universal statements and its conclusion must have been a particular statement. A typical example would be the augmented syllogism about woodworking courses at X Academy, given in §47.2. Instead of repeating that proof here, let us represent its form:

    (1)   Every $M$ is a $P$.
    (2)   Every $M$ is an $S$.
    (3)   Some $M$ exists.
∴ (4)   Some $S$ is a $P$.

How can we tell whether or not that augmented syllogism is valid? If it is valid, a complex proof will show that it is valid. In this complex proof we need use nothing but immediate inference and syllogism (*not* augmented syllogism).

What we must do is to use the added premise—in the case of our example, "Some *M* exists"—to change one of the premises in the original syllogism from a universal statement into a particular statement. Near the end of §45.6 we saw that if a universal statement (affirmative or negative) is true, and there are objects in the extension of its subject term, then the corresponding particular statement of the same quality (affirmative or negative) will be true. Then we combine the particular statement thus reached with the other premise from the original syllogism to infer by syllogism the original conclusion.

In the case of our example, the complex proof might validly take either of the following forms:

|       | (1)    | Every *M* is a *P*.    | [Premise]                        |
|-------|--------|------------------------|----------------------------------|
|       | (2)    | Every *M* is an *S*.   | [Premise]                        |
|       | (3)    | Some *M* exists.       | [Premise]                        |
| ∴     | (4)    | Some *M* is a *P*.     | [From (1), (3) by square]        |
| ∴     | (4′)   | Some *M* is an *S*.    | [From (2), (3) by square]        |
| ∴     | (5)    | Some *S* is a *P*.     | [From (2), (4) by syllogism]     |
| ∴     | (5′)   | Some *S* is a *P*.     | [From (1), (4′) by syllogism]    |

When the added premise affirms that something in the extension of the *middle term* exists, it can frequently be combined with *either* premise to get a particular statement that will combine with the other in a syllogism. This was the case in the illustration given above. But when the added premise contains some *other* term than the middle term it will combine only with the premise that contains the other term.

It was said above that the first part of this complex proof was always a case of immediate inference. In the illustration already given, that immediate inference was accomplished in one step. Sometimes, however, it will take two steps, as in the following example:

|       | (1)    | Every *P* is an *M*.   |                               |
|-------|--------|------------------------|-------------------------------|
|       | (2)    | No *M* is an *S*.      |                               |
|       | (3)    | Some *S* exists.       | [Premise]                     |
| ∴     | (4)    | No *S* is an *M*.      | [From (2) by conversion]      |
| ∴     | (5)    | Some *S* is not an *M*.| [From (3), (4) by square]     |
| ∴     | (6)    | Some *S* is not a *P*. | [From (1), (5) by syllogism]  |

Also, it was said earlier (end of §47.3) that an added premise containing *one* of the terms from the original syllogism would be appropriate, but that added premises containing either of the other terms would be inappropriate. Let us see what happens when you have an inappropriate added premise.

Suppose again we take the example of woodworking courses at X Academy, but instead of an added premise to the effect that some woodworking courses at X Academy exist, our added premise is that some courses that meet in Shaler Hall exist:

      (1)   Every $M$ is a $P$.
      (2)   Every $M$ is an $S$.
      (3)   Some $S$ exists.
 ∴ (4)   Some $S$ is a $P$.

The augmented syllogism is invalid. The evidence for this lies in the fact that we cannot combine the added premise with either of the others so as to get by immediate inference a particular conclusion. Thus we cannot even get started on the complex proof that would test the augmented syllogism.

Or take another example.

      (1)   Every $P$ is an $M$.      [Premise]
      (2)   No $M$ is an $S$.         [Premise]
      (3)   Some $P$ exists.        [Premise]
 ∴ (4)   Some $S$ is not a $P$.

This is an invalid augmented syllogism. Why? Because, although we can get the complex testing proof started, we cannot finish it. We may combine (1) and (3) by square of opposition to get

Some $P$ is an $M$.

But when we attempt to combine this with (2) so as to infer (4) by syllogism, we find that the syllogism is invalid: a term distributed in the conclusion is not distributed in the premise.

## EXERCISE

Which of the following augmented syllogisms are valid and which are invalid? Explain. (Do not forget about the first and second types of situation, discussed in §47.4.)

1.     (1)   Every $P$ is an $M$.
        (2)   Every $M$ is an $S$.
        (3)   Some $P$ exists.
    ∴ (4)   Some $S$ is a $P$.

2.  (1)  Every *P* is an *M*.
    (2)  Every *M* is an *S*.
    (3)  Some *M* exists.
∴ (4)  Some *S* is a *P*.

3.  (1)  No *M* is a *P*.
    (2)  Some *S* is an *M*.
    (3)  Some *S* exists.
∴ (4)  Some *S* is not a *P*.

4.  (1)  Every *P* is an *M*.
    (2)  Every *S* is an *M*.
    (3)  Some *S* exists.
∴ (4)  Some *S* is a *P*.

5.  (1)  Every rise in wages is an inflationary trend.
    (2)  No inflationary trend is a thing to be viewed lightly.
    (3)  Some thing to be viewed lightly exists.
∴ (4)  Some thing to be viewed lightly is not a rise in wages.

## §47.5 A Practical Shortcut

Suppose that you are considering some syllogism and that you know every one of its terms has a not-null extension. From a practical point of view, you may disregard Rule 6 and test the syllogism by the five rules given in the preceding unit. If it satisfies those five rules (and if its premises are true) its conclusion will also be true.

This does not mean that the syllogism is necessarily valid. If it violates Rule 6, it will be invalid. But we have seen that when a syllogism satisfies all the rules except Rule 6, then there is always one of its terms, *T*, such that if you add

Some *T* exists

as a third premise, you will have a valid augmented syllogism. Now the supposition at the beginning of this section was that for every term, *T*, in the syllogism, you knew that

Some *T* exists.

Hence, without waiting to figure out which would be the *appropriate* term you may confidently infer the conclusion. *Whichever* is the appropriate term, the necessary added premise will be true, and the conclusion therefore reliable.[4]

The situation described here is a very common one. More often

4  The situation discussed here is a special illustration of a general *kind* of situation considered under point vi in §41.4.

than not the terms of the syllogisms we would use have not-null extensions. And more often than not we *know* this. Hence, more often than not we can safely test our syllogisms merely by considering Rules 1 to 5, and can safely disregard Rule 6: the syllogisms will be *safe*, even though they may not be valid. This is one reason why the first five rules were considered in a group in the preceding unit and Rule 6 was separated for special study in this unit. It is probably one reason why through many centuries neither Rule 6 nor anything like it was listed among the rules for valid syllogism.

### §47.6 A Generalization of Rule 6

In Rule 6, we have stated a rule for syllogisms. But that rule may be generalized to apply to all deductive reasoning:

**If the conclusion of a valid deduction from general premises is particular, then at least one of its premises is particular.**

Notice that this rule is satisfied in valid augmented syllogisms: the added premise, "Some *S* exists." is particular. It is also satisfied in immediate inference: the only way in which we get from universal premises to particular conclusions is via the square of opposition and an additional assumption or premise of the form "Some *S* exists."

Of course, the problem confronting any reasoner is to find out *what* particular premise or premises he must add to his universal premises in order to validate the particular conclusions in which he is interested. So the general rule has, so to speak, a negative value rather than a positive one: beware of proofs that have only universal premises and yet have a particular conclusion. Either they are invalid or their author is assuming something (some additional premise) that he has not stated.

The general rule just stated could be given an even more general form that might sometimes prove useful: If the conclusion of a valid deduction from general premises is an affirmation in terms of *absolute* signs of quantity, then at least one of the premises is absolutely quantified. That is, from premises that contain only proportional quantities no conclusion that contains only absolute quantities may be validly inferred.[5]

---

[5] This rule is formulated in a rough-and-ready way and is perhaps not so useful as the earlier rule. Certain precautions must be taken in applying it. For example "no" must be interpreted always as a proportional quantifier. Again, no signs of denial must precede signs of quantity in the premises or the conclusions. Hence, the rule is more suggestive than prescriptive.

## §47.7 Syllogisms Containing a Singular Term

The remainder of this unit will be given over to a brief consideration of a miscellaneous group of special topics. In this section, we shall speak briefly of syllogisms that contain a singular term.

Traditional logic did not distinguish between singular statements of the forms, "*s* is a *P*" and "*s* is not a *P*," and corresponding universal statements of the forms, "Every *S* is a *P*" and "No *S* is a *P*." Hence, in traditional logic, proofs like, for example,

(1)   Every *M* is a *P*.
(2)   *s* is an *M*.
∴ (3)   *s* is a *P*.

were counted as syllogisms. Since we have sharply distinguished between singular statements and general statements, proofs like the above really do not satisfy the definition of a syllogism given in §46.5.

Our concern, however, is not to quarrel over names. So let us call proofs like the above **syllogisms containing a singular term.** They are structurally just like syllogisms except that one of the general terms called for in the definition of a syllogism, together with its quantifier, has been replaced by a singular term.

The only *positions* that can be meaningfully occupied by singular terms are those of subjects. As we have seen earlier, it makes no sense to write

*P* is an *s*

or

Every *P* is an *s*.

(For example, "Every man is a Judas" only *appears* to have the latter form. In it, "Judas" is a token of a general term, meaning betrayer.) Hence, not any term in a syllogism may be replaced by a singular term. None of the predicates, of the conclusion or of the premises, can be so replaced. Thus, the middle term may be replaced by a singular term only if it is the subject in both premises, as in

(1)   *s* is a *P*.
(2)   *s* is a *Q*.
∴ (3)   Some *Q* is a *P*.

In testing for validity, one should apply all five rules given in the preceding unit. In connection with the rules for distribution, regard the singular term as distributed. Thus both illustrations given above satisfy these five rules and are to be considered valid. Rule 6 is not to be employed.

## EXERCISE

Which of the following are valid and which are not? In the case of invalid forms state which rules are violated.

1.      (1)   Every $M$ is a $P$.
         (2)   $s$ is not an $M$.
   ∴ (3)   $s$ is not a $P$.

2.      (1)   No $M$ is a $P$.
         (2)   $s$ is an $M$.
   ∴ (3)   $s$ is not a $P$.

3.      (1)   $s$ is a $Q$.
         (2)   $s$ is not a $P$.
   ∴ (3)   Some $Q$ is not a $P$.

4.      (1)   $s$ is a $Q$.
         (2)   $s$ is not a $P$.
   ∴ (3)   Some $P$ is not a $Q$.

5.      (1)   $s$ is a $Q$.
         (2)   Every $Q$ is a $P$.
   ∴ (3)   $s$ is a $P$.

## §47.8 Existence Syllogisms

Of special interest are certain syllogisms that might be called "existence syllogisms." These are syllogisms that have a conclusion of the form "Some $S$ exists."

I.                         (1)   Every $S$ is a $P$.
                             (2)   Some $S$ exists.
                        ∴ (3)   Some $P$ exists.

Proof I is a valid syllogism, satisfying all six rules.

II.                        (1)   Every $S$ is a $P$.
                             (2)   Some $P'$ exists.
                        ∴ (3)   Some $S'$ exists.

Proof II is not a syllogism, but it is nevertheless valid, as may be shown in the following manner:

         (1)   Every $S$ is a $P$.          [Premise]
         (2)   Some $P'$ exists.       [Premise]

∴ (3)   No $S$ is a $P'$.      [From (1) by obversion]
∴ (4)   No $P'$ is an $S$.     [From (3) by conversion]
∴ (5)   Every $P'$ is an $S'$.   [From (4) by obversion]
∴ (6)   Some $S'$ exists.      [From (2), (5) by syllogism]

III.           (1)   No $S$ is a $P$.
              (2)   Some $S$ exists.
          ∴ (3)   Some $P'$ exists.

IV.            (1)   No $S$ is a $P$.
              (2)   Some $P$ exists.
          ∴ (3)   Some $S'$ exists.

Neither III nor IV is a syllogism, but each is valid and may be shown to be such by complex proofs more or less similar to that used above to show that Proof II is valid.

## EXERCISES

1. Why is it maintained that Proofs II, III, and IV are not syllogisms?
2. Write out a complex proof which shows that Proof III is valid.
3. Write out a complex proof which shows that Proof IV is valid.

Proof forms I, II, III, and IV show that whenever a universal statement is true and an *appropriate* one of its two terms or their negates is known to have objects in its extension, then *another* of those terms or their negates can be inferred also to have objects in its extension. But, as was said above, it must be an *appropriate* one of these terms. For example, the following syllogism is **invalid**:

          (1)   Every $S$ is a $P$.
          (2)   Some $P$ exists.
      ∴ (3)   Some $S$ exists.

## EXERCISE

Which rule or rules of valid syllogism are violated by the above invalid syllogism?

### §47.9 Some Questions About Standard Forms*

Throughout these units dealing with molecular logic and the logic of general statements, we have not discussed connections between these branches

* This section may be omitted without disturbing the continuity of the text.

of logic, nor have we discussed connections *of* them and the logic of singular statements. Yet a word must be said about these matters.

We can best begin by considering how to represent the forms of certain statements. For this purpose, let us compare the four following statements and the problems that they raise.

(1)  If John gets an A, he will receive a scholarship.
(2)  If any applicant gets an A, he will receive a scholarship.
(3)  If any applicant gets an A, the judges will be happy.
(4)  Any applicant who gets an A will receive a scholarship.

The form of statement (1) could be represented by

(1′)                               **If** $p$, **then** $q$,

where "$p$" replaces "John gets an A," and "$q$" replaces "John receives a scholarship." Notice that in giving our dictionary, we do not say that "$q$" replaces "*he* receives a scholarship." We replace "he" by "John." In this connection, see the comments accompanying the exercise at the end of §43.1.

Had we wished a more detailed analysis of the form of statement (1) we could have written

(1″)                        **If** ($s$ is a $P$), **then** ($s$ is a $Q$),

where "$s$" replaces "John," "$P$" replaces "person who gets A," and "$Q$" replaces "person who receives a scholarship." This more detailed representation shows that both clauses in the complex statement have the same subject, represented by "$s$."

On the other hand, *neither* of these kinds of representation will work for statement (2). We cannot write

                                **If** $p$, **then** $q$,

because there is no way of indicating what "$q$" replaces that does not retain a pronoun with its antecedent outside of the clause. If we let "$p$" replace "Any applicant gets an A," and "$q$" replace "Any applicant receives a scholarship," the analysis is incorrect. It would allow that *John* got the A while *George* received the scholarship. But if we let "$q$" replace "that applicant will receive a scholarship," we still have a pronoun, "that," in the dictionary explanation, and its antecedent is not in the same dictionary explanation.

We run into similar difficulties when we try to make a more detailed analysis as in (1″). Suppose we try

                        **If** (Some $S$ is a $P$), **then** (Some $S$ is a $Q$),

where "$S$" replaces "applicant" and "$P$" and "$Q$" have the meanings previously assigned. The same difficulty persists: the form does not reveal that the applicants who receive scholarships are the very ones who got A's. This kind of analysis will indeed work for statement (3). In fact we can as easily represent the form of statement (3) as we did that of statement (1):

(3′)                              If *r*, then *t*,

where "*r*" replaces "Some applicant gets an A," and "*t*" replaces "Every judge is happy." Or if we wish a more detailed analysis, we may write

(3″)                    If (Some *S* is a *P*), then (Every *J* is an *H*),

where "*S*" and "*P*" have the meanings previously assigned and "*J*" and "*H*" replace "judge" and "happy person" respectively.

This possibility of treating (1) and (3) lies in the fact that we can eliminate cross references from one clause to another in our dictionary, and the impossibility of treating (2) in the same way results from the fact that we can*not* eliminate such cross references in our dictionary.

But now notice. If we are willing to *refuse* to make a *complete* dictionary, we could represent (2) in much the same manner as we used to represent (1):

If $[(s_1$ is an *S*) and ($s_1$ is a *P*)], then ($s_1$ is a *Q*),

where "*S*," "*P*," and "*Q*" have the meanings previously assigned, but we refuse to assign a meaning to "$s_1$." This refusal to assign a meaning to "$s_1$" is our acknowledgement that statement (2) is not making an assertion specifically about John, or about Tom, or Dick, or Harry. It is rather making an assertion about *anyone*.

This refusal to assign a meaning to "$s_1$" should actually be recorded in the representation of the form of statement (2). It can be done by using a new kind of quantifier sign: one that modifies a singular term variable:

(2′)     For every $s_1$ {If $[(s_1$ is an *S*) and ($s_1$ is a *P*)], then ($s_1$ is a *Q*)}.

This quantifier, called sometimes an **unrestricted quantifier**, does not refer us to every object in the extension of the term that "$s_1$" has replaced, but instead refers us to every object in the extension of *any* term that "$s_1$" *might* replace. A great deal of modern logic depends on the use of unrestricted quantifiers—both unrestricted *universal* quantifiers like the above and unrestricted particular quantifiers, as in

(5)              For some $s_1$, $[(s_1$ is an *S*) and ($s_1$ is a *P*)].

But we shall not attempt here a further investigation of these unrestricted quantifiers.

It only remains to notice the connection between statements (2) and (4), above. When you look at these two statements, it becomes apparent that they are equivalent, are merely two different ways of making the same affirmation. Yet we have already a way of representing the form of statement (4):

(4′)                         Every ($S \frown P$) is a *Q*.[6]

---

[6]  This statement is formulated with the help of the symbol "$\frown$" mentioned in note 4, in §42.5, as a device for representing certain complex general terms.

If we let "*A*" replace "applicant who gets an A," then both (2) [that is, (2′)] and (4) [that is (4′)] can be even more simply represented:

(2″)  For every $s_1$, {**If** ($s_1$ is an *A*), **then** ($s_1$ is a *Q*)}.
(4″)  Every *A* is a *Q*.

As statements (2) and (4), and corresponding formulas (2″) and (4″) show, certain "if . . ., then . . ." forms express the same claims as do certain general statements. We may represent the forms of all these statements by using the standard forms for general statements which we have already learned, such as (4″). *Or* we may represent the forms of all of them by exploring the logic of unrestricted quantifiers followed by molecular statement forms, as in (5) and (2″). The latter method has been very highly developed in modern times. Its great merit lies in tying together the logic of singular statements ("$s_1$ is an *A*"), molecular statements ("**If** ($s_1$ is an *A*), **then** ($s_1$ is a *Q*"), and general statements ("For every $s_1$, [**If** ($s_1$ is an *A*), **then** ($s_1$ is a *Q*)]"). We shall, however, not pursue this further in the present text. The method of treating general statements throughout the last few units has certain advantages that we wish to make use of in the next unit.

# REVIEW QUESTIONS FOR UNIT 47

1. State Rule 6 for valid syllogisms.
2. Why is this sixth rule necessary?
3. What is an augmented syllogism?
4. Are all augmented syllogisms valid? Explain.
5. Describe a method for testing the validity of an augmented syllogism.
6. Under what circumstances may one, for *practical* purposes, disregard Rule 6 for valid syllogisms? Explain.
7. Discuss briefly the possibility of generalizing Rule 6 into a general rule of valid inference.
8. What is meant by a syllogism that contains a singular term? How may such syllogisms be tested for validity?
9. Illustrate the possibility of a syllogism that leads to an existence conclusion.

**48**

# *Inductive Generalization*

## §48.1 A Brief Review

We have now completed the examination and study of a few topics and problems related to the logic of deductive proof: singular statements, types of relation (symmetrical, transitive, and so on), the logic of identity, complex predicates, molecular logic, truth functions general statements, types of quantifier (absolute, proportional, definite indefinite), the square of opposition, general existence statement ("Some $S$ exists," and so on), conversion, obversion, immediate inference, syllogism.

The topics that we examined and the validating forms of proof which we noticed make up only a tiny part of what might be studied in deductive logic. For one thing, with different signs of quantity from the three which we examined, new and different validating forms of proof could be identified and studied. Second, we have not considered any validating forms of deductive proof (except augmented syllogism) that involve more than two premises.[1] And third, we have not considered the important logic of general statements that contain two or more signs of quantity.[2]

---

[1] We have, of course, seen how groups of more than two premises may be made to yield a conclusion by means of a complex proof: From one or two of the premise an intermediate conclusion is reached by the processes that we have studied. This intermediate conclusion is then combined with another premise (or another intermediate conclusion reached from one or two other premises) in order to prove a final conclusion. Most conclusions that can be validly deduced from a large number of premises can be reached by complex proofs of this sort, in which each step in the proof appeals to only one or two statements "from which" the intermediate or final conclusion is proved.

[2] Such statements have been represented by forms IV-A and IV-B in §16.5. The problems treated in the logic of such statements may be suggested in the following manner.

In §42.4, we noticed that the order of the subject terms in a *singular* statement may be reversed if we replace the given relative predicate by its converse:

$$(1) \quad s_1 \text{ is a } P \text{ of } s_2.$$
$$\therefore (2) \quad s_2 \text{ is a } \breve{P} \text{ of } s_1.$$

This sampling of the problems and theories of deductive logic will, however, have to suffice for the present text. Through its means, it is to be hoped that something will have been learned concerning, among other things, how analysis is used to establish that a *form* of proof is validating and to establish that a given proof has that form, thus how analysis opens the way to inference.

It is now high time that we turn our attention briefly to some of the characteristic forms and techniques of that other great branch of logic called *inductive logic*. (In Unit 37 the basic difference between deduction and induction was explained.) As with deduction, so here with induction —but here even to a greater degree—we can suggest only a few of the types of induction, and only a few of the problems relating to them. Perhaps, however, these few considerations will help you take a more cautious and critical attitude toward the inductive inferences that are proposed to you by others or that you are tempted to make yourself, and will help you figure out what you must attend to when you are judging the strength of an induction.

## §48.2  Inductive Generalization

Many remarks throughout this entire book have pointed toward observation and analysis as the fundamental valid grounds for belief.[3] Actualization only paves the way for an observation, and inference only selects for belief something that analysis reveals is justified on the basis of other already held beliefs.

As we just noted, inference proceeds from beliefs already held (recorded in premises) to a new belief (recorded in a conclusion). The

---

May the same thing be done validly if general terms with accompanying signs of quantity replace the singular terms?

       (1)   $x$ $S_1$ is a $P$ of $y$ $S_2$.
  ∴ (2)   $y$ $S_2$ is a $\breve{P}$ of $x$ $S_1$.

Not always! It depends on what quantities "$x$" and "$y$" replace. For example, if both of them replace "every", the proof is valid:

       (1)   Every student passed every examination.
  ∴ (2)   Every examination was passed by every student.

But if "$x$" replaces "every" and "$y$" replaces "some," the proof is invalid:

       (1)   Every student passed some examination.
  ∴ (2)   Some examination was passed by every student.

For the premise could be true and the conclusion false. In short, the *order* in which signs of quantity occur in a statement affects the meaning of the statement.

   For a review of the valid grounds for belief, see §§6.2 to 7.2.

only fundamental valid grounds for believing those premises themsel[
will have been observations or analyses: either those premises rec[
beliefs based directly on observation or on analysis, or they rec[
conclusions inferred from still other premises based on observation[
analysis.

Among the premises in many types of valid proof, we find u[
versal statements. How could these universal statements have b[
established?

Some of them, to be sure, could have been established by analy[
For example, in §23.1 we saw that "Every man has a backbon[
might have been established in this manner. By considering the st[
intensions of the terms "man" and "backbone," analysis reveals [
truth of this statement.

Some of them could have been established by observation. [
example, the statement, "Every chair in my office is made of woo[
could be so established. There are only a limited number of chairs a[
they can each of them be subjected to an independent and individ[
observational examination.[4]

But other universal statements can be established by neither of [
above means, neither merely by analysis nor merely by observati[
For example, "Every man is less than 10 feet tall," cannot be establis[
by analysis: height is not a necessary member of the total conting[
intension of "man." Nor can it be established merely by observati[
I cannot possibly hope to observe and measure the height of each a[
every man.

In the case of statements like this latter one, observation provi[
*one* ground for the belief: what I do is to observe and measure a *sampl[
of objects in the extension of the term "man." Using as premises [
statements that record my observational findings for this sample, I t[
infer something about the entire extension: that every object in it[
less than 10 feet tall.[5]

Inferences of the sort here under consideration—from observed [
otherwise known characteristics of a *sample* to a characteristic of [
*class sampled*—are known as **inductive generalizations**. These gene[
izations are inductive because it is always possible that new eviden[

---

4  Some reliance on analysis and inference occurs even in this simple kind[
generalization. But the chief dependence is on observation.
5  For a more detailed illustrative description of this process of observation a[
inference, see above, §23.1.

acquired by observing a larger sample, or another sample, will make the conclusion originally inferred to be no longer valid. (In this connection see §§37.7 and 37.8.) Yet despite this fact, this element of risk, inductive generalization is an indispensable mode of inference, continually used in the guidance of daily life and very widely used in the development of scientific theory.

In the next few sections, we shall look briefly at some of the precautions which should be taken to reduce the risk involved in making inductive inferences. Where these precautions (as well as others that we cannot mention here) have not been taken, the induction may be said to be **invalid.** Otherwise, it is **valid.**

We shall, however, not attempt to discuss all kinds of inductive inference. We shall, in fact, leave out of the discussion all reference to analogical induction (defined in §37.8) and concentrate our attention on inductive generalization (defined in §37.8). Yet this omission is not so serious as it might at first appear to be. For the thoughtful student should be able to transfer to analogical induction many of the critical considerations to be raised here in connection with inductive generalization.

In order to introduce some plan and pattern into this discussion let us put down here a preliminary representation of the proof form for inductive generalization. Then we may indicate some features of this proof form that will require special attention. Giving special attention to them will lead us eventually to replace this preliminary proof form by a small range of somewhat more complicated forms, which will more nearly represent the patterns appropriate for valid inductive generalization.

The preliminary proof form for inductive generalization is, then, as follows:

> (1)   $A$ is a fair sample of $S$.
>
> (2)   $xA$ is a $P$.
>
> ∴ (3)   $xS$ is a $P$.

For example,

> (1)   The men in this room are a fair sample of college Seniors at X University.
>
> (2)   Every man in this room speaks English.
>
> ∴ (3)   Every college Senior at X University speaks English.

Another example:

(1)  The men in this room are a fair sample of college Seniors at X University.

(2)  Twenty percent of the men in this room speak French.

∴ (3)  Twenty percent of the college Seniors at X University speak French.

The following features in the preliminary proof form will demand our attention:

(1)  The first premise and the meaning of "fair sample."

(2)  The sign of quantity, "$x$," in the second premise and the conclusion.

(3)  Variations in the type of predicate, "$P$."

Let us consider each of these matters in turn.

### §48.3  Fair Samples

Some samples of a class or group are small, and some large. For example, I might wish to find out whether or not the white crystals in a bowl are sugar or salt, and for this purpose take a relatively small sample, only a dozen or so crystals, to taste. On the other hand, when Dr. Salk was concerned to test the effectiveness of his polio vaccine, it was considered important to test the vaccine on thousands upon thousands of youngsters, so that the sample was extremely large.

It is, however, not necessarily the case that a larger sample is a better or a fairer one. In many circumstances, a very small sample might provide an effective basis, a very fair sample, for an inductive generalization.

Thus, whether or not a sample is a fair sample does not depend so much upon its size as upon certain other considerations:[6]

1.  Whether or not a sample is fair depends in part on what is being tested *for*. In the illustration near the end of the last section, the first premise affirmed that the men in this room are a fair sample of college Seniors at X University. But as the illustration proceeds, we see that what is being tested for is the ability to speak English. Now obviously if the room we had entered was that in which a Senior class in English Literature was being held, the men would *not* constitute a fair sample o

---

[6]  The question of the size of a sample is, however, not completely irrelevant to the fairness of the sample. Its relevance will be discussed in §48.8.

students generally at X University with respect to their ability to speak English: those (if any) who could not speak English would hardly have enrolled in a Senior course in English Literature, and so would not be likely to be in the room.

On the other hand, this very same group could have been a good sample of Seniors at X University with respect to their average height. Yet if the room we had entered had been the dressing room of the basketball squad, then its occupants would have offered a poor sample from which to determine the average height of the Seniors at X University.

We can infer from the above that there is no such thing as a fair sample of $S$, but only a fair sample of $S$ with respect to $P$, or of $S$ with respect to $Q$, and so on. Thus the first premise in the preliminary proof form should already be revised so as to read:

(1)   $A$ is a fair sample of $S$, relative to $P$.

2.   Whether or not $A$ is a fair sample of $S$ relative to $P$ depends on *how* the individuals $s_1$, $s_2$, $s_3$, and so on were selected for inclusion in $A$. No principle of selection should be allowed to operate which can be conceived to have any bearing on whether or not the individual selected would or would not have the property $P$. For example, suppose that we were interested in determining the average size of dried peas in a group or shipment. Now it would be desirable to draw peas from various parts of the shipment; but to accomplish this end, it would be ill-advised to shake containers in a sifting motion on the assumption that that will mix the peas in the container and thus bring to the top for selection peas that had been near the bottom. This would be ill-advised because such a shifting motion tends to bring larger particles to the top and settle smaller ones toward the bottom of the container. Thus, while one might select from the top of the shaken container peas which had been at the bottom, one is also likely to be selecting his sample from among the larger peas, so that his sample will not reflect the average size of the entire sampled group.

3.   The sample, $A$, should reflect in its composition the composition of $S$ insofar as the membership of $S$ is known to be varied in ways that would, or could, affect the occurrence or nonoccurrence of $P$. For example, suppose that Mr. Gallup is conducting a poll of the population to determine the distribution of opinions on some topic, such as popular preference for one candidate or another during a national

political campaign. He knows that a variety of factors influence the geographical distribution of opinions that might bear on candidate preferences: the South is predominantly Democratic, many of the New England states and Midwestern states tend toward Republican majorities, cities tend to be Democratic, rural areas (in the north) Republican, the East is European oriented, the Midwest more isolationist, and the Pacific coast more sensitive to Far Eastern crises and developments. With all this in mind, Mr. Gallup aims to include in his sample, $A$, of the American public, $S$, subsamples of each of these (and other) relevant geographical subdivisions of $S$. Thus, that a sample be a fair sample, it must be very carefully selected so as to sample potentially relevant subdivisions of $S$.

4. But within each subsample, the selection of individuals must be **random**. As nearly as possible, pure chance must determine which members of these subdivisions of $S$ are the ones selected for membership in $A$. This is to ensure that no possibly relevant factor is affecting the sampling of that subdivision.

It would take us too far afield here to enter into a discussion of the exact meaning of "random" or of the techniques that are employed in order to secure random selection. Suffice it to say that the aim is to eliminate any determination of the selection by a factor that could in any way be connected with the occurrence or nonoccurrence of $P$.

## EXERCISES

1. Suppose that I am interested in the question whether or not a majority of the taxpayers in my school district favor a proposal to float a $200,000 bond issue in order to build new schools. Suppose that I decide to ask the opinion of fifteen people. Those fifteen people would then be my sample of the voters. Below are listed four ways of selecting fifteen people whose opinions would be recorded. Explain why (if at all) each method of selection is likely to produce a biased (unfair) sample.

   a. I ask fifteen of my friends.
   b. I ask the fifteen people living nearest to my house.
   c. I station myself near the post office and ask the first fifteen people who come to the post office.
   d. I divide the tax lists for the school district into two lists, of rural and of urban taxpayers. I compare these two lists for length, and find two roughly proportional numbers whose sum equals 15. Let us say that these numbers are 4 and 11, there being about 4,000 rural taxpayers

and about 11,000 urban taxpayers in the district. I then pick four names from the list of rural taxpayers as follows: Open the telephone book and put my finger on a telephone number. Write down the third digit in that number. Repeat three times, until I have written four digits, for example,

0692.

Find the 692d name on the tax list. Repeat three times, so as to get four names. By a similar procedure, select eleven names from the list of urban taxpayers. Let the fifteen people whose names have been thus selected constitute my sample.

2.  Which of the four methods listed above will produce the fairest sample (for the purpose in mind), which the next fairest, and so on? Explain why you answer as you do.

## §48.4  Signs of Quantity

In the tentative proof form for inductive generalization near the end of §48.2 (as revised in consequence of §48.3), we find a sign of quantity appearing in one premise and again in the conclusion:

(1)   $A$ is a fair sample of $S$ relative to $P$.
(2)   $xA$ is a $P$.
∴ (3)   $xS$ is a $P$.

And in the illustrative examples following that proof form, the signs of quantity actually occurring were "every" and "20 percent."

1.  It must be noticed at once that the only signs of quantity which can meaningfully appear in inductive generalizations are proportional signs, such as "every." (On proportional and absolute signs of quantity, see §45.2.) It would be the height of folly to attempt to generalize on an absolute sign of quantity:

(2)   35 $A$'s are $P$.
∴ (3)   35 $S$'s are $P$.

But if the sign of quantity is a proportional one, such as "every" or "65 percent," then inductive generalization might be undertaken.

The usual procedure involves first getting an absolute sign of quantity and then, by knowing the absolute size of the sample, deductively converting that absolute quantity into a proportional one. For example:

(1)   35 $A$'s are $P$.
(2)   70 $A$'s exist.
∴ (3)   50 percent of the $A$'s are $P$.

The conclusion of this deduction is then available for use as premise (2) in the inductive generalization.

2.   In that preliminary proof form and in the example beneath it, the *same* sign of quantity appeared both in the second premise and in the conclusion. This may, indeed, be thought of as the standard pattern. But it provides only a point of departure, and various special considerations will occasionally dictate the necessity to "calculate" a different proportion for the conclusion than was found in the sample. We shall illustrate this by noticing two such types of circumstance, one of them here and one in the next section.

3.   In §48.3, under point 3, we noted that the sample, $A$, should reflect the composition of the sampled class, $S$, in ways that might bear on the characteristic, $P$, being investigated. For example, suppose we were interested in determining the average speed of automobiles on a certain stretch of highway at a certain time of day.[7] Now the automobiles traveling that highway, $S$, are some of them trucks, $S_1$, and some of them passenger cars, $S_2$. Since it is to be assumed that the average truck speeds will be different from the average passenger-car speeds, our sample, $A$, should be selected in such a manner as to include both trucks and passenger cars. Thus $A$ will contain two subsamples, $A_1$, of trucks, and $A_2$, of passenger cars. Suppose, furthermore, that in $S$, trucks are about half as numerous as passenger cars, that is, the extension of $S_1$ is one half as large as the extension of $S_2$. One way of proceeding would be to make the extension of $A_1$ about one half as large as the extension of $A_2$. But other considerations might lead us to sample equal numbers of trucks and of passenger cars, say one hundred of each. Thus, the total sample, $A$, contains two hundred vehicles.

Now suppose that upon observation, we found the following facts:

10 trucks, in $A_1$, were traveling at 35 miles per hour.

40 passenger cars, in $A_2$, were traveling at 35 miles per hour.

∴ 50 vehicles in $A$ were traveling at 35 miles per hour.

That is, 25 percent of $A$ were traveling at 35 miles per hour.

It would be invalid to infer that 25 percent of $S$ were traveling at

---

[7]   The proposed treatment of this illustrative problem is oversimplified in order to bring into prominence the point being illustrated.

35 miles per hour. For we have failed to take into account that while our subsamples, $A_1$ and $A_2$, were equal in size, they represented unequal subparts, $S_1$ and $S_2$. Rather, we should infer that 30 percent of $S$ were traveling at 35 miles per hour.

There are several ways in which this result might be explained. We shall briefly explain here only one such way:

a. Treat the inferences from $A_1$ to $S_1$ and from $A_2$ to $S_2$ independently and according to the standard form for inductive generalization:

i.      10 trucks, $A_1$, were traveling at 35 miles per hour.

There are 100 trucks in $A_1$.

∴ 10 percent of $A_1$ were traveling at 35 miles per hour.

$A_1$ is a fair sample of $S_1$.

∴ 10 percent of $S_1$ were traveling at 35 miles per hour.

ii.      40 cars, $A_2$, were traveling at 35 miles per hour.

There are 100 cars in $A_2$.

∴ 40 percent of $A_2$ were traveling at 35 miles per hour.

$A_2$ is a fair sample of $S_2$.

∴ 40 percent of $S_2$ were traveling at 35 miles per hour.

b. Combine the conclusions in i and ii, "weighting" the percentages in a ratio proportional to the sizes of $S_1$ and $S_2$. Since $S_2$ is twice as large as $S_1$, we can think of $S$ as divided into *three* equal parts: $S_1$, $S_{2a}$, and $S_{2b}$ with their percentages as given above. Then the percentage for $S$ will be the average of the percentages for $S_1$, $S_{2a}$, and $S_{2b}$:

$$
\begin{array}{r}
10 \\
40 \\
40 \\
\hline
3)\ 90 \\
\hline
30
\end{array}
$$

That is, 30 percent of $S$ was traveling at 35 miles per hour.

The incorrectness of inferring the percentage of $A$ (25 percent) to be the percentage of $S$ traveling at 35 miles per hour could have been established by noting that $A$ is not a fair sample of $S$, since its proportion of trucks to passenger cars is different from that in $S$. It is frequently preferable to work from "unfair" samples and to calculate a compensatory difference, as we did in this illustration. But this calculation, represented in 2, above, is a *deductive* proof:

(1)   10 percent of the trucks were traveling at 35 miles per hour.
(2)   40 percent of the passenger cars were traveling at 35 miles per hour.
(3)   ⅓ of the vehicles were trucks.
(4)   ⅔ of the vehicles were passenger cars.
∴ (5)   30 percent of the vehicles were traveling at 35 miles per hour.

Thus the *apparent* exception to the rule, that the same sign of quantity appears in the second premise and the conclusion, is only an apparent exception, at least insofar as the kind of problem here considered is concerned. It occurs because the proof form has not separated out certain underlying inductive generalizations that conform to the rule (from $A_1$ to $S_1$ and $A_2$ to $S_2$) and certain subsequent deductions.

4.   Finally, the inference from the sample to the sampled class, the inductive generalization, should be recognized as giving only an *approximate* value. Thus our preliminary standard form should be revised as follows:

(1)   $A$ is a fair sample of $S$, relative to $P$.
(2)   $x$ percent of $A$ is $P$.
∴ (3)   Approximately $x$ percent of $S$ is $P$.

*How close* an approximation can we assume that we have? Many factors will affect the answer to this question. A few will be mentioned later on. That branch of mathematics called *statistics* deals systematically with many of them, enabling people in many instances even to measure the closeness of the approximation.

### §48.5 Variations in the Type of the Predicate, *P*

What *kind* of predicate, *P*, one might be concerned with can also affect the manner in which one inductively generalizes from

$$x \text{ percent of } A \text{ is } P$$

to

$$\text{Approximately } x \text{ percent of } S \text{ is } P.$$

In fact, the character of *P* might well be such as to justify replacing *x* in the premise by some different value, *y*, calculated in accordance with the general principles of statistical theory. Let us look at one illustration of this point.

The predicate, $P$, might be a specific value for a measurable *variable*, such as speed, weight, height, density, I.Q., temperature, color, and so on. This was the case in the illustrative problem of the preceding section, where $P$ replaced "travels at a speed of 35 miles per hour." In such a case, we can identify $P$ as one of a class of predicates, $P$, $P_1$, $P_2$, $P_3$, and so on, each of which would represent a different value of the same predicate *form*: "travels at a speed of $k$ miles per hour."

In cases like the above, let us say that $P$ is a **variable predicate.**

On the other hand, $P$ might be an **invariable predicate,** such as "talks," "moves," "is a horse," "has a backbone," and so on. In such cases, one cannot identify a predicate form for measurement and claim that $P$ is a certain value of that measurable variable. Now whichever of these kinds of predicate $P$ might be, whether variable or invariable, the standard form for inductive generalization will be valid:

>   (1)   $A$ is a fair sample of $S$, relative to $P$.
>   (2)   $x$ percent of $A$ is $P$.
> ∴ (3)   Approximately $x$ percent of $S$ is $P$.

But you will recall from §37.7 that when valid proofs are inductive, they can be invalidated by the addition of further premises, the original premises all still being retained. In the case of invariable predicates, these additional premises would have to deal with members of $S$, either individually or in groups, that are *not* members of the given sample, $A$. An example would be

>   (1)   $A$ is a fair sample of $S$ with respect of $P$.
>   (2)   100 percent of $A$ is $P$.
>   (3)   $s$ is an $S$.
>   (4)   $s$ is not a $P$.
> ∴ (5)   Approximately 100 percent of $S$ is $P$.

Here $s$ cannot be a member of $A$, since by premise (4), $s$ is not a $P$, while by premise (2), 100 percent of $A$ is $P$. But the addition of premises (3) and (4) to the original premises (1) and (2), makes the original conclusion, (5), no longer valid.[8]

---

8   A different illustration of the same point which does not depend on $x$ taking the value 100%, would be as follows:

>   (1)   $A$ is a fair sample of $S$, relative to $P$.
>   (2)   $x\%$ of $A$ is $P$.

In contrast with the above, if $P$ is a variable predicate, then additional information that would invalidate the original conclusion might well be additional information about $A$ rather than information about members of $S$ which are not in $A$. We shall see how this might come about in the next section.

## §48.6 Statistical Distributions

Suppose that we know

$$x \text{ percent of } A \text{ is } P.$$

From this, we may deduce that

$$(100 - x) \text{ percent of } A \text{ is } P'.$$

If $P$ is an invariable predicate, this represents all that we can say about the $A$'s that are $P'$: they constitute $(100 - x)$ percent of the entire sample, $A$.

But if $P$ is a variable predicate, a value of the form "has a $Q$ of $k$" (for example "has a speed of 35 miles per hour"), we may well ask what $Q$'s the $A$'s that are not $P$ have. Organizing all this information about the various members of $A$ might very noticeably affect what we should inductively infer concerning $S$. An example of this kind of organization of data occurred in §23.1, in connection with the heights of men.

Statistical theory is developed in terms of carefully developed schemes for organizing the data gathered from examination of a given sample. It will not be practical for us to attempt here to explain in detail what methods of organization are in fact used. Let it suffice to say that, in general, instead of treating separately every value of the form "has a $Q$ of $k$," the statistician is likely to consider the form "has a $Q$ of $k \pm l$," for example, "has a speed of $(35 \pm 5)$ miles per hour." Thus, he divides the range of possible speeds into subgroups. In this

---

(3) $B$ is a fair sample of $S$ relative to $P$.
(4) $y\%$ of $B$ is $P$.
(5) $A$ and $B$ are of equal size.
∴ (6) Approximately $x\%$ of $S$ is $P$.

Here, unless $x = y$, conclusion (6), the conclusion of the original proof, is invalid. The valid conclusion would be

$$\frac{x + y}{2} \% \text{ of } S \text{ is } P.$$

fashion he can get percentages of $A$ falling within one speed range or another, rather than percentages having exactly one speed.

From a *comparison* of these percentages at different ranges, it is possible to calculate a **pattern of distribution.** By inductively inferring that this pattern of distribution is illustrated in $S$, the statistician will attribute to $S$ different percentages of certain ranges than he actually found in the sample, $A$. An example appears in §23.1, where the sample, $A$, contained a tallest man, so that 0 percent of $A$ were taller than that; but by comparing the percentages of $A$ in various height ranges, a percent greater than 0 was calculated for $S$ at the next higher height range than was illustrated in $A$.[9]

However, this kind of statistical inference, in spite of the fact that it proceeds from the consideration of a sample, $A$, to an inference concerning the sampled class, $S$, is not a case of inductive generalization. It is inductive inference, but not inductive generalization, because the pattern of distribution imputed to $S$ is not generally the pattern observed in $A$, although it is calculated on the basis of that pattern.

In fact, it would be more appropriate to think of inductive generalization as a special case of the more general inductive process of inferring a pattern of distribution described in this section. But this point cannot be further investigated here.

All that must be noted here is that when further knowledge of the sample, $A$, is available, knowledge of the sort that would permit inference of a pattern of distribution of variable predicates for $S$, then the inductive generalization might be invalid. The inference of the patterned distribution takes precedence, and its percentage is to be

[9]  Actual statistical procedures often illustrate the general principles here discussed in a manner quite different from that suggested in the text. Thus, instead of keeping constant an interval of $Q$'s and computing the *percentage* of $S$ that falls in this interval:

> 33% of $A$ is 5 ft. 10 in. to 6 ft. 2 in. tall,
> 11% of $A$ is 6 ft. 2 in. to 6 ft. 6 in. tall,
>  1% of $A$ is 6 ft. 6 in. to 6 ft. 10 in. tall,
> Etc.

the *percentages* are kept constant and the ranges of $Q$ that they occupy are computed:

> 10% of $A$ is 5 ft. 11½ in. to 6 ft. ½ in. tall,
> 10% of $A$ is 6 ft. ½ in. to 6 ft. 1½ in. tall,
> 10% of $A$ is 6 ft. 1½ in. to 6 ft. 4 in. tall,
> 10% of $A$ is 6 ft. 4 in. to 6 ft. 8 in. tall,
> Etc.

preferred for $S$ as over against the percentage inferable by inductive generalization.[10]

But in the absence of this additional information, the inductive generalization is valid.

### §48.7 Hypothesis and Verification as Inductive Generalization

It is possible to view hypothesis and verification as a case of inductive generalization. (On hypothesis and verification, see §§8.4 and 36.4.)

If any statement is true, then every statement deducible from it will be true. But equally, if all the deductive consequences of a statement are true, then that statement is true.

In the method of hypothesis and verification, one guesses at the solution to some problem. This guessed-at solution is called the *hypothesis*. The investigator then proceeds to deduce various consequences of the hypothesis, and to test these in order to discover whether they are true or false. If he finds them all to be true, he might infer that the hypothesis is true; but if he finds one or more of them false, he should infer that the hypothesis is false.

The set of consequences tested in the manner just described constitute a sample, $A$, of all the consequences, $S$, of the hypothesis. Thus the reasoning reported at the end of the last paragraph, amounts to

(1)   $A$ is a fair sample of $S$, relative to truth or falsity.
(2)   100 percent of $A$ is true.
∴ (3)   100 percent of $S$ is true.
∴ (4)   The hypothesis is true.      [From (3)]

Or:

(2)   Less than 100 percent of $A$ is true.
∴ (3)   Less than 100 percent of $S$ is true.
∴ (4)   The hypothesis is false.

Two things should be noted: First, $A$ must be a fair sample of $S$. In §48.3 we saw a number of things that must be taken into account in order to secure that $A$ will be a fair sample of $S$. Thus in the verification of hypotheses by testing samplings of their consequences, one could be using an "unfair" sample. A result would be that to find all the consequences in this "unfair" sample true, would offer very little evidence for the truth of the hypothesis.

10   However, the two procedures will usually give approximately the same results.

Let us illustrate. Suppose $H$ is the hypothesis, and suppose that

$$(1) \quad H$$
$$\therefore (2) \quad C$$

and

$$(1) \quad H$$
$$\therefore (2) \quad D$$

are both valid, so that $C$ and $D$ are two consequences of $H$. Suppose furthermore that

$$(1) \quad C$$
$$\therefore (2) \quad D$$

and

$$(1) \quad D$$
$$\therefore (2) \quad C$$

are neither of them valid, so that $C$ and $D$ are mutually *independent* consequences of $H$. Finally, let the sample of $H$'s consequences, $A$, consist of $C$ and a group of consequences of $C$. This sample, however large, would be less fair than a sample that consisted merely of the two consequences $C$ and $D$. Because if $C$ is true then every consequence in the sample, $A$, would be true (since all other consequences in the sample are consequences of $C$.) But this would not be necessarily the case if the sample consisted of $C$ and $D$.

Thus, the fairest sample of the consequences of an hypothesis $H$ will be a set of mutually independent consequences.

The second point to be noticed is that when a sampling of the consequences of $H$ turns out not to be all true, so that $H$ must be inferred to be false, nevertheless the examination of this sample may suggest a revision of $H$ that would give a true solution to our original problem. For example, suppose that all the false members of the sample were consequences of $H$ via being consequences of $C$, and that all the consequences of $D$ in the sample were true. This suggests that we might find a true substitute for $H$ by so changing $H$ that $C$ no longer is a consequence of it, while $D$ continues to be a consequence.

## §48.8  A Final Word about Fair Samples

The preceding sections seem to suggest that samples $A_1$, $A_2$, and so on may be more and less fair samples of $S$ relative to $P$; that is, one sample could be fairer than another. What can this mean and in the light of that, what can it mean to call a sample a fair one?

In the actual process of rational inquiry, one has to proceed to conclusions on the basis of the information that he actually possesses. One has a sample, $A$, of $S$, and one has some information about $A$ or can secure (by observation and deduction) some such information. He has to decide whether or not to risk an inductive generalization from this actually available sample or to abstain from making any inductive generalization at all. For he cannot make generalizations from samples that are not available to him.

On the other hand, one can *imagine* a sample of $S$, about which he presently does not have the necessary information, but about which he could reasonably well secure the relevant information so as to use it for an inductive generalization. The only samples worth considering are those that are actually available or that can be made available with a comparatively small expenditure of effort.

Of two samples, $A_1$ and $A_2$, the one is fairer than the other provided that its manner of selection avoided more of the distorting features discussed in earlier sections than the other. And of all samples more or less available, the only ones that may be called *fair* are those such that no other available ones are fairer. But this does not mean that any need be called *fair*, and hence used as a basis for an inductive generalization. One may, indeed, reject all available samples as unfair and refuse to make an inductive generalization. The discussions in the preceding sections were aimed, among other things, at pointing out circumstances in which precisely this should be done. But whether one does this or not, one should always remember that the conclusion of any inductive generalization may be subsequently falsified, either by finding a fairer sample that gives a different result (in which case, the original premise, that the original sample is fair, has been found false) or by getting more information concerning the original sample, such as a pattern of distribution for it. Thus every inductive generalization, like every induction, involves an element of risk.

One final consideration. It was said earlier, in more than one place, that the manner of selecting a sample is more important than its size in determining whether or not it is fair. And yet size does have some bearing. Here all that one can depend on is his general knowledge of the field of the inquiry. The more he knows about the field, the more effectively he can avoid biased methods of selection; and the more effectively he can avoid them, the smaller a sample he may safely use. For example, a chemist knowing a great deal about his subject in general might find that a single experiment, a sample of one, would justify an inductive generalization to 100 percent of the cases. On the other hand, should one know about a subject that the *percentage* of *S*'s that are *P* is less than 100, he will want a sample large enough to measure the *percent*, but if his general knowledge of the field is great, so that he can select the sample judiciously, he may not need a sample any larger than will measure the *percentage* to the degree of accuracy required.

## REVIEW QUESTIONS FOR UNIT 48

. What is meant by inductive generalization? By analogical induction?
. Write out a preliminary representation of the proof form for inductive generalization and state what kinds of consideration will require that this preliminary representation be modified.
. Does the fairness of a sample depend on what is being tested for? Explain and illustrate.
. Why and how must attention be given to sampling distinct subdivisions of the class being sampled for inductive generalization?
. May absolute signs of quantity modify the subject term in the premise and conclusion of an inductive generalization? Explain.
. Must the same sign of quantity appear in both the premise and the conclusion of an inductive generalization? If not, under what circumstances may the signs of quantity differ? If they do differ, will the first premise ("*A* is a fair sample . . .") be true? Explain.
. Compare statistical inference of a pattern of distribution with inductive generalization. Which method of induction, when premises for both are available, has the prior claim to validity?
. How may hypothesis and verification be viewed as a case of inductive generalization?
. What precautions must be taken to ensure that the consequences tested in using the method of hypothesis and verification are a fair sample of the consequences, relative to their truth?

# GLOSSARY

(Numbers following definitions indicate pages on which fuller explanations will be found.)

ABSOLUTE definition: one whose complete definiendum is identical with its simple definiendum, or contains in addition to it only the word "the" or "a." (320)

――sign of quantity: one that specifies a number, definitely or indefinitely, rather than a proportion. Example: "*Seven or eight* chairs," rather than "*most* of the chairs."

――term: A term that is not relative. (208)

ABSTRACT term: a term which purports to refer or apply to things that are abstract, such as properties or relations. (200)

ABSTRACTIVE substitution: replacing a term or other expression in a given statement or elsewhere by a variable so as to represent iconically the form of the given statement. (443)

AFFIRMATIVE statement: one that does not contain a sign of denial, such as "it is false that," "not," or "no." (456)

ALTERNATION: a statement or statement function having the form "$p$ or $q$." (519)

AMBIGUOUS expression: a word, sentence, question, or other sign-token that could plausibly have any one of two or more different meanings, because several conventions are associated with the sign-type to which the token belongs and nothing in the context of the token reveals which of these conventional meanings the author intended. (24)

AMPHIBOLY: an ambiguity arising out of inadequacies of grammatical structure or punctuation. (27)

ANALYSIS: 1. The study of any complex object, such as an event, a problem, proposition, statement, or proof, in order to discern what are its constituent parts and how they are related one to the other.
2. A primary ground of belief: the discernment of the truth or the falsity of a proposition or statement through its analysis in sense 1. (61)

ANALYTIC statement (or statement form): one such that analysis, or analysis and inference, suffices to establish the truth of the statement (or of every statement having the form). (486)

ANALYTICALLY false statement (or statement form): one such that analysis, or analysis and inference, suffices to establish the falsity of the statement (or of every statement having the form). (486)

ANNOTATION of a proof: explanatory remarks set opposite the individual premises and conclusions in the core of the proof. (421)

APPLIED logic: the definition of terms not defined in pure logic, according to the rules of pure logic; the determination of the logical properties (such as symmetry) of such terms and (such as analytic or valid) of statements and proofs containing such terms. Also the criticism of proposed definitions and determinations of the sort just described. (477 ff)

ASYMMETRICAL relation or relative term: a relation or term, $P$, such that the following is a validating form of proof. (475)

$$(1) \quad s_1 \text{ is a } P \text{ of } s_2.$$
$$\therefore (2) \quad s_2 \text{ is not a } P \text{ of } s_1.$$

ATTRIBUTIVE term: a term that purports to apply to, or describe, things, rather than to refer to, or name, them. An adjective, verb, or preposition, or a phrase having the force of an adjective, verb, or preposition, used as a term. (196)

AUGMENTED definitive intension of a term: any strict intension of that term which includes one of its definitive intensions and also one or more other characteristics from its total strict intension. (260)
——syllogism: a proof constituted of a syllogism to which has been added a third premise of the form "Some $S$ exists." (577)

BASIS of a definite description: the general term out of which the definite description is formed by prefixing a singularizing word. (226)
BELIEF: the holding of an attitude of acceptance toward a proposition. (46)

CATEGORICAL syllogism: a proof containing (1) two premises having forms analyzed in the square of opposition and having a common term, and (2) a conclusion having a form analyzed in the square of opposition and combining as its subject and predicate the two other terms appearing in the premises. (565)
CIRCULAR definition: one in which the simple definiendum appears in the definiens. (364)
——definitional chain: one such that some term in the definiens of some definition in the chain is also the simple definiendum of an earlier definition in the chain. (383)
CLASSIFICATORY definition: one that indicates in its definiens two or more classes (or characteristics) to *each* of which every object in the extension of the definiendum belongs (or *each* of which every object in the extension of the definiendum has). (334)
COMMON characteristic of a group: one possessed by every object in the group. (235)
COMPLETE definiendum of a definition: the entire expression whose meaning is said to be equivalent to that of the definiens. (318)
——definite description: one which purports to refer to the one and only object presumed to be in the extension of that definite description's basis. (226)
——definition: an act of definition intending completely to give the signification of its definiendum. (273)
COMPLEX proof: one containing one or more intermediate conclusions that contribute to showing how the premises justify the final conclusion. (416)
——statement (or term): one containing at least one other statement (or term) as a component functional part. (190)
CONCEPTUAL definition: a definition that at least in part analyzes (instead of merely identifying) the meaning of its definiendum. (295)
CONCLUSION of a proof: a statement listed in a proof as inferable from other statements in the same proof. (416)
CONCRETE term: 1. One purporting to refer or apply to objects or events having definite locations in space or time. (200)
2. One purporting to refer or apply to objects that are not further determinable. (200n)
CONDITIONAL definition: one whose definiens is a conditional statement (or statement form). (330)
——statement (or statement form): one having the form "if $p$, then $q$." (531)
CONJUNCTION: a statement or statement form having the form "$p$ and $q$." (517)
CONTEXTUAL definition: one that is not absolute. (320)
CONVENTIONAL sign-token: one that is like in sign-type to the tokens produced by other people when their purposes (meanings) were like those of the author of the given sign-token. (148, 163)

CONVERSE relative terms: terms in a pair such that identical claims are made by the two terms as predicates when the order of the logical subjects is reversed. Examples: "$s_1$ is *east* of $s_2$," "$s_2$ is *west* of $s_1$;" "$s_1$ *struck* $s_2$," "$s_2$ was *struck* by $s_1$." (503)

CONVERSION: a proof whose conclusion simply reverses the order of the terms in its premise, which belongs to the square of opposition. (559) Example:

          (1)   Some $S$ is a $P$.

    ∴ (2)   Some $P$ is an $S$.

CORE of a definition: the key statement presented in an act of definition. (315 f)

——of a proof: the premises and conclusion, divested of all accompanying remarks. (414 f)

COVERED definitional chain: one such that every definition in the covered chain is in the covering chain, but not vice versa. (381)

DEDUCTIVE valid proof: one such that there is no statement which, if added as a further premise, would turn the proof into an invalid proof. (432)

DEFINIENDUM of a definition: the term (or other expression) whose meaning is explained in that definition. (317)

DEFINIENS of a definition: the expression in that definition which indicates the meaning of the definiendum. (317)

DEFINITE description: a singular term formed by prefixing a singularizing word or phrase to a general term. (194)

——sign of quantity: one that specifies precisely the number or proportion of the objects in question. Examples: "*six* automobiles," "*35 percent* of the students." Counter-examples: "At least five," "ten or a dozen," "between 30 and 40 percent." (194)

DEFINITION: 1. The act of stating the signification of a word or phrase. (271)
2. A statement of the signification of a word or phrase. (271)

DEFINITIONAL chain for a term: a series of complete definitions the first of which defines the term in question, and each succeeding member of which defines some term appearing in the definiens of some definition appearing earlier in the series. (378 f)

DEFINITIVE intension of a term: any smallest intension of that term from which all the characteristics in the total strict intension of that term may be inferred. (257)

DENOTATIVE correlates of an attributive term: two denotative terms, the *first* of which purports to denote the things to which the attributive term applies, and the *second* of which purports to denote the property or characteristic whose possession makes the attributive term applicable. (198)

——term: one that purports to refer to, or name, things; a noun or noun phrase used as a term. (196)

DIRECT inference: that method of problem-solving which consists of reviewing already known facts to discover some from which a solution to the problem might be inferred. (80)

DIRECTED sign-event: one having an intended second party as a constituent. (102)

DIRECTIVE sign-type: one whose tokens tend, on receipt, to evoke action. (167)

DISTRIBUTED token of a term: any token of that term, provided the token is either the subject of a universal statement or the predicate of a negative statement. (568)

EMOTIVE sign-type: one whose tokens tend, on receipt, to arouse emotions. (167)

ENUMERATIVE definition: one in which the definiens lists one by one or group by group, or partly in one way and partly in the other, the objects belonging to the extension of the definiendum. (334)

EQUIVALENT definitional chains: chains such that every definition in either chain is also in the other chain. (381)

EXPRESSION: that aspect of meaning in which an author (or his sign-token) reveals what is the nature of his concern. (143)

EXTENSION of a term: the group or class of actual things to each of which the term refers or applies. (214)

EXTENSIONAL definition: one intended to explain (completely or incompletely) what objects are in the extension of the definiendum. (289)

FACT: a true proposition. (47)

FAIR sample: a sample of the extension of a term so selected as to justify an inductive generalization from it to the entire extension of the term. (594)

GENERAL proposition or statement: one which imputes (a) some specific property to a definitely or indefinitely indicated number or proportion of the objects in a specified group of objects or (b) some specific relational property as holding between such numbers or proportions of objects in two specified groups of objects. (179)

——term: one which purports to refer or apply to any of possibly many things. (193)

HORTATORY definition: one that recommends to its receivers that they adopt in their productive discourse the indicated meaning for the definiendum. (280)

HYPOTHESIS AND VERIFICATION: a method of problem-solving that consists of guessing at the solution to one's problem and then testing the reliability of that guess (hypothesis) by testing the truth of a sample from among the consequences of supposing the hypothesis to be true. (80 f)

HYPOTHETICAL syllogism: a proof having the following form. (537)

$$(1) \quad \text{If } p, \text{ then } q.$$
$$(2) \quad \text{If } q, \text{ then } r.$$
$$\therefore (3) \quad \text{If } p, \text{ then } r.$$

ICONIC sign-token: one that resembles the topic of concern it indicates, where this resemblance is intended as the means by which the topic of concern will be identified; hence, a picture, map, diagram, or imitative gesture, used as a sign. (147)

IMMEDIATE inference: a proof, often complex, that involves no other proof procedure than conversion, obversion, or one justified by the square of opposition. (562)

INCOMPLETE definite description: one which purports to refer to a certain, unspecified one of the presumably many things in the extension of its basis. (227)

——definition: one intended only partially to explain the signification of its definiendum. (273)

INDEFINITE sign of quantity: one that is not definite. (545)

INDETERMINANT statement form: one such that some statements having the form are true while others having the form are false. (487)

INDEXICAL intension of a term: any smallest intension of that term which is not a definitive intension of it. (262)

INDICATION: that aspect of meaning in which an author (or his sign-token) reveals the topic of his concern. (143)

INDICATIVE definition: one that is not ostensive; hence, one that is given completely in signs. (314)

INDUCTIVE generalization: a proof indicating in its premises the possession of some specified characteristic by a certain percentage of the objects in a sample of the extension of a term, and concluding that approximately the same percentage of the objects in the extension of that term have that characteristic. (590)

——valid proof: one such that there is at least one statement which, if added as a further premise, would turn the proof into an invalid one. (432)

INFERENCE: the passage of the mind from one or more already accepted beliefs to the consequent acceptance of another belief. (407)

INFORMATIVE definition: one aimed at informing its receivers as to the meaning intended by authors who use the defined expression. (281)

INTENDED second party: 1. Of a productive sign-event: the person or persons that the author intends as receivers of his message.

2. Of a receptive sign-event: the person or persons that the receiver presumes were authors of the received message. (40 ff)

INTENSION of a term: any set of characteristics that is common and jointly peculiar to the extension of that term. (240)

INTENSIONAL definition: one intended to explain (completely or incompletely) what characteristics are in the total strict intension of the definiendum. (289)

INTERMEDIARY: a person involved in the transmittal of a message from its author to its intended receiver. (95)

INTERPRETER: 1. In a productive sign-event: the author, or deliberate producer, of the sign-tokens.

2. In a receptive sign-event: the observer, or receiver, of the sign-tokens. (92)

INTRANSITIVE relation or relative term: a relation or relative term, $P$, such that the following proof form is validating. (492)

$$\text{(1)} \quad s_1 \text{ is a } P \text{ of } s_2.$$
$$\text{(2)} \quad s_2 \text{ is a } P \text{ of } s_3.$$
$$\therefore \text{(3)} \quad s_1 \text{ is not a } P \text{ of } s_3.$$

IRREFLEXIVE relation or relative term: a relation or relative term, $P$, such that every statement of the form "$s$ is a $P$ of $s$" is false. (481)

——sign-event: one that is not reflexive. (46)

JOINTLY PECULIAR set of characteristics of a group: a set such that nothing except objects in the group have all the characteristics in the set. (236)

JUSTIFYING principle of a proof (or proof form): a conditional statement whose antecedent is the conjunction of the premises in that proof (or proof form) and whose consequent is the conclusion of that proof (or proof form). (489)

LINGUISTIC definition: one intended merely to explain that a certain word or phrase has such and such a presumably already familiar signification. (295)

LOGIC: the science of exact reasoning. (11)

LOGICAL predicate: that term in a statement which is replaced by "$P$" in the conventional representation of the form of the statement. (548)

LOGICAL subject: any term (or terms) in a statement that is (or are) replaced by "$s$," "$s_1$," "$s_2$," "$S$," "$S_1$," or "$S_2$" in the conventional representation of the form of the statement. (548)

MIDDLE term: the term appearing (as subject or predicate) in each premise of a categorical syllogism. (565)

MIXED, general and singular proposition or statement: a proposition or statement one of whose subjects is a general term and one of whose subjects is a singular term. (180)

*MODUS PONENS:* the following validating form of proof. (536)

> (1) If $p$, then $q$.
> (2) $p$.
> ∴ (3) $q$.

*MODUS TOLLENS:* the following validating form of proof. (537)

> (1) If $p$, then $q$.
> (2) Not $q$.
> ∴ (3) Not $p$.

MOLECULAR logic: that branch of logic that deals with complex statements and disregards the internal analysis of the constituent statements. (510)

NATURAL sign-token: any state of nature on the observation of which one may predict or infer some other state of nature. (105)

NECESSARY member of the total contingent intension of a term: a characteristic common to the extension of a term in virtue merely of the meaning of the term. (246)

NEGATIVE statement: one that in standard form contains one sign of denial. (456)
——term: one having a sign of negation as a major constituent part. (496)

NEUTRAL sign-type: one that is neither emotive nor directive. (167)

NOMINAL definition: one intended to explain what the definer means when he uses the definiendum. (276)

NONREFLEXIVE relation or relative term: one that is neither reflexive nor irreflexive. (482)

NONSYMMETRICAL relation or relative term: one that is neither symmetrical nor asymmetrical. (476)

NONTRANSITIVE relation or relative term: one that is neither transitive nor intransitive. (492)

NULL extension: the extension of a term which does not refer or apply to any actual object. (222)

OBVERSION: a validating form of proof in which the conclusion differs from the one and only premise in only two respects: (1) one of them is affirmative and the other negative; (2) the predicate of one of them is the negative of the predicate of the other. (498) Example:

> (1) $s$ is a $P$.
> ∴ (2) $s$ is not a non-$P$.

OPERATIONAL definition: a conditional definition in which the antecedent of the definiens describes a performable experiment and the consequent describes an observable outcome of the experiment. (231)

OSTENSIVE definition: one which proceeds by simultaneously presenting the term to be defined and an actual sample of the objects in its extension: "This is a polar bear." (314)

PARTICULAR statement: one having one or the other of the two following forms: "Some $S$ is a $P$," "Some $S$ is not a $P$." (549)

PECULIAR characteristic of an object (or group of objects): a characteristic possessed by nothing other than that object (or by nothing other than objects in that group). (236)

PERSONAL sign-event: one that involves no person as a constituent other than the interpreter; hence, any reflexive or undirected sign-event. (111)

PHYSICAL sign-token: the physical object, or physical behavior of an object, which is produced as a sign in a productive sign-event or observed as a sign in a receptive sign-event. (94)

PRACTICAL problem or question: a problem or question as to what action, conduct, or behavior the person confronted with the problem or asking the question would advisedly undertake. (3)

PREMISE: any statement forming part of a proof and indicating a bit of the evidence from which the conclusion of that proof is reportedly to be inferred. (416)

PRIMARY language: a language used by authors in order directly to refer to or indicate things or situations in the world at large. (158)

PRODUCTIVE sign-event: the act of deliberately making a sign. (91)

PROOF: any linguistic structure (sign-type) which, because of an associated conventional meaning, could be presented as the record or report of an inference, this report indicating what propositions were accepted as evidence and what proposition was inferred from the evidence. (409 f)

PROPORTIONAL sign of quantity: a sign of quantity that indicates what fraction or proportion of the objects in the extension of the term the sign modifies are under consideration. Examples: "60 percent of," "a majority of." (544)

PROPOSITION: a situation or state of affairs. (171)

PURE logic: the science of the effect on the meanings of statements—and consequently on the validity of proofs—of all parts and aspects of those statements and proofs except the strict intensions of the terms contained in them. (438, 478 ff)

QUANTIFIER: a sign of quantity; i.e., a sign indicating some number or proportion. (185)

RATIONALIZATION: an invalid ground of belief consisting of the adoption of a belief merely because it would, if true, justify an already chosen, or already preferred, line of conduct. (78)

REAL definition: one intended to explain the signification of a word or phrase as that word is used by authors other than the definer. (276)

RECEPTIVE sign-event: the act of interpretatively observing a physical sign-token. (91)

RECURSIVE definition: a pair of definitional statements that have the same relative term, $D$, for their simple definiendum and that together define "the $D$ of $x$," where $x$ may range over a discrete series of objects. The general form is

(a) the $D$ of $i =$ $_{\text{Df}}$ $Y$
(b) the $D$ of $\text{n}x =$ $_{\text{Df}}$ the $R$ of (the $D$ of $x$),

where "$i$" represents the first member of the series and "$\text{n}x$" represents the next member of the series after member $x$. (399 f)

REFLEXIVE relation or relative term: a relation or relative term, $P$, such that every statement of the form "$s$ is a $P$ of $s$" is true. (110)

——sign-event: one in which the interpreter is identical with the intended second party. (46)

RELATIVE term: a term that could stand in the position of "$P$" in one of the following statement forms. (207)

$$s_1 \text{ is } P \text{ (to) } s_2.$$
$$s_1 \text{ is a } P \text{ (of) } s_2.$$

RIGHT REASON, principles of: principles drawn largely from logic, methodology, and semiotic, that will guide the more efficient and effective use of thought as an instrument of problem-solving. (7)

SECONDARY language: a language whose sign-types are used to give instructions for producing sign-tokens in another, primary language. (157)

SEMIOTIC: the science of signs and sign-making. Sometimes divided into three branches: *pragmatics*, or the science of the relations between signs and sign-users or people; *semantics*, or the science of the relations between signs and their meanings; and *syntax*, or the science of the relations of signs to one another. But these branches of semiotic cannot be sharply separated from one another. (7)

SENTENTIAL contextual definition: a contextual definition in which the complete definiendum has the form of a declarative sentence. (327)

SERIES: a set or class of object arranged in some definite order in accordance with some ordering principle. (396)

SIGN-EVENT: the act of deliberately producing or interpretatively observing a sign-token. (89)

SIGN-TOKEN: see *Physical sign-token.*

SIMPLE ambiguity: an ambiguity of a word or phrase not arising out of inadequacies of grammar or punctuation. (27)

——definiendum: that word or phrase in the definiendum of a definition for the sake of explaining which the definition occurs. (318)

——proof: one that does not contain any intermediate conclusions. (416)

——substitution: the use of a token belonging to one sign-type—for example, a pronoun—in place of a token belonging to another sign-type—for example, a term—that might have been used on that occasion. (440)

——term: one that does not contain another term as a component functional part of itself. (190)

SINGULAR proposition or statement: one whose logical subject or logical subjects are all singular terms. (176 ff, 447)

——term: a term that purports to refer to one specific thing. (193)

SOCIAL sign-event: one having an intended second party which is distinct from the interpreter. (111)

STANDARD form: a conventional arrangement of tokens in a definition, statement, or proof, by reference to which theories and rules governing these types of expression may be formulated. (418)

STATEMENT: any declarative sentence-type insofar as it is used to indicate a certain proposition. (171)

——function: a representation, containing no variables except statement variables, of a statement form. (513)

STRICT intension of a term: any intension of that term which is composed exclusively of necessary members of that term's total contingent intension. (260)

SYLLOGISM: See *Categorical syllogism* and *Hypothetical syllogism.*

SYMMETRICAL relation or relative term: a relation or relative term, $P$, such that the following form of proof is validating. (473)

$$(1) \quad s_1 \text{ is a } P \text{ of } s_2.$$
$$\therefore (2) \quad s_2 \text{ is a } P \text{ of } s_1.$$

SYNTHETICALLY true (or false): a statement—or statement form—such that observation, perhaps coupled with other grounds of belief, would suffice, while analysis and inference would not suffice, to establish the truth (or falsity) of the statement in question—or of every statement having the form in question. (486)

TACIT supplement of an incomplete definite description: an unstated characterization which, if combined with the basis of that incomplete definite description, would convert the latter into a complete definite description with the same purported referent as the original incomplete description. (228 f)

TERM: any expression-type that may be treated as a single unit insofar as its tokens may be regarded as purporting to refer or apply to one and the same object, or to any objects in one and the same class of objects. (184)

THEORETICAL definition: a definition that is real-extensional and at the same time nominal-intensional. (293)

TOPIC of concern: an analyzable constituent of a purpose, consisting of an identifiable proposition with which a person having that purpose has an identifiable concern. (140)

TOTAL contingent intension of a term: the set of all characteristics common to the extension of that term. (241)

——strict intension of a term: that intension which consists of all the necessary members of the total contingent intension of that term. (249)

TRANSITIVE relation or relative term: a relation or relative term, $P$, such that the following form of proof is validating. (491)

> (1)  $s_1$ is a $P$ of $s_2$.
> (2)  $s_2$ is a $P$ of $s_3$.
> ∴ (3)  $s_1$ is a $P$ of $s_3$.

TRANSPOSITION: the following validating form of proof. (537)

> (1)  If $p$, then $q$.
> ∴ (2)  If (not $q$), then (not $p$).

TRUTH function: a statement function such that the truth or falsity of the statements illustrating that function is always determinable merely from the truth or falsity of the statements they contain that replace the variables in the statement function. (515)

UNDIRECTED sign-event: a sign-event that has no intended second party. (99)

UNIVERSAL statement: a statement having one of the two following forms. (549)

> (a)  Every $S$ is a $P$.
> (b)  No $S$ is a $P$.

VALID inference: an inference from evidence to a conclusion logically related to the evidence in such a manner that accepting the evidence does in fact justify accepting the conclusion. (408)

——proof: a proof in which the premises and the conclusion are logically related in such a manner that, were the premises known to be true, the conclusion could be justifiably accepted as also true. (411)

——question: a question that has a correct answer; hence, one such that a method for finding the correct answer can at least be described, if not actually carried out. Minimal requirements are freedom from ambiguity, from vagueness, and from false presuppositions. (41 f)

VALIDATING form of proof: a form of proof such that every proof having that form is valid. (471)

VARIABLE: a sign-type used in place of a term (or sign of quantity) in order to represent iconically the form of a statement or other expression that might contain that term (or sign of quantity). (444)

# INDEX